Adventures in a Backwater
Government Department

# Adventures in a Backwater Government Department

. . .

*and Other Scenes from
the Unremarkable Life of a
Son of the Suburbs*

Patrick Hickman-Robertson

Matador
9 Priory Business Park,
Wistow Road, Kibworth Beauchamp,
Leicestershire, LE8 0RX
Tel: 0116 279 2299
Email: books@troubador.co.uk
Web: www.troubador.co.uk/matador
Twitter: @matadorbooks

ISBN 978 1838591 670

British Library Cataloguing in Publication Data.
A catalogue record for this book is available from the British Library.

Typeset in 11 Sabon by Troubador Publishing Ltd, Leicester, UK

Matador is an imprint of Troubador Publishing Ltd

*Illustrations by Michael Dorey*

# IN TRIBUTE

. . .

† 2<sup>nd</sup> **Lieutenant Seaborn Robertson**, aged 20, Royal Worcestershire Regiment. Killed on the Somme 18 November 1918. No known grave

† 2<sup>nd</sup> **Lieutenant Kenneth Barford**, aged 19, Royal Flying Corps. Shot down near Arras by Baron von Richtofen 27 March 1918. No known grave.

† **Surgeon Gerhard Ehrlich**, late of the Charité Hospital, Berlin, died at Gänsestrasse concentration camp, Warsaw, 5 February 1944. No known grave.

Also to the memory of all the other Germans, known and unknown, who stood up and were counted.

† **Flying Officer Dick Fairweather DFC** of Belize, British Honduras, aged 22, RAF Bomber Command. Shot down during the Wesseling Raid over Germany of 21-22 June 1944. Buried at Rheingold War Cemetery.

Also to the memory of all the other Empire volunteers who ensured that Britain never did stand alone.

. . .

*For Henry, Chloe and Emilia. May they live in*
*peace for all their days.*

# Contents

## III – BBC to Backwater

# Introduction

. . .

# 'I'VE HAD MY STRUGGLES TOO ...'

. . .

The other day I went to hear Rod Liddle speak to an adoring *Spectator* audience at a big public hall in London. Rod Liddle is the resident leftie at the otherwise impeccably right-wing *Spectator*, but cherished by the readership for the scorn he heaps upon politically correct *bien pensant* posturing metropolitan liberals. One of the reasons for his distaste for this tribe of entitled and self-regarding inheritors of the Earth is that a disproportionate number of them are alumni of public schools. Rod abhors public schools and their products. Probably the only thing he dislikes more than a braying public schoolboy is a public schoolboy who brays 'I've had my struggles too ...' when reminded of his life of ease and privilege. He was cheered to the roof on this topic by his audience, most of them public-school products well accustomed to the ease and privilege that Rod was excoriating.

As one brought up in similar circumstances, including a public school education, I am aware that what follows will fulfil all of Rod's most pronounced phobias. My only defence is this. It has not been a life of distinction and would not bear scrutiny but for one factor. I am one of those fairly rare people who lack the normal range of skills and talents with which a benevolent God has seen fit to equip most of the middle classes. I do not claim a lack of abilities in order to demonstrate a becoming modesty and win approval for touching self-deprecation – I really do have few of the basic skills that normal people need in order to function and prosper.

There aren't that many of us, the really useless ones. I have met some people who are fairly inept in a range of activities, but compensate in others. Christopher Fildes, another *Spectator* columnist, could not ride a bicycle, drive a car, hit a ball, swim, tie knots, change light bulbs or do anything of a practical nature that most people have mastered by the age of ten or so, but would tell jokes to his cat in classical Greek and could pick up the text of any line you read him from Evelyn Waugh's *Vile Bodies* and continue reciting it to the end of the chapter. Having failed to make his mark in the ladies' underwear industry, he found his feet as one of the most highly regarded financial commentators in Britain. But my incapacity was and is of a different order. The story I have to tell is not about how I overcame this abnormality by fortitude and application; rather it is about a lot of luck, combined with a degree of deception and low cunning. That and having my beloved, competent Karla at my side.

# WHO'S WHO

**Adams, Richard:** author of *Watership Down* and head of the air pollution division at the Department of the Environment, where he displayed a marked reluctance to receive the foreign visitors for whom Patrick was responsible.

**Annabelle:** ditzy former Peter Arno model in New York whose casual approach to custody of her underwear precipitated Patrick's ejection from his luxury accommodation in Mayfair.

**Archibald, Ezekiel:** Seventh Day Adventist and proprietor of Rayson Sheet Metal in Melbourne who imperilled his employees' lives as he drove them at breakneck speed through suburban streets to reach the factory before sunset marked the beginning of his Sabbath.

**Aspin, Special Agent:** member of South Africa's Bureau of State Security (BOSS) who spied on Patrick in Basutoland.

**Baden-Powell, Dowager Lady Olave:** Chief Guide, encountered by Patrick aboard the *Southern Cross* out of Perth, WA, who upset a table companion by interrogating him on Australia's balance of trade.

**Bareau, Peter:** banker and first Director of Savings appointed from outside government service. Rewrote Patrick's job description so that he was no longer eligible for his own post.

**Bartlett, Geoffrey:** under-master at Patrick's Dotheboys Hall prep school who was a beacon of light in a darkening world. Extolled on *Desert Island Discs* by his pupil and admirer John Cleese (qv).

**Beadle, Jeremy:** prankster voted by the *Sun* as the person most hated by the British public after Saddam Hussein, an assessment of his character not shared by Karla and Patrick.

**Bell, Rt Hon Lord Tim:** architect of Mrs Thatcher's Iron Lady persona who recommended Patrick for a post at No 10 that he was too scared to go for.

**Benson, Sandra:** clerk at National Savings' Lytham office who was crowned Miss Premium Bond 1972 and taken to London to meet Roger Moore, with life-changing consequences.

**Bianchi, Monsieur:** sociopathic Banqueting Manager at Melbourne's Intercontinental Hotel who kept Patrick locked in a cage 14 hours a day.

**Binney, Alec:** housemaster at Shrewsbury whose only favourable comment on Patrick in five years was that he could conduct an adult conversation at the dinner table (in contrast to his peers).

**Blackwood, George 'The Kansan' and Jim:** brothers from Buffalo, Kansas (pop. 422 and falling) who were Patrick's friends and mentors at Boston University and Baker University, Kansas, respectively.

**Botha, Helena:** daughter of Louis Botha, C-in-C of the Transvaal forces in the Boer War and first Prime Minister of South Africa. Gave Patrick a first-hand account of life in a British concentration camp, probably the one built by Hugh Rhind (qv).

**Brogger, Frederick H:** Hollywood film producer who brought Karla into major motion pictures. Lived at Patrick and Karla's Wiltshire cottage while on bail awaiting trial for fraud, forgery and perjury.

**Brooke MC, Rev Major Hugh:** Shrewsbury housemaster with John Peel and Michael Palin under his care and Patrick's form-master. Probably the only master at Shrewsbury who believed every boy had potential and that it was his job to foster it.

**Brown, David:** Patrick's first form-master at Shrewsbury whose well-intentioned initiative resulted in his being branded as 'the thickest boy in the school'.

**Burton, Kenneth:** National Savings finance director whose history of NS in WWI, written in retirement, was published by Patrick.

**Calamachi, Princess Jean Ann-Marie:** Romanian princess who had fled the communist regime with 'a handful of jewels', and whose stipulation that no woman might stay overnight at her townhouse in Mayfair proved greatly to the advantage of Patrick and his chums.

**Campbell, Dr Killie:** scion of a wealthy Durban family who devoted her wealth to building the finest collection of Africana in private hands and establishing her own private museum.

**Chamberlain, Jeffrey:** master tailor who drove Patrick up the lonely West Coast of New Zealand, regaling him with his WWII adventures when he had been released from a POW camp to travel all over Germany with a minder providing tailoring services to the Wehrmacht.

**Charlton, Christopher:** amiable and sweet-natured boy at St Peter's, Weston-super-Mare, who was brainwashed by headmaster Geoffrey Tolson into suborning the schoolboy code of *omertà*.

**Charlton, John Sills 'Toby':** elderly, louche lothario who occupied the first-floor front at 17 Oakley Street (with Patrick in the third-floor back) and made a pass at a teenage girl who was revealed to be his daughter.

**Christopher, Benjamin 'Pitch':** country lawyer in Ladysmith who, together with his wife, worked tirelessly for the betterment of the Bantu.

**Cleese, John 'Cheese':** outrageously funny schoolboy who kept the inmates of Patrick's Dotheboys Hall prep school from despair and later did much the same for the British public as a whole.

**Clinton, William Jefferson:** Oxford student , later 42nd President of the US, who was entertained by Karla at her flat in South Audley Street.

**Cook, Roger:** neophyte broadcaster who caroused with Patrick in Perth, WA, and later found fame presenting ITV's *The Cook Report*.

**Cowper, Jack:** WWI veteran and cross-generational friend of Patrick at the Public Schools Club. 'Jacko the Monkey' on *Children's Hour*, he was apprehended by Lord Reith in the act of kissing a pageboy.

**Cranko, Robin:** maverick lawyer (brother of the choreographer John Cranko) and anti-apartheid activist in exile in Basutoland.

**Culham, Sarah:** Patrick's deputy at National Savings who followed in a long line of stalwart ladies who minded his back for him.

**Curtis:** wrestling pro and fundamentalist Baptist from Chicago's Loop who shared Patrick's cabin aboard a dynamite boat crossing the Pacific.

**Dallas, Peter:** eccentric Englishman in Boston who instructed Patrick in the art of living on less than a dollar a day.

**D'Arch-Smith, Timothy 'Rubber Ears':** wise and witty bibliophile who introduced Patrick, provincial boy from the suburbs, to the lights of London.

**Davies, Norman:** Southern Pacific Railroad fireman and autodidact who was Patrick's mentor aboard an emigrant ship to America and introduced him to student life with 'Frauds at Yale' and 'Frauds at Harvard'.

**Dolman, the Rev Adolf:** paedophile master at St Peter's, Weston-super-Mare, who dispensed rationed Swiss chocolates to his pretty favourites.

**Doody, Mister:** choleric advertising manager of the *New Statesman* who plotted ways and means of dispensing with Patrick's services.

**Dixie:** 18-stone Maori chambermaid at the Hermitage in New Zealand who, under the influence of alcohol, took a flying leap onto Patrick's bed with carnal intent and fell asleep on top of him.

**Dyson, Charles:** Plato-reading Cambridge graduate with whom Patrick travelled through a war zone in the Sudan.

**Elizabeth, HM Queen:** revered sovereign whose brief exchange with Patrick left them both confused.

**Ellis, Arnold:** amiable history master at Shrewsbury who helped Patrick to rise from 551st place in the school (of 551) to 1st place.

**Ellis, Monday:** gorgeous, scantily-clad girl whose attractions upstaged Patrick's attempt to present their joint book proposal to a publisher.

**Erith, Bob:** Indian Ocean cabin-mate, later flat-mate in Ecclestone Square who took Patrick to dine with Prince William of Gloucester (qv).

**Fairweather, Donaldine 'Sistie':** Miss British Honduras 1961 with whom Patrick stepped out until she was deported by the Home Office in a shocking case of institutional racism.

**Fawcett, Michael:** National Savings clerk who, as a customer, sued his employer for £2.74 in a case that reached the High Court.

**Fergusson, Sir Bernard:** Governor-General of New Zealand with a talent for connecting with ordinary people, including Patrick.

**Fewster, Barbara:** formidable Director of Balletic Studies at the Royal Ballet School who accused Patrick of accosting a comely student.

**Filamanov, General:** Red Army commander who took over the house of Karla's family in Genthin and protected them from the fate that met so many other Germans overrun by the Russians.

**Fildes, Christopher:** brassiere manufacturer who became an acclaimed financial commentator. Cousin of Sally Hance (qv).

**Flowers, Tommy:** unhonoured Post Office engineer who built the world's first electronic computer and later designed ERNIE for National Savings. Patrick's candidate for the empty plinth in Trafalgar Square.

**Foot, Paul:** Old Salopian investigative journalist who exposed his former housemaster Chenevix-Trench as a flagellomaniac in *Private Eye* before turning his attention to Patrick's boss Bob Davy..

**Foster, Peter:** genial barman at the Hermitage in New Zealand's Southern Alps who liked everyone he met except Australians.

**Frampton, Ian:** prep school boy whose generous aunt organised drops of illegal tuck for the underfed members of Patrick's gang.

**Frost, David:** television presenter with whom Karla filmed in Iran and to whom Patrick optioned the TV rights of his first book

**Gates, Robin:** roly-poly fellow steward and best mate of Patrick's at the Hermitage Hotel in New Zealand, later sharing with him in Perth, WA.

**Gilbert, Stuart:** eccentric Director of Savings who congratulated Patrick's ad agency on showing him second-rate crap instead of their usual third-rate crap.

**Gordey, Bill:** Harvard grad-student resident at the same rooming house in Cambridge, Mass, with whom Patrick went on a 36 hr, four-day week.

**Graham, Anne:** ravishing Scottish girl in Boston who introduced Patrick to Irish revolutionaries, her own nationalist credentials including participation in the theft of the Stone of Scone from Westminster Abbey.

**Grant, Sandy:** colonial officer in Bechuanaland who worked undercover ferrying refugees from South Africa to freedom.

**Gould, JJ:** school-friend and Best Man who engineered a transformative elevation for Patrick at Shrewsbury; introduced him to Karla; and found the house in the Lambourn Valley to which he and Karla retired.

**Green, Mister:** veteran of the Spanish Civil War and lover of literature who led a wandering life until washing up as gardener at the Emerald Lake Chalet in the Canadian Rockies.

**Griffiths, Sir Eldon:** government minister who kept a pet lion and was, in Patrick's opinion, far too nice to climb the greasy pole.

**Hamilton, David:** controversial photographer whose career ended in scandal and suicide. Lured an unsuspecting Patrick and his account manager Hargreaves (qv) to a French nudist colony.

**Hamnet, Ian:** tutor to King Moshoeshoe II of Basutoland in England; later his equerry, resident at the royal palace and the only person able to control its ferocious guard-dog with a single word of command.

**Hamnet, 'Sweet' Jenny:** Bristol girl told by a clairvoyant she would marry a man who lived in a royal palace and could control the ferocious dog that guarded it with a single command. (See Hamnet, Ian above.)

**Hargreaves, Mary:** Patrick's account manager at Dorland Advertising who became a lifelong friend in spite of polar opposite political positions.

**Hart, Michael:** Anglo-German head of history at Shrewsbury who tacitly effected Patrick's belated elevation to the senior school but did not meet the beneficiary of this good deed until both had retired.

**Hawn, Goldie:** adorable chain-smoking Hollywood heroine with whom Patrick and Karla spent quality time in a tiger reserve in Madhya Pradesh.

**Heath, Edward:** Prime Minister who put Patrick's department in a spin with the unintended launch of the Clean-up London Campaign.

**Heseltine, Baron (Michael):** unpopular Salopian who became a highly unpopular minister and included Patrick in his general contempt for Government Information Officers. In spite of which Patrick still believes he was 'the best Prime Minister we never had'.

**Hill, Anthony 'Horse':** music scholar who was removed from Shrewsbury School prematurely owing to the culture of bullying that prevailed in Patrick's house. Neighbour in Islington.

**Hill, Lord (Charles) of Luton:** Chairman of the BBC, formerly celebrated as the 'Radio Doctor', who endeared himself to Patrick and the staff at News Information when he paid a flying visit in the course of greeting over 23,000 employees.

**Hoge, Warren:** patrician American aristocrat who generously arranged for Patrick and Norman Davies (qv) to masquerade as students at Yale.

**Hollings, Nigel:** diminutive and somewhat excitable flatmate of Patrick's in London and Boston whose sudden accession to wealth proved of questionable benefit.

**Holyoake, Sir Keith:** affable Prime Minister of New Zealand for whom Patrick served as relief liftman and preserved the secret that he wore elevator shoes.

**Hook, Helen:** eccentric English headmistress with whom Patrick roomed in Wellington, sharing her delight in early New Zealand history until she was expelled by the landlady for misbehaviour at breakfast.

**Horst:** houseman at Emerald Lake Chalet in the Canadian Rockies who had been the youngest member of the *Hitler Jugend* at war's end and gave a distinct impression of still being wedded to its ideology.

**Howerd, Frankie:** tortured clown who unburdened himself to Patrick on

a late-night walk across London.

**Huffs, Brother:** Pentecostal pastor who worked with Patrick at Boston University Library and enticed him to a prayer-meeting in Catholic South Boston that was violently assailed by Patrick's co-religionists.

**Hughes, Philomena:** delightful Dublin lady at National Savings with a novel approach to negotiation ('This is the British Government you're talking to – do you think we're made of money?').

**Ingrams, PJ:** prefect at Shrewsbury, brother of *Private Eye* editor Richard, who persecuted junior boys. Became a prep school headmaster.

**Jacques, Mister:** choleric manager of the Palace Hotel in Perth, WA, who held Poms in low regard and Patrick lowest of all.

**Jeen, Bloody:** malevolent Dutch waiter who tyrannised the guests at the Hermitage Hotel in New Zealand's Southern Alps.

**Jelley, Max:** amiable cripple lad from Nottingham who made his own surgical boots and invited himself to tea with Prime Minister Desai in Delhi en route to the Hermitage Hotel in New Zealand's Southern Alps.

**Jelley, Suzanne:** mouselike sole teacher at the smallest school in New Zealand who was able to write an encomium to herself as the Miss Buss and Miss Beale of NZ's Southern Alps when she received an official letter addressed to 'The Headmistress' seeking a report on Miss Jelley.

**Jerry:** American missionary in British Honduras whom Patrick persuaded to fix a soccer game when Jerry's team faced certain defeat.

**Jesus:** hitman for a Mexican drug baron who stole Patrick's poker winnings in Durango, Durango.

**Jones, Eddie:** communist Chief Steward at the Hermitage Hotel in the Southern Alps of New Zealand who signed Patrick up for the union without the formality of telling him.

**Kasterine, Dmitri:** portrait photographer whose quest for a likeness of the father he never knew was unexpectedly solved through the agency of Patrick and Karla's Backnumbers props hire business.

**Keighley, Neil:** Shrewsbury boy who became the last victim of a savage ritual flogging known as 'postering', meted out on this occasion after he had been observed speaking to a girl from the High School.

**Kimberley, Michael:** one of the 'thick boys' at St Peter's, Weston-super-Mare, lacking any potential in the eyes of headmaster Geoffrey Tolson (qv), who went on to become a Professor of English Literature.

**Kimpton, Janet:** enchanting but distracted mother of John (qv) and pillar of the Chichester Diocesan Moral Welfare Committee who dressed in haute couture of the 1930s, could invite a roomful of guests and forget about it, and lived in a state of justifiable anxiety about her wayward children.

**Kimpton, John:** Patrick's HAC chum and flatmate, son of above, who was despatched to the colonies on a one-way ticket by a wicked uncle determined to see him fail (which he spectacularly failed to do).

**King, Martin Luther:** civil rights activist whose call to a telephone in an empty office at Studio Hamburg, answered by Karla as she walked past, would take her career in a new direction.

**Lachlan, The Lovely Lily:** receptionist at the Hermitage in New Zealand's Southern Alps with an impressive embonpoint and a mysterious past, widely believed by her fellow staff to have been no better than she should be – a rush to judgement not borne out by Patrick's experience of entertaining her in his bedroom late at night (they said the rosary together).

**Lamont, Norman:** Chancellor of the Exchequer for whom Patrick unwittingly performed a service by precipitating Britain out of the ERM.

**Lancaster, Captain:** ferocious Latin teacher at Patrick's Dotheboys Hall prep school who was immortalised by fellow Old Boy Roald Dahl in both his memoir *Boy* and his novel *Danny, the Champion of the World.*

**Lisa:** diminutive Australian model who saved the day for Patrick when 49 other models auditioning for a shoot in Sydney turned out to be over six-feet tall.

**Long, Sergeant:** barber who had spent his entire army career clipping hair on a base in the mid-West and retired to live on a meagre pension in the cheap rooming-house Patrick occupied in San Francisco.

**Lumsden, Norman:** jobbing actor whose career highlight was playing JR Hartley, author of *Fly-fishing*, and later fulfilled a lifetime ambition to play a golfer when he starred in one of Patrick's commercials.

**Maggie:** enchanting and gifted English girl, granddaughter of a hansom-cab driver, who resisted Patrick's romantic overtures but became his friend and mentor in Boston.

**Mangeshkar, Lata:** Bollywood backing singer whose sell-out performace at the Albert Hall involved Patrick as a reluctant participant.

**Marsters, William:** kanaka seaman from Palmerston Island aboard the ss *Waikema* who surprised Patrick by talking in Jacobean English with a broad Gloucestershire accent.

**Mary Lou:** self-styled Californian poet who hid out with Patrick in Holywood while he was on the run from the Feds.

**Mason, Mister:** Patrick's first boss who joined S.H. Benson Advertising in 1908 and, 50 years on, had attained the modest rank of proof-reader.

**Masters, Eddie:** ex-RAF pilot who recognised the sweater Patrick had borrowed from Sweet Jenny Hamnet (qv) and offered him a lift of 2,500 miles from Bechuanaland to Tanganyika.

**Matthews, Ray:** sweet-natured older man who introduced Patrick to the open, though persecuted, homosexual world of early 60s San Francisco.

**Maxwell, Robert:** villainous media baron whose display of overweening egotism was witnessed by Patrick and Karla at his 65th birthday party.

**McRae:, Jainey, Dowager Viscountess Bolingbroke:** Receptionist from Timaru at the Hermitage in New Zealand whose mother, once courted by an Old Etonian, suggested Jainey should seek one too. Despite a shortage of OEs in the land of sheep, she found and married Kenneth St John, later 7th Viscount Bolingbroke.

**McWhirter, Norris:** editor of *The Guinness Book of Records* who helped Patrick to achieve publication of his first book.

**Mendez, Hector:** Mexican bank clerk with whom Patrick stayed in Durango at the house of his father, proprietor of a small grocery. Despite their modest circumstances, the Mendez family employed five maids at the equivalent of a pound a week each.

**Moore, Roger:** Bond actor who proved he was indeed the nicest leading man in British films when Patrick brought him together with Miss Premium Bond Sandra Benson (qv) on the 007 set at Pinewood.

**Morrison, John 'Johnnie-the-Punk':** American Peace Corps worker who set out with Patrick to hitch-hike from the Cape to Cairo and was arrested for drug-running and being a communist after the first 12 miles.

**Mueller, Miss:** pillar of the Girls' Friendly Society and niece of concentration camp architect Hugh Rhind (qv) who warned her protégée Julia Singer (qv) against associating with Patrick.

**Murdoch, Rupert:** Australian media baron who failed to ingratiate himself with Patrick's fervently feminist account manager Mary Hargreaves (qv).

**Nairac, Robert:** handsome young officer who was usher at Patrick and Karla's wedding and confided to them that he was working undercover in Ireland. Shortly afterwards he was captured by the IRA and murdered.

**Nancy from Brighton:** co-worker of Patrick in Canada who caught up with him in New Zealand and worked at a progressive school in Auckland where the underfed children were covered in running sores.

**Nash, Sir Walter:** former Prime Minister of New Zealand and architect of the world's first welfare state. Lived up to his ideals in a modest two-front, two-back bungalow in the working class district of Petone, a true socialist who won Patrick's admiration, affection and respect.

**Nicholson, Dido:** beautiful ballet dancer with whom Patrick found himself in a compromising situation in a French nudist colony.

**Olson, Neal:** charming and erudite former US Marine sergeant turned Boston University librarian who recognized Patrick as a fraud but taught him enough of the rudiments of librarianship to hang on to his job.

**Pagnamenta, PJ:** languid boy of prodigious brainpower with whom Patrick and Nicholas Walker (qv) ran a company called Information Please at Shrewsbury School, with board meetings held during chapel.

**Pahlavi, Mohammad Reza:** Shah of Iran who introduced himself to Karla after the court chamberlain had deliberately omitted to present her.

**Pape, May:** double of Dame Edith Evans, both in looks and manner, who introduced Patrick to the anti-apartheid movement in Natal.

**Parker, Ma:** Patrick's idiosyncratic Jewish landlady in Boston who denounced Winston Churchill as a pervert who had once received an American woman journalist in his bath.

**Patterson, John:** eccentric Director of Savings who ran the Department much as he had run Epsom College as head boy.

**Peel, John:** Salopian who failed to distinguish himself at Shrewsbury but whom his housemaster Major Brooke (qv) predicted would make his mark, which he did as a hugely popular and idiosyncratic DJ.

**Peterson, Jack:** inadequate headmaster of Shrewsbury School.

**Peyton, John Baron Peyton of Yeovil:** Minister of Transport Industries whose brief to Patrick for a speech on Anglo-French co-operation was 'There is no such thing as Anglo-French co-operation.'

**Pizzey, Erin:** combative activist for battered women who surprised Patrick by her distaste for *bien pensant* metropolitan leftists.

**Plomley, Roy:** founder of *Desert Island Discs* and Patrick's favourite client at BBC News Information.

**Potter, Stephen:** originator of 'Gamesmanship' and 'Lifemanship' whose influence at the BBC and close friendship with the Head of Radio was insufficient to secure preferment for a non-graduate like Patrick.

**Purnell, Leslie and Leila:** South African cousins who entertained Patrick in Durban and introduced him to the strange world of apartheid.

**Pyke Nott, Mr and Mrs:** proprietors of the Crocodile Inn in Butha-Buthe, Basutoland, and dispensers of hospitality and good cheer, not always paid for, to Africans and ex-pats alike.

**Quarmby, David 'Quaggers':** advanced mathematician paid 6d a time to answer technical questions for Patrick's Information Please company that he ran at Shrewsbury School. Later performed much the same services for Patrick at the Ministry of Transport.

**Rahmé, Madame:** Tatler-reading Home Counties wife of Monsieur below who told Patrick to 'go chase a bear' and, to his dismay, meant it.

**Rahmé, Monsieur:** Lebanese manager of Emerald Lake Chalet in the Canadian Rockies who gave Patrick a job as a lavatory cleaner when he was on the run from the FBI and the Royal Canadian Mounted Police.

**Rantzen, Dame Esther:** client of Patrick's at BBC News Information in the 60s who would greet him as 'Duhl-l-ling!' with accompanying kisses on the nose and extravagant gestures of affection.

**Razhavi, Maryam:** Savak secret service operative detailed to keep tabs on Karla in Iran.

**Read, Sir Herbert:** eminent art historian and philosopher who came to Otago University in Dunedin and eschewed the usual flattering platitudes of visitors to New Zealand, telling Kiwis that they must come out from under Britain's shadow and find their place in the world.

**Rhind, Hugh:** engineer who built the first concentration camps during the Boer War. In Basutoland, 64 years later, he recounted to Patrick his version of events, unrecorded in histories of the conflict. Uncle of Miss Mueller (qv).

**Rhys-Jones, Iona:** erudite, articulate and beauteous upper-class Welsh girl who was a welcome addition to the group of eccentrics, misfits and inadequates who were employed in BBC News Information.

**Rickards, Maurice:** founder of the Ephemera Society, whom Patrick succeeded as Chairman.

**Robertson, James 'Beast':** Scottish boy who persecuted new boy Patrick at Shrewsbury, then was remorselessly and shamefully persecuted by Patrick in retribution.

**Rushdie, Salman:** controversial novelist who won the Booker Prize for *Midnight's Children* without availing himself of Patricks proffered input.

**Rushton, Willie:** cartoonist and comedian. As head of Patrick's house at Shrewsbury School he unilaterally abolished corporal punishment

**Rutherford, Peter:** genial maitre d' of the Hermitage in New Zealand and manager of an oyster house in Melbourne, where Patrick lived on an unvarying diet of oysters for three weeks following an injudicious investment at the Melbourne Cup.

**Sabu:** impeccably mannered Zulu 'houseboy' of Patrick's Purnell cousins (qv) of whom Uncle Harry Vernon (qv) disapproved because 'you can't trust Niggers who smile at you'.

**Sandford, The Reverend Commander Lord:** £8 a week curate who became a government minister on inheriting his peerage and whom Patrick accompanied on visits to gypsy encampments.

**Sarria, José:** cross-dressing performer at the Black Cat in San Francisco who became the first openly gay man to run for public office in America.

**Seymour, James 'Jimbo' Davenport:** scion of the illustrious New York theatrical family the Davenports who earned $4,000 a week while scripting classics like *42nd Street* for Paramount and £8 a week as Ambassador Joseph Kennedy's personal aide in London. Employed by Fred Brogger (qv) as a dialogue coach, he entertained a future US President at Karla's flat in South Audley Street.

**Seymour-Higgins, Capt. Alan:** former RAF pilot officer who crossed the Atlantic aboard the airship *Hindenburg* in 1936. A member of the Public Schools Club, he became one of Patrick's cross-generational friends and warned him against other elderly members, including Jack Cowper (qv), whom he characterised as 'a bunch of faggots'.

**Shaw, Frederic Charles:** publisher of *The Ladies Directory* convicted of the new crime of 'a conspiracy to corrupt public morals' after Patrick had inadvertently prompted Janet Kimpton (qv) to bring an action.

**Shipuis, Mrs:** Patrick's landlady in Dunedin, New Zealand, indefatigable dispenser of Welsh Rabbits to fellow Lithuanian exiles, all of who had been liberated by the Russians from Nazi concentration camps only to be incarcerated again in the *gulag*.

**Simon, André:** doyen of the wine trade and *bon viveur* who showed a marked reluctance to indulge at a banquet held in his honour in Perth.

**Sinatra, Frank:** legendry 'Voice' who had his goons throw Norman Davies (qv) out on to the sidewalk.

**Singer, Julia:** clever girl deprived of a university education by her chauvinist father who took humble employment in the Government Information Service and was Patrick's best chum at DoE, despite strenuous efforts by Miss Mueller (qv) to separate them.

**Small Doglike Person:** winsome Australian waitress at New Zealand's Hermitage who divided her affections between Patrick and his best mate Robin Gates (qv) but could not be dissuaded that all Poms are 'stuck-up'.

**Soros, George:** Hungarian-American billionaire who shorted sterling after Patrick introduced his infamous FIRST Option Bond, thereby causing Britain to crash out of the ERM. Known since as 'The Man who Broke the Bank of England' (Soros, not Patrick).

**Stan and Gloria:** colourful couple who had migrated from South London to Reading, Mass, and whose generous hospitality and engaging company made Patrick realise that only in America had he been able to make working-class English friends.

**Swan, Barbara:** chatelaine of Tweedie Hall, replica of English manor house in Natal, South African cultural icon and enchanting hostess.

**Surtee, Gany:** Indian trader at Butha-Buthe in Basutoland who introduced Patrick to *dagga* (marijuana) while they sheltered from one of the worst snowstorms ever to afflict southern Africa.

**Tattersall, David:** Melbourne law student and co-worker of Patrick's at Rayson Sheet Metal who avoided the more arduous and dangerous tasks in the factory by persuading the foreman that measurements should be made by differential calculus.

**Taylor, Elizabeth:** Hollywood diva who kept the Hickman-Robertson family awake on her wedding night at the Savoy Hotel.

**Taylor, Helen:** generous British Honduran lady who rescued Patrick from a bug-ridden flop-house in Belize.

**Tiretakane, Sir Eruera:** stately Maori MP and ally of Sir Walter Nash (qv). First Maori to appear on television (BBC 1936).

**Tocock, Jack:** Sancho Panza to Patrick's Don Quixote. Rode to the rescue at National Savings whenever Patrick created 'another nice mess'.

**Tolson, Geoffrey:** paranoid headmaster of St Peter's, Weston-super-Mare, who encouraged boys to denounce each other for imagined crimes.

**Tristram, Hugh:** charming Information Officer in Basutoland who showed Patrick the better, caring side of British colonialism.

**Vernon, Uncle Harry:** dreadful old rogue in Natal, much given to the N-world, who kept his 'boys' (adult servants) in order by throwing things at them and occasionally discharging firearms in their direction.

**Walker, David:** Illiterate thug and Patrick's fag-master at Shrewsbury. One of the most unpleasant people it has been his misfortune to meet.

·

**Walker, Peter:** Secretary of State for the Environment, under whom Patrick served as a press officer. One of the most unpleasant people (no relation of the above) it has been his misfortune to meet.

**Walker, Nicholas:** Yes, this entry is out of order, but otherwise it would not be possible to juxtapose the two horrible Walkers above. Nicholas, by contrast, is still the lovely person he was when he was Patrick's best friend at Shrewsbury.

**Watson, Miss:** acerbic Scotch housekeeper at Emerald Lake Chalet in the Canadian Rockies who took a dim view of colonials but proved susceptible to Patrick's unabashed flattery. (On the run, he could not risk losing his job as lavatory cleaner.)

**Waugh, Auberon and Alexander:** father and son literary critics who had an inexplicable lack of regard for Patrick's successive books of firsts.

**Whitehead, Jessie:** daughter of illustrious Cambridge and Harvard philosopher Alfred North Whitehead with whom Patrick would breakfast in Cambridge, Mass, and listen enthralled by her evocation of pre-WWI Cambridge, England, and her unrequited passion for Rupert Brooke.

**William of Gloucester, Prince:** friend of Patrick's flat-mate Bob Erith (qv) who, over dinner, sustained an earnest conversation about antidisestablishmentarianism from the soup to the cheese.

**Williams, Ethel:** headmistress of Durban Ladies' Collegiate who bit Cecil John Rhodes. (Not when she was headmistress.)

**Williams, John:** world's highest earning composer, with a net worth of over $100 million. Persuaded Karla to relocate to England 'because the pubs have cut-glass windows'.

**Willemsen, Paul and Lucy:** Patrick's Dutch landlord and his Maltese wife with whom he lived in a shack on the edge of the Australian outback that had no books but the Bible and an outside 'dunny'.

**Winner, Michael:** idiosyncratic movie director who enjoyed driving hard bargains with Patrick and Karla while swilling their best claret.

**X, Malcolm:** Islamist revolutionary, dedicated to the overthrow of the US government, whom Patrick met in Cairo shortly before he was assassinated by co-religionists.

*The Inspector stared at me long and hard, as if trying to penetrate where I had hidden the loot.* p304

# Misspent Youth

# I

# Chapter 1

. . .

# SON OF THE SUBURBS

. . .

*1940–48*

Let's begin at the beginning, in a corner of provincial England where lies a cathedral city, Gloucester, and its leafy suburb of Tuffley in which I grew up. A quiet, leafy suburb? No, not in 1940 with long lines of tanks thundering down the Stroud Road and leaving their chain-link tracks embedded in the tarmac, and the huge formations of German bombers flying overhead on their way to bomb Bristol. Any bombs still in their bomb bays would be released over Gloucester on the return journey.

Father, a dental surgeon, was serving with the RAF in that capacity. And I was already a name at RAF High Ercall in Shropshire – not as Patrick, but as Horace. 'How is Horace getting on?' brave bomber pilots would greet my father. 'Has he spoken yet?' Horace, I should explain, was a character in the popular BBC Light Programme comedy *ITMA* who never spoke. And nor did I. Not even when I was four years of age. Naturally this caused my dear parents grave concern, however much it may have enlivened the mess at RAF High Ercall. Eventually they took me to a speech therapist. According to my elder brother Tim, who never told a lie in his life so it must be true, the specialist said that I would require an operation on my tongue, at which I immediately began jabbering nineteen to the dozen.

3

This protracted silence may have been an early intimation that not everything was going to be the same uninterrupted chronicle of cognitive success as it was in my brother Tim's life. But until I entered the competitive world of prep school, there was little to show that I differed from other kindergarten children. – except in one respect. It is said that at the age of four the great classicist and theologian Monsignor Ronald Knox would lie awake at night and think about the past. My own preoccupation with the past, which was to remain an enduring one, began at about the same age. My father's father lived with us at the family home, Wessenden, in a bedroom that he had occupied since at least the 1890s (he was born in 1866). Nothing in this room had been altered in that time other than the installation of electric light.

For the infant Patrick, entering this room was a passage into the past. And rummaging in his drawers, which grandfather did not seem to mind at all, would reveal further evidences of the past as a foreign country: wing collars, cut-throat razors and shaving mugs, pungent smelling salts, half-hunter watches, Lucifer matches, pasteboard pill boxes – some containing pills from another century – bandanna handkerchiefs, patent medicine bottles for elixirs long since outlawed, faded photographs of gentlemen in toppers and ladies with bustles, yellowing newspaper cuttings announcing engagements or weddings of people long dead, gold-rimmed half-moon spectacles, cuff protectors, tapers for lighting gas lamps, packets of lozenges bearing images of medals won at the great international exhibitions of the later nineteenth century... Even to my then unformed mind, these mundane but alien objects, and the environment in which they had been preserved, evoked the sense of a time that differed from that in which I was growing up. It also made me aware of the process of change, here represented within the small, enclosed world of family, but, as I gradually became better informed about how things used to be, also of change within a wider world.

This growing knowledge was enhanced by my daily walks with Grandfather. These were slow and stately, as befitted a Victorian gentleman now in the evening of his years. Since Grandfather had lived all his life in Gloucester, he knew most of its leading citizens, or at least those over a certain age. These we would encounter on our walks, and after much doffing of hats and formal handshakes, reminiscences would often be exchanged. To these I would listen attentively and cross question

*Great Aunt Emily was blind and Great Aunt Hyssett was senile.*
*Emily would ask if the Boy would like to see the photograph albums ...*

Grandfather afterwards about that quieter, statelier cathedral city of his and their youth. Grandfather was never less than forthcoming. The immediate post-war world was not one much to his liking. He preferred dwelling on the past and I think he enjoyed his appreciative audience, albeit one with the limited understanding of a six- or seven-year old

From time to time our walks took us to the semi-detached, red stucco villa of spinster sisters Great Aunt Emily and Great Aunt Hyssett that lay in the lea of Robinswood Hill. Emily was blind and Hyssett was senile, the former looking after her sister with the devotion and skill one might lavish on a much-loved but wayward child, her own affliction entirely unacknowledged. The interior of the house was, like Grandfather's bedroom, a portal on the past, none of its furnishings dating from after the turn of the century. It was, indeed, an even more perfect time capsule than Grandfather's eyrie, because the gas lighting had never been replaced. I was enraptured. After a substantial tea of home-made rock cakes and delicate triangular cucumber sandwiches, Emily would invariably ask whether the Boy would like to see the photograph albums. The Boy was always eager for this treat. As her wizened old hands turned the pages, Grandfather snoozed, and Hyssett rocked herself back and forth on the green-plush sofa singing some ditty of long ago in her reedy voice, Emily would recall the exact composition of each sepia-toned photograph, who was sitting next to whom, and the nature of the occasion that was commemorated in this way. None of those good Gloucester folk depicted was still alive other than those now present at the tea-table and, in the later volumes, the small boy in a sailor suit on an old-fashioned tricycle who was my father. Each character was evoked by Emily with deft touches of personality or amusing tales of eccentric manners or behaviour. The loss of her sight seemed to have been compensated for in Emily by perfect recall, a day's doings of sixty or seventy years earlier – she was older than my grandfather and her earliest memories extended back to the 1850s – being conjured up as if she was speaking of the events of last week. The Boy, her great nephew, born as *Blitzkrieg* and terror were changing for ever the world in which Emily was nurtured, feasted on these nuggets from a memory unimpaired.

This passion for the past was further developed at my prep school. The so-called 'School Library' was no more than a couple of shelves containing stirring novels of the Empire-building genre typified by boys' fiction writers GA Henty, RM Ballantyne and Mayne Reid, none dating from later than World War I. It also contained a dozen or so volumes of *The Strand Magazine* from the 1890s. *The Strand* is principally remembered today for its publication of the original Sherlock Holmes stories before they appeared as books, but it was also a window on the world way beyond Baker Street. Its imaginative use of the new halftone process of photography in the monthly 'Illustrated Interview', its stories by most of the leading writers of the day, and in-depth articles on such widespread topics as 'Life in a Military Prison', 'Saving the Lives of New-born Babies with Incubators', 'The Manufacture of Christmas Crackers' or 'The New Fashion for Alpine Sports' presented a rounded view of life during one of the most transformative decades in history – the decade that gave us automobiles, moving pictures, X-rays, wireless, the Olympic Games and the first wave of feminism. All these innovations were recorded and analysed in its pages, the perusal of which engendered in me a perspective of history quite different from the dull recital of the dates of kings and queens and battles and constitutional developments that was the classroom approach to the discipline. The information that I derived from *The Strand* encouraged me to ponder, albeit not in these words, 'What preceded this custom or practice? What followed it?'

But I have jumped ahead in this story. It is time to introduce you to the Dotheboys Hall of the sunny south-west.

# Chapter 2

. . .

# SHADES OF THE PRISON HOUSE

. . .

*1948–53*

'You go to school in Weston-super-Mare?' friends of my parents would ejaculate in the hearty voices reserved by adults for addressing the under-aged. 'What a lovely time you must have playing on the beach!'

We were not taken to the beach once during the five-year sentence I served at St Peter's, Weston-super-Mare. Our only excursions outside the not very extensive grounds of the school were the Sunday walks in crocodile to the Cabbage Patch, a destination as enticing as its name.

The school was presided over by its proprietor, Geoffrey Tolson, a tall, broad, bull-necked, bald-pated man of ferocious demeanour with massive arms strengthened by frequent exercise of the cane. Like many prep school headmasters, Tolson was a fanatical sportsman. Ability on the games field was the principal measure of a boy's worth. Academic achievement came quite a long way second. Few other accomplishments, or qualities of character, were rated at all. If you could kick a football in the direction of goal you prospered at St Peter's. If not, you languished. I was amongst the latter, with an inability on the playing field that was in no way mitigated by performance in the classroom. I could not grasp even the basic principles of Latin, French or mathematics. Other subjects scarcely counted.

I was not alone in being despised by Mister Tolson. My best friend Michael Kimberley was held in equal opprobrium, while second-best mates Christopher Charlton and Ian Frampton were held in barely higher esteem. The fifth member of our group, a tall rangy boy called 'Cheese' Cleese, was however an exception. For reasons that have never been apparent to me, he was exempted from Tolson's disdain, even though his sporting prowess was scarcely superior to those of us four pariahs. He could, however, bowl a useful leg break and prodigious height – he was six-feet tall at the age of 12 – could be a dominating factor in every sense when playing against boys a foot shorter. The fact that he was an extremely funny boy was what endeared him to the rest of the gang. Tolson did not do funny, so the mystery of his regard remains. Equally mysterious to me is John Cleese's regard for Tolson, unsuspected until I read *So, Anyway*, the memoir of his life as *Monty Python*. He even went back to teach at St Peter's for a couple of terms after he had left his public school, Clifton.

I met Cheese again at a '50 Years On' St Peter's reunion. (Another interesting thing his memoir revealed was that Cheese is actually his ancestral name – his grandfather had changed it by deed poll because it sounded comic.) He had recently been on the BBC's *Desert Island Discs* programme and he had described in a voice of anguish how he had been unmercifully bullied because of his towering height. I challenged him about this, saying that I could not remember his ever being bullied. To the contrary, he was the most popular boy in the school because he kept us in fits of laughter in a place where there wasn't much else to laugh at. Cheese hung his head and looked sheepish. 'Oh dear,' he said, 'I've been caught out. Yes, I made it up. This is terribly embarrassing to admit, but it's what is expected from celebrities. It is absolutely *de rigueur* to have had a miserable childhood. If you cannot claim more pronounced forms of abuse, it has to be bullying. I'm ashamed. I won't pretend this again.' Disarming chap, that Cheese Cleese.

. . .

Prep school masters in the post-war 1940s were a fairly undistinguished bunch, comprising mainly ex-officers who had failed to make the grade in civvy street. Headmasters like Mister Tolson looked for games-players first, academics second. Some clearly had personality disorders and every prep school seems to have had its resident paedophile. Ours was the Reverend Mister Dolman, a fat, squat, bullet-headed embodiment of the sausage-fingered German excoriated in First World War *Punch* cartoons. He had large black warts on his spreading neck, from which wiry hairs sprouted. The principal object of the Reverend's attentions was a good-looking boy called David Smith, who did nothing, I should hasten to add, to encourage them. It is a peculiarity of the *mores* of the time that Mister Dolman made no attempt to disguise his proclivities. He would come into the assembly room on a Sunday evening, one of the few times we were allowed any time for personal activities, bearing a large box of chocolates on which he must have expended several weeks' sweet-ration coupons. Approaching the matron in charge, he would greet her with a beaming smile, revealing a row of blackened teeth interspersed with gleaming gold. If the matron thought that she was to be offered a chocolate, she was soon disabused. 'Ach, Miss Findlater,' he would gush. 'I hef ein favour to ask you. May I offer one of these exquisite Swiss chocolates to David Smith?' Poor David Smith would be cringing in a corner, but was forced to consume the treat while his schoolmates stood around smirking, and then expected to make an extravagant speech of gratitude. Dolman's small piggy eyes were screwed up in ecstasy.

There was an occasion when my parents were visiting and my mother was approached by another parent, a Mrs Barton, in the lounge of the Grand Atlantic Hotel. 'Oh, Mrs Hickman-Robertson,' she wailed, 'I am so worried about Peter. May I talk to you about it?' I effaced myself behind a large potted fern. Peter Barton was an exceedingly pretty boy with a shock of blond hair and eyes of the deepest blue. This promised to be interesting. It was. The Reverend Mister Dolman had invited Peter to accompany him to the ballet in London during the holidays. The expedition would involve an overnight stay, alone with Mr Dolman. Mrs Barton was in a quandary. Mister Dolman had said he was flexible about dates, so she was unable to claim that the family would be otherwise engaged. How could she refuse without causing offence? And what reason could she give for the refusal? My mother tut-tutted, but was unable to come up with a ruse that would rescue Peter from his peril. The two mothers wrung their hands in despair. In the end Peter went to the ballet and did not return to the school

*The principal object of the Reverend Mister Dolman's*
*attentions was a good-looking boy called David Smith.*

traumatised, so it is probably safe to conclude that Mister Dolman had reined in his passions sufficiently to preserve Peter's modesty.

It is not hard to share Mrs Barton's anxiety, but in this present age when paedophiles are reviled above every other transgressor, it perhaps behoves us to bear in mind that very many of these sad and lonely men, afflicted with the one abnormality that attracts not the slightest trace of compassion or understanding, would never ever lay a hand on the objects of their transient affection. Most public school alumni recall a number of bachelor masters who tended to linger rather longer than necessary in the changing rooms after games, but none within my experience has ever been victim of a predatory schoolmaster. At Shrewsbury School there was a scandal that made the front page of the *News of the World* when a master was caught *in flagrante* with an under-age boy from the town in a public park. The master went to prison. But if any boy of the school had been as much as groped, I am sure we would have learned about it. There are few secrets within the enclosed world of the boarding school. (Revelations of systematic abuse at Ampleforth and Downside, as well as allegations about other schools, signify that there have been, and may still be, predatory masters engaged in such activity at boarding schools. While this is deplorable, I do not believe it is characteristic of the sector as a whole.)

. . .

No David Smith or Peter Barton myself, I was unlikely to attract the attention of boy-lovers. I was, however, victimised in another way by a master whose ferocity has been enshrined in literature. In his evocative memoir *Boy*, Roald Dahl, who had also served a five-year stretch at St Peter's in the 1920s, devotes a whole chapter to the choleric Captain Lancaster – 'Capio' to masters and boys alike. His outbursts of fury by no means moderated in the intervening twenty-five years, this veteran of the Western Front taught Latin, a subject he seemed to believe could only be inculcated into the dim-witted by terror. Even this tactic failed in the case of his most retarded pupil. My inability to learn Latin was total and had nothing to do with idleness or recalcitrance. I simply could not grasp the grammatical structure of the language, nor could I learn anything by rote, including vocabulary – possibly why it took me so long to learn to speak my own language. Captain Lancaster's remedy for my constant errors in translation and parsing was to pile upon me impositions, sometimes several in the course of a lesson. These were soul-destroying slabs of Latin text that had to be transcribed in one's own time. The problem was that we had very little time of our own. We played cricket or football eight times a week, including twice on Wednesdays and Saturdays. Evenings were devoted to prep. Break-times were too short to complete more than a few lines of an imposition. Sundays were spent on our knees, walking to the Cabbage Patch in crocodile, or in writing censored letters home. Consequently the backlog of uncompleted impositions grew inexorably. Soon there was no way I would ever be able to clear this constantly mounting load. At the age of ten I was burdened with levels of stress that few adults suffer before middle age brings its domestic or occupational crises.

Why didn't I tell anyone about it, I hear you say. Tell whom? Not Mister Tolson, who regarded me as idle and recalcitrant. Nor Mrs Tolson, a chilly personality who was the double of Mrs Wallis Simpson. I would not have confided in the Reverend Mister Dolman, who might have seized the opportunity for a quick grope even of one of such limited physical attributes. Certainly not the school doctor, Dr 'Awful' Alford, with his snarled 'Box on!' to cowering snivelling children during blood-bespattered bouts in the gymnasium. Matron? Miss Findlater was a kindly soul, but her authority scarcely extended beyond cough syrup and clean underwear. My parents? They had been assured by Tolson that I was a lazy and rebellious boy in need of stern measures. No, there was no refuge from emotional abuse at St Peter's.

So what to do? The only remedy that presented itself was escape.

It so happened that I had returned to school a few days late for the autumn term of 1950 owing to some childhood complaint and I had not turned over my 30 shillings termly pocket money to the headmaster. The one occasion of the week that I left the school grounds unaccompanied was for a midday Wednesday elocution lesson at a private house a few minutes' walk from the school. On the return journey I stopped at the crossroads. In one direction was the school. In the other lay the high road to Bristol. Which should I take? If I took the easier choice, I would soon confront the prospect of Captain Lancaster demanding delivery of the backlog of impositions in full. That delivery was impossible to fulfil. I turned my face towards Bristol.

I suppose the fact that I was carrying the exercise book in which I wrote notes of my elocution lessons afforded some kind of specious cover – it looked as if this small boy was heading somewhere with a legitimate purpose. Once I was outside Weston-super-Mare I began to thumb rides, fully aware that the next car that stopped might be driven by Tolson or some other pursuer from the school. I also kept a wary eye out for police cars. I got a couple of lifts, explaining to the drivers that I had been into Weston for an elocution lesson and missed the bus back. After a few miles I would need to identify a house that looked as if it might be the home of this prepubescent middle-class child. Once I was eight or nine miles out from the town, I decided that this cover story would begin to look improbable, so I resolved to walk the rest of the way. I marched on for the next fifteen miles or so. When I arrived at the outer suburbs of Bristol dusk was gathering. There were now bus stops, so I waited for the next bus into the city. By this time I was exhausted as well as hungry, frightened and cold, and had yet to reach any conclusion as to what I should do when I got there.

In the centre of Bristol I looked for a café and ordered a meal while I thought the matter through. It was growing late and a ten-year-old child wandering about on his own in the dark was going to attract attention. There really seemed to be no choice except to head for Gloucester and home. I did not expect the most cordial of welcomes.

I caught the late night bus to Gloucester, which dropped me in King's Square shortly before midnight. I then had a three-mile walk home. It says something about provincial towns in 1950 that the streets were totally deserted. No one stopped me to ask what a child was doing alone at this time of night. It had not occurred to me that my parents might not be at Wessenden. Not surprisingly they were now in Weston-super-Mare, but it so happened that my mother had an upholsterer lady staying in the house for a few days. She admitted me, put me to bed, and presumably telephoned the school.

My mother's greeting in the morning was no warmer than expected. Why should it be? I had caused her and my father immense anxiety and distress and they had no knowledge whether this latest exploit of their troublesome child was some kind of prank or whether it had a more cogent reason. It took me a long time before I could explain myself and when I did so it was on paper rather than orally. I am not sure that even then my parents understood my dilemma. From their standpoint I was a difficult pupil who would not learn his Latin and had been justly punished for it. What was my problem? Why could I not be more like my elder brother Tim, who was never in trouble at school and shone in Latin class?

I suppose that nowadays in similar circumstances I would simply have been withdrawn from St Peter's and either sent to a day school or to another, rather more humane, boarding prep. There were a few such schools, even in 1950, but they tended to be labelled as 'progressive' and my parents abhorred anything that they considered unconventional. It was explained to me that I was clearly unsuited to boarding-school education, but that all middle class children had to go away to school and there really wasn't any choice in the matter. If they sent me to a different school, I would hate it just as much. So I would have to make the best of it, as other boys did. Boys like Tim. Would I like a glass of milk and a bourbon biscuit?

I am aware that this account of my parents' reaction may make them seem callous. They weren't. They were loving parents who did what they thought was best for their children. But as I have said, they adhered to the conventional as to a religious rite, as did most provincial middle-class professional people in the stifling, closeted atmosphere of post-war Britain. My brother Tim accepted these conventions, but was a warm, engaging human being who thoroughly deserved the laurels that he won so effortlessly. I did not, and if I had any redeeming traits, they were not readily apparent to the adult eye.

I was not sent back to the school immediately. I was dispatched instead to my Aunt Lillian, my mother's elder sister, in Coventry. Married to a doctor, but having no children of her own, she was prepared to cherish her nephews indiscriminately, even the one who upset everybody so much. But after a fortnight of her tender loving care, it was time to return to St Peter's and once again confront my nemeses Mister Tolson and Captain Lancaster.

The interview with the headmaster was protracted and contained naught for my comfort. I was made fully aware of my every failing as a schoolboy and as a human being. Mister Tolson mentioned, as if citing the views of a higher authority, that the school servants were of the opinion that I should be flogged to within an inch of my life. It occurred to even my unformed, ten-year old mind that there was something singularly undignified about a headmaster who harkened to the tittle-tattle of servants for guidance on the maintenance of discipline. Happily I did not express this thought, or the servants' recommendation would surely have been fulfilled. That it was not, considering Tolson's readiness to reach for his cane, may have been simply that he was not prepared to court the risk of my doing another runner, which might reflect unfavourably on his stewardship of the school. Alternatively it could be that the quality of mercy had not been wholly extinguished in his dispensing of justice. Cheese Cleese would probably embrace this more charitable view.

I was scrupulous in delivering the full backlog of Latin impositions to Captain Lancaster, lest he should think that my escape had been motivated by no more than avoidance of an irksome task. I must acknowledge that he had the grace to look highly embarrassed. Not only that, but he welcomed me back to the school. (Not words that had been included in my conversation with Mister Tolson.) In the years that followed, my relationship with 'Capio' was to prosper. While his manner in class was never less than intimidating, a style of teaching not unusual amongst his peers, out of class he displayed a more winning side of his personality. He had a passion for natural history and from time to time he would take Michael Kimberley and me for walks in the woods behind the school, imparting to us much wisdom about their flora and fauna with an infectious enthusiasm. Looking back I think he must have been genuinely bewildered when Tolson broke it to him that his behaviour in class had been the cause of my flight. Or perhaps I am wrong. Maybe he was not so uncomprehending. Had he come to a realisation of the despair his unconsidered actions had instilled in this unhappy child and now sought to make restitution? I prefer to think so. And I am sorry for the distress I must have caused you, Capio.

· · ·

It is tempting to suppose that all prep-school masters had flawed personalities. There were exceptions. Despite their lowly status by comparison with their public school peers, and the niggardly salary they earned and the meagre prospects for promotion, many, perhaps even most, prep schools could boast of at least one master of distinctive ability. At St Peter's he was the Senior Master.

Some years ago there was a memorable television commercial for teacher recruitment that paraded before the camera a line-up of celebrities, culminating in the Prime Minister Tony Blair himself, each of whom spoke the name of a teacher who had widened their horizons or, in some cases, transformed their lives. Tony Blair named Eric Anderson, his inspirational headmaster at Fettes (later headmaster of Shrewsbury and Eton) and he was followed by the last person to appear, a fifteen-year-old black student from a 'bog standard' comp who looked shyly at the camera and whispered 'Miss Dempsey'. Rather surprisingly, out of the roster of eight or nine teachers named, I had known or encountered no fewer than three. I had been introduced to Eric Anderson by Shrewsbury's former Head of History, Michael Hart (of whom more in the following chapter). My schoolfellow the late lamented BBC disc jockey John Peel nominated Major Brooke, his housemaster and my fifth-form master at Shrewsbury. And I am relieved to say that Cheese Cleese did not award his palm to Mister Tolson. Instead he paid tribute to the Senior Master of St Peter's, Geoffrey Bartlett. (It seems to have excited little or no comment at the time that the role models featured in this highly successful and much discussed commercial, which was intended for the recruitment of teachers for state schools, came principally from the independent sector. Apart, of course, from that paragon amongst pedagogues, Miss Dempsey. Rod Liddle must have hated it.)

Geoffrey Bartlett was tall, tanned and ruggedly handsome. He looked like one of those Empire builders, pipes clenched between strong jaws beneath noble brows, that used to adorn the advertisements for Barney's Tobacco in *Wide World* magazine. He was also erudite, exquisitely courteous, and the cynosure of every woman's eyes. We lower-school brats used to speculate about a secret romance between Mister Bartlett and Matron, Miss Findlater, and would devise increasingly ludicrous stratagems to engineer accidental encounters. No such romance, nor to the best of my knowledge any other, ever came to pass in Geoffrey Bartlett's seemingly celibate life.

Cleese devotes a not inconsiderable portion of the early part of his memoir to his hero-worship of Geoffrey Bartlett when he, John, having returned as the most junior temporary master at St Peter's, was mentored by this august and saintly figure. What Cleese fails to put his finger on, and which I would dearly like to be able to discuss with him, is where did Geoffrey Bartlett come from, what was his back story, and why was he content to place his considerable talents at the disposal of this Dotheboys Hall at a salary that I doubt ever exceeded about £10 a week (John received £5). He was a figure of mystery to us all and remains so for me.

I never knew Mister Bartlett as well as did Cleese, but he was my mathematics master. As I have explained, the three most important subects at St Peter's were Latin, French and maths, and the three subects in which I was most woefully wanting were Latin, French and maths. In all three I was bottom of the class.

I have also mentioned how I was regarded as incorrigibly idle, a reputation that dogged me throughout my time at St Peter's and was to follow me to Shrewsbury.

One morning as we laboured over quadratic equations, Mister Bartlett banged the desk with his board rubber and declared despairingly 'You are a wretched bunch of boys. I do not know why I waste my time with you. None of you has the slightest grasp of the basic principles I am trying to drive into your thick heads. You don't even try. None of you!' Then he paused, and in a quieter, more temperate voice, added 'Except one.'

'Who's that, Sir?' came a chorus of childish trebles. 'Is it Sweeney, Sir?' Sweeney was head of the class. No, replied Mister Bartlett. 'Oh, Sir, is it Charlton?' Charlton was second. 'Is it Thompson minor, Sir, or Dibble, or Kimberley?' No, no, no. After the names of half the class had been proposed and rejected, Mister Bartlett held up his hand for silence. 'Enough, boys. Get on with your work.' As heads were bowed over books, Mister Bartlett stared out of the window across the playing fields, and murmured sotto voce, 'And it couldn't possibly be Hickman-Robertson ... could it?'

Unfortunately for my scholastic prospects, Geoffrey Bartlett was the only master at St Peter's who knew I wasn't idle.

* * *

The school grounds contained about five acres of playing fields, a school yard, an outdoor swimming pool, hard tennis court and gymnasium, kitchen gardens, and a wild area known as 'The Fort'. This latter was at the rear of the school, on a steep slope. It was in fact the remains of an old road, raised over the shrubbery beneath on a 12ft-high stone terrace. Behind it was the boundary wall of the school, about 15ft high, rising to a new road that ran parallel to the old. The effect was of medieval ramparts and together with the wild entanglement of the shrubbery made an ideal setting for simulated battles and other adventurous games.

So far my account of St Peter's has been bleak, but I must concede that there were a few diversions on which I look back with unalloyed pleasure. One was the termly debate, with the motion selected by the boys. Another was the monthly film show, which consisted of films of the 1910s and 1920s, since the school had yet to acquire a talkie projector. These nurtured my passion for the recent past. Then there was the end-of-term feast, during which we were allowed to make as much noise as we liked and were regaled with delicacies that must have provided Mrs Phillips, the cook, with her sternest challenge in those days of even stricter rationing than during the war. I particularly relished Russian salad on bridge rolls. But the best fun of all was the release from supervision that Kimberley, Charlton, Frampton, Cleese and I enjoyed while we rampaged through the shrubbery, built dens, and fought rival gangs for control of the Fort.

Amongst the Fort's several delights must be numbered relief from hunger. Let me paint the background to this. Apart from the end-of-term feast, the food at St Peter's was almost invariably disgusting. I say almost, because I must except some of the breakfasts. Although the porridge was horrible, full of congealed lumps that cleaved to the roof of the mouth (and nothing was allowed to be discarded), the cooked item that followed was often highly enticing, usually involving fried bread made with very thick slices fried golden in beef dripping. The topping might be baked beans, bacon, or tomatoes. Even without the topping, these half-rounds of fried bread were utterly delicious spread with marmalade. If I ever have to face a firing squad, that will be my choice of final repast. But generally the food was uneatable, not only because of the exigencies of rationing, but because no effort was made to render it appetising. The fact that there was very little of it was to do with the meagre rations, but the attitude was that we were small boys who deserved nothing better and that short commons was character-building. I should add that Mrs Phillips had an mass of unruly and unwashed hair. Nobody thought to require her to pin it up or wear a cap, and on most days one boy or other would find wisps of it adorning his plate.

So we boys were perpetually hungry. Ravenous. We used to raid the kitchen garden for raw vegetables, notwithstanding that detection would result in painful contact with Mister Tolson's whippy cane. I once came across half a pound of sugar in a bag – I cannot remember the circumstances – and took it to the latrines for a secret feast, gorging the whole mouthful by crunchy mouthful. I was later very sick. On another occasion my mother was sent two half-pound packs of Lurpak butter from a cousin in Denmark and sent me one of them. It was intercepted by the school authorities and shared out between everyone on my table in the dining room. That afforded us a dab each, just enough to excite the appetite but not enough to satisfy it. But I suppose it was fair.

It happened that Ian Frampton had an aunt in the town, a singularly generous aunt who understood and sympathised with our plight. She must also have had access to the black market or some other source of illicit goods, because every week or so she made up a parcel of sufficient goodies to give all the members of our gang one glorious feed. From the upper road above the Fort, Aunt Gladys could reach the branch of a tree growing on the Old Road below. A string was kept permanently suspended from the branch and the parcel of comestibles attached to the end, then lowered to the Old Road. And what comestibles! There were ham sandwiches (or 'sangwidges' in our parlance) and jam ditto and hard-boiled eggs and KitKat chocolate wafers and bloater paste and sardines and iced buns and Rowntrees Fruit Pastilles and hazelnuts and custard tarts. And on one memorable occasion, half a Fuller's Walnut Cake. How did Aunt Gladys communicate with us when a parcel was ready for collection? This was of course essential, lest other gangs got there before us. She would hang a scarlet ribbon from the branch the previous day and we would know that the parcel would be hanging over the Old Road by next day's break-time.

· · ·

All this bounty terminated when Mister Tolson announced one day, without preamble, that the Fort and the shrubbery were out of bounds. This was the first intimation, though we had no inkling of it at the time, of the headmaster's incipient paranoia. Over the next few weeks other announcements followed, shutting down access to various parts of the grounds piece by piece. The purpose of this curtailment of what little liberty we enjoyed became apparent when everywhere other than the School Yard had been placed under prohibition. The School Yard was a concrete square, about 100ft by 100ft, surrounded by a tall chain-link fence. Here the only activity that had official approval was football played with a tennis ball in the winter months and cricket played with a tennis ball in the summer months. Neither was compulsory, but the only alternative was to stand on the sidelines making desultory conversation with one's mates. On Sundays we all stood around aimlessly, because ball games were banned on the Holy Day. Here in the School Yard, for three months at a time, a hundred energetic children were confined. The only outdoor alternatives were daily organised games and the weekly walk to the Cabbage Patch.

A master was stationed outside the chain-link fence, surveying the scene. He was there for a purpose and it was not health and safety. It was to monitor our conversation. This was revealed when Mister Tolson called the whole school together and told us that there was a deep moral malaise in the school, an evil that he was determined to stamp out.

Most schools have their moral malaises, most often in the form of furtive sexual activity or outbreaks of bullying. Another was stealing, though this was generally perpetrated by a single boy and was often a cry for help. Our particular turpitude, we were informed, was bad language.

I had never actually heard another boy use bad language, and when I conferred with Kimberley, Frampton, Charlton and Cleese, neither had they. But surely, we reasoned, the headmaster would not have made a speech about it had he not had the evidence. Perhaps, we concluded, we simply did not recognise the bad words when they were spoken.

In an age when four-letter words are used so freely in print and on television, it may seem hard for younger people to understand how sheltered we were from obscenities and profanities. But they were not used in the home, certainly not nice middle-class homes anyway, nor anywhere in public, except perhaps by servicemen and by those who in those days our parents castigated as 'street-children'. ('Take that sweet out of your mouth, Patrick. You are not a street-child.')

A week later the school was summoned again. The evil was growing worse, the headmaster intoned sonorously. It had to be nipped in the bud or it would spread throughout the school. He was looking to every boy for support in this great endeavour. If we were prepared to back him, we could help to save the school from depravity.

There was a long pause while Mister Tolson stared out of the window over his beloved playing fields and seemed uncertain how to continue. Then he turned to us and lowered his voice as he made this appeal to our better natures. He was fully aware, he said, of the long-held convention that no boy would ever peach on another. He understood it and accepted it, when it came to ordinary schoolboy mischief. But this was something altogether more serious. This was something that imperilled the school. His voice rose again. This could imperil our very souls!

So he was asking us to set aside this outdated shibboleth. We had a choice and the choice he wanted us to make was to do the right thing. Whenever we heard another boy say a wicked word, we were to come and see him. He would guarantee total confidence. We were not to think of it as breaking the schoolboy code. That only applied to the kind of petty rule-breaking that had no consequences. On the contrary, we would be doing a noble thing. We would be saving those foul-mouthed wrongdoers from themselves. And we would be saving the school.

This was pretty heady stuff. The gang debated the issue long and hard. Should we do this thing for the sake of the school? The fact that the school had done so little to earn our loyalty did not enter into our deliberations. We were more concerned with the practical aspect. How would we recognise the foul words if we heard them? Perhaps, to be on the safe side, we should report any words that we had not heard before. 'Like shibboleth?' enquired Kimberley. 'That can't be a rude word', rejoined Charlton. 'Mister Tolson used it.' 'Yes, but if we heard a boy use a word we don't recognise, should we report it?' persisted Kimberley. 'Yes,' declared Charlton decisively. 'The headmaster will know if it is a foul word, and he would rather we got it a bit wrong than fail to catch an evil-doer.' Cleese looked doubtful.

On the third occasion that Mister Tolson addressed us on the suppression of evil, his mood had switched from sorrow to anger. Not one single boy had been to see him to report another boy. Yet he knew that sin was all around us, so we must have all agreed together to defy his wishes. We were sticking to the old schoolboy code. Didn't we know that was what prisoners in gaols did? We were middle-class boys. It was our duty to our parents, to the school, and to the great Empire of which we were all so proud, to do as he had instructed us. He was ashamed to call himself headmaster of such a school. There would be no tuck this week, he thundered, and unless we changed our ways the end-of-term feast would be cancelled.

Things were getting serious, the gang agreed. Here was all this foul language being noised abroad, and none of us five had heard it. The evil-doers must be pretty clever to keep their sins so secret. Maybe they only used the foul words to each other, when no one else was within hearing.

'Perhaps Mister Tolson should hire a detective,' suggested Frampton.

'That would be no good,' rejoined Kimberley. 'He would be a grown-up and the evil-doers wouldn't do their evil when he was about.'

While we pondered on these wise words, Charlton spoke up. 'Why don't we all go to Mister Tolson's aid? We could be his detectives. How about it, fellows?'

But for once the gang was not all of a mind. Neither Cleese nor Kimberley wanted to turn detective and spy on their school-mates.

'But you're doing just what Mister Tolson said,' protested Charlton. 'Sticking to an out-of-date idea about schoolboy honour. As he said, it's honour among thieves, like those beastly prisoners in gaols. He has asked for our help. We should give it to him.'

It still shames me to say that I volunteered. Frampton did not, so Charlton and I were the only two. Why did I do it? Was I trying to ingratiate myself with Mister Tolson, who held me in such low regard? Or did I genuinely support his crusade against the perils of foul language? Did I believe that the foul language was actually being used, rather than it being a figment of the headmaster's deranged imagination, as I now believe it was? I simply do not know.

During the ensuing days the gang divided up whenever we were in the School-Yard, with Charlton and me on our own. We spent a lot of time discussing what detectives would do in a situation where the crime to be detected was the spoken word, without coming up with any practical plan. Until one day Charlton came dashing up to me looking excited. 'I've got an idea,' he exclaimed. 'We're going about this the wrong way. It's not detectives we need. It's a posse, like in the westerns. A whole bunch of people who can chase the bad guys…'

'Hmmm…' I rejoined, not sure where this was going.

'We'll make it a club. Anyone who joins will be for the Headmaster and the school. On the side of right. Anyone who doesn't will be… '

'An enemy?' I interjected.

'No, but a suspect. We'll watch them and listen to them and wait for them to commit a crime.'

'A crime? What kind of crime?'

'Using bad language, like Mister Tolson says.'

'And what are you going to call this club.'

'How about the Anti-Crime Club?'

And so the Anti-Crime Club was born. My enthusiasm for the project had dwindled, but I felt I had to support Charlton after he had been deserted by his other chums. Or did I? Did I just lack the gumption to say no, this was not how people should order their lives even in the small world of school?

The launch of the club, with membership by personal invitation, received a surprisingly positive response. The majority of those invited agreed to join. Their motives were probably mixed. If you were not a member, you were clearly vulnerable. But as a member you would have an opportunity to pay off old scores. And you would win the favour of the headmaster.

At first Mister Tolson was delighted to be getting results in his campaign against bad language. A steady stream of crime reports came in to him and an equally steady stream of culprits emerged from his study with their faces contorted in pain. The victims, I now suspect, were not guilty of the crimes for which they had been arraigned. They had caused offence to a member of the Anti-Crime Club and they paid the penalty. It was not even necessary to repeat the bad words to the head-master. He said that he could not put us in the position of having to compound a crime in order to report it. He would accept the testimony of the officers of the Anti-Crime Club that a crime had been committed.

Caning in boys' schools largely died out in the 1970s, so only men of mature years have experienced it. I do not lament its passing. It was degrading for both the perpetrator of the punishment and for the victim. The fact that many perpetrators are known to have enjoyed inflicting pain suggests that such punishments were often unjustified. And the pain itself is not to be underrated. It was excruciating. I do not know whether Tolson was a sadist, but he seemed to derive personal satisfaction from bending others to his will.

The climate of fear that spread through the school degraded us all. Three-quarters of the boys were living in terror, one quarter were perpetrating it. Normal relationships evaporated and boys became sullen and withdrawn. Soon the revolution began to devour its own. Members of the Anti-Crime Club now turned to denouncing each other.

Unlike the headmaster, Charlton himself did not appear to derive any fulfilment from his self-appointed position of power. Whatever his personal motivation in starting the Anti-Crime Club, and I believe that he had been literally brainwashed into supporting Mister Tolson's deluded campaign against an imaginary evil, it gave him no sense of triumph. As the term advanced and the atmosphere within the school became ever unhappier, Charlton grew solitary and introverted. What he had started he could not stop and its results were not what he had sought.

As I have mentioned, one of our few diversions was a debate held on the last Saturday of each term. Unusually for a school that did not encourage self-expression, we boys were allowed to choose the topic. Normally this was one of the great issues of the day. In 1952 we were spoiled for choice: Britain becoming an atomic power, one of only three; the US detonating a hydrogen bomb; the Korean War; revolution in Egypt; the founding of the European Union's forerunner, the European Steel & Coal Community; Mau Mau disturbances in Kenya; smog bringing London to a standstill for days on end; oil crisis in the Middle East; uproar in Britain over so-called 'horror comics'; the accession of Queen Elizabeth II and the election of Eisenhower as US President. But it will probably come as no surprise that the candidate receiving the most votes was about an issue closer to home. The motion selected was 'This House believes that the Anti-Crime Club should be banned'.

In any debating society composed of prepubescent boys the quality of debate is bound to be mixed. In this instance it was not only of a high order, but also impassioned, at least on the side of those speaking for the motion. The case for 'Yea' was led by a boy called Dugdale, who had refused an invitation to join the Anti-Crime Club on moral grounds. As a result he had been targeted for denunciation, but Charlton had refused to refer the case to the headmaster on grounds of insufficient evidence. He knew that Dugdale was incapable of using bad language, being the kind of youngster who embodied the spirit of the Boy Scouts, of which he was a popular and inspiring troop leader. Dugdale was also eloquent. This was the era of the Stalinist show trials in Eastern Europe, on which this thirteen-year-old was remarkably well informed. He painted a picture of conditions in the countries under Soviet domination, countries wherein every citizen feared denunciation by a neighbour, a work colleague, or even members of their own family. The offences were usually imaginary. The arrest and punishment of people who were far too cowed to attempt any kind of rebellious behaviour was orchestrated in order to keep the populace in a permanent state of abject subjection to the will of their rulers. The Anti-Crime Club, he declared, was seeking to create a similar atmosphere of mutual suspicion, hatred and fear within our own small community. Of course our ordeal bore no comparison with the life-and-death threats to which people were subjected under Stalinism; he was not seeking to suggest any such thing, only that the psychological pressure being used to impose a rigid order bore an uncomfortable similarity. If we behaved like this as boys, what kind of leaders would we grow into as men? Perhaps wisely, Dugdale did not extend his analogy to embrace the rulers in whose name this deprivation of basic freedoms was conducted. He did not need to.

Charlton had the unenviable task of replying to such a spirited call for justice. He did so with courage in the face of an overwhelmingly hostile audience, but his arguments lacked force against Dugdale's superior rhetoric. When the motion was thrown open to the floor, speaker after speaker called for no disciplinary action without clear evidence. Several even demanded the right to defend themselves against spurious allegations, a revolutionary concept in prep school jurisprudence. No more than two or three members of the Anti-Crime Club spoke for the Nay side and they did not seek to justify its *modus operandi*, only to plead that they had simply responded to the headmaster's appeal for help from within the ranks of the school. To one such hand-wringer, a voice from the floor challenged 'Like the Nazis then? Just following orders?'

During these exchanges Mister Tolson had sat grim-faced and silent. His only intervention came when the moderator of the debate called for the vote to be taken by a show of hands. The headmaster rose to his feet. 'No,' he asserted. 'There will be no vote. I have heard enough to be satisfied that the Anti-Crime Club has run its course. I do not deny my own part in facilitating its rise, but enough is enough. The Anti-Crime Club is dissolved as of now.' He turned to Mister Bartlett and told him to carry on, then left the room without a further word. His remarks had been met by an audible, collective gasp, but now everyone had something to say. Geoffrey Bartlett raised his hand and there was an instant silence. 'Boys, you will go to your dormitories in an orderly fashion.' We began to file out of the room. 'And Dugdale, where are you? Well done.'

. . .

I left St Peter's without regret the following year. Forty years and more passed before I saw Christopher Charlton again. It was at a St Peter's reunion. By that time Mister Tolson was long dead and the school had closed. The site of so much misery was now a housing estate. Charlton the middle-aged man was as amiable as I remembered him when he was a sandy-haired, freckle-faced lad in shorts. He had done well for himself. Regarded like me as one of the thick boys, he was now professor of history at a university in the south-west. We greeted each other with pleasure and exchanged the kind of tick-list pleasantries common on such occasions, running our way through our respective biographies without too much boasting but not hiding any lights under bushels either. But for me, of course, this was just a prelude to the inevitable question I had to put to him. When there was a pause in the conversation I asked it: 'Do you remember the Anti-Crime Club?'

Charlton looked puzzled. 'Say that again. The what?'

I repeated it quietly but distinctly. 'The Anti-Crime Club. We founded it together, the year before we left.'

He was not the least discomfited. Smiling he said 'You've got me there. What was it? A cops and robbers game?'

'It was a bit more than a game,' I replied. 'It was one of the formative experiences of my early life. I thought it might have been for you too.'

I explained to him briefly about Tolson's paranoia and his attempts, sadly only too successful, to subvert the schoolboy code of *omertà*. Charlton looked slightly embarrassed, but not I think because I was treading on forbidden ground. It was the discomfort felt when someone of slight acquaintance starts to make emotional revelations. I did not pursue the story, nor did I remind him of his central role in the proceedings. I omitted any mention of the denunciations.

I think Charlton was being genuine. I do believe the episode had been wholly eliminated from his memory.

My own recall of the Anti-Crime Club is clear and detailed, except in one respect. I honestly do not remember whether I ever denounced anybody. If I did, it has been erased from my own memory. And that I find truly disturbing.

# Chapter 3

• • •

# SABRINA FAIR

• • •

## *1953–58*

I scraped into Shrewsbury School by the narrowest of margins. 'History and English exceptional', my prospective house-master Alec Binney told my parents. 'Everything else hopeless.'

I was consigned to the Third Form. There was no First or Second Form. The Third was as low as you could get. But even within the Third Form there was a pecking order, as I was soon to learn.

The Third Form was presided over by an affable youngish master in horn-rimmed spectacles called David Brown. It was his unenviable task to instil some learning into a bunch of boys who would probably not have passed the Common Entrance examination had they not been the sons or brothers of Salopians or nominees of a distinguished benefactor. For our first prep he told us to write an essay on a subject of our own choice. This was probably to assess whether his charges were literate.

Most boys chose to write on 'What I Did in the Holidays' or 'My Dog Buster'. One over-precocious idiot-child chose to compose a discourse on the inner meaning of Picasso's *The Absinthe Drinker*. That was me. My brother Tim had a picture postcard reproduction of it and I had been very taken with the pathos of the subject.

Mister Brown conceded that he had never had a Third Form essay like that before. There was not much point in my attending his English classes, he said, because I was too far in advance of the other boys. On the other hand they were so far in advance of me in Latin that I needed to catch up. While they were studying English, I was to do extra Latin.

I could have told him that there was zero prospect of my ever catching up in Latin, and that the whole thing would be a waste of time. But one did not have conversations of that nature with masters in those days, so I meekly complied. By the end of the term I was still bottom in Latin, but also bottom in English, since I was not earning any marks in those classes. That made me bottom of the Third Form, meaning I was also bottom of the school. I ranked 551st out of 551 boys.

Shrewsbury was a classical school of very high academic attainment. At some schools prestige depended solely on athletic ability, but scholarship was held in almost equally high regard at Shrewsbury. The only other quality that conferred distinction was being good-looking. I failed on all three counts. My new-found reputation as 'The Thickest Boy in the School' did nothing to enhance my self-esteem.

Life in class was challenging, life on the playing field was gruelling and without reward, while life in my boarding house, Churchill's Hall, was simply hellish. The housemaster, Alec Binney, in common with most of his peers, believed in letting the senior boys run the house with the minimum of intervention from beyond the green baize door (his private quarters). This system at public schools was time-honoured and worked well enough if the senior boys regarded their privileged status as part of a contract in which they defended the rights and wellbeing of their juniors in return for the services of those juniors as fags. Unfortunately at Churchill's Hall the incumbent prefects ('monitors') honoured only one side of the contract.

The fags (tellingly known as *douls*, the Greek word for slaves, or idiomatically as 'scum') had an uneasy time of it. Not only were they subjected to a regime of unrelenting labour on behalf of study monitors and house monitors but were physically harassed by a group of fourth-year bullies. No attempt was made by the house monitors to deter the latter.

The bullying could be casual, such as bouncing a hard fives ball on a doul's head until it bled, or organised, like making a doul stand on a dormitory mantelpiece and sing while objects were thrown at his face by the jeering third and fourth years. The house monitors themselves also indulged a penchant for inflicting pain. PJ Ingrams, whose younger brother Richard would go on to found *Private Eye*, had a bed-sheet too narrow to tuck in to the mattress on both sides of the bed. Every night he would call for the doul who had made his bed and demand to know why the bed had not been made properly. The cringing child would whimper that the sheet was not wide enough, whereupon Ingrams would exclaim 'Stuff and nonsense' and summon a third-year boy, one Jonathan Cope, to do his duty. Cope had an ambition to be a naval chaplain, and a combination of the ethos of the church militant and fine naval tradition (characterised by First Sea Lord Winston Churchill as 'rum, sodomy and the lash') encouraged him to lay on the strokes with unrestrained vigour. Ingrams later became a prep-school headmaster, an occupation in which I am confident he manifested many of the same qualities as Mister Tolson. (He came to a sorry end, falling down a crevasse on an ice field.)

My own nemesis was my study monitor, a thug called David Walker who was possibly one of the most unpleasant people I have ever encountered. Although corporal punishment was still fairly rampant in public schools, by the 1950s it had all but disappeared in the home environment – with a few exceptions, of which the Walker household in Cumberland was one. David and his younger brother Miles would be summoned to their father's study to be held accountable for their sins of omission or commission, especially on the receipt of each term's report, and the outcome was invariably painful for one or other or both. It is a well-attested trope that people who are abused become abusers, and I have sometimes wondered whether David Walker was simply cast in his father's mould. On the other hand Miles Walker was a perfectly civilised human being.

I do not think that David Walker had ever read a book, so the one place on the school site I felt safe from his victimisation was the library. Here I would skulk whenever I could evade his attentions. The library had a set of bound volumes of *Punch* from the first in 1841 to the latest, 1952. As I had two years to serve as a doul, I decided to start at the beginning and work my way through them. The text in the early volumes was rather heavy going, but the cartoons were delightful. This was more or less when the joke cartoon was invented, taking its place alongside political cartooning and caricature. Both these latter also featured in *Punch*, but it was the joke cartoons that made the era come alive for me. They served not only as a window on the manners and *mores* of their time, but also – somewhat unexpectedly – as a chronicle of innovation. *Punch* was at the cutting edge of social progress and almost as soon as something new began to penetrate daily life, *Punch* would have a cartoon about it.

A couple of examples should suffice to illustrate what I mean. In 1897 *Punch* published a cartoon about taxi-cabs. It showed a cab bowling down the road with a street urchin clinging to the back, enjoying a free ride. A passer-by calls out to the driver 'Whip behind!' The urchin yells back 'Yah! He ain't got no whip!' I was amazed. Taxis back in 1897, before my parents were even born? So I did some delving and, yes, that was the year that the Bersey Electric Cab was introduced to London.

Fast forward a few decades and the Christmas 1934 issue of *Punch* was resplendent with a double-page-spread cartoon in full colour. This depicted the Christmas of the future. On the left was a television studio in which all the traditional Christmas festivities are being enacted before the cameras. On the facing page was a cross-section of a big block of art deco flats showing the viewers slumped on their sofas as their television sets brought them Christmas cheer vicariously. Remarkably prescient, considering how many hours at Christmas nowadays are spent in a semi-comatose state staring at the box. But what intrigued me more was the depiction of the television sets. They did not appear as if they were sci-fi predictions of what a telly might look like 50 years hence. They looked here and now, the now being 1934. Were TV sets available back then? Indeed they were. The cartoonist had based his drawing on the Bush Mirror-drum Televisor, launched on 30th June 1933 at 50 guineas. Many years later I was to acquire a sales leaflet for this model, which I sold on eBay for rather more than the original price of the Bush Televisor, to the son of John Logie Baird, inventor of television. He bought it for the National Media Museum in Bradford.

What to do with all this new-found knowledge? Well, what any self-respecting thirteen-year old doul hiding in the library from the school bully would do. Write a book, of course. I had two years available, after all. In fact it took me twenty years to complete, before it burst upon an unexpecting world as *The Shell Book of Firsts*. It was the start of a lifetime's study of innovation and a series of books recording 'firsts' in Britain, Australia, the US and worldwide. I suppose I should feel grateful to David Walker, the man who had never read a book, for setting me on this path.

. . .

Recently my good friend Jeremy 'JJ' Gould, who will feature again in this story, reminded me that the years I spent skulking in the library were not wholly solitary. He tells me that I rounded up other victims of bullying in Churchill's Hall and arranged various diversions to keep us all occupied while we celebrated our temporary release from persecution. These included furtive fags in the library loos, cream-bun and sherbet-sucker feasts with provender sourced from the tuck shop, and a regular poker school for penny ante. How we carried out these activities without disturbing other people I am at a loss to remember, though I do recall that the library was not much frequented by our games-mad schoolfellows and that the School Librarian, a distinguished bibliographer called Basil Oldham, seldom penetrated the public access side, rooting around amongst the treasures contained in the closed stacks. My role as a kind of self-appointed gang leader, though, had not escaped the attention of my housemaster. Alec Binney wrote in my school report: 'If he spent less time organising his friends, and more time organising himself, he would make a more satisfactory Salopian.' My parents were not impressed with my progress at my new school.

The bullying in Churchill's Hall ended abruptly, though not before I had served out my two years as a doul. One of my contemporaries was a rather bewildered-looking red-headed boy called Anthony 'Horse' Hill. The reason for his look of perpetual bemusement was that he was stone deaf in one ear. He was also probably the most brilliant musician in the school. Both characteristics were considered perfectly sound reasons for making his life a misery. Horse's father was an eminent psychiatrist of progressive views. Why it took Horse so long to complain to his father about the bullying I know not, apart from the fact that most parents regarded bullying as something that they were fortunate not to be charged for as an 'extra', given that it was regarded as one of the character-building features of training up the next generation of Empire-builders. But Horse's father was not that kind of parent. Indeed I find it difficult to understand why he had sent his sensitive, talented son to this insensitive philistine community at all. But when Anthony finally revealed the institutionalised bullying that was rife in Churchill's Hall, Hill Senior drove up from London, gave Alec Binney what was probably the most uncomfortable hour of his life, and withdrew his son from the school without notice.

Presumably the headmaster would have to have been informed why the school's foremost musician had left overnight. Binney was an honourable man and I do not think he would have dissembled. My surmise is that, even if the headmaster and one of his most trusted housemasters regarded bullying as part of school life, it had to stop. For once Binney did not leave the matter in the hands of his prefects. He knew they had failed him. The whole house was called together in the changing rooms, out of earshot of the servants, one of only two occasions this happened during my five years at the school (the other being on the occasion that the paedophile junior master was arrested). Binney was as overwrought as any of us had ever seen this normally placid man to be. He spoke of the harm that the outbreak of bullying had done to the reputation of the House and of Shrewsbury School. He seemed more concerned about this than the effect the bullying might have had on the victims. I suppose nowadays in such a situation every doul would have been called in by a counsellor and asked how he had been personally affected. In the 1950s bullying was regarded as part of the rough and tumble of boarding-school life, unless it got out of hand. This had got out of hand. But it was seen as a breakdown of discipline, as well as a failure of trust between prefects and housemaster, rather than an assault upon defenceless children that might cause them serious and lasting damage.

And did it stop for good? During my time at Shrewsbury there was no further outbreak of *organised* bullying. By this I mean a bunch of braying fourth-years forcing a pack of terrified douls to compete against each other in wilder and ever more dangerous feats of daring with the full intention that it would continue until someone was hurt. That was, thankfully, no more. One-on-one bullying, though – yes, that persisted. I speak from first-hand knowledge. I was one of the bullies.

There was a diminutive Scottish boy called James 'Beast' Robertson (no relation) who began picking on me during my first week at the school. Why, I don't know – as I was weedy and useless at games, maybe he reckoned I was unlikely to fight back. Every time I encountered him, he would aim a flying kick at my shin. Not life-threatening, but not very life-enhancing either.

By the time I entered my second year, I decided the time had come to resist. Not with violence. That would be too crude and I was not cut out for it, but with emotional pressure. On our weekly bath-night, with half a dozen boys of the same year occupying a row of baths, it was customary to exchange ribaldry, including off-colour jokes that would have had the narrators bent over Mister Tolson's study chair in a trice. I devised a supposedly 'dirty' joke that actually made no sense and involved the use of made-up words that might plausibly have been risqué. The other four boys were warned in advance and told that they must laugh uproariously at the meaningless punch-line. They did as instructed. Beast laughed with as much gusto as the others and on a signal from me the rest fell abruptly silent. Beast went on tittering in a slightly embarrassed fashion.

'So you found that funny, Beast, did you?' I asked in a friendly tone.

'Oh, yes. Very good joke. Ha, ha.'

'And you understood what you were laughing about, did you?'

Beast began to look unsettled. 'Er, yes, of course I did. I wouldn't have laughed otherwise.'

'No, of course you wouldn't. Silly of me to ask…'

A long pause while nobody spoke. 'Then you won't mind explaining the joke for the benefit of the others, will you, Beast?'

'They know what it's about,' he rejoined. 'Otherwise they wouldn't have laughed.'

'No, they laughed because I told them to. So go ahead. Explain the point of the joke.'

'Well, it's about … I mean, it's sort of … The point is …' Beast spluttered. 'No, I don't know and I think you're being rotten, all of you.' At that point he clambered out of the bath, grabbed a towel, and made a dash for the door. My parting shot was 'Wait till I tell the chaps in your dorm about this!'

On another occasion I organised a Beast Hunt. First I invited Beast for a Sunday afternoon bike ride. Then having rounded up all the douls except Beast, I told them that the plan was to ride out to Meole Brace, a village outside Shrewsbury, as a group. 'When we get there,' I explained, 'we inform Beast that we are the huntsmen and he is the quarry.'

Come Sunday and there was not a doul remaining in Churchill's Hall. Had Beast simply refused to be hunted, and stood his ground, my plot would have come to naught. But he did as instructed, setting off back to Shrewsbury at high speed with the knowledge that in two minutes' time the pack would be in full pursuit. I had told my henchmen not to catch him. After all, what would we do to him if we did, other than let him go again? No, the object was to pursue him all the way back to Churchill's Hall and then surround him in a jeering mob. Scare the wits out of him, then demean him. It all went perfectly to plan and Beast was left in no doubt that in our small world he was the outcast. 'Care to give me a kick on the shin now, Beast?'

There were other indignities I imposed on the wretched boy, but they do not need to be chronicled here. I have related this shameful story to indicate that bullies need not conform to the Flashman stereotype, even if some of the fourth-years did. They can be mild-mannered, weedy little pricks like me. And that is one of the reasons that bullying can be so hard for school authorities to stamp out. Bullies are not always as easy to spot as uncouth louts like David Walker. (And forget that mantra about all bullies being cowards. A lot of them join the army and win medals for gallantry.)

I have read a lot of public-school memoirs and in many the author claims that his was the last generation to be bullied at that particular school. How can they tell? At Shrewsbury there was still a bullying culture fifty years after my departure. My dear godson Kristian won a music scholarship to the school and his mother Mary, whom you will encounter again in a later chapter, misguidedly placed him in Churchill's Hall. He was a chorister who also happened to be sensitive by nature as well as pretty, and according to Shrewsbury School lore of circa 2010, that meant you were gay. If you were gay, you got bullied.

I find this quite extraordinary. In the 1950s homosexuality was a criminal offence, yet nearly everyone in our single-sex school had crushes on pretty younger boys. It was regarded as wholly unexceptional, as were romantic friendships between boys of the same age. (Beast and I finally resolved our differences when we discovered we were both suffering from unrequited passion for the same boy.) Of course, if such relationships ever became physical, that meant expulsion. Ironically the previous headmaster, Lord Wolfenden, author of the government's 1957 Wolfenden Report whose recommendations led to the decriminalisation of homosexuality in England and Wales, had expelled numerous boys from Shrewsbury for this offence, but his actions seem to have achieved the desired effect, because there were no such expulsions between 1953 and 1958. My point is that the attitude towards non-physical emotional relationships between boys in the 1950s, that uptight, conformist decade, was benign. When Kistian was at the school in tolerant 2010, with the attitude towards homosexuality in the wider world wholly permissive, it was not.

My godson was bullied throughout the whole five years he was at Shrewsbury. What I find even more difficult to comprehend is that the bullying was perpetrated by a small clique of boys, though they incited others. And even more difficult to understand is why these boys were allowed to continue their persecution. Kristian's mother Mary is no shrinking violet. A militant feminist and a crusading socialist at the more strident end of the Labour Party, she does not subscribe to the public-school code that the housemaster knows best. Kristian's three housemasters over the five years were given a very hard time, yet none was able to control the boys at the centre of the problem. Was it because they feared to take the drastic action necessary lest they be branded as an adult bullying those in their charge? And was the headmaster unaware of a problem that three housemasters were unable to resolve during five years? I am in no position to cast stones. I was a bully myself. But I am bewildered that in the twenty-first century, when pastoral care is amongst the foremost of a housemaster's duties, such a dilemma should be irresolvable.

. . .

Pastoral care was not amongst the foremost of Alec Binney's priorities, nor of the headmaster's. The 'Head Man', as he was known, was Jack Peterson, selected chiefly for his classical scholarship and for having represented Oxford and England at Fives. Shy to the point of reclusiveness, he knew few of the 551 boys under his command other than the praeposters, the dozen heads of houses who ran the school. He avoided all contact with parents. I had two encounters with him during five years. One was when he took a class for a master who was indisposed. He read through the roster of names and each of us responded 'Here, Sir.' When he reached my name he looked up and asked 'Which one is Hickman-Robertson?' I raised my hand. He gave me a prolonged, searching look, then continued the call-over. Was he curious to see in person the 'Thickest Boy in the School' or had my reputation as a malcontent and troublemaker gone before me?

The other occasion arose after I had stayed in the holidays with a friend from St Peter's, Martin Pemberton, whose father was an Old

Salopian. Pemberton senior, who had joined the school in 1898, presented me with his school boater as a souvenir of my visit. Now straw boaters had been compulsory wear until 1939, when they were discontinued as a war measure. I found that the School Shop still had a stock of the ribbons in house colours that had adorned this elegant headgear. Moreover they were for sale at the 1939 price of half a crown, since no one had ever changed the tickets. And remarkably, up in the loft was a cupboard stacked with pre-war boaters. When I started wearing mine on the site I was accosted by boys asking where they could be obtained. Soon there were a couple of dozen boys sporting this handsome headgear

The boater revival only became controversial when a boy called Andy Summers in a house called Severn Hill, an athlete and school hero, took to wearing one. Severn Hill was presided over by the most leftist of the housemasters, indeed of the whole Masters' Common Room. Patrick Childs saw this flaunting of what he regarded as a symbol of pre-war class ascendency as an affront to his egalitarian principles. His remedy, somewhat inconsistent with his espousal of socialist virtue, was to subject Andy Summers to a sound flogging. Summers was outraged, since he had not contravened any school rule. He appealed to the headmaster to support his right to wear an article of clothing that was still listed as school uniform. The Head Man enquired at a housemasters' meeting how the situation had arisen and was informed that a troublemaker in Churchill's Hall was the perpetrator. The troublemaker was summoned to an interview with the headmaster.

I cannot say that there was a meeting of minds. Mister Peterson contended that there would be some boys in the school who could not afford 10s for a boater and 2s 6d for a hat ribbon. I countered that parents paying £500 a year in fees were unlikely to find an additional 12s 6d an insupportable burden, but if they did, there was no requirement for them to disburse the money. He then deposed that there had been no decree reinstating boaters and that therefore they were unauthorised. I reminded him that when boaters were withdrawn in 1939, that decree had specifically stated 'for the duration'. Therefore their reinstatement was automatic with effect from the German surrender in May 1945. The Head Man terminated the interview without further comment and an hour later a notice was posted on the school noticeboard saying that the wearing of boaters was banned forthwith.

The irony of this episode was that Peterson was a fervent upholder of tradition and it was owing to his steadfast resistance to change that Shrewsbury was still rooted in a pre-war world, *sans* boaters. Virtually nothing had changed since he had been a boy at the school forty years earlier. Other schools during the 1950s were starting slowly to adapt to a post-war environment, but Peterson harked back to the safe and secure Edwardian world in which he had distinguished himself as a classicist and on the playing fields. His unfitness to preside over a great school as the post-war world evolved was sufficiently manifest to be recognised by those who served under him. Shortly after I had left Shrewsbury, a cabal of masters led a common-room revolt in protest at his lack of leadership. Unfortunately they chose as their champion Alec Binney, presumably on the basis that as a member of the old guard he would be seen as a moderating influence and someone with whom the headmaster could negotiate without rancour. Regrettably Binney proved so moderate that Peterson was able to see off the opposition and restore his authority. He soldiered on with diminishing effectiveness (starting from a pretty low base anyway) until he was succeeded by an able moderniser, Donald Wright, in 1963 'between the Lady Chatterley trial and the Beatles' first LP'. As Philip Larkin implied, a social as well as a sexual revolution was under way and the public schools were forced to face the fact that the age of unquestioning deference to authority was over. But whereas other schools only had to drag themselves out of the rigid conformity of the 1950s, Wright's task at Shrewsbury was to compensate for several decades of stagnation.

* * *

One of the most high-profile of the reforms that took place in most public schools during the sixties and seventies was the abolition of corporal punishment, not before time. Shrewsbury followed suit, but again with some catching up to do. In my time there was still a barbarous custom known as 'postering'. Anybody who has seen Lindsay Anderson's anti-public-school cinematic diatribe *if* will have seen an exactly similar form of retribution enacted in graphic and sickening detail, though that was drawn from the imagination (his alma mater Cheltenham College having a rather more civilised regime by then). At Shrewsbury it was a reality.

*Keighley had been observed speaking to a pupil from the the
Girls' High School in the town.*

The last postering at Shrewsbury took place in 1958. The victim was
a cheerful, outgoing boy called Neil 'Lat Brush' Keighley (the sobriquet
an allusion to his hair). Keighley had been seen speaking to a pupil from
the Girls' High School in the town. Now by the time my godson Kristian
entered Shrewsbury, the High School girls were full participants in most
of Shrewsbury School's extra-curricular activities, including drama,
orchestra, choir and athletics. There were also inter-school dances. In the
1950s speaking to a girl was considered the most serious offence short
of those meriting expulsion. Accordingly a notice went up on the School
Notice Board with this terse instruction: 'NG Keighley will meet the
Praeposters in the Sixth Form Library at 6.30pm tomorrow.' The purpose
of scheduling the execution of the sentence for the following day was to
give the miscreant a sleepless night in between.

The time appointed was half an hour after lock-ups. When Keighley
made his exit from Churchill's Hall, every window overlooking the long
mall to the main School Building was packed with boys eager to see
whether the offender was already shaking with fear. They would remain

in place until his return to see whether he was still capable of walking straight.

In the Sixth Form Library the full panoply of praeposters was awaiting their victim, who had a slow climb up eight flights of stairs. Keighley was then lectured about his iniquities – though quite where they placed speaking to a member of the opposite sex in the catalogue of infamy strains the intellect – and he was then invited to bend over a chair. The proceeding, as in a Roman flagellation, advanced at a stately pace. The three executioners, the Head of School, the Head of Churchill's Hall, and the praeposter who had witnessed the depravity, then took their places at the far end of the room, flexing their bamboo canes. Each ran the length of the room and delivered a slash from on high, maximising its impact. This was then repeated. After the delivery of six strokes, Keighley was free to thank the three boys, scarcely older than himself, for the benefit of their correction. All that remained was to face the jeering faces of his school-fellows as he made his agonised journey back to Churchill's Hall.

It was said that some boys had been traumatised by postering and never fully recovered. I have no evidence of this. My cousin John Nottingham, at the school in the 1940s, was believed to have been the only boy to have been postered twice (the second time for publishing a satirical squib about the praeposters in the school magazine) and as I write is still living in Kenya with his Kikuyu wife and black Old Salopian sons, apparently in rude health.

Two years earlier Willie Rushton, a co-founder of *Private Eye* with fellow Salopians Richard Ingrams and Christopher Booker, had celebrated his elevation to Head of Churchill's Hall by abolishing corporal punishment by the house monitors. It was promptly restored by his successor. Presumably that boy had consulted the Housemaster before so doing. It is likely, therefore, that Alex Binney had an opportunity to maintain Rushton's reform and set an example that might have been followed elsewhere in the school. If so, it is an opportunity he chose not to take.

∘ ∘ ∘

At this juncture I should concede that little I have said so far has been to the credit of Shrewsbury School. I must try to redress the balance. You are reading the memoirs of a misfit. For the average boy who enjoyed his sport – probably the majority – and could hold his own in the classroom, Shrewsbury offered a sound or, on the classical side, a superlative education, with the prospect of learning early lessons in leadership as a monitor or praeposter and a smooth transition to Oxford or Cambridge thereafter. No, I did not say 'to university'. Shrewsbury did not do Red Brick. The teaching was generally competent and occasionally inspired – the inimitable Frank 'Kek' McEachran is one of the few schoolmasters other than headmasters to have earned a Wikipedia entry. Major Hugh Brooke MC, nominated by John Peel in that teacher training commercial described earlier, was another who has attracted outpourings of affection and gratitude, including from me.

And what of my housemaster, Alec Binney, not one of my most fervent cheerleaders? At almost any time during my first four years at Shrewsbury he could have expelled me for failing to attain the academic standard required or for being a disruptive influence or both. He didn't.

Shrewsbury had another estimable quality. It was, in my view, the most beautiful school in England. I have visited most of the major ones and pored over photographs of many more. Nothing compares with those lovely acres of greensward bordered by majestic oaks and the mellow loveliness of the eighteenth century School Building high on an escarpment above the town and the various ivy-clad Victorian boarding houses. Best of all is the view from the Queen's Terrace skirting the near side of the School Building, from where a panorama of one of the most unspoiled and historic towns of England unfolds over the winding, sparkling Severn (Latin *Sabrina*) with the Quarry, a verdant and immaculately maintained public park, nestling on its banks. Truly Sabrina fair.

I do believe physical environment is important in the process of growing up. To be surrounded by beauty is a civilising influence. It must be readily apparent from some of my foregoing observations that the influence of beauty did not exert itself sufficiently amongst all those who made up the Shrewsbury community, but overall it is surely a force for good. I was aware of the beauty of the school site from the day I arrived, and through all the vicissitudes of the following five years it helped to preserve me from a descent into despair.

*       *       *

Perhaps surprisingly I never lacked for friends during my schooldays. I was thick, weedy, useless at games, disorganised, opinionated and slovenly, the latter deficiency characterised by unpolished, down-at-heel shoes, inky fingers, and hair that obeyed none of the dictates of the hairbrush ('Put butter on it, Boy' commanded my maths master Colonel West). What was there to like?

I had one quality lacking in most of my school-fellows, one shared with my brother Tim. Unlikely as this may seem, it was a degree of sophistication. Now persecuting poor Beast and neglect of personal grooming may not seem the height of sophistication, so please bear with me if I digress a little to provide an explanation deriving from my home background.

My parents, dear people as they were, were not greatly attached to the diversions of childhood. Hence my brother and I were scarcely exposed to juvenile pastimes and entertainments (with the exception of *Cinderella*, to which my father, who had a horror of sex but a predilection for scatological humour, used to take us annually at Cheltenham Playhouse in the hope, seldom disappointed, that the ponies drawing the gilded coach would crap on the stage). My father, despite being tall and well-built, and with a bellicose manner when aroused, was strangely timid. I was a weakly child and subject to most of the commoner childish ailments. Our family doctor, Dr Green, was of the old school who believed that the remedy for any affliction was cold baths, fresh air and manly sports. He recommended to my parents that I should be allowed to sleep in a tent on the lawn, a proposal that delighted me, but father vetoed this on the grounds that I might be attacked by creatures of the night (in suburban Tuffley). Next time I was ill Dr Green told father to get me a canoe. Father had an easy answer to that one: I would drown myself. On another occasion he suggested shotguns for both my brother and me. Father said we would shoot each other.

Hence the recreations Tim and I were allowed were those that our parents enjoyed. Father taught us to play poker and used to win our pocket money from us with unbecoming regularity on Saturday nights. We were often taken to the country club, Shuthonger Manor near Tewkesbury, a time capsule of the 1930s presided over by three middle-aged ladies of the leisured class, one of whom, Marjorie Gibbon, adopted my brother as a personal pet, and another, Kate Dewar, adopted me. Marjorie

Gibbon was never seen without a 12-inch cigarette holder in one hand and the driest Martini in Gloucestershire in the other. I once overheard Mrs Gibbon drawl to an aristocratic looking man at the bar, 'I told her I would present her beastly daughter at Court if Duncan would take me to Ascot.' Hers was not a world I knew anything about, but I was eager to learn more. My own mentor, Kate, was a buxom lesbian with carmine lips, severely truncated hair, beautifully cut slacks, and a stentorian voice. She had served in the FANY (or 'Fannies' as they were known) during the war and had a fund of stories about London during the blackout, most of which she appeared to have spent at the Dorchester and Quaglino's. I hung on her every word.

Tim and I were also hauled along to cocktail parties from the age of about eleven. To what extent we were actually welcomed by our hosts I do not know, but my parents gave them little option in the matter. We were, however, schooled in appropriate behaviour. We were to call our host 'Sir' and our hostess 'Mrs So-and-So' (or on rare occasions 'Lady So-and-So'). We were to make polite enquiries about their families, their health, and their particular interests. Dr Neal, for example, had no interests beyond Rugby Union, so we were to inform ourselves of Gloucester Rugby Club's progress in the league. Humphrey and Denny Foster wintered every year in Jamaica, so we should ask whether the natives had stopped being restless (they hadn't). We were not to drink more than two glasses of sherry, and we were not to ask for sweet sherry, because it was a tart's drink. I don't think Father actually said 'tart' – as I explained he was very uncomfortable with sex – he probably said 'fallen woman'. The fact that we were allowed to drink alcohol at all may come as some surprise. My parents believed that if we were brought up to consume alcohol in moderation, we would never drink to excess. Persuasive as this sounds, I am not sure that either my brother's or my approach to the pleasures of the bottle in later life entirely bears out their well-intentioned theory.

When it came to culture my parents were strictly mezzo-brow and the books, plays and music that they preferred were those of their youth. Many children rebel against their parents' tastes, but Tim and I simply absorbed them. We did not go abroad because father was sea-sick on boats and, despite having spent six years in the RAF, had such a distrust of flying machines that he would not travel in one. Instead there would be a biannual trip to London. Here we stayed at the Savoy Hotel, well beyond Father's modest means, and travelled around in a chauffeur-driven limousine. On one occasion we were kept awake until the small hours by Elizabeth Taylor, who was occupying the next room with her new husband Michael Wilding. It was their wedding night and she was a very noisy lover. (Anybody else would have dined out on this episode, but Father could not bring himself to mention it.) Our meals were taken at the Ivy, Le Caprice, and – in honour of Kate Dewar – Quaglino's. In the afternoons and evenings we would see the latest West End musicals and plays by Terence Rattigan and Noël Coward. We shared one favourite performer between the four of us, the incomparable Ivor Novello, with Jack Buchanan a rather poor second.

Where my brother and I were a little in advance of our parents was literature. Father's favourite author was John Galsworthy and he seldom read anything other than *The Forsyte Saga*, beginning again at the first volume when he had finished the last. My brother was highbrow and read mainly Russian and French classics. I had embarked on Dickens when I was ten and, having polished off the major works, moved on to Evelyn Waugh, George Orwell, Arnold Bennett and George Gissing, with PG Wodehouse as lighter fare. We both read voraciously, so each of us was tolerably well-read by the age of about sixteen. My brother's contemporaries at school, Michael Heseltine, Richard Ingrams, Willie Rushton, Paul Foot, Christopher Booker *et al*, tended towards the intellectual end of the literary spectrum, so he was by no means unusual. My contemporaries, by contrast, were still on Biggles.

So, despite the fact that I was immature and juvenile in many respects, I could switch to a different mode if it seemed advantageous or appropriate to do so. (My brother Tim simply became an adult, virtually overnight, at the age of thirteen and never behaved childishly again.) So I think I had a certain attraction to those who became my friends because I knew what to do in most social situations. They did not. Mr and Mrs Binney used to invite each boy in the House to dinner on the Private Side once or twice a year. Heather Binney once told my parents that my brother and I were the only boys who could sustain an adult conversation at the table. (This was probably the sole occasion either Binney said anything even mildly complimentary about me. On another occasion Mrs Binney told my mother that I was eccentric, which alarmed her considerably as such people were prone to becoming artists or vagabonds. Pressed on how the eccentricity was manifested, Heather vouchsafed that I would spread marmalade on my kippers at breakfast. We did not even *have* kippers for breakfast.)

My chum Rusty Lewis said to me when we were both about seventeen: 'You have an advantage over the rest of us. You have already made up your mind about everything. We haven't.' I think this was something else Tim and I had inherited from our parents. No intellectuals, they were nonetheless fairly doctrinaire about most things, including politics. (My mother regarded Mrs Thatcher as dangerously left-wing.) Issues were debated at the dinner table and conclusions often arrived at about this and that. It may have helped that we did not have television as a distraction. Most middle-class homes did by the late fifties. Father said he would buy a television when colour came in. He stuck to his word and when BBC colour started in 1967, we had our first TV set. A black and white one.

· · ·

If you have friends about you, however distressing life may be it is just about supportable. Without them it can be abysmal. I was singularly fortunate in this regard, much more so than many others. There are always lonely figures at boarding schools and this is one respect in which there has been little change. I would hope that now, with pastoral care such a priority, friendless boys and girls are given whatever support is possible by those whose charge they are in. At Shrewsbury in the 1950s the only housemaster who did pastoral care was Major Brooke, not that he would ever have heard that term used. For all its shortcomings the school had a fairly broad programme of activities off the playing field, with concerts, plays, societies, expeditions, lectures, debates etc. Most boys would pair off for these events and would pour out of the House chattering and laughing together. Then would follow the strays and loners, trying not to look abandoned, refusing to acknowledge their rejection. Among their number was Beast Robertson after I had executed my revenge on him and he had been cast out from society. He, and others like him, must have hurt a lot inside.

Parents, do not send your child to boarding school if he or she has difficulty fitting in. It will not help them to adjust. It will crush their spirit.

And while I am in my pulpit, parents of thick boys and girls, I have a message for you. I know they are not called thick nowadays; they are called 'dyslexic'. But if you have a 'dyslexic' or academically challenged offspring, please do not consign him or her to a school beyond their scholastic ability. They will not prosper in that environment.

The sound of axes being ground will be audible to readers of the foregoing paragraph. There was naught for my comfort in moving from the Third Form, and my dishonourable status as 551st out of 551 boys, to the murky academic depths of the Lower IVth, a repository for those in whom the school held no expectations of betterment. It was presided over by a dismal man called Hawkesworth who looked as if he had been rather badly made up to play Fu Manchu or Charlie Chan or some other stage Chinaman. His disdain for me was fully reciprocated. Not that he had much higher regard for my classmates, being of a genus of schoolmaster, now I hope happily extinct, who actively disliked boys. They were not uncommon at the time and may have reflected the problems experienced by some ex-officers in obtaining appropriate employment after the two world wars. Though why major public schools like Shrewsbury felt the need to engage them perplexes me.

Hawkesworth's reports on my progress were so unfavourable that Alec Binney decided to flog me. He did so more in sorrow than in anger and with none of the panache of Mister Tolson indulging his favourite pastime. I think it almost hurt him more than it did me, but not quite. As at St Peter's, I was considered incorrigibly idle. Physical retribution, however, was unlikely to remedy the problem, which had nothing to do with idleness and everything to do with an inability to learn.

My spirits sank to such a low during this period that I wrote to my parents threatening to take my own life. My mother used to refer to this as 'your gas oven letter'.

The following year should have been my O-Level year, but instead of joining those preparing for the exam in the Vth form, I was consigned instead to the Upper IVth. Many of my classmates were two years younger. My form master, the Reverend Mister Furnival, who was also the School Chaplain, made no very distinct impression on me. But there was progress of a kind. I now had a form master who was indifferent to me rather than actively hostile.

The Reverend Guy Furnival was a grey man. He was grey-haired, invariably clad in a grey suit and his greyish complexion was drained of all colour. Standing against a stone wall he was scarcely visible. I do not think I learned anything at all in the Reverend's form, other than an appreciation of Victor Hugo's *Les Misérables*. He would read this to us aloud in the high, reedy monotone affected by many C of E clergymen in those days. Not a voice that one would choose for the BBC's *Book at Bedtime*, but the narrative of *Les Misérables* is so compelling that it does not demand the highs and lows, changes in emphasis, modulation and differing accents of conventional audio delivery. The protracted sufferings of galley-slave Jean Valjean helped to put my own in perspective.

.  .  .

Slowly the school year passed in quiet desperation and at its end I passed from the tutelage of one Reverend to another. The form-master of the Lower Vth, who was also housemaster of Rigg's Hall, had recently taken Holy Orders and was now the Reverend Major Hugh Brooke MC. The Lower Vth was one of the O-Level forms, and as normally these exams were taken at Shrewsbury at the age of fourteen or fifteen, I was at least two years older than most of my classmates. Major Brooke had a particular talent for conducting a class of mainly ill-informed harum-scarum lads at what is probably the least confident juncture of their teenage years. He believed passionately that every boy had something worthwhile to offer and that it was his role as their mentor to identify and foster it. We could have done with more of his kind at Shrewsbury School.

Major Brooke was also into fun, a commodity that most of his peers felt should be distanced from education. The class, freed of the restraints imposed by his more sombre colleagues, would sometimes erupt into joyful noise. To counter this, the Reverend Major commissioned a techie boy to build him a miniature working traffic signal. When the light was on green, which it was sparingly, modest pandemonium was given licence; on amber, conversation was permitted only in low voices; on red, dead silence. Boys respond to this kind of nonsense. Or at least grubby fifteen-year-olds do, and it worked. The Major also maintained discipline with a horsewhip. This was not put to the use that Mister Tolson would have favoured, but employed to instil mild terror as the Major expertly cracked its 15-foot-long thong a few inches above the heads of the boys in the rear of the classroom. On one occasion, however, his expertise momentarily deserted him and he struck a narcoleptic boy called 'Sleepy' Carmichael on the ear. Sleepy woke up with a start and shrieked at the top of his voice. A trickle of blood made its way from the victim's earlobe to his collar and the Major was overcome with anguish. He staunched the blood with his handkerchief and asked the boy if he would like to be accompanied to the sanitorium. Sleepy's face broke into a forgiving grin and he told the Major there was nothing to worry about. Ten minutes later he was asleep again.

The Major was an enthusiast for audience participation and boys were encouraged to contribute with relevant information on a subject, or even – unheard of at this level of the school – their opinions. Knowing that I collected vintage magazines and newspapers, he commissioned me to write a short history of the press in Britain and this was used as a set text for the class. I was amply rewarded in Cadbury Flakes, the Major's currency of preference in commercial transactions with his pupils. Even French lessons, in other classes a deadly recitation of the rules of grammar and syntax, were lively in Major Brooke's form. The Major did not hold the French in high regard, admiring their culture but finding them wanting in generosity of spirit. A lot of what he taught us took the form of mild ridicule. He had a particular penchant for translating English colloquial phraseology into literal French and set us exercises in this so that he could use the choicer examples to annoy the natives on his annual visit to the land of rude waiters and bad drains. 'Met une chaussette dedans' ('Put a sock in it') and 'Arrête de jouer aux bougres idiots' ('Stop playing silly buggers') each earned their *auteurs* a Cadbury Flake.

During the holidays preceding the dreaded O-Level examinations, I embarked on an heroic programme of revision. I set myself a target of twelve hours cramming a day, and if I was placed on cocktail party duty by my parents or subject to other unavoidable distractions, I made up the hours the following day. Neither Major Brooke's kindly attentions nor my own efforts to justify them had much impact on the outcome. My results were abysmal. When Alec Binney summoned me to his study to review them, he told me that I had brought shame on Shrewsbury School by achieving the lowest ever recorded mark in the mathematics papers. He dismissed the result on the English Language paper on which I had scored 90%, as 'what was expected'. The fact that this also constituted a record, though at the other end of the scale as the highest mark achieved at any school in the country, did not seem worthy of comment.

My prospects held little cheer. I was destined to spend my final year in the form called the Remove, which covered the first year of the A-Level syllabus. But the A-Level course was two years, so I would leave school with no qualifications other than my woefully meagre clutch of O-Levels; hardly the most promising basis on which to seek employment.

At about this stage of our progress through the school we were encouraged to seek the advice of the Careers Master, so that he could set us on the right path for seizing those glittering prizes that were within most Salopians' expectations. It cannot have been a particularly demanding role. Many boys would be going on to Oxford or Cambridge, so it was a matter of advising what they would read at the varsity to best equip them for the Bar, for medicine, the Church, the Home Civil Service, the Diplomatic Corps or, for arty types, the more distinguished publishing houses and fine art auctioneers. The guidance was the same in each case: read the classics. Those opting for agriculture scarcely needed his advice (you obviously went to Cirencester), nor those headed for the military (you obviously went into your father's regiment). Others whose uncles were chairmen of merchant banks headed towards the City without the intervention of the Careers Master. Thick boys went into the family business – a lot of Salopians were from the north of England and were destined for dark, satanic mills, though in the rather less dark and satanic environment of the board room. Or they went into the colonial police, but you had to be sporty for that. The default position for those without the talent or the family connections for any of these career paths was accountancy, though that was clearly closed to someone who had scored 2% at O-Level maths. When I told the Careers Master that I was toying with the possibility of either journalism or advertising, his advice was succinct. 'Don't.'

One day Major Brooke came into the Vth Form brandishing a letter. He switched the traffic signal on his desk to red and put on his reading glasses. 'Boys,' he declaimed, 'I am going to read you a letter from one of the boys in my House. It's from John Ravenscroft. Some of you knew him and you will remember he left the school early. Well, he's now in America, in a place called the Deep South, wherever that might be, and I want you to hear what he says.'

The letter was a testament of gratitude to Major Brooke for the years Ravenscroft had spent under his care, and for the fact that he had never felt discriminated against because he was a duffer at work and a waste of space on the playing field. But as the Major explained, these compliments were not the reason he was reading it to us. 'Boys, some of you may get discouraged sometimes. Ravenscroft was often discouraged and we had long talks about it. He left school early because his parents didn't think he was getting anywhere. Well, he's gone to this Deep South place to 'find himself' as he puts it. And I think he will. Notice how literate, how well phrased this letter is. Being able to communicate like that should stand him in good stead. I don't know what his career path is going to be, but I really think we may all hear the name John Ravenscroft again.'

In that last sentiment, the Major was wrong. By the time the former pupil had registered in the public consciousness, he had changed his name to John Peel. Not only did the maverick disc jockey nominate his old house-master as a formative influence in the teacher-recruitment television commercial alluded to earlier, but when he was interviewed on the BBC's *Desert Island Discs* he spoke movingly about this other maverick. Would that the Major could still have been alive to know that his regard for even the 'useless' boys had sustained them through troubled times.

At the time of this incident with Ravenscroft's letter, the Major had recently welcomed a New Boy to Rigg's Hall. An unremarkable little chap, who would probably also need a bit of care and attention. The sort who might get potato chips stuffed up his nostrils by a big bad boy. His name was Michael Palin.

. . .

Shortly before the end of term and the school year I was summoned again to Alec Binney's study. I was surprised to be asked to sit down, the first occasion in my four years at Churchill's Hall that I had received such an invitation. Normally the chair by Binney's desk was strictly for bending over.

Binney looked uncomfortable and sucked vigorously on his pipe as though seeking inspiration from the noxious weed. 'I have had a visit from Mr Hart,' he ventured. Michael Hart was Head of the History Side, known to me only by sight. 'He has made a somewhat unusual proposition.' He paused. ' Concerning your future,' he added bleakly.

'My future, Sir? But Mr Hart does not know me.'

'Be that as it may. It has been suggested that you should not go into the Remove next year, but join the History Side. That would mean missing the first year of the A Level syllabus, and taking the examination after one year. Most irregular. It has never been done before.'

There was more furious sucking of the pipe. I was nonplussed and could think of nothing constructive to say.

'I doubt that you would pass History A Level,' Binney continued. 'I know that you have done better in history than in other subjects, but the syllabus is a demanding one. Unlike O Level, which only requires you to know a range of facts, at A Level you have to be able to interpret. It is a preparation for university and we know you aren't varsity material.'

Where was this leading? Surely he had not called me in to hold out the prospect of a glittering prize and then tell me that I was not going to be allowed to compete?

He peered at me through a haze of smoke. 'You have done little during your time at this school to deserve special consideration. What is proposed could establish a precedent – other boys in your position, though happily there aren't many of them, might demand similar treatment. I don't mind admitting it gives me great unease ....'

More billows of smoke. 'But then do I have a right to deny you this opportunity? I am not sure that I do. Reluctantly – very reluctantly, because you have done nothing to deserve this – I am going to authorise your placement in the History Lower VIth under Mr Ellis. Try not to let me down, Hickman-Robertson. You'd be letting down Mr Hart as well.'

'Sir,' I ventured, 'I have never met Mr Hart. Did someone speak to him about me? Major Brooke perhaps?'

'It wasn't Major Brooke, though he tells me he supports the proposal. Seems to have more faith in you than I do. No, it was a boy....'

'A boy, Sir?' I echoed unbelievingly.

Schoolboys in the 1950s simply did not interfere in the way those set in authority over them chose to run the school. Or make suggestions. It was not a participatory democracy.

A pained look crossed Mr Binney's face. 'Yes, I know, it is highly unusual. Not something I would wish to encourage. But Mr Hart is of a new generation of masters. He is ... how, should I put it? Forward thinking. He seemed to think he should listen to what the boy had to say and pass it on to me.'

'Am I allowed to know the name of the boy who interceded, Sir?'

'I suppose so. It was Gould.' Binney sighed. 'Such a sensible boy usually.'

I thanked my house-master and took my leave. Jeremy Gould had done this for me? I sought JJ out and reported the outcome of the interview. He was delighted at the news. 'But what made you do it?' I asked.

'Oh,' he said airily. 'It just seemed to me that you had loafed around in the Lower School for long enough. I reckoned you were capable of something better.' He chuckled. 'Let's hope you are.'

I asked him about Michael Hart, who had taken the unusual step of interceding on my behalf. To me he was no more than a shadowy figure with a close resemblance to Roger Bannister. JJ told me that he was half-German, with an English mother, but that he had been with his German father in Berlin in 1939 when the war began. He spent the duration in that city and went to school there. As the Russian guns became audible to the east, the seventeen-year-old slipped out of the city and made his way towards the Americans in the west. He passed through Nazi lines at great personal risk and succeeded in making contact with the Allies. Having persuaded them that he was not a spy or a saboteur, he was taken on as an interpreter. Several months after the end of the war he was repatriated and reunited with his mother for the first time in nearly seven years. An athlete at Oxford, he became accustomed to being mistaken for his *doppelgänger* at the Iffley Road track and being quizzed about his prospects of breaking the four-minute barrier. After graduating from Oxford with a First in history, he was appointed Head of History at Sherborne at the improbably young age of twenty-four. From there he went on to head the history faculty at Shrewsbury, still in his twenties.

I looked forward to discussing this remarkable life with its protagonist. It was to be a long wait. I never had the privilege of an encounter with Michael Hart during the rest of my sojourn at Shrewsbury. More than half a century passed and then my benefactor, who had enjoyed a distinguished career as Headmaster of Mill Hill and subsequently of the huge International School in Luxembourg, retired to the small market town of Marlborough. Karla and I had retired nearby in the Lambourn Valley. We became close friends with Michael, much to our delight. When I had got to know him well enough, I broached the matter of his proposition to Binney. Why, I enquired, had he never made contact with me? Michael explained. To have done so before consulting my housemaster would have been improper. To do so after consultation with him was unnecessary. While it is difficult to fault either the logic or the rectitude of this, I cannot help feeling, dear Michael, that you are exposing the more teutonic side of your estimable character.

. . .

I joined the History Lower VIth together with my best friend in Churchill's Hall, Nicholas Walker. (No relation to my ghastly fag-master, but younger brother of Sykes Walker, the Head of House who reintroduced corporal punishment after it had been abolished by Willie Rushton. Sykes sentenced his own brother to a flogging after he and I had been caught riding bicycles on a weekday.)

Nicholas was a year younger than me, the son of a Yorkshire mill-owner who also hobby-farmed in Gloucestershire. Together with another Gloucestershire boy, John Hance, whose sister would become my first adult girlfriend, we would make expeditions to London in the holidays to sow wild oats and mark the passage from adolescence to the onset of manhood. Mrs Walker did not consider her son ready for such ventures, nor did she want him exposed to the temptations of city life. She disapproved not only of his bid for personal independence but also of the slightly older boy who she believed was leading him astray. Thus I was cast in the kind of role played in the uplifting school novels of Dean Farrar of *Eric, or Little by Little* fame, by which a boy who smokes and plays cards proves a malign influence on the hero, a boy of hitherto untrammelled innocence and virtue. I had a huge admiration for Mrs Walker, who was pretty and accomplished and a practically perfect mum, but my attempts to exercise the superficial charms that won over my parents' cocktail party chums had absolutely no impact on Nicholas's fiercely protective parent. I was not invited to visit the farm.

Our new form-master, Arnold Ellis, was not an inspiring teacher, but he was diligent, kindly, committed and treated his pupils like adults. He fostered a collegiate atmosphere in class and his teaching methods were a foretaste of the university life that some of us would go on to enjoy. We were set one or two essays a week and shown how to conduct the research they necessitated. Our essays would then be reviewed during fireside tutorials held at his home in the evenings. Arnold's delightful wife Margaret was on hand to dispense cocoa and good cheer. She called Nicholas and me, who were seldom seen apart, 'the heavenly twins', a sentiment to which I do not think Mrs Walker would have subscribed.

The History Lower VIth was, I believe, the only form in the school in which the class-mates addressed each other by their Christian names. I think this was a response to the relaxed though disciplined atmosphere that Arnold Ellis cultivated. It certainly helped to foster kinship and a mutual desire to absorb everything that Arnold was offering us. We all wanted to be a credit to him. Among his other virtues as our mentor was a becoming modesty. On one occasion he told me to take over the class because he said I probably knew more about the Boer War than he did.

Amongst my classmates two of the more conspicuous in the free-wheeling debates on historical topics that Arnold encouraged were Michael Balfour and Martin Hall. Curiously, both were to become friends of Karla's independently of me. Michael founded a small publishing house called the Garnstone Press and was wont to use the 'French' pub in Dean Street (the York Minster, watering hole of the Free French during WWII) as an extension of his office. Karla would drink there with her raffish mates in the film industry and she and Michael bonded. Martin Hall was one of these raffish mates, whom she had met while making David Frost's *Crossroads of Civilisation* in Iran just before the revolution there.

Less conspicuous in debate, because he found talking an effort, was the languid PJ Pagnamenta, later editor of the BBC's *Panorama*. Nicholas and I had come up with what we thought was a brilliant notion for augmenting our meagre pocket money and earning enough for those lively jaunts up the Smoke. It occurred to us that the school numbered amongst its staff and senior boys an expert on almost every subject. If we set ourselves up as an information bureau, advertising our services in the literary weeklies like *The Spectator*, *The New Statesman* and *Time and Tide*, we could call on this resource to answer any question that readers cared to pay two shillings (10p) to have answered. We needed Pagnamenta on board because he was the cleverest boy in the class. The three of us had a letterhead printed on the school printing press, calling ourselves 'Information Please'. It was Google in embryo.

The very first question to come in, accompanied by a two-shilling postal order, was a quite fiendish one evidently designed to test our mettle, especially since the questioner said he would claim his two bob back if the answer failed to satisfy. It concerned the coefficient of restitution when one billiard ball travelling at such-and-such a speed and at so-and-so velocity struck another travelling at this-and-that ditto. I am not sure that there wasn't a third ball in there somewhere. We took this to David 'Quaggers' Quarmby, a bespectacled brainbox in Oldham's Hall who was the *non pareil* of the Mathematics Upper VIth. We offered him sixpence (2½p) for the task, contingent on the questioner letting us keep our fee. Quaggers returned the following day with several sheets covered in those arcane symbols that are the language of advanced mathematics. 'Here's your answer,' he said. 'Would you like to know how long it took me? Four hours.'

The questioner did not ask for his fee back and we were in business. Incidentally a few years later Quaggers and I found ourselves employed together at the Ministry of Transport. As I was a press officer I had occasion to call on his services again from time to time when I received questions from specialist journalists of a highly technical nature. He never failed me.

Board meetings for 'Information Please' were held in chapel during the Reverend Mister Furnival's more protracted sermons. We soon had a stable of experts who enjoyed the challenges thrown at them, and in the case of the masters we called on it was below their dignity to accept any part of the fees we earned through their efforts. Quaggers, though, demanded a shilling and we had no option but to meet the demands of the Alan Turing of Shrewsbury School. The enterprise continued to prosper until a rival organisation called 'You Ask We Answer' began to advertise in the same weeklies that we used. They had the audacity to undercut us, with any question answered for 1s 6d. We lost no time in dispatching the billiard ball question to them. When we received their reply, we took it to Quaggers for appraisal. He conceded that they had arrived at the correct answer, but found their proofs wanting in lucidity. He suggested that we withhold half the fee. A little sleuthing revealed that the address of our rivals was that of a well known girls' school. In the end they ran us into the ground, but that was probably just as well as A-Levels loomed ever closer.

Despite these diversions, there were few out-of-school hours that we did not devote to feverish revision. Occasionally we felt we had to take a break from our arduous studies and have a bit of excitement. What better than the races? We broke bounds to attend Chester Races and inveigled my mother into meeting us at the end of a country bus route and driving us to Ludlow Races. Nicholas was indiscreet enough to reveal these escapades to his mother. Mrs Walker was appalled. She wrote to Alec Binney a furious letter demanding that Nicholas should be forbidden to associate with this depraved youth Hickman-Robertson who was turning him from the path of righteousness. She was too honourable to reveal the particular depravity that had so aroused her ire, so Binney must have wondered what had suddenly occasioned such outrage. Much to my amazement when I learned of it later, Binney had leaped to my defence. He wrote an emollient letter to Mrs Walker sympathising with her concern for the welfare of her younger son, but pointing out that there had been a transformation in his attitude to school-work. Never previously noted for application, Nicholas had a new-found work ethic and, according to his form master Mr Ellis, his enhanced performance in class seemed entirely to do with the spirit of competition between him and Hickman-Robertson. While doing all their work together, they each urged the other on to achieving the best results. He even referred, in a jocular manner, to Mrs Ellis's calling us 'the heavenly twins'. That must have really set Mrs Walker's teeth on edge. (It saddens me that she and I were never reconciled, because I admired and respected her sterling qualities. Had she known that her son and I would enjoy a lifelong friendship, and that our wives would have an instinctive rapport, I think she would have accepted that I was not going to be an impediment to his later undoubted success in life.)

A year passed and the A-Levels were upon us. The history papers were challenging, particularly European history – I had never been riveted by constant eddies of the balance of power – but gave plenty of scope for combining a detailed knowledge of the periods covered with an assessment of cause and effect. The General Paper, though, was unexpectedly difficult. This was principally about current affairs, and was a salutary counterweight to the received notion, prevalent then, that history terminated in 1914. The issue that dominated the press and airwaves at that time was the aftermath of Suez, an event that polarised the nation and marked a sea-change in Britain's world role and her relationship with the United States. Arnold Ellis had warned us that this would be the main subject on which we would be interrogated and did his best to prepare us, but I do not think any of his pupils, with the possible exception of Pagnamenta, grasped the overwhelming complexities of this wide-ranging topic.

There was, however, an escape route in the form of an alternative topic. Not, as one might expect, the birth a few months earlier of what would become the European Union. That was ignored. The other choice was 'The Loch Ness Monster', evidently slipped in by an examiner rather more given to levity than most of his kind. Now I knew no more about the fabled monster of the deep than anyone else in the class ... but then, not many people do, including most examiners. If I was going to wing it, I had one advantage. The previous year I had enjoyed a walking holiday at Loch Ness with my brother Tim, then doing his National Service, and two of his army friends. We had traversed most of the perimeter and I knew all the place names. That would lend veracity to what I wrote. Or what I made up. For make it up I did, with a complete history of the Monster since its first sighting (in my version) by a professor of zoology from Chicago University called Dr Hiram Schoenberg in April 1934 to recent attempts to locate the creature with sonic detectors lent by the Royal Dutch Navy (I was nothing if not inventive). Nowadays all you would have to do to blow a story like this out of the water would be to Google it. But what ready access had an examiner in 1958 to a handy reference on the Loch Ness Monster?

I was the only member of either the Lower or the Upper History VIth to opt for the Monster over Suez. I was the only member of either History VIth to pass the A-Level General Paper. Even Pagnamenta must have been having an off-day.

But this was a relatively minor achievement. Most of us passed the History exams, but I was the only one to be awarded a Distinction. Now the normal marks awarded for class work did not apply in the A-Level forms. Your exam results determined your end-year place in the form. So I concluded my time at Shrewsbury with not only first place in the History Lower VIth, but first place in the whole History Side. I had gone from bottom of the school to (equal) top. From 551st to 1st.

This news caused something of a sensation in the Masters' Common Room, as gleefully reported to me by a notoriously indiscreet young master called 'Squeaker' Brooks. Binney's courageous decision to elevate me to the Sixth Form had not met with universal approbation. Many of the greyer heads had been wagged in disapproval of indulging a thick and unprepossessing troublemaker in this way and some predicted that it would end in grief and humiliation. The experiment had proved a success, but my first form-master David Brown, unwitting architect of my rapid descent to the bottom of the school five years earlier, opined 'Shrewsbury has failed that boy'. I prefer to think that the generous spirit of a schoolboy, the enlightenment of a young master, and the reluctant decision of an older, more traditional master to take a risk on an unpromising prospect, meant that the school had proved itself capable of dealing with a situation that lay outside the norm.

• • •

The term drew to its end and with it my schooldays. Together with Stuart Alexander, who had joined Churchill's Hall on the same day, I organised an auction in the changing room to dispose of the detritus accumulated over five years. John Hance and I arranged a party in my dormitory with printed invitations and, for entertainment, a film show with a hired projector. We even invited some girls, which would have been a first for any social occasion at Shrewsbury, but sadly they failed to appear. Trunks were packed. Goodbyes were said. Addresses were exchanged. And then, just as I was preparing to leave for the station, there came a summons to Alec Binney's study. I had already performed a dutiful farewell and thanked him for the chance he had given me, so what final message could he have at this late hour?

For the second time in my school career I was invited to be seated. There was much sucking on the pipe and shuffling of papers, before my former housemaster peered at me over the top of the roll-top desk and observed, 'I have been having another look at your A-Level results'. Puff, puff. 'I think you had better come back next term. We could put you in for a history scholarship to Oxford.'

More puffing. 'You won't get the scholarship of course. But we might find a college that would let you in on the strength of the scholarship papers without you having to take College Entrance. It goes without saying you would never pass that.'

Clouds of smoke swirled around his head. 'The only problem is that you would need Maths O-Level. It is a basic qualification and there's no way round it for either Oxford or Cambridge. But we could get you extra tuition.'

The dreaming spires! What a heady prospect. What a joy to follow in the footsteps of literary heroes like TE Lawrence, John Betjeman, Evelyn Waugh...

But I had packed my bags, said my farewells. I had a job interview in London the next week. And there was the insuperable hurdle of Maths O-Level. I was frankly more likely to win an Oxford scholarship than pass the algebra paper on which I had previously scored 2%. It was a lovely, enticing dream. But all too likely to remain just that – an elusive dream.

I thanked Alec Binney for his interest and concern and expressed my regrets. Then I left his study for the last time, gathered up my bags, walked out of Churchill's Hall, tipped my banned and battered boater to the statue of old boy Sir Philip Sidney, then strode purposefully towards the school gates and passed through them to my uncertain future.

# Chapter 4

• • •

# LIFE IN LONDON ON FIVE GUINEAS A WEEK

• • •

*1958–61*

As the alumnus of a public school in the 1950s, there was really only one way of seeking employment. You pulled strings.

So: it was not what you knew, it was who you knew. It is sometimes observed that the malaise that brought the British economy nearly to its knees less than twenty years later was a direct result of this recruitment policy in the management grades. Managers could not manage.

I reserve judgement. There were certainly exceptions. Nicholas Walker joined his father's mill soon after leaving school and learned the trade from the bottom up, eventually becoming sales manager. Unexceptional, perhaps, for a scion of the founder? So far, yes. But in 1980 the business was taken over and all the family members summarily ejected. Nicholas obtained a post in another mill, becoming a director. By 1987 the former Walker family business was in severe trouble and he was headhunted as managing director, solely on merit. Over the next fifteen years or so he restored it to profitability and built it up into one of the most successful textile firms in the West Riding.

Most Shrewsbury parents had a network of business contacts who could be called on for support when it came to facilitating their sons' first steps on to the career ladder. My father, as a professional man, knew principally other professional men. His only close friends in the world of business were the manufacturer of England's Glory matches and a man who had built a substantial fortune from hiring out sacks to farmers at a penny a week each. Neither matches nor sacks had much allure for me. Besides, I was desperate to leave the confined, provincial world of Gloucester and make a new life in London. I had set my heart on a career in advertising.

The only contact we had with that world was an extremely tenuous one. Back in the 1920s my mother had 'walked out' with a young man who was later one of the founders of More O'Ferrall, destined to become the largest billboard company in Britain. They had maintained Christmas card contact so now she wrote to him and sought his guidance on the placement of her second son in the advertising business. He replied that he would recommend me to an agency, and within days an interview had been arranged with S.H. Benson Ltd, the agency for Guinness, Woodbine cigarettes, Bovril and many other leading brands. This was accomplished without Mother's old admirer having met me. In what terms he had couched his recommendation was not disclosed.

I remember little about the interview, other than the interviewer asking me if I had a private income. I was hired as a trainee at £6 a week, from which it was explained that there would be deductions of 5s (25p) for income tax and 10s (50p) for National Insurance. That left me with 5 guineas a week, not a princely sum on which to sustain life in London, even in 1958. (Hence the question about a private income.)

My bed-sitting room in Beauchamp Place in Knightsbridge cost three guineas a week. It might seem strange for someone earning an office boy's wage to choose to live in the shadow of Harrods. The fact is that nearly all young middle-class boys and girls living away from home in London did settle in the West End. Before the explosion in house prices, the difference in rents between rented accommodation in the smarter areas of London and the suburbs was not great. I made a chum at Benson's called Roger Wigram who lived in Streatham for economy and walked an hour to and from work to save an 8d (3p) tube fare. His rent was £2 15s, only marginally less than mine.

Although I had been taken on as a trainee, it rapidly became apparent that there were two varieties of trainee and that their destinies were very different. Graduate trainees were trained in management once they had mastered the basics. If considered to have potential, early on they joined an account team in a junior capacity with a view to becoming account managers and account directors. The other type of trainee, including my kind, were fresh-faced public schoolboys recruited as general dogsbodies because, unlike many products of the state education system, they never answered back and would work without complaint for low wages. There was some attempt to teach us a craft, but it was strictly the technical side of the business. Those who stuck it – most dropped out within a year or two – were consigned to a Gehenna called 'Production'. There it was possible to pass an entire working life without ever encountering a client. None of this had been revealed at the somewhat perfunctory interview. On that occasion the interviewer had nodded as if in compliance when I revealed my ambition to become a copywriter. I started my new career as a filing clerk.

Most young people coming to London had a network of social contacts through their parents' friends or their own school chums. My parents had no family or other connections in London and Shrewsbury had drawn its pupils mainly from the North and Midlands. I started with just two contacts, one of whom was the sister of my Gloucestershire schoolmate John Hance. Sally was a secretary living with three other girls in a mews house off Edgware Road and she became my first girlfriend. The other was my brother's army chum, Timothy 'Rubber Ears' d'Arch Smith, whom I had met on the Loch Ness holiday. He was gay and introduced me to a circle of somewhat extravagant personalities, many of them bibliophiles like himself. I joined the Public Schools Club, as it was the only club in London that would accept members under the age of twenty-one. Some of my fellow members were equally colourful, many of the more senior ones being of the same orientation as the bibliophiles. They would warn me against each other in hushed voices behind the potted palms.

. . .

An altogether different environment was the Honourable Artillery Company. Sally Hance had taken me to visit a friend who lived in

Hereford Square. Towards the end of the evening the friend's flatmate came stumbling in lugging an army kitbag, which he flung down with a groan as he collapsed on to a sofa and began whimpering for gin. It was explained to me that this was John Kimpton, who had just attended his first Honourable Artillery Company (HAC) parade at Armoury House. I asked him what it had been like. 'Hell,' he replied. 'Would you like to join?' Though I had failed as spectacularly in the school Combined Cadet Corps as I did in everything else requiring coordination or dexterity, I did at least know how to present arms and how to strip a Bren gun. 'Yes please', I said.

The HAC required you to turn up to a weekly parade on Thursdays (though you could miss some), attend weekend exercises every couple of months or so at the Brigade of Guards depot, and do a week's camp with other Territorials in wild places like Wales and Norfolk. For this you were paid: not much, but anything on top of five guineas a week was welcome. The weekly parades were quite arduous, since our NCOs were retired Guardsmen, but dinner afterwards in the mess at Armoury House was highly convivial. Officers and men came together in the bar and the dining room on terms of equality, although many of the private soldiers were the social superiors of their commanders. These occasions cemented my friendship with John Kimpton, and it has survived to this day.

That was Thursday nights taken care of, and on Wednesdays John Hance came to London for an evening class. He was working for a paper mill in Oxfordshire. Every Wednesday night we met up at his sister Sally's little mews house and the girls would cook up pasta or a stew while John and I contributed a bottle each of the cheapest available retsina (7s 6d, or a third of a day's pay). Alternatively we might go ice skating at Queen's Ice Rink in Bayswater or, if we were feeling flush, took a box at the Metropolitan Palace of Varieties in the Edgware Road. As Collins Music Hall in Islington had been burned down just before I came to London, the 'Old Met' was now the only music hall surviving in the capital. A box seated six people and cost 30s (£1.50), so we only had to cough up five bob each (the girls earned more as secretaries than John or me, and did not expect to be treated). The acts were variety and some of the older performers harked back to the Edwardian heyday of music hall. Within a few more years variety itself succumbed to the lure of television.

Tuesday night was poker night. This was at the rooming house in Tregunter Road in Chelsea where John Kimpton had his bed-sitter (and where the rents were collected by an Old Salopian with a startling shock of golden hair called Michael Heseltine). Kimpton and his fellows had the luxury of a common room for their enjoyment, a rare luxury in such establishments. We commandeered the big round table in the bay window for our tournament. At a penny ante, the most you were likely to win or lose of an evening was about a week's pay. I played cautiously and strictly to the odds, because I really could not afford to lose. On average I would come away a couple of guineas to the good, increasing my weekly income to nearly £8, or just over if I was attending HAC parade on Thursday. On the rare occasions that I lost a couple of guineas, woe! That was a hungry week.

After one particularly successful night at the table in Tregunter Road, I decided to buy a car. No, not that successful. The car would be co-owned by Sally's flat-mate Annette Horne (whose typing speeds were higher than the others' and earned more) and we set off together to deepest Coulsdon to inspect the 1934 Humber Vogue that we had seen advertised in *Exchange & Mart* for £20. The engine started, so we bought it. Annette drove it back, as I had not mastered the art. I did not do so until I was forty-seven. As she and I were the only car owners within our social circle, there was no lack of volunteer drivers. Wherever I wanted to go, there was usually someone happy to come along for the ride.

The Vogue performed reliably if slowly, though it did have a disconcerting habit of dropping odd pieces of ironmongery from its innards on to the road. At first we used to pick these up and store them on the back seat against the day we might be rich enough to take the Vogue to a repair-shop. That day never came, and as the car still seemed to function without these bits and pieces, we carried on regardless. When Kimpton and I attended HAC camp in Pembrokeshire, it got us all the way to that far-off coast. And half the way back. On reaching my parents' home in Gloucester for a pit-stop on that return journey, it gave what sounded like a huge metallic sigh and subsided into the gravel on the driveway. The Vogue never moved under its own power again. Annette and I sold the hulk for scrap and received £5.

With that large white fiver burning a hole in our pockets we reinvested in an even newer model. This was a 1935 Austin landaulet taxi with a hood that let down so that the passengers could ride in the open. Now even in 1959 there was a limit to what you got for £5, so there was one slight downside to this bargain. Our cab would not start by any conventional means. It so happened, though, that the girls' next door neighbour knew how to hotwire cars – he had learned it while serving with the SAS, he told us. We could only go for a ride when he was in and available. And on reaching our destination, we had to keep the engine running until ready to return.

One day the taxi had disappeared and so had the ex-SAS man. It occurred to us that he might have learned his hotwiring skills in some other occupation. Some months later I was walking to the Public Schools Club through Shepherd Market and a shady-looking character in a grubby raincoat sidled up to me and whispered behind his hand, 'Pssst. Wanna buy a taxi going cheap?' 'Show me,' I said. He led me round the corner and there was my taxi. Changed number plates of course. 'Special price to you,' hissed the raincoat. 'A five pun' note and she's yours.' I declined the generous offer.

On the evenings when other diversions were not on offer, I repaired to the club for tea and toast, usually in the company of Captain Seymour-Higgins. The gallant Captain, a veteran of World War I, was the most unpopular member of the club, probably on account of a very prickly temper and a low tolerance of fools, foreigners and faggots (he had lived in America), the latter of which the club had more than its fair share. Why he liked me I am not sure, though perhaps it was on account of the courtesies my parents had taught me to extend to my elders and my genuine interest in his memories of service in the trenches, of the Indian Army in the 1920s, of New York of the prohibition era, of upper-crust London life in the 1930s, and of flying with the RAF in World War II. He had been one of the first passengers to cross the Atlantic in the giant Hindenburg airship in 1936, three years before transatlantic airliner service began. All these tales kept me enthralled, but they were punctuated from time to time with the abuse he directed at 'furriners' or faggots who had the temerity to encroach on our corner of the lounge overlooking Green Park.

One of the faggots was a delightful silver-haired old darling called Jack Cowper, also a First World War veteran, who would buy me a drink in the bar provided Captain Seymour-Higgins was nowhere to be seen. He once offered to let me read his diary of the trenches and I leaped at the opportunity. Alas, it was no *Goodbye to All That*. Each entry recorded the weather (usually rain) and nothing but the weather. Jack had lived through Armageddon and all he had to say about it was that it rained?

Jack was one of those slightly feckless young men who, come peacetime, had no very clear direction in life and ended up, like other feckless young men (as this memoir will attest), at the BBC. In the pioneer days of the BBC at Savoy Hill, he became Jacko the Monkey on *Children's Hour*. In 1932 the BBC moved to its magnificent new headquarters in Broadcasting House, and it was in the marble foyer of the new flagship building that Jack, having done an evening rehearsal which may have terminated with alcoholic refreshment, had a late-night encounter with a particularly fetching pageboy in tight trousers and a bum freezer jacket. Jack plonked a slobbery kiss on the boy's startled pink face just as the swing doors opened and Lord Reith appeared in the foyer. (According to the version he told Rubber Ears d'Arch Smith, he took the boy's lower lip between his teeth and bit it. Is this conventional behaviour among gay people?)

The miscreant was summoned the following day by the Head of Light Entertainment and told that he was being transferred to the Midland Region. That meant Birmingham. There was no harsher penalty at the Corporation than this until BBC Television began in 1936. Reith hated television, so then the Alexandra Palace studios became the gulag to which you were sent for improper behaviour; as, for example, a secretary who was spotted in Great Portland Street with bare legs (she had laddered her stockings and taken them off). Jack's offence and the secretary's misdeed were probably rated about equal in the BBC's hierarchy of sin.

. . .

Bed-sitting rooms scarcely exist today, so it is probably hard for the younger generation to imagine life in a room probably no bigger than, say, 12 ft by 8 ft, in which you slept, cooked, did your ablutions, studied, made love (possibly) and in which all your clothes and other worldly goods were stored. Cooking was performed on a gas-ring (fed by a shilling meter) and so tended to be limited to anything that could be fried or boiled in a single utensil. Dinner was not an enticing prospect in such circumstances, but eating in restaurants was generally outside the budget of bedsit dwellers. A bunch of young members of the Public Schools Club found an alternative to gas-ring meals that we could just about afford once a week or so. This was tea at the Ritz.

At the time of writing, the cost of tea at the Ritz is 'from £54 per person'. In the late 1950s it was 5s (25p). Nowadays they bring large silver salvers of goodies and dispense a single item from each – quite sufficient for most people in a diet-conscious age. Then they used to deposit the silver salvers around the table and leave us to help ourselves. (I am not sure that other guests got quite such liberal treatment. We were privileged regulars.) So for five bob we were able to stuff our faces with delicately cut crustless sandwiches with wonderful fillings like smoked salmon and prawns and ox tongue and breast of chicken before moving on to teacakes and crumpets dripping with butter, followed by cream cakes galore, éclairs, brandy snaps and scones. We were usually the last to leave the tearoom, but even in the knowledge that the tip wouldn't exceed 6d the Swiss waiters were extraordinarily indulgent.

One day over tea two of the chaps, Henry Ashby and Kenelm Bennett, said they were fed up with bedsit life and what if we pooled our meagre resources and looked for a property to rent? It seemed a good idea and we fell to discussing where. It was agreed that really it should be Mayfair, so that we could walk to the club. I do not know whether very young men were more idiotic then than they are now, but I think it is probable (friends' grown-up grandchildren all seem so together). Mayfair was, of course, way out of our league. But fortune sometimes favours the foolish.

The first few estate agents we visited had responded with hollow laughter on learning of our resources, but with the boundless optimism of youth we persisted. Then we met an agent who did not throw up his hands in mocking disbelief, but said that he had a single property on his books that might meet our needs. If, he added, we were prepared to meet the needs of the owner. It was a five-storey Georgian property in Culross Street, which is a quiet thoroughfare that runs for about 150 yards from the back of the old American Embassy in Grosvenor Square to Park Lane. The club would be less than ten minutes' walk away. The rent, the agent explained, was exceptionally low because of the somewhat unusual condition the owner had imposed for the tenancy. He lowered his voice before confiding, 'No woman is ever to spend a night under its roof.'

This condition, the agent went on to say, had made letting the house very difficult. It had gone on the market at 35 gns a week, and he had lowered the price by progressive steps of 5 gns till he reached the present offer of 20 gns. We asked if he was at liberty to reveal the reason for the condition. He said he must phone the owner for her permission. When this was done, he came back into the room and told us this story.

The house, the agent informed us, belonged to the Princess Jean Ann-Marie Calamachi, who had fled Romania on the eve of the 1947 communist revolution 'clutching a handful of jewels'. It must have been quite a capacious handful, as it bought her a large farmhouse in Kent and the townhouse in Mayfair. The latter she let. In recent months, however, the Princess had begun to have complaints from neighbours. There were constant comings and goings through the night and some of the visitors to the house were of an unsavoury appearance. The Princess hired a private detective and his report shocked her to the core. Her elegant house was being run as a brothel. The madam was swiftly dispatched and the house put on the market with the proviso that not only could no female inhabit it, but nor could they stay even for a single night.

This was long before boys and girls shared flats, so the condition was really no impediment to us. Girlfriends? Well, if any of us struck lucky, it would have to be at her place.

Not that we conceded this to the agent. We sucked our lower lips and said that it was going to be mighty inconvenient. How about 15 gns? The agent said he could not insult the Princess with such a low offer. We settled at 18 gns.

There were five bedrooms. Henry and Kenelm were going to share and I had offered John Kimpton the other half of my double room. The three other rooms we let out at 5 gns a week each, leaving us with 3 gns to pay between four of us. That left us sufficient in hand to hire a maid. A live-out maid, naturally.

Besides the five bedrooms, there were a ground-floor sitting room, a dining room and a spacious drawing room that occupied the whole of the first floor. At the rear was a communal garden which ran the length of the half dozen or so houses on our side of Culross Street as far as Park Street. Amongst the select group with whom we shared this amenity were our next-door neighbours, Lord Astor on one side and the Hon. Angus Ogilvy on the other, and Daphne du Maurier a couple of doors down. Opposite us was Michael Wilding, whose bride Elizabeth Taylor had kept the Hickman-Robertsons awake at the Savoy. She had long since departed the scene, after *Confidential* magazine revealed that he had entertained strippers at Culross Street while she was filming *Giant* in America.

The strippers must have seemed fairly tame compared to the shenanigans that went on across the road from Mr Wilding's abode. The first thing that I encountered on taking possession of the room that I was to share with Kimpton was a cupboard full of whips, canes and chains. It seems that the madam had fled the wrath of Princess Calamachi in something of a hurry.

We had certainly moved up in the world. One day I arrived home to find a ragged looking man contemplating the oily, begrimed moped that was my means of getting around London at minimal cost. He offered to clean it for me and it was immediately apparent from the way he spoke that his social progress had been downwards. While he swabbed and polished, he told me that he used to visit our house in the 1920s. It was then the residence of the Marquis of something whose name has escaped me. One day he arrived for a cocktail and was told by a clearly embarrassed butler that he could not be admitted. The Prince of Wales had dropped by unexpectedly.

I would dearly like to have known what misfortune had reduced this cultured gentleman to such a low point in his fortunes. Homeless, he was unable to draw any benefits because he lacked a fixed address. He told me that he was staying in a hostel in Chiswick and later, discussing the incident with a Salopian chum, Dominick Grundy, we determined to find him and see if there was anything we could do to finance the three weeks' residence somewhere that would entitle him to draw the dole. Together we visited the refuge in Chiswick, but sadly he had departed. We were shown round the refuge and the sight of twenty or so mainly elderly men slumped in upright chairs round the peeling walls of the day-room, staring into space with a look of total defeat on their faces, was quite sufficient to instil in me a proper realisation of the privileges I enjoyed.

. . .

John Kimpton proved an engaging room-mate. He worked for an import-export business in the City that was run by his father and uncle. The uncle, an overbearing character who had devoted much of his life to worldly pleasures, particularly those of the table and the bottle, had been born again at the Billy Graham Crusade in Wembley Stadium. Now he felt impelled to bring the staff of his company to righteousness. Every morning began with the staff having to kneel at their desks while he led them in prayer. Woe betide any sinner who had the temerity to arrive late. Forbearance did not loom large in Uncle Tony's fire and brimstone campaign to save their souls.

John himself had enjoyed a school career that bore comparison with mine. He had succeeded in getting expelled from the über progressive Bryanston, which is not an easy thing to do. He and his sister and brother boasted a single O-Level between them, in carpentry. Kimpton had never read a book, and I mean this in the literal sense rather than the figure of speech that I used in respect of school bully David Walker. He suffered (as I do) from OCD, Obsessive-Compulsive Disorder, which in his case manifested itself as an inability to reach the end of a page of printed text without going back to the top in case he had omitted a line or a word. Happily I was instrumental in curing him of this (not the OCD but the reading disability) when I lent him Horace Annesley Vachell's evocative story of Harrovian life in the 1890s, *The Hill*. He was so enthralled from the first paragraph that he forgot to obsess when he reached the bottom of the first page and turned straight over. The book was devoured in a sitting and Kimpton found that he was cured of this particular affliction.

Not surprisingly, Kimpton caused his parents a good deal of anxiety. His mother came of an upper-class background but had married into trade, albeit the kind of trade that ensures a life of ease and comfort. She and Mr Kimpton, always addressed as 'Sir' by his two sons, lived in an elegant Georgian manor near Hassocks in Sussex, Knowles Tooth, wherein Nelson had reputedly had his wicked way with Emma Hamilton. Mrs Kimpton, a strikingly handsome woman but wholly indifferent to her personal appearance – the haute couture clothes she habitually wore dated from before the war – combined fervent passions with a delightful, other worldly vagueness. She had a tendency to invite people to the house and forget about it. On one occasion when I was staying at Knowles Tooth for the weekend she returned from church and enquired whether anybody had 'dropped by'. I was able to inform her that there were thirty-seven people in the drawing room and that I had taken the liberty of dispensing drinks. 'Oh, dear me,' she exclaimed, 'Are they staying for lunch?'

Two hours later several people still present displayed no inclination to go home and elected to stay for lunch. This was not a problem because Mrs Kimpton had left a steak-and-kidney pie large enough to feed a small troop of cavalry in the oven before departing to worship. I remarked on the pastry, a beautiful golden crust but unusually sweet-tasting. 'Oh it's not pastry,' Mrs Kimpton declared without a trace of discomfiture, 'I put almond paste on the pie by mistake.'

Mrs Kimpton's passions were Mr Kimpton, literature, her garden, friendship, Godliness, and the reformation of ladies of easy virtue. I told her one weekend about a publication I had seen in the window of a surgical appliance store in the Edgware Road titled *The Ladies' Directory*. This little book did what it said on the can, providing a guide to diverse services available in central London with prices accordingly. Mrs Kimpton exclaimed in horror, 'I shall write to the Bishop of Chichester immediately!' It did occur to me to wonder what interest the Bishop of Chichester might have in what seemed a metropolitan matter, but I did not press the point.

All was revealed a month or so later when it was reported that the Chichester Diocesan Moral Welfare Committee had brought an action against one Frederic Charles Shaw for the publication of *The Ladies' Directory*. The case caused a sensation and before it came to court had been taken over by the Director of Public Prosecutions. Judge Maxwell Turner found Shaw guilty of a conspiracy to corrupt public morals and sent him down for nine months. Shaw appealed on the grounds that there was no such offence in common law and took his case all the way to the House of Lords. Controversially, their Lordships dismissed his appeal and it was alleged that they had in effect created a new offence where none existed before. I am sure Mrs Kimpton meant well, but after that I was a little more cautious in revealing to her the depravity to which young men like her son John might be exposed in the Great Wen.

'John dear,' Mrs Kimpton appealed to him plaintively one evening over dinner, 'Don't you lie awake at night worrying about me lying awake at night worrying about you?'

She worried that John wasn't getting enough sleep, that he didn't eat during the week, that he smoked too much, and that he might not marry the lovely Christine Young, heiress to a potted shrimps fortune. (In all these respects she did indeed have something to worry about, and we both still sigh over the lovely Christine, now a grandmother many times over, whenever we see her.) But the chief worry was whether his talents would ever be properly recognised in the office. What exactly these talents were may not have been immediately discernible to the chief executive of Kimpton, Kimpton, Kimpton & Kimpton, the exacting Uncle Tony, because John's attempts to sell exotic imports from the Spice Islands to hard-faced traders in the grimier purlieus of the capital had met with limited success. He confided to me that every time he stood in front of a hard-faced trader's door, his hand poised to rap on the smoked-glass panel, his only inclination was to run and hide. His prospects were not enhanced by the fact that Uncle Tony had a son, the beautiful Andrew Kimpton, Head of Pop at Eton, Oxford graduate, charm personified, and possessor of all the talents an ambitious businessman father seeks in a son marked down for occupation of his chair in the fullness of time.

There came the day when John was summoned to Uncle Tony's office. Fearful that his employment in the family firm was about to be terminated, he was surprised to be informed by the chief executive that he had been selected for a senior post. John was overwhelmed – him, in a senior post?

'Yes,' Uncle Tony assured him. 'It is in one of our subsidiaries and you will be head of the company.' John asked which company.

'It is called Woods & Woods and it is in Australia,' his uncle replied. 'You will be in sole charge.'

'How many staff will I have?' ventured John. 'None' said Uncle Tony with finality. 'When I said sole charge, the operative word is *sole*. You'll be on your own. We want you to take over as soon as possible.'

'Do I have to fly out immediately?' stammered John. 'You don't fly out. You'll be going by boat. So I suggest you go over to the Australian High Commission and apply for your passage now. You're going out as a ten-pound-pom.' This was the assisted passages scheme run by the Australian government to attract British migrants – Australians did not always welcome the newcomers, who attracted this disparaging sobriquet.

'But what if I want to come back?' John persisted.

'If you chuck in the job, you're on your own. There will be nothing back here for you. And you'll pay your own return trip. Good luck.'

I have already jumped forward a few years, and I am going to jump a lot more to give you the *dénouement* to this story, as I don't expect you want to riffle through to the end to find out what happened to my old friend Kimpton. Reader, he made good. Within a few years he was able to buy Woods & Woods from the parent company and it went from strength to strength. Given that his previous record had not suggested the making of a captain of industry, you may well ask what brought the change in his fortunes. Faced with the daunting prospect of rescuing a moribund company in a strange country, he rose to the challenge. I do not think it diminishes his achievement in any way, though, to say he was in the right place at the right time. Supermarkets came late to Australia, but at the time that John emigrated in the mid-1960s, they were beginning to edge the traditional corner grocery out of business. With the supermarkets came ready-meals and processed food. The various preservatives, enhancers and flavourings that Woods & Woods imported in their raw state were exactly what were needed by the food processors. John responded to this demand with imagination and enterprise, flying all over the world to find new sources of supply. No longer did he cringe in outer offices. He was somebody people wanted to do business with.

After twenty-five years of growing the business, including opening a branch in Melbourne, John was ready to sell out and take early retirement. He was now a multi-millionaire, married to the former Sally Windeyer from one of the oldest families in New South Wales and with a family of four. Having never passed an exam, he enrolled at Macquarie University and took a degree in Australian history. With the proceeds of the sale of the company, John began to speculate in real estate at a time when there was a huge growth in demand for high-end property in Sydney and built a substantial portfolio. His own home stands on the North Shore overlooking the Harbour Bridge and the Sydney Opera House. The lovely Christine of his Sussex youth lives up the road.

. . .

Not all of our group enjoyed the same advance up the career ladder. One of our chums in the HAC was a diminutive lad called Nigel Hollings, who would stand on the large kitchen table at Knowles Tooth and sing opera arias in a remarkable falsetto, much to the delight of Mrs Kimpton and the disgust of Mr Kimpton. Nigel had stopped growing when he was about twelve but was always beautifully turned out in tailor-made three-piece suits and a miniature bowler hat, probably one of the smallest Locke's had ever made. At our invitation he occupied one of the three single rooms at the Culross Street house. His occupation was something indefinable in the City, a job that he gave up on his twenty-first birthday without informing his parents. Nigel had come into a fortune.

Not a substantial fortune, but sufficient to keep him in idleness and fund a monster Rolls Royce, the first purchase he made on coming into his inheritance. The amount of his bequest was £30,000 and that needs to be put in context. I do not know how it was invested, but supposing that he was earning at least 5% from the capital, that would mean an annual income of £1,500 or more. So he probably had nearly four times as much as John and I were earning. We had an older friend who occupied a middle-ranking executive post at Lord Rothermere's Associated Newspapers and he earned £1,000 pa. The capital sum would have been just about sufficient to buy our house in Culross Street – it sold for £32,000 in 1962. (The current Zoopla value is £7.1 million.)

Nigel now embarked on a life of luxury and ease. Parking meters had just been introduced in Westminster (6d an hour – 2½p). Nigel would come down to the street at 8 am in an exquisitely embroidered silk dressing gown and ring next door's bell. When Lord Astor's stately butler answered the door, Nigel would hand him a fistful of sixpences to feed the meter and then trot off back to bed. He rose again at noon and drove the Royce to whichever expensive restaurant he had selected for lunch. His company on these occasions comprised a widening circle of rather louche characters either with no visible means of support or with jobs that did not demand attendance at regular hours. Luncheon would often continue until drinks time. Nigel always signed the bill.

Among the chancers who feasted at Nigel's table was a man who owned, or had access to, a professional-size roulette wheel. Now the drawing room at Culross Street occupied an entire floor. It was just about large enough to host a private casino and Nigel proposed that we should convert it to this use and watch the money roll in. The fact that casinos at this date were illegal in Britain counted little against the huge profits we believed could be made. We would serve free liquor as an attraction and there would be a pianist to serenade the gamblers. In those days it seems that there was always someone who knew somebody who could source this or that. We obtained the loan of a grand piano from the friend of a friend, but the problem was getting it to the first floor. There was no option but to remove the window casement and swing it into the drawing room by crane. Amazingly, we also found someone willing to lend us a crane for nothing at the weekend. The police magnanimously held up the traffic while we made these preparations for infringing the law.

The bank was chiefly funded by Nigel, to the tune of £600. John chipped in £100 and I contributed my life savings of £27. Obviously my rewards would be commensurate with my share, so the risk I was taking – including the possibility of gaol – was way out of proportion to any prospect of reward. Such is the idiocy of callow youth released from the constraints of home and school.

Invitations to the grand opening night were by word of mouth, many of the players being our fellow warriors from the HAC and their chums. We began play at about nine and for the first three or four hours the bank's assets steadily mounted. We had imposed a limit of £5 on any single bet, so that a win on an individual number would cost us a maximum of £180. But not many of our punters were affluent enough to risk the better part of a week's wages on a single bet. All went well until about one o'clock in the morning, when someone looked out of the window and said, 'Here come the Weybridge heavy mob!' Well, at least it wasn't the Flying Squad. Who, I enquired, were these Weybridge heavies? They were, it seemed, a bunch of young men who lived with wealthy parents in the Surrey suburb and mainly worked for their fathers' stockbroking firms in the City. These youngsters were, in the terminology of the day, 'fast'. They wore coloured waistcoats and bow ties, drove noisy sports cars, talked much louder than necessary, and bore adoring silky-haired blondes on their arms. I took an instant dislike to the whole lot of them.

The £5 limit was no impediment to these new arrivals. They peeled fivers from the rolls of notes they extracted from their hip pockets and scattered them with abandon across the board. Half a dozen of them struck lucky at 36-1. By two o'clock they had broken the bank and departed into the darkness whooping and singing lustily, waking the distinguished neighbours as they went. Doubtless we would be hearing from the Princess's agent.

Nigel had dropped the equivalent of the average annual industrial wage in the course of these few hours. His fortune was diminishing at a pace that even he found alarming. His parents were still unaware that he was unemployed. When John Kimpton took off for Canada (see next chapter), Nigel followed. He rented an expensive flat in Toronto and became an habitué of the city's late night bars. Always known to be good for a drink or three, he attracted a coterie of demi-monde characters ready to keep him company. One of these sidled up to him in the small hours of a morning and, perching himself on the neighbouring barstool, glanced furtively around, then whispered behind his hand, 'Psst. Wanna be put on to a good thing?'

The good thing, it transpired, was a parcel of land north of Toronto going for a knock-down price. All Nigel had to do was write a cheque for the amount specified and the chancer would do the rest. Nigel had no need to trouble himself about the legal details. All was above board and the deeds would be in Nigel's hands as soon as the cheque had cleared.

Everything progressed as the chancer had promised. It was too dark to read the deeds in the bar when they were delivered later in the week, so Nigel left that until the light of day. It was then that he found that he was proprietor of a substantial tract of virgin forest to which there were no access roads.

Several months later Nigel received a communication from the Toronto City Council. It informed him that the forest that encompassed his land had been scheduled for housing development. Nigel's land would be subject to a compulsory purchase order, at a rate to be determined by the assessors. A follow-up letter informed him of the sum payable, a five-figure sum that was several times the amount of his investment.

It took very little time for the chancer to renew Nigel's acquaintance at the late night bar. He slid on to the stool next to him, placed his hand in front of his mouth, then hissed, 'Wanna know the next big thing? Night car-washes.'

I do not know how the night car-washes panned out, but there came a time when the fortune had dwindled to a point where the burden of employment could no longer be repudiated. The problem was that Nigel had not worked for several years and had no skills or accomplishments other than the ability to sing falsetto. He eventually obtained work with the Toronto Post Office as a night telephone operator. His Post Office employment, in various capacities, continued until he retired on a modest pension. Nigel never considered that life had dealt him a bad hand and his spirits remained as irrepressible as they had been in his misspent youth. He now lives with his adoring wife Gillian in a mountain fastness somewhere in Ontario and seemingly has no regrets.

. . .

And what of my own progress up the slippery ladder of success? I was still teetering on the bottom rung. I learned little at S.H. Benson Ltd other than proof-reading, a very useful art, and about life in the trenches in WWI. My mentor in both respects was Mr Mason, a small man with a wizened face like a monkey who had joined the firm in 1908 at the age of fifteen – exactly fifty years before my own arrival. He and I sat on either side of a desk all day reading the proofs of advertisements. The fact that he had progressed no further in half a century's devoted service says quite a lot about social mobility and its lack in the first half of the twentieth century. He was highly intelligent and quick on the uptake. On one occasion he spotted that an advertisement headed 'Drink Bovril today!' was scheduled for insertion in an Irish newspaper on a Friday. An obvious solecism? None of the suits upstairs had noticed and we were the longstops.

Mr Mason had no resentment of those who had denied him preferment. He would tell me tales of Philip Benson, son of the founder, for whom he worked as personal assistant in the 1920s. Mr Philip was a stickler for correct dress. One Saturday (a half-day in the office), Mr Mason arrived wearing a soft collar. 'M-M-M-Mason,' Mr Philip expostulated with his habitual stammer, 'when you see m-m-m-me come into the office at a weekend without a proper stiff collar, then you m-m-m-may.' (We still wore stiff collars in my day and the London air was so polluted that the ridge of the collar would be black by the end of a working day. I used to buy paper collars at 1s 9d for six. After the first day I would clean the collar with a lump of compressed bread and wear it the following day. Then I turned it inside out and wore it for another two days.)

Mr Philip enjoyed an extravagant lifestyle. He had a yacht to which he invited select members of the staff at weekends. I asked Mr Mason if he had ever been one of them. He chuckled. 'It wasn't the likes of me that got invited. You had to have been to a public school.' He paused, ruminating. 'It was only the young men who got asked,' he added thoughtfully. 'Good-looking young men.'

But as I said, Mr Mason had no grudge against these gilded, entitled youths. 'If I was in charge of recruitment for S.H. Benson,' he confided to me over a cup of tea between proof-reads, 'I would always hire public schoolboys for the account teams.' They were the people who dealt with clients.

'Why is that, Mr Mason?' I asked, genuinely curious as to why he was prepared to exclude himself from the role. His monkey face creased into a wide grin. 'They're much better liars.'

Mr Mason had joined up in 1914 and had spent four years in the trenches, being wounded twice. He was one of Kitchener's 'First Hundred Thousand', of whom there were few survivors by 1918. There was no reticence about sharing the horrors of the Western Front with me. As I observed in the first chapter, I seldom found any reluctance in WWI veterans to talk about what they had witnessed and the oft-repeated saw that no one who had survived the carnage would ever talk about it is, to my personal knowledge, simply not true. Of course there were those who were so traumatised by their experiences that they could not bring themselves to reveal what they had endured, but most veterans' reluctance to talk – according to their own testimony – was either because they did not think that anyone who had not been there could comprehend this worst of all wars or, simpler still, because most British soldiers in the trenches lived a life of privation, boredom, discomfort and terror little different from the nine million of their fellows who served between 1914 and 1918. So what was there to tell? They could, however, be coaxed into sharing their memories by a show of genuine interest (and choosing the right questions to ask).

Knowing what he knew now, would he have volunteered with such alacrity in 1914, I asked Mr Mason. Yes, he told me, he would. The camaraderie of the trenches has been so often evoked in fiction that it has become something of a cliché, but it was undoubtedly what gave men like Mr Mason and his fellow volunteers the spirit to endure. The friendships he described were clearly the most meaningful of his life. And the most tragic, in those cases where the friends were parted from him by death.

Of course I should have written down what Mr Mason told me, because much has faded with the years. Some aspects of his war were unfamiliar to me from other sources. For example, he told me that no one in the trenches ever caught a cold. There they were standing in icy water with leaking boots, soaked by the incessant downpour of a Flanders winter, warmed by nothing more than stubs of candle in a mess-tin, yet nobody suffered coughs and sneezes. I mentioned this the other day to my neighbour, the distinguished military historian Sir Michael Howard, and he was most intrigued, never having heard it reported either.

Time came for me to move on from Mr Mason and there followed a succession of progressively dispiriting jobs that could only end with the supposed completion of my illusory 'training' and consignment to the dreaded Production Department. From thence there was no known way out until the 9-carat gold watch. I decided to jump ship.

Rubber Ears d'Arch Smith had a chum at the *New Statesman* called Michael Roberts who looked after book advertising. A Mr Doody looked after general advertising and they were seeking someone to take charge of classifieds. The wage was £10 a week.

Michael Roberts was a florid, tweedy, bibulous, but affable gay man with socialist principles wholly in line with the weekly he represented. Mr Doody, by contrast, wore striped trousers with a black jacket and wing collar topped by a matching homburg hat. He had bristling moustaches and I never knew him to smile, let alone laugh, during the six months I persevered in the soul-destroying job of persuading capitalists to advertise in an anti-capitalist paper. The only thing he and I had in common was our politics. We were the sole Tories on the paper and my guess is that, if we had ever sustained a conversation for long enough, we would have found ourselves both about as far to the right of the political spectrum as Michael was to the left. Sadly, though, this community of interest did nothing to endear me to him. Mr Doody never spoke to me in a normal voice. He barked at me. And he never looked at me with anything other than a glower. Why this should have been so remains a mystery still. I was unfailingly polite and deferential to him, I worked diligently, and although he was not technically my boss, I permitted him to order me around as if he was. He showed no such animosity to Michael, whose homosexuality, drinking habits and Trotskyite brand of socialism were all abhorrent to him.

There came a day when Michael and I were alone together in the office and he warned me that Mr Doody was planning to have me sacked. He was unable to tell me what offence I was supposed to have committed, but he thought it would be in my own interest to seek alternative employment.

. . .

Meanwhile there had been an upset at Culross Street. I was still going out with Sally Hance, who had now moved to a bijou residence in Polygon Mews off Baker Street. One of her flat-mates was a bubbly blonde called Annabelle, recently returned from New York. Annabelle looked exactly like one of the saucer-eyed blondes depicted by Peter Arno in those marvellous *New Yorker* cartoons in which he reflected the hedonism of the mighty metropolis's extravagant post-war years. To cite a single example, saucer-eyed young blonde with impressive embonpoint and pencil-slim skirt perches atop a bar stool while her sleek, tuxedoed, middle-aged escort commands the barman 'Fill 'er up.' It is perhaps not surprising that Annabelle resembled a Peter Arno girl, because she had modelled for the great man in New York.

Annabelle had a somewhat stolid boyfriend called Andrew, newly qualified as a dental surgeon, who was frequently absent overseas. On one occasion when he was in Borneo – why was a neophyte dental surgeon visiting Borneo? – she asked me if I would take her on a day trip to Eastbourne that Sunday. Sally, who was also away that weekend, assented and off we went. We had a lovely day, eating cockles, wearing kiss-me-quick hats, rolling around on the beach and giggling a lot. We came back to London in time for a modest supper at a trattoria and were making our farewells when Annabelle looked in her handbag and exclaimed that she had left her key behind. All the other girls at Polygon Mews were away. Could she come home with me?

Now this will sound like a put-up job, but I firmly believe that it was completely kosher. Annabelle adored Andrew (for reasons never evident to me) and would not have cheated on him. Also, it was wholly in character. Annabelle lost everything and was as daffy as the characters she modelled for Peter Arno. And there simply was not much promiscuity amongst well brought-up girls in 1960 – there were still three years to run before the invention of sexual intercourse per Philip Larkin.

Annabelle knew all about the ban on women staying overnight at Culross Street. She knew that we would have to creep upstairs in our stockinged feet, not speak above a whisper, and that she must not leave in the morning until the house was empty. John Kimpton was down at Knowles Tooth, so his bed was available. There was a lot of whispering, much barely suppressed giggling and then all that sea air and cheap Italian wine took its toll and we slept.

*'Can you account for these?', he asked.*

In the morning I left for work early and Annabelle promised not to make a sound until she heard the last lodger leave the house.

On my return in the evening I was met by Henry Ashby and Kenelm Bennett. They asked to speak to me in private. We went into the drawing room, long since restored from its temporary makeover as a casino, and I was invited to sit. They both stood. The atmosphere bristled with ill-concealed hostility. Kenelm walked over to a bureau, opened the drawer, and with a somewhat theatrical flourish held aloft a pair of pale pink, silk cami-knickers.

'Can you account for these?' he asked, holding the offending garment at arm's reach. Henry looked on with a sneer on his face.

'Never seen them before in my life,' I answered with more confidence than I felt.

'Then what were they doing on the floor of your room?'

'And what were you doing in my room?'

'We had a reasonable suspicion....'

'Of what?'

'That you were harbouring a woman in your room.'

That daffy, adorable, scatterbrained Annabelle had truly dropped me in it. And had she really gone off to work without any knickers? Of course she had. (When pressed on this later, she pleaded innocently that she had been 'thinking about other things'. Bloody Andrew most likely.)

Henry and Kenelm now informed me that, as I had broken the terms of the lease, I must leave. They would not have been able to enforce this had I been a signatory to the lease, but I was under age. In spite of this, we had a 'gentlemen's agreement' that I was an equal partner with equal proprietorial rights. My erstwhile friends chose not to honour it.

• • •

So, back to bed-sitterland. Moreover, this particular bed-sitter was in grimy Paddington. Would I ever live in marvellous Mayfair again? It seemed unlikely.

Life began a downward spiral. Having left the *New Statesman*, my next job did little to enhance my career prospects. Another of Rubber Ears's chums, fellow Old Cheltonian Jeremy Kauntze, was working at an outfit in Marylebone called The Shepherd Press. On hearing about Mr Doody's threat, Jeremy told me he could get me in there.

The ease with which this transfer of employment was engineered should have served as a warning. The Shepherd Press published a stable of magazines, of which the flagship was *Mother and Baby*. Flagship because it was the only one that had a newsstand sale. The others were trade or specialist publications. Jeremy sold space for *Women's Wear Weekly*. I was assigned to *Technical Book Review*.

The proprietor Mr Shepherd suffered delusions of grandeur, imagining himself the Beaverbrook of the trade press and forever lecturing his sycophantic staff about 'the power of the press' and 'our mission to inform'. None of this translated into a glimmer of reality. The editorial staff, few in number, were ill-paid and wholly lacking in skills and experience. The editor of *Mother & Baby* was a nineteen-year old proto-hippie who lived in a squat with a boyfriend whose nose may not have been a total stranger to illegal substances. Her knowledge of babycare was about on a par with mine. One of her columns – she had to write the whole magazine herself – was called 'Nurse Ackroyd Advises'. One can only hope that readers did not follow the advice too closely.

The editor of *Women's Wear Weekly* was a very genteel girl from Surbiton called Pamela Snook who had been hired as a typist and promoted to her new post on her second day in the office. She also had to write the whole magazine single-handed, including a column whose title, 'London Undie-world', caused her acute embarrassment. Mr Shepherd refused to change it. At first Pamela took great pride in her elevated position in the office hierarchy, but disillusionment began to set in on a day when the telephonist was dragged drunk from her switchboard soon after lunch and Pamela was instructed to take over. A call came in from Condé Nast Publications saying that the editor of Vogue, Audrey Withers, would like to be put on to the editor of *Women's Wear Weekly*.

'Speaking', chirped Pamela.

'But I thought I was speaking to the switchboard?' said Condé Nast.

'You are,' replied Pamela. 'I'm operating it this afternoon.'

'Thank you,' rejoined Condé Nast. 'I don't think Miss Withers will require to speak to you after all.'

*Technical Book Review* was a moribund publication for whose title Mr Shepherd had been offered £200 by a Fleet Street combine. Typically, Mr Shepherd thought he could leverage this offer by reviving the magazine. He hired a man called Ronald Ramsay as editor, his task being to write reviews of the most prominent new scientific and technical books. My job was to persuade the publishers to supplement these reviews by advertising, there being an unspoken *coda* that the booking of space would ensure a favourable review. This should have been like shooting fish in a barrel, but for the fact that publishers had an unwelcome habit of asking about Ronald Ramsay's credentials. I was certainly not going to reveal that he was a former sweetshop proprietor, but unfortunately there was not a lot that I could say that would instil confidence in a man who had no kind of scientific qualifications whatever. Sadly there was very little advertising to support Ramsay's glowing reviews.

None of The Shepherd Press's publications had audited circulation figures. The circulations we quoted were backed only by a printer's certificate. Now *Technical Book Review* had a quoted circulation of 6,000, whereas I knew that only 2,000 copies were actually distributed (mainly to a free list). One day in the pub I nobbled Joe, our print production man, about this.

'What happens to the other 4,000 copies, Joe?'

'You know where the printers are, young Sir, sarf of the River? Well, I collects the print run in the small hours of the morning and brings 'em back.'

'Yes, Joe?'

'Across Vauxhall Bridge.'

'Yes Joe?'

'Well, there's six farsand copies in the back of the van when I comes on to the bridge and there's two farsand when I comes orf it.'

'You don't mean...?'

'I don't mean anyfink, young Sir. Now drink up and mine's anuvver pint of wallop.'

I had only been at The Shepherd Press a few months when Jeremy Kauntze got his marching orders. Someone had revealed to Mr Shepherd that he was moonlighting. As space salesmen, we were only expected to be in the office at the beginning of the day and at its end. He would leave the premises about 9.30 and by 10.00 was ensconced behind his desk at the juvenile casting agency of which he was a partner. He would leave his office at 4.30 and be back at The Shepherd Press by 5.00. Once a fortnight he would devote a whole day to selling space for *Women's Wear Weekly* and, being a highly accomplished salesman, was able to bring in enough orders to satisfy Mr Shepherd.

I now found myself 'promoted' (there was no increase in salary) to Jeremy's former job. This was my undoing. My sales figures working full time being so much inferior to his sales figures for one day in ten, the writing was on the wall. I was duly sacked.

The day of my dismissal was 21st March 1961, which also happened to be my 21st birthday. Chums from the HAC and the Public Schools Club threw a dinner and an all-night poker party for me at the Reform Club (of which another chum was a member). The dinner was magnificent. It was the only occasion I have ever witnessed the archaic practice of bewigged footmen standing behind each diner's chair. It is slightly disconcerting when everyone at table is laughing and joking and the footmen's faces never crack a smile, but then you would hardly expect them to join in.

So much luxury and privilege lavished on a humble member of the unemployed. When I revealed my new status to John Kimpton and Nigel Hollings, they told me they were heading off to Canada. Why didn't I join them?

It was a tempting offer. But they were going to be staying with important friends of their parents, from whom John at least hoped to solicit offers of temporary employment. I would be a bit of an appendage, and besides it was permanent employment I was seeking. But here I was, having reached man's estate, and all I had to show for it was no job and a crummy bedsit in Paddington. Why not go West? But not to Canada.

I was on my way to America.

# Young Man
# Going West

# Chapter 5

. . .

# KENNEDY'S CAMELOT

. . .

*1961–62*

I sailed from Southampton on 20th May 1961 aboard the Holland America Line's *SS Maasdam*, one of the last emigrant ships to ply the Atlantic. The fare, at £65, was the cheapest way of getting to America. Since 1958, the year that transatlantic jet service was introduced, more passengers had crossed the Atlantic by air than by sea. But the cheapest single air fare was £90, quite a significant difference. The *Maasdam* had been built in 1952 specifically to cater to the bottom end of the market – there were thirty-nine first class passengers to 880 in steerage, with nothing in between. (Other than large barriers – I never spotted one of these gilded creatures from the Top Deck during the whole nine-day voyage.) On my trip the *Maasdam* was pretty nearly full, but within four years the decline in maritime passenger traffic on the Atlantic route was so great that she and her sister ship the *Rijsdam* were converted into student cruise ships, catering to perhaps the most impecunious travellers of all.

Accommodation was rudimentary. I shared a cabin with fifteen other passengers. Two of these were young Americans who boarded at Southampton. The remainder of my cabin-mates came aboard at Cobh. They were peasant boys from Connemara and I was unable to understand anything they said. Whether they were speaking Irish, or a particularly strong West Coast dialect, I never learned and I do wonder how they fared on arrival in the promised land.

One of the Americans in the cabin became an instant chum. Norman Davies was from Watsonville, California, and worked for the Southern Pacific Railroad as a fireman. As all the SPR's locomotives were diesel, this was not a particularly arduous job. Norman worked in a shunting yard and his only task was to jump down from the footplate and change the points when the train switched tracks. The grizzled old driver, put out to pasture in the shunting yard pending retirement, would sing out 'Points ahead, Norman!' to arouse his assistant, whose head was invariably deep in a book. Norman had built a library on the footplate, erecting shelves wherever there was a space. As often as not the driver would then say, 'Stay where you are, Norman. I'll do it. You're getting yourself an eddication.' He was indeed, having flunked out of five colleges because he did not like the set books, becoming an autodidact instead.

The deal between the SPR and the all-powerful rail union was that the firemen would be kept in full employment for seven months of the year at $125 a week and laid off for five months at $50 a week. Norman was not only of a literary bent, but also a committed traveller (unusual in a nation where fewer than 10% owned a passport). There was at that time a popular guidebook called *Europe on $5 a Day*. Now $125 was about double the average clerical wage, so Norman was able to put quite a lot by. Even the $50 a week was sufficient to finance his annual travels in Europe. (Technically the firemen were on stand-by, subject to immediate recall, and were not allowed to leave California. Norman said he doubted that any fireman had ever been recalled.)

There was a window of a couple of weeks between the arrival of the *Maasdam* at Hoboken, New Jersey, and the resumption of Norman's duties in the shunting yard and he proposed that we should join forces. Knowing not a single person in the United States, I was delighted to comply.

We spent a day and a night in New York, starting in Greenwich Village where Norman wanted to check out some of the hang-outs of the beat poets. We then went up-market, enjoying cocktails at the Waldorf Astoria. Although Norman was dressed in a costume that combined elements of both working man's and student attire, I was outfitted, at Norman's decree, in a three-piece suit with bowler hat and furled umbrella. This was sufficient to gain both of us entry through the hallowed portals of New York's most luxurious hotel. From there we descended to Gotham's depths, ending the evening in a succession of the low dives that lined the Bowery. We slept in a flop-house which cost rather less than one of the Waldorf Astoria's cocktails.

In the morning I enjoyed the first of what was to become, and still is, one of my greatest pleasures in America – breakfast in a diner. We British witter on about our breakfasts, but frankly the Americans outdistance us when it comes to the first meal of the day. For lunch and dinner stateside, the results are, at best, variable. But breakfast! The freshly squeezed orange, the crispy bacon, the eggs over-easy (never hard, never a broken yolk), the golden home-made hash-browns (in Britain these are frozen and from a packet, even in leading West End hotels). Somerset Maugham famously said that if you want to eat well in Britain, have three breakfasts a day. If you want to eat well in America....

The inner man replete, Norman inspected the outer man and found it a bit dishevelled after the evening's shenanigans. He marched me off to a shoeshine stand to have my Chelsea boots properly buffed. The proprietor of the enterprise was a twelve-year old negro boy who restored my footwear to gleaming perfection for 25c. As I handed over the coin, the little lad looked up at me with big round eyes and, cocking his head on one side, ventured, 'Are you a dook?'

My attire also attracted attention on Broadway. A tour bus halted a few yards ahead of me and I heard the guide call out 'Quick photo op, folks. Get a load of the crazy European coming up the sidewalk.' There was, however, a point to my stereotypical City gent costume. Norman had decreed that our next adventure would be 'Frauds at Yale'. We were on our way to Grand Central Station to board a train for New Haven, Connecticut.

'Frauds at Yale', Norman explained to me, was our passport to free accommodation and other delights over the next few days. All we had to do was start on one side of the campus and progress towards the other side. With me in my City finery, Norman predicted that before we were halfway across we would have made contact with our prospective hosts. It was a sure thing, he assured me. I was a great deal less certain. If you started walking through Oxford or Cambridge dressed as a matador, say,

*'Frauds at Yale', Norman explained, 'was our passport to free*
*accommodation and other delights …'*

or wearing *lederhosen* and a hat with a feather in it, eyes would be averted
and you would be studiously ignored.

They do things differently in America. We started on our progress, me
with bowler hat, gold watch chain across my weskit, and a copy of *The
Times* under my arm, Norman in his Sloppy Joe outfit walking a dozen paces
behind, and within minutes we had a result. A bunch of what I later learned
are called 'Preppies', attired in button-down polo shirts, cashmere sweaters
and penny loafers, hailed me and asked if I was visiting. Their leader, tall,
patrician and casually elegant, introduced himself as Warren Hoge. Would
I, Warren asked, like to come back to the dorm with them. There was only
the most momentary discomfiture expressed in his handsome features as
I revealed that not only was I accompanied, but by someone who did not

look entirely in tune with the gilded youth strutting the serene and verdant Yale campus, but he instantly recovered his composure and greeted Norman with the sangfroid of one well accustomed to daily intercourse with railroad firemen. While the contrast between the Waldorf Astoria and the Bowery had given me some intimation of gradations of wealth and status in the US, this was my first opportunity to observe different classes interacting in a supposedly classless society. Both sides handled themselves with aplomb and over the following days Warren's group of friends, all of them, like himself, alumni of America's most prestigious prep schools, acknowledged that Norman was far better read than any of them.

A 'dorm' in England is, or was, an unheated, sparsely furnished chamber in which boarding school children sleep on iron bedsteads. A dorm in America is something else. The one inhabited by Warren and his friends, one of twelve at Yale, was called Calhoun College. It was a stately, gabled Elizabethan-style edifice with a fortress-like castellated tower at one end and a courtyard. It was, indeed, much like an Oxford or Cambridge college, though with rather superior accommodation. Here Norman and I were found two vacant beds and invited to join our new friends in the refectory for meals. Whether this liberality was generally extended to visitors, or whether it was assumed that we were bona fide students, I never discovered. On the first evening we were entertained at the Yale Club, which was furnished like a nineteenth-century London chop-house and provided traditional fare to match.

Other diversions included attending rehearsals of Warren's glee club, the Spizzwinks, who were to spend the vacation touring South America, and the opening concert preceding the tour. The glee club singers all wore tails. At a punch party for parents given on the lawn of Calhoun College I helped the Master's wife to serve the drinks. Here I had my second encounter with the class divide in America. Most of the parents exuded the quiet discretion that accompanies wealth and privilege, but there was one father with a loud voice and coarse features who stuck out from the rest. He consumed no fewer than fifteen glasses of the punch, which was mainly champagne, and his behaviour deteriorated progressively. The Master's wife was seething.

Most of the students owned cars (forbidden at English universities even for the few who could afford them) and we made various forays into neighbouring states. One of these was to Smith College in Massachusetts, one of New England's leading girls-only universities, for the graduation ceremony. Afterwards we spent a raucous evening in the company of four exceptionally pretty girls and arrived back at Yale as dawn was breaking. Another was to Choate, alma mater of one of Warren's chums as well as President John F Kennedy. *It is very like an English public school, I wrote home, except that everything is in a better state of repair, and all the rooms are superbly furnished, rather in a club style.*

Norman and I agreed that we should take our departure before outstaying our welcome. 'Where next?' I asked him. 'How about 'Frauds at Harvard'?' he suggested.

So it was that I found myself ensconced in Wigglesworth Hall for a week, indulging in many of the pleasures of life at Harvard. Norman set off for California and his literary life on the footplate, but before he left we agreed to spend the following winter in Mexico, fixing a date in January when we would meet on the steps of the General Post Office in El Paso, Texas. I needed to start looking for work, but first I had a date with Warren in New York before he embarked for South America. There I was to stay with the Hoges in their apartment on Park Avenue.

Due to some confusion over dates, I arrived a day before Warren. He kindly arranged for me to spend the evening with one of the pretty girls from Smith, called Diana. Now the Hoges' apartment was quite unlike any flat I had ever seen in London. It was enormous, sumptuous, grandiose, and yet in exquisite taste. But this was a mere taster for Diana's parents' apartment on Sutton Place. This was even more capacious, and even more gorgeous, with contents that resembled a saleroom at Christie's. Diana's father, a self-made man, sat me down on something probably Louis Quinze and put a tumbler of something probably as rare as it was expensive in my hand, before enquiring: 'You wanna give my dotter a good time?' I agreed that that was the general idea.

'Listen up,' he said. 'I'll tell you what you wanna do. You start at the Champagne Bar at the Plaza Hotel. That's on Fifth Avenue. Hold the cab.'

Hold the cab? How much would that cost while we sipped the most expensive champagne in town?

'Then you go on to eat at the Four Seasons. That's in the Seagram Building. You'll need a reservation, but I'll call Luigi and fix it. Hold the cab.'

This was going from bad to worse. I had arrived in America with $420, which needed to last until I secured gainful employment. Although I had been living rent-free at Yale and Harvard, naturally I had needed to repay hospitality. Funds were already depleted.

Diana's father turned to her. 'You like the Four Seasons, don't you Sweetie?'

'Yes Daddy. But isn't it rather expensive?'

'Nothing's too good for my dotter. Isn't that so, Mister … er, Mister … er?'

I concurred that nothing was too good for Diana. But her daddy wasn't finished.

'After that you'll wanna do some dancing. Head for the Stork Club. They have a great band. Hold the cab.'

He took another swig of his Chivas Regal before delivering the *coup de grâce*. 'Then to finish up the evening, you go on to El Morocco. Diana knows the people there. They'll look after you.'

'Do I hold the cab, Sir?'

'Of course you HOLD THE CAB. How else do you think you are going to get my dotter home at that time in the morning? She don't wanna wait around while they summon a cab from downtown. Do you, honey?'

Diana didn't reply. She gave me a nod to signify drink up, and we were on our way. The last words from Daddy were 'Don't forget to hold the cab.'

Descending in the elevator I did some rapid calculations. If my 300-odd dollars was sufficient to pay for these entertainments, plus several hours' waiting time for the cab, I would be starting life in America stony broke and with nowhere to live. This was a lesson not to play out of my league.

When we were on the sidewalk I looked up and down Sutton Place for a yellow cab. I was about to hail one when Diana put her hand on my arm. 'Do you really want to do all those things Daddy suggested?' she asked. 'Well,' I replied, 'I thought perhaps it was what you wanted to do?'

She chuckled. 'No, it's what Daddy wants me to do. I would much rather grab a burger and a shake. Have you been to a real New York burger joint yet, Patrick? And as it's a lovely evening we could go for a stroll in Central Park afterwards. There's probably a concert or a play on. They have an open-air auditorium where anyone can put on a show, but they're not allowed to charge for admission.'

Dear Diana. You gave me one of the happiest evenings I spent in America. And it cost a total of $4.28.

. . .

Warren arrived the next day. After an enjoyable stay with the charming and hospitable Hoges, I flew back to Boston prepared to begin the search for suitable employment. I had glimpsed how the rich live in America and I had learned that the 'American Dream' meant the opportunity to acquire wealth and position regardless of origin or background. While my prospects in battered old Blighty had been dim, here in shiny new America nothing could stand in my way.

Could it?

I found myself a bed-sitter for $10 a week in a rooming house on Mount Auburn Street in Cambridge, just off Harvard Square. The communal kitchen had been put off limits because the tenants left it in such an appalling state, but there was a connecting door to my room and a fellow lodger obligingly picked the lock in return for 'visiting rights'. The kitchen contained a television set. Now, I had never lived in a house with television before. This gave me another window on America, not all of it to that great country's credit. The highs of American television were inspiring; the more frequent lows betrayed a poverty of imagination and creativity that were a sad reflection of the power that sponsors wielded over programme makers. Incidentally, I was frequently asked whether I had ever seen television before, on the assumption that it did not exist outside the United States. My protestations that BBC Television had been in operation since 1936, three years before NBC introduced TV in America, were met with scepticism.

The principal reason for choosing Boston as my place of residence was that it was the home of the HAC's sister regiment, the Ancient & Honorable Artillery Company. Unlike the HAC, this was no longer a functioning military unit, but a combination of gentlemen's club and fraternal organisation. Much of its activity comprised very convivial dinners, varied from time to time by appearances in uniform at parades and processions. Whereas the HAC was drilled by Guards' NCOs to standards not far below that of the Brigade of Guards itself, the drill performed by the Ancient & Honorables owed more to the tutelage of Fred Karno's Army. I have never witnessed such a shambles on a parade ground. None of this caused the Ancient & Honorables the slightest discomfiture. When they marched as a unit in processions most of them were out of step and a number were puffing on stogies.

Many of the members, however, were from the upper echelons of Boston society and enjoyed power and status in the city. My hope was that suitable introductions might lead to lucrative employment. Several members were very generous in their hospitality and optimistic about my prospects of securing a position commensurate with my supposed superior background. One of them speculated that he could find me a placement on the *Boston Globe*. My letters home were full of the glorious prospects opening before me.

Then the Ancient & Honorable Artillery Company went into recess for the summer. Contacts began to dwindle and few of the promises of introductions came to fruition. No more was heard of the *Boston Globe*. I signed up with an executive employment agency and they pronounced that I should have no difficulty obtaining a position in marketing or communications. A number of interviews were arranged. Several prospective employers turned me down on grounds that I was not an American citizen. Any kind of state-run enterprise had a ban on employing non-citizens, and this included all educational institutions that were supported by public funds, but there were private enterprises like shipping companies that rejected me on the same grounds. Other prospects reported back that they would be delighted to employ me after I had lived in America for a year or so.

It looked as if I might have to lower my sights and settle for clerical work, just as an interim. It transpired, though, that this was a somewhat overcrowded market. By 1961 almost half of the American population, male and female, went on to college after graduating high school. The problem was that there were insufficient management-level positions to absorb such a number, and many had to settle for routine office work. Not surprisingly, with such a wealth of talent available, employers were more likely to select the native-born or American-educated.

So my sights sank lower still. Perhaps, being well-spoken ('We just love your cute accent'), I might find a job in retail. Having exhausted the possibilities of Filene's, Gilchrist's and Jordan Marsh, who all loved the accent but required previous experience behind the counter, I embarked on a round of the supermarkets. Alas, anything that involved monetary transactions required an ability to compute dollars and cents. Not that even I, with zero mathematical ability, found much difficulty in adding or subtracting in a decimal currency. But employers seemed to think that, coming from the land of £ s and d, I would be baffled by the complexity of a hundred cents to a dollar. I assured them that I would not. They told me to apply again in a year or two's time.

Climbing even further down the ladder of ambition, I threw myself on to the resources of the job centre. They were sure they could find me something gainful, provided I was not too selective. First I would need to take an aptitude test, then they would match my abilities to the work most suitable. Was I prepared to work in a factory? I was. Good, the aptitude test would reveal what kind of manufacturing I was most attuned to. Several days later I was summoned back to hear the results. The job centre manager greeted me affably enough in his austere little office, but he was plainly not at ease.

'I am not sure how to tell you this, Mr Robertson. Your aptitude test results are not quite like any other we have ever had.' He looked up at the ceiling, as if seeking inspiration from the cracked lines in the plaster. Then he looked over my shoulder to the frosted glass door, as if hoping it would open of its own accord to release him. 'The fact is, Mr Robertson ... well, the results indicate that you aren't really fitted for any kind of employment. Not the kind that we deal with here. I hope you won't be too discouraged by this. Have you considered the army?'

The alternative to being trained up as cannon fodder was catering, which required minimal skills. I was sent for a number of interviews, but with the same negative results as I had received in the retail sector. I would not understand their money, I was assured. I did not look strong enough to be a kitchen porter. That left dish-washer and bus-boy, the spotty youth who clears the tables. Neither paid a living wage but I was rejected anyway. I was told I was over-qualified.

Then one day in the *Boston Globe* there was an ad which offered a number of placements in the advertising and marketing department of the Grolier Society at $97 per week. The Grolier Society was a huge publishing conglomerate. I had previous experience in advertising. This was my chance!

I was hired with surprising ease and told that there would be a three-day training session. The purpose of the training was to instruct the new inductees in the promotion of a teaching machine that would be launched on the market after field trials. Our job as inductees was to select people to receive free teaching machines worth $150 each, together with a free set of the *Grolier Encyclopedia*, so that they could report back on its functionality. We were warned during training that some people might mistake us for salesmen. If we were asked if we were selling something we were to apologise that we were unable to oblige them. We could only give away our machines, in return for their invaluable input.

Now $97 a week was less than a fireman on the Southern Pacific Railroad earned, but it was not to be sniffed at. It was nearly ten times my weekly rent. In London I had earned less than three times my weekly rent. The only slight fly in the ointment was that the generous emolument was contingent on placing so many teaching machines a week, but how difficult could it be to give valuable things away for free? I reported for work on the first day following training with high hopes and expectations. About a dozen inductees were to be taken in a mini-van to the city of Worcester. There we were to ring on door bells in select neighbourhoods and distribute our largesse to grateful recipients.

I remarked to the young man sitting next to me on the bus that I found it remarkable that the Grolier Society, huge and successful as it was, could afford to give away $150 teaching machines and expensive encyclopaedias all in the interests of market research. My neighbour looked at me quizzically. 'Are you being serious?' he asked. 'C'mon,' he said 'you didn't really fall for all that guff they spun us in the training classes did you? We're not giving away anything. We are selling encyclopaedias.'

'But what about the free $150 teaching machines?' I urged, 'and the encyclopaedias are free too, aren't they?'

My neighbour looked at me with a mixture of amusement and contempt. 'That $150 teaching machine costs the Grolier Society about $3.50 per unit. They can afford to give that away. The encyclopaedia isn't really free. You remember from the training session that we have to tell the punters that in order to be sure that they are really going to use the machines and the encyclopaedia, all that we require is that they pay a small subscription for the annual yearbook? Well, that not-so-small subscription amply covers the cost of these giveaways, plus our wages, and provides the Grolier Society with a nice fat profit. It's simply a clever marketing wheeze.'

On arrival in Worcester we were each dropped off in a different scrubbed and manicured suburb and given a roster of streets to cover. It was now 6.30 pm and most Americans are finishing their evening meal by then. My heart was thumping as I rang the first doorbell. 'Now remember,

Patrick, to say that you aren't selling anything,' I told myself with more confidence than I felt.

The door was opened by an amiable middle-aged man sucking on a pipe. 'Good evening, Sir. I am here from the Grolier Society to invite you to be one of a select few to participate in a test of our new teaching machine. If you agree to be on our panel, you will receive a $150 teaching machine and the latest edition of the *Grolier Encyclopedia* absolutely free of charge.'

The pipe-smoker took a couple of puffs and then enquired: 'Before we go any further, tell me this. Does your generous proposition involve, at any stage of the proceedings, the transfer of funds from me to you?'

He had me. He had not asked if I was selling anything. There was only one truthful answer to his question.

'It does', I declared. 'And I have just decided that I am not cut out for this job. I no longer represent the Grolier Society.'

He gave me a big grin. 'Come inside and meet the wife. You from England? Yes, sounds like it. What would you like to drink?'

After a couple of noggins, my new friend asked if I would like to see Worcester. For the next couple of hours he drove me round all the sights and told me the turbulent history of a city that had been settled and abandoned several times over during the Indian wars of the late seventeenth century. At nine o'clock he dropped me on the corner where I was to meet the van and wished me well in my renewed quest for work.

\* \* \*

Being unemployed meant that I could not afford any kind of social life outside the rooming house, where I became friendly with the young man who had picked the kitchen lock, a Harvard post-graduate student called Bill Gordey. He had been cast in Harvard's production of Bernard Shaw's *Misalliance* and sought my help in polishing up his English accent. I became his dialogue coach and we bonded. Apart from when I had job interviews – which were becoming alarmingly sparse – he and I both tended to keep late hours and sleep until lunchtime. We came to the conclusion that a twenty-four-hour day did not really suit people of our waking and sleeping habits and that we would do better with a thirty-six-hour day. With the week divided into four-and-a-half days, our times of rising and going to bed would vary considerably each day. In Harvard Square there was a 24/7 eatery called the Waldorf Cafeteria whither we would repair for breakfast, which might be at any time of day or night. Another habituée of this establishment was Miss Whitehead, a very elderly English lady who dressed in clothes of another era and had a cockatoo permanently seated on her shoulder. She treated this attendant as if he was a family retainer and severely discouraged Americans from talking to him in baby language. 'Who's a pretty boy then?' was met with a frosty stare and the observation 'I don't think we have the privilege of an introduction.' She was forthcoming with Bill and me, though, as we accorded her the deference due to the daughter of the illustrious Harvard philosopher Alfred North Whitehead.

Miss Jessie Whitehead had been born and raised in the other Cambridge, where her distinguished father was a fellow of Trinity College. She herself was a graduate of Newnham. While there she met the poet Rupert Brooke, then an undergraduate at King's and described by WB Yeats as 'the handsomest young man in England'.

'All of us girls were in love with him', Miss Whitehead recalled. 'Of course we all knew he liked boys as well as girls, but it didn't make any difference. People nowadays assume we were all so innocent back then, before the Great War. But that's rubbish. We knew perfectly well about sexual orientation in its several forms.'

But the man she fell properly in love with was George Mallory, one of the gilded youths who belonged to what would later be dubbed the Bloomsbury Group – the Strachey brothers, James and Lytton, Duncan Grant, JM Keynes. In 1909, which was probably the year that Jessie Whitehead met her inamorato for the first time, Lytton Strachey wrote: 'Mon dieu! – George Mallory …! He's six foot high, with the body of an athlete by Praxiteles, and a face – oh incredible – the mystery of Botticelli, the refinement and delicacy of a Chinese print, the youth and delicacy of an unimaginable English boy.' Alas for Jessie, the following year this godlike creature left Cambridge to become a master at Charterhouse and there met his future wife, Ruth Turner. Shortly after Mallory and Old Salopian Sandy Irvine had disappeared near the summit of Everest in 1924, Jessie Whitehead followed her father to Cambridge, Massachusetts. She never returned to the land where she had loved and lost.

When I was not looking for work I spent a lot of time in the numerous second-hand bookshops of Cambridge and Boston, where I was surprised to find that about half the books were by English authors. I doubt that new bookshops would have reflected the same division. At this time many of the books sold in second-hand bookshops were pre-war, when almost any English novel with literary pretensions would find a US publisher. Paperbacks usually started at 10c and hardbacks at a quarter, so even with my dwindling resources I was able to indulge myself with two or three books a week. The American booksellers were almost without exception charming to do business with, unlike English booksellers who seemed to hate their customers. (And some of them seemed to hate books too.) The only unfriendly bookseller I met in North America was English – he said he would send for the police if I did not get out of his shop. The Cambridge booksellers were delightful. One lovely lady suddenly leaped up from her counter and announced that as it was a very hot day she was going to buy choc ices for everyone in the shop. I helped her price some Victorian children's games – if you were English you were assumed by Americans to be an expert on anything old – and in return she gave me all the books I had intended to buy. Not the kind of experience I have ever had in an English bookshop.

When I had been job hunting in Boston, I often indulged myself with the price of a cinema ticket. Cambridge had a very good arts cinema, the Brattle Theater, but by this time I could no longer afford regular-priced cinema tickets, generally in the $1.25–$2.50 range. In downtown Boston, though, in areas frequented by down-and-outs and winoes, there were fleapit cinemas that offered you three features, a newsreel and a one-reel comedy for 35c. They were open twenty-four hours a day and were used by the homeless as a cheap alternative to the flop-house. One of the three features would always be English. The Americans may have had a taste for English literature, but this did not extend to films. The inclusion of at least one, and sometimes two, English features was simply because distributors charged very little for their rental. The customers were indifferent. Most of them were there to get a few hours' sleep. (I had a nagging anxiety that I might soon be among their number.)

The cheapest entertainment was television, which in Boston operated until three in the morning and resumed at six. I wrote home that on the whole it was more entertaining than British television, as there were far fewer interviews with politicians. I singled out *The Jack Paar Show* as my favourite. This was a late-night chat show presided over by the supremely affable Jack Paar, assisted by his hyper-intelligent sidekick Hugh Downes, and it surprised me on rereading this letter to my parents that I needed to explain what a chat show was. I had forgotten that they emerged in Britain only around the mid-sixties. Hence those endless interviews with evasive politicians to fill up airtime.

This may sound like a relatively carefree life, but it was not. I was now down to my last $50 and faced the very real prospect of homelessness. Could I not ask my parents for support? Yes, and they would have helped. But if I had done that, it would have been an admission that I had failed in America. There would have been no alternative other than to return to England and suffer the humiliation of responding to friends and family's queries of 'Back so soon?' My state of mind at the time may be judged by the fact that I still, in my eightieth year, have anxiety dreams in which I am in a far away country and broke, either homeless or facing the prospect of eviction. Often in these nightmares I shed articles of clothing progressively until I am left standing only in socks and underpants. Fortunately that did not happen to me in America.

I reached my lowest point in the quest for work when I attempted to become a leaflet distributor. This involved standing on the sidewalk and thrusting flyers for pizza joints, loan sharks or bail bondsmen into the hands of reluctant recipients. In order to be selected for this task, which paid $1.25 an hour, you had to present yourself at a warehouse in downtown Boston at five in the morning. For me this involved a four-mile walk from Cambridge, starting about 3.30 am. It is indicative of the scarcity of employment in one of the greatest metropolises of Kennedy's Camelot, indeed the President's own home town, that on each occasion I presented myself ready for work there were at least a hundred other applicants. Only twenty fortunates were picked, seemingly at random, though it now occurs to me that they may have been personally known to the foreman, and I was never amongst their number. The four-mile walks home as dawn broke over the Charles River are amongst the most despondent memories I have of the new life I had chosen.

. . .

I had now reached the nadir of my fortunes. While I was having a moan to Bill Gordey one day, he asked if I had tried the Harvard personnel office.

Had I thought of applying to the largest employer in Cambridge? No, I had not. Being desperate is no antidote to being stupid.

Harvard had no vacancies but helpfully suggested that I try Boston University's personnel office. This I did. As I was wearing a three-piece suit, it was assumed that I was seeking a professional position. I asked what was available. 'We need an in-house lawyer,' the personnel lady told me. 'You a lawyer?' Sadly that is not a job where you can wing it. 'We need an accountant. You a certified accountant?' I demurred. 'There are a couple of vacancies in the library. You a librarian?' Now that *was* something I might be able to wing. It's mainly about books and I had picked up odd bits of bibliographic jargon from Rubber Ears d'Arch Smith. 'Yes,' I said emphatically.

And so it was that I found myself ushered into the office of the Head Librarian and seated before the great man himself. I was fully aware that the interview might be brief, once I had revealed that my only experience in this field was as school librarian at Shrewsbury. To my surprise this information received a positive response. As the conversation developed it became apparent that the Head Librarian was under the misapprehension that Shrewsbury was a university – the term 'school' is often used in American English to signify a place of tertiary education. (The question 'Where did you go to school?' does not mean which high school did you attend.) He asked me how many staff I employed. I told him, truthfully, that I had a dozen assistants. I did not feel it necessary to add that each house was required to provide a boy to spend half an hour a week putting returned books back on to the shelves. His next question was more difficult to answer: 'How many books did you have in your Shrewsbury College library?' Well, we had never actually counted them. I drew a bow at a venture and replied 350,000. (In fact it was probably fewer than 10,000.) The Head Librarian owned himself impressed that I had run such a large library with only twelve staff.

Then came the killer question. 'What kind of classification system did you use at Shrewsbury College?' I gulped and sought inspiration. There was a silence while I collected my thoughts. If I said Dewey Decimal, which I was aware was the most widely used system, he would probably ask me technical questions about it. But I did not know the name of any other system. I looked him straight in the eye and spoke slowly and deliberately. 'Shrewsbury was founded by King Edward VI,' I said, 'and the Library dates from the 1560s, which as you know is a long time before the Dewey Decimal System was introduced. So we still use an Elizabethan classification unique to the Library.'

The Head Librarian waved a hand towards a colleague who was passing the door. 'Hank, come in here.' I thought perhaps Hank was a security guard summoned to throw me out. 'I got a fella here from Shrewsbury College in England looking for a job with us,' he said as Hank entered. 'And do you know what he just told me. At his university library they use an Elizabethan classification system! Waddayaknow?' Hank shook me warmly by the hand and introduced himself as the Deputy Head. Turning to the Head, he said 'Chuck, that is somp'n else. You gotta hire this guy.'

. . .

I acquired a job, a new residence and a girlfriend all in the same week. In order to be close to my place of work, I moved across the River Charles and into Ma Parker's rooming house on Bay State Road, a couple of minutes from Boston University's main building on Commonwealth Avenue. There were about a dozen lodgers, all of them students or otherwise connected with the university. Ma Parker was a small roly-poly person of pronounced views on every subject who was not inhibited from expressing them by large reservoirs of ignorance. She was, however, very good-natured and welcoming and on the night of my arrival entertained me to a prodigious dinner of corn-on-the-cob, ham, tongue, chicken, cakes and Jewish pastries.

I met the new girl in my life at the English Speaking Union, in theory a club for bringing Americans and Brits closer together, but in practice a place where the British, Irish and the odd colonial could get together to consume copious draughts of tea and complain about the host country to each other. It was a curious feature of Boston life that the Irish – and I am speaking here of immigrants, not Irish-Americans – buried the hatchet with their former oppressors to forge a united front against the boisterous, braggart Yanks. I have to say it was neither becoming nor generous-spirited of us to repay our host's hospitality in this way, but it was good to get to know the Irish on neutral ground with old animosities at least temporarily suspended.

Maggie, the girl who had won my heart, was a working-class English autodidact, whose grandfather was one of the last hansom-cab drivers. She had a cut-glass accent (presumably acquired though it sounded not the least forced), a compelling laugh and a golden aureole of hair. She also had effortless charm and was universally adored by the English, Scots, Irish and colonials who frequented the ESU. The night we met I was invited back to her flat on Beacon Street with a crowd of others and we all enjoyed a hastily concocted supper of scraps in an atmosphere reminiscent of bohemian hang-outs in Chelsea. Smitten, I returned on Sunday and boldly rang her doorbell, to which there was no answer. The lovesick swain spent seven hours waiting in the street in the hope that she would return but, as I learned later, she was at her sister's house upstate. The next day I found her at home and was invited to accompany her to the launderette. Never before had I become so intimately acquainted with a lady's underwear so early in our relationship. Back at the house, she made me a tuna and mayonnaise sandwich. My least favourite filling, but I was too delirious with joy to notice the taste.

The next Saturday I took Maggie to the opening night of the Harvard Players' production of Shaw's *Misalliance*. The accents tended towards the Dick Van Dyke delivery of the Queen's English, but we both agreed that Bill Gordey was the honourable exception. Under my tutelage he had perfected his diction and was the one Harvard Player who might have been mistaken for a Brit. Afterwards I spent some of my remaining $40 – I would not be paid until the end of the month – in wooing Maggie over a candlelit dinner. In a letter home I remarked that she ate rather a lot, which I think was probably a reference more to my anxiety about the bill than a criticism of her appetite.

The following day Maggie drove me to Gloucester, a small fishing town on the Massachusetts coast named after my own place of birth. Here we ate seafood direct from the ocean. At an opportune moment Maggie revealed to me that there was a gentleman in Leicester with whom she had an understanding. Looking back, she did exactly the right thing in stopping me from becoming too ardent. She was ten years older than me, I had no profession, and I was too young to settle down anyway. I curbed my rapidly developing passion and replaced it with an affectionate regard that burgeoned over the coming months into the warmest of friendships.

The sister, Mary, who was also to become a good friend, was a GI bride married to a mailman, David, with a daughter of twelve, who was wholly English in speech and manner, and a son of nine who was just as resolutely American. Maggie's niece declared her intention of 'returning' to England, which she had never seen, as soon as she was of age. I would love to know whether she fulfilled this dream. Or did she go native as a teenager?

My first encounter with Mary was when I was invited to join the whole family, plus their friends from Balham, Stan and Gloria, on a trip to a lake in the Maine woods. Maggie drove me to Mary's home in Wakefield, a manufacturing town whose principal industry, curiously, was model aeroplanes, and from thence we set forth in a string of vehicles carrying about twenty people. Until now I had only seen what lay between New York and Boston, some 250 miles of mainly suburban sprawl. (It was claimed that before the tramways closed, you could travel from New York City to Boston by streetcar, never having to walk more than a mile or so from the outer terminus of one network to that of another.) Now I experienced the kind of countryside for which northern New England is renowned and saw for myself that there really are idyllic villages and winding lanes. It was that part of America celebrated by Norman Rockwell, and having bathed in the warm, limpid waters of the lovely, forested lake that was our destination, I could testify that you did not need to venture far beyond one of the most densely populated areas of America to find the wilderness that Americans cherish so dearly.

*   *   *

Amongst Maggie's coterie of devoted admirers was an unusual young man called Peter Dallas. He claimed to be the American correspondent of the *Shrewsbury Chronicle*, which sounded a bit improbable. I think they had published some of his articles about American life, but I doubt that he was paid for them. The reason he made an impression on me was because he had developed a skill for survival in the United States on virtually no money at all. Peter lived in the basement of a junk shop in a poor part of Boston, sleeping on a couch bearing a ticket saying $8. If it found a buyer, Peter would be on the floor. The shop was owned by a female artist who allowed him to overnight there in return for his services as janitor.

There were no cooking facilities, so Peter ate in the canteens at Harvard and Boston University. Here you could purchase two slices of white bread for 5c. The canteens had an immense range of pickles, dips, sauces and relishes that patrons added to their burgers or hot dogs. These were free. Peter would pile the relishes on top of his two slices of bread until they formed a mini-Snowdonia and had a meal, albeit a not very appetising one, for a nickel. Other than this he relied on the hospitality of friends and Maggie was particularly generous in providing him with at least two hot meals a week. For transport he had a rusty old bicycle.

Peter was keen on exercise, in which he indulged at minimal expense. One Sunday he took me to a lido which was one of Boston's best bargains at 10c a head. After some vigorous swimming in icily cold water, our next stop was the historic and very exclusive Union Boat Club on Chestnut Street. Peter announced that we were visiting oarsmen from England, and he as a member of London Rowing Club and I as a member of Royal Shrewsbury School Boat Club would like to use a couple of sculling boats. The Secretary looked a bit nonplussed and asked whether the LRC and the RSSBC had reciprocity with the UBC, as he could not recall any such arrangement. Peter assured him that reciprocal membership was of very long standing and may have been overlooked as no one had invoked it for some time. The Secretary, in the absence of any proof that no such arrangement existed, allowed us to take two shells out on to the River Charles. It is amazing what you can get away with by brazenness and a superior manner, though I would not have had the nerve to act as Peter had. We had a delightful scull as far as Boston University and back, whereupon Peter informed the Secretary that we would return on Tuesday for a further outing on the Charles.

Peter was but one of several unusual personalities who foregathered at the ESU on Friday nights, or at other times at Maggie's Beacon Street apartment, for tea and gossip. One was a man called Finlay Featherstonehaugh who made his living by importing kippers. As I never encountered a kipper on any breakfast plate in Boston, and as few Americans would have been able to identify a kipper as something you ate, it must have been a precarious enterprise. I was particularly taken by a soft-spoken, gentle and very lovely Scots girl called Anne Graham, who revealed herself as a militant Scottish nationalist. The militancy took the form of blowing up English pillarboxes, an enterprise in which she was abetted by an English scientist who knew how to make bombs. He was, she explained, indifferent to the cause, but enjoyed tinkering with detonators and timers and fuses. I enquired jocularly if she had been instrumental in the theft of the Stone of Scone. She told me she had not been a member of the party who spirited it out of Westminster Abbey, but she had been one of the plotters. It was she who had hidden the Stone under the floorboards in a pub near Loch Lomond and, when the police mounted a raid after a tip-off, she was interrogated by a detective who was standing right on top of it. Anne was engaged to an Irish nationalist called Barry. It must have been an explosive relationship in every sense.

* * *

My new job in the library at Boston University gave me the opportunity of meeting some real North Americans. I had been designated for the new library of BU's School of Public Relations & Communications, but pending the appointment of a qualified librarian (I was to be his deputy) I was assigned to the Order Department. This was headed up by a Canadian called Mr Butler, who had thrown up a successful job in business to go to Library School, accepting a much reduced salary for the love of books. His PA was a stunningly beautiful Lithuanian-American called Justina with exceptionally slender ankles. These attributes were enhanced by the fact that she habitually came to work in white sneakers and bare-legged. I had never ever observed girls without stockings in any of the London offices I worked in, and on that side of the Atlantic it was not to become commonplace until at least twenty years later and then only in progressive work places like advertising agencies. I suspect that Mr Butler had selected Justina neither for her bibliographic skills nor her typing speeds. Once when she fluttered her eyelashes at me, I observed that she had very mobile eyes. 'Does it bother you?' she enquired silkily.

Miss Newman was Jewish and her florid pink face was adorned with rather more chins than is general. She was a martyr to her weight and would loudly lament the ineffectiveness of the latest in a long line of stringent diets while sucking on the straw in her fourth or fifth Coke. Miss Winn was a spinster of uncertain years who collected art. She allocated part of her modest salary each month to the purchase of modern paintings, which she was able to do on hire purchase – not an amenity I had ever encountered in the Old Country. As this was the era in which Jackson Pollock, Cy Twombly, Jasper Johns, Roy Lichtenstein and Andy Warhol were beginning to make a name for themselves, I like to think that one day Miss Winn woke to find herself the richest librarian in Boston.

Of the male members of the Order Department, Mr Webber was very silent and the only time I remember him speaking was when he revealed that he had run out of money after two years at the University of Miami. He was working at BU until he had enough to return to Miami and complete the other two years. This self-financing of university education, known as 'working your way through college' and by no means unusual, was another feature of American life that was novel to me. The Department's complement was completed by two pastors, neither of whom was paid a living wage by their church. Mr Widuff was a Unitarian and told me that he did not believe in God. Apparently this was not an impediment to his ministry. Mr Huffs was a Pentecostal who held revival meetings at which he was regularly assailed with eggs and ripe tomatoes. He seemed to welcome this as an opportunity to display spiritual resolution.

I wrote home: *Religious controversy is rife in the office as everybody belongs to a different sect, and Mr Huffs is busy converting us all. So the other day Miss Winn and I told him we would visit one of his meetings. I particularly wanted to go, as Mr Huffs reckoned it was the Catholics who were throwing eggs at him and I wanted to investigate this for myself. When we arrived in Charlestown, where the meetings are held, I found that here was a new aspect of America I had not met before. Slums. It was about as rough as Bermondsey, mainly poor Irish, with quite a strong peasant Italian element too. The meeting house was a disused shop looking as if it had been blitzed. The windows were broken, purportedly by flying brickbats from Catholics, and the door had been kicked in. Around its remains there was a milling crowd jeering and yelling for Mr Huffs's blood. We passed inside and this was worse than the outside. There was a rickety piano, a few broken sticks of furniture, and two dilapidated couches. The congregation consisted of about eight little boys, all yelling their heads off, and an old woman whom I learnt to be Sister Zonzani, a Polish peasant. This small number was soon swelled by a band of roughs and toughs who invaded the room and sprawled about on the couches. When we entered an earnest-looking young man called Brother Thomas, dressed in a new but damaged grey suit, and sneakers, was extolling and exhorting. The reason for the suit's condition is that a belligerent Catholic had set fire to it the night before (while Brother Thomas was in it). After some very dismal hymns had been sung, extempore prayers were said, while every few moments Brother Huffs and Brother Maclean would intone Hallelujah in a voice of doom, and Sister Zonzani would raise her hand and mumble 'Yes, my Jesus. O yes indeed my Jesus.'*

*The little boys and the big men merely went on yelling and catcalling. This was a period of comparative calm, for when Brother Huffs gave his address the children started fighting, the youths and men began booing and from outside the first missiles fell among us: pieces of wood, bottles, bricks and anything else to hand. One very hostile person put a match to the curtains, which provided an exciting interlude. The atmosphere of worship was not greatly enhanced by the altar, which was merely an erection of whisky crates, an unhappy choice as the Pentecostals are teetotal. There was a temporary lull in hostilities when Brother Huffs welcomed his workmates to the meeting. He drew the attention of the crowd to Mr Robertson in particular (growls and hostile grunts) all the way from London England (expressions of interest) who had been brought up as an Episcopalian (sic) but had become a Roman Catholic (wild and resounding cheers from all except Brother Thomas, Brother Maclean and Sister Zonzani).*

*After that the meeting really got out of hand and there was pandemonium. Brother Huffs evicted several small boys, posted Brother Thomas to withhold the mob outside, and tried to continue. Not a single sentence could he get out. A lot of the interruptions stemmed from a gentleman who introduced himself as Al Capone's great-nephew, and thereafter regaled the congregation with his sallies in a wonderful Mafia accent. 'Noa, I donta believe eet, it nona be,' and so on. He began as a declared atheist, but must have experienced a lightning conversion to the opposing forces, for when a disparaging remark was made about the Mother Church, he claimed definite allegiance and deep personal offence. Brother Huffs struggled on manfully, but his cause was not helped by derogatory comments about the Catholics he was aiming to convert. He also had to contend with Sister Zonzani, who kept racing round the room shouting – 'The Policja, I getta da Policja, have dem all shut up in da Policja Station. I cannot stand dis, getta da Policja.' Miss Winn and I decided that this might be an appropriate moment for a strategic withdrawal.*

*As we left I heard a girl confide to her pal about Mr Huffs 'I'm a goin'*
*to kill 'im when he comes out!' We felt quite anxious till we saw him*
*breeze into the office again next morning, bright-eyed and bushy-tailed as*
*ever. He hasn't much sense but he is certainly very brave.*

. . .

Shortly after this episode I left the Order Department for the School of Public
Relations & Communications Library, where the new head, Neal Olson, had
now taken up his post. Mister Olson was an ex-Marine Corps sergeant. Now
most of us are familiar with US Marine Corps sergeants by virtue of having
seen them played on the big screen, usually by Lee Marvin. Since Hollywood
cherishes its stereotypes, there is only one kind of Marine Corps sergeant.
Grizzled. A man of mature years and wise in the ways of the Corps that
is his only home, he barks at the new recruits, treats his officers as if they
are on probation, and drives the wisecracking Italian, the moody Polak, the
farmboy from Iowa, the scrawny Jewish intellectual, and the bug-eyed Negro
in his platoon with a ferocity that they deeply resent until they come to the
realisation, in the heat of battle, that all this pain is to weld them into an
efficient fighting machine and that in reality he cares for each one of them as
an individual as well as a Marine. Recognise the picture? Well, for starters,
Neal Olson was not grizzled. He was sort of pink and white, with the rather
dreamy expression of a poet. Which was probably because he was a poet,
author of a slim volume of verse that he would shyly produce from an inside
pocket should the conversation happen to be diverted from, say, the Marine
Corps's participation in the bloody Battle of Iwo Jima to matters of iambic
pentameter. On leaving the Marine Corps he had taken advantage of the
benefits offered by the GI Bill to enrol at library school and cast aside the arts
of war for the somewhat calmer study of bibliography.

My role in the Order Department had been undemanding, consisting
chiefly of transferring catalogue entries from white cards to blue cards.
In the School of Public Relations & Communications Library, however, I
was deputy to Neal Olson and in charge of half a dozen student assistants
who were working their way through college. I had been recommended
to Mr Olson by Chuck the Head Librarian with a glowing testimonial
that included my supposed expertise in Elizabethan classification systems.
About lunchtime on my first day, Mr Olson summoned me into his office.

'I've been watching you,' was his not too encouraging opening gambit.

'Indeed, Mr Olson,' I gulped. 'I will of course endeavour to give satisfaction....'

Mr Olson waved this aside. 'From what I've seen,' he continued, 'I would say that you have never worked in a library in your life. Have you?'

The game was up. Well, at least I had three weeks pay owing. I could pay my rent for a couple of months, even if I would not be able to eat much.

'No, Mister Olson, I haven't. I think the Head Librarian misinterpreted what I said about my previous experience. Anyway, I'll get my coat and be on my way.'

'Hold it!' enjoined Mr Olson. 'Siddown. Let's talk.' He then asked me about Shrewsbury School Library and how I had talked my way into the job. He seemed to find this mildly amusing.

'Look,' he said. 'I spent four years at library school and I have to tell you that an awful lot of that is taken up with theory. If you are prepared to knuckle down and work really hard, I can probably teach you the practical essentials in about three weeks. Enough to pull the wool over old Chuck's eyes anyway. Waddaya say?'

And so it was that Neal became my mentor and I his acolyte. I did work hard and I did master the basics sufficiently to survive not only Chuck's occasional forays across Commonwealth Avenue from the Main Library, but also to convince my student assistants that I was what I purported to be, a trained librarian from England. My relationship with Neal prospered, for we shared many of the same tastes, and in one of my letters I reported that he was the nicest American I had met. Eventually I was invited to his home, a rare honour in America, and enjoyed meeting his delightful wife and family. I still have that slim volume of verse with Neal's personal dedication.

. . .

Vying for the Nicest American title was the Kansan, aka George D Blackwood of Buffalo City (pop. 402), alumnus of Baker University at Baldwin, Kansas, now reading African Studies at BU and a fellow lodger at Ma Parker's. In fact he already possessed a title, confiding to me and Nigel Hollings – who had turned up from Canada and was now sharing my room – that he was voted BMC at Baker U. 'What on earth is that, Kansan?' Nigel and I queried. 'Big Man on Campus,' George declared proudly. Nigel and I collapsed on the bed and were unable to contain our howls of laughter for several minutes. The Kansan looked a little put-out.

Nigel's arrival had been precipitated by a falling out with the manager of the Emerald Lake Chalet in British Columbia. Nigel and John Kimpton and two other well-heeled Englishmen had arrived in Toronto with a list of addresses of various movers and shakers who were friends of their parents. At first all went swimmingly. They were deluged with invitations and spent their time moving from one mansion to another enjoying the lavish hospitality of their generous hosts. They also spent liberally, not, as far as I am able to ascertain, on reciprocating the hospitality, but in bars and nightclubs and impressing girlfriends. When the funds started to run out, they began enquiring of their hosts about suitable openings in whichever banks or brokerages sustained the mansions, the manicured lawns and the chauffeur-driven limousines. There were no openings and the invitations, once so frequent that they were spoiled for choice, ceased abruptly.

Despite Nigel's wild lifestyle, he still had much of his inheritance on deposit in London. But it was not transferable to Canada, as these were the days of severe exchange controls. Eventually the situation became so dire that the quartet of over-privileged young Englishmen, having pawned everything of value that they had with them, were forced to consign themselves to the mercy of the Canadian social security department. They were allowed $1 a day for rent and $1 a day for subsistence. Now you could probably have eaten reasonably well on a dollar a day in Toronto in 1961 if you exercised a modicum of common sense – a can of baked beans was 15c, potatoes 10c a kilo, bread 25c a loaf – but none of the four had been endowed with that quality. They ate but once a day, spending most of the daylight hours in bed, then venturing out in the evening for an 85c burger and fries and a 15c Coke.

Pleading messages left at the various mansions at which they had formerly been entertained went unanswered. Eventually desperation and an ultimatum from Social Security drove them to draw lots for who was to hitch-hike to the Golden West and seek work for all four of them. John Kimpton drew the short straw. The other three gave him all their remaining money, which amounted to four dollars and some odd cents, and wished him well as he set off on the 3,500-mile journey to British Columbia. The destination was Vancouver, though why the four young idiots thought they were any more likely to find work on the West Coast than the East I know not. Maybe their parents had more rich friends on that side of the continent.

John did not reach Vancouver. After a week crossing the endless prairies, he found himself at nightfall outside the township of Kamloops in the Rocky Mountains. Having no money for a bed, he wrapped himself in the tartan rug he had thoughtfully packed in his rucksack and settled down in a ditch to await the dawn. He was awakened by a flashlight shining in his eyes. A sallow, oriental face was scrutinising him from behind it. 'Who are you?' enquired the oriental gentleman. John identified himself. 'You looking for work?' asked the other. John conceded that that was the general idea. 'You know anyone else looking for work?' was the next question. John said he happened to know three people in such a situation. 'Good,' said the oriental gentleman. 'My name is Monsieur Rhamé. I am manager of the Emerald Lake Chalet – that's near here. I need four peoples for work in kitchen. You OK for kitchen work?'

So it was that the four feckless friends found work unexpectedly easily, Monsieur Rhamé sending the other three their bus fares from Toronto against future earnings. John did well at Emerald Lake, being retained as janitor when the hotel closed for the winter – living alone in a cabin and walking eight miles down the frozen track to the valley to buy stores once a week. Nigel was the lesser acquisition as a dishwasher, as I explained in a letter home: *He leaps about all day smashing crockery and doing imitations to amuse the natives, and the boss is getting a bit narked and doesn't like Nigel drying plates standing on his head and so forth. Apparently he nearly incited a strike of all the kitchen staff the other day because Monsieur Rhamé does not see why he should pay Nigel double overtime just to entertain the cooks.*

Shortly after writing this, I received notification that Nigel was on his way to Boston. Any fond imaginings that Nigel had missed my company were dispelled when it became apparent that his principal motive was to draw on my unexpended exchange control allowance. (Nigel transferred funds to my London bank, which were then wired to his acccount in Boston.) Ebullient as ever, he became an instant hit with Ma Parker and was soon firm friends with my fellow lodgers, known as the Kansan –

that was George 'Big Man on Campus Blackwood – the Texan and the Vermonter. (The Kansan, who has not seen Nigel in nearly sixty years, still seeks news of him whenever we are in contact.) Maggie, who probably found his antics a little wearing at times, welcomed him into Boston's English/Irish fold with all the warmth of her generous heart.

. . .

As summer gave way to fall, and fall to winter, life in Boston offered many pleasures. My weekly stipend of $57 did not allow for luxurious living, but I allocated $5 for books and every Saturday was devoted to a round of the city's many second-hand bookshops. My favourite was the Cornhill Bookshop, founded 1828 and the oldest booksellers in America. My principal quest was vintage American magazines, especially glossies from the twenties and thirties with wonderful art deco covers. On one occasion I found a 1771 copy of the *Universal Magazine* in original wrappers. This was older than any other magazine in my collection – any eighteenth century magazines that have not been disbound are exceptionally rare. Now it occurred to me that it was probably going to exceed my self-imposed allowance of $5 by quite a bit, so I resorted to a ruse, the probity of which occasionally still pricks my conscience (but not very hard). I made a large pile of miscellaneous magazines of all dates, including some which were clearly of very little value, and placed the eighteenth century treasure about halfway down. I then asked the bookseller if he would quote a price for the lot. The bookseller skimmed through the half dozen on top and grunted '$5 to you, Bub.'

When I counted my acquisitions back at 179 Bay Street Road, there were exactly fifty, so I had obtained the *Universal Magazine* for 10c along with a fair amount of dross, of which one was a very dull looking magazine in faded beige wrappers called *The Triangle* of January 1892. It was the house journal of the YMCA physical training college at Springfield, Mass, and looked too uninteresting to be worth perusing. But as I tossed it back on the pile, *The Triangle* fell open at a drawing of young men propelling a soccer ball into a peach basket suspended from a gallery. Underneath ran the legend 'The Rules of Basket Ball, by James Naismith'. As a collector of 'firsts' I knew who James Naismith was: the Canadian inventor of what was to become one of the three sports that dominate American life

– not just its sporting life, but life in general. The game means little in this country, but in the United States it is so huge that in some areas – North Carolina, for example, where I was to spend six months researching a book – there is hardly any other topic of conversation. I do not know how much *The Triangle* for January 1892 would have fetched if I had offered it for sale as 'the first printed rules of basketball' at the time I acquired it. In fact I waited half a century before putting it into an auction of sports memorabilia in Texas. It sold for $7,450 – not a bad return for a 10c outlay! (When I eventually sold the 1771 *Universal Magazine* it fetched £100. Meagre by comparison, but still not a bad way of investing a dime.)

. . .

This was the year of the failed Bay of Pigs invasion – the Cuban Missile crisis was soon to follow. The United States was on high alert and there was considerable anxiety amongst the population in general. All the main roads out of Boston had 'Evacuation Route' signs on them, and people who owned their own homes were busy installing nuclear fall-out shelters. Public information programmes on radio and television gave streams of advice on what to do in the event of a Soviet attack – much of it witless, such as 'Get under a table and shield your face with your arms'. In my letters home I encouraged my parents to have the World War II shelter at Wessenden restored and nuclear-proofed, but it seems that Britons were a bit more relaxed about impending Armageddon than their American cousins. My parents took the attitude that if an atomic weapon were unleashed on Britain, it was better to be extinguished right away.

The perception of imminent attack and potential obliteration heightened people's desire to make the most of whatever time remained to us. I was caught up in this feverish atmosphere and, while I had little money to spend, I look back on those uncertain months of 1961 as full of fun and frolic. There were expeditions to Duxbury in what was once the original Plymouth Colony of *Mayflower* fame with a group of avant-garde artists to whom Peter Dallas had attached himself, and excursions with Maggie to other places in Massachusetts of historical renown: Salem of the notorious witch-hunt; the whaling port of New Bedford; and Lexington and Concord, where the first shots of the Revolutionary War were exchanged. Each of these two scenes of battle has a memorial worthy of note. That in Lexington, erected in 1799, I believe from subsequent researches to have been the earliest war memorial in any country to record the names of the dead. The somewhat later memorial erected in Concord is the only war memorial I have ever seen that honours the enemy dead. It seems to me wholly characteristic of the Americans that they should have had the generosity of spirit to accord this tribute to the British troops who laid down their lives so far from home. (There is at least one other British war memorial in the US – dating from World War II, it is on the Outer Banks of North Carolina and is the smallest Commonwealth War Graves cemetery anywhere. It has four graves in which lie the bodies of seamen washed ashore after their ships had been sunk by U-boats.)

After-work diversions tended to the cheap and cheerful. Many hours were spent with Nigel at the Bellevue on Beacon Street, Boston's only English-style pub, debating JF Kennedy's Soviet policy with the natives. At three times the English price, a pint of Bass had to be nursed through the evening. Back at 179 Bay State Road we had musical soirées in Ma Parker's large vestibule with the Kansan, the Texan and the Vermonter each contributing songs from their native states and Ma herself providing exotic Jewish eats. A fellow post-grad colleague of the Kansan accompanied on his guitar and performed his own solos. My favourite was about a cat that 'would not stay ... away'. Efforts are made to exterminate him, but he always turns up again. Eventually the Soviets drop their bombs and every living thing in Western Europe, Britain and the USA is wiped out. Except the cat. A song very much of its time – I wish I knew what it was called and who it was by. (On reading this my village neighbour David, proof reader *extraordinaire* and fount of all knowledge, informs me that it is titled 'The Cat Came Back', written by Harry S Miller in 1893. But this must have been an update, with its allusions to impending nuclear destruction.)

It was during one of these convivial get-togethers that the Kansan related this story about his grandfather George, a farm-boy from Marion County, Mo, who had joined the Union Army in 1862 when he was only fourteen-years-old, though big for his age. 'Gran'pappy was marchin' through Missouri,' recounted Kansan, 'when by the side of the road he sees this girl perched up in a tree pickin' cherries. On perceivin' that she wuz a comely lass, he called out above the din of marching feet for her name. Her answer led to a correspondence throughout the War between the States. When it was concluded he made his way once again to the cherry tree. There by arrangement he was reunited with the cherry picker, Electa Jane Carley, who became his bride and my ole great grandmammy.' (By the miracle of the internet I have been able to call up a portrait of the happy couple on the occasion of their fiftieth wedding anniversary in 1917. The *Buffalo Blade* reported that George was at this time the youngest veteran of the Civil War. He survived Electa by nine years, dying in 1931.)

Boston University's Homecoming was always celebrated with a football match against Boston College, to which the Kansan took me together with two flasks of scalding tea put up by Ma Parker. The Kansan was very anxious that I understood exactly what was going on and painstakingly explained the rules to me, several times to ensure I was taking them in, but the spectacle was so colourful and so unlike anything that takes place on an English football pitch that I think a comprehension of the technicalities might actually have detracted from my enjoyment of the game. This was my first encounter with that peerless American invention of cheerleaders and I was enthralled by their acrobatic routines and high-pitched, squeaky chants. 'Two – Four – Six – Eight, Who Do We Appreciate? B – O – S – T – O – N ... Boston!!!' I loved the team mascots that were paraded around the field (BC had a live bald eagle) and the oompah oompah marching bands. During the interval an over zealous Boston College supporter ran on to the field towards BU's band and swept the tall shako off the drum major's head. The enraged drum major swung his heavy baton into the small of the receding BC supporter's back, at which that worthy turned and hit the drum major hard in the face. There followed a melee in which BC and BU supporters and BU bandsmen slugged it out together until the police intervened and rescued the perpetrator from certain BU retribution. We learned next day that the offender had been summarily dismissed from Boston College. I am sorry his education was terminated so abruptly, but grateful to him for the most fun I have ever had at a sporting occasion.

Maggie and I would buy seats in the gallery, whenever we could afford it, for the new shows that came to town, taking such diverse theatrical fare as Eugene O'Neill's sombre *The Great God Brown* (played in masks) and the pre-Broadway try-out of Frederick Knott's engaging romp *Write Me a Murder* with a cast that included veteran actress Ethel Griffies. She had made her debut in the stage version of *East Lynne* in London in 1881! We were able to forsake the gods for superior seating when the fetching Anne Graham, she of the predilection for blowing up pillarboxes, invited us to accompany her and her fiancé to Micheál MacLiammoir's one-man show *The Importance of Being Oscar*, one of the most memorable nights I have ever spent at the theatre.

. . .

It was through the enticing Anne that I became an honorary member of the Irish ex-pat community in Boston. (Maggie as a Londoner born and bred tended to regard the Irish as troublemakers.) Anne was in the process of turning Catholic in order to marry her romantic revolutionary fiancé Barry O'Flanagan and I had already converted, so we had that experience in common. She would take me to revolutionary meetings, which I suppose were in aid of Sinn Fein, though I was yet too ignorant about Irish politics to know one faction from another. The IRA was at a low ebb and the Northern Ireland Troubles were still nearly ten years in the future. On the first occasion I attended, there was a spirited debate about whether I should be charged double as an English oppressor, or admitted gratis as a sympathiser to the Cause. It was characteristically Irish that the majority vote was for the latter: 'He's called Patrick and he's a Catholic – give him a big welcome.'

Meetings were invariably followed by parties. These were often presided over by a beautiful girl from the Irish consulate in Boston called Kay O'Hearn. She sat at a silver samovar dispensing 'cups o' tay' and blarney to a line of devoted swains. Alcoholic refreshment came later. She it was who led the songs, mostly of a revolutionary nature, though 'I've Left my Heart in an English Garden' and 'Maybe It's Because I'm a Londoner' were performed on my first visit as a gesture to the London visitors, of whom the other was a Chinaman, the only other person in Boston to sport a bowler hat. This was worn with a Savile Row suit and kid gloves. Wang was an authority on all things connected with the British Army, but particularly the Brigade of Guards, service with which was his most fervent ambition. There were also two Americans on this occasion, but as we departed with the dawn Kay told me that they would not be invited again. They had committed the solecism of leaving the party before midnight and one of them had had the temerity to call for 'When Irish Eyes are Smiling' as a request number. I must have looked a little perplexed, because Kay enlightened me with a snort 'It's an *American* song!'

Anne Graham's best party, at which she brought all the English, Scots and Irish together, was a fancy-dress ball. The latter were instructed that they had to come as leprechauns (like many beautiful girls Anne could be a mischief-maker). I went as a cavalry officer in the 1917 American Expeditionary Force and Maggie accompanied me as my flapper, perfectly attired as a Strand Palace Girl of the time. (It was alleged that officers booking into the Strand Palace Hotel would find a girl in their beds.) Our costumes, which were the genuine article, were sourced from the wardrobe department of the Quannapowitt Players, to which Maggie lent her thespian talents. Mine comprised a tunic with epaulettes, breeches, cheese-cutter hat, Sam Browne belt, holster, canteen, gas mask and steel helmet, and best of all the cavalry boots with gleaming steel spurs. Only the khaki shirt and tie did I need to borrow from a member of the Boston University ROTC. Maggie's heavily rouged cheeks, fur tippet, picture hat and high button boots made her the kind of saucy minx who was the undoing of many a young officer. We had a dress rehearsal the night before the dance, crossing Boston Common in our costumes to test reaction from the natives. Most of them just stood staring wide-eyed with their jaws dropping, but there were a few catcalls of the 'Jeez, doncha know it's the 1960s?' variety. Maggie had a lightning reply to each and every sally, in perfect cockney, perfect 1917, and perfect flapper. She shook them rigid.

Anne Graham greeted us at the ball in shining armour as a somewhat fanciful Joan of Arc. The outfit emphasised all her physical attributes without too strict a regard for historical accuracy. We mingled with a Mephistopheles, firefighters, pirates, a druid, two stone age men and a stone-age woman, a Roman emperor, a pussycat, an assortment of American presidents, including a Lincoln and a Theodore Roosevelt, as well as a Jackie Kennedy. Finlay Featherstonehaugh might have looked heroic as a matador but for his Harold Lloyd spectacles. I congratulated a circus fat lady on the realism of her fat-suit, but Barry O'Flanagan drew me aside and hissed that she was not wearing one. My personal favourite was a girl dressed as a baked potato with an outsize pat of butter on her head, but when it came to couples there was a general consensus that the Yankee Division captain and his World War I English floozie were unsurpassed. The Irish Consul-General, having imbibed perhaps too freely of the Jameson's, expressed his admiration to Maggie in terms that she considered transgressed the limits of propriety. He was firmly rebuffed with a reminder that just because she was costumed as a lady of easy virtue did not mean that she was one.

We danced until dawn to a string quartet, by which time Anne Graham had shed most of her armour and acquired bits and pieces of other people's costumes, including a silvery mermaid's tail, Finlay Featherstonehaugh's matador jacket and my cavalry captain's hat. She still looked stunning. Maggie and I walked back across the deserted Common as the sun rose. We bought eggs and bacon from a milk roundsman in Beacon Street and made a capital breakfast at her flat, before I left for early mass at the Pauline Chapel.

For Thanksgiving Maggie and I were invited to the Reading home of Stan and Gloria, the cockney friends of Maggie's sister Mary, her extended family being the other guests. Reading is a manufacturing town ten miles north of Boston, noted for clocks, organ pipes, furniture, shoes, neckties and coffins. Stan, a joiner, and hair-stylist Gloria had escaped austerity Britain to start a new life in America at the height of its post-war prosperity. Apart from this observance of America's principal national holiday, neither had been the least affected by the change of culture and spoke, dressed and conducted themselves as if they were still living in their terraced house in Balham. Mary and mailman husband David and Stan and Gloria were my first working-class friends. (Maggie was classless.) There had been little opportunity for friendships across the class divide during my early working years in London. Working-class people of my age whom I encountered at work all lived with their parents, mainly in the outer suburbs; only middle-class youngsters lived away from home, usually in Kensington, Chelsea or Fulham. The only working-class members of the HAC were the NCOs – the private soldiers were upper middle or upper class (the Colonel's driver, a private, was a former brigadier in the regular army). And living in Mayfair, you did not meet many workers down at the pub....

So it was that I had to come to America to enjoy the fellowship of English people of a different social background from my own.

Gloria was a card. She enjoyed a nip of the cooking sherry and was not averse to a glass or two of the ruby red to accompany the magnificent turkey and its cohorts, the roast potatoes, the squash, the cranberry sauce, the stuffing and the bangers. The last is not a traditional accompaniment to a Thanksgiving turkey, but folks from South London would not serve the noble bird with anything else. When all our plates were set before us like so many mini-Mount Kilimanjaros, and with her tongue loosened by a replenishment of her wine glass, she revealed what had transpired at the previous Thanksgiving. Her parents, strict chapel folk, had arrived for a visit, the first since Stan and Gloria had emigrated. No wine was served on that occasion. But there were home movies of their life in America, which Gloria was eager to display for confirmation that the move from Balham had not been the descent into perdition that her strait-laced parents feared. But unbeknown to her or Stan, a prankster chum of her husband, invited for the occasion, had switched the reels for some blue movies. All her mother and father's worst imaginings about the depravity of this licentious land were amply confirmed as soon as the images of squirming naked bodies flickered on to the silver screen. There were no plans for a repeat visit.

The magnificent repast was crowned with a delicious dessert comprising a lattice of sponge fingers enclosing a cornucopia of scarlet strawberries embedded in an ocean of whipped cream. We had scarcely finished this delight when Gloria exclaimed that she had quite forgot, she had invited the neighbours round for tea. This was not just a cup of Rosie Lee, but a full-dress sit-down affair with cakes and sandwiches and buns as befits a proper South London celebration of the settlement of the New World. The neighbours participated with slightly bewildered expressions on their faces, but everyone relaxed when Maggie's various nieces and nephews cajoled us into a riotous game of Murder. Maggie made an accomplished detective and in her cross examination nearly convinced us that we each had an ulterior reason for knowing the others. Gloria declared that she was just like 'somethink on the halls'.

As a skilled tradesman Stan would have earned two to three times as much in Massachusetts as he did in London. Prices were 50–100% higher, with the exception of gasoline, cigarettes and property. He and Gloria lived in a shoebox in Reading, but the likelihood is that they enjoyed a generally higher standard of living than they did at home, though medical insurance would have taken a big bite out of Stan's wages. Were they better off overall, though, I wonder? With globalisation many of these Massachusetts towns that had spearheaded America's industrial revolution lost their manufacturing base – Reading actually declined in population during the 1980s. If Stan and Gloria had held on to the freehold of that bijou terraced house in Balham, they would have been property millionaires (in $ if not £) by the time Stan retired. The property in Reading, by contrast, may actually have declined in value in real terms.

They were a lovely couple and they deserved to have happy lives. I just hope Stan had invested in a good pension.

Nigel missed the Thanksgiving party because he had gone to New York. I wrote home: *Apparently he has been with a crowd of Harvard people and is disgusted. He said they were all long-haired intellectual left-wing pansies and he couldn't stand them. His latest venture is a partnership in a French Dressing company. The manufacturing plant is in the other partners' drawing room. So he will either prosper or have some 'ORRIBLE calamity.* (The venture veered more towards the latter. Interesting that Harvard liberals were wearing their hair long as early as 1961, though 'long' may have been relative in this era of the crew cut.)

. . .

The approach of Christmas was marked by the unveiling of Jordan Marsh's Teddy Bear House. Jordan Marsh were the Macy's of Boston and, like Macy's, their Christmas window displays drew crowds from all over the city. Each window was a room – there were elegant Teddies in a drawing room, feasting Teddies in a dining room, industrious Teddies in a kitchen, and adorable baby Teddies in a nursery. In the bedroom the recumbent Teddies had separate beds – after all, this *was* Boston. All the Teddies had white fur (probably to the disapproval of those long-haired Harvard liberals) and highly intelligent faces cast in appropriate expressions. The crowds blocked the sidewalks.

Christmas celebrations for Maggie and me began with a performance of Handel's *Messiah* by a massed choir at Lexington, and two days later there was a party at the English Speaking Union where we were regaled with Smoking Bishop, the beverage with which a reformed Scrooge seals his Christmas compact with the downtrodden Bob Cratchit in *A Christmas Carol*. Peter Dallas told us a rather involved story about an old man in his Shropshire youth who spoke in Chaucerian Middle English and then we all sang carols and became sentimental about Christmases past in the Old Country.

There were more carols when Maggie and Nigel and I were invited to join Herr Anton Winkler's waits for their annual tour of Cambridge, singing from house to house. By this time, the day before Christmas Eve, the whole Bay area was thickly blanketed in snow. There was a proper rehearsal beforehand and Herr Winkler, from Salzburg, was an exacting taskmaster. He had been doing this for eighteen years and each year had to surpass the previous one. When Herr Winkler was eventually satisfied, we were each given a lighted candle and, well muffled against the frosty night, the twenty-three-strong choir set forth to serenade the good people of Cambridge. Besides the avenues of eighteenth and early nineteenth century mansions that characterise Cambridge, there are, or were then, numerous inter-war apartment blocks built around courtyards. These made an ideal platform from which to perform, and the surrounding walls amplified our voices so that we sounded like the massed *Messiah* choir in Lexington. People threw open their windows to listen and at the conclusion of a set it was heartwarming to be rousingly cheered by the apartment dwellers, an audience sometimes a hundred strong or more. Afterwards we returned to Herr Winkler's for hot punch from a wassail bowl and further singing, more secular this time, around the piano.

On Christmas Eve Nigel and I clambered through the newly fallen snow on Beacon Hill to lovely Louisburg Square. Here all the elegant brownstone houses were illuminated, each window having lights of a different colour. At one end of the square Cornish handbell ringers were performing carol tunes, and a crowd had gathered round them to add the vocal accompaniment. The inhabitants of Louisburg Square kept open house on Christmas Eve. You could perambulate from one to the next, having a glass of something at each, but Nigel and I had been invited to join Elizabeth Parker, doyenne of the English Speaking Union socials, at Number 20, her beautiful, bow-fronted Greek Revival townhouse. Here I was persuaded to read the Christmas chapter of *The Wind in the Willows* to the assembled company and Nigel performed an aria in his fine tenor voice, startlingly powerful emanating from one so small. I departed for High Mass at St Anthony's Shrine at midnight. There was no sign of Nigel when I got to bed at 4 am.

At 11.30 am on Christmas morning the little chap was very much in evidence. I wrote home: *He came in tight as a lord and started beating me over the head with a saucepan. It took a long time to restrain him, especially as he was trying to impart his evening adventures in broken fragments between blows. It seems that on his way back from Louisburg Square he had met a man who invited him home for some whisky. He had something to do with a local church choir and after Nigel had been fed two baked eggs he had had his voice tested. His host was so delighted he marched him down to the church at dawn and put him into the choir for the first service of the day. Afterwards they returned for more whisky, quite a lot more I should imagine. I finally got him to bed and an hour and a half later Maggie arrived to take us to Christmas lunch at her sister's.*

*I did everything I could to rouse him. I reclaimed the saucepan and banged it on the headboard. I leaped on him, shook him, pulled off the bedclothes, poured cold water on his face, placed the wireless on full volume just by his ear and finally covered his head with a lampshade and put the ringing alarm clock inside. All to no avail. So Maggie and I left without him.*

We sat down seventeen to Christmas lunch at Mary's house. Stan and Gloria from Balham were there, plus two sweet New Zealanders, and a beautiful girl from Wiltshire, whom I had met before in Boston, called Audrey, with a voice like Joan Greenwood, together with her very big but benevolent businessman husband. It was nice to meet an American for a change. The enormous turkey was accompanied by a dressed ham and eight different vegetables, to be followed by a choice of four puddings. Mary told us stories of her days during the war working in munitions. Afterwards the girls repaired to the kitchen and their menfolk joined the kids on the carpet to play with their Christmas gifts. The best ones were clockwork: a puppy that chased a ball round and round, a pig in chef's costume who tossed a fried egg over easy in a frying pan, and the *pièce de résistance*, a bear in check trousers who blew his nose on a white pocket handkerchief. The kids hardly got a look in.

The festivities continued until three in the morning. When I arrived back at Bay State Road Nigel was sitting up in bed in his silk dressing gown looking disconsolate. 'You're a beastly beast,' he exclaimed petulantly. 'Why didn't you wake me up?'

I explained my efforts to do so, but he was not to be mollified. 'Do you know what I had for Christmas dinner?'

'Tell me.'

'A boiled egg!' he whimpered in disgust.

. . .

In the New Year I gave in my notice at the Library. It was nearly time for my rendezvous with Norman Davies on the steps of the main post office in El Paso, Texas. That was what we had agreed when he left me at Harvard to return to his seven-month stint in the shunting yards of the Southern

Pacific Railroad. The plan was to cross the Rio Grande into Mexico and settle down there to write our books, his the Great American Novel, mine a successor to Evelyn Waugh. There's nothing like aspiration.

On the eve of my departure Maggie took me to a rehearsal of her new play at the Quannapowitt Players, whose members had all become chums over the course of the year. Afterwards she invited me to come with her to her sister Mary's nearby to hear the latest Peter Sellers record. I recorded what happened next in a letter home: *I walked in and said O Hello Mary and wandered into the dining room and found myself in pitch dark and then suddenly the lights snapped on and there were all the Quannapowitt Players who had said tearful goodbyes but ten minutes before. And the room was all decorated, streamers and balloons and funny quips in Spanish on the walls and 'ADIOS' in big letters and a Mexican Guy Fawkes with presents heaped all over him and dollar bills pinned to the lampshade. Then everybody sang Happy Mexico to You and yelped and leaped about and made whoopee.... I was very touched and felt like sitting down and having a good cry but I couldn't really could I? And then I saw on the sofa the fabulous Anne Graham with her fiancé Barry and I think Maggie must have realised my admiration for Anne and she had arranged for her to come along though she is not a Quannapowitt Player. What a dear, unselfish girl she is. Then Anne told me that she and Barry are going to be married at the end of this month and I would have been an usher. There was also a cake in the shape of a sombrero. And I was presented with the cavalry boots and spurs from the 1917 Yankee Division officer's uniform I had borrowed from the Quannapowitt Players' wardrobe for Anne's fancy-dress party. What could be better for tramping through the Sierra Madre?*

The next day Maggie saw me off on the Greyhound bus and on that occasion I could not restrain the tears.

. . .

# Chapter 6

• • •

# WITH THE NOMADS

• • •

*January–June 1962*

The first stop on my journey west was at New Haven, where I met up with my Yale chums and stayed overnight in Calhoun College. Changing buses in New York, my route was via Philadelphia to Pittsburgh, then through West Virginia, Ohio, Indiana, Illinois and Missouri. As we approached Kansas the ends of barns were emblazoned with the command 'Chew Mail Pouch Tobacco'. This was truly the Middle West or, as the Kansan would have it, the Great Beating Heart of America.

In Kansas City I caught another bus to Baldwin City (pop. 2,000), home to the Kansan's alma mater Baker University. Here I was met by the Kansan's younger brother Jim and led to the Delta Tau Delta fraternity house, my residence for the following few days. I was invited to watch the initiation ceremony for the Pledges, known as hazing. This consisted of humiliating the postulants for membership in various ingenious and usually disgusting ways. A number of them threw up after being made to drink horrible concoctions and then made to lick their vomit from the floor. Those reluctant to do so were offered the alternative of consuming another victim's puke. I was assured it was all good clean fun and the Pledges were having a wonderful time.

Baker University is a Methodist foundation that serves principally the rural population of Douglas County and neighbouring counties, though it is not an agricultural college as such. The undergraduates I met were mainly farm boys who were allowed this four-year gap between graduating high school and returning to the grinding labour of the family farm. For them this was a time of fun and frolic and not too much was demanded by way of book learning, the Kansan being an exception in going on to graduate studies at a major Eastern university. According to the present day Wikipedia entry on Baker, it is the top-rated university in Kansas among Midwest Regional Universities (whatever that might mean), but at the time of my visit the priorities were sporting activities, dating co-eds and raisin' hell.

The day after my arrival it was announced by the frat secretary that we were going tobogganing that evening. As Douglas County is as flat as the rest of Kansas, this seemed an interesting proposition. The toboggan turned out to be the upturned bonnet of a car which was attached by a cord to another car. About eight of us piled into the bonnet and we were dragged through the snowy streets of Baldwin at hair-raising speed. Whenever we turned a corner the bonnet would slew across the snow until we were riding on the sidewalk, before sliding back again in a huge skid. Parked vehicles had to be fended off with gloved hands. Once we turned over in a snowdrift, and after the bonnet had been righted and we were hurtling forward again, our navigator drove us straight into a tree. So we abandoned the bonnet and rode behind the car in a crouching position, holding on to the bumpers and with the soles of our boots substituting for skis. At 40 miles an hour down Main Street that felt like travelling on a rocket sled.

Such were the simple diversions that kept Jim and his classmates and their English visitor entertained and, yes, it was glorious fun. I saw my first game of basketball and afterwards paired off with one of the cheerleaders to attend the Saturday night hop. Her name was Robertson and I showed her the family crest to which she was entitled on my signet ring. She stared at me as if I was demented and made no comment. I do not think they went in for heraldry much in the cornfields of Kansas.

Few of the farm boys had ever been farther than Kansas City and none had ever encountered an Englishman before. They asked me a string of questions, some of which would seem to have little relevance to anyone in Douglas County. For example, they wanted to know where in England was farthest from the sea. Jim confided to me that when I told them it was Coventry, they had gone off and measured it on an atlas. The fact that there is some small town near Coventry that is slightly farther from the sea proved to their satisfaction that I was an impostor. What followed was a game of cat and mouse. They kept thinking of devious reasons for wanting to see my passport. I kept fobbing them off with equally tendentious reasons for not being able to produce it. Jim fuelled their suspicions by reporting that his brother George, the Kansan, claimed never to have heard of me.

I was using the Public Schools Club address as my London *poste restante* while I travelled. The farm boys were very suspicious about this, 100 Piccadilly sounding somewhat grandiose as the supposed residence of a young man with no apparent means of support. They managed to find the phone number and telephoned to enquire if I lived there. On learning that it was the Public Schools Club, they interpreted this information from their own limited knowledge of clubs (fairly sparse on the prairie). 100 Piccadilly must be a bar, and if it had a club licence that meant a bar with strippers!

Two theories about my presence at Baker U were advanced. One was that I was an American post-graduate student doing Anglo-American studies at Boston University. The other was that I was a spy from the national headquarters of Delta Tau Delta sent to check up on their activities. There was some anxiety that I might be reporting on the hazing of the Pledges. When the time came for my departure I left behind, as if inadvertently, a large envelope, unsealed, addressed to the fraternity's headquarters in Indianapolis. Inside was a photocopy of my passport details, on which I had inscribed a big question mark. I had been picked up by a friend of George's, a Baker U alumnus called Dick Driver. As we pulled away, a horde of farm boys came cascading out of the frat house, waving the photocopy and baying for my blood. I asked Dick to drive just faster than they could run, and so we progressed down Main Street, the boys slithering and sliding on the snow and calling out for us to stop. The only one left behind was Jim. He was leaning out of a top-floor window of the frat house with a big grin creasing his homely features.

Dick was a schoolteacher in Osage County and he told me that the headmaster wanted me to address the children. This turned out to be a full day affair, taking each class in turn for a 45-minute session, then addressing the whole school in assembly. Dick had warned me that none of the children had been farther than the neighbouring county and that their knowledge of a world beyond this tightly-knit farming community would be very limited. Most of the farms had television by 1962, but apart from children's programming it was unlikely that the pupils were exposed to much beyond sport and game shows and *I Love Lucy*. There were no national newspapers in America and local newspapers focused on local events. Few adult Americans had much awareness of what was happening outside the US, other than the threat from the Soviet Union, so it was unsurprising that the youngsters of Osage County had little comprehension of alternative cultures. To get by I concentrated on leisure activities and food and school, all things that they could relate to. The Q and A sessions tended to dwell heavily on dating practices. In the United States then, and probably still, the passage towards maturity was marked by the most elaborate courtship rituals, conditioned by the fact that those who did not go on to college tended to marry high-school sweethearts as soon as they left school. Dating began much earlier than in England, usually around the age of twelve. Given that I had attended a single-sex school, and that dating in the sense of steady relationships scarcely existed between middle-class teenagers in England, I was at something of a disadvantage. If the sexually precocious young people of Osage County were left with the impression that England was a very backward country, particularly in matters of the heart, then they were probably right.

After a pleasant stay with the Drivers I moved on to George's Aunt Katy, who presided over all things cultural in the city of Chanute. She farmed me out to the grade school, where I talked to nine- and ten-year-olds, and to the Neosho County Community College, equivalent I suppose to what were then called polytechnics in Britain. At the grade school one bright little girl asked me to speak English. I was nonplussed for a moment or two, until I grasped that she was unaware that Britain and the US had a common language. I gave her several bits of choice cockney rhyming slang, delivered in the nearest I could approximate to East End diction, and there are probably people in their sixties in Neosho County today who are still convinced that English is a foreign language.

The teachers at the Community College had evidently been led to expect someone academic by Aunt Katy and I was somewhat startled to be invited to lecture impromptu on Elizabethan drama. Happily it transpired that I was not required to make any textual analysis of the works of Shakespeare, Marlowe and Ben Jonson, as it was the social ambience of early English theatre that the professor of literature wanted me to explain. I recalled just enough of those diagrams of the Globe Theatre that English masters at Shrewsbury used to draw on the blackboard to be able to reproduce something approximating to them and padded out my discourse with accounts of spectators soaked by deluges of rain, the consumption of oranges and nuts and the secondary use of this provender as missiles aimed at the stage, and the practice of casting winsome boys in the female roles. This latter piece of information was received with gasps of horrified incredulity, and more so when I told them it was still the practice in English boarding-schools. If the kids of Osage and Neosho Counties exchanged notes on their visitor, the absence of dating rituals in English schools and the proclivity of the prettier boys for cross-dressing probably confirmed the widespread belief beyond our shores that English men generally have a preference for their own sex.

I loved the Midwest. Having written the passages above, I was reflecting on its virtues when, quite coincidentally, I came across these words by the Turkish-born writer Melik Kaylan after he had visited for the first time: 'The widespread feeling of friendliness, the innate and palpable optimism, the bright transparency of manner, the indelible impression of Americanness as something irreducible and constant. A sort of eternal America.' At this present time there is a widespread cult of diversity – the notion that any place is improved by the introduction of alien customs and ideas (Provence, Tuscany anyone?). The rural Midwest must be one of the least diverse areas of the Western world, yet I cannot accept that it compares unfavourably with places elsewhere, whether in the New World or old, that are populated by significant numbers of newcomers. I cherish the 'eternal America' of those broad, sweeping flatlands.

Before we head south from Kansas, there is just one more tale of Baker University to relate. For this we must travel forward thirty-five years to the mid-nineties. Baker, though a religious foundation, had never had its own chapel. Worship took place in the assembly hall. This was remedied when a wealthy alumnus, Robert Osborne, donated funds to purchase a disused Methodist chapel and transport it to Baldwin. The chapel selected was in Sproxton, Leicestershire, and owing to declining population it had been closed in 1988. Here it was that Methodist lay-preacher Alderman George Roberts of nearby Grantham used to preach when his daughter Margaret, future prime minister, was a slip of a girl. George Blackwood, the Kansan, now a successful lawyer in Kansas City, was commissioned by his alma mater to make the purchase and arrange for transatlantic shipment.

George purchased the building for £20,000. He then spent a further million dollars on having it dismantled stone by stone and tile by tile, each stone and tile being numbered, and having it shipped from Leicestershire to Douglas County. When the initial funding was exhausted, Mr Osborne put his hand in his pocket again to finance the rebuilding. Margaret Thatcher made the pilgrimage to Baldwin in 1996 to dedicate the chapel on behalf of its new congregation. George was present on that occasion and the two of us followed in her footsteps a few years later so that he could show me the end result of one of the most fulfilling episodes in his legal career. It stands solitary on a greensward backed by trees and is, unusually for a Victorian chapel, quite extraordinarily beautiful in its new setting. And there was one other thing George accomplished with Mr Osborne's support. With the removal of the chapel, Baker University found itself proprietor of a piece of land in Sproxton. It could have been sold for development but Mr Osborne needed little persuasion by George to have it landscaped as a public garden and presented to the village.

Methodists. Midwesterners. Like George says, the great beating heart of America.

. . .

Amazingly Norman Davies and I succeeded in meeting up as arranged, on the appointed day, on the steps of the general post office in El Paso, Texas. Not at the appointed hour, though, as Norman was seven hours late. He advanced no explanation for his tardiness and I did not seek one. The next day we crossed the Rio Grande into Mexico, caught a bus in Ciudad Juarez and headed through cactus-studded desert for Durango in the state of Durango. There we were to meet up with Norman's friends René and Hector, who were cashiers at a bank in the town. We were invited to stay at Hector's family home.

Hector's father kept a general store, not large but successful enough for him to maintain a substantial property, surrounding a paved courtyard, in the centre of town. Here Hector dwelled with his four brothers and two sisters, attended by five maids. The maids, I learned, earned the equivalent of a pound a week, with board and lodging. Hector earned £6 a week at the bank. I found it interesting that a small shopkeeper was able to maintain an establishment on this scale. René's family also lived comfortably and the impression I received was that while agricultural workers and the unskilled lived a pretty hand-to-mouth existence, anyone above this level – what we would call the lower middle class – enjoyed a perhaps surprising level of prosperity.

Both René and Hector were keen poker players. The first night we played amongst ourselves, with the whole of Hector's family looking on. The next night there were two guest players, one of them a swarthy, pockmarked individual with a Zapata moustache who looked like the stereotypical Mexican bandit of Hollywood films. His name was Jesus and he was not one of the friendlier Mexicans I encountered. During the course of the game we drank mescal, an evil potion comprising fermented cactus juice. The custom was to pour salt on to your hand, lick it, take a bite from a segment of lemon, then down the mescal in a single gulp. Everyone did this in unison and to omit a round would be to prove yourself lacking in manhood as well as an insult to the host. It tasted like cough medicine laced with methylated spirits, but not as nice.

As observed earlier, I am lacking in skills. The only competitive skill in which my performance is above the average is poker. As the game progressed, the pile of chips in front of me grew at a satisfying rate. The pile in front of Jesus steadily diminished. Jesus was not a man to turn the other cheek. As he grew wilder and more aggressive in his style of play (a sure way of losing at poker), he also increased the rate at which the ritual glasses of mescal were consumed. I have a reasonable head for alcohol, but this was a drink to which I was unaccustomed. Round about midnight, my face fell into my mountain of chips and I passed out.

What happened next was recounted later by René and Hector. Jesus rose, grabbed me up by the collar and flung me back to the wall, where I crumpled on to the floor. He then scooped up all my chips, added them to his own meagre pile, and after counting them all, extracted that amount from the kitty. As he weaved drunkenly towards the door he waved a hand in my direction, and declared, 'El Inglés, he quit the game.'

*Jesus rose ... and flung me back to the wall, where I crumpled on the floor.*

I was outraged when the boys told me this. 'You let him go with all my money?' I expostulated. Hector looked shamefaced. 'C'mon, we're a couple of bank clerks. Jesus works for a drug baron. He's got a gun.' I saw their point.

Apparently the boys had carried me back to my room and put me on the bed. I awoke that night with the most raging thirst I have ever experienced. I staggered off my bed to head across the courtyard to where I knew there was a water faucet. I had forgotten about Pariah Dog, the ferocious beast that guarded the compound. I just made it back to my room as it lunged at me, snarling and snapping, eyes red with fury. I spent the rest of the night with my swollen tongue cleaving to the roof of my mouth.

The following day we attended a wedding. After the ceremony we repaired to the courtyard of the bride's father's house, where an ox was being roasted on a spit. I was asked what I would like to drink. I said I thought I would just stick to something soft. René handed me a glass of mescal. I shuddered. 'This is just for the toast,' he assured me. 'You would not want to insult the bride's father by refusing his hospitality?' I assured him nothing was farther from my thoughts and, in concert with the other guests, downed it in one. Ugh! I retched. René handed me another glass. 'What's this for?'

'That was the toast to the first bridesmaid. Now we drink to the second bridesmaid.'

'But there are six bridesmaids!' I pleaded.

'We must honour each of them. And the bride and groom of course. And the bride's mother. And her father....'

. . .

When I was sufficiently recovered, Norman and I set forth for Mazatlan, a port city on the Pacific coast. Mazatlan has a claim to history that has been generally overlooked. I will try to avoid embroidering these memoirs with too many 'firsts', but this is one that I think is so significant it deserves to be better known. On 6th May 1914 Gustavo Salinas, piloting a Glenn Martin pusher biplane, missed the military target in Mazatlan that he had been instructed to bomb by revolutionary general Alvaro Obregon. Instead he dropped the bomb, a cluster of dynamite sticks and nails wrapped in a pigskin, on to the busy shopping street La Calle de Carnaval. Four people were killed and eight injured, including the French consul. These were the first civilian casualties in the history of aerial warfare. (And no, World War I was not the first aerial war. Aeroplanes had been used in no fewer than six earlier conflicts.)

Norman and I stood on a rooftop in Mazatlan looking over the bay as the sun set on a shimmering sea. We were deep in argument. There was a detail that we had failed to settle in advance about the writing of the Great American Novel and the successor to the works of Evelyn Waugh: where we were going to wield our pens. Norman wanted to take rooms in a big city, Guadalajara or Chihuahua for preference, and immerse ourselves in the local arts and student scene. I hankered after a mountain-top village of ancient, honey-hued stone, in which the only English speaker would be Señor el Padrón, with whom we would while away the hours in a vine-clad taverna. The only point that these two fantasies had in common was that both involved a bewitching, slender-waisted, olive-skinned peasant girl with flashing black eyes who would minister to our wants for a pound a week. Alas, we were unable to agree on anything else and we reluctantly agreed to go our separate ways, he back to San Francisco, I to Panama with a view to finding a ship crossing the Pacific. The world of literature would have to hold itself in patience.

. . .

I bought a bus ticket for the equivalent of $20 to take me from Mazatlan via Mexico City and Vera Cruz to Quintana Roo, the last territory in Mexico. (As in the US, territories could not attain statehood until they had reached a certain level of political and economic development. It would be another twelve years before the wild and primitive Quintana Roo achieved this.) The distance was 2,000 miles, the cost of transport 1c a mile.

A week later I arrived at Chetumal, capital of Quintana Roo, at five o'clock in the morning. It was an unprepossessing little town, shabby, dusty and litter-strewn, its inhabitants mired in poverty. I had run out of English cigarettes (Mexican cigarettes were made of a foul, coarse shag with a flavour so acrid that I preferred to go without) and, even worse, I had finished the last book I had with me. I went to the street market when it opened in search of reading matter. The only publication in English on any of the stalls was a dog-eared five-year-old copy of *Reader's Digest*. The market lady, well practised in spotting a sucker, charged me four times the original cover price.

Chetumal lies close to the River Hondo, the border that separates Mexico from Belize, then British Honduras. I was anxious to leave this last outpost of Mexico on the first bus across the border. The bus station was unmanned when I had arrived, but now I went to enquire after the cross-border buses. The next one, I was told, would leave in 'una hora'. I returned in good time, but was informed that it had already left. The next would be in 'una hora'. Every time I returned the answer was the same. So now I remained at the bus station. 'Una hora' after 'una hora' passed and no bus arrived. Darkness fell and at ten o'clock, hot, hungry and exhausted, I repaired to the main square to find something to eat.

There were no vacant tables at the open-air café, so I asked a black man by himself if I might join him. He responded in English, the first person I had encountered in Quintana Roo who could do so. Moreover he was from British Honduras himself. Over a plate of refried beans, the cheapest item on the menu, I recounted the tribulations of the day. My new friend laughed heartily. 'There aren't any Mexican buses across the Hondo,' he said. 'The bus station people only told you there were because Mexicans don't do negatives. They tell you what you want to hear.'

'So how do people get to British Honduras?'

'On the cinema bus. British Hondurans are crazy about movies. When people on the other side of the Hondo have seen the film that's on at their local cinema, they come to Chetumal to see whatever is on here. On a special weekly cinema bus.' He pointed across the plaza. 'There's the cinema. And today's the day of the bus run.'

My heart leaped. 'Can anyone travel on the bus?' I asked.

'Anyone with 50 BH cents. The film's nearly over. When you see a whole bunch of English people leave the cinema, follow them and they will lead you to the bus.'

'How do I know which people coming out of the cinema are English?'

'Easy,' declared my table companion. 'They're black, like me.'

It worked out exactly as he said. I was ushered on to the bus by the conductor, a ten year old boy who marshalled us like a company sergeant major. The driver did not look a lot older. Not all my fellow passengers were 'English', as I found myself surrounded by a group of Maya Indians. They took charge of me when we arrived at the border and insisted that I was placed at the head of the queue. The border post on the Mexican side of the Hondo had a portrait of the Queen at Balmoral surrounded by corgis. The border post on the British side had a portrait of President Lopez. A pleasant exchange of courtesies.

After we had crossed the Hondo on a ferry and had our passports stamped, the Maya cracked open a bottle of something that happily was not mescal. We drove through the jungle in a pleasant alcoholic haze and about a mile outside Corozal the bus stopped to let the Maya off. I could hear the rhythmic beating of drums deep into the rainforest and the Maya told me they were attending a tribal dance. They insisted that I joined them.

We walked down a track, the drums growing steadily louder, and emerged into a clearing where about 300 other Maya were already gathered. Our arrival was the signal for the festivities to begin. I was prepared for the kind of gyrating native dances witnessed in innumerable Burton Holmes travelogues and newsreels of the Queen watching stony-faced, the Duke yawning, on their visits around the Empire. But this was different. This was British Honduras. The dances were foxtrots and quicksteps and even the latest craze, the twist.

Corozal is a coastal town on the Caribbean. I arrived in time for early mass at a Catholic church that had been all but blown away by the recent Hurricane Hattie. We worshipped in the ruins, enjoying a wonderful view of palm-fringed beaches and an azure sea. The young man I was sitting next to introduced himself as Jerry, an American doing a year's missionary work in BH, and he invited me back to his villa for scrambled eggs. Afterwards he showed me around the school in which he taught, St Francis Xavier's, which had a surprisingly eclectic library. Amongst the books was an Edwardian album of Gibson Girls, the statuesque all-American beauties created by illustrator Charles Dana Gibson who embody the era. Jerry sought my advice. Should he destroy it lest it corrupt the morals of his pupils?

At one o'clock we bundled said pupils on to the back of the school truck and set off to Orange Walk, where St Francis Xavier's were to play a major soccer fixture against La Immaculata. After a bone-crushing journey over unmade roads for thirty miles through the jungle, during which there was no sign of human habitation or any indication that we were in the twentieth century, suddenly a sign rose up out of the dense vegetation. 'Ovaltine – The World's Best Night-Cap', it proclaimed.

The match was hotly contested, with the whole population of Orange Walk bellowing their support for La Immaculata in English and Spanish and me, sole supporter of the visiting side, doing my best to outshout them on behalf of St Francis Xavier's. Both sides had an equal disadvantage: their coaches were American missionaries who had never seen a game of soccer, let alone played in one themselves. Things were not going well for Corozal though. Jerry rushed up to me, flapping his arms. 'Wadda I do? Wadda I do?' he pleaded.

There was probably not an Englishman in the whole of the New World who knew less about soccer than I, but it was not a time for hiding lights under bushels. 'Put an extra man on each wing', I replied decisively.

Jerry looked uncertain. 'Are you sure that's allowed, Patrick?'

'Do you want to win this match, Jerry?' I adjured him sternly.

Jerry strode over to the truck, and plucked a couple of younger brothers off the tailboard. They had no boots, but neither did any of the other players. Everyone played barefoot.

Corozal won the match 2–1.

I spent that night with the Orange Walk missionaries, which was forgiving of them as I had probably lost them the match. I added further insult to injury by beating them in a marathon game of poker.

In the morning I caught the carrier truck bound for the capital, Belize City. I wrote home: *The truck is what passes for a bus in BH. A big Bedford cattle lorry, carrying merchandise and grain in the middle, and with a couple of wooden school benches at each end for passengers. The winding jungle tracks that lead to the capital have 1930s English traffic signs donated by the British government when they were replaced. There are no villages as such, only clusters of palm-thatched huts.*

*After a two-hour drive we arrived at the capital, the completion of my 5,600-mile bus journey from Boston. Belize City was struck by a hurricane in October* [four months earlier] *and still looks as if it has been blitzed. Utter shambles – houses turned over and smashed to matchwood, debris and uncollected rubbish obstructing the sidewalks. The roads are bordered by open sewers from which a putrid stench pervades the atmosphere. Nearly all the buildings are wooden and Belize City has the look of a stricken shanty town. It is significant that you can't buy a postcard of it even pre-hurricane – there just isn't an angle you could take it from that would make it look like a civilised town. And yet when you are in the midst of all this chaos, it has a certain charm. It is not unlike the towns you see in Westerns: false fronts, saloons with batwing doors and general stores with open frontages, unpaved streets.*

*The population is 30,000, a third of the population of the colony as a whole. It boasts three cinemas, an SPCK bookshop, half a dozen restaurants, all offering the same menu of fried chicken or ham and eggs, and a fire station, where the engines are magnificent forty-year-old Rolls Royces dripping with brasswork. Also a barracks, base for men of the Hampshire Regiment and the local Defence Force, a good boys' secondary school and a good girls' secondary school, both Roman Catholic, a superb hotel, the Fort George, quite out of keeping with the rest of the town and very expensive, $20 BH or £5 a day including meals. There are no tourists in BH apart from me, so the only people who can afford to stay there are British officials on government business and American academics studying Maya ruins. There is also a well-appointed cultural centre, the Baron Bliss Institute, named after an eccentric millionaire who died aboard his* *yacht in the harbour without ever stepping foot on BH soil. He left his entire fortune to the colony to give them literature and the arts. The radio station, by contrast, is housed in a shack, but is ambitious enough to be rehearsing for a live presentation of Shaw's* The Devil's Disciple.

*There are two newspapers, execrably printed and with no photographs, though one of them does have 'The Gambols' comic strip.* [About suburban life in the Home Counties, which must have been instructive for the colonists.] *Belize City has three terrific assets: Brodie's Store, where Player's cigarettes are two bob a packet, almost half-price; restaurants where you can get a decent cup of tea, unlike America where I sometimes invaded the kitchens to make it myself; and the SPCK bookshop which sells English Penguins at English prices – the American Penguins cost double.*

The only alternative to the swanky Fort George were $2 a night flop-houses. I endured one of these my first night in the capital, but had no wish to repeat the experience. I was enjoying a cup of tea at Sandy's Spanish Restaurant the following morning when I saw a white woman with a packet of Player's cigarettes. I enquired where she bought them and she told me about Brodie's Store, a cornucopia of good things including tinned Fray Bentos Steak & Kidney Pies and Wall's Sausages. She invited me to join her and introduced herself as Helen Taylor, a native British Honduran whose military family had settled in the colony in 1860. Sadly the family house had been totally flattened by the hurricane. A tidal wave had completely overturned a huge 10ft by 10ft iron water tank weighing several tons, yet a Georgian claret jug had survived and not one of the champagne glasses had been broken.

Miss Taylor was now living with her mother and her great-aunt in a rented flat. Where was I staying. she enquired. I told her. 'But that's a dreadful place,' she exclaimed. 'Full of cockroaches. I have a spare room with a camp bed. Come back with me and meet the family.'

Which I did. Mother was a frail little silver-haired lady of great sweetness; the Great-Aunt a large, formidably erudite woman who had been born in the colony in the 1860s. Miss Taylor was prominent in the National Independent Party, which formed the opposition in the British Honduran Assembly, and over the next fortnight I was introduced to the leading luminaries of the party, as well as various pillars of the colonial establishment. Miss Taylor made several rousing speeches agin' the government and in particular the premier, George Price, whom she considered to be complicit with the Guatemalans in their efforts to seize their small neighbour in order to gain access to the sea. Although Miss Taylor's accusations of treachery were probably baseless, the threat from Guatemala was an ever present and very real one. Only the small British garrison prevented an armed incursion. This meant that it was not possible for BH to become independent unless Britain was prepared to guarantee its security, something to which no government could bind future governments. Consequently it was nearly twenty years before the colony attained its sovereignty, one of the very last to do so (followed only by Antigua, St Kitts and Brunei).

As an unreconstructed Imperialist (albeit one wholly committed to self-determination), I was enchanted by BH. The dissolution of the Empire can be dated to a number of junctures, from the loss of the American colonies in 1783 or the handover in India and Pakistan in 1947, but really began as a sustained progress towards the self-determination of subject peoples with the sovereignty of Ghana in 1957, followed by Nigeria in 1960 – Macmillan's famous 'wind of change'. At the time that I was in BH in early 1962 no Caribbean colony had become a sovereign nation, though that was shortly to change with the accession of Jamaica later that year. The whole process of dissolution was to take only twenty-seven years, barring the return of Hong Kong to China in 1997.

I was to visit many colonies and newly independent former British territories in my travels, but BH was the first and, I think, the most typical of the British Empire of popular imagination. I wrote home: *There is the most tremendous atmosphere of unchanging tradition – all the colonial administrators are lean brown men with sandy moustaches and khaki shorts and people really do wear solar topees. And one of the most delightful things about this little country is that everybody seems to know everybody else.*

That is a lost world which even then was not to everybody's taste. But BH was a true melting pot, most of the population deriving from several out of thirteen different ethnic or national origins, ranging in colour from very black to light brown. There was a small white minority, not all of them like Helen Taylor of privileged backgrounds. There was a tow-haired, blue-eyed boy with ragged shorts and bare feet whom I used to see in the street most days selling *The Belize Times*. And contrary to received views about Empire, there was a good deal of mixing between races and between Governors and governed. Most of the people I met, admittedly the more prosperous citizens, knew His Excellency personally and were frequent visitors to Government House. This was the practice throughout the Empire. When the racist Duke of Windsor was appointed Governor of the Bahamas during World War II, he refused to admit black Bahamanians to Government House. The Colonial Secretary of the day issued the sternest warning that unless he dropped his colour bar forthwith he would be recalled to London and dismissed.

There was one other attribute of BH that I took for granted until one night I was enjoying a rum in some backstreet bar. A local with whom I fell into conversation asked if I felt safe walking the streets of the city after dark. It had not occurred to me that I might be in any danger. My drinking companion told me that Belize was the only large city in the whole of the Caribbean in which violence and random criminality were almost unknown. Sadly, I am informed that this no longer obtains and that the introduction of a drug culture to this once so peaceful city means its people now face the same threats to person and property as elsewhere in that unsettled region.

. . .

My plan had been to follow the Pan American Highway to Panama and there take ship to New Zealand. My route had been planned with the help of a Methuen School Atlas, perhaps not the best choice. It transpired that the Pan American Highway, intended to run the entire length of the American continent, petered out somewhere in the Central American jungle. I tried to find a boat heading down the coast without success, and the air fare to Panama on top of the cost of crossing the Pacific was beyond my resources. There was nothing for it but to return to the US. Norman was back in California. Why not join him?

I flew out from Stanley Field International on the weekly flight to San Pedro in the Republic of Honduras. I am not sure whether this was the only destination served, or whether there might have been flights to somewhere in Mexico too, but I think it must have had a good claim to be the world's smallest international airport. The airport terminal consisted of a hut about the size of the more commodious kind of garden shed. The airliner, of unidentified marque, looked as if it had probably done service with Imperial Airways on one of their lesser routes before following all those discarded traffic signs to find a further lease of life in BH.

At San Pedro in the Republic of Honduras I encountered the *Evening Standard*'s foreign correspondent, who had been assigned to a two month tour of Central and South America. He was a languid young man who lived in South Audley Street in Mayfair (round the corner from Culross Street) and despite first-class travel, generous expenses, and VIP treatment wherever he went, did not seem to be enjoying the experience. It struck me as strange that I, living from hand to mouth, was having the time of my life, whereas he, travelling in luxury, was weary of his journey before it had scarcely begun. His cables home, he told me, were each of 800 words. At a shilling a word, that was £40 a telegram. As he was a young man of expensive tastes, his articles must have been costly. A close relative of the *Standard*'s proprietor perhaps?

From San Pedro I flew to Guatemala City, where I was surprised to see little evidence of the endemic poverty of Mexico. The streets were clean, the shops modern and full of attractive goods, the smart-looking restaurants bustling, and the people well dressed. So these were BH's enemies? They did not need to invade. They could have just bought up the colony.

The night flight to LA and San Francisco was a revelation to me. It was the first time I had been on a large jet airliner. This was a Pan American Clipper and I wrote home that it was like an hotel inside. I was seated on the end of a long row of Russians, or possibly Ukrainians, all wearing picturesque national costume. I imagine they were performers of some kind, probably of folk dancing, the men attired in Cossack shirts outside their breeches and knee-high boots, the women, whose plain faces looked as if they had been scrubbed with carbolic soap, in very bright prints. None spoke a word of English, but they were voluble in their efforts at communicating with me in sign language. There was a baby on the lap of the woman next to me, its face just like that of the infants in Giles cartoons, creased in a happy idiotic grin. The immaculately coiffured and tailored Pan Am stewardess, no better natured than American cabin staff today, came up to me with a clipboard, pointed at the baby, and snapped, 'What sex is it?' I told her I had no idea. 'Find out,' she commanded. What was I expected to do – undress the child and inspect its more intimate parts? The stewardess returned and demanded 'Well?'

'It's a boy,' I assured her.

. . .

Arriving in San Francisco at 3.30 am I spent the few remaining hours of the night at a YMCA before venturing out to seek accommodation. At 328 Hayes Street in downtown I found a rather sparsely furnished room with shared use of kitchen for a modest $35 a month, rather less than I had been accustomed to paying in Boston. It was well situated, just off Union Square with the Opera House round the corner. My kitchen-mates were both homosexuals, not surprisingly in the gay capital of America. Trevor was a supercilious Englishman in his mid-twenties given to wandering about clad only in a towel and making waspish comments to the detriment of most people and most things. He worked in a gay bath-house, so I suppose what he wore in the kitchen was his normal workwear. I took an instant dislike to him, a sentiment that was reciprocated with interest.

The other gay man was a middle-aged poet with a seraphic smile and gentle manner, a happy contrast to my countryman. Mister Matthews was a computer programmer by day, a fairly recondite calling at that time. He was bohemian in his tastes, which included generous consumption of Californian red wine bought in flagons at a dollar a gallon. Rotgut, as we called it. Californian wines now have such a cachet that it is hard to imagine that there was a time when they were synonymous with the winos and derelicts that were so common in Kennedy's Camelot, a facet of the world's richest country at the height of its power and self-confidence that sometimes tends to be forgotten. Mister Matthews would consume most of a gallon flagon before passing out on the floor. He sometimes awoke in the night, and other times lay there till morning. Either way he never seemed the worse for wear.

Having laid in a stock of provisions, I set out to explore, riding a cable car to the harbour, inspecting Alcatraz through a telescope, and touring an historic clipper ship that had been built on Clydeside. I ended the day at America's only English restaurant, the Coachman. Here I was regaled with a steak and kidney pie, with a pie crust that the maitre d' informed me was made with a pound of butter to a pound of flour. It was so good that I asked to pay my compliments to the chef. Somewhat to my surprise he was an American. The maitre d' explained that they had advertised extensively for an English chef, including in London, but it seemed that chefs trained in England only knew how to cook French or Italian cuisine.

Elizabeth David has much to answer for. The compromise position was to engage an American, but limit the menu to two items and train him to produce both of these to perfection. The alternative choice was mixed grill. San Francisco restaurants were eclectic. I was particularly taken with one that had the unusual name of We're Itching to Get Out of Portland, Oregon.

Another side of San Francisco life that was very appealing was the bohemian quarter and its denizens. The day after my arrival Mister Matthews took me up to North Beach to visit the various hang-outs of the beat poets who were then putting SF on the cultural map. We had Viennese coffee with brandy and whipped cream at the Bocce Ball, where the patrons are serenaded by opera singers. We then took tea at Enrico's Sidewalk Café, the place for listening to traditional jazz in the open air. We finished the evening in a pub with Mister Matthews tickling the ivories. He could play any request number from the past forty years.

The complement of 328 Hayes was swelled by the arrival of Norman and a retired US Army sergeant called Mister Long. There were now more heterosexual lodgers than homosexuals, quite unusual for San Francisco. Ever since encountering the delightful Mister Olson I had found it difficult to reconcile the popular image of the United States military, all blood and guts, with the reality. Mister Long was a sad little man who had spent his thirty-five years serving Uncle Sam in the capacity of barber. He had no tales of World War II or Korean War heroics and I do not think he had often been off his base somewhere in the mid-west. He had no relatives other than a niece in Denver and, seemingly, few acquaintances. He was probably still in his fifties and how was he proposing to spend the next twenty or thirty years? It seemed a dismal prospect, staring out of the window of a cheap rented room at the traffic passing below.

Norman and Mister Matthews and I would take Sergeant Long with us on some of our outings, to Golden Gate Park, to the zoo and the funfair, and to Sutro's palace of wonders at Land's End, the westernmost point of the continental United States. But Mister Long hated spending money and so he would agree to accompany us only provided expenditure was kept to the barest minimum. He did enjoy the funfair though. He did not go on any of the rides but he stood there with his face wreathed in smiles while Norman and I and Mister Matthews cavorted on the dodgems and the whirligig. He said it reminded him of a leave when he had taken his little niece to a funfair and how happy it had made her. Looking back, I think perhaps we were his only friends.

Sergeant Long did not accompany us, though, on our pilgrimages to hear the immortal Sonny Rollins conjure magic from his tenor sax at the Jazz Cellar, nor on our Sunday expeditions to the notorious Black Cat Café on Montgomery Street. The latter was the haunt of San Francisco's drag queens, as well as such luminaries as Allen Ginsberg, William Saroyan and John Steinbeck. The Sunday entertainments were presided over by José Sarria, who had started at the Black Cat as a waiter but had elevated himself to master of ceremonies, as well as baiter-in-chief of the Federal Agents who frequented the bar in the hope of gathering enough evidence to close it on moral grounds. (They succeeded the following year.) José became our chum, always welcoming, forever funny, frolicsome and fantastic in its literal sense. His fantasies depended on his extraordinary talent for singing in any register, as well as an ability to switch from male to female persona and back again in a trice. Thus he could perform both sides of a male-female dialogue, whether spoken or sung. His *pièce de résistance* was a modern-day *Carmen*, set in San Francisco with the feds as villains and the queens as heroes/heroines, in which he would play every role. Dressed as a man, he would slip behind a screen and emerge a nanosecond later as a woman. We were all enraptured.

The evenings would end with the whole cast (José) and audience, gay and straight, joining in 'God Save Us Nelly Queens' sung to the tune of the British national anthem. The Federal Agents would move their lips without singing the words.

José was already famous, at least within the queer world of San Francisco. The previous October he had stood for a seat on the San Francisco Board of Supervisors (the city council), the first openly gay man to stand for public office in the United States. He was not elected, and it was the much more celebrated gay activist Harvey Milk who eventually succeeded in being elected to the Board, sixteen years later. But it was the fact that José had offered himself for election, seeking the votes of the straight community, that had put heart into the increasingly vociferous community of gays and lesbians in the Golden Gate City. They had already shown that the gay vote mattered. When Mayor Christopher had been re-elected in 1960, the margin by which he won was less than the estimated number of homosexual voters. His Democrat opponent was stridently anti-gay and wanted to close down all the gay bars in San Francisco. George Christopher was not pro-gay, but he won the gay vote by default. No Republican has been elected Mayor of SF since then. What was historic about José Sarria's candidacy was that the Nelly Queens had someone to vote for who represented their constituency. It was probably the starting point of gay power in the United States.

And how was the job-hunting progressing, I hear you ask, while you were swanning around San Francisco spending more than you could afford? Not well. I thought I would be able to walk into a job in any university library now that I understood the Dewey Decimal System, and there were thirteen universities in San Francisco to choose from. Alas, twelve of those thirteen were state-funded in greater or lesser degree and therefore were not permitted to employ anyone who was not an American Citizen. The thirteenth, not state-funded, declined my services.

My employment prospects were not enhanced by the fact that San Francisco had the highest unemployment rate of any metropolitan centre in the US. While evenings and weekends were full of fun and frolic, the long days were spent trudging the streets knocking on doors and suffering the humiliation of recurrent rejection. Come back, I was told over and over, when you have lived here for five years.

The pot of money I had saved in Boston was shrinking rapidly. I had never yet suffered actual hunger, but this now became a real and alarming prospect. When things started to look fairly desperate, I was saved by the fact that Mister Matthews decided that the immediate threat of nuclear annihilation had passed (the Cuban missile crisis was three months in the future). Whenever he visited the shops it was his habit to buy an extra tin of something to store in his Nuclear Annihilation Cupboard. This was to sustain him for several weeks following the dropping of an atomic bomb on San Francisco, on the assumption that all fresh food would be contaminated. Mind you, if the bomb were dropped anywhere near Union Square, it is unlikely that Mister Matthews would have had any need of sustenance. (San Francisco was, according to a world map published in *Life* magazine, one of the primary targets for Soviet attack. The cities of the world were colour coded with red for 'Probable', blue for 'Possible' and yellow for 'Low Risk'. Belize City and London were rated as being at the same level of risk, both coloured yellow. Americans, even those occupying editorial chairs at *Life*, were largely unaware that Britain was one of the world's four nuclear powers.)

The Nuclear Annihilation Cupboard was now full and Mister Matthews deemed it time for a cull. We decided to make an heroic stew out of the whole lot, then comprising (with some additions of fresh produce): onions, butter beans, carrots, mushroom gravy, baked beans, tomatoes, beef gravy, chicken soup, bouillon, green lima beans, peas, potatoes, a whole cabbage, spaghetti, several pounds of stewing steak, a dozen rashers of bacon, a pound of cheese and a bottle of burgundy. There was no pot large enough to contain all this so we found an old hip bath and heaved it on to the hob. Norman and Mister Matthews went off for preprandial drinks while I slaved over a hot stove.

The result, though I say it as shouldn't, was magnificent. It did have a somewhat piquant flavour, which Norman and Mister Matthews thought to be not unconnected to the burnt bits on the bottom, but which I preferred to attribute to the flavour-enhancing effect of the burgundy. We invited Mister Long to join us for its debut and he was delighted to enjoy a meal that he did not have to pay for. We ate it again for breakfast, lunch and again for dinner. This was repeated on the third day. On the fourth day Mister Matthews suggested that we tip the rest of it down the lavatory. I firmly rejected any such wanton waste of scarce resources.

The upshot was that Norman and Mister Matthews took themselves off to a diner at the end of Hayes Street, while Mister Long and I continued on a diet that even we had to concede had a certain sameness about it. At the end of the first week the piquant flavour had intensified. Indeed, the stew could be said to have become pungent. We even offered some to Trevor, but he treated our generosity with the same contempt as he responded to any overtures of goodwill. On the eighth day we abandoned it and Norman and Mister Matthews returned to our communal dining table. Sadly, there was all too little that I could afford to place on it.

It was shortly after the stew saga, and when my savings had diminished to a point of penury, that an official-looking envelope addressed to me and with a Washington postmark was delivered to 328 Hayes. It was from the Selective Service Board. It informed me that I was to await formal induction into the United States Army and that in the meantime I was not to attempt to leave the country.

It may seem strange that the US Army drafted foreign nationals, but it made perfect sense to the Pentagon. The more expendable foreigners who could be pressed into service as cannon fodder, the fewer all-American boys needed to be called upon to make the supreme sacrifice.

This aspect of the matter, however, had not occurred to me, and the prospect of $28 a week and all found seemed quite alluring until Norman put me wise.

Norman's best friend Murphy wrote to him regularly from Vietnam, where he was doing his army service. 'Murph' wrote that the reports in the American press that the Americans were there simply as advisers to train the South Vietnamese troops were quite untrue. He and his buddies, he told Norman, were in the front line and taking the brunt of the action. New drafts were arriving in Saigon regularly and Murph believed that this was a build-up to full-scale war. So it turned out to be. How it could be that in the early 1960s a state secret known to Norman and me had not been revealed to the American public, and could be so successfully concealed by the Kennedy administration, is an historical mystery that I am still pondering. Were the press and broadcasting media colluding in this deception? And the Republican opposition in Congress?

I decided to appeal against my call-up, not on the grounds that I objected to fighting in a war of doubtful legality that had nothing to do with me or my country, because the Selective Service Board would simply have denied that any such war was being fought. My objection was on what I believed to be the much firmer grounds that I was already a serving soldier in a foreign army. I explained that I was on leave of absence from the Honourable Artillery Company and that if I did not return at the end of it, the Ministry of Defence and the Foreign Office would seek my extradition (a pardonable exaggeration, I felt, in the circumstances). If this was refused, it would probably cause a diplomatic incident. Did the Kennedy administration wish to incur a rupture with its wartime ally in a matter of such trifling importance to the American military?

Apparently the Kennedy administration was happy to take this risk, because my appeal was summarily rejected. Norman had received another letter from Murph in which this reluctant warrior recounted the casualties his unit was suffering. Norman's advice to me was terse: 'Get your tail over the border into Canada pronto.'

I did not have the fare to Canada. Norman, however, was possessed of a beat-up 1951 Buick. The only problem was that neither of us had the wherewithal for gasoline.

The reasons for this were self-inflicted. I must confess that my present poverty was not wholly unconnected to a trip that Norman and I had seen advertised in the *San Francisco Examiner*. Harrah's Casino in Lake Tahoe, just over the border from California in the gambling state of Nevada, would reimburse your return coach fare on presentation of the ticket stub. There was free food on offer too, as well as welcoming drinks. How could I visit the west coast of America and never try my luck at the tables? Why, it might solve my solvency problems for months to come!

It did not, and it also deprived Norman of all his ready cash until his next monthly retainer check arrived from the Southern Pacific Railroad. But the resourceful Norman had a solution to the problem of how to finance my escape to Canada. We would join the nomads who followed the inland route from Tijuana north to the Canadian border.

These were the Mexican nomadic workers who crossed the Rio Grande in the spring to work their way up the western seaboard of the United States toiling in the fields, starting with spring sowing and terminating with the Idaho potato harvest in the autumn. In between, there was vine cultivation in the vineyards, hop training, peach thinning, strawberry picking, hoeing and tilling and all the stoop labour and other arduous tasks that gringos were unwilling to perform under a gruelling sun for the minimum wage (or below). Norman was confident that he could talk our way on to a gang and we would earn sufficient to pay our way to the border and his return trip. It would be an experience that would contribute to the Great American Novel, which he had embarked upon soon after his arrival at 328 Hayes Street.

· · ·

We left San Francisco having bidden José and Mister Long sad farewells. I wished Trevor well and he sneered back. Mister Matthews accompanied us to Bodega Bay, where we planned to spend the first night, he returning on the bus. He brought with him a gallon flagon of his usual rotgut and we had a jolly goodbye party on the beach, roasting wieners on sticks in front of a driftwood fire. Had Hitchcock's terrifying *The Birds*, which was shot at Bodega Bay, been made a year earlier I think we might have chosen some other beach. As it was, we spent a night lying on the still warm sand under a canopy of stars, undisturbed by killer seagulls. Mister Matthews left at first light. Dear Ray: you were also one of my favourite Americans and it would have saddened me to know, as you turned and waved from the top of the breakwater, that I would never see you again.

We lost no time in seeking work. Norman, who had high-school Spanish, did the talking. We were engaged to work with a gang who were hop training and the next morning, in the dawn light, we joined them at the appointed place. The hours were long, the sun was hot, the pay was low. At sunset we wound our weary way through the fields to the pay table – wages were on a daily basis for casuals like ourselves – and Norman told the foreman he would not be returning in the morning. He knew the retainer cheque would be arriving soon after he got back to Hayes Street. I did not enjoy such a choice.

Our days and nights fell into a routine. Norman slept in a sleeping bag in the front of the car, I under a rug in the back. The 1951 Buick was not wide enough to stretch out one's legs, so sleep tended to be in snatches of an hour or two. At first light we breakfasted on peanut butter-and-jelly sandwiches and I made another one to take with me to the fields. Norman, meanwhile, was preparing for his day's labour at the typewriter. He sat himself sideways on the driving seat with his feet on the ground outside and the typewriter on his lap. Before I left he would already be clacking away, brows furrowed as he concentrated on the lyric passages that would light up the pages of the Great American Novel.

On my return from the fields, sweat-stained, famished and exhausted, we would prepare supper together. This was the same every evening. We had a stockpile of Dinty Moore Beef Stews in the trunk. These came in family-sized tins and contained carrots, turnips and potato, so they were a complete meal. We did not possess a saucepan, so when we had removed the lid, we placed the open tin on top of the fire that Norman had lit earlier and had now died down to embers. When the stew was hot enough, we ate it with a spoon straight from the tin. The spoons were our only eating utensils and we did not indulge in the luxury of crockery. For a while we had the solace of the remainder of Ray's rotgut wine, after which the flagon served for our water supply.

After supper Norman would recount progress with the GAN. I would respond with the highlights of my day, which might be someone falling off a ladder, or a desultory fight between two Mexicans over a matter of honour. Once it was a petty thief suffering summary justice with the foreman's belt before he was jeered out of the field by his compatriots. We retired to our makeshift beds without washing and rose the next morning to embrace a new day with the dirt of the previous one undisturbed by soap and water.

On Saturday night the permanent members of the work gang received their week's pay and hit town for a night of carousal. It was time for us to move on. As we drove slowly down Main Street the whoops and hollering from every bar informed us that our erstwhile Mexican colleagues were having the good time they deserved.

After we had crossed the state line into Oregon, we drove on for half an hour or so and stopped at a roadside diner with a neon sign proclaiming 'Joe's Place'. As we entered the twenty or thirty men seated at the counter and at tables fell silent. Twenty or thirty pairs of male eyes followed us as we approached the counter and greeted our host, presumably Joe. He grunted in response, looked us up and down, rolled his stogie to the corner of his lips, then muttered 'You fellas from outta state?'

'Yessir,' I responded brightly. 'I'm from London, England.'

Joe ruminated on this information. 'London, England, huh?' He rolled the stogie to the other side of his mouth and nodded to Norman. 'Where you from, Bub?'

'I'm from Watsonville, California,' said Norman, adding 'We're travelling north to the border.'

Joe stared at Norman for a few seconds, then slapped the counter with the flat of his hand and called out to the room in a loud voice:

'Hey, youse guys, listen up. This is somp'n else.' He slapped the bar counter again for emphasis. 'There's a fella here what's come all the way from Californy!'

The long hours in the car were passed with games of 'Who Am I', in which you declare whether you are dead or alive, male or female, and the other person has twenty 'Yes' or 'No' questions to guess your identity. If you play this with a woman your first question should be 'Are you Mary Queen of Scots?' because they nearly always are. I like to think our selections were a bit more imaginative: Mona Lisa, The Real McCoy, Dinty Moore (of beef stew repute), Virginia Dare, Peter Rabbit, The Unknown Warrior. Others were drawn from our recent experiences: The Man Who Stared at Us in Yuba City, The Woman in Sonora Who Knelt on the Sidewalk to Pray, Mister Long, Agent O'Brien (most bitter of the Feds who pursued the Nelly Queens at the Black Cat), Pariah Dog in Durango....

Alternatively I would recount stories from my schooldays, the fagging, the ritual bullying, the cold baths, the beatings, fascinating and repelling Norman, product of a carefree Californian education, in equal measure. In return he told me anecdotes of his life that were equally alien. I enjoyed this one. After he had completed his two years' army service, during which he trained as a cook, he applied for a job as a deep-fry cook in a short-order restaurant. He was rejected with the words 'Son, you're not old enough for deep-fry.'

And this. Norman hero-worshipped Frank Sinatra. On a trip to Vegas with his army gratuity, he went into a casino bar to assuage his grief at its rapid loss. He sat himself at the bar counter next to the only other patron. There was something familiar about the hunched shoulders, the fedora hat worn at a distinctive angle ... it couldn't be, could it be? It was! Norman leaned over and squeaked, 'Gee whiz Mister Sinatra. I'm your greatest ever fan....'

A pair of bleary blue eyes were half turned towards him. 'Beat it, Kid' uttered the world's most acclaimed singer.

'But Mister Sinatra, I only wanted to tell you ...' persisted Norman.

With infinite weariness the great man swivelled on his bar stool and clicked his fingers. Two enormous henchmen loomed out of the shadows. They spoke not a word; each inserted a massive forearm under Norman's armpit and lifted him bodily from his stool. They then marched him across the floor, Norman's feet pedalling the air, flung open the doors on to the street, and threw him across the sidewalk into the gutter. The Voice did not look up from his dry martini.

I was also taken with a little story Murph had told his friend Norman. He was working in a fruit cannery in Monterey – on the original Cannery Row – his job being to insert peeled pears into cans and seal them. One day on the production line, he observed the youth next to him take a large bite out of a pear, drop it into the can, and close the lid. It is the thought of the look on the housewife's face when she emptied out the pears that so appeals to me.

My next job with the nomads was peach thinning. I had been no great shakes at hop training, but I was a sight worse at this new task. It involved standing on a high ladder against a tree and thinning out the

*The Voice did not look up from his dry martini.*

young peaches to allow them space for growth. If you were Mexican you did this with both hands, and at high speed, balancing on the ladder by knee pressure alone. If you were me you held on to the ladder for dear life with one hand while you groped the peaches clumsily with the other.

We were on piece rates. At the end of my first day, when it came to pay-out time, I received just $6. The big swarthy Mexican ahead of me in the queue had just been handed $22.

As I turned to go, the foreman called out, 'Hey, Gringo! Come over here.' I stood in front of him, feeling as I did at St Peter's when invited by Mr Tolson for one of his 'little chats'.

He looked me up and down and did not seem very impressed with what he saw.

'You too slow for this job,' he began. 'You really wanna work for 50c an hour?'

I hung my head in shame.

'Gringos don't work like Mexicans,' he ventured. I was inclined to agree. 'You stand on top of that ladder like a girl.' I did not demur.

'I figure that's it then,' I said. 'I guess I'd better be moving on....'

'Momento, Gringo. Not so fast. I reckon you need the work, no?'

I assented.

'You gringos not much use in the fields, but I like your face. You can work flat rate. I pay you ten dollar a day. Deal?'

'Deal!'

        * * *

It took us three weeks to reach Portland, Oregon. Three weeks without soap and water or brushing our teeth. Three weeks without a change of clothes. Indeed we had slept in them all this while. On the sidewalks of Portland people gave us a wide berth.

We made for the University of Oregon. There we were not a lot grubbier than some of the more radical students and were able to pass ourselves off quite easily as two of their number. We made for a dorm and enjoyed the luxury of its showers. Nobody challenged our right to be there.

Another week's travel and stop-offs for work brought us to Seattle. The World's Fair was the biggest event in Seattle's relatively brief history and we joined the other rubberneckers. Although this was one of the last of the World Fairs, I have to confess that I have no memory of anything we saw at the Fair itself. I dimly recollect that it was mainly about the world of the future and heavy on the kind of industrial technology that requires an insider's knowledge to appreciate. Downtown, though, there was one exhibit that did make an impression on me. At the city's top department store, Frederick & Nelson, they were holding a British Week in association with the World's Fair. The windows were given over to British fashions and other products, the most striking being one that exhibited a Rolls Royce Silver Cloud balanced on four delicate Royal Worcester teacups in their saucers.

We were nearing journey's end, but first we had to pay a visit to Ray Matthews's friend Roy in Manchester, a fishing village on the other side of the Puget Sound from Seattle. Roy lived in a wooden house on stilts driven into the waters of the Sound. It was accessed by a rickety footbridge.

I suspect that Ray and Roy had been lovers in their younger days. They had lived together in San Francisco but now Roy had retired to his dwelling on the water. There was very little furniture, other than beds, a table and a few chairs. Tea-chests and packing cases were piled up in every room and there were no carpets or curtains. It was very cold. I asked Roy if he had just moved in. He said yes, he had, and there really had not been time to get things straight yet. 'When was that?' I enquired. 'Four years ago,' he replied.

Despite the discomfort and the chill, we were living rent-free, and Roy, who I think was lonely, seemed content to feed us in return for our company. For myself, I was in no particular hurry to face the rigours of job-hunting in a new and alien environment. I spent the days walking the banks of the Sound or sitting in the kitchen with a good book, the oven on full with its door open to provide some warmth. It was a strange, detached kind of existence and I wondered what had made Roy desert the pleasures of city life for this literal backwater. Welcoming and friendly as he was, his personal life was not for sharing.

This peaceful interlude concluded when Norman announced it was time for him to return to San Francisco. He would drive me the 160 miles to the Canadian border and then I would be on my own again.

At the border there was a Greyhound bus disgorging its passengers on the Canadian side. Among the motley crew of passengers there was one strikingly beautiful girl with the poise and grace of a professional dancer. Norman stood there with his mouth hanging open and a glazed expression in his eyes. 'Norman, pull yourself together. She's out of our league,' I admonished him. He did. Starting forward, he went up to the girl, spoke a few words, then took her suitcase. They walked towards me and Norman turned to her and said, 'This is my English friend Patrick. He's crossing into Canada. Where are you going?'

'I'm heading to San Francisco,' she replied. 'I want to get into one of the dance companies. My name is Maria.'

After a brief conversation, it was time for me to thank Norman for aiding my escape from the draft and bid him a fond farewell. As I walked towards the border post I turned and saw Norman stowing Maria's bags into the back of the Buick and shepherding her towards the passenger seat. I wondered whether anything would come of this instant romance.

Well, it did.

Reader, she married him!

Maria was Russian-Canadian, Norman was Australian-American. They had a beautiful Russian-Canadian-Australian-American daughter and they called her Carla.

# Chapter 7

. . .

# WANTED IN TWO COUNTRIES

. . .

## *June–October 1962*

What induced me to tell the immigration officer at the Canadian border post that I was a buyer for the Times Bookshop of Wigmore Street? Now it is true that I had a roving commission from Rubber Ears d'Arch Smith, head of the Times Bookshop's antiquarian department, to source saleable books for them, but I was dressed like a tramp in soiled work-clothes with a sweat-stained bandanna kerchief round my neck, a straggly beard, and 1917 cavalry boots. The fact that many English book dealers do indeed dress like tramps may not have been known to an immigration officer on the British Columbian border.

I can only put it down to the idiocy of youth. It cost me dear, because the officer stamped my passport with a twenty-four-hour visa. 'If you are not back in the United States by noon tomorrow,' he warned, 'you will be on a wanted list as an illegal immigrant.'

On arrival in Vancouver I sat in a café over a pot of tea and contemplated my immediate future. I had $15 and some odd cents. I could not apply for legitimate work in Canada. If I returned to America I would be on the run from the Feds. It did not look very promising.

The only contact name I had in British Columbia was Monsieur Rahmé, John Kimpton's saviour who had employed him and Nigel at the Emerald Lake Chalet in the Rocky Mountains. I finished the tea, went over to the public phone, checked the number of Emerald Lake with Directory, and dialled Monsieur Rahmé. The conversation was brief. It was the beginning of the season and he was fully staffed. Yes, there might be vacancies later on, but there was no telling when. Yes, I could call in if I was passing, but not to make the journey specially. Have a nice day.

I went into the restaurant's rest-room and had a thorough wash, shaved off my beard, stowed my work-clothes into my suitcase and put on my three-piece suit, a stiff collar and the HAC tie, and exchanged the 1917 cavalry boots for a gleaming pair of Oxfords. Mother had told me you must always look immaculate for a job interview. Then I sought directions to the station and bought a one-way ticket to Field, the nearest stop for Emerald Lake. It cost $13. At least I could sleep overnight on the train and tomorrow was another day.

Field was a one-horse town with little to detain me. There was no public transport to Emerald Lake, but after I had waited by the side of the road for a couple of hours a truck stopped. It was the Emerald Lake Chalet truck returning from Banff with the laundry. The jovial driver, a Finn called Risto, drove me the eight miles up the winding mountain road to the Chalet and led me to Monsieur Rahmé's office. It was now dusk and I caught him just as he was leaving. He did not look overjoyed to see me and less so when I introduced myself.

I stated my business. He expressed surprise that I 'happened to be passing' so soon after our telephone conversation. There were, he declared, no jobs.

'No jobs at all….?' I pressed. 'No jobs of any kind,' he rejoined with marked emphasis.

'Not even something in the scullery, washing up, or something dirty no-one else wants to do….?' If I had to leave empty-handed, I was only too conscious of the fact that I was 550 miles from Vancouver and I had $2 in my pocket. Monsieur Rahmé looked at my three-piece suit with distaste and sighed. 'Not in those clothes,' he replied.

'You mean,' I responded, 'that there might be something I could do if I got out of these clothes?'

'You're not the right type,' he said. 'Go to Vancouver and look for something clean and tidy in an office.'

'So there is something!' I urged.

The manager checked his watch, not I think because he needed to know the time, but to signify that I was detaining him beyond office hours. 'There's only one opening at the moment and you aren't suitable. You're the most unsuitable-looking candidate for rough work I've ever had.'

'Monsier Rahmé,' I pleaded, 'let me get out of these clothes and give me a chance to prove myself. Please tell me what this unsuitable opening is. Please....'

'Very well,' he sniffed. 'I need a lavatory cleaner. Now have you ever seen a lavatory cleaner in a stiff collar and a waistcoat?'

I solemnly removed my jacket, took off the collar and tie, and divested myself of the offending waistcoat.

'Monsieur Rahmé,' I declared 'I am ready for work. I *really, really* want to clean lavatories.'

He sent me off to see the Housekeeper, on the understanding that if she was not satisfied with my lavatory-cleaning performance I would have to leave at the end of next day. At least I had a bed for the night. When I knocked on Miss Watson's door it was already dark. She was a Scots lady, matron at a boarding school in the east as I later learned, and a stickler for good manners, in which she considered most young Canadians, including the chambermaids and housemen in her present charge, woefully deficient. I treated her with the deference I had been brought up to accord to my elders and apologised profusely for troubling her after hours. This, apparently, was what secured my employment against Monsieur Rahmé's better judgement, because my accomplishment with a mop and pail was comparable to my ability to perform other practical skills. Happily my frequently expressed concern for Miss Watson's state of health – she was a martyr to draughts – and effusive admiration for all things Caledonian saved me from any of the wrath visited on idle or incompetent colonial members of the staff.

I did, however, have occasional lapses from grace. One was occasioned by a houseman a few years older than me, Horst, who had escaped from an East German prison and then succeeded in fleeing the DDR itself. He had been a member of the Hitler Jugend as a boy, indeed he claimed to be its youngest member, having joined at the age of nine just as the Third Reich was collapsing. The normal age for enlistment in the Hitler Jugend was eleven, but Horst was such an ardent little Nazi that they let him in two years under age. It is interesting to reflect that, should he live to a great age, Horst could become the last living Nazi – the last, that is, who wore the swastika in an official capacity.

I had one day off a week and Horst was detailed to stand in for me. I took him to one side and told him to pay close attention. I explained that the cleaning of the lavatories took from breakfast to lunch, the afternoon being devoted to other domestic pursuits, and that he was not to let me down by some whirlwind of teutonic efficiency resulting in the lavatories being finished by coffee-break. Did he understand? 'Jawohl, Patricklein', Horst assured me, with a big grin on his oafish face.

'Horst, I am serious. You could get me into serious trouble. Do you promise to work at my steady pace and not like a whirling dervish?'

'Patricklein, you can trust me. I always obey orders!'

I'll bet you do, I thought, but probably only when they come from an *Obergruppenführer*.

The following morning on my way to breakfast I was intercepted by Miss Watson. She had a face like a stormy day in her hometown, Aberdeen.

'Horst finished *all* the lavatories well before coffee-break,' she informed me. 'And he had completed *all* your afternoon duties by lunchtime. How do you explain that?'

'I'm sure he can't have been as thorough, Miss Watson....'

'Horst is the most thorough worker we have at Emerald Lake. You must know that?'

I did, indeed I did. If Horst had been a year or so older, I dare say the fall of Berlin would have been postponed at least till the Yanks arrived.

For the next couple of days I kept well out of Miss Watson's way and sought to emulate Horst's heroic levels of productivity, though with meagre success. Then suddenly the clouds parted and the sun shone through again. Horst had been rude to Miss Watson. Apparently he had called her a *Schottische Hackfresse* and although she did not know what it meant, she got the Scottish bit and surmised the rest was not intended as a compliment. (According to the net, it means having a face like squashed-up mincemeat. It was not a wholly inaccurate appellation.) Anyway, I was restored to Miss Watson's affections and the most thorough worker at Emerald Lake was banished from her circle of acolytes. I got Risto to bring me back a bunch of flowers from Banff to give her on the anniversary of Bonnie Prince Charlie's landing in Scotland. Brown-nosing? Certainly not! It was an insurance policy against future misdemeanours.

. . .

We were a fairly cosmopolitan lot at the Emerald Lake Chalet. Risto from Helsinki and Heil Hitler Horst you have already met and Monsieur Rhamé was Lebanese, while his wife was from the Yorkshire squirearchy. After she had asked to borrow an old copy of *The Times* from me, I ingratiated myself by getting my parents to send over copies of *The Tatler* for her to wallow in. The staff I described in a letter home: *Mister Gauweiler is the chef, huge and Swiss. Temperamental, and a terror in the kitchen, but very nice out of it. He charged a waitress the price of a dinner for eating some cake crumbs. Rao and Oscar are Swiss and German cooks respectively. Al is the pastry cook and a great gambler. Mrs Johanssen is Canadian-Swedish, and very fat and jolly. She looks after the coffee shop.*

*There are three carpenters, an Aussie called Don who never speaks and never smiles, a Scot called Angus who never speaks but is always smiling, and Gunther from Bavaria who speaks a great deal between bellows of laughter. Mister Green and Mister Baker are the staff philosophers. Mister Green is Welsh, Mister Baker a Canadian. Mister Green dislikes women and Americans and anything to do with America. He has been a wanderer since his youth and likes all the finer things of life, good music, good books etc. He is very cagey about where he was educated. It was near London and sounds like a boarding school. I suspect he is an old Harrovian who got into disgrace and was sent to the colonies.'* [I later learned that he had fought with the International Brigade in the Spanish Civil War. During the winter months he would go to Vancouver and live in one of the cheap hotels for transients and the homeless that existed all over North America in those days. They cost \$1.50–\$3.00 per night and were very rudimentary, usually with worn linoleum on the floors or just bare boards, and a musty smell of dust and grime and unwashed bodies. There wouldn't be a restaurant – there was usually a diner on the block where you could get a bowl of chilli for 35c – but there was always a foyer with scuffed and greasy armchairs lining the walls. Here the denizens would sit all day, a few of them listlessly turning the pages of yesterday's paper (retrieved from a bin), but most just staring into space. Nobody spoke. Here, or somewhere like it, Mr Green would sit out the five months before Emerald Lake Chalet reopened. He deserved better.]

*Kay comes from Warwickshire and works in the still room. She is very brassy and common and I like her a lot. She is one for the gay life, and has a lot of titled friends who I think are Birmingham war profiteers.*

*Nancy is from Brighton and a housemaid. She is a schoolteacher and the world treats her very hard. She is always complaining, which made me cross at first, but now I see that her grumbling is only the sort soldiers enjoy so much, so Nancy is alright.*

*The waitresses are all very pretty. Most of them are Canadian students on summer vacation. One who is not is a French-Canadian who looks like Brigitte Bardot. Her name is Elise.*

*On the desk are Beryl from Leicestershire, Martin from Acton, and a Canadian girl called Louise who sort of shakes in a very charming way. I am very fond of Louise. She thinks Mister Green and Mister Baker and myself are all very intellectual. When Louise is around Mister Green and Mister Baker and I become very intellectual indeed.*

*Neil McPherson is my room-mate. He is a Nova Scotian and an undergraduate at Acadia University. Tall and angular and has a diffident something which the girls go for. The waitresses and the housemaids are all goofy about him, and he brushes them off with a half shy, half come-back-again air, and this fetches them. Perhaps if I wore horn-rimmed spectacles and had a sweater with a big letter on the back they would be delirious over me too. But I do not begrudge Neil his success with the fair sex because he is a very loyal chap and makes my bed every day. He says he does not mind making beds. This is beyond my comprehension.*

Not only was I relieved of making my bed – neither I nor anyone else was required to do any dusting. I asked Miss Watson about this one day. 'You've never lived in the mountains before, have you Patrick?' she replied. 'There isn't any dust here. We are too high up.'

. . .

One day I was leaning on my broom contemplating the shimmering beauty of the Emerald Lake in the sunshine when Madame Rahmé called out 'Patrick, go chase a bear.' I took this to be Rocky Mountain parlance for make yourself scarce, and began to saunter off. 'It's not over there, it's in that direction', Madame Rhamé said, pointing her finger. It certainly was. A great big fierce-looking brown bear of the kind that we read about

*It was apparent that Madame Rhamé's command 'Patrick, go chase a bear'*
*was not intended as a figure of speech.*

in the local newspaper. Usually after someone had been mauled. I began
making a rapid exit. Madame Rahmé summoned me back. 'Get rid of
it,' she commanded. I hesitated. There had been no mention of danger
money in my terms of employment and I had no desire to confront the
snarling beast. At that point, though, it ascended a tree. I thought that let
me off the hook, but apparently not. 'Get it down!' was Madame Rahmé's
next instruction. I hoped this might be a shaft of Yorkshire humour, but I
was mistaken. She sighed. 'You've never done this before, I suppose?'

I was tempted to say that there had not been many bears in Mayfair
to practise on, but held my counsel. Madame Rahmé explained to me
precisely and clearly the art and science of getting bears down from trees
without sacrificing yourself in the process. I was told to throw pebbles
at the trunk of the tree just above the bear's head. This would drive it a
few feet down the trunk and I was to continue the bombardment until
the animal reached terra firma. Try not to hit the bears – it tends to
annoy them, she added helpfully. Next came the tricky bit. The thrower
must position himself in such a way that the bear could exit stage left, to

paraphrase Shakespeare. If the bear thinks you are blocking its passage, it will attack. Then you are likely to become the subject of a brief report in the *Banff Bugle* or the *Kamloops Mining Record & World Herald Enquirer*, concluding with the date of the interment.

Keeping the estate clear of bears now became part of my regular duties. Whenever I had to 'go chase a bear', the routine was to call the Ranger and get him to come over with a bear trap. This was a big iron cylinder on wheels with a sliding door suspended like the blade of a guillotine above the entrance. A piece of honeycomb was placed at the end of the tube on a counterweight and when the bear ate it he triggered a mechanism that brought the door crashing down behind him. I would then call the Ranger again and he would come with a pot of orange paint and paint the bear's behind with a circle about the size of a football. If the same bear was captured a second time he was put down. This was a humane measure, because being caught twice meant that the beast had become dependent on garbage for its sustenance. Such a diet did not build up sufficient reserves of fat and the bear would wake up during winter hibernation and die of starvation. So we had to be cruel to be kind.

Nearly all our guests were Americans and they came in two varieties as far as the control of bears was concerned. Some, generally ladies of a certain age with blue-rinsed hair, would flee shrieking from the scene. This was not good because it could frighten the bear and a scared bear is a dangerous bear. The other kind, often overweight men in pork-pie hats with stogies between their fat lips, would stand gawping in unsuitable places, such as the base of the tree I was trying to coax a bear down from. 'Would you mind stepping aside, Sir?' had little effect. 'Do you want to be MAULED BY THAT BEAR, Sir?' sometimes persuaded the cannier ones to shift themselves.

It was hard to persuade our American guests that they were in a foreign country. Among my household duties was emptying the mailbox. It was generally full of the guests' picture postcards, invariably with American stamps on them. If the guests were still in residence I would go to their cabin and explain the necessity for applying Canadian stamps when in Canada. The most frequent response was 'Why? Doesn't Canada belong to the good old US of A?'

It was difficult to resist the temptation of teasing the American guests. They would often enquire why the Emerald Lake was so green. All the staff had the same practised routine on this one. It was necessary to deliver it with a straight face and in the tone of a lecturer in aquatic studies.

'At the end of each season, Sir or Madam,' we would begin, 'a couple of us row out to the middle of the lake. Now if you look carefully you will see that there is a small buoy exactly in the centre. Can you see it, Sir, Madam?'

Sir or Madam would shield their eyes with their hands, peer across the water, and assure us that they could see the non-existent buoy.

'That buoy has a long chain attached to it, the other end of which is attached to a plug, like a bath plug but obviously a lot bigger. We haul up the plug and that drains the lake of water. Once it is empty all the staff get cracking and paint the basin of the lake an emerald green colour. That's why it is called the Emerald Lake.'

Provided you did not start smirking while you were spouting this nonsense, the guests would nearly always respond with the anticipated exclamations of amazement. Sometimes they would ask supplementary questions like how much paint was needed, allowing for almost unlimited flights of fancy.

Before leaving the American touri, as we called them, here is something Martin on the reception desk told me. When he handed a tourist some stamps, the American peered at them, did a double-take, and exclaimed 'Jeez. Your stamps have pretty gals on them!' I am sure Her Majesty would have been very flattered.

Life at Emerald Lake settled into a steady routine, enlivened by occasional upsets of one kind or another. It was not unlike being back at school, happily without the institutionalised brutality. You did as you were told and kept your nose clean and generally that meant $22 a week and three meals a day (better than school food except when the chef tried to imitate American cuisine). As at school, though, there were some who failed to make the grade.

I wrote home: *This week a very sweet girl who worked in the still-room was sacked. However, Monsieur Rahmé, having dismissed her, rang up Chateau Lake Louise and got her a job there. Query: is he a clot to sack her and then find her another situation, or a jolly good chap to be so compassionate?*

*Kay, the brassy gay-lifer, walked out after a screaming match with the chef. She told him she would go back to school-teaching and he said 'You, school teach? A slag like you shouldn't be put in charge of other people's children.' Kay packed her bags.*

*Ray the French-Canadian sous-chef, left yesterday. He said the chef and the chief cook, both of whom are Swiss, could jolly well get another Swiss because he wasn't staying in the kitchen to be pushed around.*

*'Who next?' we all ask.*

Not all the involuntary departures were at the behest of management. About once every couple of weeks or so a Royal Canadian Mounted Police car would come snaking up the road from the Kicking Horse Pass. There would be one fewer of our number at supper that night. They were most often kitchen staff, usually wanted for petty larceny or drugs or deserting their wives. But whenever I saw the men in the scarlet tunics interviewing Monsieur Rahmé, I was in dread that this time they were seeking a lavatory cleaner unencumbered with a work permit.

Apart from these moments of high anxiety, I enjoyed this placid life carrying out menial tasks that required no mental and not a lot of physical exertion. The air was probably as clean as anywhere in the world, the landscape was of majestic beauty, and my companions congenial, a mixture of bright and effervescent students and life's drifters with colourful pasts. The days passed pleasantly, with a lot of laughter and good cheer, together with that staple of every closed community: gossip. Miss Watson deplored gossip. She also depended on me to pass the more interesting nuggets on to her. And once a week there was the luxury of a day off.

* * *

Transport on days off was restricted to the laundry truck, if it was mobile that day, and hitch-hiking. I hitch-hiked to Golden, the nearest town with a cobbler, to have my 1917 cavalry boots fixed. The cobbler was a Londoner. He asked me if I knew Greenwich and had it changed much. I said it may have, it depends when you last saw Greenwich. '1885,' he replied through a mouthful of nails. In that case, I assured him, there would be one or two things that might be unfamiliar, like supermarkets and cars, but also he would find that much of Greenwich had been rebuilt after the blitz. Apparently he was fifteen when he emigrated to Canada and came out west. This was a man who would have been too old to have served in the

First World War! A couple of years ago Karla and I attended an exhibition of photographs of Greenwich, all taken by a single photographer and all in the same year. That year was 1885. Many were street scenes with groups of young people staring at the camera with that slightly bewildered look that the Victorians evinced when confronted by a photographer. I searched the faces looking for the cobbler of Golden. Of course he could have been any of the young men or none of them, but it was fascinating to look back at the world that he had last looked at before embarking on his great adventure.

Our nearest city was Calgary, a distance of 150 miles and across the provincial border in Alberta. This was the nearest place with a proper bookshop and I had already exhausted the somewhat slender literary resources of the Chalet. A housemaid called Gale whose family lived there had the same day off as I and the evening before we decided on an impulse to hitch-hike together. We swallowed a quick cup of tea and set off, Gale having succeeded in getting herself ready faster than any female person contemplating a journey has ever done in recorded history. Two cowboys picked us up in the Kicking Horse Pass and drove us to Lake Louise, from where an Irish construction engineer gave us a ride in his truck all the way to Calgary. We made it in four hours and slept at Gale's house, which we had to ourselves as her family were away.

The following morning Gale showed me her home town. This was a large city, with a population of a quarter of a million people. The most striking thing was that if you stood on the main drag below the Hudson Bay Company footbridge, this being the centre of town, you could see open prairie in both directions. I doubt that there is a city of comparable size elsewhere in the world where it is possible to see beyond its boundaries to open country.

Much of the day was spent perusing the bookshops and Gale, should you ever read this, thank you for being so forbearing. I came away with a good haul: Surtees's *Hawbuck Grange,* Norman Collins's *London Belongs to Me*, Michael Sadleir's *The Noblest Frailty,* Dr Ivan Bloch's *Sexual Life in England Past and Present,* and most joyous of all, *The Boy's Own Paper Annual* for 1909. My Uncle Seaborn, sadly killed on the Somme aged twenty-one, had possessed the 1910 volume of *BOP* and it had come down to me. It gave me so many happy hours as a schoolboy, and was so evocative of a lost Edwardian twilight, that it gave me enormous pleasure to be able to look again through that window into my heroic uncle's boyhood. It might have tarnished the pleasure somewhat had I to hitch-hike bearing this large and heavy volume together with my other acquisitions, but the benevolent Irish engineer collected us at Gale's house after we had enjoyed a scrumptious salmon supper and drove us all the way back to the Chalet. It was one of those exceptional outings where nothing, but nothing at all, went wrong.

There was another Gale on the staff, a Canadian student-waitress known as Glorious Gale owing to her gorgeous mane of golden hair and her lovely face and figure. She and I made a date to attend the Big Bend Rodeo, which is held in the Big Bend of the Columbia River between Golden and Revelstoke. I wrote home:

*Fortified by a tomato sandwich and a large cuppa, set out at 10.30 and rode a tour bus down to the Trans Canada Highway. Here we started thumbing. Gale always gets despondent after the first two cars have gone by and started calculating how many hours it would take to walk to Golden. Indeed it must have been 200 cars which passed before we were picked up by two jolly cowboys, professional bronco riders, who were on their way to the rodeo. These professionals tour from rodeo to rodeo all over Canada and the US, making their living on prize money. It must be a somewhat precarious existence, as they have to pay to enter the competitions, $10 at a small rodeo, as much as $200 or $300 at the Calgary Stampede. Prize money at the Big Bend rodeo was $1,150 all told, about 200 dollars for each winner. At the Stampede it runs into thousands for each competition.*

*We rode into Golden in style, sitting on hay bales on the back of the cowboys' truck, wind whipping the hair into our eyes, and with their two horses peering out of their box at us. The country between Field and Golden is some of the most spectacular in the Rocky Mountains. At half past twelve we met Joe Turner at the Canadian Pacific station in Golden. Joe Turner was in my study at school, and I received a letter from him forwarded from San Francisco the other day, saying he was coming down from Banff and could he stay with me. I rang him up, told him I was 50 miles away, not 1,750, and we arranged this rendezvous. Gale said afterwards she had no idea the reserved stiff upper lip English greeted each other so effusively. I had to explain the difference between any two Englishmen, and two Englishmen who were at school together. Poor girl, what she had to put up with, with all that 'I wonder what happened to old Bouncer, did you hear about Bertie? No, how disgusting, what about Benjie and Bird?'*

*After two poached eggs on toast with chips and tea we walked to the rodeo ground, which was about a mile out of town. The rodeo consisted of a corral, like you see in Western movies, a grandstand, no more than a few planks knocked together, a judges' stand, the horse and cattle runs, and some dozen side-shows, including a try-your-strength ring-the-bell apparatus run by the strongest and brownest man I have ever seen. He was able to hit the bell every time, though he was the only one who could.*

*We were just in time for bare-back bronco riding, and were able to see one of our two friendly cowboys perform. The great advantage of a small rodeo is that you can climb the corral fence and sit on the top, so that you are right in the thick of it. For the next event we hung over it, so that we could make a hasty descent every time a wild steer plunged in our direction, which was frequently, for it seems that I am like a magnet to wild steers. All the crowd, except us, were dressed Western style, and there were a large number of Indians about. They are very handsome people in this part of the world.*

*Besides the bronco riding, both bareback and with saddle (only one hand allowed), we witnessed steer decorating, calf roping and Brahma Bull riding. Calf roping involves lassooing the calf from the horse, then leaping to the ground, wrestling the animal prone and tying three of its legs together. Steer decorating is very exciting. The cowboy leaps from the saddle on to the steer, grapples with it till he has it on the ground, and then fixes a riband onto its horns. Extremely dangerous. Brahma Bulls, those hump backed bulls they have in India, are most bad tempered. Even more so when they are being ridden. Brahma Bull riding is always the climax to a rodeo.*

*I should have mentioned the Grand Parade through the streets of Golden. This was very droll. It was a straggly line of about twenty floats, or exhibits, or just people, in various stages of moth-eaten fancy costume, and seemed to consist mainly of flags, of which one was the Canadian flag and all the rest were Union Jacks. Even the solitary Canadian Standard was hemmed in on both sides by four Union Jacks. Joe and I were delighted. Gale was too busy trying to explain that Canada is not a colony. Gale is sweet.*

. . .

As the season drew towards its end, and the college students started leaving, I found my duties expanding. I became a bell-hop for two days a week, which meant the welcome addition of tips to my $22 a week. I learned quite a lot about the psychology of the tip, I wrote home. *For one thing people who work for tips would rather perform a service for someone who is civil and courteous for 25c, than put up with disobliging behaviour for a dollar. Also that women and young people are the best tippers. They are nervous of undertipping. The English tip badly or not at all. Californians are the most generous, and are also genial. And a big tip* does *inspire better service. When people tip a dollar you really feel like doing something extra for them. For instance the honeymoon couple who gave me a dollar to put their champagne on ice for them. I managed to purloin the only two champagne glasses on the premises by some swift cajolery of one of the waitresses, and I arranged them under soft light with a wild flower entwined round the stem of one glass. Not for 25c I wouldn't have, though!*

The tips amounted to as much as $20 for the two days a week, nearly doubling my income. Bell-hops at Chateau Lake Louise, the pearl of the Rocky Mountain hotels, could earn sufficient in a summer season to pay their college fees for the year.

My largest tip for performing a single service was the result of the visit of a Pentecostal congregation led by their dour and unsmiling minister. He wanted to hold a service in the ballroom, but it was a chilly day and he demanded a fire. The laying of fires was one of the new skills I acquired at the Emerald Lake Chalet and, unlike most other duties, one for which I found I had a natural ability. I built up a pile of kindling and then arranged sticks of equal length around it in a wigwam effect. This took a while and all the time I was working the minister was chivvying me, 'Get on with it, Boy. We haven't all day. Hurry up!' I could see that his flock were beginning to look embarrassed at this graceless behaviour.

Now a classic Canadian wigwam fire takes a while to combust. I lit it and stood back to observe progress. The minister began to caper up and down. 'There! It hasn't lit. You are useless, Boy. Get out of here. Go, go, go....' I walked slowly towards the door and before I reached it there was a satisfactory 'Whoosh!' as huge flames gushed upwards into the chimney. There was an audible gasp from the congregation.

Afterwards each member of the congregation presented me with 50c or a dollar, a total of $18, the only recusant being the minister. 'I am so glad you had a nice warm room for your service,' I murmured to him sweetly as he pushed roughly past me.

My other source of income was collecting beer bottles. Emerald Lake Chalet was dry, which explains those elaborate machinations over the champagne. That was a bottle of champagne the happy couple had brought with them. Most of the guests brought six-packs of beer. As I doubled up as garbage-man, the empties were my perquisite. By the end of the season I had over a thousand. Horst, the unrepentant Nazi, had a contact in Banff who dealt in empty bottles of all kinds. This rather shady character – most of Horst's contacts in the outside world appeared to live on the margins of the law – paid 20c a dozen, and sold them on to a scrap dealer in Calgary at 25c a dozen. This slender margin apparently provided him with a reasonable standard of living, though given that he was a chum of Horst's there may have been other sources of income of less reputable provenance.

The point of my story is that these bottles, shipped to Banff on Risto's laundry truck, were make or break for me. As will be related, I would not have escaped the clutches of the Feds without the vital extra $23 I made from this source.

I reported the departures in my letters home: *They're all going in dribs and drabs. The Lovely Louise, Big Bertha, Saucy Susannah, Beryl the Peril, Greek Goddess, Public Enemy No 1, La Belle Elise, Goofy, Teacher, Duster, Glorious Gale, all splendid girls and it is very sad to say goodbye to them.* A result of this exodus from the dining room was that I ceased to be a housemaid and became a waitress. A word of explanation. As a lavatory cleaner, I was brigaded with the Housemaids' Department. As far as pay and rations were concerned, that was my designation: 'housemaid'. Emerald Lake did not employ waiters, so when I was drafted to the dining room my new designation, as per my pay slips, was 'waitress'.

My debut in this capacity was not auspicious. I got very confused and brought the wrong orders and often my mind would switch off when confronted with a table of diners chopping and changing their orders. When one person did it, or rather when one woman did it – for I have to say this was an almost exclusively female characteristic – all the other women on the table would follow suit, sometimes changing their orders more than once. If I found myself at the serving hatch holding a blank order pad, as happened on occasion, I would load up my tray with a random selection of different dishes and returning to the table, sing out gaily 'Who's for the steak?' Who's for the chicken?' It was remarkable how often I cleared my tray. I think most of the lady guests had already forgotten what it was that they had changed their orders to.

I did have one small triumph. I was serving the president of Philadelphia's Merion Cricket Club – for those unfamiliar with the City of Brotherly Love I should explain that this is their most exclusive country club, the appellation being honoured with a single annual cricket match – and at the end of the meal he summoned me over and declared in those rich, deep tones that characterise the American male elite, 'My friend tells me I have grossly over-tipped you. I have done so because you have been so nice to us.' He then proffered me his card and said that there was a job open to me at Merion Cricket Club should I care to take it. I thanked him profusely but thought it prudent not to mention that should I avail myself of his kind offer, I would probably be dragged from the dining room by a posse of FBI agents. It tickled me that I had created such a favourable impression; it was, fortuitously, the first table I had served without mixing up the orders.

• • •

From time to time I received letters from my anxious parents enquiring whether I was proposing to embark on a career as a lavatory cleaner, bear chaser or bell-hop, the implication being that they had not invested in ten years' boarding education to such an end. I sought to reassure them that I would, in due course, settle down in some occupation involving a stiff collar and a waistcoat. But not just yet. I was planning to follow Kimpton to New Zealand, a fact that I only vouchsafed after I had booked the ticket. There was no question of flying across the Pacific, nor indeed of travelling by liner. My savings, including tips and beer bottle money, would only run to a freighter that carried a few passengers. The cheapest on offer was a dynamite boat, the *SS Waikema*, which apart from one obvious disadvantage also had another: it left from Long Beach, California. There were no freighters out of Vancouver.

By this time the Selective Service Board in Washington DC had written to my parents enquiring after my whereabouts. My mother, having no idea what the Selective Service Board was, and not knowing that her son was on the run from the Feds, had helpfully responded with my Canadian address. By now my name would have been posted at all British Columbian border crossings.

In the meantime I had several weeks to kill before the boat sailed. Monsieur Rahmé kindly allowed me to stay on an extra week after the Chalet had closed, as a member of the cabin-painting crew. This also put a few extra and very welcome dollars in my pocket. Although my painting skills barely exceeded my attributes as a waitress, Monsieur Rahmé was demob happy by now, looking forward to wintering in sunny Beirut, and largely indifferent to cabin renovation.

Nancy the teacher from Brighton had also stayed on to cook for the paint-crew and as she was also planning to visit New Zealand, we hooked up together when it was time to leave. I recounted our progress:

*We hitch-hiked from Emerald Lake to Vancouver, covering the 550 miles in two days, and spending the night at the small town of Kamloops. We had quite a large number of rides, though the last two hundred miles was with one driver. It was during this one that we saw a rather exciting, and spine chilling spectacle – a car coming down the road towards us at seventy miles an hour suddenly collapsed as an axle broke and the front left hand wheel buckled so that it was nearly flat on the road. It was 150 yards before the car came to a screeching halt a few feet in front of us. We noticed that the driver was still clutching a bottle of beer in one hand. No one was hurt.*

*We passed through three types of countryside – the high sierras of the Rockies, then through desert country, and finally lowland foothills sloping down to a plain round Vancouver. The desert was a surprise – I had no idea there was any in Canada, but apparently it is a continuation of the desert which runs down through Utah, Arizona, into Mexico to Durango. So I have been in it before, but over three thousand miles further south.*

*It was here that we saw the valley which in 1907 was cultivated by a colony of young Englishmen, who built a wooden trough several miles long to carry water down the mountain side and irrigate their fruit orchards. The English settlement prospered until 1914, when as a body, they all left to serve in the First World War. Few survived, for nearly all fell with Kitchener's mob, the first 100,000, and so the settlement was abandoned and the fertile valley returned to desert and the buildings rotted away.*

*The trough can still be seen winding down the bare hillside, but wind and weather have battered its timbers and now it is the only memorial of that green English valley so far away from England.*

*After spending the first night at the YMCA we searched for lodgings in Vancouver, and were disappointed to discover that the city has hardly any accommodation for residents, everyone living out in the suburbs. We eventually, for want of better, took rooms in a dingy hotel called the Lyle House, and spent a week being peered at by our fellow lodgers, all of whom were old biddies of over seventy, mainly English, but of the English 'We Disapprove' (of everything) type. The first night we despaired of using the kitchen, which was a sort of Old Ladies Natter Circle, so we went out and bought a jar of caviar and a punnet of raspberries. We sat in Nancy's depressing room, with scuffed linoleum floor and no lamp-shade, and devoured caviar in these incongruous surroundings.*

My next letter reported that we had moved over to Victoria on Vancouver Island and were enjoying it so much more than Vancouver. In those days Vancouver was a grimy, dreary city with little to recommend it, far removed from the hip, happening place that is such a go-to destination now. I wrote: *We are staying in a hotel in the city centre called the York and have two housekeeping rooms. We are leading a quiet life and trying not to spend too much money, so mostly it revolves round sleeping, eating and reading. Norman is in Vancouver with his girl friend Maria. Beryl, the Emerald Lake girl from Market Harborough, is leaving for New Zealand on the next sailing from Vancouver. She has a plum job in the meantime, living in the house of a very rich family called the Millers so that she can keep an eye on the teenage daughter (who is at school all day anyway) while Mom and Pop are off on yachting trips. For this she gets $20 a week and all found. The only work involved is keeping the house clean and cooking breakfast and dinner for herself and Betty, the girl. We have been over there to spend the day twice and it is a fabulous house of the ultra-modern kind. We had brunch sitting at a window overlooking the Pacific Ocean, and with the water lapping on the shore not ten yards outside.* [In the *Daily Telegraph* on the day I transcribe this passage there is an article about nannies for teenage children, claimed as a wholly new phenomenon amongst the busy rich. Not all that new apparently.]

*The three of us went to Sandown Park races the other day. Yes, Sandown Park. Everything round Victoria has an English flavour. Of course it was* *nothing so good as our Sandown Park, and the track is cinders, not turf. The starting gate is different too, as each horse is lined up in a separate trap, and the 'gate' is literally a series of gates which all fly open at the same time. There are no bookmakers, only the tote, which is government controlled and gives very low odds. The minimum bet is $2 (14 shillings) so we agreed on a horse for each race and split the bet three ways, which works out at 66 2/3 cents each, nice round figure! We had a very jolly day and were only a dollar each down at the end, and our entrance money, another dollar.*

*Our day's routine is late breakfast, cooked by the maestro of the tin can opener, sightseeing, tea, reading, dinner, Rummy, reading, and bed. Lots of bed of course, as I have not got over having to get up at seven at Emerald yet. I am sure it has left a permanent blemish on my well-being.*

What, no television? Different days, different ways.

. . .

I was in a state of high tension when I crossed the border back into the United States, but if they had my name on a list they did not bother to consult it. I had been careful this time to look clean and decent and I told the immigration officer that I was visiting a sick aunt in Seattle.

There was no question of hitch-hiking to Long Beach, my port of embarkation south of Los Angeles. On the way up to Canada I had been stopped by the police no fewer than fourteen times. This was more or less whenever Norman and I were walking anywhere, if only to the supermarket to buy bread and peanut butter. True, we looked thoroughly disreputable, but the real cause of suspicion was the fact that we were *walking*. No one walks more than a block in the United States. Many years later, when I had become respectable, I was stopped by police in Beverly Hills, my temporary residence at the time. When I asked what I had done to merit this attention, the cop said that the only people who walk in Beverly Hills are the domestics or people preparing to burgle rich people's houses. As I was not black he very reasonably concluded that I belonged in the latter category.

So it had to be the train and that exhausted most of what remained of my savings after paying for my fare across the Pacific and subsistence in Vancouver and Victoria. The problem was that I did not have a firm date for the departure of the *Waikema*. Dynamite boats, which are tricky to load and unload, do not run to fixed schedules. That is why they are cheap, besides the fact that you might never arrive at your destination. You are given an 'earliest possible date' and you need to sit it out until the boat arrives. Some people have to spend as much as a week or ten days in an hotel. I did not have the wherewithal for any nights in an hotel.

Train travel in America differs from its counterpart in Britain in that people converse with each other. A pleasant couple from Pasadena asked me where I was bound for and expressed interest when I told them New Zealand. A dialogue followed:

Fair Californian: You will be careful of the New Zealanders, won't you?

Me: Most cautious.

FC: I hear they are very savage.

Me: Especially the rugger types.

FC: And please don't penetrate too far into the interior.

Me: Wouldn't think of it.

FC: So easy to get lost in the jungle.

Me: Jungle?

FC: And all those head hunters.

Husband of FC (drily): I think you are confusing New Zealand with New Guinea, dear.

Collapse of Fair Party.

A single lady from San Luis Obispo overheard and continued the conversation, introducing herself as Mary Lou. I do not think that she was any the wiser about the whereabouts of New Zealand than the first lady, but she was very interested in England. She was, she revealed to me, a poet, and she thought that our romantic poets were 'just wunnerful'. I shared her picnic and she pressed me to accept a couple of drinks even though I explained that I was in no position to return her hospitality. The drinks seemed to have a liberating effect on her and she announced to me that she had decided not to get off at San Luis Obispo, but to accompany me to Los Angeles.

I had mixed feelings about this. I felt I might be getting myself into the kind of entanglement that can take a bit of explaining to Father

Doolan in the confessional; on the other hand she might have access to accommodation. A week on the streets in Long Beach did not appeal, especially as I dared not walk them.

Mary Lou thought we should make a base in Hollywood. She led me to a motel on the corner of Hollywood and Vine and we spent a pleasant afternoon rubbernecking the 'homes of the stars' with other tourists. The next two days were spent in the motel room, meals being delivered by room service. In between meals we watched television – and daytime TV was as execrable in 1962 as it is now – or Mary Lou read me her poetry. Neither diversion would be among my prime choices for whiling away the hours in the world's most celebrated entertainment hub.

The poems tended towards the sentimental end of the spectrum and one could discern the influence of Lakeland poets on an untutored mind. One of them, newly inscribed, was about me. It began with the line 'Fair Patrick from Cornwall's far-flung shore....' (I think Cornwall was the only place in England that Mary Lou had heard of; she had probably read Daphne du Maurier.) It was then that I decided that life on the streets of Long Beach was possibly a more attractive option.

I had rung the New Zealand Steamship Line each day to enquire whether the *Waikema* had come into port. Each time I was told that it was still on the high seas. I rang again and when my query was once again answered in the negative I replied 'Oh, the ship's in is it? Good. I will be there first thing tomorrow.' The query clerk must have thought that I was deranged.

Mary Lou and I celebrated our last night together with champagne, charged to the room. In case you should think that we then slipped between silken sheets, arms entwined, we didn't: she spent most of the night reading to me more of her poems. Just before switching off the light she leant over and told me that she had an urgent appointment in San Luis Obispo on the morrow and we would need to leave at 5 am. I reminded her that the desk clerk did not come on till six. She said not to worry about that, she would take care of the check in due course.

We crept out of the motel in the pale light of dawn. I had evaded the clutches of the Mounties; I was still under threat from the Feds; now I would be wanted by the LAPD for welching on a motel bill. What a good thing that my saintly parents knew nothing of this.

Mary Lou bade me a tearful farewell at the bus stop for Long Beach and pressed the poem about Cornwall into my unresisting hand. The bus arrived, I paid my bus fare, then counted my remaining cash-in-hand. I had three dollar bills and two quarters.

Arriving in Long Beach I could think of nothing better to do than go down to the docks and seek out the New Zealand Steamship Line berth. What I would do after that I had no idea. Sit on a bollard and read a book till nightfall perhaps. Then sleep under the stars. For how many days and nights could I do that?

When I reached the New Zealand Steamship Line berth there was a ship tied up alongside. I asked the man on the gate what ship it was. 'That's a dynamite boat, buddy,' replied the gateman. 'She's the SS *Waikema*. Just in from Auckland.'

Reader, there are many types of joy. The joy of relief must be one of the sweetest. It was for me on that October morn.

I stumbled up the gangway and was met at the top by the purser. 'Good-dye, Sport,' he greeted me. 'What can I do for youse?'

This was my first New Zealander. He was only a couple of years older than me, chubby, and with twinkly eyes below a thatch of somewhat unruly hair. He looked dependable. I explained that I was a passenger and asked him which day we would be allowed on board.

'You can come on now, Sport, 'slong as you don't get in the way of the unloading. Want a cuppa tea and some tucker?'

Somehow it felt like being home again.

# Chapter 8

. . .

# THE LAND OF
# THE LONG WHITE CLOUD

. . .

*October 1962–May 1963*

The *Waikema* lay at anchor in the docks at Long Beach for three days. I kept a wary eye on the dock gates for any sign of the Feds. Not until we had put out to sea and were beyond the three-mile limit was I able to relax and start enjoying my surroundings.

There were six passengers aboard: a schoolteacher couple, a sheep farmer and a teddy-boy, all New Zealanders. The ted had been on a goodwill mission from the teds of Auckland, of whom he appeared to be one of a very select number – the youth cult not having yet taken hold in NZ – to the teds of South London. (Teds, for those who were not around in the fifties, were urban working-class youths with heavily brilliantined hair, velvet jackets that reached just above the knees, drainpipe trousers and brothel-creeper shoes. They hung about in coffee bars or skiffle clubs, sometimes played in pop groups, and often rode motorcycles or motorscooters. They evolved into the mods and rockers of the sixties.)

Non-New Zealanders were represented by my cabin-mate and me. Curtis was a semi-pro wrestler from the Loop in Chicago who had engagements to fight in NZ. He was also a fundamentalist Baptist

181

of pronounced views. He had never drunk alcohol, danced, or been to a cinema. How wrestling had managed to evade the Strict Baptists' prohibited list I do not know. He was an amiable fellow except when aroused on the subject of religion. I should probably not have revealed that I was a Catholic. Curtis regarded this as a direct challenge to his own deeply held beliefs. He would lean over the side of the top bunk and demand, 'So what's wid da Voigin Mary, punk, huh?' or 'All dem smells and bells. Waddaya trying to say to the Man Upstairs? Huh, punk, huh?' I could usually avert these forays into doctrinal debate by enquiring into such niceties of wrestling practice as to whether it was better to break your opponent's nose with a forearm smash or by stamping on his face.

The officers were either Scots or New Zealanders. We shared their mess with them and they proved pleasant company, full of the wisdom of the sea and salty tales of the perils of the deep. The food was fairly basic, probably the same as you would have enjoyed as a shearer on a sheep station: basically mutton in various forms, or pies with lots of gravy. The breakfasts were heroic, as befits the appetites of men who have been on the bridge all night in a force eight gale.

The crew of the *Waikema* were kanakas, South Sea Islanders. Few spoke English, so my communication with them was limited. But I did establish contact with one man after I had overheard him conversing in the familiar Gloucester accent of my childhood. I asked him if he was from Gloucester. He said no, he was from Palmerston Atoll in the Cook Islands. But his grandfather, William Marsters, who had settled there in the 1860s with four Polynesian wives, had come originally from Bibury in Gloucestershire. All fifty of the inhabitants were descendants, other than two or three wives, and spoke as he did. I noted that a lot of his speech was archaic to modern ears and gently probed about this. He explained that his grandfather had taught his children from the *English Book of Common Prayer*; consequently they grew up speaking a seventeenth century form of English in their Gloucester accents.

I was so taken with this tale that I wrote an article for the *Gloucester Citizen* titled 'Gloucester's Forgotten Island'. This was my first appearance in print, unpaid. I suppose it was fairly typical of provincial newspapers of the early sixties that, on receiving an unsolicited contribution from Samoa (where I posted it), they were happy to publish it, but did not think to enquire what their contributor, presumably someone with local ties, was doing in the South Seas. I should not be too smug, though. My publishing debut was a travel article about a place I had not visited.

A dynamite boat is not a hub of entertainment. Apart from watching the flying fishes arching over the stern and talking to Purse the purser about life in the Land of the Long White Cloud, there was little on offer other than the pleasures of the ship's library. This contained no books published later than 1914 and I think must have been transferred from an earlier New Zealand Steamship Line vessel. It was housed in the officers' mess, since it was deemed improbable that any member of the crew would ever seek access to it.

I imagine that the creation of the library had been the work of the wife of a ship's captain in the days when it was customary for such ladies to accompany their husbands on voyages. The selection definitely suggested female choice, because the majority of the books were romances. Prominent amongst them were the works of Marie Corelli, an immensely popular author of tales of love and mysticism amongst the Victorian and Edwardian upper classes whose works were said to outsell those of Sir Arthur Conan Doyle, HG Wells and Rudyard Kipling combined. She had overcome the disadvantage of being born out of wedlock to a servant girl who had been ravished by her master to become immensely rich and influential and to lead a life of luxury and connubial bliss with her lesbian lover Bertha, former housekeeper to the ravisher. There were distinct undertones of this emotional baggage in the novels. I set myself the task of reading her entire oeuvre – I believe the complete canon was contained on those creaking shelves. I doubt that any of the dusty volumes had been opened since the demise or departure of my imagined captain's wife. Purse declared that I was possibly the only living person in the southern hemisphere to have achieved this doubtful distinction. Myself I think it more probable that I was the only one in either hemisphere.

We had a single stop during our month-long voyage and that was at Apia, capital of the newly independent Western Samoa (now simply Samoa). The colony had won its independence not from Britain, but from New Zealand. Formerly it had been a German colony, but the Germans had been ousted by the NZ Navy in August 1914. At the end of the war it had been mandated to NZ by the League of Nations.

Apia was a sleepy little town with a single main street dotted with white wooden houses and shops and a palm-fringed sea-front. Apart from Government House, the only buildings of interest were the Immaculate

Conception of Mary Cathedral, Aggie Grey's Hotel, celebrated throughout the South Pacific, and Robert Louis Stevenson's bungalow. It was a pleasant, easy-going place.

Purse took all the passengers to a lagoon he knew near Apia. Here we were able to swim in limpid, turquoise waters beneath a canopy of palms. It was the quintessential Pacific experience of picture books or Hollywood movies, except that in the latter there would have been dusky damsels disporting themselves in the shining waters. Half a century later Karla and I were staying at Aggie Grey's and I took her to find this magical place, this dreamscape from my lost youth. Alas, I could find nothing that remotely resembled it.

In the arvo, as Purse had taught me to call it, I visited the national library in Apia. This was about the size of a village library in Britain, but it had the estimable benefit of a full run of *Samoanische Zeitung* aka *Samoa Times*. I was curious to see how the newspaper, a loyal servant and supporter of German suzerainty, handled the sudden change in Samoa's governance. The issue for 29th August 1914, the day of the bloodless invasion by New Zealand troops, was in German. The following issue, dated 5th September 1914, was in English. The lead story recounted how the German Governor had absented himself from Apia as the invasion force was sighted to confer with the native chiefs. They had instructed him not to oppose the New Zealand forces and to submit gracefully and with honour to the new administration. This he did and was lauded by the *Samoa Times* for avoiding the spilling of blood.

A day or two distant from Auckland, Purse asked me if I was ready for the immigration board when we dropped anchor. This was the first I had heard of such a thing and my heart missed a couple of beats. It was nothing to worry about, Purse assured me. A panel of three immigration officers would come aboard from the pilot boat and would interview each of the passengers in the Captain's cabin. Just simple, routine questions, said Purse. 'They just need to know you've got enough money to support yourself. They don't want any Pommy bludgers living off the state. But you'll be alright. You've got plenty of dosh, haven't you?'

I swallowed. This was not the moment to reveal that my monetary assets totalled 25 shillings. 'Oh, plenty,' I shrilled gaily. 'But seriously, Purse, what would they do to some Pommy bludger who didn't have the wherewithal?'

Purse gave me a searching glance. 'We'd take him back to Long Beach,' he replied. 'And when he landed he would find himself with a bill from the New Zealand Steamship Line for his return fare.'

'Before he was led away in handcuffs by the Feds,' was my silent addendum.

I had a couple of restless nights before the day of the inquisition dawned. As we sailed towards Auckland Harbour we were met by the pilot boat and I watched the three officials from the Immigration Department mount the gangplank. They looked purposeful.

We passengers were instructed to get in line on the deck outside the Captain's Cabin. I was last in the queue. The schoolteacher couple, the farmer and the ted, Kiwis all, passed through immigration as the merest formality. Curtis spent several minutes in the Captain's Cabin but emerged with a big grin between his cauliflower ears. Then it was my turn.

The three immigration officers were busy with their papers as I entered. There was a prolonged silence, before the one with the most gold braid, seated in the centre behind a blanket-draped table, glanced up and said 'Good-dye.'

'Good morning, Sir.'

'Nime?'

'Hickman-Robertson, Sir.'

He looked down at the papers before him and there was an even longer silence. One of his colleagues was staring out of the port-hole at the seagulls swooping and diving overhead.

I could not stand this suspense. I must know my fate. 'Excuse me, Sir,' I mouthed unctuously, 'but could you tell me the next question, please?'

The arbiter of my future fortunes leaned over the table and extended a large, bronzed paw.

'There isn't a next question. Welcome to New Zealand, Sport.'

. . .

While my many quests for work in America had been a sorry repetition of disappointment and rejection, now the work came to me. New Zealand, possibly uniquely in the free world, had full employment. The 500 or so workless out of a population of two and a half million were probably, in the majority of cases, unemployable. On one occasion in a park in Christchurch I was approached by a loafer who asked me for money. I fumbled for a florin and, as I handed it to him, he said 'You needn't look so embarrassed about it mate. This is how I choose to lead my life.'

Work came to me by the good offices of John Kimpton, who had arranged an interview for a job at the Hermitage Hotel at Mount Cook, where he was employed as barman, the following day in Christchurch. Kimpton had sent me the money for the fare *poste restante* Auckland. He met me in Christchurch and I spent a couple of days in that most English of New Zealand cities before travelling across the Canterbury Plain and into the Southern Alps to take up my new job. The manager who was to have interviewed me had been detained and I was told to just turn up. I think technically I was on probation, but this nicety seemed to have been forgotten once I started work.

Christchurch was very different from American or Canadian cities, despite having been settled at much the same time as many of those in the North American west. The buildings were almost wholly Victorian and the shops very small: no supermarkets, and if there were any department stores I did not see them. It was like entering the world of HG Wells's *Kipps* and *The History of Mr Polly*. Unlike American cities, built on the grid system, the streets of Christchurch ran haphazardly, which made it more exciting to explore. The exploration revealed four antiquarian bookshops, as well as the magnificent Anglican cathedral (sadly destroyed in the 2010 earthquake) and the lovely Avon river, bordered by weeping willows, which wound through the city and its parks. Also a revelation so far from home was Christ's College, which might have been any Victorian public school in England – a Radley, or Lancing, or Cheltenham transplanted to these southern climes. The only architectural features betraying the fact that it stood 12,000 miles from the majority of its fellow members of the Headmasters' Conference were the classrooms, which were open on one side. Very practical and pleasant in summer, but did they have sliding walls for winter?

The resemblance to an English provincial city between the wars extended to Christchurch's culinary amenities. On my first evening Kimpton and I sought a good restaurant to celebrate my arrival, but everything in the city, including the pubs, seemed to close at 6 pm. Eventually we asked a bobby, whose helmet and blue serge uniform made him look exactly like a London copper, and who had a cockney accent to boot, and he directed us to a backstreet workman's café where we were regaled with the first egg and chips I had eaten since leaving England. When we returned to the YMCA through deserted streets at the wicked hour of 10.30, the doors were firmly locked against us. We had to phone to rouse the warden from his bed.

The cars in Christchurch, I noted, were nearly all Vauxhalls, Austins and Morrises. A remarkable proportion dated from the 1930s or earlier, so standing in Cathedral Square and watching the traffic pass was rather like attending a vintage car rally. New Zealander men dressed conservatively in brogues, light suits or flannel trousers with tweed jackets, woollen ties and broad-brimmed trilby hats. By this date, 1962, the wearing of hats, other than on formal occasions, was rapidly nearing extinction in England. Not so Down Under. Women wore print dresses, with hats and gloves if they were going visiting. Casual wear as we now know it, then already prevalent in North America and emerging in Britain, was almost unknown. Young adults and teenagers wore the same as their parents, and jeans had yet to make an appearance. (The odd cluster of teddy-boys on the streets of Christchurch seemed incongruous.) Schoolchildren wore English-style school uniforms, the same for all the schools in one area, those for girls, with English-style pudding-basin hats, being particularly hideous. Christ's College boys, unlike Salopians, wore straw boaters. Out of school, children ran barefoot with no taint of poverty.

I was impressed by the wide range of magazines of New Zealand provenance, not all of them about sheep. They had to compete with Australian imports, just as in Canada they had to compete with a huge influx of American publications, the difference being that there were only about a dozen mainstream Canadian periodicals. New Zealand could even boast its only scandal weekly, titled *New Zealand Truth*. There was evidently a problem about finding sufficient scandal in NZ, however, as most of the stories of errant vicars and dodgy doctors emanated from the Old Country. For 3d you could purchase from the post office a listing of every periodical published in New Zealand – why, I am not sure, but as a collector of magazines I was delighted to have it.

I reported home that '£1 notes are huge and look worth £5. There are £10 notes as big as table napkins.'

. . .

It was important to me to gather as many impressions of NZ as I could during my brief stay in Christchurch, because Mount Cook was distant from any centres of population. The nearest village was 65 miles away; the nearest town, Timaru, 140 miles. Kimpton had already flown back to resume duty in the bar. I caught a bus that took me the whole way, entering the spectacular Mackenzie Country on the last lap of the journey.

The Hermitage was the most luxurious hotel in New Zealand (not that there was a lot of competition). Unusually it was owned by the government. New Zealand, known in the nineteenth century as 'the social laboratory of the world' for its progressive policies towards workers and women (who gained the franchise twenty-five years earlier than their English sisters), was innovative in other ways too, one of which was the official sponsorship of tourism. As early as 1898 the colonial government established the world's first Department of Tourism and by 1902 had opened what may have been the world's first Tourist Information Offices (the hesitancy of my 'may have been' is occasioned by a rival claim from Hawaii). You may well ask, who were these intrepid travellers visiting NZ purely for pleasure even while Queen Victoria was still on the throne? Mainly rich English and Americans on world tours, so obviously the numbers were not great. There were also naturalists and outdoorsmen of private means who sought out the natural wonders of the far-off colony and it was for all these pioneers, who included mountaineers, that the Hermitage opened its prestigious doors in 1914.

The Hermitage that I knew was not that historic edifice. The original building had burned down and it had been rebuilt in 1958, not the best of architectural periods. Happily New Zealand was twenty years behind Europe in its architectural styles, so the resulting building was pleasing, comfortable and at ease with the surrounding grandeur. The lounge, which was my principal area of activity, overlooked one of the great views of the world: New Zealand's highest mountain, Mount Cook. Not just the majestic mountain itself, but also the Tasman Glacier and the Hooker Glacier's moraine lake.

For the privilege of staying at this wondrous place, our top-end customers, those occupying a suite, paid £5 12s 6d a day. This compared with West End prices. They did, however, have all their meals included in this overall price, as I explained in my first letter home:

*We feed the beasts six times a day. Brekker, morning tea, lunch, afternoon tea, dinner (which is called TEA by the Aussies and the Kiwis) and supper. Two of these bun fights I am in sole charge of, afternoon tea and supper. Would you trust your offspring with getting tea for a hundred people, and doing all the washing up as well? Not on your \*\*\*! And you should see them when they are allowed at the trough. Eat anything you put in front of them. Eddie, the Chief Steward, from Tottenham, gave me solemn warning. 'Don't putcher 'and anywheres near the supper table – it will get bit.'*

*I am a Steward. This is definitely socially superior to Lavatory Cleaner, so I seem to have progressed up the hotel scale. It involves more or less what a ship's steward job involves, though one does not wait at table excepting wines. I wear black trousers, crisp white shirt (the crispness is theoretical – everybody else's are crisp), bow tie, O horrors, a made-up one, and I should wear a black cummerbund, but I have not got one. All this is set off by a starched white pea jacket with silver buttons.*

*The hours are ideally suited to my caprice. I do not start till 1.30 pm, which means I can lie in bed till noon every day. This is not as degenerate as it sounds, because I work until eleven, and then from eleven to two or three am is my 'evening'. So the timetable runs as follows:*

| | |
|---|---|
| *Noon* | *Stagger forth.* |
| | *Lunch.* |
| *12.30–1.30* | *Forty winks.* |
| *1.30* | *Proceed to Servery, and serve after-luncheon coffees to mixed assortment of Americans, Australians and Englishmen. Few Kiwis stay at this hotel because they cannot afford it. Wash up coffee cups.* |
| *3.00* | *Serve tea to office staff.* |
| *3.15* | *Serve tea to Manager.* |
| *4.00* | *Fill feeding troughs for guests' tea. Wash up.* |
| *5.30* | *Knock off for supper.* |
| *6.00* | *Prepare games room for film show.* |
| *6.15–7.15* | *Serve cocktails in bar. Natter to Kimpton behind bar.* |
| *7.20* | *Serve after dinner coffee and wash up.* |
| *9.30* | *Serve guests' supper. Wash up.* |
| *11.00* | *Tidy up and lock up.* |
| *11.30* | *Poker!* |

*Wage scale I am not sure about. They have a very casual method of employment here. No word passed between myself and the management, I just arrived at Kimpton's bidding, signed a tax form, and that was it. No discussion of hours, duties, experience, suitability, sobriety, honesty or WAGES. So at the end of the first week. the pay packet was veiled in dark mystery. It proved to contain £12 5s 10d, and as I had made about £3 in tips, with no outgoing expenses, I am well satisfied. I think that must have included some overtime though.*

*The Hermitage is not unlike Emerald Lake Chalet, being a mountain resort hotel. It is though, BIGGER and BETTER. Bigger in size and accommodation, holding 140 guests, to ELC's 90–100. Better from the guests' point of view, in that it has far higher standards of service. I always felt that at Emerald Lake there was a sort of conspiracy between the management and staff against the guests. Here everything is much more professional, and though it is nice to be part of a very efficient and well run organisation, there is not quite the happy family atmosphere of Emerald Lake. At ELC most of the staff were students, while here they are professionals.*

*At ELC we had dreadful old staff quarters but they were very cosy; here we have the most up to date and well appointed staff quarters in New Zealand. Nevertheless the comparison is like that of the decaying and delightful old studies in Churchill's [my house at Shrewsbury School] and the new and totally characterless ones that replaced them. If this is a CON, then I think the work is a PRO, because serving guests is considerably more fun than cleaning out lavatories, and I have met some delightful people. We have a lot of Californians, and as they are the most genial and breezy of Americans I like them a lot. They have much trouble with the money, so when I serve them with a one-and-sixpenny Bourbon on the rocks I tell them it is 20c and then they are radiant. They are always thrilled to hear I am from San Francisco and there ensues much discussion of San Mateo, San Rafael, San Bernardino, San Diego, San Luis Obispo and San Fairy Ann.*

*The Australians are fun too and they take their coffee 'blick' or 'whoite'. Topping up whisky is 'say win' rather than 'when'. They are very plain speaking. There is, as Norman used to remind me, being half-Australian himself, no subtlety in the Australian character. The New Zealand staff try to avoid them, as they cannot resist telling Kiwis how much bigger and better things are in God's Own. The other day I was helping out in the bar and overheard an encounter between Kimpton's bartender colleague Peter Foster, a laconic Irish-New Zealander from the West Coast, and an Australian guest who had already imbibed a few. The latter wagged his finger at Peter and said 'Shall I tell you something, Sport....' Peter leant over the bar, thrust his face within a few inches of the Australian's, and hissed, 'If it's anything about bleedin' Hostralia, Mate, I don't want to hear it.'*

*The English are terribly stiff upper lipped and look as if they have walked straight out of a drawing room comedy. We agree that it is a jolly good show, what what, that I am travelling round the world and have I been to Brunei, Sarawak and British North Borneo? No, I have not – Well, I must drop by if I am ever in Bulawayo, Nairobi, Calcutta or Singapore.*

*Nancy from Brighton turned up last week but after two days she said she could not stand it and gave her notice in. The poor girl has had rather a rough time in New Zealand. After we missed each other in Seattle (we were scheduled to meet at the YWCA and then found there were five YWCAs) she flew down here and arrived three weeks before me. She had very little money and took the first job offered, which was in a progressive school near Auckland. They had nothing to eat except dates, nuts, grapefruit and dark, sour-tasting bread (baked by the children). The kids, both sexes, all ran about stark naked, there were no rules and no punishments, the children all had open sores on their bodies, there was no medical attention, and Nancy was paid a pound a day for 12¼ hours' work. She stuck it for a month and then took flight. She is returning to England in July and never wants to leave its friendly shores again. The thing which has apparently disillusioned her most about 'abroad' is that she could never get a cup of tea in a bone china teacup. I must say I have always been thankful if I can just get a cup of tea that's hot and wet.*

· · ·

The nightly poker game referred to in the timetable above was a ritual that could only begin once the maitre d', an urbane Englishman called Peter Rutherford, was satisfied that his dining room, cleared of the detritus of dinner, was ready prepared for the morrow's breakfast. The other regular players were Kimpton and Peter Foster, and we were usually joined by odd members of the kitchen staff. These latter could usually be relied upon to drink too much during the game and start to play recklessly. We would play until four and Peter Rutherford had to be back on duty by 6.30 am. How he managed this I do not know. Peter, wherever you are, I salute you.

Since I breakfasted when my colleagues lunched, and lunched when they dined, by the time we had played the last hand I was usually pretty peckish. Fortunately the small hamlet at Mount Cook that included the school and the manager's and the rangers' houses also had a shop from which I could source provisions. The selection was not extensive, but there was beef stew, lamb and green peas, steak and kidney pudding, various soups and Watties' Creamed Corn (highly recommended, but no longer available in England since the New Zealand Shop off the Haymarket closed down). I had managed to source a Peek Frean biscuit tin from the kitchens and this was the basis of my cooker. I placed an empty Nescafé tin in each corner, and four candles in the central space between them. A saucepan of water placed on the Nescafé tins over the lighted candles would boil in about fifteen minutes. You could not use more than four candles because they would melt. I needed a spatula for fried eggs and this was something that was beyond the limited stock of Mount Cook Shop, but Richard the proprietor, a skilful handyman, fashioned one for me by flattening a jam tin and cutting it out with shears. My room became known as 'Patrick's Pie Palace' and was a popular venue for any night-hawks who happened to be up and about in the small hours.

My mentor and immediate boss at the Hermitage was the Chief Steward, Edward Jones. He was a communist whose political allegiance had grown out of his experiences growing up on a traditional Norfolk estate before World War II. His father had been an agricultural labourer whose livelihood and wellbeing, together with that of his family, was wholly dependent on the whim of the squire, a man of uncertain temper and capricious moods. Eddie had never forgotten what it was like to be at the bottom of a hierarchy, nor forgiven the ritualised humiliations of his youth, and on leaving school at 14 he had headed for London to train as a waiter. Here he had succumbed to the lure of socialism. My fellow steward Robin Gates and I agreed that if the red, red revolution for which Eddie yearned ever came about, he would probably be one of the first to be liquidated. He had the fatal flaw, for a Marxist, of being a man of goodwill and honour.

He was, of course, a faithful upholder of worker democracy. A lady journalist came up to the Hermitage to do a feature on government-run hotels, and she interviewed me in the Servery. Eddie stood guard to ensure that I did not regurgitate any running dog capitalist lies in favour of the privately run alternative. Was I, the lady journalist enquired, a member of a union, to which I replied in the negative. 'Yes you are,' chirruped Eddie from the wings. 'You're a member of the Canterbury Hotel Workers Union.'

'First I've heard of it,' I said.

'I signed you up myself,' Eddie explained.

'But I don't pay any dues,' I expostulated.

'Yes, you do,' said Eddie. 'I arranged for them to be deducted from your pay.'

The lady journalist cut short the interview and departed with a bemused expression on her face.

Robin Gates was also English and my china plate (New Zealand rhyming slang for mate). Like Eddie he had grown up in the country, but unlike that refugee from rural life, was determined to make his career on the land. Before he came to New Zealand he had worked on the Somerset farm owned by a Farmer Dibble, whose son Tony had been the Fat Boy at my old school St Peter's, Weston-super-Mare. When we were incarcerated there together, Tony's favourite holiday food had been mashed potatoes and cream, at the time that rationing was at its most stringent and the sale of cream was still illegal. Not surprisingly, the adult Tony Dibble had grown huge and Robin told me that in an altercation with the cowman he had broken his jaw and three ribs with just two mighty blows.

Robin and I shared a girlfriend, a diminutive but very pretty Australian called Small Doglike Person. She was warm-hearted and delightful in every way except for one rather curious prejudice, not untypical of Australians. We asked her one day if she would visit us in England. She said no, she had no desire ever to visit England, because everybody there lived in castles and looked down upon people. We pointed out that there were at least a dozen English staff at the Hermitage and not one of them put on airs, least of all her admirers Robin and me, but she was unconvinced. Fifty-five years on, this prejudice still persists among some Australians. A Senator recently declared that all the Poms in Australia were 'stuck-up', a display of bigotry contradicted in a personal statement by the Prime Minister. Common sense suggests that stuck-up people would neither choose to reside in such an egalitarian society, nor flourish if they did so.

I wrote home about some of my other co-workers. *There is a girl here who works as a housemaid, her name is Liana. She is of Aborigine stock and comes from one of the half-savage islands north of Australia. One of fourteen children, her family live in a grass hut in a semi-wild state.*

*Then there is Sharon, also a housemaid. She is heiress to the Phillips-Ferranti fortune. Such a contrast of social position and yet if you were a guest at the Hermitage, and had either as your chambermaid, it would probably be difficult to distinguish which was the child of nature and which the heiress.*

Definitely not stuck-up, Sharon, or I doubt that she would have been working as a housemaid.

*Dixie, a Maori, is also a housemaid. She weighs in at 18 stone. She is so tough that at a staff party when a drunken driver made some ill-timed remarks about Maoris she hit him so hard she knocked him out cold. After that she got very drunk herself. Long after I had departed for bed she decided she would like to make love to the* pakeha *boy from England. She burst into my room at four in the morning bellowing what I assume were overtures of romance in Maori and took a flying leap from the doorway on to my recumbent body. She then passed out. The weight was so great that I was unable to heave her off me and had to lie there for the rest of the night, the breath being pressed out of me and listening to snores like the call of bull moose at rutting time.*

*Ronald Singleton, assistant cook, heir to a baronetcy, who the week his girlfriend, a waitress, left the Hermitage, bought a bottle of champagne every night and two on the last night.*

*Lennie Lomax, bus driver, who, having spent all his own money on grog, has now spent all the petrol allowance as well, so he will have to stay here till he can pay it off.*

*Liesl, an American waitress from Wisconsin. She greets the guests with a breezy 'Hi, folks!' Maitre d' Peter Rutherford says even the American guests are a bit shaken by this. I thought she had the most enormous eyes I had ever seen till I met her cousin, Toni.*

*Cliff, a cook, and what is known over here as a 'no-hoper'. He had had four jobs in a fortnight before he came to us, and had been sacked from them all. As employers have to pay two days' wages in lieu of notice, and as he only survived two days in each job, he had made sixteen days' pay for eight days work in fourteen days. He lasted three days with us, his final rupture with the management involving orders to the barmen to serve him no more liquor and a serious threat from the chef that he would have the police up if Cliff was not out on the next bus.*

*Peter Rutherford, maitre d', from Lyme Regis, purveyor of tall stories, favourite expression 'Gospel Honest Truth'. Adored by all the guests, and liked by all the staff. Played snooker for seven days and seven nights at the European Club in Accra on the Gold Coast and lost £40, but his partner won £2,000, which they blued together in five days in Jo'burg. This story I am prepared to believe. I have watched Peter in action.*

*Max Jelley, a crippled boy from Nottingham, waiter. Father owns a boot factory. Friends here at Mount Cook tried to persuade him to take up skiing. No boots to fit his lame foot. Undeterred, he made his own surgical ski-boots. Every piece hand done beneath our noses from the sole to the laces. Max is the most can-do person I know. He arrived in NZ via India. Passing through New Delhi he rang the Prime Minister's residence and asked if he could have an audience. The PM happened to be walking through the diary secretary's office and overheard. He invited Max to tea the following afternoon and they spent forty-five minutes together over the cucumber sandwiches, sitting out on the lawn. Max said that there were about a hundred peasants lolling around on the verandahs. He asked Mr Desai who they were and the PM said they were all nieces, nephews, aunts and uncles, and cousins of every stripe: they expected to be looked after by their prominent relative.*

*Peter Foster, barman. Likes everybody, he even liked Cliff. Was going to be a priest. While at the seminary there was a fête, in which there was a competition to guess the number of dried peas in a jar. The prize was a huge bottle of humbugs. He and his chum had a special weakness for humbugs. Determined to win, by fair means or foul, they secured a jar of the same size, bought a sack of dried peas, and having filled it up, counted the peas. On the day of the fête they brought 3d tickets for the competition and very cunningly, registered their estimates forty off their calculated number, confident that no one would get so close (there being over a thousand peas in the jar). As it was the Abbot won the humbugs, his own honest guess being within two of the right number! And Peter says their calculation had been dead correct.*

*Peter is engaged to Rita, a charming Irish waitress, full of the blarney and the kindest girl on the staff. Peter and Rita and I are amongst those who attend a weekly session of the rosary, the nearest Catholic church being 140 miles distant, together with …*

*The lovely Lily Lachlan, receptionist, who has a dark and mysterious past. She is said to have abandoned her husband of only six months in Auckland. With her smouldering looks and ample embonpoint, it is widely believed that she is no better than she should be. There is much tittle-tattle, but the truth is probably known only to her best friend and confidante…*

*Jainey McRae, fellow receptionist. Whatever reason the Lovely Mrs Lachlan had for coming to the Hermitage, Jainie has a quest of her own. Before meeting her father, Jainey's mother was stepping out with an Old Etonian. This was quite a distinction in sleepy Timaru in the 1930s. But the war intervened and the OE sailed for home and duty. Had he not, there would have been no Jainey, but her mother brought up her only child in the belief that her destiny was to marry an Old Etonian. The chances do not seem that favourable, given that there are fewer than a dozen OEs in New Zealand, but others may visit and the Hermitage is as likely a place as any to encounter them. Especially on the Reception Desk.*

Would you like to hear the outcome of Jainey's quirky ambition? Since she became a close friend, and we later met up in London, I am in a position to enlighten you. She did meet her OE, Kenneth Oliver Musgrave St John, not at the Hermitage, but at a travel agency in Christchurch where he worked. Not only had he been to the right school, but he was heir to his father the 6th Viscount Bolingbroke. The family fortune had long been squandered, and the family seat, Lydiard in Wiltshire, sold to the Swindon Corporation for a knock-down £4,500 in 1943, but in far-away New Zealand the name itself carried sufficient lustre even without the allure of an ancestral home and broad acres.

Reader, she married him. In 1974, when Kenneth succeeded, the little girl from Timaru became Viscountess Bolingbroke, Baroness St John.

I wish I could report a happy outcome for this unusual marriage. When the Bolingbrokes dined with Karla and me in Islington, we could well understand how Jainey had fallen under the spell of Kenneth's insouciant charm. But his easy grace was lubricated with frequent recourse to both the wine and the whisky bottle and ultimately it was habitual over-indulgence that was to precipitate the dissolution of their union. After the divorce Jainey came to live in London with her two boys, Nicholas and Oliver, and here she established a warm relationship with an entrepreneur from Hampstead whose prodigious wealth compensated for lack of an Eton education. He was also brought to Islington for inspection and was deemed by both of us to be definite husband material. The question was duly popped, but there was a condition attached. Her intended had resolved to spend his retirement in the sun and Florida was his chosen destination. Jainey abhorred Florida.

The compromise agreed was to delay the marriage until Jainey had spent six months amongst the orange groves.

Florida turned out to be as abhorrent as Jainey had feared. After six months she bade her former intended a fond farewell and headed home to New Zealand. He wasted little time in finding a substitute for her affections. He was wedded to his new inamorata the following year and three months after the nuptials suffered a massive heart attack and dropped dead. His relict found herself one of the wealthiest widows in Florida. Back in Christchurch and stony-broke, Viscountess Bolingbroke was living in a small bungalow in the outer suburbs and taking in lodgers.

At the time of writing Jainey is the Dowager Viscountess. Kenneth's son by his first marriage, Henry, succeeded to the title in 2010. Sadly he was severely brain-damaged and died the following year without ever knowing who or what he was. Jainey's youngest son Nicholas, who lives in Sydney, is the 8th Viscount Bolingbroke. Reportedly he does not use the title. The elder boy could not inherit it as his parents were not married at the time of his birth.

. . .

I made no mention in my list of co-workers of my two least favourite colleagues, Bloody Jeen and his only friend Jorst. In addition to Chief Steward Eddie Jones, there were four of us in the Servery, Robin and me and these two Dutchmen. Now I yield to no one in my affection and admiration for the Dutch. With only two exceptions.

Bloody Jeen was a misanthrope. I do not know what brought him to New Zealand, but I suspect it was because he hated the Dutch. Then he found he hated the Kiwis even more, but not as much as he reviled our American, Australian and English guests. I never saw him smile once in the eight months we worked together and Jorst was not exactly a barrel of laughs either.

Robin and I vied with each other as to which of us could extract the largest tips by exuding charm and bonhomie. Bloody Jeen was listening to our friendly banter on the topic one day and growled that he and Jorst earned bigger tips than either of us. 'How come?' we chorused. 'The guests hate being served by either of you. You intimidate them.'

'That's why,' Bloody Jeen replied. 'They are too frightened of how we will react if they don't tip enough. So they overtip us. Your guests think you're both soft. They undertip you.'

So the great tipping contest was born. We agreed to record all tips over the course of a week and see which approach brought the richer returns: *joie d'esprit*, or service with a frown.

I wish I could report to you that excellence of service reaps the greater rewards. But at the end of the week, the final tally, presided over by Chief Steward Eddie to see fair play, showed Jeen and Jorst's combined total to be almost exactly equal to mine and Robin's. There may have been half a crown either side, but nothing of significance. All we had succeeded in proving is that tipping, sadly, does not rise or fall in line with quality of service.

It could, however, be enhanced in other ways. Robin and I would endeavour to find out where our guests were from early in our relationship with them. Wherever it was, it was either our favourite place or, if we had not been there, the place we most wanted to visit. Now North Americans drink coffee with or after every meal and Australasians, in those days, drank only tea. We stewards were not allowed to serve tea at morning coffee or following lunch and dinner, nor were we permitted to serve coffee at teatime or supper. When Americans asked for coffee and Australasians for tea, we would purse our lips, roll our eyes and reiterate those deathless words 'more'n-my-jobs-wurf'. Then we would look conspiratorially around us as if seeking such enemies of the rights of coffee and tea drinkers as the Chief Steward or Mr Dennis the Manager and, if the coast was clear, say in a whisper: 'Seeing as you are from Omaha/Poughkeepsie/Moose Jaw' – or it might be Hobart, Wagga Wagga or Invercargill – 'I will take the risk just this once. Don't tell anyone or they will all want us to break the rules.' This rigmarole would be worth at least a couple of bob and, repeated several times a day, yielded a useful addition to our income. We only developed the technique after the great tipping contest, otherwise the result would have been different.

Tips also increased when I became a temporary wine waiter. I wrote home: *People are funny over their wines, it is mainly a matter of national characteristics. The English are wine snobs. There is a great display over choosing the wine, involving the describing of circles in the air with pince-nez, and the preening of moustaches, and deviation into long-winded stories of wines sampled at the Savoy or the Georges Cinq, or in Hamburg, the Loire, or Alsace-Lorraine. Needless to say the English take a very long time to order their wine.*

*The Americans consider wine vastly inferior to iced water.*

*The Australians tend to become facetious over wine ordering. They make no pretence of knowing anything about it, and either ask for the recommended wine on the menu, or flip over the wine list as if it was a telephone directory, and settle for the cheapest. Tasting the wine is accompanied by roguish winks and declamations of total ignorance, 'Well I don't know nothink abaht this wine caper, Sport, but it smells a bit of orright.'*

*The New Zealander, loyal as always, chooses an Empire wine. Preferably a sparkling McWilliams, the Bollinger of New Zealand.* [This was before NZ developed a wine culture. Wine was regarded as something you took as a tonic if you were a bit under the weather, and its quality was commensurate with this medicinal approach.]

*There is a New Yorker cartoon by Thurber in which a supercilious wine waiter is saying to a guest, 'This is but a naïve domestic burgundy, but I think you may find its presumption amusing.' I was determined to repeat this line, but I needed the right kind of guest. My opportunity came last week when I had two chaps just down from Oxford who looked as if they had walked out of the pages of* Brideshead Revisited. *They said they had only recently arrived in New Zealand and could I recommend a local wine. I pointed to one of the few just about drinkable offerings on our wine list. 'It is but a naïve colonial burgundy,' I intoned sonorously, 'but I think you may find its presumption amusing.' I had to maintain a rigidly straight face while they fell about laughing. Very satisfactory, as was their generous tip.*

The day I had my first order for champagne, Eddie was radiant as a schoolgirl. He seemed to regard the occasion more as if I was tasting it for the first time rather than serving it. Fortunately the cork came off with a gentle plop and no wine spilled.

The second time was not quite so easy. The cork resisted valiantly, and then decided to take me by surprise, cascading into the air with a report like a shotgun. It struck the wall, rebounded, described a beautiful arc right into a gentleman's soup, rose again covered in Brown Windsor and hit another gentleman in the face. This caused something of a sensation. Eddie said, well it was not so bad as the time a steward poured half a litre of Burgundy down the shirt-front of Mister Satterwaite, the Chairman of the Government Hotels, when he was making his annual inspection.

I was also to encounter this formidable individual and found him as intimidating as did my peers. *Very big brass and most unpopular as he never tips and usually sacks about half a dozen people on each visit if they fail to tug their forelocks hard enough, I reported home. In fact last time he was here, Peter Rutherford, the maitre d', spoke to Mister Dennis the Manager, saying of course he would be having Mister Satterwaite at his table at dinner, and the Old Man replied that rather than eat at the same table as Mister Satterwaite he would have dinner at home. Anyway, I had to serve Mister Satterwaite a lot, which I did in fear and trepidation and he asked me a lot of searching questions and stared at me awfully hard while I was serving coffees, which was disconcerting. He went away yesterday, big sighs of relief throughout the Hermitage, and then the Assistant Manager calls me on one side and says how long am I staying in New Zealand, as Mister Satterwaite would like me to join the Hotel Corporation permanently on the managerial side. I cannot believe that I was singled out in this way because I was more capable than my colleagues, as the reverse is truer. Robin said it was because I walk around with 'that silly grin' on my face and Mister Satterwaite is so unaccustomed to anyone looking cheerful in his presence that he mistakenly concluded that this bespoke managerial potential.*

• • •

Off-duty hours in this very closed little community of seventy-two (staff, management and guides) were spent in usually innocent pleasures: the staff bar, the staff weekly film show (no television), the nightly poker school, writing letters home, reading, gossiping about management or the Lovely Mrs Lachlan and, more surprisingly, handicrafts. The latter I did not participate in, but my description of others' efforts showed an impressive range of skills. *Fritz, the Swiss Alpine guide who looks like Neolithic Man, has just come in with a magnificent pair of après-ski loafers which he has made himself. They are of white kid, with fleece interiors, and braided with scarlet cord. John Commins the sous-chef has built himself a motor boat, Eddie Jones has constructed a patent bird cage with a copper floor for his canaries, Alex the Hungarian cook invented a cabbage cutting machine (he has since taken himself and his contrivance off to Sydney to open a Hungarian restaurant), Henry the Austrian cook makes dresses, and another Austrian makes beautiful boxes of beaten copper into which he sets unusual coins. We had a kitchen hand who was an expert at painting photographs so that they looked as if they had been taken in colour, and then there is Max the crippled Nottingham boot maker, who made himself surgical ski-boots, a waitress who is writing a book, a window cleaner who mounts antlers, and there have been many more besides.*

And of course there were parties, sometimes attended by the guests in this demotic, cosmopolitan hideaway. Christmas and New Year parties, leaving parties, birthday parties, engagement parties, even a winning the daily double party. That one was thrown by Dorrie the Housekeeper, a bit less strait-laced than Miss Watson at Emerald Lake, in conjunction with the German head chef Herr Winkler, who had each ventured half-a-crown on a pair of rank outsiders for the daily double and reaped an unexpected, possibly unprecedented, reward of £564. Never had so much champagne been consumed at a Hermitage staff party. Another memorable occasion was John Kimpton's leaving party, which was the only time I have witnessed someone drinking champagne from a lady's slipper. The someone was Kimpton himself and the slipper had been removed from the slender foot of a very pretty Australian waitress called Venetia for whom he nursed an undeclared passion. Since she was not wearing stockings, this gesture denoted a degree of devotion that I doubt I would have emulated.

Robin Gates's 21st birthday was another occasion that demanded worthy celebration. *He came into the Pie Palace the week previous to discuss ways and means. After exhaustive discussion we decided that it should be called an Easter Dubonnet Party. Everyone was to wear a hilarious Easter Dubonnet, and the prize would be a bottle of Dubonnet. This clever play on words was incorporated into a notice displayed in the dining room and staff quarters. The rich humour of which was completely lost on our less well informed brethren, but after careful explanations in words of a single syllable of the meaning of Easter Bonnet to the continentals, and more explanations about the nature of Dubonnet to the Aussies and Kiwis, light and smiles dawned.*

*Robin was thrown into feverish activity buying quantities of liquor, and arranging for food to be sent up from Timaru for preparation in the kitchens.*

*Rustic Richard, the Worcestershire farmer he came out with, had a cake made in Timaru.*

*Much furtive discussion about presents. Everybody told everybody else to leave it to them, and so nobody did anything at all until the day itself, when there was a run on the hotel shop.*

*I gave him a book called* From N to Z, *which is one of the few books on New Zealand which is devoted neither to flora and fauna, nor to Maori Customs and Crafts.* From N to Z *is a much truer picture of New Zealand life, being mainly about pubs.*

*Also much secretive preparation of funny Easter bonnets. I made mine at four o'clock in the morning the night before the party, the hour I have the most artistic inspiration. I found a piece of wallpaper, out of which I fashioned a crown, and taped on to its rim a fan of three playing cards, denomination 7 (3 x 7 = 21) and on the back a pontoon of the King and the Ace, which also equals 21. Then I cut out the letters from a Rothmans cigarette advertisement and pasted them onto a colourful strip cut from* Australian Woman's Own *to form the words 'Vingt et Un', which I affixed on the front of the crown. I was quite pleased with this creation, though it turned out there are far fewer devotees of Vingt et Un than I imagined, and my numerical permutations went uncomprehended.*

*Miss Shanks insisted on dancing a somewhat revealing shimmy
on top of the Ping Pong table.*

*The party began at eleven, and a most wonderful assortment of spirituous liquors, ales and punch there was. I soon found myself with Miss Shanks on one arm and the Lovely Mrs Lachlan on the other, which was very agreeable. Miss Shanks went a bit doolally and insisted on dancing a somewhat revealing shimmy on top of the Ping Pong table. It was very 1920s.*

*At twelve o'clock Mrs Hogg, an American guest from Hawaii, judged the hats, and the bottle of Dubonnet was won by an Australian housemaid who had made a most marvellous creation out of a picture hat decked with Ajax, Harpic, Lux Liquid, Mansion Polish, a feather duster, and other aids to the domestic arts. She well deserved to win it, though there was other most ingenious headgear. Robin himself wore a tin wastepaper basket veiled with Miss Shanks's black frilly underwear and with the inscriptions 'Tit for...' on the front, and 'T'at' on the back. Irish Rita looked delightful underneath a lampshade bearing a legend asserting that she would not be left out of the shade. Trevor, a somewhat louche waiter, had an assemblage of chickens and bunny rabbits and things on his head which I believe must have had some slightly obscene connotation. The Lovely Mrs Lachlan had offset her raven black hair with a turban of black feathers, and looked like Theda Bara. I was particularly struck by a 1900 motoring veil worn by an Australian waitress.*

*Small Doglike Person, our girlfriend (Robin's and mine), was going to paint her nose black and wear a large bone in her hair, but it was discovered at the last moment that the bone still had pieces of festering meat on it. She is very pretty (like a Chihuahua) and would have made such an attractive dog's dinner. After the award we presented Robin with the Stewards' present, a lovely rug emblazoned with a huge representation of Mount Cook. Very vulgar of course, but as Robin is going to have a farmhouse when he gets home we thought that that would not matter.*

*Edward Jones the Chief Steward spoke a few carefully prepared words absolutely spontaneously and shook Robin's hand six times while he was doing it. Eddie loves oratory, and is never happier than when he is being unaccustomed to public speaking.*

*Robin blew all the candles out at the first puff, and the cake was cut. I don't know what he wished for, but it may have been that Edward will start remembering to put his overtime in.*

*The pie-cart* [this was my biscuit-tin and candles stove] *having been rigged up by the sink, I started to brew up soup and made ham and pea, oxtail, and tomato in succession. The dancing went on till about three o'clock.*

*Robin told me next day that every waitress he had asked had been ill (tangibly) during or after the party, so it was voted a great success.*

*Miss Shanks had only the haziest memory of where she had spent the evening and woke up beneath a table.*

There were frequent informal parties in the Pie Palace, as there were usually nighthawks drifting around the staff quarters in the small hours. These were even attended, on occasion, by the guests. One who invited himself was Monsieur Armand, manager of the Clarendon Hotel, the only four-star hotel in Christchurch, who was doing a little light industrial espionage at his establishment's principal rival. He had heard from Peter Rutherford about a stew concocted by Robin and me on the candle burner that had the distinction of being brandy based, the brandy being a fine and rare one given to Robin for his 21st. M. Armand was eager to try it. I must say he was a very appreciative guest, and not only of the stew. He sat eating it with a spoon in one hand while the other hand stroked Miss Shanks's knee. Meanwhile his eyes never left the cleavage in the Lovely Mrs Lachlan's impressive embonpoint.

Miss Shanks, Small Doglike Person and the Lovely Mrs Lachlan were our most frequent night-time visitors, and their presence in the Pie Palace excited no comment. Except on one occasion when the Lovely Mrs Lachlan was observed leaving my room at three in the morning, the other regular visitors having been seen retiring to their beds at an earlier hour. The Hermitage being a hotbed of gossip, and the Lovely Mrs Lachlan being the centre of much lurid conjecture about both her past and her present, there was quite a buzz about this. The staff bar, Robin informed me, was rife with rumours about the supposed liaison between her and me. Their illusions, sadly, were unlikely to be dispelled by the truth of the matter. She and I had been in close proximity, as the scandal-mongers insisted, but it was in a kneeling rather than a prone position. We had been reciting the rosary together.

• • •

Readers may have noted a preponderance of young female Australian employees at the Hermitage. Long before the gap year emerged in Britain (earliest citation in the *Oxford English Dictionary* is 1978), Australians and New Zealanders were spending a year or more travelling before settling down to careers or domesticity. By the end of the fifties the Earl's Court area of London was already known as Kangaroo Valley. Those who headed halfway across the world to the Old Country were predominantly male, girls on the whole opting for somewhere closer to home. Closest was NZ, and Kiwi girls ventured the other way, across the Tasman Sea to Oz. The US did not attract many of these proto-backpackers, because the visa requirements of the time meant that the only way you could work was by applying for permanent residence: the Green Card. And Canada was too cold for them.

Although I ran across a lot of Brits on my travels, they were mainly footloose young refugees from the stifling conformity and rigid manners of fifties and early sixties Britain. Unlike most other areas of British life, class hardly entered into it; they were from nearly all backgrounds. Most conspicuous by their absence were students. They began to undertake extended journeys outside Europe only with the advent of mass (and cheap) air travel.

Americans scarcely featured amongst these cohorts of globetrotters, perhaps because half the population of student age attended college and most college courses lasted four years. The puritan work ethic may also have curbed extended travels for pleasure. The odd exceptions like Norman were usually college drop-outs and unburdened by a work ethic. Young Americans did start travelling in the 1970s – again with the inception of mass air travel – but their overseas excursions tended to be structured and purposeful: as members of the Peace Corps or other voluntary organisations operating in what Americans referred to as 'underdeveloped countries' (many of them thought this applied to anywhere outside North America) or as part of a college scheme for study abroad. According to Wikipedia, the annual number of American students now embarking on a gap year is 40,000, including these latter. It is not a huge number out of a student population approaching 21 million. There are probably that number of peripatetic Aussies, Kiwis and South Africans just working in British pubs.

◦ ◦ ◦

Among Mount Cook's several distinctions was having the smallest, as well as the highest, school in the Southern Hemisphere. The pupils consisted of the Manager's two children and the Ranger's two children and another two miscellaneous children. The teacher was Miss Suzanne Jelley, no relation of Max Jelley, the remarkable crippled boy from Nottingham, but also English. Being small of stature and mouselike, she looked as if she would collapse if you poked her to emphasise a point, but within her own domain, the classroom, she was a female Doctor Arnold.

Suzanne originally obtained this job through an advertisement in the *Christchurch Press*, which had asked for an uncertified teacher, keen disciplinarian etc. She answered it and was called for an interview before the Board. The Board was a charming and somewhat vague man who discussed a number of interesting subjects – the best way to make a Welsh Rabbit was one – before telling her that she would be ideal for the job. He omitted to ask her if she had any qualifications (which she had not), previous experience (neither) or academic passes (none). The only question she herself asked was 'Where is it?'

'On a sheep station,' she was told.

Arriving at the Hermitage, after a thirty-mile ride along a cart track, was a disconcerting experience for anyone (most of the guests flew in), but when you were expecting a sheep station and arrived to find snowcapped mountains and glaciers, with not a sheep nearer than the Canterbury Plain, it must have been a bit of a culture shock. Nor did the fact that no one had told her what to teach the children help matters. Fortunately she had equipped herself, on her own initiative, with some question and answer books for each age group.

All this I learnt on my second day at the Hermitage when I met Suzanne at a party in the administration quarters. She told me that one of her main problems was to keep the six children, who were divided by age into four classes, all in the same one room, occupied and interested for the long school day. I breezily said, 'Oh I'll come and give them a long lecture on some very abstruse subject that'll keep them quiet.' Suzanne looked thoughtful. I dismissed the matter from my mind.

A week later Suzanne came to me and said, 'Have you decided what you are going to give your lecture on?'

'What lecture?' I asked.

Suzanne was stern. 'You're not backing out of it now. The children love lectures. We had the sheep-dip man, and the man from the Ceylon Tea Board, and Jungle Doctor....'

'What!' I exclaimed, 'Do you expect me to be able to compete with Jungle Doctor?' I had read all Jungle Doctor's books, which recounted this colonial medical officer's thrilling experiences in West Africa and had the most disgusting pictures of native diseases, when I was about ten.

But Suzanne prevailed. We decided the title of my lecture should be 'Nineteenth-Century Education'. I had till the next day to prepare it.

On examining the literary resources of the Hermitage, which tended towards fiction of the more sensational stripe, I could find nothing relating to Nineteenth-Century Education other than Winnie the Pooh artist Ernest Shepard's memoir of his days as an art student.

Several hours of hard thinking modified the original subject to 'The Story of Schools'. I would have to rely on whatever I could remember about monastic schools, grammar schools, endowed schools, charity schools, board schools, state schools and whatever I could piece together about early education in New Zealand. I had visited Christ's College in Christchurch and been told its early history, and my reading up on New Zealand's early settlement had given me an outline of Bishop Selwyn's pioneering efforts to bring education to a new land.

The pupils of Mount Cook School led an extraordinarily isolated existence. I doubt whether they had all been to the local market town, Timaru, 140 miles away. They could have little conception of what traffic looked like, would never have seen a ship, never been to a cinema, hardly have entered a shop, certainly not a department store, have no idea of soldiers or politicians or scientists, nor public bodies and institutions, entertainments and sports, all of which a town child automatically becomes aware from about the age of seven or so. Thus I was never sure, as I was speaking to them, whether they knew what I was talking about. Ranging as they did from early kindergarten to secondary school age, I was sure I had failed to reach all of them, and whether I had reached any of them was in doubt. I was heartened to hear from a somewhat distraught Suzanne next day that the kids had been subjecting each other to some of the bizarre and barbarous punishments of yesteryear that I had described. An elaborate attempt had been made to haul one of the younger pupils up to the ceiling strapped in a chair. So some of it may have made an impression.

Suzanne faced the prospect of tending these developing minds on a daily basis, in circumstances that must have been as challenging as they were novel. She did, however, receive the highest commendation of her work from the Canterbury Education Authority. One day a letter had arrived from this august body addressed to 'The Headmistress'. It requested a secret and confidential report on Miss Suzanne Jelley. Needless to say the Headmistress of Mount Cook School responded with what was probably the highest praise any teacher in the Canterbury Province had ever received.

. . .

My happy days at the Hermitage were drawing to a close. I wrote home that I had served 15,000 cups of tea and 20,000 cups of coffee. I had dispensed some 3,750 alcoholic drinks and cut 32,500 sandwiches. I had carried 4,500 suitcases for guests who came from the US, UK, Australia, Ireland, France, Germany, Holland, South America, Hungary, Canada, South Africa, Rhodesia, Austria, Czechoslovakia, Switzerland, Italy, New Caledonia, the Solomon Islands and Norfolk Island. There may even have been a few from New Zealand. Daily tips had ranged from one shilling to £2 8s, with an average of 17s 6d to a pound. The lowest individual tip was one penny from a rich American who thought this large copper coin was worth a dollar. My poker winnings, deposited in the NZ Post Office Savings Bank, exceeded the amount I was allowed to take out of the country. I had read forty books, had a snowball fight on the Tasman Glacier, and climbed a total of no mountains.

My own leaving party was something of a come-down. It was a secret, one kept so diligently that nobody remembered to invite me. I was entertaining Miss Baxter, the new schoolteacher, and her beau the Strong Silent Ranger, to cream of tomato in the Pie Palace when Robin burst in and demanded to know why I was not at the celebration. By the time I arrived, most of my colleagues were too inebriated to utter coherent farewells.

No matter, there was a greater celebration to come. Peter Foster and his Irish fiancée Rita were already in Christchurch and I was to join them on the morrow, the eve of their nuptial mass at the Catholic cathedral.

One of the cooks, a nice lad called Don Evans, drove me to Christchurch. We stopped at Timaru for lunch. There was little choice other than the

Grosvenor Hotel. In those days there were no restaurants in New Zealand outside the provincial capitals and even in quite a large town like Timaru the choice would be between a greasy spoon and the commercial hotel. The Grosvenor offered a choice of three mains: there was mutton, or there was hogget, or there was colonial goose. Since the staff at the Hermitage had been fed on an unremitting diet of mutton, I opted for hogget. 'What is it exactly?' I asked the waitress. 'Mutton' she replied. 'In that case I'll have the colonial goose,' I declared. 'I hope it hasn't been hanging since 1907,' I added facetiously, in an allusion to the year that New Zealand was accorded dominion status. The waitress treated my sally with the scorn it deserved. 'It isn't colonial,' she pronounced with a heavy sigh, 'and it isn't a goose. It's mutton.'

On arrival in Christchurch I proceeded to my rendezvous with the groom at the United Services, a large pub in Cathedral Square. Outside it on a low platform stood a man called Carrington Minge, who had been there since the previous day attempting to break the world hand-shaking record. He had been soaking his right hand in methylated spirits for weeks to harden it. By the time I gently pressed the flesh he had already passed the existing record of 15,000 shakes and was aiming for 20,000 by nine o'clock. (I have just googled Carrington Minge to see whether he was a New Zealander and did he do that kind of thing for a living. There is no trace of him. Sad to think that so much effort should be expended with so little mark made on posterity.)

I had been instructed to meet up with Peter at five sharp, in order not to waste any drinking time. This was the first occasion that I had witnessed the notorious male-only 'Six O'Clock Swill', all New Zealand pubs being required to close at 6 pm. Hardened Kiwi drinkers would have a dozen glasses lined up on the bar just before the clock struck five, and as it did so the barmen would start filling glasses from a hose with a trigger nozzle like that of a petrol pump. While we were drinking one of the group surrounding Peter was approached by a detective and, after some *sotto voce* questions and monosyllabic replies, led away. Though there was a certain amount of speculation about what he had done, this episode evoked little surprise; the assembled company seemed to regard odd brushes with the law as one of those sad inevitabilities of life. When the bar closed on the dot of six, there was a noisy exodus of all but those in our group. As soon as the doors had been barred and bolted, Peter and his mates crept behind the bar to join the barmen for more grog in a private parlour at the rear.

*All the barmen are personal friends of Peter's, I wrote home. Actually most of the barmen throughout the country are friends of Peter's. Now I like my beer in the same quantities as I like my tea, just a sociable amount and enough to quench the thirst. But New Zealanders treat the stuff with a sense of desperate haste and urgency. You do not go to the pub to have a drink, but to drink, and this means from the time it opens to the time you are forcibly ejected.*

Peter and I were billeted together, but as the dining room of our hotel was closed by the time we left the United Services we went to the Regent Café instead, where he ordered each of us three poached eggs with chips. I was ravenous and polished mine off in no time while Peter dawdled over a cigarette. Looking conspiratorial, he leaned over to whisper in my ear that he did not like to boast, but he had once laid out a fella right over the table next to ours. Pressed for details, he confessed to a full-scale brawl, resulting from him and his cobber objecting to two teds who refused to pay the waitress. Peter and friend had championed the waitress, but the teds remaining in a recalcitrant mood, they met and closed. Peter lifted one of them across the table with an upper-cut. The police had eventually broken up the fight, and the teds had been taken away to gaol.

Peter abandoned his poached eggs to return to the United Services, where we joined Robin and Peter's brother and sister for another lengthy session of illegal drinks. The back parlour was full and on the table in the centre of the room was a man holding a glass of ale in each hand while he sang 'The Wild Colonial Boy' in a melodious tenor. I was told that he was a safe-cracker who had been released from Mount Eden Gaol that very morning. Having had only three hours' sleep the previous night, I excused myself after a couple of midis (small measures of ale) and returned to the New Wellington Hotel.

I awoke at half past seven and there was no sign of the prospective bridegroom in the other bed. This was disturbing. I felt sure that there must have been a brawl and Peter was behind bars. I did, however, fall asleep again, until re-awakened by a pale and haggard Peter. He had been locked out of the room all night. There had been no second key, and I had slept serenely through all the battering on the door.

The groom looked terrible. He had not eaten for three days, was dead on his feet, and afflicted by acute prenuptial nerves. As we bundled him into a taxi he looked as if he were due to attend his own execution. Robin and I took another taxi and followed.

On arrival we went straight into the cathedral and sat down amongst the other guests, who viewed us suspiciously and even with some hostility. The reason for this became apparent as the bride appeared. Robin leant over and whispered that Rita wasn't looking herself. He was quite right, she wasn't. Moreover, she wasn't even Rita. Then we knew that we were at the wrong wedding.

It turned out that this was the previous fixture, and presently we were surrounded by a new lot of guests. The Wedding March struck up again and Rita came down the isle at a gallop on the arm of Peter's enormous brother Joe, who was obviously in a hurry to get his part over with. Rita arrived at the altar panting but looking lovely and very Irish. Peter brightened up considerably.

I felt it was very poignant that Rita was given away by her about-to-be brother-in-law and that she had not a single relative in attendance, and only two friends. But Ireland was not a prosperous country in the 1960s and Christchurch was a long way from County Limerick. It was also a long way from Ross on New Zealand's West Coast, as far as Peter's mother was concerned. This was the first time she had been to the metropolis of the South Island. After the mass, Peter and Rita departed in a taxi emblazoned with white ribbons to see his auntie and his cousin, both of them nuns in a Christchurch convent. How they must have thrilled to see Peter's blushing, smiling Irish bride in her white satin gown worn with a tulle veil and a clasp of arum lilies in her hair. But as it was an enclosed order, they could only admire Rita's radiant beauty through the grille that separated them from the outside world.

Father O'Reilly presided over the wedding breakfast at Warner's Hotel with the same grace as he had over the nuptial mass. The guests, many of whom had been fretting in unaccustomed tight collars and ties, began to relax when the good Father signalled that they were permitted to loosen them. Ale was taken, with sweet sherry for the ladies, and the conversation swelled from a low hum into hearty exchanges the length of the table and lots of laughs. Following the soup, the fish, and the chicken and ham, I was myself feeling an air of contentment and good cheer when Father O'Reilly leant over and muttered in my ear.

'Could you repeat that, Father, I am not sure I heard you right.'

'I was just sayin', Patrick, that I think it is time for your speech.'

I felt a chill. 'My what, Father?'

'Your speech, Patrick. And the toast. I don't think our friends from Ross are really the speechifyin' kind, do you? Now you're an eddicated fella, comin' from England and all that. It would be a small return for the friendship Peter and Rita have extended to you. Don't you think so, Patrick?'

At that moment the strawberries arrived. This gave me about ten minutes to compose a suitable speech while continuing to make polite conversation to my neighbours. When the last strawberry had been consumed, Father O'Reilly banged on the table with his spoon and I struggled to my feet amidst an expectant hush.

I need not have worried. This was an Irish wedding, albeit one held twelve and a half thousand miles from the Ould Sod and attended by an Irish family and their Irish friends who had never seen Ireland. To be sure, ale had been taken. But the generous spirit of my audience would have given me a warm hearing even if it had not. As I looked into Peter and Rita's eyes, I knew that all I had to say was how happy they both were, and how happy their lives together would be. Because if ever there were two people, born 12,500 miles apart but sharing the same heritage, who were destined to spend their lives together and create a new, brave Catholic family, here they were....

It does not do to get too sentimental about these occasions. Before the happy couple departed on the bus for their honeymoon, the groom had been stripped of his wedding finery and deposited on it stark naked. His ever-so-proper fellow passengers looked on with faces rigid in disbelief. Rita, sweet virginal Rita, was howling with laughter and egging on her big brother-in-law to further excesses. Fortunately Father O'Reilly had already said his farewells and returned to his solitary room in the presbytery.

# Chapter 9

• • •

# DUNEDIN DAYS

• • •

*May 1963*

*Dear Mater and Pater*, began my letter from Heathfield, a little corner of Lithuania in the otherwise resolutely Caledonian city of Dunedin, capital of NZ's southern province of Otago. *We have just finished a very excellent lunch, a festive board, presided over by my landlady the excellent Mrs Shipuis, around which sat five Lithuanians, one Czech, one Kiwi and one Pommie (me). This was highly entertaining and just like something out of Hyman Kaplan* [American humorous tales about a mittel-European migrant failing to master the English language in New York]. *Not only am I regaled on all sides with 'Ven I vas a leedle gurl, mine grandmodder she say to me' and 'Vonderfool contry dis New Zeelant' and vells and ver' gutts but also the Twist* [popular dance] *becomes the Tvist. The Lithuanians all speak six languages almost fluently and can make themselves understood in Serbo-Croat and Slovene and possibly Sanskrit as well. Despite fourteen years residence in New Zealand they still cannot distinguish between a V and W or between singular and plural. Not that I would want them to. 'Zer is much gravies on my pea' is much more picturesque than the conventional form. Now Mrs Shipuis has gone over to South Dunedin on a visit, and her parting* words to daughter Yhani were, 'Now mind you not be cheeky to Meestair Roberdzhon.'

I came to Dunedin from Christchurch station, which is roughly the size of the British Museum with the same kind of monumental architecture and services about three trains a day. It is the pride and joy of the city, second only to the Victorian gothic cathedral. The train was hauled by a marvellous great black monster of a locomotive with a cowcatcher in front and a vast bulbous chimney stack. I think it must have been bought in a job lot from America when they replaced steam trains with diesels.

The train did not go very fast (it was the express) and every few miles it stopped for tea. This is a very laudable arrangement. There are no dining cars, but the danger of a New Zealander suffering dehydration is averted by these tea stops, with a consequent mad rush into the station tea-room. The canteen staff are waiting in a crouching position and start pouring from big chipped enamel pots as soon as the engine grinds to a halt. The length of the stop is calculated according to the time it takes for the average New Zealander to swallow four cups of tea at 8d each. (This seems expensive but the cups are about the size of paint pots.) Ordinary stops for discharging and collecting passengers last only a minute.

The railways are not popular with the awkward minority who want to get someplace in a hurry.

At first we were passing through the pastoral country of the Canterbury Plain. It is flat, and so I was able to get a better view of it from the train than I had in a car. I had not realised that there were so many cottages. Most of these are colonial, and are small wooden structures with a door and one window on either side. Sometimes the roof has an overhang to form a verandah. I doubt they contain baths.

We also passed through a number of pretty little towns.

Otago is a country of hills and valleys and rugged coastline reminiscent of Cornwall. The train runs right along the shore for many miles, and at one point, actually goes over the sea. One quaint sight was a row of telegraph poles planted in the water from one side of a bay to the other. It had evidently been more economic than using twice as many round the curvature of the bay.

We passed through Port Chalmers, wherefrom departed the good ship Dunedin *with the first cargo of frozen meat in 1882.* [This transformed the New Zealand economy, the frozen meat trade bringing New Zealand unprecedented prosperity and enabling the government to undertake the various welfare innovations that earned the colony the sobriquets 'the social laboratory of the world' and 'the working-man's paradise'.] *Seven miles inland lies Dunedin, on a wide reach of water which flows in from the sea. The Edinburgh of the South they call it. I was in dread of a fake and sham pastiche of Scotland, akin to the phoney Englishness of Victoria, BC. Actually I have never known a city capitalise less on its popular image. Though the streets are all named after Edinburgh streets, and the people are mainly Scots, and the buildings are heavy granite, there is not a single Scottish gift shoppe, not one Rabbie Burns Tea Rooms, and I have not seen a square inch of tartan in the week I have been here, other than one man in a kilt.*

*I alighted at a very beautiful station in mid-Victorian gothic.*

*My first impression of Dunedin was one of narrow streets, imposing architecture, and a confusion of traffic. I made my way down Princes Street, inspecting the hostelries. I walked as far as the Scott Memorial, then returned up it again. New Zealand does not offer a very high standard of hotel accommodation. The hotels are drab and dingy, old fashioned in their appointments, depressed and decaying. Nevertheless they offer quite good service. And charge you accordingly.* [This has changed. New Zealand embraced the motel some time in the eighties and nineties and, coming to the idea late, did it better than motels are done in the country of their origin. They are luxurious, well furnished, spotlessly clean, and equipped with every kind of mod con you could wish for. In one motel in the South Island where Karla and I stayed in 2007 there was even a sunken bath next to the bed – you could descend straight into it.]

*Having spent the night at the over-priced Excelsior, in the morning I checked through the guest houses in the* Otago Daily Times, *and settled for Heathfield as it had TV. I found the late Victorian terraced house perched on top of a steep hill, commanding a spectacular view of Dunedin and the bay, the ships' red funnels contrasting with grey towers and spires.*

*'Allo you come in what you want yes I do bedanbrekfus gut you stay ave a cop o'tea.' Thus was I greeted by Mrs Shipuis as the first of many kettles was put on the hob. And what a hob. A great black cast-iron affair which must have escaped the vigilance of the Otago Early Settlers Museum Committee. Made in Dunedin ninety years ago, as an inscription testified.*

*With this one concession to Otago's illustrious pioneer past the rest of Heathfield is very up-to-date and clean and polished with shiny white paint and artificial roses everywhere. Bedanbrekfus costs 25s, which compares favourably with the Excelsior's daily tariff of three guineas. It includes about a dozen pots of tea at various junctures of the day, such as getting up, going out, coming in, going to bed, switching on the TV, or sneezing.*

*Mr Shipuis belongs to* The Good Soldier Schweik. *I think he may have sold dirty postcards in his far off Lithuanian youth. He opens his mouth to let out a flood of totally unintelligible English, but it is always cut short by a sharp command from Madame. She has just returned from South Dunedin and her first question was 'Vas they girls cheeky?' She is a despot to her family, but the guests are treated like visiting Saxe-Coburg-Gotha royalty. She takes a real pride in running the best house in Dunedin and works like a Trojan – perhaps I should say a Baltic peasant woman, for that is what she is. Her country has been overrun by the Russians, and her family scattered. Most of them are in Russia. She has not heard from them for three years. The last letter she received was from her sister, who wrote, 'We have just spent a seven-month holiday in Siberia to see Uncle.' Mrs Shipuis has no uncle. She wrote back guardedly, asking which Uncle. She has not heard from her sister since.*

*The day she opened Heathfield she had 10s in her pocket. That was last year. She is still heavily in the red, but has the most ambitious plans for expansion. Coupled with her ability to do a week's work in one sixteen-hour day and determination to give her guests genuine value, she should go a long way.*

*Provided, that is, that she does not dissipate the takings on her generosity to her fellow Lithuanian refugees and the odd visiting Englishman. On Tuesday and Friday nights the front parlour is occupied by up to a dozen of Mrs Shipuis's fellow countrymen, consuming Welsh Rabbits and smoking rank shag tobacco. (Whether Welsh Rabbit is a Lithuanian national dish – perhaps known as Latvian Rabbit – or whether they have acquired a taste for it in NZ I do not know. The Kiwis have a novel version of their own: the bread is spread with melted cheese and rolled into something like a swiss roll before being toasted a golden brown. I do not know why it has not spread beyond these shores.)*

*Conversation around the table is mainly about concentration camps. They all served in Nazi ones, and on being 'liberated' were incarcerated in Russian ones. In terms of debasement of humanity, the Russians had nothing to learn from the Nazis. You had a month to learn Russian. If*

217

*you could not understand the orders barked at you after that period of grace, you were liquidated. Somehow all these brave men – there are no women, possibly because they did not survive their liberation – had escaped the Soviet Union and found refuge in New Zealand. While I am treated to Welsh Rabbit by Mrs Shipuis along with the rest, I have nothing to contribute to the conversation. They speak in English out of politeness to Mrs Shipuis's guest, but what have I to say in a group of exiles who have suffered and survived monstrous persecution by the two most evil tyrannies in the world?*

*The first day of my Dunedin stay I devoted to Newbold's bookshop, the largest in the Southern Hemisphere. I unearthed a veritable treasure trove of early New Zealand magazines, including the first issue of* New Zealand Punch *of 1888. I was thrilled to bits. On subsequent days I examined the First Church, the Art Gallery, the Otago Boys' High School, Otago University, the Hocken Library, the Early Settlers Museum and the Cathedral. But what has impressed me most is the wealth of colonial architecture. I am enchanted with Dunedin's buildings. I have given some thought to these splendid structures and have determined a classification:*

*Aberdonian – Heavy granite: Law Courts, Stock Exchange etc. Very substantial. Will outlast generations of worthy Dunedin Scots.*

*Seaside Terrace Villas – Late Victorian, richly ornamented with baubles and balustrades. Found only at seaside resorts in England – Brighton, Bournemouth etc. Select abodes for Elders of the Kirk.*

*Colonial Cottage – Built to remind Colonists of their cottages in the Old Country, but with wood as a substitute for stone. Picturesque verandahs of bowed corrugated iron painted in bold primary colours.*

*Artisan Dwellings – Probably inspired by Prince Consort's design for Model Dwellings (1851). Slate roofs, wrought ironwork balconies, aspidistras in windows. Wooden gates that creak with age and pocket handkerchief front gardens.*

*Elephant and Castle – Traditional English public house style, applied to both hotels and shops. Frosted glass, iron lamp brackets, old oak counters, steam, sawdust and gaslight. Few have been refronted.*

*I have been rising early, breakfasting and devoting the hours till eleven in reading Osbert Sitwell and Compton McKenzie, then out to explore, buy books, and research. Eat economically in one of the city's very scarce restaurants. Return around six and glue face to television screen. I am very fond of television.*

*New Zealand television is quite good. Most of the programmes are imported from America and England of course. Native efforts on the Otago channel include gardening talks, interviews with Elders of the Kirk, New Zealand News, discussions between Elders of the Kirk, racing and rugby, and talks by Elders of the Kirk. There are no panel games, which is a good thing. Soap operas are popular, especially a new one from England called* Coronation Street, *about day-to-day working class life in Salford. Strange that New Zealanders should find that interesting.*

*I went to the Otago University Capping Ceremony in the Town Hall yesterday. The Town Hall is very large and imposing and the procession of dignitaries was long and very colourful, with every hue imaginable in the academic gowns from all over the world. Bringing up the rear were the Pro-Chancellor and the guest of honour, the English art critic, poet and philosopher Sir Herbert Read.*

*The ceremony began with 'God Save the Queen', and I always find that very moving a long way from home. Then the degrees were awarded, and the poor old Pro-Chancellor, a recent appointment, got things a bit mixed up and turned to the audience to say 'You know, I've never done anything like this before.'*

*Sir Herbert Read was most impressive. He is a white-haired elderly gentleman, with a face rather like Bertrand Russell. He began by saying he was unable to offer any advice to young graduates about to commence life, as he did not believe in universities, did not like them, and considered them worthless institutions, stifling to creativity and originality. That certainly made the dons sit up and the Pro-Chancellor nearly fell off his throne.*

*He continued by saying that he would address his remarks to the audience as New Zealanders. He now proceeded to give poor inoffensive New Zealand a good going-over, castigating it as 'A nation of a million bungalows and ten thousand tabernacles.' They were culturally stagnant, they made no effort to carve out a way of life of their own, they looked to Europe for all their inspiration. It was imperative they find something individual for themselves. 'Whatever you do, make it a NEW Zealand,' Sir Herbert urged. 'No matter what course you pursue, see that it is new, NEW.'*

*It was really a terrifically good speech and a welcome change from the usual platitudes on such occasions. (Sir Herbert did not once say that it was a pleasure for him to be there.) Instead of handing out a lot of empty and meaningless compliments, he did suggest a constructive redirecting of intentions. But there was no sugar on the pill.*

*Last night he appeared on television in an interview during which he substantiated his remarks to the university, and expanded his theme to embrace the everyday life of ordinary people in NZ. He said that he considered everyone should practise an art or craft. I am not sure that I agree with him there. It is too much like those people who say that every man in his senses must play some healthy invigorating sport, whether he like it or not, and regardless of his aptitude.*

. . .

Did I agree with Sir Herbert's strictures? New Zealand was certainly parochial, it was excessively conformist, and for the majority of male Kiwis, life outside the workplace was generally confined to drinking (often to excess) and sport; women seldom ventured beyond the domestic sphere. So far, so bad. But a lot of this was negated by the sheer good nature of New Zealanders and their laconic disregard for some of the drearier aspects of the Protestant work ethic. Sir Herbert's wake-up call, though, was timely. A youth revolution would sweep North America and Europe very soon after this notable speech and while New Zealand never succumbed to its wilder excesses, there was a transformation in New Zealand society, one all the more marked for the fact that formerly the country seemed to have been in a time warp. (Not that I personally saw anything wrong with that.) Britain joining the EEC was another seminal change for New Zealand. Instead of the child leaving home, the parent had abandoned its youngest offspring. New Zealand was now on her own and she had to modernise and look to her neighbours in the Pacific Rim for her economic future. In the process this lovely land stopped being like a somewhat fractious teenager and became an adult nation.

. . .

One night in the Pie Palace at the Hermitage, Peter Foster had held my attention between the hours of eleven and four with tales of a misspent youth among his wild Irish kindred in the remote village of Ross on the West Coast. This latter is not simply a coast to the west of the Southern Alps, but a distinct region of New Zealand, its lawless inhabitants known as 'Coasters', and in those days probably the least visited of any in New Zealand. Its remoteness was on account of the Southern Alps that divided the populated east coast of the South Island from the underpopulated west. Peter's village of Ross lay only twenty miles or so from Mount Cook, but beyond impenetrable mountain ranges. To get there you needed to go via Timaru and Christchurch up to Nelson at the top of the South Island, then down the west coast to the West Coast and Ross, a distance of 550 miles. The road petered out at a lumber camp a few miles to the south of Ross, so no one went to the little town unless they had a compelling need to do so. I had no such need, so of course I had to go. This was my destination when I left Dunedin.

It took me three days to get to Ross. The first night I spent at the Grosvenor Hotel in Timaru; despite its limited menu of three kinds of mutton, there were not many other options. But I was glad I did, because who should be emerging as I entered but the Lovely Mrs Lachlan, swathed in black. She always looked best in black; it complemented her smouldering black eyes. We fell into each other's arms.

I have described earlier how Mrs Lachlan, with her turbulent past and a broken marriage behind her, was regarded by our more censorious colleagues at the Hermitage as a wanton. The twenty-four hours we spent together at Timaru hardly bore this out. We dined together, and my expectations that the dinner menu might be more varied than the lunch menu were not fulfilled: the choices were still mutton, mutton or mutton. Then we attended Timaru's sole cinema and giggled together over Stanley Holloway's antics in the Ealing comedy *The Titfield Thunderbolt*. After that the only nightlife on offer in Timaru was a coffee bar in which, at that late hour of 10 o'clock, we were the only patrons. Mrs Lachlan recounted tales of the terrible fates that had befallen various of her closer relatives, her own troubled youth being only an extension of wider family misfortune. I was so absorbed by this narrative that I was scarcely aware of the waitress making very loud and obvious preparations for locking up. As Mrs Lachlan's detractors at the Hermitage would have predicted, I did end up in her room that night. The tryst, however, was only to bring her boiling water from downstairs for her hotwater-bottle.

The now sleepy village of Ross had been a rip-roaring goldfields town during the West Coast Gold Rush of 1865–67. While other mushroom towns had faded back into the bush when the gold ran out and the prospectors left, Ross survived as a centre for tree felling. At its height during the gold rush, the West Coast had contained a quarter of the population of New Zealand. Nearly a century on it was less than one per cent.

I arrived at Ross as it was growing dark and made for the Empire Hotel, as instructed by Peter Foster. The term 'Hotel' may suggest something a little more grandiose than the actuality. It was a large green wooden structure, but definitely a pub. There was a law in New Zealand (and I think in Australia too) that licences in rural areas were dependent on the licensee providing accommodation for travellers. This may well account for the fact that pubs in Australasia are nearly always called 'The Somethingorother Hotel'. Few have the kind of names you would expect in countries where the settlers generally tended to try to replicate 'home' – White Hart, Red Lion, Queen's Arms etc. So when I asked for a room at the Empire Hotel the reaction was a kind of stunned disbelief. The room I was shown into was neat and clean, if somewhat sparsely furnished, but had an atmosphere of having been long unoccupied.

When I went down to dinner I found a surprisingly large dining room and sat myself at an empty table. Indeed all the tables were empty. I waited for ten minutes or so and nobody having appeared I began scraping the chair, coughing, rattling cutlery etc to try to attract attention. This succeeded, for a surprised face peered round the kitchen door. 'Oh!' exclaimed the landlady. 'I should have explained. We only use the dining room for the annual Firemen's Dinner. Would you mind eating with us in the kitchen?' So dinner was *en famille*, together with the padre and the schoolteacher, bachelors both, who were able to enlighten me on many singular facets of West Coast life.

*By the time I had dined, it was closing time,* I wrote home, *but actually there is no such thing on the West Coast. Official closing is 6.15, but the West Coast pubs keep open till the last Coaster has gone home or been carried out. This is usually about two o'clock in the morning.*

*I met Peter's brother Joe in the bar, and it took no time to be introduced to all the leading lights of Ross. Such as Verdon, who claims to speak a dozen languages, though none that is actually intelligible. And Lofty, the Maori Chieftain, who as the evening progresses becomes overwhelmed with a mad desire for human flesh. His forefathers, he tells us, were accustomed to a diet of missionaries. And Old Bob, who had drunk all his pension by mid-month, and had £2 10s to last the three weeks till June, unless he can pan some gold.*

*A lot of Coasters still go gold-digging, and make enough for beer money out of it. All the rich deposits have been tapped, but one prospector reckoned he could fill an Aspro bottle in a day. The same man has a paint pot which he keeps under his bed. It contains £400 worth of gold. A few still make their living at it, but it is a far cry from the days when the great West Coast Gold Rush brought 5,000 diggers to Ross.*

*Now the population of Ross is 450. The old houses have been cleared away, but even so there are a number of deserted shops, fast becoming decaying shells. All the Coast towns have a decreasing population. Coasters are not house-proud people, and some will live in a broken-down shanty a quarter of the value of the motor car outside. Those are the single men. The wives are good housekeepers, but being frontier people, have no desire for any luxuries. Besides which there is no money to be spent on refrigerators or washing machines as the Coasters, like the Irish from whom they are descended, tend to spend their money as soon as they have got it. Enormous sums go on gambling. There is a carrier who goes up to Westport once a week to bring back supplies. He takes the bets with him and the following week brings back the winnings, if there are any. This is, of course, all strictly illegal.*

*Ross consists of:*

- *Town Hall, Public Library, Community Hall.*
- *Volunteer Fire Station (complete with antique fire engine, and two alarm bells, one cast in 1868, a gold rush year).*
- *Empire Hotel and City Hotel (City is the oldest pub on Coast, dating back to 1860).*
- *Three sawmills and a lime quarry.*
- *Railway station. (Closed down shortly after I left Ross.)*
- *Draper's shop, kept by Peter's sister, tea room, two general stores, a stationer's, and a garage, which also sells agricultural implements, the price of a plough being, I noted, £97 10s.*
- *A yellow school-house, with three teachers and 74 pupils.*
- *Three churches, Catholic, C of E, Presbyterian. The Father is Irish, and much loved, the C of E vicar is High-Anglican, very Popish and highly disapproved of, and the Minister is one of those very dedicated nonconformists with high ideals, respected by all faiths.*

*Of the ten lunches and dinners I had at the hotel one was fish and the other nine mutton. I despair of New Zealand gastronomy. I must add that on the fish day there was an alternative offered. Mutton.* [Happily this has changed. When mass tourism began in the seventies and eighties, NZ had to up its game. No longer was the only choice between a hotel dining room and a greasy spoon café: proper restaurants opened wherever there were tourists to support them. And for the first time this sea-girt nation realised that it had a natural resource just waiting to be exploited: seafood. The only negative in all this, though I acknowledge it is a purely personal viewpoint, is that New Zealanders switched from a nation of tea-drinkers to being almost exclusively coffee-drinkers. All the restaurants and coffee shops have the same make of Italian coffee-making machine, so it would appear that the hot beverage preferences of an entire nation were radically changed by the astuteness of a single entrepreneur.]

*I spent a very leisurely five days, but was never bored as there was so much to watch and to think about. The bar was always open, and as I could not possibly compete with the Coasters at their principal pastime, I would read my book in front of the fire, and then join them for a few beers before eating or going out or going to bed. They drink at fantastic speed, so that you are bound to consume seven or eight glasses of ale in half an hour. That is sufficient for me. The Coasters will keep this up for five or six hours at a time.*

*Meanwhile there is usually a game of forty-fives going on, a very intricate card game played only on the Coast, and nowhere else in the world, except where four Coasters find themselves together. Also music. Stan Johnstone's bar has a couple of pianos and these are played at the same time, one by the headmaster, and the other by a grizzled old rogue with two fingers missing on his right hand. Chopped off in the sawmill. Other entertainments include fights and raids. There is a tacit agreement with the Constabulary that ample notice should be given of a raid, which normally take place once a week.*

*I did not witness an actual raid, but was privileged to participate in a raid rehearsal. Mine Host called for silence and we were all told to line up outside the lavatory door. There is a strict rule that this always has to be kept open when the khazi is unoccupied. Now the local Constable habitually waits for thirty seconds from the time he raps loudly on the*

*When the Constable knocked on the door, the entire bar could be cleared in 30 seconds.*

*front door to the time he enters. So for this rehearsal, somebody knocked on the door and that was the signal for everyone else to move. You leap on to the lid of the lavatory seat and dive head first through the window, rolling yourself into a ball as you reach the ground so that you don't impede the man following. This way the entire bar can be cleared in half a minute. In a real raid the Constable then makes his entrance and, without a glance at the open lavatory door and wide open window, greets the Landlord. There is a time-honoured ritual. 'Just clearing up?' he enquires, this being probably four or five hours after closing time. 'Just clearing up, Officer,' the Landlord assures him. 'But I see there is a bottle open here. Would you join me in it, Constable?' After ale has been partaken, and cordial good-nights exchanged, the recumbent bodies in the vegetable patch rise to their feet and make their stealthy way back through the lavatory window. Meanwhile Plod is back at the nick filling in his report for Police Headquarters in Greymouth about this latest raid, all carried out strictly according to regulations.*

*One day I spent out in the bush with the loggers, huge men in singlets. I went out with Peter's uncle 'Digger' Foster on his truck, and watched the tree-trunks being lifted into place on a cable. These trucks take immense loads, seventy and eighty feet long, over the worst and roughest bush tracks. We ate our lunch of meat pies on the winch, refreshing ourselves with cold tea. In the afternoon I watched the logs being cut up in the sawmill with a band-saw. This is a saw which is literally a band, a great steel belt with huge teeth which runs round at high speed and goes through a sixty-foot log in a few seconds, end to end. The lengths are passed down to the men operating the smaller circular saws, who fashion them into planks. Most of this wood, red pine, is used for building. Nearly all NZ houses are wooden, even in cities.*

*On the Saturday we went to a village rugby match at Hari-Hari, some twenty miles from Ross. There were ten injuries during this game, one third of the players being carried off the field. Rugby is not considered worthwhile unless an odd ear or two are left on the pitch to commemorate a noble contest. The game is comparatively short, in order to leave the rest of the afternoon free for serious drinking. The crush in the taproom of the local was tremendous, 150 at least.*

*Other activities included Sunday lunch with Peter's mother Mrs Foster; a marvellous walk along a totally deserted shore with great breakers crashing onto the beach – my first sight of the Tasman Sea – and an untimely encounter with a bull in a lane; a visit to Phil May, the celebrated New Zealand historian, who has just published his monumental 600-page history of the West Coast; attendance at a Volunteer Fire Brigade meeting; a bun fight at the Community Hall, which included among its attractions a second-hand book-stall; and the appealing sight of all these terrible West Coasters with whom I had spent the week soberly and reverently making their devotions at Mass.*

. . .

I left Ross with regret. It had fully lived up to Peter Foster's colourful descriptions of it. They say never go back to places which have a place in your heart. I made that mistake when Karla and I visited NZ in 2007. I took her to see this extraordinary isolated township, inhabited by rambunctious, larger-than-life Coasters who never left town from one year to the next. And of course that Ross was no longer there. The road has now been extended as far as Queenstown in the south, so the village has become easily accessible and is on the tourist circuit for people visiting Milford Sound (as all foreigners do). There is no longer anything very distinctive about it. But the Empire Hotel is still there. You can even watch a video on YouTube showing Friday night revelry (now perfectly legal since NZ revised its draconian licensing hours). The revellers, though, are the same kind of amiable tourists you encounter in any other pub in any other pretty part of New Zealand. The Landlord that Karla and I met was not even a Coaster. I did not reveal that I had been probably the first tourist ever to visit the Empire Hotel. I don't think he would have known what I was talking about.

# Chapter 10

. . .

# WINDY CITY

. . .

*June–October 1963*

Why head for Windy Wellington? I frankly cannot remember. It may have been a feeling that in order to know a country, you need to have spent time in its capital. Or it may be because Wellington was where Katherine Mansfield was born and brought up. Some of her finest stories are set there.

I left Ross in the company of Mr Chamberlain, who drove me as far as Westport. That is where the West Coast meets New Zealand (or that's how the Coasters regarded it – you didn't go beyond Westport other than to get married or watch the All Blacks). I had met Mr Chamberlain in the bar of the Empire Hotel. He is still the only ex-PoW I have ever known who enjoyed the experience. Some of the officer johnnies who were inside say it wasn't as bad as prep school, but that is hardly an encomium.

Mr Chamberlain was a tailor who had been captured on Crete. He was banged up on the island before escaping to the Greek mainland. He spent eighteen months wandering about Greece before being recaptured and taken to Germany. This represented a turn in his fortunes, and not for the worse. As most German tailors were serving in the Wehrmacht, there was a shortage of them in the Fatherland. Mr Chamberlain was let out of the camp on day release to work for a master tailor over military age. As his keeper's services were in such demand, Mr Chamberlain travelled all over Germany with him, enjoying comparative liberty and seeing wartime Germany in a way that none of his compatriots was privileged to do. He and his keeper even went to the pictures together. Mr Chamberlain remembers one that was in German and Yiddish. This must have been the notorious *Jud Süss*, one of the few openly anti-semitic films made by the Nazis. Goebbels was savvy enough to realise that ordinary German people did not want propaganda, they wanted entertainment, and he gave it to them. But *Jud Süss* is a terrific story, even when retold in such a prejudicial way. All that was completely lost on Mr Chamberlain, who had little German at his command. He just thought it was a rattling good film.

He also told me about life inside the camp, including the watery Crosse & Blackwell's jam they got in the Red Cross parcels and the fish-cheese the Germans served up on Fridays. What was fish-cheese? A Google search fails to reveal any information. But Mr Chamberlain seldom had to worry about short commons within the wire, because he was generally outside it. It was only towards the end of his four-and-a-half years in captivity that food shortages became acute for everyone in Germany. I wonder whether he ever wrote any of this down, or have his unusual adventures been lost to posterity?

We stopped in Charleston, a ghost town from the West Coast's gold rush frenzy. Once it served a population of 5,000, now it was empty. Mr Chamberlain and I visited the celebrated European Hotel, one of the largest entertainment centres on the goldfields, where Melbourne dancing girls and San Francisco gamblers rubbed shoulders with diggers from Bendigo, Ballarat, Otago and the Fraser River Canyon and sought to separate them from their gold dust. We explored its decaying interior, where layers of peeling wallpaper marked the passage of time like the rings of a tree trunk. It was the only monument to those dead diggers and their dreams of sudden wealth. Sadly, no longer so. Only five years after our visit, the authorities pulled down what they considered a dangerous eyesore. But something of Charleston survived. When Karla and I passed through it in 2007 it had been reinvented as a 'heritage adventure experience'. Mr Chamberlain and I had explored the ruins of the town alone and without impediment. Now it was thronged with tourists, but with anything genuinely old cut off from physical contact.

Mr Chamberlain dropped me off in the unassuming little town of Westport. I stayed overnight at the only place with accommodation, the Melbourne Hotel. The one other guest was an English maiden lady of mature years who introduced herself to me as Miss Hook. Over our mutton that evening she revealed that she had been on the fringes of the Bloomsbury Group in the 1920s. We resolved to meet up in Wellington.

My first stop in the Windy City was to pick up my mail from the GPO. There was a letter from Kimpton's original travelling companion Rory Richmond Collins, a languid fellow whose life hitherto had been dedicated to the avoidance of exertion, but now found himself in one of the most energetic occupations known to man as a jackaroo in New South Wales. Not only was he being worked to exhaustion, he wailed, but on his wages of £5 a week he would never be able to repay the fare from Vancouver to Sydney that he had borrowed from the opulent Nigel Hollings.

When my heart had stopped bleeding for Rory, I examined the other missives. There was one from Maggie, about to depart home to England to marry her fiancé after much soul-searching (could she settle down in provincial England after six years in the US?), from the Kansan, now graduated from Boston University and also about to be married, from Nancy from Brighton, embroiled in an unhappy love affair, from Mister Matthews, still battling with the odious Trevor for mastery of the kitchen at 328 Hayes Street, and from Miss Watson at the Emerald Lake Chalet. I marvel now that I was able to sustain such a widespread correspondence with these and many other friends and relatives, despite having to depend on *poste restante* addresses in the cities that I visited. But looking back, what surprises me most was that I seemed to be penpals with the forbidding Scotch housekeeper at Emerald Lake. Had all that unctuous flattery, motivated by a desire to keep my job at any cost, really developed into a friendship across the ocean? What did we write to each other about and how long did the correspondence continue? Along with so many other memories, it has all gone.

* * *

The search for somewhere affordable to live was not a happy experience. I had done enough of these quests in London to know how substandard a lot of furnished accommodation can be, but I was shocked by the seedy, run-down bedsitters and flatlets that confronted me in Wellington, the so called Empire City. After spending the first night in a decrepit hotel called The Duke of Edinburgh at which the execrable dinner was stone cold, I suffered equally the following night at a guest house described as 'beautifully furnished'. The bed was sagging, the chest of drawers was made from packing cases, and the wardrobe consisted of a soiled curtain on a string. For seating there was a kitchen chair. The whole house reeked of overcooked cabbage. The next morning I went to inspect a house claimed in the advertisement to have 'breathtaking panoramic views from every window'. The room I was shown looked on to a high fence of rusty corrugated iron only eighteen inches from the window.

Miss Hook had given me the address of the bed and breakfast establishment at which she was the only permanent resident. I left it till last because I thought it was in the outer suburbs, but 166 Sydney Street West proved to be anything but. It lay on a hill behind the Houses of Parliament and just below the Botanic Gardens. I rang the bell and the first positive sign was that the landlady was not wearing a dressing-gown, nor did she have the butt end of a fag in the corner of her mouth. I walked into the hall and sniffed. There were no alien odours. I was conducted upstairs. The place gleamed with new paint. I was shown a small room with fitted carpet and a well scrubbed appearance. The coverlet on the bed did not have stains on it. The window had a delightful outlook on to a tree-fringed early colonial graveyard.

This became my base while I continued the quest, but nothing I saw in the ensuing days came within measurable distance of No 166. The problem was that, as a B & B, it charged a nightly rate, and this made it more expensive than I could easily afford. My daily reports of the horrors of rented accommodation elsewhere in Wellington had, however, worn Mr and Mrs Hill down, besides which I think they were flattered by a comparison so favourable to their own establishment. Eventually an agreement was reached by which I would pay a weekly rate of £5 10s, more than the slum tenements that I had been viewing but well worth the extra. It included a substantial breakfast with a different hot dish each day of the week.

Miss Hook and I now joined forces to explore the city. It was, we opined, a metropolis, albeit a modest one, whereas Christchurch was more of a large country town. We examined Victoria University, which we deplored as dingy, and the Houses of Parliament – impressive and based on our own with a Bellamy's (members' dining room) and an Annie's Bar – as well as the Government Buildings, claimed by Wellingtonians to be the largest wooden structure in the world; rode a scarlet cable car to a high ridge overlooking Oriental Bay and marvelled at the view; and checked out what was on offer at Wellington's three theatres. Fortunately Miss Hook was an indefatigable walker, as most of Wellington is built on hills, save the reclaimed Lambton Quay and a central square or two, and you gravitated from one level to the next via flights of stone steps and from one residential area to another via funny little paths, bordered by wild flowers, winding round the gaily painted wooden houses. We particularly admired the freshly painted white wooden railings on the curves of roads. Wellington, we agreed, was built to a human scale. Its exterior appearance belied the poverty of too many interiors.

It was, I suppose, a curious cross-generational friendship that developed between Miss Hook and me, one based almost wholly on exploration of the past. We were both passionate about the history of settlement in New Zealand and for much the same reason: we were curious to find out how the early settlers had succeeded in replicating English life and, in the case of Otago, Scottish life, so far from home, more so in this colony than any other. Miss Hook would disappear to her room after breakfast each morning to delve into a high stack of books sourced from the Alexander Turnbull Library and would emerge into our shared kitchen only to solicit my views on the Wakefield System and its effect on class attitudes, or on Governor Grey's approach to the land question. I noted in one of my letters home that despite the extent of her researches, she never seemed to get beyond 1843. As NZ had only been settled by pahekas (persons of European descent) in 1840, this tended to give her studies a rather narrow focus.

For my part, while I was happy to engage in these spirited discussions (we both had the grace to shut up when Mr and Mrs Hill had other guests in the house), I wanted to mine as much as I could of her memories of bohemian life in London in the 1920s and 1930s. She was very willing to talk about this, but just as New Zealand history seemed to stop, for her, in 1843, her personal history came to an abrupt halt at the end of World War Two. She could not be drawn out on her life or career after that. She was one of the most private people I have ever met. Indeed we had quite a serious falling out after I had looked through the mail on the hall table and seen an envelope addressed to her and inscribed Association of Headmistresses. I joshingly remarked that I now knew her closely guarded secret, that she had headed some eminent girls' school, and to my dismay she reacted with nothing short of fury. She accused me of prying into her affairs and invading her privacy. In vain did I protest that the envelope with its inscription had been lying in plain view. There followed a week of muttered 'good mornings' and dark looks before normal relations were resumed. But I was careful now to make no reference to anything personal that had occurred after 1945.

. . .

Now that I had a place to live, I set forth to find a means of paying for it. I aimed high to start with, applying for a job as an interviewer with NZBC. I had heard of other footloose Englishmen who had secured jobs with colonial broadcasters simply on the strength of a plummy voice. Maybe mine wasn't plummy enough.... I then lowered my sights to a vacancy for librarian at the Government Tourist Department. I was told I was overqualified, as it was a dead-end job with no prospects. This surprisingly frank assessment from the head of personnel could be interpreted, I think, to mean that they expected to employ a woman in the job. My ambitions shrank, as they had on previous searches for employment, until they reached the level of messenger. Not any kind of messenger, though, but a Parliamentary Messenger.

I was hired, the youngest messenger in the House of Representatives. Most of my colleagues in the Messengers' Room were new to the job too, though they were almost all of them some fifty years my senior. It transpired that there had been a wholesale clear-out of Boer War veterans after the previous Parliamentary Session, and the incomers were veterans of World War One. The reason for the cull was this. When on duty in the chamber, messengers sat on high seats like bar stools, elevated so that they could see across the heads of the Members they served. One of the Boer War veterans had fallen asleep during some especially soporific debate, fallen off his stool, and gently rolled down the carpeted steps until he came to a halt in front of the Mace. There he continued to slumber, emitting peaceful snores, until the Sergeant-at-Arms could arrange his removal. It was then decreed that the Boer War veterans must go. There was an immediate national outcry about this discrimination against these gallant ex-soldiers who had stood shoulder-to-shoulder with their British Army comrades against the deadly sniper fire of the Boer commandos. The Government was adamant. It was time to give youth a chance. As the white-headed retirees who now filled the Messengers' Room could hardly be so described, I suppose I was the youth Her Majesty's Government had in mind.

The duties of a messenger were not onerous, and the recompense of £13 10s clear for a four-day week not ungenerous. Parliament sat only from Monday until Thursday, which gave me a three-day weekend. Sundays were spent rambling in the countryside with Miss Hook, often following in Katherine Mansfield's footsteps to discover the scenes of the stories based on her Wellington childhood, but the other two days I determined to put to purposeful use. Readers may recall that I had begun compiling a book of 'firsts' when I was a fag at Shrewsbury. That had had to be put on one side when O- and A-Levels intervened, and London life had been too busy for literary endeavour. But now I had no excuse not to return to the project. Every Friday and Saturday was spent in Wellington Public Library, systematically working through the Reference and Non-Fiction sections. My initial task was to establish a base of all the firsts that could be easily culled from other people's books; there was no point in undertaking original research on such well-documented topics as, for example, railways or military advances or the development of education. This, then, was the spadework. The gaps, demanding the use of primary sources, could be filled in later. (Had I known that the filling in would take ten years, I might have re-embarked on the project less blithely.)

News of my new employment was not well received at home. In describing my daily round, I had mentioned the smart blue serge uniform with silver crown buttons that I wore in the House. A pained letter from my mother requested me not to refer to the uniform again. To have a younger son proclaiming his menial status in this way had upset my father too much. There was a follow-up letter a week later demanding to know whether I was giving serious thought to a career. Being a waiter had been bad enough; now it was apparent that I had taken a further step downward in the social scale and I did not even seem to feel any shame about it.

Those I served in the House were somewhat more tolerant. I was fortunate enough to be assigned to the messenger's station that overlooked the Cabinet. When the House adjourned at the end of my first day, a tall, good-looking man came up to me and introduced himself as Harry Lake, Minister of Finance. He welcomed me to the House and asked if I had met the Hon. Mr McKay, the Minister of Health? And this is the Hon. Mr Goosens, Minister of Works, and that is the Hon. Mr Tallboys – come over here, Jim, and meet our new messenger from England – he's our Minister of Agriculture. And here is the Senior Whip, Mr Scott.... And so it went on until I had met nearly all of the cabinet, excepting the PM who had made a dash for it when the House rose. Now where in the world, I asked myself, would the senior ministers of a government bother to make themselves known to the newest, youngest, and most junior employee of the House? Except in New Zealand.

Members of Her Majesty's Loyal Opposition were rather less forthcoming. I think this may have been to do with class. The Labour Members tended to come from the same social background as the majority of the messengers and the impression I had at the time was that these political placemen despised those of their own kind who had failed to attain such status. I have to say that the House was one of the few institutions in New Zealand that did seem divided by class. On the whole NZ was the classless country it liked to claim to be; there were very few rich people and very few poor. The gap between the top and the bottom of society was a lot narrower than it was in the Old Country or, indeed, the United States. But politics seemed to divide people by class rather more than in Britain, perhaps the only respect in which this was so.

One marked exception to the general aloofness of the Labour members was the former Prime Minister (1957–60) Sir Walter Nash. He came bounding up to me in the Lobby and pumped my arm, exclaiming, 'I hear you're from Blighty. Whereabouts?' I told him and added that I knew he was from Kidderminster, where I had often stayed with a schoolfriend. There ensued an animated conversation about the West Midlands, which Sir Walter had left in 1909 for NZ. As Minister of Finance in the 1935 Labour Government, he had been one of the principal architects of New Zealand's welfare state, which preceded Britain's by a full decade. Whenever I saw him in the House, Sir Walter would give me a cheery wave and stop for a word or two if he was not on urgent affairs of state. One Sunday I was invited to Petone, across the bay from Wellington, by a fellow messenger who was the town's former mayor. His guided tour of the rather drab little town of which he was so proud included Sir Walter Nash's house. This was a 1920s stucco bungalow with two rooms in front and two rooms at the back. Even by New Zealand standards it was humble. Sir Walter was a socialist who lived up to his political creed in every way, and sought nothing for himself but the satisfaction of bettering the condition of his fellow man.

Another exception in the Labour ranks when it came to courtesy and modesty was Sir Eruera Tirekatene, senior of the four Maori MPs. He had a special bond with Sir Walter, as the latter had been instrumental in overturning the shocking restrictions on Maori welfare during the Depression. Maori were not entitled to dole payments, nor eligible for work on relief programmes; they were expected to subsist from the land, even if they had none. Sir Eruera led the campaign for reform and, when Labour was elected, Sir Walter responded.

It may seem strange that the four Maori constituencies were separate from the white voter roll. In fact in a House that had only sixty MPs it made a lot of sense. There was a guarantee that the number of Maori MPs approximated to Maoris' incidence in the general population, and their bloc of four, although nearly always representing Labour, made a powerful grouping that could exert pressure in policy areas with particular resonance for the Maori people. It allowed them to punch above their weight.

The Prime Minster, the Rt Hon. Keith Holyoake, I only got to know later, when I was drafted in as his relief liftman. On the first occasion we met, he asked me if I happened to be going anywhere near the third floor – where his Private Office was situated. I assured him it would be no trouble to make a special journey. He was an impressive figure in a country in which people were not encouraged to look impressive: it smacked of tall poppy syndrome. The more so because he compensated for his middling height by wearing elevator shoes. I may have been the only person outside the Holyoake family to be privy to this curious fact. And he was a good orator in a country where oratory was not cultivated. It seemed, in the unsolicited view of the most junior person within those walls, that he was the right man for the job.

Another routine task was standing guard on committee rooms. I was on this duty when I had my initial encounter with the Governor-General,

Sir Bernard Fergusson, war hero and last British-born Governor-General of New Zealand. Both his grandfathers had served as Governor of the colony, and his father as Governor-General. His only child was to become British High Commissioner. Sir Bernard was another of those people in high places who had the art of communicating with others on another level without patronising them. He stopped as he came out of the committee room, asked who I was, and then engaged in a fairly lengthy conversation about my experiences in New Zealand. I would have liked to ask him about his, and did he think it had achieved the expectations of his grandfathers, but there is a time and a place.

A fortnight later I happened to be posted outside the same room when he came processing down the corridor in tailcoat and striped trousers, a shining topper in his hand and monocle in eye, followed by a retinue of aides, attachés and government advisers. As he reached where I was standing, he broke off his conversation with an enrobed Mister Speaker and turned towards me. The whole retinue juddered to a halt behind him. 'Good heavens!' he exclaimed. '*Still* here?'

The quality of debates was not high, unless the PM or the belicose future PM Robert Muldoon was on the floor. Indeed it was so inferior on the Opposition benches that the Labour Party ran a school of public speaking to try to improve matters. Coming from a country where there is never sufficient time for the full legislative programme during a session of Parliament, it surprised and rather amused me that the House sometimes ran out of things to talk about before it rose on a Thursday. Or would have done, but for the fortunate insertion into that session's programme of the Indecent Publications Bill. Now there were no indecent publications in New Zealand. (As a collector of colonial books and periodicals I could be fairly certain of that.) Not only were there none published in New Zealand, but it was highly doubtful that 'this threat to the youth of the country', as Honourable Members kept repeating, existed at all. But every Honourable Member, on either side of the House, was a self-appointed expert on the subject. Not that they had ever read any of these foul publications themselves, they were hasty to assure fellow Honourable Members, but they knew someone who had. They could not name any of these publications, but they knew for a certainty that they were unspeakably vile. And a threat to the youth of this great country of ours.

After some weeks of this, the on-and-off debate was flagging a bit for lack of any hard evidence of the vileness of the threat, and the fact that both sides of the House were united in the need for strong action meant that there was little difference of view other than the severity of penalties to be imposed: harsh, very harsh, or draconian. Then a blessing from heaven fanned the flames of everyone's condemnation and revived the passion of the debate. Not from heaven exactly, but left on the front steps of Parliament by an anonymous protector of the nation's virtue: a genuine pornographic book! It was found by the first messenger to arrive that morning and borne in triumph to the Messengers' Room, where it was passed from hand to hand, or indeed wrenched from each pair of hands. To be truthful it was not *that* porno, just one of those Olympia Press books that you could buy openly in Paris and from under the counter in London, but it was a lot steamier than anything to be found at Whitcombe & Tombs' bookshop on Lambton Quay.

As soon as the Chief Messenger, an ex-RSM, heard about it, the wicked thing was whisked away to the Sergeant-at-Arms. He, holding it between thumb and forefinger, marched it at arm's length to the Senior Whip's office. The Senior Whip decided that he needed to examine it before deciding what to do. Several hours later he consigned it to Mister Speaker, the mild-mannered and fervently Christian Sir Ronald Algie, who recoiled in horror. It could not be allowed to stay in the Speaker's Apartments, he declared, and the offending object was consigned to the Deputy Speaker to convey to the Prime Minister's Private Office. At this point we messengers lost track of it, but the consensus in the Messengers' Room was that the Badger (aka Kiwi Keith Holyoake) would be staying in the House late that night.

Reinvigorated by this fresh evidence of the extent to which not only the youth of our great country but even humble parliamentary messengers were being exposed to lewd and depraved literature, the debate gathered pace and the Indecent Publications Act received Sir Bernard's assent on 22nd October 1963. Its principal innovation – there were already powers for customs officers to seize anything they deemed indecent – was the setting up of an Indecent Publications Tribunal. Thus, three years after the verdict in the *Lady Chatterley* case had virtually ended the suppression of obscene literature in Britain, New Zealand had established a court to deal solely with pornography in a country that did not have any. It was to survive, remarkably, for thirty years.

*As soon as the Chief Messenger heard about it, the wicked thing was whisked away to the Sergeant-at-Arms …*

Since the Honourable Members often found debates on more mundane topics tedious in the extreme, they looked for other ways of passing the time. They occupied double seats and each seat had a small writing bureau in front, so it was easy enough to conceal diversionary items. I found Mister Hauman, a Tory Member of long standing, reading a sevenpenny shocker titled *The Kelly Gang of Bushrangers* under the desk, while his colleagues maundered on about local government audits. The Hon. John McAlpine, Minister of Railways, secreted a radio inside the desk, connected to a small speaker in his ear which he fondly imagined would be mistaken for a hearing aid. It might have been, had he switched the audio to the earplug. He hadn't, and the wireless blasted hot-diggity jazz music throughout the Chamber, while he sat with his eyes closed oblivious to colleagues gesticulating and waving at him and Mister Speaker's outraged command. As all parliamentary debates were broadcast, this may have been the first time the radio had broadcast a radio.

Cartoons of Britain's Parliament often show Members snoozing, but this was a reality in the New Zealand House of Representatives. The Minister of Housing was a very short man and when his neighbour on their double seat was absent from the Chamber, he would curl up on it for some gentle repose. My partner Albie Newman – we took turn and turn about looking after the Cabinet – told me that on one occasion he had seen the Prime Minister, the Deputy Prime Minister and the Chief Whip all asleep at the same time.

. . .

Relations with Mr and Mrs Hill at 166 Sydney Street West became somewhat strained. Mr Hill was agoraphobic and could never leave the house; Mrs Hill was highly sensitive to a weight problem that was getting out of control. Neither was blessed with a developed sense of humour and the stress occasioned by their circumscribed life in a small house surrounded by strangers began to tell. It culminated in the expulsion of poor Miss Hook. Her offence had been to enquire at breakfast whether an overnight guest would prefer hot milk in her coffee. This was overheard by Mrs Hill, who summoned the miscreant after breakfast and denounced her for interfering in the way she ran her B & B. She was told to pack her bags and be gone. Miss Hook was very upset, but her profuse apologies and promises of reform were rejected out of hand.

Miss Hook proposed to me that we should share a flat together. Some years later it would become relatively common in London for boys and girls to share, but not at this time and certainly not in New Zealand. I was tempted, partly because I felt that I was probably next on the Hills' hit-list but also because I relished the idea of the reaction to a maiden lady in her seventies living with a fresh-faced youth in his early twenties. What would the straight-laced bourgeoisie of Wellington's suburbs have made of that? But Miss Hook herself could be prickly, as the episode over the letter had revealed, and I decided against her novel proposal. We remained friends and I used to visit her at her cottage in Alton, Hampshire, to which she retired on returning to England.

. . .

My pleasantest task in the House was showing visitors around. In the rather casual manner in which most things were run in and out of government, we were given no training for this somewhat specialist role. You watched other people doing it, noted what not to do as well as what worked best, and read up on the history of how this colonial backwater had become one of the world's first true democracies (arguably the very first if you accept universal suffrage as the cornerstone of a democracy). It helped to have some knowledge of the Mother of Parliaments, because not only was the House of Representatives closely modelled on it in respect of its layout and appointments, but the procedure was based largely on Erskine May. There were one or two respects, though, in which the offspring had pre-empted the parent. I enjoyed telling British visitors that Hansard had become the official record of the parliamentary debates in NZ long before it received the same recognition from the House of Commons. In 1936 New Zealand became the first country in the world to allow the regular broadcasting of legislative proceedings, an example that was not followed in Britain until 1975. Another respect in which NZ practice differed from that of the Old Country was applause. Strictly prohibited in the House of Commons, in NZ's House of Representatives clapping was permitted after a maiden speech and to honour the promoter of a Private Member's Bill on the rare occasions that one of these reached the statute book.

There was an occasion when I was told that there was a young lady in the foyer wishing to see round the House. I trotted along to collect her and as we were about to set off, another girl, about the same age, arrived at the entrance with the same request. They were not known to each other. I asked if they would like to go round together and they assented.

As we walked down a corridor past the group portraits of previous parliamentary sessions, one of the girls said she would like to see the group for 1889–1890. The other girl said she was also looking for a particular group, one in which a member called Holmes appeared, her great-uncle. The first girl expressed amazement. Holmes was the very person she was looking for in the 1889–1890 group. He was also her great-uncle. Of course it did not take long for the girls to compare families and establish that they were cousins. Up to that day they had never met, nor even known of each other's existence. I met them in town later for lunch, and they were both able to tell me the same family legend, which had been handed down the branches independently, that Great-Uncle Holmes had had to resign his seat when it was found he had won the election by getting the whole Maori electorate drunk.

Despite my parents' aversion to my menial occupation, I recounted tales of my fellow messengers in my letters home. *The other day,* I wrote soon after my arrival, *I went into the Members' billiard room to have a look at this place where great men spend their leisure and plot the downfall of other great men. There were two messengers in charge, an old hand and a new one. The old hand was a barrel-chested man with waxed moustaches, clearly a retired NCO; the new messenger was a pipsqueak. I passed the time of day and asked to look round.*

*The old sweat acquiesced. He mopped his brow. He was obviously under severe mental strain. 'I 'ave been tryin' to impress on this 'ere' – he jerked a thumb at the new messenger, 'that this place is NOT a Billiard Saloon or a Pool Hall.'*

*I understood him. After all, the PM himself comes in here. 'Quite,' I agreed, 'It is more of a club.'*

*'Eggzackly!' affirmed the Old Sweat. 'That's what it is. A club. Like the Military Club on Lambton Quay ...'*

*'Or the Wellington Club', I suggested.*

*'Or the Wellington Club, certainly,' agreed the Old Sweat.*

*'Or the Lower Hutt Working Men's Club,' piped up the new messenger.*

'*O my Gawd,*' bellowed the Old Sweat, rolling his eyes in exasperation. '*YOU 'ORRIBLE LITTLE MAN!*'

Debates in the Messengers' Room were as spirited as any taking place on the floor above. My colleagues who had survived the Gallipoli Landings and the Western Front tended to be men of strong and wide-ranging opinions. Despite their common adherence to the Labour Party and the trade union movement, there was seldom unanimity of opinion. On the one occasion there was, I felt the matter worth writing home about: *The messengers are outraged at news of Auckland Art Gallery's decision to spend £9,600 on a shapeless lump of clay through which Barbara Hepworth has poked a quite becoming hole. A spokesman for the gallery defended their action by stating that the citizens of Auckland needed to be elevated, as they have a taste in art which reaches to the very lowest of Victorian standards. In that case, agreed my colleagues, why not give them something of that low Victorian standard which they will enjoy and appreciate? Jock, a Scottish messenger, who is still almost unintelligible after forty years residence in New Zealand, was of the opinion that 'The Stag at Bay' would be the most welcome addition to Auckland Art Gallery. This was endorsed by all the other art-minded messengers, who were unanimous in considering 'The Stag at Bay' beyond aesthetic reproach. I am sure many art lovers in England would be delighted if its custodians were to send 'The Stag At Bay' to Auckland. They could hardly send it any farther.*

I did not stay till the end of the Session, because I had booked passage aboard the *Oriana* to New South Wales on 20th October, a few days before the House rose. The farewell party in the Messengers' Room was most affecting, with speeches and toasts and farewell gifts – the girls in the Government Printing Office had clubbed together to buy me a leather-bound address book embossed with a greenstone Tiki, which touched my heart. The principal speech was made by one of my more colourful colleagues, Cyril Maws, who had been a rum runner for Fatty Arbuckle in Hollywood during Prohibition. His encomium was backed up by Mr Wright, Marxist firebrand and scourge of the idle rich (of whom there were disappointingly few in New Zealand), who declared that I had come to this great country to rectify the mistakes of an over-privileged English education and was making encouraging progress.

The Rt Hon. the Prime Minister, when I told him I was leaving and wished him well in the upcoming general election, thumped me hard on the left shoulder and called me a 'Damn Tory, begad!' I don't think he encountered many of those from the Messengers' Room.

. . .

I left Wellington the following morning for the thirteen-hour bus journey to Auckland. I seldom comment on scenery in this memoir, because you need to *see* it, but crave your indulgence for the prettiest village in New Zealand – Cambridge, seat not of a university but of a leading prep school called St Peter's, confusingly one of two schools of the same name in this small community – and renowned for its geysers. Now the North Island is full of geysers and I can take 'em or leave 'em, but these were pretty special geysers because they had been harnessed to generate a public electricity supply. Moreover, Cambridge's geysers had silencers fitted to them. Without the silencers, I was credibly informed, they could be heard at a distance of fifteen miles and sounded like the more martial Greek gods of antiquity breaking wind.

After devoting the following morning to the bookshops of Auckland, I met with Miss Shanks from the Hermitage for tea on a balcony in an arcade at which we gorged ourselves on éclairs and brandy snaps stuffed with cream. That evening I dined with the Lovely Mrs Lachlan and lunched with her the next day. After lunch she sprang her surprise on me. The sweet girl had hired a cab for the whole afternoon, driven by a chum, so that I should see her home town in style. The Lovely Mrs L had an engagement in the evening, but Mr Fraser the cab driver scooped me up and carried me off to a birthday party in Epsom.

*This was very interesting*, I wrote home, *as it was a largely working-class gathering, and showed what a high standard of living the New Zealand worker enjoys. Not all workers live this well; I have been into houses in Wellington which equal anything in Bermondsey for filth and disrepair. How best to describe the sort of people there? – well I think the women were the sort you see in large crowds at seaside resorts of the middling kind like Worthing or Ramsgate. The men were the kind you see on bowling greens on a Saturday afternoon. Solid respectability, but fond of a glass of milk stout and a good laugh when George Formby is on at the pictures. Amongst these good plain folk, though, was a very pukka woman who is something in the colonial service (New Zealand has acquired its own colonies), and her friend, a highly sophisticated and very smart Australian woman. Also present was the Hon. Hugh Watt, the Deputy Leader of the Opposition. He was as surprised to see me there as I was to see him.*

After the Lovely Mrs Lachlan and I had attended mass at the cathedral next morning, we met up with Miss Shanks and visited the zoo. The girls were delighted by the giraffes. I recounted to them how Osbert Sitwell, on joining his Guards regiment in World War I, was asked by the colonel whether he was keen on horses. 'Not especially,' responded the aesthete, 'but I adore giraffes.'

Then it was time to embark on the *Oriana*. I had a problem. My poker winnings from the Hermitage, harvested to make a good start in Australia, exceeded the maximum amount allowed to be taken out of the country by £60. The Lovely Mrs L had a solution. I may have had occasion to mention her ample embonpoint. She suggested that I should secrete the roll of notes between its constituent parts. No New Zealand customs officer, she assured me, would be brazen enough to search in such a place. I accepted her proposal eagerly and moved towards her to effect the transfer. The Lovely Mrs L gently extracted the roll from my hand and inserted it herself. Then she kissed me on the nose.

Having boarded together, and successfully effected the transfer of funds while evading the attention of the customs officers, we bade each other farewell in my cabin as the ship's hooters sounded their mournful knell for departure. Dear, darling Lily Lachlan. I was unable to find you when I returned to NZ with Karla. Your friend Jainey, Dowager Viscountess Bolingbroke, searched for you too. I still miss your throaty laugh.

# Chapter 11

. . .

# THE LUCKY COUNTRY

. . .

## *October 1963–April 64*

To my surprise and pleasure I was met at Circular Quay in Sydney by Robin Gates and his chum Rustic Richard and carried off to their new abode in Croydon, a largely Edwardian suburb lying some six miles to the west. They were working as hospital orderlies at Concord Hospital, which they seemed to enjoy despite being charged with the duty of incinerating amputated limbs. The boys were living in a garage that they rented from a vet, the interior of which I described in my first Australian letter home as 'having the atmosphere and appearance of an army hut when the sergeant is away on leave'. Robin was moonlighting in the evenings helping the vet to perform operations on dogs. He invited me to help myself to a beer from the fridge and when I opened it I found it full of carcasses of patients who had failed to survive Robin's and the vet's ministrations.

*I think I have lost my heart to Sydney, I reported in my letter home, that is all except the Waratah House Hotel, which is truly the most sordid lodging it has been my misfortune to occupy. I am soon going to shake the dust, of which there is a great deal, from my heels, so don't address any mail here. It would probably be steamed open anyway.*

*Sydney is like London with sunshine. My first view of it was from the deck of the* Oriana *soon after dawn, steaming through the Heads and right up to the Harbour Bridge. It is vast – 2½ million souls – rambling, old, dirty, and delightful. Sydney has four periods: Georgian, Victorian, Federation (from the federation of the autonomous colonies in 1901 to c.1920) and modern. Victorian predominates in the inner city. Most of the private houses are Victorian and abound in Sydney Lace. This does not refer to curtains, but to the beautiful lace-like wrought iron balconies on all these terrace houses. Some of these have been done up and have a Chelsea smartness about them, while others are virtually slums.*

*Place names are familiar to a Londoner: Oxford Street, Hyde Park, Paddington, King's Cross (where I am now – the Soho of Sydney), Smithfield and suburbs such as Woolwich, Greenwich, Kensington, Richmond, Chiswick, Mortlake, Stanmore, Dulwich, Lewisham and Enfield. I have heard Sydney likened to an American city, but few cities are less so. For one thing it is not built on a grid system, but sprawls haphazardly. So there is always something exciting round a corner: sometimes an elegant row of Georgian townhouses or maybe a sweeping vista of the harbour. Or, joy of joys, one of Sydney's ten second-hand bookshops.*

My most exciting discovery in Sydney was the Rocks, where the original settlement of 1788 grew up on either side of the Tank Stream. The streets and alleyways had been hewn from solid rock foundations and the houses built on the tops of the cuttings, reached by flights of well-worn stone stairs with ancient iron balustrades. Here was the oldest house in Sydney, dating from 1816. Most of the houses were built in the 1840s and were little changed; the area was a classic slum, Dickensian not only in its tumbledown appearance but also for its raffish inhabitants. Kent Street when it was built must have been a cut above its surroundings, as the fine multi-storey stone-built houses had early nineteenth-century firemarks attached to the walls, signifying that their owners were insured and could call on the services of the company fire appliance. Now they were tenements. There was little or no traffic and the streets in the Rocks were a playground for barefoot larrikins, often wielding a bat and ball before a chalked wicket on a crumbling wall. At that time the area attracted few visitors and did not feature in any tourist guide. There were various municipal initiatives for sweeping the whole lot away and replacing it with office blocks. Happily none of these came to fruition before the heritage movement began its belated progress in the seventies and eighties. The Rocks was saved, restored, scrubbed and manicured, and given a total makeover as a kind of Colonial Sydney theme park. In the process it was gentrified, with the working classes moving out and hip young middle class entrepreneurs moving in to open gourmet restaurants, coffee houses and chic 'period' bars with lots of frosted glass. Saved in one way, lost for ever in another.

To find the oldest house in Australia, Robin and I set out for Parramatta by train. This was Australia's second settlement, established a year after Sydney. We knew the name of the house, Elizabeth Farm, and that it had been built in 1793 for the notorious John Macarthur, but not its whereabouts. Nor could any of the natives of Parramatta tell us how to get there. Most had not heard of it; a few knew of its existence but had never seen it. Eventually we came across a recently arrived Scotsman who knew exactly where it was located, at the end of a row of ugly modern bungalows. It looked derelict, but was apparently occupied. The galvanised iron roof was rusted and sagging and no paint had been applied to the doors or windows in generations. The fine sandstone walls, however, were intact. The garden was a thicket of brambles, weeds and nettles within a thick cordon of barbed wire. This prevented us from a closer scrutiny and the gate was firmly padlocked.

It was not until fifteen years later that the State Government of New South Wales became concerned that the oldest house in Australia was in danger of collapse. They bought it, restored it admirably, and made it over to the Historic Houses Trust, which opened it to the public in 1984. This was about the time that Australians woke up to the value of their heritage. Hitherto there had been a conscious effort to suppress a history that many found shameful, but by the 1980s people no longer wanted to draw a veil over convict origins and realised that they should celebrate the fact that a wretched penal colony had become an envied nation with one of the highest living standards in the world. Go into the outback nowadays and nearly every village has a sign with its name prefaced by 'Historic' and usually there is a local museum full of quaint relics donated by locals. The closing years of the twentieth century, when Australia was discovering the value of its early built environment, were also the time that the Australian film industry saw its renaissance, and most of the films that garnered awards all over the world – *Picnic at Hanging Rock, My Beautiful Career,*

*The Getting of Wisdom, Caddie* etc – were period movies. Publishing also saw a huge increase in historical works on every facet of Australian society and Robert Hughes's 1986 study of transportation *The Fatal Shore* became a worldwide bestseller, rated by *Time* as one of the 100 best non-fiction works in the last fifty years. But all this was in the future when I was there. Shortly after I returned home the Australian Tourist Board ran a series of advertisements in upmarket English magazines that declared 'If you're interested in history, don't come to Australia. But if it's sun and sand you want …' or words to that effect. Many things have changed for the better in Australia since the sixties. From my perspective, this change of attitude towards the nation's past is one of them.

A postscript. While Robin and I were searching the countryside around Parramatta for Elizabeth Farm, we passed a five-bar gate on which were perched two tow-haired larrikins of about ten, sucking straws. As we sauntered by, one boy inclined his head to the other and muttered, 'There go a couple of Pommie poofdahs'. The word 'Pommie' was already familiar, usually in a disparaging context. But 'poofdah' (nowadays anglicised as 'poofter') was new to me. 'What do they mean?', I asked Robin. He explained. I was outraged. 'Shouldn't we go back and knock them off that gate?' I suggested. 'Nah,' said Robin. 'You'll soon get used to it. Australians think that all Poms are homosexual. It lets them to feel superior to us. Get used to it.'

. . .

Sydney was a city of newcomers. One day I was crossing George Street, dodging in and out of the traffic to reach the other side. As I stepped on to the pavement, I was confronted by a policewoman of menacing aspect. 'You're jaywalking,' she proclaimed, 'and that's an offence.' I endeavoured to compose my features into a suitably contrite expression. 'I'm terribly sorry, Officer,' I declared. 'But I've only been in Sydney for a fortnight and I did not know the law.' The policewoman drew herself up to her full 5ft 2ins and responded in a pure Glaswegian accent: 'Is that so? I've been in Sydney for a week now and I DO know the law!'

. . .

Robin departed for Perth, while I set off for Melbourne and the Cup. The first night I spent in the Hotel Victoria, an immense barrack-like structure with 690 rooms and the atmosphere of a YMCA but the prices of a four star hotel. Where could I go? Did I know anyone in Melbourne? I did! I knew Peter Rutherford, maitre d' at the Hermitage, stalwart of the early hours poker school. I knew he was running an oyster bar. The number of such establishments in Melbourne is limited and I tracked him down in Parkville, a pleasant suburb that hosted Melbourne University and where Peter had a flat on whose floor I was welcome to crash. He also accommodated a cash-flow problem occasioned by an injudicious choice for the Melbourne Cup. There were twenty-six runners and I put a fair amount from the roll of notes extracted from the Lovely Mrs Lachlan's embonpoint on the nag that came second, Ilumquh. Peter allowed me to eat at the oyster bar for nothing until I could find a job. Now oysters are a delicious luxury and one that I had seldom indulged. But oysters for breakfast, oysters for lunch, and oysters for dinner seven days a week can become a tad monotonous. It was an incentive to find gainful employment without delay.

The oysters were served by a waitress from Bradford called Red. I mention this because she was the only person I have met who really did run away to live with the gypsies. This was when she was fourteen and she travelled with them for six weeks before a Romany child who resented the presence of a *gorgio* denounced her to the social workers. Red had an informant at one of the leading Melbourne stables and came to us one day with a hot tip for a certain winner. My lack of funds meant that I could only invest £1, but Peter ventured £10, Red herself £120, and a rather louche friend of Peter's called Beth, determined to make enough to give up work, ponied up £2,000. The race was at three o'clock and by ten minutes past our friendly illegal corner bookmaker found himself, much to his relief, richer by £2,131.

I also saw my first test match in Peter's company, together with a mob of Melbourne University students who frequented the oyster bar. It was Australia versus South Africa and outside the Melbourne Cricket Ground there was a large group of picketers making a loud and vigorous protest about the South Africans' exclusion of non-white players from their team. This was a lot more exciting than anything happening within the stadium. It was possibly the dullest seven hours I had experienced since watching flying fish arcing over the stern of the *Waikema*, but as I had diverted myself then with Marie Corelli, I now turned to JB Priestley's *Bright Day* and lost myself in the cobbled streets of industrial Yorkshire on the eve of World War I. The Melbourne students were outraged.

As the seemingly endless match drew towards a blessed close, there was a debate about the pleasures of the evening. The students were all of one mind: to go to the pub and get wasted, then on to the students' union to drink some more. As the only two topics of conversation during the match had been cricket and their sexual conquests real or imagined, the prospect of more of the same did not fill my heart with joy. I proffered an alternative. I had never been to a drive-in movie during my time in America and had learned with interest that they flourished in Australia too. Peter had never been to one either and was keen to go. The suggestion was met by the students with a lot of tittering and smirking and innuendo, all totally lost on me. They set off for the pub and Peter and I drove out to Toorak to see Dirk Bogarde and Capucine in *Song without End*. On the way Peter explained to me what all the sniggering had been about. Apparently couples went to the drive-in to neck and pet and sometimes to indulge in other activities of a more advanced nature. If two Pommie men were going to a drive-in, it was obvious to a bunch of Melbourne University students what they would do when they got there. It grieves me to say that these young men, despite their privileged background, were fairly representative of most of the Australian males of their age that I encountered, puerile and immature and coarse. Young Australian females and older Australians of both sexes were mainly delightful but, sad to say, the larrikin element, decried by social commentators as early as the 1880s, had survived into the 1960s.

* * *

The urgent need for gainful employment precipitated me into the embrace of Melbourne's Southern Cross Hotel, one of the Intercontinental chain of luxury hotels. I was posted to the Banqueting Department and installed in the Dispensary. This was a cage, kept locked all the time I was in it, from which I dispensed bottles of liquor through an aperture in the wire in fulfilment of orders dispatched by any of several bosses in the Banqueting Department. I was kept in there for an average of fourteen hours a day, during which there were no comfort breaks let alone mealtimes. I was only paid for eight of these hours. Most of my colleagues in the Department worked equally extended hours and I asked one of the friendlier ones why the union did not make representations on our behalf. He looked at me with a pitying smile. 'This is the State of Victoria, Sport,' he reminded me. 'The management pays off the union not to make trouble.'

I wrote home with an account of my new working life. *The trouble is too many bosses. There are five in the Banqueting Department and whatever one says do, another says don't do. It is a department run mainly on shouting. The bosses do not actually do any work. They just stand and yell at people in various European languages, often Hungarian. Or sometimes Serbo Croat or Estonian, Rumanian, and Czech. The day to day business of the department, though, is conducted in Italian. This seems to be a sort of universal language in the hotel business. They all speak it except the English and the Australians, and as the hotel employs hardly any Australians it makes no difference to them. The English can only converse with each other.*

*Monsieur Bianchi is Head of all the Heads of the Banqueting Department. He behaves as if also head of the whole Southern Cross, except that Mister Sutherland, the Manager, seems to think he is. Prime Minister Robert Menzies might want to watch his back. Monsieur Bianchi is immense and he can curse volubly in seven different languages and eleven dialects. He never stops eating. My first day he ate his way through a seven-course banquet standing up, eating not only the set courses but all the a la carte as well. Then he suddenly espied a waiter taking a plate of food out of an oven. Swallowing the portion of strawberry shortcake he was masticating, he roared at the wretched waiter 'Put that down, Carrion rejected by Vulture. THAT is my DINNER!'*

*We have a very small and very portly Yugoslavian called Mchza who has been sacked by Monsieur Bianchi forty times. Each time he is dismissed he returns the next day and is re-employed. Came one day worse than all the rest and Mchza was fired thirteen times during the course of one banquet. Mchza has his own way of contending with Monsieur Bianchi. Every time M. Bianchi pours himself out a drink, which is frequently, and is called to the phone, just as frequently, Mchza emerges suddenly from some hiding place and drains the glass. By the time M. Bianchi has finished yelling into the phone there is no drink and no Mchza.*

*One day I watched M. Bianchi telephone the electricians. 'Why hast mine lights not been turn down?' he bellowed. Splutter splutter from phone. 'Don't gimme excuses I don't want to 'ear dem. So OK. You no come up and fix my lides, heh? I DON'T WANT TO KNOW WHY. I ring Meester Sutherland now. I tell him you no goot. DON'T TALK TO ME I DON'T VANT TO EER. Get off der line and leef me in peece and tranquillity. LISSEN TO ME YOU EER! Youse is a no goot outfit cara mia del pinto fiasci nona etc etc.' Then he crashed the receiver down with a thundering slam, paused for thought, picked it up again and shouted into it 'TANK YOU.' Next day I watched him phone the electricians again. 'Dey tell me you nona like being abused by me', he said sweetly. 'Dat you nona stand for it, heh? Vell, HOW YOU LIKA PUNCH ON DA NOSE?' Crash.*

After I had been in my cage dispensing for a week, they told me I had been moved to waiting. Now the cage was relatively safe from the casual abuse meted out to my fellow wage-slaves in the Banqueting Department. I gave Monsieur le Chef his hourly tot of whisky and he gave me great big plates of lovely food. I gave Monsieur Alex the Head Waiter the rum he needed to sustain his sanity and he rewarded me with one of his rare apologies for a smile. I didn't actually give Monsieur Bianchi anything because he just walked in, stepped over me, and took it. But I was secure there. Being a waiter in that madhouse spelled trouble and strife and so I quit.

• • •

I secured my next job by attaching myself to another friend of Peter's, a charming English boy called David Tattersall who was studying law at Melbourne University. He found vacation jobs for us both through the University Appointments Bureau at a sheet metal factory called Rayson's. This was about twelve miles from the centre of the city, a lengthy commute from Parkville, but on my first day a Dutch worker called Paul Willemsen offered me a room at his house in Keilor, a village two or three miles further out right on the outskirts of Melbourne. If you stood in Paul's pocket-handkerchief garden facing south, you had fifteen miles of suburbs and city in front of you. Turn around and there lay the bush, with not a lot between you and Cape York except 1,867 miles of parched red earth.

Paul had a Maltese wife, Lucy, and two children, both of whom were born with club feet. The chances of a second child having the affliction is remote and they were exceptionally unlucky. Moreover, they had moved from Holland, a country with a comprehensive health service, to a country with no free health service. Paul had spent £2,500 in the previous two years on specialists. The surgical boots, which the children grew out of every three months, were so expensive at 24 guineas a pair (four times the cost of the Chelsea boots I habitually wore) that Paul who, unlike Max Jelley in New Zealand, had no shoe-making experience, taught himself to make his own.

The cottage with its red galvanised iron roof was a fairly representative working-class Australian dwelling and I suppose the Willemsens, club feet apart, were a fairly representative working class migrant family. The house did not have hot running water and the weekly bath was taken in a tin tub that we filled with buckets of water drawn from the copper outside. Nor was there any other indoor sanitation. The call of nature was met by a wooden 'dunny' at the bottom of the garden. In after years, if I was accused by socialists or their ilk of having enjoyed a cotton-wool existence, I would enquire whether they had ever lived in a house with an outdoor lavatory.

There were no books in the house other than the Holy Bible – we were all Catholics – and a complete set of the latest edition of the *Encyclopedia Britannica*. These were in their original cartons and had never been removed from them, but I was assured that as soon as the children were old enough they would be introduced to this cornucopia of learning. The Willemsens had a touching faith in the power of the printed word to effect self-improvement, and I did not voice my doubts that children brought up in a non-reading household would find their own way through the twenty-two volumes of the world's knowledge without guidance. We worked long hours at Rayson's and when we arrived home, Paul's cultural wants were met by whatever cowboy movie was on our black and white telly in the living room. Jeff Chandler was his favourite, usually playing a tough hombre whose fists spoke louder than words. That was Paul's kind of man.

The hours at Rayson's were twelve a day from Monday to Thursday and eight on Fridays and Sundays. We did not work on Saturdays because Ezekial Archibald, the proprietor, was a Seventh Day Adventist. Rayson's had won a contract to install an air duct system for the paint shop of the Ford factory at Niddrie, running halfway across the roof, then through it and underneath. This was to provide an environment free of dust in which the finished cars could be paint sprayed. The contract had to be completed by 15th January, with escalating penalties for every day over. Mister Archibald and his foreman kept us all pretty busy.

In my various hotel jobs there had been a simple them-and-us divide between management and staff. In this strange new world of the factory I found that status depended on your trade. Whenever I met someone for the first time, the opening question was not 'Where are you from?' or 'Have you worked in sheet metal before?' but 'What's your trade, Sport?' I would confess that I did not have a trade and the 'Oh … uh huh?' in response spoke volumes. I was, for the first time in my experience, at the very bottom of the social heap. I was unskilled labour in an environment in which craft skills were highly prized.

*I am constantly amazed at the complex and difficult tasks assigned to untrained workers*, I reported home. I was pleasantly surprised, though, to find my fellow workers, most of whom did have a trade, to be friendly and welcoming. I had read of neophytes being put through embarrassing and sometimes painful initiation rites in factories, but there was nothing of that kind at Rayson's. In a way I think my lowly position in the hierarchy of labour helped: I was no threat to them. Also unexpected was the range of their interests and how well informed they seemed to be on matters far removed from their personal experience. I have already castigated the Melbourne University students I had met, who only talked about sport and sex. There was also a group of schoolteachers who were habitués of Peter's oyster house. They only talked about sex. On my first day at Rayson's a dozen or so of my fellow workers sat around a work-bench to eat their sandwiches at lunchtime. The conversation turned to the Boer War and whether Britain had provoked it in order to annex the Transvaal. The sort of conversation one might anticipate in the company of university students or schoolteachers, in fact.

My first few days were spent on the factory floor, but then I was moved to the Ford factory, where it was my job to push quarter-ton sections of air ducting across the thirteen acre roof, the largest in Australia. It was like working in a giant frying-pan. Now mid-summer, the temperature each day was a scarcely varying 104°–106°F. To obtain water you had to clatter down four flights of metal stairs to where there was a single faucet. This was out of order and you could only extract a few drops at a time from it, just sufficient to wet your lips and make you yearn for a long draught of ice cold water. Daily complaints were made to Ford's management. Nothing was done about it.

Meanwhile David, having spent one blistering twelve hour day on the rooftop, had found himself a cosy niche back at the Rayson factory. There were a number of calculations that needed to be made for most of our constructions. Many of these could be performed by simple arithmetic. David produced the same results by differential calculus and somehow convinced the foreman that this was essential to Rayson's productivity and ability to deliver the Ford contract by 15th January. Thereafter he was closeted in a snug little out-house, away from the banging and crashing and heat and dust of the factory, and had endless mugs of tea and sometime a bologna sandwich delivered to him by the foreman to keep his brain cells functioning.

Meanwhile we had laid the air ducts across the vast roof of the Ford factory and were busy making a big hole in its surface to bring them from outside to inside. Our next task was to extend the duct under the roof as far as the paint shop.

There was nothing on the underside of the roof except narrow girders in a criss-cross pattern. We were to lay the duct across these and, balancing ourselves on the cross-girders, rivet the sections together. Have you ever used a rivet gun? They recoil. So picture this. Me, barely able to change a light bulb, balancing on a three-inch-wide girder forty feet above a concrete floor, with nothing to hold on to, and needing both hands to operate the rivet gun. And did I mention the hard-hats? There weren't any. Not that they would have been much protection if you fell forty feet on to a concrete floor.

The recoil of the rivet gun threw you backwards about half a foot. So you leaned forward six inches, squeezed the trigger of the rivet gun, and if you had judged the distance right, ended up in a vertical position on your narrow strip of girder. Then you would lean forward again and inject the next rivet. For twelve hours a day, in 104° heat and rising.

This is the kind of thing factory workers do to earn a living. It is why most of the population would prefer to be middle-class and sit at a desk in a comfortable chair slurping coffee and exchanging banter with mini-skirted office girls.

*The recoil of the rivet gun threw you back about half a foot ...*

. . .

Our short, eight-hour days on Fridays were so that Mister Archibald could close the factory gates before sunset. That was when his Sabbath began. The short day on Sunday was to enable those of other faiths to worship in the evening. Paul and I would attend St Albans, the Catholic church in Sydenham (Melbourne also replicated London place names). Lucy had attended earlier with the children. About three weeks before Christmas Father Driscoll announced that there would be the customary Christmas stockings for the orphans of the parish. He would give out slips at the end of mass and these would tell us whether our orphan was male or female and how old. My slip told me that I had to fill a stocking for a fourteen-year old boy. It also assured me that I would receive a personal letter from the recipient.

A lot has been written since then about the terrible abuse suffered by children in Australian orphanages, some of the worst afflictions being those perpetrated in Catholic institutions. I am glad that at least the poor little perishers each got a stocking at the end of their bed on Christmas morning. I spent the following couple of free Saturdays ransacking the chain stores in Fitzroy and Yarra for the kind of things I would have liked to have found in my stocking when I was fourteen. There was a small Bakelite camera, I recollect, and a die-cast model Spitfire and a moulded relief map of Australia with the mountain ranges sticking up, and several practical jokes like the bleeding finger and the dog turd, and a kaleidoscope and a bow tie that lit up when you pressed a concealed bulb and some miniature comics and some poker dice and a kazoo and I don't know what else, but lots of things, and wherever there was an inch of space left in the stocking I rammed in another candy bar or chocolate money. Everything was wrapped in a different design of Christmas paper, because that is what I liked when I was a kid. Don't know why.

Meanwhile Lucy was having palpitations about the turkey. Paul had never tasted turkey before and in previous years they had been too poor to buy one. Lucy did not know how to cook it but was determined to learn. Paul bought a live turkey three months prior to Christmas and then spent large sums of money on fattening it up. On 23rd December he left work at noon to spend the afternoon first slaughtering, then plucking the bird, but as that cost him £6 in lost wages, altogether it would probably have been cheaper to have gone to the Victoria Market and bought Melbourne's champion dressed turkey. Lucy incurred further expenditure on a roasting tin capacious enough to harbour the giant bird and an American cookbook of turkey recipes. This latter contained detailed instructions on how to cook turkey in every conceivable way except simply roasting it. But as Lucy could not read English anyway, this was an additional expenditure that might have been better forgone. I was relieved when the recipe book joined the unread *Encyclopedia Britannica*s though; otherwise we might have had deep-fried turkey with hominy grits and hush puppy sauce.

Never having cooked a turkey myself, but having watched my mother do it, I now proffered my advice. 'Shove it in the roasting tin, rub some butter over the crown, bang it in the oven. Baste every 20 minutes. Remove when it is golden brown all over.'

'Is that all there is to it?' asked a relieved looking Lucy.

'Except the trimmings,' said I.

'Trimmings?' repeated Lucy falteringly.

'Essential trimmings: roast potatoes, gravy, brussels sprouts, chestnut stuffing, chipolata sausages, bacon rolls, bread sauce, cranberry sauce. Some people like to have a ham on the side....'

Lucy's face fell. Paul came to her rescue. 'The turkey's the thing,' he declared. 'None of that other stuff matters.'

I tried to make him see the light. You cannot eat a roast turkey on its own. We argued each trimming and one by one they were eliminated from the menu until we got to the cranberry sauce. I think Paul only agreed to that because he knew cranberries were unobtainable in Australia. I set off on a cranberry sauce quest that took me from one end of Collins Street to the other. Every high-class grocery was canvassed. Few had ever heard of cranberry sauce, but there was one that did stock it. Normally. This year their supply had been held up in Canada. Then somebody told me that Qantas served cranberry sauce on Christmas flights to England. I went out to Essendon Airport and tracked down the Qantas catering manager. He confirmed that they did serve cranberry sauce at Christmas, but they did not stock it themselves. They sourced it from a Chinese grocery near the airport who had it flown out once a year from London to supply Qantas. (Flown out by Qantas? Why didn't Qantas simply buy some in London for their own use?) I found the Chinese grocery and they had three pots over, surplus to the reserve they were holding for Qantas. I returned to Keilor in triumph.

The turkey was also a triumph. Paul declared that if he found that he didn't enjoy turkey after all that preparation, he was going to throw the darnn thing over the back fence for the dingoes to scavenge. In the event he ate enough for three or four average trenchermen. The magnificent bird was accompanied by a rather untraditional Asian dish of chopped cabbage and prawns, plus the cranberry sauce – scarcely touched by my host and hostess – and iced beer for the men, Marsala for Lucy. She, poor girl, had stopped looking haggard and careworn for the first time since the Christmas decorations went up. This was the Willemsens' first proper Australian Christmas and everything was new to her. I had found her wrapping the children's stockings in Christmas paper and had to explain that the empty stocking was hung at the end of the child's bed on Christmas Eve and would be filled by Father Christmas, with a bit of help from Mum and Dad, after the little ones had gone to sleep. They did not have Christmas stockings in Malta.

On Boxing Day we drove to the historic gold-rush town of Ballarat and took photographs of each of us standing on his or her head to send to our relatives in our respective Old Countries. (Just to prove that we were upside down of course.)

Then it was back to work. I confess I did watch the post over the next few days, as I was eager to know how my fourteen-year old orphan had enjoyed his mammoth Christmas stocking. But no letter came. It was well into the New Year before I hesitantly asked Father Driscoll about it. 'Ah, Patrick,' he exclaimed, looking a trifle uneasy, 'I've been meanin' to talk to you about that, indade I have. You see, your stocking was twice as big as anyone else's and it had three times as many presents in it. So we thought it would be fairest if we divided your presents up among the other stockings, to make them all about the same. You don't mind do you now, Patrick?'

Of course I minded. I wanted my fourteen-year old orphan to have his best Christmas stocking ever.

'Not at all, Father,' I replied. 'I am sure you did what was best.'

. . .


We were now nearing the deadline for completion of the Ford contract and Mister Archibald, one of the most energetic men I have ever met, drove himself and his overworked employees to ever greater feats of productivity. I wrote home: *Only ten days to go. I have never been so cut and bruised and blistered and calloused. Working on construction is very fatiguing, and believe me factory operatives are worth every penny they earn. It is also very humbling to see the way that men who can scarcely write their own names are able to mould and bend and weld a lump of metal into a useful, complete and finished product. And that we, people like David and me, who are supposed to be clever and educated and fit to lead, can only stand by and hold things and try not to get in the way. Big Bill from Denmark said to me the other day, apropos a heavy piece of ductwork that had to be raised – 'This time you do the liftin' and I'll do the gruntin',' which I thought was rather droll.*

The completion deadline was midnight on a Saturday, after which Mister Archibald had to pay penalties for every day over. But Saturday was his Sabbath, which began at sunset on Friday.

That final week was more arduous than any other I had worked. Mister Archibald began to reveal his inner Simon Legree as he strove to complete about two weeks of remaining work in only five days. The last day was the worst, with not a single minute of relief from lifting, cutting, sanding, bolting, grinding, welding, riveting and sealing. That morning we had driven to the Ford factory in the dark to begin work with first light just after 6 am. Sunset was at 8.43 pm, but according to Seventh Day Adventist doctrine, the workday was only completed when the doors of the Rayson factory were closed and bolted. The distance from Niddrie to Rayson's was about five miles. By the superhuman efforts of Mister Archibald and the rather more human efforts of the rest of us, the whole job was finished at just after 8.30 pm. But we still had to get back to Rayson's and stow the gear before sunset.

Mister Archibald drove the five-ton truck back through the industrial suburbs that separated Ford's and Rayson's in fading light at speeds that never dipped below 80 mph except when he was screeching round corners on two wheels amidst a stench of scorched rubber. The foreman in the passenger seat gripped his arm in an effort to slow him down but to no avail. In the back of the truck the rest of us crouched on the floor watching the houses and factories passing in a blur and wondering whether each moment was to be our last. I could see that the lips of several of my companions were moving and I have no doubt who they were addressing, as He was the same as the One whose favour Mister Archibald sought by imperilling all our lives. Paul and all we other Catholics crossed ourselves.

With a squeal of brakes Mister Archibald brought the truck to a dead stop on the forecourt of the factory, hurling us all backwards and on top of each other. The foreman sustained a nasty bump on his head from the windscreen. As we sorted ourselves out, Mister Archibald had already flung himself from the cab and was rolling back the doors. The sun now displayed but the merest slither; within seconds it was going to disappear from view and it would be the Sabbath. 'Don't go into the factory,' Mister Archibald commanded. 'Throw the gear in from here.' We did as we were told. Expensive items of precision-made equipment, drills and sanders and rivet guns and welding arcs, were thrown from the back of the truck about fifteen or twenty feet on to the concrete floor of the factory. Several broke in the process, but Mister Archibald urged us not to falter. As the last one crashed on to the floor with a scream of splintering metal, Mister Archibald lunged at one of the sliding doors and hurled it along its groove in the concrete as the foreman did the same with the other. They came together with a thunderclap and Mister Archibald bounded towards the clasp that held the two together and snapped the padlock shut. As he did so the last faint glimmer of the sun was extinguished.

. . .

When I had finished recalling that frightening and bizarre episode for this memoir, I did a quick Google to see if Rayson's was still going. There it is in the Yellow Pages: Rayson Sheet Metal Fabricators, 203 Princes Highway, Hallam, Vic. Hallam is in South Melbourne, so they have moved, but still going after fifty-five years. What happened to Mister Archibald, I wonder? I have very mixed feelings about him. I admired him tremendously for his skill and vigour; he could perform any of the tasks that our skilled tradesmen in the factory carried out, and often quicker and better. He was a demanding employer, as he needed to be in such a competitive business, but scrupulously fair to his men. He treated unskilled hoi-polloi like David and me with the same respect as he did his aristocrats of labour. And yet he could have killed us, or other road users, in that mad dash to be back before sunset. What would his standing with his co-religionists have been had he done so? Would he have been applauded for placing the tenets of his faith before all other considerations, above even life itself, or would he have been condemned for behaving in a way that most would see not only as sociopathic but also as unchristian? Would he himself have regarded death or injury as a worthy price to be paid, as the will of God? I remain mystified.

. . .

I left Melbourne and returned to Sydney and spent a month there, living in a cheap hotel in Kings Cross. I made excursions to the towns that had grown up in Sydney's wake when the first generation of emancipists started receiving land grants and the pioneer free settlers began to arrive, places like Windsor and Richmond, Liverpool and Camden. This was during the Regency period, the time of Jane Austen's novels. The horrors of transportation and the penal system have been so graphically described by Robert Hughes *et al* that there is a common belief, both in Britain and Australia, that all convicts were innocent victims, transported for stealing a rabbit to feed their starving children, and that the penal colony itself was a place of unrelieved cruelty and misery. There is another side to this partial view of Australia's extraordinary beginnings.

Few of the convicts were transported for minor crimes; most were recidivists, professional criminals of whom many had been convicted of violent crimes. Those starving poachers? Out of 164,000 people transported, only twelve were poachers. Eleven of those had killed a gamekeeper. Yet despite this unpromising material, the policy of successive governors was to give those who kept out of trouble in the colony a second chance. Land grants enabled those with a will to work to become farmers and with large numbers of convicts to be fed there was a ready market for their produce. Others became entrepreneurs, opening pubs and shops or small manufacturing ventures like sawmills and ropeworks, or operating as traders, sometimes with their own ships. Sydney's first two restaurants were opened as early as 1803, both by ex-convicts (one of them a woman).

Of course not all convicts prospered; some were reconvicted for secondary crimes (often committed against fellow prisoners) and of those who won their freedom, many fell into destitution and want. But the opportunities were there for those with the energy and enterprise to seize them, opportunities that did not exist for the labouring classes in England.

Their children were the first generation of native-born white Australians, whose descendants, along with descendants of free settlers, transformed a penal colony into a nation.

. . .

Many of my excursions into Sydney's hinterland were made in the company of Rustic Richard Williams, now parted from Robin who had crossed over to Perth in Western Australia. Robin invited me to join him. Much as I loved Sydney and its historic environs, unemployment was high. Perth was in the right direction for home. I decided to accept.

I wanted to travel across the continent by train, but was informed at Central Station that you needed to book six months ahead. Why, if there was such demand, did they not run additional trains? Australia in the 1960s was an extraordinarily inefficient country. A surprising number of travellers whom I encountered did not enjoy their new life in the sun. Robin was one of them; he disliked almost everything about it, particularly the hostility of some Australians to the English and the fact that many basic services functioned so poorly. All that has changed. Australians have stopped being hostile and learned to run efficient services. It is hard to find any visitor today who does not fall in love with the sunburned country. How did this transformation come about? I have studied Australia's 20th century history in some detail and yet I am at a loss to explain it, though thankful that ultimately this nation with such a tainted beginning has become such a laudable success.

With no rail option available, I flew to Perth. I had a stopover in Adelaide, which I was eager to see as my Uncle Louis had visited it before the First World War and had praised its beautiful parks encircling the inner city and the stately mansions that bordered them. Parks and mansions were still largely as they had been in Uncle's day and the city, unlike busy, bustling Sydney and Melbourne, was pleasingly somnolent in the hazy sunshine. The flight from there to Perth was some 1,500 miles and we flew below the clouds, so I had a view of that seemingly endless emptiness. There were occasional tracks in the bare, reddish-brown earth, but they disappeared over the horizon and served no apparent destination. After 400 miles we passed over a farmstead, then again nothing. How did these farmers survive in such isolation? Another 400 miles and we passed over a small town. I have examined the map and the flight path suggests that it may have been Rawlinna, a speck in the desert with a post office and a neighbouring 2½-million-acre sheep station of the same name. I checked the next nearest place, wondering where you would go from Rawlinna if you wanted a pint. The answer is Kambalda, a quick spin of 217 miles and there you will find, per Wikipedia, a choice of two pubs as well as a supermarket and a public library. So, only an eight hour round trip when you needed to return your library book.

Another 450 miles of barren nothingness and we alighted at Perth, the world's most remote metropolis. If you live in Perth you are as cut off from the world as you are in Rawlinna. Your nearest city is Adelaide, 1,674 miles away and, as my flight had shown me, with precious little in between.

So what of Perth itself as a place in which to spend a lifetime? 'Perth is very beautiful', everybody in Sydney intoned when I told them I was heading west. Looking back, I now realise that these were people who had never been to Perth. They had been told by other people that Perth was very beautiful, but these others hadn't been to Perth either. Very few people had. There wasn't a lot to go there for unless you were into yachting. And I am now going to reveal Perth's best-kept secret.

Perth isn't beautiful.

The Swan River is beautiful. Kings Park, which overlooks the Swan River and is the largest city park in the world (150 acres bigger than Central Park), is beautiful. The rest of Perth has all the loveliness of a very large Swindon.

It was certainly sizeable. When I arrived the population was 500,000 – it is now over two million. The city centre comprised three commercial streets running in one direction and two commercial streets crossing them. Within this area were two substantial hotels, the Adelphi and the Palace, a branch of David Jones department store, His Majesty's Theatre, two or three cinemas, City Hall and assorted churches. I do not remember any restaurants, though I am sure there were places you could get a good meat pie. I guess the nearest proper restaurant was in Adelaide. The rest of Perth consisted of suburbs, almost identical in appearance, for the fourteen miles between the city centre and Fremantle. I have a Betjemanesque regard for suburbs and I loved the concentric rings that surrounded Sydney, so that coming in on the train you receded in time from modern to inter-war, then Federation, and finally monumental Victorian with traces of Georgian as you entered the city proper. But Perth was just a huge conglomeration of undistinguished little box-like houses of indeterminate period, lacking any distinction. It was in one of these featureless suburbs, Mount Lawley, that Robin lived and I joined him there. Mount Lawley had a single claim to fame: an absence of pubs. When this former bushland was designated as a suburb in 1901, Lady Lawley agreed to it being named after her husband, a former governor of Western Australia, only if no licensed premises were allowed.

I had left Sydney, with which I was enchanted, because of the high unemployment, only to find myself in a city singularly lacking in enchantment with an even higher rate of unemployment. There were no vacancies at Robin's hotel, the Adelphi, but I found a berth at Perth's No. 2 hotel, the Palace. This was a majestic Victorian pile in St George's Terrace, with a wealth of mahogany empanelling its interior, a naked marble Venus in the foyer, a profusion of ferns shielding the bits of Venus that might have over-excited the more sheltered West Australians, and an effusion of brass, most of which it was my task to polish. I also operated the antique lift, reputedly the first in Western Australia, dating from the opening of the hotel in 1897. Elsewhere in the world lifts had by then been in use for thirty years, enabling cities like Chicago and New York to build upwards instead of outwards, but at the time that the three-storey Palace was built, there were few other buildings in Perth with more than two storeys and the majority were bungaloid.

Apart from polishing and elevating, I had little to do other than serve drinks. Perth had yet to become a tourist destination, so the guests were businessmen, airline crews and visiting sportsmen. The latter included the Australian cricket team, tongue-tied young men who blushed every time they were addressed by ravishing blonde Kathy in Reception. There were also a few resident guests, including a wealthy widow called Mrs Macfarlane who occupied the largest guest suite in the hotel. She would meet Mister Jacques, the manager, each evening at six for a glass of cream sherry before dinner and each Saturday afternoon a gleaming Daimler would glide to a halt at the bottom of our entrance steps and Mrs Macfarlane would depart for the races in an elegant hat and a cloud of Chanel. Apart from this weekly exeat, she never left the hotel and she received no visitors. It must have been a lonely existence, scarcely relieved by the fawning attentions of Mister Jacques.

The manager was a small, rotund Dickensian character who spent most of his working hours harassing his staff and criticising everything they did. He probably had a complex about being so small. One day when there were six stewards on duty to serve only eleven guests he stared at me hard for a long time trying to find some fault. Eventually he ventured, 'You walk like Felix the Cat.' There was quite a long interval before he had a further inspiration. 'Don't.'

The tedium of life at the Palace and in Mount Lawley was occasionally interrupted by casual work at the Adelphi. Until 1936 the Palace used to play host to most of the banquets and other junkets of the great and good that took place in the remote post-colonial capital, when the splendid art deco Adelphi, co-designed by Western Australia's first woman architect Margaret Pitt Morison, usurped its position as the go-to place in Perth. One of these functions was for the West Australian dairy farmers, relaxing after a hard day conferring about milk yields. All I was required to do was circulate with a tray of drinks for an hour and a half and then wash up the glasses while the dairy farmers made speeches congratulating each other on their butter and cheese output. The washing up became a party, as we casual waiters finished off all the part-empty bottles of wine and spirits. After that we were given a hot meal and then led into the mezzanine bar to fill in our time sheets, which we were told could include the time spent eating. This seemed very generous of the Adelphi, or maybe of the unwitting Western Australian dairy farmers, and our gratification knew no bounds when management sent in several jugs of beer to top the evening off. We had catered for one party and enjoyed two of our own. I have to say that this liberal approach to the labour force and bestowal of just rewards was not uncommon in the comparatively relaxed atmosphere of the Australian workplace, though not in the one presided over by that undersized tyrant Mister Jacques.

An altogether grander occasion was the celebration of the eighty-seventh birthday of Wine & Food Society founder André Simon by the West Australian Wine & Food Society. It came as something of a surprise that Western Australia had such a thing, given that it was based in a city without restaurants and that Australian viticulture at this time had scarcely advanced beyond that favourite of the anaemic, Emu Tonic Wine. Nevertheless its members gave a good account of themselves, swilling an average of six cream sherries each before progressing to a substantial dinner that was accompanied by three white wines, two red wines and a champagne, and concluded with port. Monsieur Simon, one of the few Frenchmen who has distinguished himself on the cricket pitch, scarcely touched his wine glasses. Whether this was to keep himself in training for the wicket or a commentary on the quality of the wine I know not. I reported home that, despite this modest intake, he made a very voluble speech and sounded just like Maurice Chevalier, while in appearance he had Mark Twain's head on GK Chesterton's body. He was, I opined, 'an old dear'.

Monsieur Simon revealed to the assembled company that he had been a winebibber for eighty-six of his eighty-seven years and that he always smelt his food before tasting it. Moreover, if he did not like it when he had tasted it, he spat it out. 'Nobody has to swallow food to be polite,' he declared. Hmm, not sure about that one. One other idiosyncrasy attracted my attention: he pronounced the Bordeaux wine *Graves* in the same way as pits for the consignment of corpses. As we washed up afterwards we counted over 500 glasses, a remarkable number for sixty or seventy diners.

I worked split shifts, so did not get off until late. It was too far to return to Mount Lawley during the afternoon, so I tended to flop around in the stewards' room, which had day-beds, as there was so little to do in Perth. One day, however, finding that an English boy called Michael was off at the same time as me, and that he had just acquired a rattly old Holden, I suggested we went bush together. I had been told by another steward about a monastery at New Norcia, eighty-two miles to the north, where the Benedictine monks made a raw wine in the Spanish style, and which was sold at the local hostelry. There was nothing to be seen at New Norcia, he said, but it was worth going to taste this local firewater at the pub, which unusually was run by aboriginals. (Aboriginals were banned from drinking in pubs, so this would be a bit like having an English pub run by the Band of Hope.) Michael was up for it, so we doffed our white jackets and bow ties and leaped into the Holden.

*I have had very little chance to see much of the bush, so I was as pleased as Punch to be going for a drive,* I wrote home. *Most of it consisted of parched undulating country, wooded with gum trees, many of them blackened stumps. It is very monotonous. We crossed the Darling Ranges, which are a low range of hills you could just about run up if you had a lot of puff. We made the eighty-two miles in just over two hours. The country here was just like the bush in Victoria and, Michael assures me, like every other part of Australia. New Norcia proved to be an extraordinary settlement. We had expected to see a cluster of shacks and a service station like the other villages we had passed through. But this consisted of half a dozen enormous palaces and a Spanish church, a shop, a mill and a dilapidated hotel about the size of Gleneagles.*

*The palaces were built in a variety of styles. One looked like the Hollywood conception of an English public school, another like a Foreign Legion fort in the Sahara, another like a Moroccan harem, or a huge pink birthday cake, and another, vast but less palatial, like a row of towering Glasgow tenements. We went up to the hotel, where we found no abos and no wine. The wine was sold only in Perth, we were informed. However, we had a pie and a glass of beer and learned that New Norcia is the Vatican State of Western Australia, and here there was a boys' boarding school, St Ildephonsus', a girls' boarding school, St Gertrude's, an aboriginal boys' orphanage, St Mary's, an aboriginal girls' orphanage, St Joseph's, and a monastery. Some bushies in leather hats with the brims turned down against the sun were discussing hedge posts. Conversation in New Norcia tended towards the pastoral in either sense.*

*We walked down to the mission church, passing a number of semi-naked aboriginals on the way. The church was of the Spanish adobe style seen in California. It was built by Father Salvado in 1847 and had a rude beauty. The rough walls inside were painted in brilliant greens and golds. It was very strange and remote from anything Australian. The bush, for all its monotony of landscape, has many surprises, so contrary to what the steward told me, there was no wine but much to see*

Having consulted Google images, I think the 'palaces', of such architectural distinction and so detached from their habitat, must have been the boarding schools and the orphanages. There is a sad and sinister coda to my description of this happy day out. In 2017 Australia's Royal Commission into Institutional Responses to Child Sexual Abuse revealed that the incidence of tacitly sanctioned abuse by Roman Catholic priests and members of religious orders had been over three times more prevalent at New Norcia than Australia as a whole. Seven per cent of RC priests and brothers in Australia have been accused of abuse between 1950 and 2010. In New Norcia the figure was 21.5%. Who knows what horrors were being perpetrated behind the high walls of these strange buildings while

Michael and I ambled around them marvelling at their alien presence in the desert landscape.

. . .

By now Robin had saved sufficient for his passage back to England and he departed with heartfelt expressions of relief at leaving Australia. Despite his antipathy to the country, though, it was to make his fortune. His plan had been to buy a farm on his return home, for which he estimated he would need the loan of £12,000 from his father. When this was not forthcoming, he did something much more enterprising. Robin had noticed that in Australia and New Zealand there were more qualified herd testers than there was demand for their services, whereas in Britain the reverse was true. So he set up an agency to bring these young colonials to Blighty on short-term contracts. He arranged with the Foreign Office to fast-track their visas, which they were willing to do because the scheme had eager backing from the Ministry of Agriculture. My roly-poly little friend, with his teapot-handle ears and limping gait, now cut a deal with British Airways' head of passenger traffic to fly his protégés to London at cut-price fares. Robin received a commission on every booking. He built up a large and prosperous business.

I wish I could report that Robin lived happily ever after. Sadly not. He married a very beautiful but wayward working-class girl who began having affairs not long after the wedding. Robin was devastated and fell into a deep depression. His wife left him and he was living alone in a farm cottage in Warwickshire. One night he consumed several glasses of whisky, then placed a plastic carrier bag over his head and tightened it round his neck. His body was found two days latter. It must have required enormous courage, or singular desperation, not to tear off the bag as the air in it was exhausted.

. . .

After Robin had left Perth, his place was taken during my leisure hours by Gérard, the Mauritian cadet manager at the Adelphi and a keen poker player. Robin had introduced us the night before his departure from Fremantle aboard the *Marconi*. Our new poker school also comprised an

Englishman called Andrew Wise who had been a crocodile-hunter in New Guinea, a cherubic pink-and-white young New Zealander called Roger Cook, a neophyte producer with ABC and later to earn fame and fortune in Britain with ITV's long-running *The Cook Report*, and a swashbuckling adventurer from Texas called Bob Nelson. Bob, generally known as Tex, was deeply envious of Andrew for having blasted so many crocs out of the swamps of New Guinea (as well for his tall, elegant girlfriend perversely named Dumpy), but Andrew could not compete with Tex's record as a diamond prospector in Venezuela, a bullfighter in Mexico, and a freelance fighter pilot for Fidel Castro during the Cuban revolution. The poker games were lively affairs, offering rather more fun and frolic than was on offer elsewhere in Perth.

It was not uncommon in those days to hear Australia castigated as a cultural desert. This was unfair. Sydney and Melbourne, and to a lesser extent Adelaide, had vibrant art and literary circles. Australian publishers had a remarkable output for a country with a limited market. But all this activity took place on the other side of the country. None of it touched Perth, let alone anywhere else in Western Australia. Tex would fulminate about this over the poker table, protesting that he had been in some pretty isolated places in his time, but none so far from civilisation and the creative life. (Tex, like my friend Norman, had ambitions to be America's next Ernest Hemingway – hence the bullfighting exploits.)

There were, however, people who worked in related fields in Perth. People like Roger Cook, turning out his own radio programmes at the age of twenty, and his square-eyed colleagues over at Television Western Australia (TVW), where Rolf Harris had been the first live performer. TVW was owned by the venerable *West Australian*, another sanctuary for the kind of people who wore their hair half an inch longer than the customary short-back-and-sides. Added to that there were aspiring poets, novelists and painters, even if none of them had yet to knock Patrick White or Sydney Nolan off their pedestals. But whereas in Melbourne and Sydney the whole arts coterie tended to congregate, straddling the disciplines with musicians hanging out with writers and thespians with painters, in Perth the small number of creatives was not only isolated from the wider world of the arts but also from each other. Where were the smoky dives, the attic clubs, the back-alley bars that proliferated in other metropolitan cities, demanded Tex.

'Don't just moan about it,' we urged Tex. 'Do something about it.'
And much to our surprise he did.

It was called the Melpomene Club, a name that might have suggested
it was for singers and dancers had prospective members known what the
name meant, but not many Perthians had been subjected to a classical
education (a blessing I envied them). Usually the first requirement for the
aspirant club-owner is some working capital, but Tex hadn't any. In fact,
after a couple of poor nights at the poker table, he was broke. Properly
broke, cleaned out, after his knave-high full-house had succumbed to a
king-high ditto. Andrew, principal beneficiary of Tex's misfortune, kindly
advanced him £30. It was not a huge amount on which to float a new
commercial venture in an environment as conservative as Perth's.

The budding entrepreneur simply ignored the normal dictates of
success or failure. He found a disused and partly derelict restaurant in
Subiaco that he was able to lease against future earnings because nobody
else would have contemplated its use. There was no hot water, no cooking
facilities, and no electric light. Nor did the premises have a licence and
the prospect of obtaining one from the uptight Perth licensing authorities
was nil.

None of this deterred Tex for an instant. His fellow poker players
and Dumpy were enlisted to give the place a paint job and repair the bits
that were admitting the elements. He spent most of the borrowed £30 on
buying a large log, which he proceeded to cut into two-foot sections and
three-foot sections. The former served as seats and the latter as tables.
On the tables he placed candles in Chianti bottles. For lampshades he
procured several dozen children's balloons, inflated them, and then stuck
one-inch squares of coloured tissue paper over them, an arduous task for
which I was conscripted. When you pricked a pin in the balloon, you were
left with a perfect tissue paper globe to place over the candles. Fire hazard
was not in Tex's vocabulary.

Once the place was clean and relatively decent, Tex announced that
the membership list was open to anyone who was active in the creative
arts. This was given a fairly broad interpretation. I was eligible because I
was writing a book of firsts. Gérard got in because he had had a painting
displayed in the 'Under 16' section at the 1955 Mauritian Société des Arts
et Métiers *vernissage* in Port Louis. Andrew Wise produced a copy of
the *Old Harrovian* containing an ode to sardines on toast that he had

contributed and Dumpy's admission was approved because she had come second in a dance contest in Coolgardie. Roger Cook was one of the few members with a bona fide creative provenance.

The subscription fee was three guineas and this allowed you use of the club for nine months. After that, Tex said, it would close. The reason for this cut-off date was that Tex had already been in Perth for three months and he declared that he would never stay in a domicile for more than a year. There were too many places in the world to see and experience. By opening night he had managed to attract nearly 200 members, so he was able to repay Andrew's £30, re-engage in the poker school, and live for the next nine months on the paid-up subscriptions while devoting himself by day to the Great American Novel.

The club itself provided a further income stream. The lack of a licence was got round by allowing the members to keep their own stash of liquor on the premises. In practice any member in good standing with Tex could buy liquor from under the counter. The police made regular raids but never succeeded in catching Tex in the act and everyone found drinking swore that the liquor came from their private locker. Hot food was more difficult, but we contrived some primitive biscuit tin-and-candle cookers of the kind I had used in 'Patrick's Pie Palace' at Mount Cook and were able to offer soup and stew with crusty bread. The stew contained potatoes and vegetables, so was a one-pot meal. Dumpy and I were alternately chef of the day.

While the Melpomene Club took care of Tex's temporary financial embarrassment, I am not sure that it fully achieved its loftier aim of stimulating the intellectual life of Western Australia with the kind of discussion of new directions in the world of art and letters, drama and music that he had been accustomed to on the boulevards of Paris. The prevailingly English clientele had a distressing tendency to talk about their cars, while it was hard to divert the Australians to the contemplation of verse or painting from two standard topics, sport and their sexual adventures, real or imagined. I tried to persuade Tex that if that was what educated young men talked about without respite in Sydney and Melbourne, his prospects of elevating their conversational interchange in Perth were unfavourable. He was not easily dissuaded, and would corral anyone with some kind of performing talent to entertain the members. Dumpy did a somewhat provocative dance on one of the log tables, while Gérard would stand on the bar and sing Mauritian folk-songs.

I have never been much of a public performer, being unable to learn lines and having a singing voice like a corncrake, but I was not to be let off. Tex would stand me on a log table and invite any member to challenge me with the date and place of a famous first. This turned out to be surprisingly successful and I was able to answer questions as diverse as the first air stewardess (Ellen Church, United Airways, 1930), the first author to submit a typewritten manuscript (Mark Twain, *Life on the Mississippi*, 1883), the first crossword puzzle (*New York World*, 21st December 1913), the first raincoat (French Guiana, 1749) and the world's first full-length feature film (*The Story of the Kelly Gang*, Melbourne, 1906). Roger Cook was particularly taken with this memory act and invited me to the ABC studios to perform it on radio. The £8 that I was paid for this was the beginning of what would eventually become a fairly lucrative speciality in firsts. I would later repeat the 'Memory Man' jig on LBC whenever Jeremy Beadle ran out of more enticing guests for his late-night show.

Tex was the consummate host. I was particularly impressed with his ability to remember the members' names, but he informed me privately that most Australians share half a dozen between them, and whenever a group came through the door he would sing out 'Hi Dave, Hi Bruce, Hi Jim, Hi Dick, Hi Don,' and they usually responded enthusiastically. An out-of-the-way one like Egbert he remembered by association, shape of ears etc, but generally this was only necessary with the English members.

Tex's valiant efforts to bring Parnassus to Perth may have been mostly ill-rewarded, but these were jolly nights that we spent in the flickering candle-light of the Melpomene Club. For me, though, they were soon to end, because I had booked passage aboard the *Southern Cross* to Durban.

. . .

While the nights were full of fun, my days were not. The Palace Hotel employed a moon-faced, flap-eared simpleton called Albert to do the worst job in the place, cleaning the floors of the public bar. Like most antipodean hotels catering to the upper crust, the Palace also provided for an ocker clientele with a spit-and-sawdust tap-room letting directly on to the street (so that the likes of Mrs Macfarlane would not have to cross their path). It was time for Albert's annual holiday. Whither he departed, since he had no family, I know not, and there were not many options in

West Australia. But off he went. And Mister Jacques, perhaps dissatisfied that I still walked like Felix the Cat, appointed me in his place.

It was, I think, the worst, and certainly the most degrading job I have ever had to perform. Public bars in Australia are, or were then, all-male places of resort, and the habits of their denizens were what you would expect, ranging from coarse to unspeakable. It was my twice-daily task to swab the floors on hands and knees, clearing them of spit and mucus and urine and vomit and occasionally other forms of human waste. Mister Jacques would often stand over me, pointing to some blood or snot that I had passed over or making me pick up soggy cigarette butts in my bare hands. Why he had such a dislike for me he never revealed, though I think it more likely because I was a Pom rather than because I was middle-class. Aussies, to their credit, seldom made class distinctions. I was several times tempted to lift my bucket of filthy water above his head, which would not have required raising it very far, and upturn it over his little bullet head and his immaculate manager's suit, and it was only the sacrifice of my remaining few weeks' wages, essential to pay the bond required by the South African authorities, that restrained me.

It was without sorrow then that I left Western Australia. Peter and Michael, the English stewards, threw a farewell party and came to see me off at Fremantle. While we waited for embarkation to begin, we went to a tea-room by the dock. The tea came in one of those stainless steel pots with a spout designed to channel the tea down the side of the pot and over your jumper and your crotch. I exclaimed in mild despair, 'You'd think they could make a teapot that poured the tea into the cup!' At once a voice from behind me, couched in the nasal whine that signified the young Australian male with a grievance, shrilled 'If you don't like our bleedin' teapots, why don't you go back to your own bleedin' country?'

I picked up the tea-pot and scanned its base. The inscription confirmed, as I suspected, that it came from Birmingham. 'There wouldn't be much point, Sport,' I observed to my interlocutor, 'in going back to the bleedin' country where this bleedin' teapot was made.' I did not give him the satisfaction of knowing that I was about to set sail on the first leg of my journey back to that bleedin' country.

. . .

It was not infrequently remarked, back then, that Australians had chips on both shoulders. Of course it was not true of all, but there was enough truth in the allegation to create an atmosphere of discomfort bordering on hostility in ordinary, everyday social interchange. I am thankful to say that it is a syndrome that scarcely applies anymore. In the previous chapter I said that the New Zealand of the early sixties was something like an unruly teenager. If that was so, then Australia was like that teenager's truculent elder brother. Both countries matured into nations which are everywhere held in the highest regard. Each punches well above its weight in the councils of the world. They have both made notable contributions to culture well beyond their own shores.

I was to make many return visits to Australia, and each enhanced my respect and admiration for its people and their achievements. I have written a book about their notable innovations, ranging from the domestic refrigerator to the container ship. On one of my excursions down under, I drove with a book-collector friend the whole 20,000-kilometer perimeter of the continent, from Darwin back to Darwin, visiting 189 second-hand bookshops on the way. I have probably seen more of its cities, country towns and outback than most people, including many Australians. And I have come to accept this spirited people's own contention that they have the good fortune to occupy God's Own, the lucky country.

# Chapter 12

. . .

# APARTHEID IN CLOSE-UP

. . .

*May–June 1964*

I do not think that many of my fellow passengers aboard the *Southern Cross* would have aspired to membership of the Melpomene Club. Among the few whom I characterised in a letter home as 'cultivated' was the Dowager Lady Baden-Powell, Chief Guide and widow of the founder of the Scout movement. An Australian asked to be moved from her table on the second day out after she had interrogated him at dinner about Australia's balance of trade.

There were three others with the Queen's English and they happened to be my cabin-mates. One was named Jonas Asplin, a recently qualified lawyer who seldom spoke other than to recount anecdotes about the Duke of Devonshire. I think there may have been some kind of family connection. Then there was Robert Erith, 6ft 4in tall and the double of the Duke of Kent, under whom he had served with the Scots Greys in Hong Kong, much to the confusion of visiting top brass. He became accustomed, he told me later, to being saluted by generals. The self-appointed leader of the team, who were planning to drive from the Cape to Cairo in a Land Rover, was one Campbell Gordon Douglas, a smooth-talking Lothario who devoted the days at sea to shipboard conquests and his nights to doing whatever it is that heirs to Scottish estates do with smitten colonial maidens.

At first this trio were a bit aloof, probably thinking, correctly, that a provincial boy from the suburbs would be far removed from the glamorous world of debs' delights that they inhabited in London and would have little in common with them. On the third day out Robert Erith came into the cabin holding a month-old copy of *The Times* that he had open at the court circular. 'Is your father a friend of the Prime Minister?' he ventured.

A recent letter from home had suggested what this might be about. 'Not a close friend,' I responded cautiously.

'Close enough to get invited to Number 10 for lunch, though,' he chuckled, pointing to an item below the court circular.

My father did not habitually break bread with the likes of Sir Alec Douglas-Home. It so happened that his best friend from boyhood, Jim Fielding, who was CEO of Gloucester steel-makers Fielding & Platt, had that year been elected Chairman of the Iron & Steel Federation and the invitation to No. 10 was in recognition of this. Those invited were allowed to bring a male guest (why not their wives?) and 'Uncle Jim' invited his old chum to accompany him. I think my father met only two famous people during his life, the other being the character actor Laurence Naismith in the 1920s. So this was pretty special for him.

As indeed it seemed to be for Robert. 'Splendid, splendid!' he exclaimed, folding up *The Times*. 'Are you free to join me and the other chaps in the bar on A Deck tonight?'

Now you, dear reader, would have probably said 'Shove it! You didn't want to know me yesterday, why do you want to know me today?' But we suburban boys from the provinces are made of lesser stuff, so I meekly thanked Robert for his kind invitation and agreed to meet at six. And so the trio became a quartet.

. . .

It was for this reason that when I disembarked at Durban, I failed to meet up with my long-lost cousins, the Purnells. The four of us rushed down the gang-plank and hailed a couple of rickshaws to take us to the Royal Hotel, where we relaxed under the sporting prints in an oak panelled bar being ministered to by a magnificent Sikh barman in a bejewelled turban.

Meanwhile the Purnells, expecting to meet a lone traveller, were scouring the docks for me. Suffice to say that before nightfall we had found each other.

Hitherto in this travelogue there has been no odyssey of moving from one distinguished family to another. And indeed this is not about to change, because the long-lost cousins were distinguished in no way except their utter respectability – an African version of my own suburban heritage – and their overwhelming niceness. I make no apology for the fact that this chapter of my story is about people who led very ordinary lives in a very conventional environment. Because those ordinary lives were led in the conventional environment of apartheid.

Most of what follows will be verbatim transcripts from my letters home. These give a white middle-class perspective of apartheid, but I think have a certain interest in depicting the racial conflict as it was perceived by English-speaking South Africans of my cousins' background. In essence, they did not see it in terms of white versus black, but Afrikaner versus their own people. (Strange that there is no generic for English-speaking South Africans.) The division between the two white races had long historical antecedents, but by the time of which I was speaking was largely about class (as is nearly anything that involves the British) and of course politics. The white working classes in SA were largely Afrikaner; the professional classes were largely English-speaking. Government, and government employment, was dominated by the Afrikaners and had been since the inception of the Union of South Africa in 1910.

Although the Union, a federation of the former Boer republics of Transvaal and the Orange Free State and the British colonies of Natal and the Cape, had given SA dominion status – in effect independence – only eight years after the defeat of the Boers, every government from then until the accession of Mandela was lead by an Afrikaner. Until 1948 the political parties they headed had represented both white races, but the National Party that came into power that year and launched the policy of 'different separate development' – *apartheid* – was almost exclusively Afrikaner. The opposition United Party was almost exclusively English-speaking. The attitude of the UP's adherents towards apartheid was confused; they were broadly in favour of a racial division allowing white hegemony, but deplored the casual cruelty with which the agencies of the Afrikaner state – government, police, military – enforced it. There were three parties that opposed apartheid, the Liberal Party, the Progressive Party and the illegal Communist Party of South Africa. The first two were predominantly English-speaking, whilst the latter was inter-racial and also had a strong Jewish following.

I came to South Africa with an open mind about apartheid. Given what we now know about the excesses of the ruling National Party's treatment of the non-white races, such indecision may seem naïve. Bear in mind, though, that this was the year in which the Rivonia Trial found Mandela and his fellow proponents of the 'armed struggle' guilty of terrorist acts. The whites had good reason to fear this relatively new departure in the ANC's resistance to apartheid. Consider also that South Africa, despite its fanatically hard-line government, had preserved, and would do so until its eventual downfall in 1994, an independent judiciary and a free press. It could not, therefore, be characterised as a totalitarian state. And despite their deprivation of liberty under apartheid, the non-white races enjoyed a higher standard of living than the indigenous population of any other African country. There were even millionaire entrepreneurs (mainly Indian), so it appeared that they were not denied every opportunity for advancement.

It did not take long for the scales to fall from my eyes, as the letters reveal. Two points about them that I should mention. References to 'the Dutch' signify Afrikaners. I cannot remember whether my cousins and other English-speaking South Africans called them that. It is certainly a misnomer. Prime Minister Verwoerd, whose family emigrated to South Africa from the Netherlands in 1903 when he was an infant, launched a campaign to entice well-educated Dutch emigrants to South Africa because he thought they would assimilate with the Afrikaners and dilute English-speaking dominance of the professions, media and arts. The real Dutch were horrified both by the cultural poverty of their Afrikaner cousins and their extremist politics and became UP supporters to a man and a woman.

The other point relates to Uncle Harry and his use of the forbidden N-word. Uncle Harry was amongst a small minority of English-speaking South Africans who supported the Government and its excessive racial policies. He was also in a minority with his use of the N-word. Afrikaners called black people 'kaffirs' or 'munts' – probably no better, but more allowable because liberal Americans, ignorant of these words, are not offended by them. If you are an American reader, it is probably safer to skip the rest of this chapter.

. . .

My cousin Leslie Purnell's family had emigrated to South Africa in 1902, as soon as the Boer War had finished. There was already a connection with Natal through some other relatives, the Cullingworths, pioneers who had come out two generations earlier in 1850. Leslie was the first member of his family born in Natal and was known to his siblings, much to his disgust, as 'the Little Colonial'. He was an accountant, married to Leila, a small dumpy woman of forty-five who had spent her youth representing Natal on the hockey field. There were two well-behaved children, John aged six and Peta aged four. Their comfortable family home was at 392 St Thomas Road on the Berea, a select suburb on a ridge overlooking the city and harbour.

The Purnell residence was an Edwardian villa that might have been in Virginia Water or Sunningdale. *There is nothing about it to indicate you are in Africa*, I noted, *except three native servants padding about. Their names are Sabu, who had his hand cut off by a street gang, but manages well with the other, and Dora and Lulu, both very fat and indistinguishable. They are very deferential, but appear to be happy. They are paid £5 a month and live in the servants' quarters at the back of the house. Each has a small room with whitewashed walls and stone floor, with an iron school-bed standing on bricks. Dora is a Catholic, but still has recourse to the witch doctor in moments of panic. (She lost her first child due to his ministrations.) Sabu is a heathen. He had a look at all the Christian churches with a view to joining, but does not care for any of them. His chief love is boxing, and he holds a boxing school in the backyard every night, which Leslie encourages, helping to buy their gloves.*

*The servants start at half six in the morning and finish about seven at night. They have a half-day on Sundays. Leila says it is more than a half day, because they do not have to come back in the evening, but I don't see that this follows. Their diet is mealies, boys' meat* [inferior meat fit only for 'boys', as male bantu of all ages were known] *and a variety of vegetables. These they make into hashes and stews, boys' meat needing a lot of cooking to be edible. They also eat a lot of avocado pears and aubergines and things that in England are an expensive luxury. There is always a sack of avocados in the garage and this costs two shillings. I asked Leila what happens when they start to go black and she told me they throw the rest away and buy another sack. The servants are very fond of tea, which is sold in special sixpenny packets for them.*

*Domestics are improvident and don't save much money, but most of them send some home to their families. Their general conditions seem much the same as that of English domestics before WWI. They spend money on clothes, as bright and varied as possible, musical instruments, native beer and gambling. The girls also buy native magazines, which are published in both English and Afrikaans, and books of picture strips in photographs, the characters all being natives of course. These are quite pricey at 1s 6d.*

*The servants are very polite and always smile when they say good morning. They move silently and serve silently. They never snatch a plate nor bang it in front of you. The food is spirited to the table and wafted away again. They do not wear shoes in the house. Sabu has a uniform of white ducks and white jacket. When he converses with Leslie he bends on one knee. Leslie takes a paternal and somewhat feudal interest in their well-being and activities. When Sabu had his hand cut off he and Leila nursed him for a month.*

*On my first night in SA there was a stabbing case on the premises. A 'boy' had been eating an apple when another 'boy' asked him for one. He said he did not have a second one. Whereupon Boy No. 2 drew a throwing knife on the end of a piece of string, and threw it at No. 1 whose cheek it penetrated right through to the gums, damaging two teeth. Thereupon there was a chase, and No. 2 ran into our backyard, where Sabu was conducting his boxing class. Boy No. 1 followed and seeing his aggressor, shouted in Zulu 'Lay hands on him!' No. 2 tried to escape but was overpowered. At this point we entered the picture and Leslie rang the police. They came and took No. 2 away. It appears that this was his third assault of the evening, and that he is also suspected of murdering a policeman. Thus I have come face to face with violence right at the outset.*

*Penalties are very severe for natives. Only this week a 'boy' was sentenced to ten lashes for 'wearing a police button'. There was no question of impersonation. He was merely wearing it for decoration. The magistrate said that he considered ten lashes a lenient sentence. If you inflict ten lashes for such an offence, how do you punish a thief? Flog him to death perhaps. The South Africans insist that harsh retribution is the only practical course in a deteriorating racial situation. Whether this be so or not, surely there can be no justification for flagrant cruelty and abuse of the natives.*

*Leslie told me about Uncle Harry, who throws things at his 'boys'. He shied a shooting-stick at an errant gardener so hard that it bent; he hurled it at him again to straighten it out. This sort of thing is considered uproariously funny. I wonder.*

. . .

First impressions of this turbulent country had been mixed; the peace and calm of a quiet suburban household suddenly disrupted by an apparently senseless crime, but what kind of society breeds such meaningless violence?

The day after my arrival there was a report in the *Natal Mercury* about the nine-year old child of white parents who had been reclassified by the Race Classification Board as 'coloured' (ie mixed race). This was in response to a complaint from a parent at the child's school who objected to her own child having to consort with a non-white. There was no record of miscegenation in the child's ancestry, but it is biologically possible for black genes to skip several generations. The child was not allowed to sleep under the same roof as its parents, so had to be accommodated in the separate servants' quarters. The insensitivity with which the authorities handled the case turned it into a *cause célèbre* and recently there has been a very compelling film based on it.

On my first weekend with them, the Purnells drove me to Pietermaritzburg, capital of Natal and a bastion of British values within the recently created Republic. Leslie drove me past the venerable Victoria Club so that I could see the Union Jack flapping in the breeze on its rooftop. Or rather the Victoria Club ensign, since that is what a combination of the flags of St George, St Andrew and St Patrick were designated by unanimous vote of the club committee when the Afrikaner authorities sought to ban it following the declaration of the Republic.

It was arranged that we should have a *braaivleis* in the attractive public park. This park, Cousin Leslie explained, was open to all races. Since the introduction of apartheid, however, it had been necessary to make separate recreational arrangements for whites and non-whites. The important thing, he told me, was that there were facilities for all – that was what separate development meant.

John and Peta were keen to play on the swings and we made our way to the white children's playground. This was laid out immaculately on a green sward. The kids were soon happily swinging and squealing (not allowed at home) in the busy playground, evidently a popular venue for Maritzburgers, and I wandered off to find the non-white children's playground. It was in a far-away corner of the park. A meagre collection of rusting swings and slides stood in a large clump of stinging nettles. As few black children wore socks or stockings, access would have been at the cost of stung legs. Not surprisingly the playground was deserted.

When the children were sated with swings, we began the *braai*. While we were munching away, a solemn little black girl came and stood a few yards away from us and stared at our food with hungry eyes. Peta was chewing on a bun. 'Give the little girl the rest of your bun, Peta,' admonished Leila. Peta, obedient child, did as she was told and held out the half-eaten bun. The child took it in both hands, as was the custom among her people. She stared at it for a few moments in seeming disbelief at her good fortune before stuffing it in her mouth and, suddenly shy, turning and running speedily away. I watched this trivial incident transfixed. It was like some nineteenth-century morality tale about the obligation of rich children to the poor. But I think what disturbed me was that the bun was *half eaten*. Would well-meaning Leila have instructed Peta to give a partly consumed bun to a needy white child?

On the way home John pronounced that he would like to be a duck. After thinking about this for a while, he added, 'Provided I could be a white duck.'

. . .

*South Africans are very preoccupied with politics,* I wrote home. *Perhaps this is an understatement. They burn with zealous political fervour which lights the wrongs of the world and the rectitude of South Africa by day and by night. They are intensely concerned with their image overseas. Uncle Harry happened to remark, as one does, that he had shot a damn nigger that afternoon and Cousin Peter was deeply concerned. 'Harry', he remonstrated, 'you must not use that word in front of an Englishman.'*

*(The victim? He survived.) Political discussions don't get far, though, because all the participants agree with each other. The Boers vote one way, the English-speaking South Africans another, and the damn niggers not at all. So there is little room for argument unless you are on calling terms with an Afrikaner, which few seem to be. Nevertheless the government is minutely dissected over every tea table. Apartheid is never mentioned by name. It is referred to as 'our policy'.*

The reference to Africans not having a vote will cause no surprise, but it may enlighten some to learn that under Cecil John Rhodes, excoriated in recent times in Britain as an arch-racist, they did have the vote. When the Afrikaners came to power with the creation of the Union of South Africa in 1910, their first act was to disenfranchise the blacks in national elections. Yet in the Cape, Rhodes's old fiefdom, an African was elected to the Provincial Parliament only a few weeks later and held his seat for five years until defeated in a democratic vote – by another African. Racism was never far from the surface in pre-apartheid South Africa, but was not as all-pervasive as some would like us to believe.

The wicked N-word was not the only one prohibited in front of overseas visitors. Leila reproved Leslie for saying he had been to the bioscope lest I, or any other foreigner, should perceive South Africans as old fashioned. (I am happy to say that 'bioscope' and its diminutive 'the bio' have survived into the twenty-first century.)

I was still struggling to be open-minded about apartheid. *The whites' main justification for 'our policy' is that the natives are far better off in SA than in other parts of Africa. To which I would say – so they should, as this is the most prosperous part. But then I do think they should be given credit for the efforts which are being made in housing, education, and provision of amenities. The slum clearance schemes are particularly impressive. At present a big drive is being made for better schools for the blacks and higher education, but the appropriation is pitiful compared to that for white education. There are 75,000 native nurses, 70 doctors, 70 librarians, and 50 lawyers. It seems painfully small out of a population of 13 million but then it is probably better to grant higher education on a strictly selective basis, than to any too-clever-by-half young firebrand who might become a willing tool for communism.*

Cousin Leslie had doubts about educating Africans above their station, as he believed the unsophisticated tribesman was more dependable. This view seemed to be derived mainly from his relationship with Sabu the houseboy. I recounted this anecdote from Leslie's repertoire: *The first time that he went on leave back to his kraal, Sabu arrived back here a week early. 'Why have you come back before your holiday is up?' Leslie asked him. 'Well Baas,' Sabu explained, 'I didn't know how long a month is, and I didn't want to return late.' The next year when he went away Leslie noticed that his luggage had been reduced from all his possessions in brown paper parcels, as per the previous year, to the bare necessities in a single suitcase. Leslie asked why. 'It's like this, Baas, the first time you have a whole month to yourself, it seems like a very, very long time. Then you go away and find that a month is a very, very short time.'*

*Uncle Harry says he does not care for Sabu because he smiles too much. Friendly niggers, according to Uncle Harry, are no damn good.*

• • •

Uncle Harry lived at Umhlanga Rocks, north of Durban, with his daughter, Cousin Pam. I was invited to stay, and as I had never met anyone quite like Uncle Harry before, I complied. It was a small household, with just one outdoor servant and one indoor. *The houseboy has been with Uncle Harry for forty years*, I reported home, *which only goes to show that if you treat them badly enough they will stay with you until their dying day.* One day I referred to the Kaffirs, which I thought was acceptable parlance because the Kaffir Wars were still called that and the language spoken to the servants by their mistresses was Kitchen Kaffir. 'You mustn't use that word, Patrick', Uncle Harry admonished me. 'The niggers don't like it.'

*Uncle Harry declares that whatever people say about South Africa not being a free country*, I wrote, *it is free if you don't go about making trouble. And all the trouble-makers are Jew-boys. All Jew-boys are communist. Life is uncomplicated to Uncle Harry.*

Generally Uncle Harry was an unspeakable old rogue, steeped in the attitudes of a generation prior to his own. He roundly pronounced that he would never shake hands with a DN, at which Cousin Pam and her Cousin Bobby, who was visiting, said of course nowadays you must extend the normal courtesies to a native. They are human, Pam added, and have the same feelings as us. Uncle Harry snorted and Pam said that was the difference between the generations, and with changing attitudes she saw hope for South Africa. Uncle Harry snorted again.

They say there is good in everybody and even Uncle Harry could behave out of character. He had gone out into the garden to throw things at the DN there, but found him asleep under a tree. Instead of taking a sjambok to him, Uncle Harry tip-toed back into the house. 'Ach, it's such a warm day,' he explained. 'Who wouldn't want a nap in the shade?' I wondered whether Cousin Pam and Cousin Bobby would have been so indulgent.

*Cousin Pam knows someone who bit Cecil John Rhodes,* I reported home. Rhodes had died in 1901, so we are talking serious history here. *Moreover it was the Headmistress of Durban Ladies Collegiate (for the Daughters of Gentlefolk). When Miss Williams was a small girl she wore her hair very short. Cecil Rhodes, a frequent visitor to her home, thought she was a boy, and always used to greet her with 'Hullo Little Feller.' This made Miss Williams very disgruntled. She repeatedly asserted that she was a girl, but the Prime Minister either couldn't or wouldn't take this in.*

*Came the day when the architect of modern Africa said Hullo Little Feller once too often, and Miss Williams went for him, fastened on to his ankle with her sharp little teeth, and bit him hard.*

*As Rhodes died the same year Miss Williams can probably also claim to be the very last person to have bitten him.*

*Cousin Pam took me to see Cousin Bobby's sister Cousin Barbara. Her houseboy is a witch doctor,* I reported. *I have never met a witch doctor before. Cousin Barbara allows him to see his patients at the house. He charges five guineas for a consultation, a little more than the monthly wage of a domestic. The Zulus are very reluctant to entrust themselves to an MD and prefer to have their evil spirits cast out by a real witch doctor. There is a witch doctor in the Transkei whose fortune is estimated at R6 million (£3 million). Very few Africans become rich any other way. Of course the Transkei millionaire has multiplied his fortune by speculation, and he has twelve trading stores and sixteen farms as well as his lucrative practice. There are some as say he knows where the Kruger millions are hidden; it is not impossible, for his father was Oom Paul's ox-driver.* (Paul Kruger was President of the Transvaal.)

* * *

On my return to Durban, Cousin Leila, aware of my interest in South African history, conducted me to Dr Killie Campbell's private museum – admission by appointment only. Dr Campbell, heiress to an immense sugar fortune, had spent the whole of her long life – she was at this time eighty-three – pursuing her passion for Africana, building a library and a collection of South African antiquities that was without rival. In her youth she would travel to London regularly with her mother and spend halcyon days roaming the back streets in search of second-hand bookshops and frequenting the auction houses, where she frequently paid over the odds until she learned about market values. By World War II her immense library had swelled to 20,000 volumes. She had the life that every collector dreams of: being able to devote all your waking hours to the pursuit of new acquisitions and the conservation of old ones in an environment dedicated to the collection. In Dr Killie's case, it was her grandiose mansion in Marshall Road on the Berea, a lovely neo-Cape Dutch edifice built by her father in 1914.

*It is a fantastic collection*, I reported, *and includes Napoleon's dinner service and Marie Antoinette's toilet mirror (which her father used to shave in). Home and museum are one, so there are no red ropes or 'Do Not Enter' signs. The Doctor is surrounded by a coterie of fawning maiden ladies who do part-time duty and worship her like adolescent schoolgirls do their games mistress. 'Dr Killie says this ... Dr Killie says that...' they whisper in awed undertones. When we had been shown round by one of the minions (there was also a staff of fifteen servants, including an imposing black butler of stately mien) we were escorted to Dr Campbell's boudoir, where we were entertained to tea on wafer-thin bone china by the goddess herself. Besides Leila and me and the American minion, who is clearly in love with her mentor, there was a young authoress, a very silly Dutch woman and her English husband, tomato and egg sandwiches and cup cakes. The silly Dutch woman proceeded to monopolise the conversation, which was all about her distinguished relatives, and her distinguished self. Her undistinguished husband never opened his mouth.*

One of the difficulties of writing a memoir at more than half a century's distance is the tricks memory plays. I distinctly remember meeting an Afrikaner for the first time, none of the many social gatherings at which the Purnells had introduced me having included anything as exotic. And not just any Afrikaner, but General Botha's daughter. Surely she cannot have been the silly Dutch woman who prattled on about her distinguished relatives? They were indeed distinguished: her father, after a meteoric rise to high command during the Boer War, had become the first Prime Minister of the Union of South Africa and one of Britain's staunchest allies during World War II, while her Irish mother Annie had helped to broker the peace negotiations that ended the Boer War. But which daughter did I meet? There were two, Helena and Minnie. I have checked out a portrait of Helena at about the time that I encountered a Botha daughter at Dr Killie Campbell's, and the stately *grande dame* depicted, with whom in her youth Winston Churchill is reputed to have had a dalliance, does not accord with my description of a silly Dutch woman. The other daughter Minnie? Possibly, but the mystery lies in the fact that the lady I met made a very distinct impression on me for a very particular reason. On either the first or second occasion that I was entertained to tea by Dr Campbell – I was invited back on another day to inspect her collection of nineteenth-century century South African periodicals – I met a daughter of General Botha who told me that her father had taken her mother, her sister and herself to the British lines under a flag of truce and asked that they be placed in a concentration camp.

The concentration camps of the Boer War are notorious and are widely though erroneously believed to have served as a blueprint for the death camps established by the Nazis. It was singularly unfortunate that the British chose this designation for what were in fact internment camps, but the very high death toll has given them the reputation of being dedicated to the extermination of Boer women and children. A total of 4,000 Boer women and 22,000 children died in the camps, mainly of enteric fever, and this is indeed shocking – the reason it may have happened, largely overlooked by historians, is examined in the next chapter in my account of meeting the engineer who built the concentration camp at Pretoria. It was probably this camp in which Annie Botha and her daughters were interned. The daughter that I met explained that her father had asked for them to be taken into custody because with all the Boer men engaged in hostilities, there was no one to ensure their safety in what was at that time a battle zone.

The General himself recorded, 'One is only too grateful nowadays to know that our wives are under British protection', an unusual sentiment coming from perhaps the most prominent of those who were seeking the downfall and destruction of these same British, but then it was an unusual war in many respects. The General's daughter told me that as a child in the camp she was largely unaware of the high mortality rate – possibly as a family of distinction they were afforded special treatment – and had never felt bitterness towards her captors. But all this comes from memory. Although my letters home reported every encounter of significance, they bypassed this one, other than the references to the silly Dutch woman. I have no explanation for the oversight.

One day Leslie told me that Cousin May from Pietermaritzburg, of the Cullingworth branch of the family, was coming to lunch next week and it was hinted in a roundabout kind of way that it would be a good thing were I to be on my best behaviour, not that I was ever on anything else, they hastened to assure me. An almost visible air of tension began to overtake the Purnell household during the days leading up to the visit. It was rather as if Queen Mary had announced that she would be dropping by. When Cousin May arrived in a chauffeur-driven car of great antiquity I began to see what all the fuss was about. She was a distinguished old bird with a ramrod-straight back, gloves to her elbows, and a choker of diamonds. Perhaps more Lady Bracknell than Queen Mary, though I am sure she would have regarded the latter as a social equal.

As instructed I did not throw bread rolls at the dinner table or wipe my nose on my sleeve. The visit passed without any noticeable upsets, the servants were becomingly obsequious, and the children conducted themselves as if they had stepped out of the pages of Kate Greenaway. The ancient but gleaming limousine glided away amidst mutual protestations of goodwill.

That evening Cousin Leslie took a telephone call and by the way he stiffened on hearing the voice at the other end I guessed it was Cousin May. Leslie's end of the conversation sounded like a subaltern conversing with a general. When it was over he turned from the phone and declared with a look of relief, 'You passed!'

'I passed what?' I enquired.

'The test. I thought you might have guessed that Cousin May's visit today was to inspect you. She wanted to see if you held your knife like a pen, that kind of thing. Anyway you didn't, thank goodness. So you've been invited to stay with her in Maritzburg.'

He paused. 'Well, I wouldn't call it an invitation exactly. It was more like a summons.'

Cousin May's son Cousin John, who lived in Durban, motored me up to Maritzburg and gave me some useful family background on the way. The South African patriarch was Jeremiah Cullingworth, who had come out from Coventry in 1850 and started the *Natal Times* the following year, soon to be superseded by the *Natal Mercury*, which survived apartheid and is still with us today. His daughter, Cousin May, was married to Septimus Pape, headmaster of Maritzburg College from 1925 to 1937, a classical scholar who was wont to converse with his deputy in Latin. Besides John they had an elder boy, Cousin Lewis, who had recently emigrated to Australia.

Given Cousin May's regal manner and appearance, it came as something of a shock to learn that she was regarded by the Afrikaner authorities as one of the most dangerous leftists in Pietermaritzburg. She and both her sons were very active members of the Progressive Party. Indeed the reason for Lewis's abrupt departure was that he was likely to have been arrested had he stayed. John was also under surveillance.

*Cousin May was looking very stately and grey and gracious,* I reported of our arrival. *She is one of the grandes dames of Pietermaritzburg society and her domestic environment reflects this. Her new house, which she designed herself, is groaning with antiques. Not only superb furniture, including a Stuart chair with the Crown carved on the top, but also Ming china, Raphael drawings, Battersea enamel, sixteenth century Italian pottery, eighteenth-century English silver, Meissen porcelain and a collection of rare Africana, including three of only four known copies of the* Natal Times, *the first newspaper published in Durban.*

Over lunch, served by a butler only marginally less stately than the majestic figure who presided over Dr Killie Campbell's household, Cousin May explained some of her political philosophy. The English-speakers who supported the United Party – the official opposition – were preoccupied with a strongly held belief that the Afrikaners were seeking to marginalise them in South African society and their chief aim was to counter that. They saw this as a higher priority than securing human rights for the Africans, justifying their stance with the assertion that with a significant English-speaking element in government, the betterment of Bantu peoples would automatically follow. Cousin May and her fellow activists in the Progressive and Liberal Parties believed that the UP were expending their political energies wastefully, because nothing short of revolution was going to dislodge the National Party from its unassailable position of total power. But the Progressives were confident that revolution could be engineered peacefully by winning the support of world opinion and bringing diplomatic pressure on the government. The alternative was armed insurrection and the direction the African National Congress had taken since 1961 suggested that this could be the shape of the future.

There was, of course, an element of self-interest in this posture; May and other liberally-minded whites wanted to preserve the South Africa they loved. In order to do so they were prepared to share power with the non-white races. As history unfolded, and Mandela achieved the peaceful transition to majority rule, it was this prognosis by the Progressive Party, which never had more than seven MPs at one time in parliament, that proved to have a greater validity than that of the official opposition party supported by my Cousin Leslie and most other English-speaking whites.

Much of the time political debate was conducted at a rather less elevated level than the kind of measured discussion exchanged over the Papes' elegant luncheon table. Cousin May was frequently asked whether her opposition to apartheid meant that she wanted the butler to sit down with them at luncheon. To which she would enquire of her challenger whether they believed that the avoidance of such a social solecism necessitated the apparatus of a police state and the denial of human rights? No wonder she evoked the ire of the Afrikaner establishment in Maritzburg, adding fuel to the fire with her fervent devotion to the Empire. On 24th May, the Old Queen's birthday, she had led a cohort of ladies who presided over the teatime salons of Maritzburg to the leafy square where Queen Victoria's statue still looked out imperiously over the town and here they all raised their voices in the National Anthem – the one that had been discarded on South Africa's declaring itself a republic. Being left-wing in South Africa did not always involve a commitment to socialism.

On that busy first day of my visit we attended an antiques fair at Maritzburg's art gallery, then drove out of town for a tour of Hilton School, one of SA's two major public schools, and thence to Howich Falls, which are deeper than Niagara though of rather more modest volume. The excursion concluded with a tea party that I described in a letter home, since it epitomised for me the way of life that Cousin May so ardently sought to preserve, though within a multi-racial free society.

*We drove on through the rolling Sussex countryside (which is just what it looks like) past copses and spinneys, the Zulus on the road looking quite out of place. Eventually we arrived at a gorgeous house, Tweedie Hall, the home of Howard and Barbara Swan. It was long and low and whitewashed and thatched. I estimated probably late seventeenth-century, until I was told it was built last year. The Swans built it themselves, disclaiming a professional architect, which probably accounts for why it is such a beautiful house. (One architect told Barbara that the charm of it lay in all the mistakes.) Inside it was all chintz and* South African Tatler. *The drawing room windows commanded a sweeping view of the Wye Valley. I was sure it was the Wye Valley, and that somehow the drawing room looked out on to England. But there were Zulu kraals dotted about on the slopes of the pastures, so it can't have been. We went out on to a billiard table lawn, and inspected the swimming pool, which was about Olympic size. We went through a door into a walled garden, where large dogs with floppy ears were romping on the grass.*

*During a scrumptious tea we all listened entranced to Barbara who is one of those amazing mortals who does everything brilliantly and yet remains adorable in all respects. She has a very clever way of addressing her remarks to one person by name, but omitting nobody. This makes you feel as if you are being singled out for special attention. So one anecdote is retailed in sequence to each listener, rather than to them all as a group. I think I must try this and see if I too can be adored.*

*After tea we were shown the house, or rather we were consulted about the house. A priceless mahogany table was not merely displayed for our admiration, but each was singled out for his or her special appraisal. We were not mere guests called upon to gape, but connoisseurs of fine art called in for a consultation.*

*Upstairs there is a loft with an enormous picture window. The roof has been left untended, so that the ceiling is the underside of the thatch. Most fascinating. This room is devoted to the art of making a mess graciously, for they have two boys at Michaelhouse, SA's leading public school. Apparently they gave a teenagers' party in it, and decorated it as a Parisian boulevard. No mere spatter-dashing of French travel posters, but an authentic reconstruction of a continental street scene.*

*When time allows, Barbara has myriad activities outside this amazing household. She makes films. The Swaziland Government commissioned her to make a film. Now herein lies the art of how to be expert at something without appearing superior. Various professional film producers and Barbara were invited to display examples of their work to the government. After her demonstration they asked Barbara how much she would charge to make them a 1,000-feet film, i.e. a one-reeler of about twelve minutes. She said (to one of us) that she blushed to the roots of her hair, and then (to another of us) that she asked if ten guineas would be too much. Afterwards she discovered that the standard professional charge is 22s 6d a foot, thus £1,125 for a 1,000 ft film. She got the job, and when the Swazi government saw the finished film they were so delighted that they paid her a proper rate for the job. I decided afterwards that the reason she manages not to be superior despite her manifold talents is because in every field that she is an expert, there is always some aspect of which she is woefully ignorant. Or so she would have us believe.*

This enticing 'Sussex in Africa' was one side of my Cousin May's life, the other side being her political activism, to which I was introduced when we attended a protest meeting at Pietermaritzburg Town Hall. I reported: *The measure was the 90-day Act, by which anyone suspected of having any connection with, or knowledge of sabotage against the government can be arrested by any policeman without warrant, and held in solitary confinement for any number of ninety-day periods. The terrible thing about this Act is that any person, guilty or not guilty, can be held in prison WITHOUT CHARGE and WITHOUT TRIAL. The Chair was held by Professor Edgar Brookes of Natal University, and the platform consisted of representatives of all the major Christian Churches, and leaders of the Hindoos and the Muslims.*

*The speeches made by the Church leaders were horrifying. It appears that suspects are detained in isolation in a cell of no prescribed size, without legal, medical, or Christian aid. They are allowed to see nobody, neither doctor nor priest nor visitor, except their gaoler, their inquisitor, and once a week a visiting magistrate. At the end of the ninety days they can be detained another ninety days, and so on. No writing materials and no book other than the Bible is allowed. As one worthy churchman said, even his brother clerics might find that the Bible palled after three months of no other diversion. It was pointed out that the maximum solitary confinement allowed under the Geneva Convention is thirty days, and under British Law the maximum is two days in any one week. There is no reason to suppose that physical coercion is not resorted to, and if it is there is no redress.*

*The meeting was very well attended, there being some 400–500 of all races present. The vote in favour of the motion was 'carried unanimously except for two members of the Special Branch'. These two secret police were sitting right in front of us, and they looked a very sinister pair indeed. I would not care to be interrogated by them. Afterwards Cousin May introduced me to a woman whose husband has been in and out of prison for four years. He is leader of the Liberal Party. When he was first arrested they surrounded his home and flashed torches in all the windows. They took him away by night, and he was held for over three months without being charged. This was before the ninety-day clause had been enacted. He is in prison at the moment.*

The fact that such inter-race meetings were permitted, and moreover at the Town Hall, reflects the oddity of this state in which a certain degree of dissent was tolerated, yet only as far as an invisible red line. Cross that line and you were in serious trouble. Cousin May's son Lewis had already decided that life in South Africa as an opponent of the regime was intolerable and had decamped to Australia. Cousin John, at the time of which I write, had decided to abandon his job in government service. He had campaigned for the monarchy in the 1960 Republic Referendum and since then had been consistently passed over for promotion. He came to the attention of the authorities again when he very publicly resigned as a judge at the Royal Natal Agricultural Show in protest at a decision to exclude non-white farmers from participating. Soon after I left Natal, Cousin John was secretly warned that he was going to be detained under the 90-day Act. Rather than follow his brother down under, as a self-avowed leftist he decided to relocate to London, centre of the anti-apartheid struggle overseas.

On arrival John immediately sought out his fellow-leftists in the anti-apartheid movement. Disillusion was quick to follow. He had assumed that leftists in London would be similar to his own family, all of them proud to stand on the left in South Africa's very broad political spectrum while remaining ardent monarchists and upholders of British values. His new associates in London were equally ardent republicans and despised the traditional values of their own country as bourgeois and decadent. Many looked to the Soviet Union for a political lead. And while there were a few dedicated activists whose opposition to apartheid was genuine and founded on a sincere desire for racial equality, for the majority, as John found to his profound disappointment, the cause was no more than an opportunity to strike a pose as a dangerous revolutionary and to foment riots outside sports stadiums. Their knowledge of South Africa was minimal and empathy with people of other races non-existent. Sadly John packed his bags once more and set out for New Zealand. There, much to my regret, I lost track of him.

My fairly protracted visit to Cousin May was a restful and restorative interlude as I prepared to make my way north to Cairo, then home. There were visits to numerous estates and their owners in the neighbourhood, one of which featured a mansion in the Elizabethan style occupied by an elderly bachelor and his ten servants, one of whom had been with the family for sixty-four years. (He told me that he had no need for so many servants, but he loved them all so that he could not bear to see any depart.) There was a trip to Michaelhouse, SA's Eton to Hilton's Harrow, where I was regaled with tales of savagery and deprivation that evoked unwelcome memories of my own not very distant schooldays. And there were long, idle afternoons stretched out in an ancient armchair, losing much of its horsehair stuffing, in the faded lounge of the Victoria Club while I devoured buttered toast, *Punch* and *The Illustrated London News*. Around me senior members snoozed, perhaps dreaming of the Natal of their youth before the war. The Boer War.

It took little time for me to realise that Cousin May's somewhat forbidding demeanour and her imperious manner were a mask, perhaps assumed originally in order to deter presumptuous Afrikaners who thought they had a right to run Natal. Underneath was a warm heart and a surprisingly developed sense of humour. The latter first manifested itself over her business enterprise. The remnants of what had once been a quite substantial publishing business, including the flagship *Natal Mercury*, were two slender volumes titled *Cullingworth's Zulu Dictionary* and *Cullingworth's Zulu Phrase Book*.

Neither of these publications had been updated in forty years or so, but both were among the set books prescribed by the Natal Board of Education for use in all non-white schools. As such they provided a steady income stream. I came across them when I mistakenly opened a door in the hall thinking it was the loo and found that it let on to a cupboard filled to the ceiling with the volumes in question. The *Phrase Book* in particular I found very engaging. It contained phrases like *We English expect you Bantu to do what you are told when you are told* and *Stand up straight when you address your mistress.* John should have taken some to show to his fellow-leftists in London. The illustrations were charming, having no connection with the text but selected from a job lot of old printers' decorative devices of the late Victorian and Edwardian periods. I particularly liked one of a soldier in uniform and goggles tearing over a battlefield helter-skelter on a primitive motorcycle.

I told Cousin May that Cullingworth's Publications was probably the smallest publishing house in the world, certainly in a literal sense if you took the dimensions of the cupboard. I signified an intention to notify the McWhirter Twins of this new superlative for *The Guinness Book of Records* and she found this wryly amusing, shedding her Lady Bracknell persona to become more of a Margaret Rutherford. Thereon we shared all kinds of jokes and when we were not laughing together, she was telling me of some of the trials and tribulations of being a headmaster's wife and all about the growing pains of her two adored sons, one now in exile, the other probably even then contemplating his flight to safety. What had begun as a duty visit soon deepened into one of those cross-generational friendships that so enriched my youth. Now that I have reached the age that dear Cousin May was then, I strive to reach out to present-day millennials, though in an age that has become obsessed with 'inappropriate' relationships this can present its own challenges. (Our efforts, Karla's and mine, are sometimes rewarded. We are thrilled that Pieter, a young gay Afrikaner from the Northern Transvaal – they don't do gay in the Northern Transvaal – has invited himself to spend New Year with us.)

. . .

I have always been a timid traveller; my ideal is an escorted bus tour led by a charming, erudite and ultra-competent guide who allows you to disengage the practical side of your brain for the duration. Unfortunately this was not on offer on the Cape to Cairo route. You could fly if you had a lot of money or, if you did not have a car, you could hitch-hike. What I needed was a travelling companion, preferably one who was charming, erudite and ultra-competent, but I probably could not afford to be too choosy. I cannot remember what made me think that I might find this paragon – or a lesser paragon, or indeed anyone at all nuts enough to hitch-hike 7,000 miles to Cairo – in Basutoland. Why Basutoland, I hear you exclaim. Why indeed? This remote enclave, entirely surrounded by the hostile Republic of South Africa, was a mountain kingdom under British protection with some fairly scary local customs, of which ritual murder was one to try to avoid. It was certainly not a tourist destination and the only white people there were ex-pats working for the Basutoland government, rival groups of English Catholic and French Protestant missionaries, and refugees who had fled from apartheid South Africa together with SA government agents who flitted across the border to spy on them. Oh, plus a few Americans serving with the Peace Corps. But with the impetuosity and heady optimism of youth I set forth on this seemingly misguided quest.

The way to Maseru, Basutoland's capital in miniature, lay via Ladysmith, locale of the 118-day siege at the outset of the Boer War, when the invading forces of the Transvaal and the Orange Free State invested this small railway town and most of the British expeditionary force. One of the Boer commanders was General Louis Botha, whose daughter I had recently encountered over Dr Killie Campbell's best bone china. Less prominent in the campaign, but an even greater future leader on the world stage, was a humble stretcher-bearer named Mohandas Gandhi. This was the siege where hostilities were suspended on Sundays, and where neither side fired on stretcher-bearers like Gandhi removing the dead and wounded from the battlefield. This also was the siege at which the Boers, not normally noted for their sense of humour, lobbed over a mortar shell on Christmas Day containing a Christmas pudding, two Union Jacks and a message reading 'Compliments of the Season' (preserved in a glass case at Ladysmith Town Hall). The scene of all this I had to see.

My first letter home after leaving Pietermaritzburg not only reported what I saw but tried also to disentangle the topsy-turvy world of South Africa's race relations for the benefit of parents who found it difficult to comprehend how well-mannered, educated middle-class people could set their faces against authority and the forces of law and order.

*I travelled from Pietermaritzburg to Ladysmith on the train. It was a very nice train with compartments like English trains, so you don't have to travel with other people. Green leather seats and a wash-basin in each. Every compartment converts into a sleeping cabin, because most SA journeys involve at least a night on the train. My trip was only a full day though. Took sad farewell of dear Cousin May at the station, and soon we were puffing away across the Veldt. I had a nice cuppa tea and a piece of railway fruitcake and then settled down to read* Goodbye Dolly Gray, *Rayne Kruger's compelling history of the Boer War, and when I looked out of the window it was on to the scenes recorded in the book. I passed through Moon River, Estcourt, and Colenso, each a battlefield. I saw the place where Winston Churchill was captured by the Boers.*

*The Veldt is more undulating than I had imagined, and apparently in the summer it is as green as England. It is brown now in wintertime, but again not quite so desolate and barren as I had conceived. Very rocky though and with kopjes sticking out all over the place. Alongside the railway line there were little cemeteries and sometimes a solitary grave of some forgotten hero who fell for Queen and Country. I arrived at the little town of Ladysmith at half past three, and repaired to the Royal Hotel (there are Royal Hotels everywhere, and none seem to have changed their names). I had a not very nice cup of tea, and collected a letter from Mrs Benjamin Christopher, to whom I had an introduction, inviting me to dinner. Her husband 'Pitch' collected me and drove me through the sleepy town to their house on a hill. This house was Sir Frederick White's headquarters during the siege, and it was here that the young war correspondent Winston Churchill had an interview with the Commander. The room in which it took place is now the children's nursery. A short while ago the Christophers found Sir Frederick's dispatches in the attic. What a treasure.*

*I am anticipating. Before we went to the house Pitch took me up on to the top of a hill which commanded a view of the whole town, the British defences, and the Boer laagers. He is Ladysmith's foremost exponent of the siege, and he could tell me the exact placement of all the regiments, and where the Boer guns were based. Looking over this great panorama of town and veldt and hills it was easy to project back sixty-four years and see the conflict raging. Of course there are still many inhabitants of Ladysmith who remember the siege, and even some who fought in it.*

*I was introduced to Mrs Christopher, who appeared somewhat formidable, having red hair and horn-rimmed glasses, but turned out to be absolutely charming. She is a great humanitarian, and both she and Pitch are Liberal Party. Pitch has a secret service agent to shadow him. It is ridiculous, because Pitch knows him and when he comes out of his office and sees the agent lurking he goes up to him and says, 'I am just going up to so-and-so, if you would like to follow me. We will be turning off at the so-and-so road.' So far away in England this cloak and dagger business may seem unreal and you will think of the Christophers as sinister London School of Economics Ban the Bomb types. But they are so like any of your friends that if you were asked to place them, you would say 'Ah, they must be Painswick people.'* [Before Chipping Norton usurped its supremacy, Painswick was the epicentre of Cotswold high Toryism.] *Here, though, it is the working classes who are right-wing and the upper class and professional people who are left.*

*The reason for this is that if the Africans are elevated and given basic rights the first people to be affected will be the Dutch working classes. The Dutch do jobs which could quite easily be performed by Africans, but they are restricted to menial occupations by the Reserved Occupation Act. So naturally the Dutch are fighting every move towards equal opportunity tooth and nail, for even if they do not lose their own job to someone better qualified, they do not want to work beside Africans, nor even to have their fellow Boers doing so. Although it is possible to understand their fears, it is impossible to condone the methods by which they protect themselves. Dr Verwoerd was a Nazi sympathiser during the war, and he has chosen to use Nazi means to maintain his regime.* (Their fears were not entirely misplaced. In post-apartheid South Africa it is not uncommon to see working-class Afrikaners begging at intersections.)

*On the morrow Pitch took me out in the car to the bottom of a kopje a mile or so out of Ladysmith. I was soon struggling through dense thorn bushes and over huge unbroken boulders. However it was not a very high kopje, and on the top I found the grave of one Sergeant Webb. I walked along the ridge to Wagon Hill and saw the monument to the Devons; then down to Caesar's Camp, where lies the cemetery for those who died in the great battle fought here. It is well kept and the white crosses are clean and easily legible. Nearby is the grave of the Earl of Ava, who also fell in the battle of 6th January. The remains of the Manchester Fort are still there, and probably much as it was then. Scattered about in the scrub there were rusty corroding pieces of tin. Later Pitch told me they were Maconochie tins, and they have lain there decomposing ever since the battles of sixty-four years age.* [Maconochie Beef Stews were the original ready-meal, introduced in 1894 for campers and explorers as a one-pot dish – the vegetables were included – that could be easily prepared on a primus or open fire. It was soon adopted by the military.]

*At the bottom of the hill I walked through the Indian Village, and a couple of Indians gave me a lift into town. Over lunch Pitch entertained me with an account of his appointment as US Vice-Consul in Ladysmith. Once a year the US Ambassador does a round of his Consuls and Vice-Consuls to check that American interests are being properly served within their domains. The same interview takes place on each of these occasions. 'How many Americans have stopped in Ladysmith in the past year, Mr Christopher?' 'None, Your Excellency.' 'Very good, Mr Christopher. The United States is grateful to you. Keep up the good work.'* [Eventually Consul Christopher did receive an American calling on his aid. In the late 1970s the distinguished historical novelist James A Michener stopped by while he was researching *The Covenant*, his epic of South African life through the generations. The acknowledgements in the book include Benjamin and Eileen Christopher for all the background information on the Siege of Ladysmith. I am sure the Ambassador was gratified.]

*Afterwards I drove out with Mrs C to the Location. This is a slum township of poor Bantu. Mrs C has organised a welfare depot to look after their most pressing needs. First we went to the school, which is run by the organisation. The children all ran to the fence when we drove up and squealed and squeaked in unison. I was introduced to the Bantu teachers, and Mrs C whispered would I shake hands with them because it pleased them so much. The school was bare but very clean and there were the usual child paintings and pieces of handicraft displayed on the walls. I asked Mrs C if the children liked school and if they were amenable to discipline. She said yes and they were far too amenable. They do not get up to mischief like ordinary children. They have no will to be naughty. When we emerged the teachers had arranged a dance in my honour. The children love dancing and have a natural flair. I expected to see a Zulu war dance, but no such thing. Four little piccaninnies started to twist.* [Popular dance of the early sixties.] *The others all clapped in rhythm. We had two more teams of four and they performed with huge delight. I asked the teacher to tell the children that they danced much better than English children. She did so in Zulu, and I expect she said 'the children over the water' because they have no knowledge of England. When we left there was vociferous cheering and waving. They seemed happy little creatures, but Mrs C pointed out one or two who had a ginger streak in their hair, and this she told me is a sign of malnutrition.* (Fifty-something years on I visited a similar school in Pretoria. Although this was a state school, there was the same dependency on white Lady Bountifuls and the same slightly cringe-making deference from the children. Not everything has changed with majority rule.)

*Next we visited the soup kitchen. A huge copper makes forty gallons of rich vegetable soup at a time. The people queue before an open frame in the wall and they receive a pint of soup and a fortified biscuit for one cent. The soup has two spoonfuls of Pro-nutro wheat-germ added to it. It is manufactured by a firm in Durban who sell it to all the welfare organisations at cost price. It contains all the essential vitamins, and is supposed to be eaten like porridge, but the Zulu do not like it, so it has to be put in the soup. A meal like this every day can maintain a person in health whose only other diet is a few handfuls of mealies.*

*We went on to the welfare centre for blanket distribution. A collection of gnarled and grizzled old women were seated outside patiently waiting. They were brought in one at a time and handed a blanket out of the box containing two dozen beautiful new blankets donated by the Indian community. Their expressions of gratitude were most touching. We were literally blessed in Zulu. Somehow I had expected them to clutch the blankets to them and scuttle out without a word. But no, they seized their blankets with great glee, and flung them about their shoulders with gusto, then bowed and grinned and said a few gracious words. Whoever are the 'sullen poor' it is not the Zulus.*

*A report came in about an old man who was demented. He was living in a tool-shed and had no covering for the night. The problem was that if we gave him a blanket it would be stolen. So we drove down to the copse where stood the tool-shed. He was not at home, but we found him begging at the Bantu Beer Hall. Mr Soames, the welfare officer, interviewed him. What would he do with the blanket if we gave him one? He assured Mr Soames that he would never leave it in the tool-shed but would carry it with him wherever he went. So he was put in the back of the truck and taken away to be fed and blanketed. Now he will come to the soup kitchen every day where he will receive soup and biscuits free of charge.*

*Mrs C explained to me the problem of these old people. The Zulu love old people, in the way that Americans love children and English people love animals. In the kraal no old person is ever left in want. Somebody is made responsible for the old one, and he or she must be fed and looked after and given affection. But in urbanised communities, the old tribal ways have no place and the old are left destitute. There is only one home for Bantu old folk in the whole of S. Africa, and that is run by another small welfare organisation.*

*Mr Soames came up and said he was going to have a door put on the tool-shed so that the old man could keep his few things locked up when he is out. This seems to me the most wonderful example of completely circumnavigating bureaucracy. The old man has no right in the tool-shed and Mr Soames knows it. Mr Soames has no right to put a door on the tool-shed, but he does not care about that. Thus is humanity served. He is very concerned about these old people and their terrible plight. He has even faked up false charges in an effort to have them committed to gaol where the state will have to look after them.*

*The Orange Free State train left at 3.30 in the morning, so Mrs C had decided that I was to hitchhike. I was not consulted on the matter. She drove me to the National Road after a strong fortification of several cups of tea, and dumped me with strict instructions to come back for lunch if I had not got a ride by then. I waited about twenty-five minutes and then a Boer farmer in a pick-up stopped for me. He was going right through to Bethlehem. He was a nice old Boer, and spoke English quite well. I was careful to keep well away from politics. After crossing the Drakensbergs into the Free State, we stopped at Harrismith for lunch. General Sir Harry Smith, for whom the town was named, was the husband of Juana, Lady Smith, for whom Ladysmith is named. She was a Spanish girl, descended from Ponce de León, discoverer of what is now the US, whom he rescued on the field of battle in the Peninsular War and married when she was fourteen. She was much beloved by everyone from the Iron Duke himself, who dubbed her 'Juanita', to the humblest private, for she cared equally for all. Juanita accompanied her husband to South Africa when he was appointed Governor of the Cape, and is one of the few women other than royalty to have had a town named after her, Alice Springs being another. The Boer told me that 'Ven it is cold at nights, ve vonder vhy Harrismith is not closer to Ladysmith, heh heh heh!' Very droll. Harrismith is a pleasant little town full of historic buildings and with a main street broad enough to outspan an ox wagon.* [I returned to Harrismith recently. It is now an ugly little town with not a single building that was there on my first visit other than the church and the Town Hall. I have also revisited Ladysmith, now a large, bustling town crowded with tourists visiting for 'the Battlefield Experience'. There is a Visitors' Centre, a state of the art museum, and guided tours of the battlefields every hour. When I was there in 1964 I was the sole pilgrim.]

*I booked in for the night at Bethlehem and after an early dinner went to see the new James Bond film at the bioscope called* From Russia with Love. *All highly improbable with a very confusing storyline, but good nonsense entertainment for all that. In the morning I continued hitch-hiking. Got a car to Paul Roux, another to Senekal, then a truck carrying tyres down the dirt road to Marquant. Here I picked up the main road again, but had to wait much longer for a lift. I spent two hours standing on the side of the road throwing stones at a signpost on the other side. About one in every twenty shots I hit it. At last I got a ride to a dirty little town called Clocolan. Here it was not long before an African picked me up in a battered old Chevrolet and took me down to Ladybrand. 'My goodness', he said, 'my friends won't believe me when I tell them who I had as a passenger! I've never given a lift to a white man before.' The Orange Free State is the most backward of all the provinces.*

Ladybrand proved to be a classic high-veldt *dorp* (inconsequential small town), with no main road and very wide, unmade streets. There was no traffic and just a few chickens scrabbling in the dirt and mangy-looking dogs lying in the sun. It had been established by Johannes Brand, President of the Orange Free State, as a buffer against Basutoland following the second Basuto War, and named after his wife Johanna (another of those rare towns named after women). It also became the railhead for Basutoland and that is why I was here, to make the 12-mile journey to the capital, Maseru, of what was then a British Protectorate – now the Kingdom of Lesotho. Hitch-hiking, I had been told, was inadvisable, as there was so little traffic into the Protectorate from the Free State.

*'The next train to Maseru left nine years ago, Baas."*

First I had to find the station, which you would think would be easy enough in a *dorp* of only 1,000 population, but Ladybrand was spread out over several square miles. Under a blistering sun I lugged my suitcase down a long dirt road in the direction a not very friendly Afrikaner had pointed. After a couple of miles a rather friendlier Bantu pointed me in the opposite direction, back the way I had come. It seems I had been standing a hundred yards from it when the Afrikaner had his little joke at the expense of the *rooinek* (Englishmen were recognisable by their sun-stricken necks).

The station was deserted except for a solitary Bantu idly pushing a broad broom up and down the platform. I asked him when the next train to Maseru was due.

'The next train to Maseru has already gone, Baas', he replied cheerfully.

'When was that?', I asked.

His face creased into a cheeky grin. 'Nine years ago, Baas.'

# Chapter 13

. . .

# BRAVO BASUTOLAND!

. . .

*June–July 1964*

'What you need,' said Mac the Scotchman behind the bar at Ladybrand's Pretorius Inn, 'is a Portuguese. They're the only people going through to Maseru at this time of night.'

'What do the Portuguese do in Maseru?' I asked innocently.

The Scot gave me what in any other nationality would be a leery look. With him it was more of a squint with a bit of eye-rolling thrown in. 'What they're not allowed to do in Zuid Afrika,' he responded. I must have looked blank, because he sighed, examined a couple of glasses he was polishing against the light, then muttered out of the side of his mouth. 'Have a roll in the hay with the Munts. Where have you *been* since you got here?'

The Portuguese, it transpired, were whites from Mozambique who had settled in SA for its greater economic opportunities, but found the draconian laws against inter-racial sexual congress particularly irksome. No such laws obtained over the border. Mac told me to hang around in the bar and if a Portuguese came in, he would point him out to me.

It was not until nearly closing time that I heard Mac say, 'Toni, there's an English bloke over there wants to meet you.' Toni introduced himself.

He was a Portuguese grocer who, unusually, had married the Bantu lady of his choice, something that would have resulted in imprisonment in SA. He and she had emigrated to Basutoland and now ran a grocery and tea-room in Maseru, to which Toni was on his way back after a trip into the Republic to buy stock. All this he explained to me as we bumped and bounced over the unmade road that was one of the few links between the two nations. I explained to him my reason for going to Basutoland: to find somebody willing to hitch-hike with me to Cairo. Toni evidently thought my chances of succeeding in this quest were somewhere between nil and zero, but suggested that I hang around in the bar of the Lancers Inn and keep my ear to the ground.

We crested the brow of a hill and Toni sang out, 'Look! The lights of the mighty capital.' What lay below appeared to be about the size of a small English market town, though only the main street was fully lit and the softer glow on the fringes of the town, Toni told me, signified the Locations, their huts lit only by kerosene lamps.

At the border the South African authorities examined my passport at length, perhaps hoping that I was one of their illegal countrymen travelling on false papers. A couple of hundred yards on lay the frontier. A smartly dressed dismounted trooper in a Boer War uniform with puttees and a wide-awake hat snapped to attention and raised the barrier. Nobody examined our papers. We drove under a triumphant arch emblazoned with the royal arms, up a short rise, and we were entering the city. In the main street Toni's shop and his Select Tea-room lay opposite the Lancers Inn, an old-fashioned colonial hostelry from which the hum of conversation spilled out into the street. I thanked Toni, grasped my single suitcase and strode across to its welcoming entrance. In a burst of exultation I sang 'Rule Britannia' into the night.

There was, thankfully, no segregation at the Lancers Inn, but there was a bar for Basotho in blankets, and another bar for all races *sans* blankets. I made my way into the latter. It was very crowded and very noisy. A single seat at the bar, the only empty one in the room, beckoned. I found myself sitting between a sweet-faced girl on my left and a rather weary-looking young man on my right, hunched over his beer in the way that Americans in bars hunch in movies. The sweet-faced girl, who sat very upright, introduced herself as Jenny from Bristol. She was working for a tour outfit in Maseru that arranged treks into the Drakensbergs, but ate all her meals at the Lancers Inn. 'And this,' she said, indicating my neighbour to the right, 'is John Morrison from New York. He's been working up in the Maluti Mountains with the Peace Corps, but he's finished now.'

I introduced myself to them both and asked the American what he was going to do next. 'I've been sitting on this goddam bar stool for the last coupla weeks,' he replied, 'waiting for someone to come in who wants to hitch-hike to Cairo. But I'm not waiting much longer. I guess I'll just have to fly home to New York from Jo'burg.' He took a long pull at his ale, then turned to me and wiped the foam from his lips.

'And what brings you to this outpost of Empire?' he asked.

. . .

For all John Morrison's impatience to be on his way north, it transpired that we could not leave right away as he was waiting for a transit visa for South Africa. The SA authorities did all in their power to impede people travelling from the Protectorate. I liked the cosy atmosphere of the Lancers Inn, I liked the little I had seen of sweet-faced Jenny and I was keen to see something of one of the last British colonies in Africa, so the delay did not disturb me. My first letter home from Maseru gave a thumbnail sketch of the Protectorate and the trappings of Empire.

. . .

*It is about the size of Wales, and is entirely surrounded by the Republic of South Africa. It has absolutely no connection with the Republic other than that South African currency is used here. Also of course most imports come from the Republic, as there are no industries here other than, strangely enough, two publishing houses. The resident population is estimated at 900,000 and there are another 150,000 Basotho working on the Witwatersrand.*

*There are nine so-called towns, including the capital Maseru. Of these, five have a population of over 1,000 and have a range of civic amenities; the others, in the 400-600 range, are villages.*

*Most of the population lives out in the bush, many on the tops of mountains. This was originally for protection, but has now become a habit. They are engaged in subsistence farming. Although the standard of living is very low, the educational standards are high. Basutoland has the highest literacy rate in the whole of Africa at 80%. It also has the highest percentage of African university graduates. The tragedy is that when they return to Basutoland there is so little for them to do with their learning, and few are prepared to live under the oppression of the Republic.*

*The country is very cold. For this reason the Basotho wear their famous blankets. These are not made in Basutoland, but in Birmingham and Witney. Basutoland forms a special market, because the blankets must have gorgeous, multi-coloured designs. When the blanket is worn well it assumes the majesty of a Roman toga, as well as being exceedingly practical for the climate.*

*Maseru, the capital, is not just a petrol pump, as sceptical South Africans told me. It has some 8,000 souls (mainly Catholic ones). About 1,000 Europeans live here, and there are another 1,000 scattered about the rest of the Colony. It has a fine cathedral (RC), a Parliament building, hospital, law courts, GPO, prison, police barracks, two hotels, a city square, a Residency, Paramount Chief's Palace, library, club, two department stores and a supermarket, numerous trading stores, a large football stadium, a showground, a number of government departments including the Treasury, and half a dozen tea-rooms. The streets are broad and rough, for there are few motor cars. Most ride horses, and even the most modern shops have hitching rails outside.*

*There are two weekly newspapers, the* Basutoland Times *and the* Basutoland News. *the* Times *is issued by the government and the* News *is published over the border in Ladybrand.*

*There is no Apartheid. Most Europeans have African friends, though there are some Dutch people living here who are shocked and repulsed at the idea of sitting next to an African in the bar. Many of the Europeans in Maseru are political refugees, together with many Bantu. Some have sacrificed everything to come here and live in freedom. Robin Cranko, brother of the famous choreographer John Cranko, gave up a lawyer's practice in Durban to come to Maseru so that his children would not be indoctrinated. He has established a new practice amongst the Africans here, and he receives many of his fees in cattle. His wife, whom I met at the Lancers Inn, has asked me to dine with them.*

*My first morning in Basutoland dawned upon the Queen's Birthday. I wasn't sure where the celebrations were to be held, but when I saw a troop* of mounted policemen in khaki uniforms and wide-awake hats jingling and trotting up the main street I scampered after them. Mr Pomeroy, the hotel manager, picked me up in his motor car, and took me to the showground where great events take place. A large crowd had already gathered, and I stationed myself on a dais to the left of the grandstand, where I could get a good view of the nobs: the Resident Commissioner, his lady, the Chief of Police in the most dashing cavalry uniform and Sam Browne belt, the Governor of the Prison, heads of the Civil Service, local dignitaries, missionaries, and the tribal chiefs. The Colonial Service chaps were looking gorgeous in Persil-white uniforms and solar topees. Chaps tripped over dress swords. Chaps fingered moustachios to ensure that they were bristling. Chaps looked as languid as is possible when the spine is being held like a ramrod.

Then the band struck up and everybody, chaps included, rustled with carefully controlled anticipation. Then on to the field rode the Basutoland Mounted Police, their lances flashing in the sun, pennants streaming in the breeze. The horses gleamed, the silver bits and snaffles and curbs gleamed, even the black faces under the slouch hats gleamed.

Behind the mounted police drove a long low sleek black motor car, flying the standard of the Paramount Chief. It halted before the stand, and the Chief stepped out and was greeted by head chap. Then came the hoisting of the Union Jack, and a squad of unmounted troopers did the present. Their drill movements would have done credit to the HAC. After this came the inspection – troopers, prison warders, boy scouts and girl guides and others.

The Union Jack was lowered, and with great ceremony the Royal Standard unfurled at the head of the flagpole. Then the Birthday Honours were read out, first in English, then in Sesotho. The recipients came forward to the stand and had their medals pinned on them. Marvellous to think that in other small colonies scattered over the globe similar ceremonies are taking place.

Finally, the grand march past. First the mounted troopers, then the unmounted marching like Grenadiers. Everybody was in step except the cub scouts, whose socks kept falling down because they had lost their garters.

Back in the pub Johnnie-the-Punk, as John Morrison is known among his lowlier associates, said he had never seen anything like it before. He has *leftist leanings, so naturally he did not approve, but I don't think he could help being just a wee bit impressed. Bravo Basutoland! It may be the last Queen's Birthday Parade, as next year Basutoland becomes independent.*

*It is now snowing hard. Not something you expect in Africa.*

*After lunch Robin Cranko drove me out to see his selection. First we dropped in to see the witch doctor, and had a chat with him. Very charming chap. One of his huts is labelled 'Surgery'. Like something in a Punch cartoon. Over the road Robin has fenced off his selection. There is no land tenure in Basutoland. All the land belongs to the people, and no one can purchase any. If you wish to acquire a plot of building land you go to the local Chief and apply to join his tribe. (Robin has taken an oath of allegiance to his Chief.) The chief will then apportion you land according to what he considers are your needs. When you die your heir inherits it from you, but only the right to live on, or cultivate, the land. If you have no heir the Chief will re-apportion it. The Chief has no rights of tenure either, only the privilege of distribution. It is believed that Basutoland is the only country in the Western world where there is no ownership of land. Robin is building a house on his selection. The foundations are already dug. It is a circular house. Robin is not the type of person to live in a rectangular house like everybody else.*

*Back in Maseru we went to a party in the Location. This was most interesting for me, as we were the only Europeans present. The Basotho people are very social and very punctilious. When you are introduced you shake hands with everybody, and each and everyone is Mister so-and-so. They are the most extraordinarily well-travelled people. It is curious to walk into a tin roofed shack and be introduced to a man who has lived in America, Britain and Russia, toured Africa and Europe, and speaks nine languages. If it was not for apartheid these men would be in the Republic, as leaders of government, commerce or professions. But they prefer to live in poverty in Basutoland. Robin has taken me into dozens of African homes, and everywhere you see similar sights. A few rough pieces of second-hand furniture, and a shelf full of Oxford University Press books. One cannot help feeling sympathy for their aspirations, though I had the impression that there is still a tendency to defer to Europeans. I told one learned gentleman with a goatee beard that he looked like Jan Christian Smuts. He was thrilled – not because I had likened him to a great statesman, but to a white man.*

*After the party I went to have dinner with the Crankos. They have two children, Robyn (six) and Frederick (five), who are being brought up on yoghurt and self-expression. I must say they seem very intelligent and well behaved, but I cannot help feeling that this unremitting diet of politics will have some strange effects.* [Frederick I cannot find on Google, but Robyn is a schoolteacher for special needs children in Fairlawn, Ohio, married to a man called Tobias, possibly Jewish, as Robyn seems to have reverted to her Jewish roots. She is also vegan, which seems about par for the course, but her photograph on Facebook reveals a happy-looking attractive woman who seems to have emerged from her unusual upbringing pretty well adjusted.] *The Crankos live in one of those incredibly untidy houses where everything is just flung on the floor. After dinner Robin played me tape recordings of political meetings until I fell into a deep slumber.*

*In the morning I went to Mass at the Cathedral. Passed a woman carrying her missal on her head. In the Cathedral the men all sit on one side and the women on the other. There was a large congregation, but only three other Europeans. The sermon was in Sesotho, and very long. The Basotho are an excellent congregation, for they join in the Mass most vociferously. The Catholics are in the majority in Basutoland, being over a third of the population. Another third are pagans, and the next largest denomination is Calvinist. Most of the education is in the hands of the English Catholic missionaries and French Protestant missionaries, whose fierce rivalry accounts for the very high level of literacy. I asked Hugh Tristram, the Government Information Officer, how Calvinism affects a naturally joyous people like the Basotho. He said the Basotho Calvinists he knew were very dour.*

*After Mass Robin collected me to take me to Julius Gandhi Mali's birthday party. First we had to find Robin's servants, who had disappeared. They were collected from their homes dead to the world. They had both been to an orgy the night before and were suffering from prodigious hangovers. After dumping the miscreants back at the Crankos', we drove to Julius's house. The party was most convivial. Fifteen sat down to luncheon, in a room about 10ft by 8ft. Among those present were Mister Cheeseman of the Treasury and Ian Hamnet, anthropologist and equerry to the Paramount Chief. The guest of honour was Chief Plin, resplendent in a scarlet blanket. He made Ian and myself a special little speech in Sesotho, which was interpreted for us. We had roast beef and curried mutton with green peas and roast potatoes, followed by apricots and gloriously sloppy jelly. The party was all male. I don't think Basotho women attend parties. The Chief did not speak at all until he had finished his meal, when he rose and made a long speech in Sesotho, translated sentence by sentence by his interpreter n-chou-chou. It was a very good speech, even in translation. When the Chief had made his departure amongst affirmations of respect and goodwill, we all retired to another house where there was more room to talk politics. A good time and a lot of whisky were had by all.*

*Robin and I left the party some hours later with n-chou-chou and another Chief. We drove out to Teyateyaneng, known as TY to its friends. A most enjoyable drive through rugged country, dotted with clusters of square huts. The Basotho hut, unlike the Zulu, has corners. Also doors and windows, these latter sticking out from the roof. There are many interesting sights on the road. Native buses chugging along, fierce-looking horsemen, small boys on donkeys, oxen dragging sledges, women with hundredweight bags of mealies on their heads. TY is a small town compared with Maseru, but it has a club and an hotel. First we went to see Mofolo, whose father, still alive at ninety-one, is known as the Shakespeare of Basutoland. He wrote three bestsellers, which were translated into fifteen languages. His fourth book was accidentally burnt when the printing press caught fire. We had a nice cup of tea and a chat about Basutoland literature, and then repaired to the bar of the hotel. Here I met the Superintendent of Police, who had been on a Hendon Police College course, and was very fond of England. He looked a bit like Louis Armstrong. Mofolo conducted me into the lavatory to warn me that Robin is a Communist. Everyone in Basutoland is a Communist to everyone else. Later a religious argument commenced between Mrs Mofolo, who is an ardent Catholic, and Robin, who is a humanist. It was rather one-sided, as every time Robin opened his mouth to defend himself Mrs Mofolo told him to shut up and listen. We arrived back in the capital rather late.*

*In the morning I went with Robin to the Courts to hear him in a case. In Basutoland he is both solicitor and barrister. Most of the Courts' business has to be done through an interpreter. It was a most interesting Magistrates' Court, because of course it is not just an interminable succession of motoring offences. Juicy things like stock theft and culpable homicide. One was for aiding an arrested man to escape. Friends and relatives sat unhappily at the back practically submerged in their blankets.*

*After the Court I had an appointment at Parliament. I had met the Sergeant at Arms while gaping over the wall at a Residency tea party. He had promised to show me round. Actually he wasn't there, but one of the Hansard translators who is a bar-room chum of mine at the Lancers Inn took me to see the Chamber. It is hexagonal, with benches running round a well in the centre for the sixty elected MPs and twenty-two Chiefs and ex-officio members. (Next year there will be a House of Lords, in which the Chiefs will sit in solitary splendour.) There is also a special throne for the Paramount Chief. Being their monarch, he cannot sit in Parliament, but he attends on special occasions by invitation. Hansard is published in English and Sesotho. I was given a copy and, judging by the text, the debates must be very lively affairs.*

*I have met quite a number of the MPs at the Lancers Inn, one of whom invited me to visit him at one at the MPs' hostels. These are two blocks of flats built to accommodate the country members during the session. A 'flat' consists of one very small room, in which the MP lives sometimes alongside his family. My MP was in bed with something – may have been a cold, more likely the demon rum. His wife was sitting on a kitchen chair. It was a very bare comfortless room with a concrete floor. The MPs living here eat their meals in a communal dining hall.*

*On leaving the House of Commons I went to the Government Information Department, where I collected some data on Basutoland, and some back numbers of the* Basutoland Times. *Hugh Tristram the Information Officer dashed in and dashed out in a great hurry. That evening in the bar he apologised for being so brusque, and said would I like to come for drinks tomorrow? I would. Would I also like to visit the University at Roma? I would also. It was arranged. He also introduced me to my first rabid Nat (member of the South African National Party), a striking beauty called Fiona who said she hated the Basotho, the Zulus, and all other Bantu. Johnnie-the-Punk asked her to explain why. She got very cross and sulky, and said no one knew them like the South Africans, and no one else was qualified to give an opinion. The SAs always say this, and it is very silly, because the only Bantu they ever meet are their servants. South Africans particularly dislike the Basotho, because they are not servile like the South African Bantu. They do not call you Baas or Master. Some of them even expect to shake hands with you.*

*Next day Hugh Tristram, the GIO, drove me out to Roma. It was a Catholic university until last year, when it was bought by the government and it is now the University of Basutoland, Bechuanaland, and Swaziland (the three British Protectorates bordering South Africa). The buildings are austere, but dignified, of rough-hewn Basutoland stone. We also toured the monastery, hospital, two seminaries, Catholic Centre, chapel, two high schools, two primary schools, convent, mission etc. Roma is a little Vatican. Children come from the mountains to board at the schools.*

*Hugh collected me again in the evening and took me to the Club. A most depressing establishment, with a lot of junior civil servants flopping about in sweaters and no ties. Barmen in scruffy day clothes, no white jackets and cummerbunds. We were drawn into a prolonged debate about Gatwick Airport, which went on and on, on and on. I was not impressed. When I asked Johnnie-the-Punk whether this was what they normally talked about at the club, he said, 'No, it's usually the women who take the lead. Then it's the three Ks – Kids, Kitchens and Kaffirs.' There are three African members of the Club, elected at great protest from the South Africans. I was quite glad to get out of it.*

*Hugh told me about an occasion when the Maseru Club put on a very bad amateur performance of an Agatha Christie play and he had to review it for the* Basutoland Times. *Rather than deplore the acting, which would have caused offence, he wrote a mild criticism of Agatha Christie's abilities as a playwright; her characters Hugh felt tended towards stereotype. The next time he entered the Club, he was advanced upon by a furious old colonial quaking with rage. 'You you you you …' he spluttered in Hugh's face, 'You blackguard! You dared to make an attack on a white woman in your paper. And it is read by AFRICANS!' Hugh said it was such an incredible remark that he thought the man was joking. When Hugh chuckled jocularly it added the blackest insult to the deepest injury.*

*At Hugh's house we had a pleasant dinner, with Mrs T and daughter Caroline, who is stunningly beautiful to look at but stone deaf poor dear. She lip-reads, but it is a real struggle. Her speech is very grotesque, consisting of grunts and honking noises. The only person who can understand everything she says is Hugh himself.*

Hugh's lovely daughter Caroline must have led a very isolated and lonely existence in this quaint colonial capital where half the population did not speak English and the other half could not converse with her anyway. But there was a happy outcome, I am delighted to report. One day an Afrikaner engineer came to Maseru on assignment. He too was stone deaf and a lip-reader. For the first time Caroline could communicate freely with someone besides her father. The two fell in love and when Hugh wrote to me after I had returned to England, a marriage had been arranged.

. . .

When I was not dining with the Crankos or the Tristrams, I generally ate with the sweet-faced Jenny in the dining-room of the Lancers Inn. She was a down-to-earth, sensible girl, very good at her job organising treks into the Drakensbergs, so I was somewhat surprised by her answer when I asked her how she had come to Basutoland. It was because of a clairvoyant in Edinburgh, she told me. She had always wanted to visit Africa, but in the early sixties it was not a continent that many well-brought up gels from the shires would travel to on their own. So being of a practical turn of mind, she decided it would be a good idea to find out whether she would ever succeed in her ambition before abandoning her job and her flat and making preparations. She did not tell the clairvoyant that this was the reason for her patronage; only that she wanted to know what the immediate future held in store for her.

This is what the clairvoyant told her. You will travel to a far distant country (Africa was not mentioned). In that country you will meet a man who works for the King and lives in his palace. You will be invited to the palace. When you get there you will cross a bridge into a courtyard and there you will hear the baying of a ferocious hound. This hound will emerge into the courtyard and make towards you as if about to attack. You will be rigid with fear. Then you will hear a man give a single command. The dog will instantly stop in its tracks. Then the man will come forward to greet you.

That man you will marry.

There was a codicil. After they were married, she and the palace functionary would go to America and work at the top of a high building. Fortified in the knowledge that she was not wasting her time in planning to go to Africa, even if the stuff about kings and palaces and fierce guard-dogs was all a bit fanciful, Jenny bought her ticket. My next letter home threw some further light on this curious tale.

. . .

*By the time I had finished my last there was already a thin layer of snow on the ground. The snowfall gathered in intensity, and continued all day and all night. It also got colder and colder, and then even colder. Dear sweet Jenny, a delightful table companion, insisted on giving me her sweater. She had two. So with two shirts, half a pair of pyjamas, the waistcoat from my best suit, and Jenny's voluminous sweater, I was something like warm again. When I went across the road to get cigarettes I threw a lovely big snowball at Toni the Portuguese grocer. My first African snowball! I was supposed to be going to Buthe Butha with Hugh Tristram, but the roads soon became impassable. So I spent the afternoon lying in front of a hoozing great log fire talking to the lovely Jenny and watching the soft white snowflakes fluttering down outside.*

*After twenty-four hours, that is yesterday morning, it stopped. The snow was a foot deep all over Maseru. Hugh Tristram said he had written over thirty letters to enquirers saying that winter sports were quite impracticable in Basutoland. Now it would be easy to ski down the main street of the capital. Jenny thought she had better go to work because the English always do, regardless of bombs, strikes and disaster. A foot of snow wasn't going to keep any Gloucestershire girl from her duty. So I set off with her to pull her out of snowdrifts. We waded up to our knees down the road, and every time a jeep or Land Rover slithered past we had to jump into a drift. At length we reached Maluti Treks, Jenny's office, but of course it was all shut up and closed. Honour having been satisfied, Jenny was very pleased to find she had a holiday, so I suggested we go up to the Palace to see Ian, Jenny's bf, who used to be the Paramount Chief's tutor at Oxford and is now his equerry.* (The Paramount Chief was crowned King Moshoeshoe II in 1966.)

*Much puffing and blowing and flapping of arms, and when we had almost arrived at the Palace Jenny remembered the royal dog, which is a great brute mastiff trained to go straight for the throat. This was not reassuring, but Jenny went first, while I clambered on to the wall for safety. The hulking creature came tearing into the courtyard baying for*

*Jenny went first, while I climbed on to the wall of the Palace for safety.*

*blood and Jenny called out to Ian in a somewhat urgent tone. He came wandering out into the snow wearing Newmarket boots beneath a silk smoking jacket and puffing a cigarette in a long black holder. He was looking rather like Noël Coward. At a single, low command from Ian, the slathering beast froze in its tracks like in the Road Runner cartoons and began to whimper, probably in disappointment at being deprived of one of Patrick's limbs for lunch. Ian chained up the animal, whose name is Tiger. I gather he lives up to it.*

*Inside the warm kitchen Margaret the parlourmaid bobbed us a curtsey and set about making tea. So we all sat on kitchen chairs in front of the fender and sipped strong tea and discussed the snow, which has even ousted politics in Maseru. It seems that the snow had blanketed the whole of the continent south of the equator, and even the Kalahari Desert. Basutoland seems to have got it heaviest, for it is the deepest. After tea Ian showed me round the Palace. It is a large Victorian house, very draughty, but with a lovely view over the hills from the veranda. It* is kept immaculately clean by the convict women who are assigned there for hard labour. Every week they polish all the floors with beeswax, not only the part which shows, but under all the carpets as well. Ian says the government stores send up ten large tins of wax at a time and they don't last long. All this energy only really contributes to Ian's comfort, because the Paramount Chief never sleeps at the Palace, preferring to drive back the thirty miles to his country estate. When he holds a dinner party at the Palace, and has to be in Maseru again at nine in the morning, he still goes home to sleep. Ian says the dinner parties are crashingly boring and last an interminably long time. The meal usually takes two hours because of the long delays between courses. There are not enough forks to go round, and so at the end of each course the used forks have to be washed and returned to the table. As Ian remarked, if it was not so stiff and formal you could have a good laugh about it, but with four crystal wine glasses at every place setting it seems ridiculous that there isn't adequate cutlery.

We repaired to the royal study, where Ian does his anthropology work. Nice hoozing fire in the grate, and coffee was brought in. He explained about the convicts. They are all murderers or assault cases. Violent criminals are considered safe to be allowed out to work. Thieves are kept in prison. This is reasonable enough. Obviously they would not let out a homicidal maniac, but a common or garden murderer isn't going to start killing everybody he comes into contact with, whereas a thief might well steal anything that is lying around. Ian is uncertain what the men prisoners are supposed to do at the Palace. A whole squad of them comes up, and they are left in the charge of Paul the houseboy. The warder goes home. One lays the fire, another cleans Ian's shoes. The rest sit about in the garden and play a complicated form of Basotho noughts and crosses. Margaret makes them tea and Ian gives them cigarettes. They have a lovely time, and express regret when it is time to cease Hard Labour and go back to the prison again.

We all walked back to the Inn for lunch. On the way we passed a splendid snowman. No ordinary snowman, but an African snowman. He had a couple of squash for eyes, lemon quarters for eyebrows, a cucumber nose and a slice of pumpkin for a mouth. He was outside Toni the grocers, so perhaps he was a bit of sly advertising as well. We noticed that all the telephone lines were down. Then we found that all the electricity had stopped too. That afternoon we faced a crisis when the wood ran out, and we sat in the darkening lounge and shivered.

. . .

Tempers became frayed as these deprivations intensified. There was a fight in the public bar at the Lancers Inn and the police had to be called. Disputes in the saloon bar may have been a little more circumspect, but involved even this timid traveller. I had a run-in with a discourteous South African and told him to mend his manners. I asked Curtis, a friendly African, who he was. 'He's called Aspin. He's BOSS', replied Curtis. 'Boss of what?' I asked. Curtis raised his eyes towards the rafters. 'BOSS is the Bureau of State Security in Pretoria. Don't you know anything, Patrick? Aspin is a secret agent, but not very secret. He could be here to spy on me, or he might even be here to spy on you. After all, you're a known associate of Robin Cranko and he's ANC.' African National Congress – I knew that much. After this incident Aspin used to sit himself beside me at the bar and make notes of what I said, particularly to Africans. This may have been simply to intimidate me. Or possibly there is a file somewhere in the archives in Pretoria detailing Patrick's opinions about the lunch menu, his quest for extra woollies since the electricity failed, or his latest attempt to evade the attentions of the Paramount Chief's horrible hound.

My other fracas was with Mister Rhind, the oldest white man in Maseru at eighty-eight (and eventually to become the oldest inhabitant of Basutoland of any race). He was a former engineer turned trader and had lived in Basutoland for sixty-six years. I liked to talk to old people and our discussion began amiably enough with his observation that this was the heaviest snowfall he had known since the great blizzard of 1881. Mister Rhind was then five and he was, of course, talking about the Old Country. He got very cross, however, when he saw some small boys outside throwing snowballs and insisted, without empirical evidence, that these contained stones. There followed a tirade about the modern generation, followed by the assertion that such things never happened in his youth. Ardent student of the great age of Victoria as I was, I could not let this pass. 'Mister Rhind,' I expostulated, 'you know as well as I do that small boys threw stones in the glorious 1880s. And not always with snow around them. That was the age when *Punch* thought that someone getting a stone in the eye or half a brick on the back of the head was the height of hilarity.' Mr Rhind continued to insist that the small boys of his Victorian youth led lives of unblemished virtue, to which I retorted, 'Only in *Eric, or Little by Little,*' which did little to assuage his passion. We parted with mutual growls of disavowal.

Hostilities were resumed when Mister Rhind saw me conversing with two Basotho politicians suspected of Marxist affiliations. He denounced them and me with vigour. When tea-time arrived I decided that it was quite ridiculous for two admirers of the Victorians to fall out, as indeed it was for two people who probably shared much the same political perspective to quarrel about whom one of them talked to. I fetched him a cup of tea with two extra large spoonfuls of sugar – I knew he had a sweet tooth – and a toasted teacake with strawberry jam. He invited me to join him and in an effort to bury the hatchet I asked after his experiences in the Boer War. What he told me was illuminating.

The so-called concentration camps were built as part of Kitchener's 'scorched earth' policy after the capture of Pretoria, epicentre of the Boer war effort. The conflict entered a new phase, moving on from sieges and pitched battles to guerrilla warfare waged by the sharpshooters of the Boer commandos. The commandos lived off the land, provisioned from the farmsteads on the veldt. The British strategy was to lay waste the land, destroy the crops, burn the farmsteads (in many cases) and intern the Boer women and children. It was in pursuance of the internment policy that the young Hugh Rhind, a civil engineer lately arrived from England, was called in to build the first camp at Pretoria – another was built at Bloemfontein about the same time. Unlike the later camps these camps were for Boer families and single men over military age who had surrendered voluntarily and they were not enclosed. It was only the following year, after a Boer commando had rustled a herd of cattle intended for feeding the inmates of a camp at Sanderton in the Transvaal, that the camps were enclosed within barbed-wire fences. This was the first use of barbed wire in detention camps, later in the century to become symbolic of the excesses of the Nazi holocaust and Stalin's Gulag. The open camp at Pretoria was the one in which Louis Botha's Irish wife and his two daughters were interned.

The high mortality rate in the camps evoked worldwide protest, compounded by the intense dislike many Europeans felt for the British. (As I write we are living through this again with Brexit.) There was certainly a lot to criticise about the manner in which the camps were run in the early stages – those in command were used to military encampments, not to a community of hostile civilians only too ready to defy orders – but Mister

Rhind threw an interesting light on the death toll that I have not seen rehearsed in any published history. He told me that he had built latrines according to the best sanitary principles, together with a proper sewage system to dispose of the effluent. The Boer women, however, refused to use them. Their farmsteads had no sanitation and they were accustomed to doing their business out on the veldt and covering it with earth. The women persisted in the same habit within the confines of the camp, and the deposits attracted vast swarms of flies. These insects spread enteric fever (typhoid), which killed more people during the war, both soldiers and civilians, than died on the battlefield.

Could this have been averted? Probably, but only by imposing military discipline. The camps were not intended to be punitive and any attempts to coerce the Boer women would have inevitably resulted in organised resistance. Putting civilians in camps, whether as refugees or internees, was a new idea in 1900. The British got it wrong. It is a black mark in the annals of Empire, but it behoves historians to review all the facts. Mr Rhind was a witness to history, but he died just as Boer War studies were beginning to acquire their modern cachet.

. . .

When the snows melted, it was time for Johnnie-the-Punk and me to start our long trek north. Robin Cranko had a complicated plan for us that involved him taking us to his friend Gany Surtee's trading store in Butha-Buthe where we would wait for a friend of Gany's, a commercial traveller, who would give us a lift to Jo'burg. That may sound fairly straightforward, but Robin's plans seldom were when it came to their execution. This occasion was no exception. Somewhere the other side of Leribe, in the pitch dark of a starless night and with the temperature well below freezing, the lights failed on Robin's rattletrap motor. Robin drove on regardless, into stygian blackness. A few miles further on he eased his juddering jalopy down a steep defile and gunned the motor for the steep ascent the other side. The engine gave a short succession of coughs as if in protest and then died. The car did not have a self-starter. A push-start on that gradient was not an option. We emptied our cases of everything that might provide extra protection against the bitter night and started upwards and onwards.

We had no idea how far it might be to Butha-Buthe and the prospect of walking all night was a frightening one. Would hypothermia fell us before we reached civilisation? After only half a mile we encountered, much to our amazement, a tribesman striding in the opposite direction. We asked the way and he told us that we were only another half-mile from Gany Surtee's main trading store. He insisted on showing us the way and, on our arrival, would not even stay for a hot toddy.

Gany was the most welcoming of hosts and we were soon ensconced in front of a blazing fire of chopped-up packing cases and dried cow-dung, hot toddies in hand and large plates of fiery curry on our knees.

*Gany is most amusing, I reported. Like most Indians he pleads poverty. To listen to Gany you would imagine that nothing stood between him and the workhouse but a handful of rice a day. At the moment he is busying himself with a plot to send his son to an expensive English public school. I say plot advisedly as the simplest Indian transactions take on an aura of mystery and intrigue. His house is opulent and shambolic. An enormous number of people live in it. You keep seeing new ones, who drift in and drift out. Most of them are Gany's cousins.*

*Meals are in two shifts. The men eat first, and when they have finished the table is re-laid, and the women, children and servants have their food. Curry is served at every meal, with an enormous mountain of rice. They eat with the fingers, no cutlery being used. If you want a knife you must bring your own, because they are never supplied in a Basutoland home. This is to prevent you stabbing your host with his own knife. Apparently it is all right if you stab him with the one you have brought with you. After the curry (there is no pudding) tea is poured, and served with boiled milk. This latter is not to my taste.*

*We sleep in an outhouse under such a mound of blankets as I have never seen before. The blankets are doubled over on both sides, and when you are in you let the sides down. The sheets are green, of thick woolly material. They are called 'winter sheets'.*

*On Saturday we went into Butha-Buthe on the truck to see the grand opening of the new District Council Buildings. We had to be there for the ceremony at nine o'clock sharp, so having arrived at half past ten we only had an hour to wait. We took our seats among all the nobs, with a good view of the new building so long as Mister Stores, the District Commissioner, did not move his head. Union Jack fluttering nicely in* the breeze. We awaited the arrival of the Paramount Chief with eager anticipation. When it became clear that the Paramount Chief wasn't coming the ceremony started.

First we had a selection of what I was told was Basotho native music played by the Band of the Basutoland Mounted Police. This included 'My Bonnie Lies over the Ocean', 'The British Grenadiers' and 'America the Beautiful'. Then came the speeches. These were in Sesotho and very long. A choir sang in Sesotho. I don't know what they sang but it sounded as if it might be the local version of 'Hang out the Washing on the Siegfried Line'. More speeches, and then the laying of the Foundation Stone. The Stone was actually already laid, but it had a big piece of sticky paper over it, and this was swept off with a flourish and one of the nobs daubed some cement round it. He did not do it very expertly because it began to slither down. I noticed that when the speeches had started again a chap in overalls came and scraped it all off.

Following speeches, more band, more speeches, more choir, more speeches, came the cutting of the tape stretched across the doors of the new building. Important chap attacked it with a pair of scissors, and the two ends sprang apart with a satisfying springiness. The important chap opened the doors, walked inside, turned round several times, and walked out again.

Speeches, then a dance troupe. They looked savage and impressive. Their legs were wrapped in coloured straw and they wore skins. They all carried knobkerries, shillelaghs, or broom handles. The men danced very fiercely in the middle, and the women cavorted round them wailing and blowing whistles. Rather like a sort of tribal Paul Jones. I must say native dancing is much more enjoyable in the flesh than at the bioscope. Still, a little goes a long way and I shall not be stricken if I leave Africa without witnessing another. I wouldn't mind seeing a fertility dance.

In the evening Robin and Johnnie-the-Punk decided to go on a blind. I get awfully bored standing around in bars for hours on end, so I decided that I would find out whether Gany has any books, and if not I would go with them to the pub and listen to the never-ending political debate. To my delight Gany has a whole library at the side of the store, so my evening was arranged. I found myself a nice JB Priestley novel, and repaired to the store to read it. They were stocktaking. This is an annual event and goes on for a week. All Gany's brothers and cousins were busy reading out lists of goods, and the African 'boys' were checking them. Gany sat like *a potentate amidst all these labours and dispensed tea and his personal philosophy. I noted that while Indians received cups of tea at hourly intervals, the Africans went without. Stocktaking is evidently a pleasantly social occasion. No one worked too hard and there were many pauses for discussion.*

*I went to bed at something past midnight and the revellers had not returned. When I awoke in the morning their beds were empty. After breakfast Gany's brother Rezak turned up. He took me into Butha-Buthe and we searched the town for them. At the Crocodile Inn we learnt that they had been seen in the bar wearing Basotho blankets, that witnesses had observed their departure at half past ten, and that they were in the company of African women. It sounded bad. Rezak thought the police might have them in the cells, so he went off to the police station while I stayed and had tea with Mr and Mrs Pyke Nott, who run the inn, and are Gloucestershire people. Mister is very Cheltenham and Mrs is very Glarster.* [The social demographic of Cheltenham was several steps up from its neighbour of nine miles away, the industrial inland port of Gloucester.] *They are both adored by the Basotho. In Africa for over thirty years and they are the very best type of colonials. Regard the Africans as friends and equals, but never fail to set a good example. I have been in and out of the Crocodile quite a bit in the last few days, and it is very nice to have a yarn about home. You don't meet many Gloucester people abroad. People who travel seem to be mainly from the home counties.*

*Rezak came back reporting failure, and most disturbed because it seemed that the errant pair were definitely in a kraal the other side of the mountain. He thought some breakfast would be the best course. (It was now lunchtime.) So we went to Rezak's mud hut and his sister was commandeered to fry eggs. Rezak is the eldest of Gany's brothers and sisters, and unashamedly admits to being the black sheep. The Pyke Notts are very fond of him. The mud hut has a door and two windows and a thatched roof. It contains two beds and a child's cot and a chest of drawers and a wardrobe and a rickety chair. There is a primus stove for cooking and a coloured wedding portrait of a man who may or may not be Rezak with his bride. Rezak has two wives but they have both gone back to their mothers. He is toying with the idea of a third.*

*The eggs were excellent. There was no pan so they were cooked in the tin plate I ate them from. Then Rezak cooked some curried scrambled eggs which were also good. After that we sat outside the hut with half a bottle of brandy and commiserated about our friends' lost reputations.*

*On returning to Gany's in his brother-in-law's motor bus (which is a bus body slung on to the chassis of a lorry) there was still no sign of the prodigals. We spent the rest of the day stocktaking. It was not until the following afternoon, when I was having a pleasant nap between the blankets, that they pitched up. It was a sad story they had to relate.*

*There had been no Basotho blankets and no African women. On leaving the pub they had been prevailed on to give a Chief a lift back to his kraal, which was, he assured them, only six miles away. This turned out to be twenty-seven miles. After about an hour's driving Robin mistook a turning and they plunged into a ravine. No one was hurt, and Robin spent the night freezing on the back seat of the car while Johnnie-the-Punk hoofed it to a kraal a mile distant and froze on the floor of a hut. In the morning they recruited twenty men to haul the car out of the ravine, and on the way back to town they had a puncture. The spare wheel was also flat. When they got the car into Butha-Buthe, the Calvinist garage owner would not mend the puncture on a Sunday. They had to spend the night at the Crocodile; in the morning the Pyke Notts refused to accept any payment for dinner, bed and breakfast.*

*When they were all set to return to Pitch's Nek the clutch broke, and they were held up until after lunch. It was a sorry pair who crept back to Gany's place with a car and a reputation to mend. Rezak will be gratified to hear that none of the awful rumours circulating in Butha-Buthe were true of his good friends Lawyer Cranko and Mistah Johnnie-the-Punk.*

*Now it is the eve of departure. Tomorrow the Punk and I are determined to cross the border and head for Jo'burg, then north to Bechuanaland.*

* * *

My letters home seldom recounted the *whole* story. During the evenings at Gany's house we had idled away the hours playing gin rummy, a game new to Johnnie-the-Punk. While we played we smoked dope. Dagga, the local name for marijuana, was freely available in Basutoland, used by nearly everybody in the non-white community, and tolerated by the law. Indeed there was no law in respect of soft drugs. I did not myself find it a particularly elevating experience. Gany's Golden Ganja, as his own rub was known, tasted of liquorice, which I do not like, and the effect was much the same as schoolboy drunkenness. I became light-headed, silly and giggly, which I prefer not to be, and nor did it enhance my gin rummy skills. It does occur to me, though, that politicians faced with that dreaded Catch-22 question 'Have you ever smoked dope?' – you're a wimp if you haven't and a self-confessed criminal if you have – could well improve on Bill Clinton's feeble claim that he had done so in his distant youth, but had not inhaled. The perfect answer is: 'Yes, in Basutoland, where it was legal.'

. . .

Americans do not travel light. Johnnie-the-Punk was no exception. Whereas my worldly goods were contained in a single small suitcase which nowadays would be eligible to be flown as hand luggage, the Punk's four months' absence in Africa necessitated a mound of bags that would only just fit into Archie's fairly capacious car. Archie was the commercial traveller who had kindly offered to take us to Jo'burg, where Punk was going to forward most of the mound back to New York.

We set off in a festive mood, feeling as if it was the first day of the holidays. Archie proved a very amiable companion, with a fund of commercial traveller tales. As soon as we had got across the border at Fourisburg, we would be able to relax, we told each other. That was just twelve miles from our pick-up point, Gany's house at Pitch's Nek.

Hopes that the customs and immigration officials at the South African border post would wave us through were rapidly disappointed. Archie and I had no difficulties, but Johnnie-the-Punk's transit visa exercised the attention of the Afrikaner immigration officer, who kept changing his mind about the terms under which our American friend would be permitted to pass through the country. Finally he declared that the visa would only be good for transit directly to Johannesburg International, and that J-the-P must exit the country from there. When Punk protested loudly and volubly, the officer said he would have to ring Pretoria for further instructions.

The conversation with Pretoria was protracted. When the officer emerged from the small booth that constituted his office he was grim-faced. Without looking at us he commanded the customs officer to search all the bags. That worthy merely glanced into my suitcase, and unzipped and zipped Archie's single bag in one movement, before setting to work on Punk's possessions. From each bag every item was laid out on the dusty road. There was a large packet of pamphlets that J-the-P had collected from all the political parties in Basutoland. As there were 22 parties in this emerging democracy, the collection was voluminous. It was when the customs officer began writing down the title of each, very slowly and laboriously with a pencil whose lead he paused to lick after each title, that Archie said he was sorry, but he had to be in Jo'burg by six and needed to leave without further delay. I offered to stay with the Punk, but the generous fellow urged me to accompany Archie to Jo'burg. Archie left Punk his number and it was arranged that if he did not call, we would contact the American Embassy.

And so I departed Basutoland, having achieved just twelve miles of the 7,500 miles overland to London, and with no certainty that I still had a travelling companion. I determined to waste no time in exiting South Africa myself.

. . .

They say you should never return to the places you have loved. I loved Maseru and I had been enchanted by Basutoland and the Basotho people. I had been stimulated by the wide variety of people I had met since Toni the Portuguese grocer had dropped me in front of the Lancers Inn: Jenny and Ian and Ian's jolly convicts, Johnnie-the-Punk, Julius and Curtis, the Crankos and Tristrams and Pyke Notts, Mister Rhind, Gany and Rezak, even Special Agent Aspin. It was 1997 before I returned. Basutoland was now Lesotho, independent for over thirty years. Maseru, that dusty little capital of just 8,000 souls, down the centre of whose main street you could saunter in the confident knowledge that any traffic would circumvent you, was now a steamy metropolis of over a quarter of a million population. Like many rapid-growth African cities, it was not a pretty sight. The streets were clogged with vehicles frantically honking their horns, the buildings were of uniform concrete blocks topped with rusty tin, many of them unfinished. The Lancers Inn was still there, but it had been totally rebuilt in the international style that characterises the cheaper hotels surrounding the seedier airports. Nothing of that weather-worn, thatched colonial hostelry remained and there was no bar for Basotho in blankets. Of Toni's Grocery and Select Tea-room there was not a trace; a giant service station bathed in orange fluorescent light occupied its space. Karla looked around and exclaimed, 'This was the place you were so happy?' I told her no, that was a different place. And I quoted her Robin Cranko's dictum: 'Basutoland is a fictitious country where mythical things happen.'

. . .

Robin Cranko, exile. He could not return to South Africa without immediate arrest, but he made his mark from beyond her borders. Dianne Stewart, *Durban in a Word*, said that he was 'one of those liberation icons who have now gone down in history as the relentless fighters for democracy'.

And Ian and Jenny? They returned to Britain and married as the soothsayer had predicted they would. When Karla and I stayed with them in Clifton we slept under the magnificent bed-cover of water-buffalo skins that King Moshoeshoe II had presented to his former tutor as a wedding gift. I wish I could report that they had a long and happy life together and a thriving family. Alas, it was not to be. Ian died at a comparatively early age and Jenny did not live out a full life-span either. They had no children. Nor did they ever go to America and work together at the top of a high building. I wonder if the clairvoyant had added that flourish from her imagination because there was not a lot to say after the fulfilment of the prophecy about Basutoland? I mourn them both still.

# Chapter 14

• • •

# CAPE TO CAIRO

• • •

## *July–September 1964*

rchie dropped me at the Grand National Hotel in Jo'burg, which he recommended as clean and inexpensive, and then hurried back to his flat to call the American Embassy. He telephoned early the next morning to say that he had heard back from the Embassy and that things did not look good for Johnnie-the-Punk. He had been arrested on two charges. The first was drug-running and the second was membership of the Communist Party. Archie said that the Embassy had been sympathetic when he had first alerted them to the Punk's plight, but that their attitude had now changed. Drug-running was a federal offence in the US, attracting up to ten years' imprisonment for a first offence. No American committing such an crime in a foreign country could expect aid from the US State Department, which would only intervene in cases where the human rights of a US citizen were in jeopardy.

We had both enjoyed a narrow escape, Archie told me. If we had stayed with J Punk until his arrest, he and I would also have been arrested for aiding and abetting. Moreover, Archie's car would have been impounded as the vehicle employed for the commission of the crime. In such cases, he told me, the vehicle was seldom restored to its owner, even in the event of an acquittal. Not that an acquittal, the US Embassy official added sternly, was a likely outcome.

In Archie's view I was particularly vulnerable, as I was a known associate of the ANC renegade Robin Cranko, and Johnnie-the-Punk had lived with Robin during his time in Maseru. I had already told Archie about the attention I had received from Secret Agent Aspin. He recommended that I get out of South Africa as fast as possible, preferably through Bechuanaland. If I took the direct route north, the authorities would probably apprehend me on the border between the Transvaal and Rhodesia. Meanwhile he would monitor the Punk's situation and let me know the outcome when I arrived at the Rhodesian capital, Salisbury.

. . .

I would still need to hitch-hike, in order to conserve my rapidly diminishing capital. Jo'burg covers a vast geographical area, and it was not practical or safe to hitch lifts within the conurbation, so I took a train to Rustenburg in the Western Cape. I walked out of the town carrying my single suitcase and positioned myself under a sign that read 'London 6,479 miles'. I was soon picked up by an elderly Boer farmer, who was not going that far, but kindly regaled me with a hot steak and kidney pie and a eulogy to the Nationalist government. He took me to Swartruggens, where we repaired to the pub and drank Guinness together until another Boer farmer, a friend of my benefactor, joined us and was prevailed upon to take me on to Groot Marico. He bundled me into the back of his car next to his tribe of little Boers, who were very affable and passed the time telling me about the iniquities of 'de broddy Kaffirs'. My host volunteered the information that 'De only gut Kaffir, Robbi, ist de dead Kaffir, he he he!' When they turned off at Groot Marico they wished me well and sought a promise that I would tell 'de Englischers de troot about de broddy Kaffirs'. Uncle Harry would have told them off for using such a rude word.

My next lift took me to Zeerust: a young Boer with his girlfriend. The girlfriend had an aunt whose husband was military attaché at the SA High Commission in London. When she arrived she was given a big house by the government, and a couple of days later a British official turned up leading a young woman by the hand and said, 'this is your servant.' 'It can't be,' declared the aunt. 'Why not?,' asked the official. 'She's white,' exclaimed the aunt. 'Of course she is white,' replied the official. 'We don't have black servants in England.' 'This is impossible,' pronounced the aunt. 'Back in Pretoria, if my servant does something wrong I hit her. But I can't hit a European.' So the servant was sent away and auntie Boer got down on her hands and knees and scrubbed all the floors herself. *Which goes to show, I wrote home, the sort of indomitable spirit that has served the gallant Boers to keep the Kaffirs in a proper subjection for the last 300 years. The girlfriend told me that de broddy Kaffirs are dirty, lazy, and would steal de melk out of your koffie. I said this was interesting because in England it is your tea out of which no-goods steal de melk.*

I spent the night in Mafeking, a town of singularly few attractions but in those days a unique distinction. It was the only capital in the world that was not situated in the country which it administered. This was the capital of Bechuanaland, despite being a full twenty miles from the border of the Protectorate. I assume this was because the largest town in Bechuanaland, Francistown, was in the far north of the Protectorate and it was deemed necessary to have access to the communications and other amenities offered in South Africa. Gaborones had already been scheduled as the post-independence capital, which indeed it became, but the building programme had yet to begin.

The next day two lifts took me to the border and another one brought me to Lobatse, a pleasant little town boasting Bechuanaland's only bioscope and its only bookshop. It also had the only paved road in the Protectorate, a three-and-a-half-mile stretch from the station to the High Court that was macadamised in 1947 to celebrate the visit of Princess Elizabeth. A long afternoon in a cold wind passed before a car stopped and took me the forty-five miles to Gaborones. The future capital comprised a station, an hotel, two banks, two trading stores, four European houses and a cluster of rondavels. How much banking activity took place I know not, but doubtless the two banks had been opened in anticipation of business generated by the expansion of the new capital.

Gaborone (it has lost the 's') is now a city of nearly a quarter of a million people and has been immortalised in the *No. 1 Ladies Detective Agency* novels of master storyteller Alexander McCall Smith. Most African literature tends to be about tribal life or, in a city setting, about poverty, violence and corruption. McCall Smith's enchanting stories paint a picture of day-to-day 21st century life for relatively prosperous lower middle-class urban Africans as represented by 'traditionally-built' Mma Ramotswe, a private detective whose cases revolve round domestic situations requiring a female perspective, and her undemonstrative but ever-loyal admirer Mr JLB Matekoni, proprietor of Tlokweng Road Speedy Motors. It is perhaps significant that the tales take place in the only country in Africa that is virtually free of corruption.

There is much to criticise about Britain's custody of her African possessions, but one singular blessing was that corruption for personal gain was unknown. That valuable legacy was rapidly squandered in every former British territory except Botswana, as Bechuanaland became on attaining independence in 1966. When Seretse Khama became the country's first president, he set it as one of his principal objectives to have a government and public services in which bribery had no part. He enforced this rigidly and made it clear that no one who succumbed could remain in public life. His successors have continued this admirable policy, never diluted as the nation, originally one of the poorest in Africa, acquired wealth first from the discovery of diamonds and later by the development of a thriving tourist industry. The underdeveloped Bechuanaland I knew was the only country in the world other than Bhutan that had no newspaper. The advanced Botswana to which I returned in 2001 was a beacon of hope and an exemplar for those other African nations in which democracy has failed.

The Gaborones of 1964 had yet to come to terms with its glittering future. The hotel, which had no lounge, expected its guests to double up. I shared with an Afrikaner railwayman on his way to a cattle halt twenty miles up the line to which he had been posted for a month. He told me he had brought two books with him. I hope he was a slow reader.

After an indifferent breakfast I began thumbing lifts north. Three cars passed during the course of the morning, none stopping for me. The traffic count declined in the afternoon, with only two vehicles, but thankfully the second picked me up. The driver and his companion were young Voluntary Service Overseas (VSO) workers from England who were driving around the whole of Bechuanaland to recruit enumerators for the forthcoming elections. They were spending the night at Mochudi, then continuing up the Great North Road for seventy miles before turning off into the Kalahari to visit the desert tribes. Would I like to stay the night and ride with them tomorrow as far as the turn-off? I would.

At Mochudi the VSO boys said that we would go and see the District Commissioner and get it fixed up. I wrote home: *The DC was charming and just like a DC out of Somerset Maugham. (All DCs are. Perhaps the selection boards read Maugham carefully before choosing chaps.) The boys were lent an empty government house to camp in, and I was to be lodged with one Sandy Grant, a welfare worker. I wondered whether Mr Grant would mind being told he had a guest for the night, but apparently it is quite normal in the remoter areas, for strangers are few and a new face always welcome. The government-owned house was very empty and bare but for the government furniture, comfortable but plain: beds, a couple of tables and half a dozen chairs upholstered but with wooden arms. All in regulation government brown. No carpets, curtains, or bits and pieces.*

*After we had unloaded the pickup, we sought out Mr Grant. He loomed up behind his garden fence and proved to be a tall bespectacled young gentleman with a somewhat learned air but a humorous mouth. He seemed delighted to see us. He invited us in and we scrambled over the fence.*

*After a couple of sundowners we cooked up all the rations in the house, supplemented by some out of the pick-up, and fared very well. Sandy Grant is a Cambridge man who went into publishing and became disaffected with it. He worked for Harraps and said he had a lot of good ideas but they were always squashed. There is a large market for British books abroad – we have the highest book export figures in the world – but Harraps only send books abroad if they are specifically ordered. Mr Grant contacted one of Harraps' foreign agents and found that they were unaware that they handled the agency. But when he put forward a constructive plan for increasing overseas sales he was told it was not for young men to put forward suggestions. So he left and joined Nelsons, where he was given a desk and a chair and nothing to do. After a few years of this aimless existence he threw up his London life and came out to Bechuanaland as a community development worker. He is very happy out here and thinks he may have found his niche.*

*Unfortunately there was nearly a row. One of the VSO workers opined that he considered it was childish to consider that the protectorates were riddled with spies. (He had plainly disbelieved what I had said about the spy situation in Basutoland.) Sandy nearly went off his nut. Not only was Bechuanaland spied on but it was riddled with saboteurs, he said, and cited examples of planes being blown up and trains derailed.*

*I later found out that the reason Sandy feels so strongly on this matter is that one of his jobs is to ferry South African refugees through Bechuanaland (unofficially). So the SA Special Branch take a keen interest in him. As he said, for all he knew his servants might be reporting this conversation we were having to a man with a Dutch accent who paid them money.*

*After this altercation the VSO boy, having insisted that everybody exaggerated about South Africa (he has not actually been there), took himself off to bed. The other three of us remained talking until three o'clock. It is regrettable that wherever you are in southern Africa, and I believe all over Africa, politics divides friends and relatives and people of the same blood and under the same flag. Divides not only on opinion, but so often foments hatred and conflict. And yet it is difficult, well nigh impossible, to stand apart from the issues involved. I suppose this is always so when the issues boil down to a matter of liberty.*

. . .

In the morning we drove along the sandy road to the vet post where the boys were turning off. The country was absolutely flat and all you could see on either side of the road was thorn bush. The speed at which we drove was regulated by the depth of sand, which was variable. Occasionally we passed an African on a bicycle, going whither it was hard to guess, the distances between settlements being great.

I traded my last remaining book, which I had just finished, for Laurens van der Post's *The Lost World of the Kalahari* before the boys drove off into that lost world. I sat down on a dusty bit of it, leant against my suitcase, and started to read, hoping that I would shortly be interrupted by the arrival of a vehicle. The sun grew higher in the sky and no vehicles approached. A number of hours passed. Laurens van der Post's descriptions of the utter desolation of the Kalahari were not reassuring. I had nothing to eat and, more importantly, nothing to drink. Why had I made reading matter my first priority as always?

As a lunchless lunchtime came and went, I rose and started jumping up and down to distract my mind's eye from visions of whitened bones found in the desert scrub. I read some more, jumped some more, strode up and down, and sang *Floreat Salopia* in Latin. The sun was now beginning to descend in the sky. I considered what extra clothes I could put on if I had to spend the night by the roadside in the desert cold. I also fell to wondering what kind of wild animals came out at night.

There is scarcely any dusk at this latitude. A fiery sunset is succeeded by rapid, inky darkness. I shivered in anticipation. There could not be many more minutes of light remaining.

You could see up and down the Great North Road for miles. I stared longingly to the south. Then in the gloaming, at the very farthest distance that visibility allowed, there was what appeared to be a puff on dust on the horizon. It grew bigger as it advanced towards me, until it assumed the unmistakable shape of a car. Nearer, yet nearer. Was I saved?

I extended my arm, thumb skywards, and assumed what Robin Gates used to characterise as the 'silly grin' that got me out of scrapes and ingratiated me with those from whom I sought favours. On this occasion it appeared that those from whom I sought favour were unimpressed. To my horror I realised that the vehicle was accelerating.

I then did what I have only ever done on this single occasion. I walked into the middle of the road and waved my arms frantically. The car ground to a halt. As I walked round its side, and leaned down to importune the driver, I saw to my alarm that he was already putting the car into gear. I did not speak to the driver. Instead I wrenched open the rear door, threw my suitcase in, and dived after it as the car began to move forward.

How to introduce oneself and initiate lively chit chat in these circumstances? My unwilling hosts, two elderly Boer farmers, emitted no more than grunts, and these not in the most amicable of tones, during the first hour of their involuntary association with me. My main concern, though, overriding any about the social niceties of our situation, was whether they were going to halt the car and order me out of it. This, happily, did not happen. Eventually the passenger Boer leant over the back of his seat and asked where I was from. I told him I was English. 'English South African?' he queried. I explained my provenance, which seemed to satisfy him, because he turned to the driver and pronounced 'He's not English. He's a Britischer.'

The conversation that ensued, at first haltingly, but as the long hours passed, increasingly volubly, was notable chiefly for its absence of denigratory remarks about 'de broddy Kaffirs'. It was 'de broddy Englischers' who blighted the lives of my two companions. 'You would not believe it, Robbi' – by this time they were Johann and Piet and they had conferred this diminutive on me – 'you would not believe how these Englischers treat us. It is our country and yet they push us around and take all the best jobs and they have all the money. And the way they talk about us, like we were ignorant peasants. It is shameful, Robbi! They even call us broddy Boers behind our backs.'

There was a lot more in the same strain, punctuated by copious drafts from the bottle of South African brandy that Piet passed around. (Drink driving was not a problem in the Kalahari; there was nothing to hit.) None of it was very surprising, as it was simply the mirror image of how I had repeatedly heard English-speaking South Africans characterise Afrikaners. It was also a stark reminder that during the many weeks I had spent in South Africa I had never encountered an Afrikaner socially, only in their capacity as (usually minor) officials. I suspect that Johann and Piet had lived in the same isolation from the English-speaking half of the white population.

I did not return to South Africa until several years after the bloodless revolution that brought an end to apartheid and the peaceful transition of power to the Bantu, Indian and Coloured populations. In all the acres of newsprint devoted to the enormous cultural changes that accompanied the new political dispensation, little or no attention was devoted to what I found one of its most remarkable and least expected consequences, the rapprochement between Afrikaner and English-speaking South Africans. They first came together in the wake of Mandela's release for mutual protection – we now celebrate the 'Rainbow Nation', but at the time that the ANC was preparing to assume power there was no certainty that democratic institutions, the rule of law and the rights of property holders would be preserved. Initial contacts between these old enemies were held in an atmosphere of mutual suspicion. Gradually Afrikaners began to realise that not all English-speaking South Africans were the sons and daughters of privilege; Englischers began to learn that not all Afrikaners were bigoted, ignorant, racist religious fanatics. Move forward a few more years and they were not only working together, but forming friendships. There was even inter-marriage. And now when I visit South Africa I meet as many Afrikaners as I do Englischers. Regretfully I cannot say I meet as many Bantu in social situations. Race relations in SA have advanced immeasurably; there is still a way to go.

Johann and Piet dropped me outside the Kalahari Inn at Mahalapye with admonitions to 'tell de Britischers de troot about de broddy Englischers'. Belatedly I am now fulfilling that promise.

. . .

Breakfasting late the next morning, I was alone in the dining room except for a chap in the opposite corner with a handlebar moustache and an RAF tie. I presumed he must be English, but there was nobody to effect an introduction. Finishing his toast and marmalade, he strode towards the door, then paused, turned in my direction and with his eyes directed at my chest, enquired in a tone more of curiosity than challenge, 'Is that Jennifer's sweater you're wearing?'

I choked on my tea, to the detriment of the sweater in question. 'Yes,' I affirmed. 'I borrowed it from her during the big freeze in Maseru. Were you there?'

'I was staying at the Lancers Inn. I arrived shortly before you left. I used to watch you and Jennifer giggling together at dinner. Do you think she is going to marry Ian? Or do you have ambitions in that area yourself?'

After responding 'Yes' to the first question and 'No' to the second, I invited my new chum to join me and another pot of tea was ordered. His name was Eddie and he had been running an airfield in Zanzibar until the revolution earlier that year, when he had been given twelve hours to get out by the new socialist government. He now had a new job in Dar es Salaam and was currently on leave. He had never visited Basutoland or Bechuanaland and had decided to take a tour. Now he was on his way home. He was going to spend three days in Francistown, the metropolis of Bechuanaland (pop. 2,300, two hotels, no bio), then a week in Salisbury before heading up to Dar. What were my plans? I told him. Would I like to come along? I was keen to see a bit of Rhodesia, though I would have to watch expenses. And a lift of 2,500 miles would be a great blessing. I accepted Eddie's invitation eagerly.

Francistown proved to have few distinctions, other than a strong claim to be the only town outside Australia named after an Australian. (John Kimpton was so enthused by this abstruse piece of knowledge that he wrote to the *Sydney Morning Herald* about it. Their readers were unable to come up with another.) Eddie was disappointed by its lack of attractions and we spent most of the first two days in the billiard room of the cheaper and shabbier of the two hotels, Eddie muttering, 'Fancy coming to the bloody Kalahari to play bloody snooker!' The next day we visited the annual Francistown Show, where the most interesting exhibit was, unexpectedly, the Public Works Department stand. This showed a scale model of the new capital city of Gaborone, as it would be on completion of the initial phase of building. Then there would be 5,000 inhabitants (the 1964 population was about 200; it is now 230,000) housed, by the good offices of the PWD, in three levels of accommodation, priced at £400 for the most affordable to £1,000 for the most luxurious. Do these homes still exist, I wonder, and what do they go for now?

Francistown lay only an hour from the Rhodesian border. After a short, uneventful ride we pulled up at the frontier. An immigration officer was speaking on the phone in the adjacent booth and we could just overhear his words: 'KJ3 to be stopped and sent back? I'll attend to it immediately.' Eddie turned to me a stricken look on his face. 'That's our car!,' he hissed. The immigration officer emerged from the booth, but strode past our car and started checking the line of cars – half a dozen or so – that stood behind us. At that moment another official lifted the barrier and waved us through. Eddie took off like a jack rabbit on skates and we shot forward in a cloud of red dust. I turned to look through the rear window. The immigration officer was running up the road gesticulating at us. I suggested to Eddie that he keep the accelerator flat on the floor.

Once we were out of sight of the frontier post, Eddie relaxed a little and told me that a week ago in Lobatse he had got into conversation in the hotel bar and revealed that he was carrying some animal skins on which he did not propose to pay duty. One of the people in the bar was a policeman's wife. He thought she may have overheard him. I had my own suspicions as to why our car was to be apprehended. The South African authorities worked closely with their Rhodesian counterparts, whereas there was no such co-operation with Bechuanaland. There were, however, South African secret agents in Bechuanaland, as Sandy Grant had attested. My belief was that there was an APB out on the known associate of the renegade Robin Cranko and the drug-runner John Morrison alias Johnnie-the-Punk.

Twenty miles further on my feeling of relief that I had evaded Rhodesian justice was dissipated by the sight of a police road-block up ahead. This time, I was confident, there would be no such slip-up as had occurred at the frontier post. Eddie was now in a state of high anxiety (though a police road-block for the evasion of a few shillings' duty was surely doubtful). My anxiety was even higher.

But when our papers were checked we were told to drive on. I have wondered ever since what the explanation was. Assuming the road-block was for us, and it seems to me most likely that it was, I can think of only one. Many of the BSAP, the Rhodesian police force, were British. By no means were all of them supporters of the South African regime. I believe that I struck lucky with a police officer of integrity who had been ordered to mount a road-block and did so, but had no intention of delivering the British suspect into the hands of the notoriously brutal South African police. I did not voice this to Eddie. Once he had recovered from the shock of these events, he was swelled with pride that he had succeeded in smuggling his animal skins past both the customs officers and the police. And saved himself fifteen bob in duty!

Looking back now I find it quite extraordinary that such a law abiding person as myself, timid by nature and generally inclined to defer to authority, should have attracted the attention of the Federal Bureau of Investigation, the Royal Canadian Mounted Police, the Los Angeles Police Department, the South African Bureau of State Security and Rhodesia's BSAP, the British South Africa Police. Not to speak of my time in the custody of the Tanganyika Police and being deported from Kenya (see later in this chapter). Where had my poor dear mother and father gone wrong?

. . .

Bulawayo, I noted, was a city of wide avenues and attractive buildings, very green and spacious. As is my wont on visiting any colonial city for the first time, I went in search of the oldest building. The oldest I could find with a date on it was a three-storey office building of 1895. As the city was only settled by Europeans at the end of 1893, it must have developed at remarkable speed. There were also a lot of old brick shanties with thatched roofs that must have dated from the earliest pioneer days (now all long gone). By striking contrast was a high-rise apartment block in the most *moderne* of art deco designs. What sort of Rhodesians, circa late

1920s or early 1930s, lived in a luxury, ultra-modern flat resembling the one occupied by Hercule Poirot in the popular TV series? Remarkably, it was still there in 2015, looking a bit dowdy and down-at-heel. What kind of Zimbabweans live there now?

Our next stop was Victoria Falls. I hope you have noted, dear reader, and appreciated, the absence of sightseeing in this travelogue. Neither Eddie nor I were fond of tourist attractions, but you can hardly omit the world's largest waterfall when you visit either of the Rhodesias, so we made the detour. All I have to tell you is that it was mainly spray that we saw. If you visit, take a mac. It was Founders' Day, the biggest public holiday in Rhodesia, and all the hotels had been booked up nine months earlier. The nearest place we would find a bed, we were informed, was Wankie.

There were two hotels in Wankie. The Baobab was full up. The other one, we were warned, was multiracial. Eddie said as far as he was concerned this was an attribute. I wrote home:

*Wankie is a coal mining town and a railway depot. The view from the Railway Hotel was like looking out over Barnsley. The hotel was remarkably clean, though the language in the bar was not. It was quite a lesson in semantics. Nor did it come from the African customers. Although there is no legal colour bar in Rhodesia, it is up to individual proprietors to make their own rules. The manageress of the hotel we stayed at in Bulawayo said she only imposed a ban when the Africans completely took over one of her two bars. When they started coming in to the other one, she said no – as they had taken over one and would not let Europeans enter it, so be it. They had imposed their own discrimination. She was a most reasonable woman and most interesting to listen to. She could talk of the virtues and the vices of the Africans without this virulent hate which removes all logic and reason from most discussions on race relations south of the Zambezi. It seems that many Rhodesians are in favour of establishing apartheid here. In South Africa few English-speaking South Africans were wholeheartedly in favour of the policy. Rhodesians are more towards the Boer way of thinking. I wonder why this is. If Rhodesia succeeds in obtaining the sort of independence that most white people are asking for, I only hope they are not allowed to remain in the Commonwealth.* (Rhodesia was indeed expelled in 1965 and only restored to membership with majority rule. Gross violations of human rights resulted in suspension of Zimbabwe's membership in 2002.)

Eddie and I spent another two days in Bulawayo and then drove on to Salisbury. My first stop was at the GPO, where there were two letters and a telegram for me. The first was from the Lovely Mrs Lachlan, very worried that Jainey McCrae, late receptionist at the Hermitage, who was on her way to Britain, was unprepared for what she, the Lovely Mrs L, characterised as the overwhelming experience that was London. 'Does she realise, Patrick,' Mrs L wailed, 'that the population of the capital is nearly four times that of the whole of New Zealand? Will she ever find her way to Earl's Court?' Mrs L, if you are reading this, let me assure you that the future Dowager Countess Bolingbroke took to London life as if it was just a bigger, brighter version of Timaru.

The telegram read: FREE AGAIN STOP DEPORTED STOP LETTER FOLLOWING STOP PUNK.

Johnnie-the-Punk's letter, written from Archie's address in Jo'burg, revealed all that had transpired after our American friend had told us to leg it. In the last case that he had opened, the fat South African customs official had found a matchbox containing a small amount of *dagga*, probably enough for half a dozen spliffs. Punk explained to me how he had acquired this. On his last night in the Maluti Mountains, the tribesmen that he had been assisting had slaughtered a goat in his honour and held a feast. A lot of maize beer was consumed, several spliffs smoked and a good time had by all. Before he departed, the Chief had gathered up the remaining shreds of *dagga* and put them in the matchbox. He handed this to the Punk with the words 'Take this back to New York with you as a souvenir and think of us when you smoke it!' Punk said that by the time we left Basutoland, he had forgotten all about it.

After the fat customs officer had made his triumphant find, all the Punk's luggage was impounded, the police were summoned, he was cuffed and bundled into a van and driven off to police cells in Ladybrand. The fat customs officer had handed over his list of the Punk's collection of political ephemera to the police, pointing out as he did so the pamphlets from the Communist Party of Basutoland. Punk was arraigned on two charges: attempted drug-running across international borders and membership of a banned organisation. Both offences carried maximum sentences of several years.

Punk was then thrown into the slammer with only a Bible in Afrikaans for reading matter. He rattled the bars and shouted for the guard to let him call the American Embassy. This was refused. He then demanded a lawyer. That was also refused.

The days that followed, Punk declared, were the worst he had ever spent in his life. There were no communications from the outside world. He was totally isolated. Twice a day the guard would slam a tin plate and a rusted enamel mug down in front of him. The food on his plate was always *boerewors*. The water in his mug had insects floating on the surface. The cold was piercing and he was not allowed to access his bags for warm clothing. The bags, he was told, were evidence.

When an attorney did appear, he made it clear that he was not acting for the defence. He had been sent to inform the Punk that if he pleaded guilty the sentence might be half that imposed for a not guilty plea. There was no point in making a not guilty plea, he informed the Punk menacingly, because the evidence was incontrovertible

A week later Punk was told to get ready for court. He was driven to Bloemfontein, capital of the Orange Free State, the most Afrikaner, the most rigidly authoritarian province in the Republic. Nearly all the judges were Afrikaners and few were noted for their leniency, least of all to foreign offenders. But here Punk got his first lucky break. He came up before one of the Freistaat's small minority of English-speaking judges. He pleaded not guilty to the charge of drug-trafficking, but guilty to possession. On the charge of belonging to a banned organisation he also pleaded not guilty. It did not take long to present the evidence. Punk did not dispute that the matchbox of *dagga* had been in his luggage. He could not say for sure whether he meant to take it over the border; he had forgotten about it by then.

The defendant strongly contested the evidence that he was a member of a banned organisation. He was a student of politics, he claimed, and the Communist Party pamphlet was amongst literature issued by no fewer than twenty-two political parties in Basutoland.

The proceedings had not advanced very far when the judge called a halt. He declared that he had heard sufficient of the evidence to come to a verdict. He then addressed the prosecuting counsel and said that his remarks should also be noted by the police who had brought the case. Much of the evidence presented was, in his opinion, deeply flawed. While accepting that Mr Morrison had attempted to bring a matchbox containing *dagga* across the border, there was nothing to suggest that he proposed to sell it either in South Africa or elsewhere. On the other charge, the judge pronounced that there was no case to answer. Possession of a pamphlet published by the Communist Party of Basutoland did not signify membership; and even if Mr Morrison was a member, the Communist Party of Basutoland was not a banned organization in South Africa.

Since Mr Morrison had pleaded guilty to one of the drugs charges, possession, he had no option but to impose the minimum penalty: a fine of ten rand and deportation within seven days. The other charges were dismissed. He then summoned the police witnesses to approach the bench. He admonished them to consider very carefully whether the bringing of these charges against a national from a friendly country had been a constructive use of police time and, moreover, that of the court. Finally he turned to the defendant and wished him a safe return to the United States.

. . .

*This truly is a very beautiful city, and of all modern cities I think the most attractive I have seen,* I reported from Salisbury. *In the downtown area there are a host of miniature skyscrapers, not drab and grey, but dazzling white. Everywhere you look there is grass. Here as in Bulawayo early single-storey buildings still stand in places, looking so out of place next to their twenty-storey neighbours. Eddie pointed to one, an ancient store with weathered rough cut stone walls whitewashed, and a low shingled roof overhanging a veranda supported by wooden props. 'You would schedule that for preservation I suppose?' he remarked. 'Naturally', I replied. 'Ah, how I would love to get the grappling irons on to it', he gloated maliciously. Eddie is staying with his sister-in-law and I am at the Mayfair Hotel, a small private establishment which for 27s 6d a day offers a six-course dinner, which last night included turkey and bread sauce and four veg.*

You got a lot for 27s 6d in Rhodesia in 1964. It was part of the attraction for sun-starved Britons who had returned from wartime service to find that life in a prefab in austerity Britain left much to be desired. They flocked to Rhodesia in the late 1940s and 1950s, where working-class and lower-middle-class toilers with dead-end jobs at home were able to hold down supervisory jobs because being white gave them an automatic right to give orders to black workers. It was said at the time that the officer class went out to Kenya and the NCOs to Rhodesia. Of course the social demographics of the colony were more complex than that, but there was a modicum of truth in it. While there was no formal system of apartheid in the colony, the manner in which white Rhodesians, many of them British migrants, treated the Bantu was far more imperious and lacking in common courtesy than the behaviour of most English-speaking South Africans to servants and black workers. This was compounded by the fact that a large element of the white population were Afrikaners, a fact often overlooked when Lord Salisbury's appeals for Britain to support 'our kith and kin' were quoted in English media. They treated the Bantu much the same as they did at home, which was not the best example to set before new arrivals. My feeling then, little changed since, was that the stereotype of the English overseas treating the natives with contempt and opprobrium was largely false, but sadly less so in Rhodesia than in other British territories.

A codicil. These strictures, and those quoted below, apply to urban white Rhodesians, who were, contrary to popular perception, the vast majority of the 250,000-strong white population. I do not doubt for a moment the raw courage of those farmers who in later years were to face bitter persecution by the tyrant Mugabe with such fortitude. Nor do I doubt their genuine commitment to the wellbeing of their farm workers, a large segment of the Bantu population, for which there is ample testimony.

I expressed myself with rather less restraint in a letter home. I quote it here for what it is worth, the initial impression of an observer of a country in transition (UDI was declared the following year): *I cannot say I am impressed with the attitude of the white inhabitants. They seem to have a virulent hatred for the Africans, and no idea of working with them, only against them... I was curious to find that they do not regard themselves as British, but rather as South Africans. There is a strong faction in favour of merging with South Africa. I think it would probably be a good thing if they did. They are no ornament to the British Commonwealth.*

There were, however, striking differences between South Africa and its neighbour. The occupational choices of blacks were not restricted by law (though they doubtless were by custom) and there were no formal bans on blacks and whites mixing for social, professional or political purposes. The most striking difference became apparent when I visited Parliament. This was housed in a converted hotel and from the outside it still looked like a place where you might find a pint and a pie. The interior, however, had all the panoply of responsible government, granted forty years earlier. It was the House of Commons in miniature, the chief difference being that the green leather benches had arm-rests. But a much greater distinction was those who occupied them. There were sixty-five Members of Parliament, and of these fifteen seats were reserved for Bantu Members. Since the 1961 Constitution there had been qualified voting by a black electorate. There were two ways a Bantu could qualify for the vote: by education or by property. The reasoning behind this was that if you were a literate person, you were qualified to participate in the governance of the country. And even if you were not literate, you were qualified if you owned a certain amount of property because you had a stake in the country. (In neither case was the bar set impossibly high.) Now you might argue that this was about as advanced as Britain's franchise following the 1867 Reform Act; I would rejoin that it was a darnn sight better than what they had south of the border.

. . .

It was time to head north of the border. Johnnie-the-Punk, busy in Jo'burg with despatching his restored luggage to New York and obtaining visas for various African countries, arrived somewhat breathlessly in Salisbury only a few minutes before Eddie and I were due to leave for Mozambique.

*We crossed the border in the late afternoon,* I wrote home, *and spent the night at the Hotel Zambezi in Tete. Tete is a town about the size of Stroud and distinctively Portuguese. The architecture is quite unlike that in any other part of Africa I have seen, and like everything in Tete, has a continental atmosphere about it. The hotel was excellent, very clean and well appointed. There was a colourful bar, and we had some drinks with a couple of Portuguese whom we had helped with a puncture a few miles out of town. The conversation was mostly in sign language. The beer was most interesting, as it was not ale but stout. I had no idea stout was brewed in Portugal, let alone in Mozambique. Along with the nuts and crisps a dish of spiced beans in sauce was served with each drink. Round the dish were cubes of bread to mop it up with, though a spoon was provided. By the time you had consumed several of these there was not much need of dinner.*

However, dinner was good even on a diminished appetite. Soup followed by something that looked like Yorkshire pudding, tasted of fish, and was made from eggs. After this the main dish which was a mess of meat Portuguesa. Then followed cold victuals, slender slices of sausage and ham. Finished with pawpaw and a nice pot of tea. I must say the Portuguese make a very decent cup.

In the morning we strolled round the town and looked in the shops. All most strange and foreign and interesting. I imagine the Portuguese live very comfortably in their dominions. At noon the streets are deserted and remain so until three: siesta time.

We crossed the mighty Zambezi by ferry, leaving Southern Africa behind and heading up into Central Africa. It was lunchtime now so we went to a cantina and had cheese and ham rolls. Then back in the road and in a few hours we had left Mozambique and were entering Malawi.

We put up for the night at Nash's Private Hotel in Blantyre. The second largest city in Malawi, Blantyre is a town of singular charm, partly because the streets ramble up and down and over and around. It is very colourful, and must contain hundreds of shops. I have never seen so many shops next to each other all selling the same things, and with few gaps for other sorts of building. There is however a handsome edifice inscribed in familiar lettering 'The Times Bookshop'. It really was like a small replica of our Times Bookshop in Wigmore Street where Rubber Ears d'Arch Smith works, evidently catering, as he does, to a refined and cultivated clientele. The range of books was excellent, and it also sold the other bits and pieces as in Wigmore Street, such as leather blotters and gramophone records. Most impressive was its range of glossy magazines – in French, German, Spanish and Italian as well as the English and South African ones: I have no idea who buys them. Even more unexpected were the Beano and the Dandy. I like the idea of little black Blantyre kids being brought up on a diet of Biffo the Bear and Korky the Kat. The only other patron in the shop was an elderly lady of superior aspect; probably a pillar of strength on the Church Flower Arrangement Committee, and I expect she was looking for books on gardening. I gather this shop has no connection with the Times of Wigmore Street, other than trying to look as if it does. Blantyre also has a newspaper called The Times. Not the Blantyre Times. Just The Times.

The Punk is cross because he was shaken awake at six o'clock in the morning by a big black man at Nash's Private Hotel and forced to drink a *cup of tea which he didn't want and doesn't like. The big fella stood over him till it was drained to the last drop. Punk lectured me for a long time on the insidious influence the British have had on their former colonies, so that even when these colonies have thrown off the yoke of imperialism they remain rooted in such barbarous customs as early morning tea. It is no good explaining that Africans like tea, especially in the early morning – he believes that these new nations should be defiantly African.* [Malawi had become independent twelve months earlier.]

*We all three agree on South Africa though, so we each in turn fell out with the proprietress, a Scots woman and strong admirer of Dr Verwoerd and his band of swell-mobsmen. She cornered us one at a time and extracted our opinions of South Africa. She told us how nice Nyasaland had been on her arrival in 1919, when the Africans had been happy and contented, obedient and respectful. Now they were insolent and refractory. Her main complaint was that there were no longer jobs for young Europeans, as young educated Africans were taking them. I am not sure whether this demonstrated the evils of education or the evils of the Africans.*

*We headed north again mid-morning, and stopped at a roadside hotel for lunch. To our surprise we found everybody in the hotel was Portuguese, and our luncheon of steak and eggs done à la Portuguesa. 'You are in Portugal!' they explained to us. 'But where is the border?' we asked. They pointed out of the window. That side of the road was in Malawi, but this side of the road was in Mozambique, for the centreline marked the border. Back in Malawi we spent the night at a very plush and very expensive hotel in the bush, miles from anywhere. It is the last hotel on the road north, so weary travellers have little option but to pay its fancy rates. Punk curled up for the night in the back of Eddie's car.*

The absence of hotels meant that the next night we were obliged to use a Government Rest House, originally intended for government officials travelling in the remoter areas, but now open to all travellers. This one had most of the amenities of a small hotel, for there was a resident cook (you supplied your own food) and bedding. Other rest-houses sometimes required you to provide your own bedding and do your own cooking. What was on offer was not unlike the menu provided by a transport café: eggs, sausages and beans, with pint mugs of tea. Afterwards Eddie made a killing at gin rummy, 1,500 up.

The friendly cook advised us the road north was impassable, and that we would need to take a detour past Lake Nyasa, 150 miles from the Rest House, and head up through Northern Rhodesia (now Zambia) to the Tanganyika border. We did as he advised, stopping at Ngata Bay on this vast inland sea to enjoy a large canned steak and kidney pudding that we had procured at a police canteen. I reported: *The beach was lovely, pale sand and white crested breakers. Had a most delightful bathe. Afterwards on the beach we watched a native doing the three card trick. He had a dupe who was 'winning' a lot of money at it in order to pull in the suckers. The trickster was lightning quick in his movements and had soon attracted quite a crowd of beachcombers, layabouts, and two pink bank managers from SA. The Punk was greatly enthused by this performance and afterwards he pursued the trickster and inveigled him into revealing the secret. He promised to send the trickster half his profits if he operated it successfully on the sidewalks of New York. So he learnt the age-old secrets of Find the Lady, which are indeed most ingenious, and took the trickster's name, which was Mr Rich Banda. He said he was a grandson of Doctor Banda, the President of Malawi.*

I think the Punk would have discovered that Three Card Monte, as they call it over there, had already preceded him to the sidewalks of the Lower East Side. I am distressed that I can no longer remember the secret of this most classic of all scams. A Google search failed to reveal Mr Rich Banda's secret. Was Rich short for Richard or did the cognomen signify the reward reaped by his endeavours?

We crossed into Northern Rhodesia shortly after breakfast and drove the whole day, crossing into Tanganyika at dusk. It speaks of the vast emptiness of Africa that we could drive a whole day through a country that none of us had visited before, without seeing anything, not a solitary thing, worthy of comment. Wild animals? Just a monkey or two.

At dinner that night at a modest guest-house called the Tundaman Hotel, where a tempting chicken fricassée was served, we shared the single dining table with six English people on their way to Kilimanjaro. Johnnie-the-Punk engaged a particularly silly young woman in a fierce debate about Southern Rhodesia. When she declared that the whole Bantu population, all 2½ million of them, should be expelled from the country, he stormed out into the night. I had a fairly good idea where he had gone, as there had been absences on other evenings. When he stumbled into our room at three in the morning smelling of maize beer and *amour*, I asked him whether the lady of his choice had succeeded in assuaging his anger. She had. And was the price of her favours the same as it was further south? It was: the standard fee of one shilling. How would Punk have fared in a Southern Rhodesia bereft of bashful Bantu maidens?

After we had been driving for some time the next morning, we found ourselves in a long line of vehicles, somewhat unexpected so deep in the bush. The line moved very slowly and only after about twenty minutes or so did we see that there was a road-block up ahead. A lot of very officious looking policemen were inspecting the passengers in each car and asking questions. This was tiresome, but as I remarked jocularly to Eddie, this time it could not be us they were after. Eventually it was our turn and we expected to be through the barrier and out on the open road as soon as we had given our names. Somewhat to our dismay one of the police pointed to our number plate and then they all began jabbering in Swahili in a state of great excitement. The largest policeman, who seemed to be in charge, stuck his bullet head through the open window and surveyed us one by one with a malevolent glare. Then he growled, 'Which one is Hickman-Robertson?' I shrank as far as I could into the upholstery before squeaking 'Me Sir.' 'Get out,' he commanded. I hesitated. 'Now!' he thundered. I did as bidden. Two of the big man's goons were summoned and they seized both my arms. I was then pushed into the back of a police car with a downward thrust on the head, just like in Hollywood movies. The big man climbed into the front. 'Is there some kind of a problem, Officer?' I ventured. 'Shaddup', he growled.

We drove for what seemed to me a very long time, no one speaking. Eventually we reached a town and pulled up in the main street outside a police post. I was hauled out of the back and frog-marched inside. The big man knocked on a door and opened it. 'We've got him, Sir', he said to whoever was inside. Then he turned and beckoned to the goons, who hustled me into a small room furnished only with a desk, a filing cabinet, and the single chair in which sat an urbane-looking black police officer sporting a good deal of gold braid. He looked me up and down, then snapped 'Passport'. I proffered it. He spent a long time inspecting each page, then looked up and asked where I was going and what was my business in Tanganyika. I complied and there followed a silence while he stared at me long and hard, as if trying to penetrate where I had hidden the loot. Then he slowly reached down to the bottom drawer of his desk and began to slide it open, inch by inch. 'Ohmighad he's going to get out the handcuffs,' flashed through my mind, followed immediately by 'What if it's not handcuffs. It could be a gag. Or a gun. That's it. He's going to shoot me!'

What he drew out of the drawer was something made of white linen. He shook it and it unfolded to reveal a shirt. A not unfamiliar shirt. He turned the collar inside out towards me and pointed to the Cash's woven nametape that had been lovingly sewn there by my mother. 'That you?' he grunted. 'That's me,' I tried to say, but managed only a splutter and a nod of the head. For the first time my interrogator relaxed, and there was even the ghost of a smile playing about his sable lips as he leaned back in his chair. 'We are a very new nation, Mr Robertson. We want people to think well of us. Everyone's property is safe in Tanganyika. Here ... take your shirt. You left it at the Tundaman Hotel last night. Enjoy the rest of your stay in our beautiful country.' With that, he gestured to the big man, who was hovering in the doorway. 'You letting him go, Baas?' he asked in a disappointed tone. 'Of course we're letting him go, Sergeant. Mr Robertson is an honoured guest of our country.'

With that I took my farewell of Tanganyika's rural constabulary and emerged into the sunlight. Happily Eddie and the Punk were leaning against the car at the curb slurping Tusker Lager from green bottles. They had not bought one for me and explained that they thought I might be absent for a number of years.

. . .

We drove on to a town called Iringa, where the Railway Hotel, a very fly-blown commercial, cost 42 shillings, ten shillings more than the Tundaman and nearly double the hotel prices in southern Africa. The next night at Morogoro I joined the Punk, who had already taken refuge from high prices on the back seat of the car. It was a most uncomfortable night, despite the fact that I won the toss and the goatskin blanket. The gear-stick rubbed against my ribcage and if I raised my head without thinking I cracked it against the steering wheel.

Next day a short run of 120 miles brought us to Dar es Salaam on the Indian Ocean. We drove through the Southern Highlands, which were shrouded in mist and had the same eerie aspect as the Highlands of Scotland. The bush country had changed from the arid browns of Northern Rhodesia to the most vivid greens, and when we reached the coast there were forests of tall coconut palms. Dar was a city of the most exotic and foreign appearance, but short of amenities. This was journey's end for Eddie. We thanked him profusely for the longest lift – 2,500 miles – either of us had ever enjoyed in our several years of hitch-hiking. After saying our farewells we booked ourselves into a pleasant hotel on the sea, and the Punk had a few beers while I went in search of a tailor. In every African town, large or small, there are sewing-machine operators who sit under the verandah canopies that shade the shops and minister to customers who bring them clothes for repair. For some reason they are all male, but then so are Savile Row tailors. A button on my jacket had worked loose. The jacket had three buttons and this was the third time I had had recourse to these cheerful make-do-and-mend merchants during my journey north. Neither of the first two had accepted payment for this small but invaluable service. Nor did the wielder of needle and thread in Dar. How can people who live so close to the poverty line afford such generosity?

Our next destination was Kilimanjaro and on hearing that the trains were cheap in East Africa, unlike the hotels, we booked ourselves third-class tickets to Moshi, the small town that is the gateway to Africa's highest mountain. The fare for a distance of 500 miles was 16s 6d. For lunch we had a 2½d (1p) loaf and a penny orange each, but for dinner we treated ourselves to the first-class dining car. Duck à l'orange for two was brought forth on a silver platter and the Punk swept the whole lot on to his plate. The waiter looked somewhat startled, but brought another silver platter from which to serve me. The Punk seized this and was about to pile a further helping on to his plate when it was wrenched from his hands by the outraged waiter, who addressed my embarrassing friend in a flood of Swahili not all of which I took to be complimentary.

The night was long. I wrapped myself in the goatskin and read Beverley Nichols's *The Sweet and Twenties*, describing the glamorous world of his youth that seemed very distant from my present surroundings. Some of the more experienced travellers commandeered the luggage racks, in which they were able to sleep fully stretched out. Johnnie-the-Punk anaesthetised himself with a flagon of maize beer. We disembarked at

Moshi in the dawn after twenty-three hours on the train and set off in quest of poached eggs on toast.

The remainder of the day was spent looking for Mount Kilimanjaro. None of its 17,000-foot elevation was visible, the whole shrouded in mist. By late afternoon we were becoming sceptical whether it was really there at all. The Punk declared that it was something made up by Ernest Hemingway. Other folk go to Kilimanjaro to find themselves, or a deeper spiritual truth, in the struggle to attain its snow-topped summit. J Punk and I went to Kilimanjaro and ended up in the bio. We saw Albert Finney and Susannah York in Tony Richardson's *Tom Jones* and a cracking good movie it was too.

We stayed overnight in an Indian hotel that charged 7s 6d a night, including an uneatable breakfast that I removed in a paper bag, in order to avoid offence, and discarded in an open sewer. There was still no sign of Kilimanjaro, so we set off for Arusha, leaving Moshi behind in a trail of dust and a 5-cwt van. There were two other hitch-hikers, Africans, in the van and every mile or two we stopped to pick up locals going into market. They would stand patiently by the roadside with all their produce and wait for someone to stop for them. As the road was studded with these hopefuls, on a bad day they must have had to wait a very long time. This was a red-letter day as they all got picked up by the same vehicle.

Arusha was a pleasant little town that even boasted a theatre. How such a very small place could support a theatre was a mystery. We had lunch in a restaurant kept by an unhappy Czech woman. She was doleful because all the Europeans had gone away and she was lonely. The restaurant looked pretty prosperous despite this and the Punk remarked to that effect. 'Oh, vot is moneys if you are not heppy', wailed the poor lady. 'Now I go to Amerika, ver is mine modder and mine brodder and mine seesters. Zhen I be heppy agen.' She had been in Tanganyika for twenty-three years, she said, and never wanted to see the place again. I should have enquired how she had made her way across war-ravaged Europe and the battlefields of North Africa to reach Tanganyika in 1941.

A Land Rover stopped for us on the Nairobi road. It was driven by a furious-looking Englishman with a bristling white moustache and a relaxed, smiling Irishman called Paddy. We climbed into the open rear and enjoyed the bush and the breeze. After about six miles the Land Rover stopped and there was a lot of muffled cursing by the Englishman and invocations to the saints by the Irishman. The matter mended, we proceeded another mile and then halted again. I lost track of how many times this happened but after an hour and a half we were only eight miles out of Arusha. The final breakdown took place in a narrow defile between steep walls of rock. The Punk and I were sunning ourselves on the back when he suddenly remarked, 'Don't look now but we are being watched', so of course I did and we were. A head had arisen over the side of the cutting and was peering down at us intently. Two more heads appeared on the other side, and after a while several spears also became visible. As the owners of the weapons emerged into a standing position it became apparent that these were Masai warriors, the famous tribe of giants who plait their hair and daub it with red ochre to inspire fear and awe in their enemies. There was plenty of fear and awe in the back of the Land Rover too, as we had no knowledge of the warriors' intentions. Presently one of the giants appeared on the road. He trotted up to the Land Rover and stood staring at the engine which the Englishman and the Irishman were fiddling with and cursing. After a minute had passed he began to chuckle, then laugh uproariously. The Punk and I laughed too. The Englishman and the Irishman did not.

The whole band of Masai were clustered round the Land Rover whooping and grinning and having a good time when a Volkswagen Beetle made its appearance. On learning of the problem, its Australian driver offered to take Punk and me on to Nairobi. He was driving from Mombasa via Arusha to call on his girlfriend in Nairobi and take her back with him for the weekend. He was doing this because he had written to her and the mail had been held up, so he had decided to run over and see her on the off-chance. If she wasn't in he would turn round and drive straight back to Mombasa. The distance for the round trip was nearly 700 miles. I told him that I thought no girl could be paid a higher compliment.

. . .

The border with Kenya was unmanned. A five-bar gate straddled the unmade road and on it was a notice saying that non-residents of Kenya must make themselves known to the immigration authorities on arrival in Nairobi. The lush greenness of Tanganyika gave way to the thorn trees and high grassland of Kenya and soon after nightfall we could see the distant lights of the capital glimmering through a light shower of rain. On arrival our lovesick Australian driver dropped us at the YMCA and set off to find his girl. I do hope she was in.

Next morning I suggested to Punk that we go and register with immigration. He looked at me in surprise and politely enquired whether I was nuts. I assured him I was not; my dear mother had brought me up to obey the dictates of the law wherever you were. Punk asked if my mother was nuts too, a bit less politely I thought. While Punk set off for the Stanley Hotel to imbibe some Tusker Lager (it was here that the famous Kenyan beer had made its debut), I went off to fulfil my promise to mother always to do the bidding of those set in authority over me. The interview with the immigration officer was brief. He asked me how much money I had. I told him. He told me that I was a prospective burden on the Kenyan state and I must leave the country within seven days. He then issued me with a Deportation Order. As he stamped it with his official seal he informed me genially that to the best of his knowledge I was the first white man to be deported by the new nation state. I can well believe this, as it is doubtful that any other white traveller would have been idiotic enough to obey the instruction posted at the border.

Fast forward a decade. I happened to relate this anecdote to Maurice Rickards, founder of the Ephemera Society. He asked me whether I still had the Deportation Order. I dug it out at his request and he was quite excited by this unimpressive-looking scrap of officialese. He said it represented the transfer to power from white to black, the transition from colonialism to self-determination. Could he exhibit it? At the Ephemera Society's inaugural exhibition in 1975, *This is Ephemera*, the humble document was one of the star attractions, illustrating how contemporary items of what Maurice characterised as 'the minor, transient documents of everyday life' could illustrate history in the making. This one, I thought ruefully, could also illustrate the maxim 'don't always do what your doting parents tell you'.

Nairobi took my breath away. It was almost entirely modern, its dignified buildings were huge and surprisingly graceful. Some were even beautiful, which could not be said of any London buildings of that period. Evidently they employed architects with some imagination in prosperous post-war Nairobi. These edifices were mainly a gleaming white, but with broad splashes of colour, and what with that and the palm trees and the coloured lights and the ultra-smart and sophisticated people walking about, Nairobi seemed to me an African jewel. I had never seen so many well-dressed people outside the West End, not even in Manhattan. It was not only the Europeans who looked sleek and prosperous; many of the African men sported beautifully tailored suits and hand-made shoes. The shops were lovely and full of expensive and luxurious items. There were some very chic couturiers, and hairstylists late of Mayfair. Bookshops abounded, including an antiquarian dealer in Africana from whom I purchased a photographic history of the city published for its fiftieth anniversary in 1950. This was revealing; it had started as little more than a shanty town and continued to have a frontier air until civic improvements were made in the 1930s, presumably as depression-era work relief. After the war it burgeoned into the glorious, vibrant metropolis that I now beheld. Nairobi today has, sadly, gone full circle. Much of it has become the neglected, decaying third world urban African nightmare of popular imagination.

For culture there were two theatres, a National Museum, a conservatoire, a spacious park, and about eight or nine luxurious bioscopes, half of which catered to the significant Indian population. Concerts and conferences were held in the magnificent 1935 City Hall. The Punk eschewed any of these diversions in favour of a day at the races. Ngong Racecourse could have stood in for Royal Ascot on Ladies' Day. My companion had, unfortunately, come dressed as he would for an American racecourse, so although we just scraped into the Enclosure, with some disapproving looks from its guardian at the gate, the Luncheon Tent, its enticing entrance flanked by two Hussars in full dress, was a step too far. The Punk was not abashed, as he arrived back at our modest Indian hostel considerably richer than he left it. He had put ten bob on a rank outsider called Cinderella, selected solely because that had been the name of Gany Surtee's dog in Basutoland (I doubt that Punk was familiar with the winsome lass in the glass slippers). It had romped home by seven lengths.

Not all the denizens of Nairobi were friends of Lord Delamere or members of the Muthaiga Club. I took sweet Jenny's sweater in for dry cleaning and fell into conversation with the proprietress. She had emigrated from South London only recently and I enquired what had made her and her husband decide to set up a dry cleaners in Nairobi. She said that there were already too many dry cleaners in South London and it was difficult to make a living. She and her husband had investigated the potential of Australia, New Zealand and Canada, but it seemed there was a superfluity of dry cleaners there too. So they then had the bright idea of checking out colonial capitals and Nairobi scored highest on an index of rising prosperity and a lack of rival establishments. She and her husband enjoyed the lifestyle and were earning more than they had in South London. How did they feel about *uhuru* (independence)? They reckoned Kenyatta was a wily old bird and he wasn't going to drive out Europeans prepared to invest in the new nation.

We met another enterprising couple when we set off from Nairobi on the Uganda Railway taking us north across the border to Gulu. Jim was a GPO engineer who had volunteered for service in Kenya and his wife Pat was an interpreter. Punk and I had a second-class compartment with two green leather seats convertible into beds. Jim and Pat had booked the same accommodation, but their compartment was flooded by a leaking faucet and they were upgraded to first-class. They were so thrilled by this 'bit of the high life', as Pat characterised it in her chirpy cockney accent, that they invited us to come and join them. I was intrigued how someone clearly of fairly basic education had become a linguist. She told us that she had applied to join the Post Office as a trainee telephonist when she was sixteen and one of the questions at the interview had been whether she spoke French. She said she could even though she couldn't, deeming it unlikely that this compromise with the truth would be put to the test. It was only when she got the job that she learned that she had been recruited for work on the switchboard at the British Embassy in Paris. Instead of reassigning her in London, the Post Office offered to send her to language school. She became fluent, went to Paris with an overseas allowance of £500 pa on top of her salary, had a wonderful time, met Jim at a Post Office social, and was now using her language skills as a freelance on behalf of Kenyan businessmen and officials interacting with their opposite numbers from the Congo.

The whole of the second day on the train we passed in a cut-throat game of rummy. This was a continuation of the contest that had started in Basutoland and I was now 12,500 points and several hundred dollars ahead. It was the day we reached the equator, which was signified by a circular steel plaque on a post by the railway track that proclaimed 'The

Equator'. There was no white line running across the horizon. Either just before we left the southern hemisphere, or just after we arrived in the Northern hemisphere, Johnnie-the-Punk had an epiphany. He suddenly got the hang of the game, of how you play to win at gin rummy. From henceforth, all the way to Cairo, the game would be as one-sided in his favour as it had hitherto been in mine. I still owe Punk something like 10,000 East African shillings.

We arrived at Gulu that evening and were allowed to stay the night in the stationary train, saving ourselves a 42-shilling hotel bill. In the morning we boarded the native bus that would carry us seventy miles through northern Uganda to the Sudanese border. The only other white man on the bus was an Englishman of about my own age, but I did not speak to him as he was carrying a rucksack – usually a bad sign – and nor was there anyone to perform an introduction.

• • •

On the Sudanese border there was a delay while we awaited a military escort. Apparently there was fighting in the area we were to pass through on our way to Juba, where we would board the Nile steamer. The buses were no longer running and we were told we would have to take a taxi for the 123-mile distance. Punk tried to bribe a Sudanese army officer to let us ride on one of the escort trucks, but either the Sudanese military are incorruptible (doubtful) or he had miscalculated the going price. He then tried threats, but this was a place so remote from the wider world that even American power and prestige had failed to penetrate it. I hustled my embarrassing friend away and squatting in the red dust we continued our rummy marathon. The Englishman sat on his rucksack and perused a paperback Plato. Presently two other white travellers joined us, American Peace Corps volunteers, which meant that we could divide the prodigious £25 fare between five.

The escort when it arrived proved to comprise two trucks each of twelve soldiers, bristling with weapons. These troops wore US-style pudding-basin steel helmets, French denim uniforms, and basketball boots. They would not have been my No. 1 choice of bodyguards on my first venture into a war zone.

We set off with one truck in advance of us and the other behind. Since there were five of us crammed into a space intended for two, it seemed churlish not to address my fellow Englishman when brought together so intimately. His name was Charles Dyson, a Trinity Hall man (my brother's old college at Cambridge), filling in time between coming down from the varsity and embarking on a career. It seemed he was up with Pagnamenta, the Salopian with whom I had run an 'Information Please' business at school and held board meetings with during chapel. Charles also knew Fairfax Lucy, an Old Etonian chum who was spearheading the fight for homosexual law reform. (He later revealed that this mutual acquaintance made him wonder about the preferences of the fellow countryman with whom he was now pressed thigh to thigh; I confessed to him that I had entertained the same anxiety about his.) And he knew Egerton Smith, who still owed me 30 shillings from the last time we had played poker together.

These pleasantries were interrupted by a cry of 'Oh my Gahd!' from one of the Americans. A thick plume of black smoke was rising from a village lying ahead of us. The meagre crops in the fields bordering the road outside the village had been laid waste. The village itself was deserted and flames rose from the rondavels. There was an eerie silence other than the crackling of the flames. We stared out from the windows of the taxi at the devastation all around us without comment; there was nothing to say.

There were other burning villages as we progressed along the road. From time to time the convoy would stop and the soldiers from one of the trucks would saunter off into the bush for what may have been either a smoko or a somewhat desultory patrol. About an hour into our journey we stopped again. There was a cleft stick driven into the middle of the road containing a note. The officer commanding read it with a frown. I went up to him and asked who it was from.

'The rebels,' he responded tersely.

'What does it say?'

'Their commander says he is going to ambush the convoy and kill us all if we don't turn back.'

'Should we turn back?'

'No. If we turn back, how are we going to get you to Juba?'

'If the rebels kill us, we aren't going to get to Juba anyway. Maybe you could radio for reinforcements?'

'There aren't any reinforcements. I am going to lead my men in pursuit of the rebels.'

'What, all your men? What about us?'

*'What if the rebels are on the other side?' I protested.*

'You stay here. We're going to scour the bush this side.' He waved his arm vaguely towards the left side of the road.

'What if the rebels are on the other side?', I protested.

The commander's lips parted in a malevolent smile and he slowly drew a finger across his throat. With that he gave me a laconic salute and turned towards his sergeant. 'Prepare for action,' he instructed.

The soldiers shambled off in a ragged line. We passengers stood in the road under the glaring equatorial sun conferring in low voices while our driver leant against the bonnet of the taxi nonchalantly dragging on a spliff. The minutes passed. Conversation flagged. We listened in the silence for the snapping of a twig or the flutter of a startled bird. Nothing. After an hour and a half the soldiers sloped out of the bush, wiping the sweat from their faces with grimy sleeves. I doubted that it had been occasioned by the heat of battle.

The commander sauntered over to us. 'You lot still here?' he remarked cheerfully. 'I thought you'd been hacked to pieces by now.'

• • •

At Juba we bought Native-Class tickets on the Nile River Steamer and set off in search of bedding. We paid 28 shillings for mattresses and eight shillings for sheets, blankets being superfluous. The bunks in Native Class were made of steel slats, very uncomfortable until we later acquired reed mats to place under our mattresses. There were about a hundred bunks, arranged in three tiers, in each of the five lighters. These were lashed to a steam vessel that also accommodated the European passengers, the whole cumbersome vessel forming a rectangle about the size of a football pitch.

The atmosphere below decks was fetid and the lavatories, of the squatting Asian type, were six inches deep in faeces from the previous voyage, or possibly the one before that. There was a lot of shouting, much spitting on the floor, and an overpowering stench of unwashed bodies. The Americans surveyed the scene in horror. For the English it was no worse than the first day of term at their boarding schools.

The deck was like a stockyard. The Sudanese brought their food with them, principally alive. They would slaughter goats and chickens as needed and cook them on charcoal fires made in kerosene tins with holes punched in the side. The animal blood running over the decks crawled with flies.

There was one other white man in Native Class, a German hitch-hiker called Helmut who was circling the globe for the fourth time. While my taxi companions and I escaped to the haven of the saloon for meals, Helmut was self sufficient. He lived on a single, enormous loaf of *Brot* that he kept under his shirt next to his skin lest it should be purloined by someone even hungrier. Towards the end of the voyage it was very stale and very sweat-stained. The other Europeans were saloon passengers, a delightful couple from Kenya called Mr and Mrs Nicholson. They were going on leave and were driving back to Blighty from Cairo via Algiers and across to Marseilles. These good-hearted people made copious draughts of tea for us on their Primus and let us share their picnic lunches.

*There is damn-all nothing to do on a Nile River Steamer, except complain, I complained. For the first three days we have passed through the Sud, which is flat swamp country and you can see nothing over the papyrus which chokes the river banks. The surface is clogged with water hyacinth. We were held up for a whole day in one place where this broad river was completely blocked by them from bank to bank. On one occasion, we've been told, the steamer was held up for fifty-seven days when the river was impassable for ten miles. The passengers had to wait on the steamer all this time as there was no way of getting out.*

*We start our day with breakfast in the saloon. Fruit juice, fish omelette and toast and jam and tea. This costs five bob and is quite good value. Then we sit in the saloon until the purser turns us out. If we don't go back to Native Class, he pursues us. Half go round the deck one way and half the other, so he can never catch us all at once. When his patience is completely exhausted, and he threatens us with exclusion from the saloon for the rest of the voyage, we climb over the railings back on to our lighter and wait till he is gone. Then we climb back and repair to the Nicholsons' Land Rover and talk until those sweet people feed us at lunchtime. Afterwards we play gin rummy and lie in our bunks reading till dinner in the saloon. Sometimes we relinquish dinner in favour of eating something out of a tin – corned beef or cold baked beans. This saves us seven shillings. Helmut always offers us some of his ageing Brot. We decline gracefully.*

*While we were passing through the Sud, from time to time we would stop at a landing stage and then all the villagers from miles around came to greet us and sell their wares, mainly fish and eggs and reed mats. The mats we bought to put under our mattresses were brought to the river bank by naked Nubians, who we were told had walked for a week from their village. It was the first time that I have seen tribesmen completely nude, though their dangly bits were secreted in a sheath. They sold about a dozen mats at a shilling each, then set off at a lope on their week's journey home. Where are they able to spend the twelve bob I wonder?*

*Later, when we were out of the Sud, there were Arab towns. These consisted of mud buildings and open shops. No roads nor motor vehicles. Once when we were sitting with the Nicholsons a crocodile reared up a few feet away from us in the reeds. A man with a .303 shot it and it was dragged up on deck to be skinned. The carcass was cut up and there was great feasting in Native Class.*

On arrival at the rail-head after ten days we boarded the train for Khartoum. It was so packed that there was no room in the third class even on the floor, so we – Charles, Helmut, the three Americans and I – sat on the floor of the second class. It was a most uncomfortable night, with bodies and baggage crammed into the small space between two open doors. Most of the next day was spent in and out of the buffet car, as we attempted to prolong our stays in it over a coffee or a rock cake until eviction by the officious head waiter. The train stopped at every station on the line and often between stations for half an hour or so, once for two hours, while the driver waited for the rails to dry after a shower. The train, we were told by the driver, was once held up for a week by the rain. I enquired why the train needed to make these unscheduled stops. He explained that it was because it would jump off the rails if they were slippery. I suspect that when the original Sudan Railways line from Wadi Haifa to Khartoum was completed on New Year's Eve 1899, some Scots engineer who had taken a dram too many told the Sudanese this in the spirit of Hogmanay revelry. Unfortunately they did not understand Caledonian humour and the trains had been delayed ever since.

Khartoum was a brown, dusty city of few attractions. The shops were poky, cafés few and flyblown, and the roads in a state of disrepair. The few Europeans looked as if they had been sent out as secret agents by AEW Mason and forgotten about. It was hot and sultry. Our Arab hotel was quite pleasant, though, with beds in the courtyard and more beds in a room with fans. It was relatively clean and the price was only fifteen piastres (three shillings). In the afternoon we walked along the banks of the Nile to the Palace to see the steps on which Gordon fell. The Palace was guarded by soldiers in uniforms of gorgeous array. Punk said he thought they were dressed up like that for the tourists. I pointed out that there weren't any. Americans abroad often seem to think that all attractions are designed to extract their dollars. I met one once who thought the Queen's Guard outside Buckingham Palace were out-of-work actors.

Next morning we boarded the Sudan Airways flight for Cairo. We had hoped to travel overland but the Aswan Dam had caused all transport to be suspended. We flew over trackless desert dunes, completely empty as far as the horizon, the most forbidding landscape I have ever seen. As we descended over the Pyramids I reflected how Cairo had been the gateway to Africa for so many generations of travellers. For me, approaching from the south, it was the gateway to Europe … and home.

# Chapter 15

. . .

# BACK TO BLIGHTY

. . .

## *September 1964*

My friend Johnnie-the-Punk was an ardent supporter of revolutionary movements. More or less any inflammatory cause won his adherence, provided it was anti-Imperialist, anti-American, anti-bourgeoisie and agin' most things that I held dear. It was therefore with great excitement that he read that Black Muslim leader Malcolm X was in Cairo and staying at Shepheard's Hotel. (As you do if you are dedicated to the overthrow of society in the name of the poor and dispossessed, Shepheard's being the most luxurious and costly hotel in the whole of Africa.) Punk was on the phone to Shepheard's in a trice. I expected to hear a smooth disembodied voice repeating a mantra that Mr X was unavailable or had just checked out but, much to my surprise, Punk was put through to his suite. To my much greater surprise another disembodied voice said that Malcolm X would be very pleased to meet Mr Morrison and Mr Hickman-Robertson for a drink. It suggested six o'clock the same evening.

I wrote home: *We put on our suits and scrubbed our faces shiny and did our best to straighten out the Punk into a semblance of something human. Thence to Shepheard's. There were several Negroes waiting in the lobby but none of them looked dangerous enough to be the leader of the notorious Nation of Islam. Then a somewhat shy, diffident black man in a very elegant suit and silk tie rose from a chair and identified himself as the architect of armed revolution that we were seeking. He had beautiful manners and when he had ordered a freshly squeezed orange juice, and Punk had asked if he minded if we had something stronger, he replied that consumption of alcohol was contrary to his religion but he would not challenge our own beliefs in this regard. We found him very affable and good-natured and he explained his aims so rationally and dispassionately that he made murder, rapine and revolution sound really quite constitutional. The Punk was nodding his head enthusiastically at all this, but looked mildly alarmed when Mr X declared that separation of the races was one of the cornerstones of his political philosophy. He saw no future for integration in the United States; the white and black races should live entirely separate lives. So, just like South Africa then.*

The only precise words that I recall Malcolm X saying were apropos violent change: 'If a house is rotten, what do you do? You don't try to patch it up. You tear it down and build something better.' The analogy I find, with hindsight, a particularly interesting one, because that was exactly what corporations and developers were doing at the time – pulling down historic buildings and raising concrete bunkers in their stead. Distressed housing that could have been repaired and resuscitated, keeping communities together, was replaced by tower blocks. Now of course Malcolm X was not talking about redevelopment, he was extolling revolution. But the inverse analogy is instructive. We eventually, post-1970s, gave up destroying heritage buildings in favour of improving them. Similarly the solution to the racial wrongs of the 1960s was not revolution but reform, most notably through the agency of the non-violent civil rights movement. This much should be said for Malcolm X. He was an extremist, but he put such fear of God into the white American population that they were prepared to give a hearing to the more moderate voice of Martin Luther King Jr.

On bidding us farewell Malcolm X told me he was hoping to come to England. A vision of my parents entertaining this firebrand to tea and cucumber sandwiches at Standish Court flashed through my mind, but I dismissed it as a fantasy that, however delightful, was more than I could expect my dear ones to indulge. Instead I assured him that he would receive an open-hearted welcome from those who had a genuine desire to hear alternative points of view. (Hot-buttered toast at the Public Schools Club mebbe...?)

In the event Malcolm X's visit to England was unscheduled. He had been due to speak in Paris in February 1965 but was refused admission as an 'undesirable person'. The Home Office allowed him to divert to London provided he restricted his visit to LSE, Birmingham University and Stetchford in response to specific invitations. No opportunity to instil revolutionary fervour into the chaps at the Public Schools Club then.

At the time of our meeting in Cairo Malcolm X had recently repudiated the Nation of Islam and it was during this extended tour of Muslim nations that he embraced the Sunni version of his religion. Exactly six months after our meeting in Cairo and nine days after his flying visit to England he was assassinated by three members of the Nation of Islam.

· · ·

Johnnie-the-Punk did not attempt to convert Charles or me or the two Peace Corps boys, Bennet and Gary, to his revolutionary brand of international socialism, but he did lecture us on our way to Cairo on the need to immerse ourselves in the lives of the native population and adapt ourselves fully to their customs and cuisine. On arrival he went to the American Express office to collect a remittance from his parents for the fare to New York. As this proved to be unexpectedly generous he promptly removed himself from our Arab hostel with its communal dormitories and disorderly plumbing to less spartan accommodation at the Hilton and spent the week stuffing himself with hamburgers in its squeaky-clean, all-American coffee shop. From time to time we were invited to join him in these repasts. The downside of accepting this much-needed hospitality – our resources were dwindling rapidly – was that we could not seek his advice on where in Cairo to go for the best sheep's eyes or enquire when he was going to don the *djellaba*.

We paupers found refuge at a small Greek *taverna*. The food was indifferent, but the proprietor could speak comprehensible English, unlike the locals, and did not add imaginary items to the bill, unlike the locals. I had little enough money left anyway when we arrived in Cairo, but it was depleted by about half during our stay. In those pre-credit-card days you either carried cash or travellers' cheques, but cash was the only option for the kind of remote areas we had travelled through. I had hidden some reserves in the lining of my suitcase, but this was rifled and I lost it all. I was cheated at the *bureau de change* and short-changed everywhere I went, even buying stamps at the post office. Appropriate bribes had to be paid to secure any service, official or otherwise. Our sojourn in Cairo was protracted because it took so long to transact any business: booking tickets, changing money, obtaining visas etc. The queues in every kind of establishment providing these services were so long, and the heat so oppressive, that they employed waiters to bring cooling drinks and other refreshments. It was prudent to tender the exact money.

There was one thing I liked in Cairo – the horse-drawn *fiacres* jingling through the busy streets at night with their oil-lamps glowing softly. Ah, to be accompanied in a *fiacre* trotting alongside the moonlit Nile accompanied by Maggie. Or the Lovely Mrs Lachlan. Or sweet Jenny.

. . .

I booked passage on the *SS Lydia* bound for Naples via Piraeus and the Greek islands. Johnnie-the-Punk was flying out the same day as Gary and I were leaving by bus across the desert sands to Alexandria. I was sorry to see him go. We had absolutely nothing in common, and I am sure I had been marked down for liquidation as soon as his cherished world revolution was achieved, but we had enjoyed some good times together and he was an amiable companion despite our many differences. I knew I would not see him again. I would be arrested, jailed, then inducted into the US Army if I set foot on American soil.

Gary and I had a jolly time in Athens and a miserable time in Naples, whose natives could have taught the Egyptians a thing or two about parting *Americani* and *Inglesi* from their money. It was now touch and go whether I would make it to London and Gary had little enough to spare. We hitch-hiked to Rome, where the locals had a good stab at extracting from us the little that remained. The cheapest rail ticket to London was £13. That left me with a total of nine shillings and sixpence.

It looked as if we would be going hungry on the two-day journey across Europe, but a generous Italian *madre* opened her picnic basket and insisted that we shared the good things therein. I particularly remember a cold omelette shaped like a *tortilla* but containing pasta. Thank you lovely Italian lady, your kindness to strangers is remembered with gratitude 55 years on.

I was quite overcome when the White Cliffs of Dover appeared through a morning mist as a smudge on the horizon. On landing the immigration officer asked me where I had started my journey. I was tempted to say London, but desisted lest he think me a smart-arse. So I said 'Basutoland' instead. He still thought I was being a smart-arse.

. . .

In London I expended three shillings on a telegram to my parents announcing my imminent arrival. The other six shillings and sixpence was spent on a stiff collar. I was now without any money at all, so I walked to St John's Wood to interview the mother of my friend Rubber Ears d'Arch Smith. Happily she was in and she lent me the 30 shillings fare to Stonehouse and an extra shilling for the tube to Paddington. The dear woman also gave me a good feed and let me use Rubber's room to change out of my travel-stained clothes, bathe and shave. I donned my three-piece suit with crisp white shirt and my shiny new collar with the regimental tie. I polished my Chelsea boots until they gleamed and was ready to set off on the very last leg of my journey around the world.

Only two passengers got off the train at Stonehouse and there was only one couple waiting on the platform. The other passenger, who alighted from the far end of the train, was an unkempt beatnik with long, matted, unwashed hair and a straggly beard, a soiled duffel coat and broken shoes. My mother called out 'Patrick! Patrick!' and ran towards him. She was about to fling herself into his arms when she realised her error and stopped dead in her tracks. Confused, she turned about. Then I ran towards her.

. . .

I had been absent for three years and four months. Had I gained in wisdom, self-reliance, insight and empathy during that time? I doubt it. I was three-and-a-half years older, so I hope commensurately more mature, but I have never been a great believer in that tired truism 'Travel broadens the

*My mother called out 'Patrick! Patrick!' and ran towards him.*

mind'. I am not sure that I would wholly endorse Malcolm Muggeridge's converse 'Travel narrows the mind', though there is indeed some evidence that travel involving beaches and *trattorie* does little more than reinforce cultural stereotypes about the host nation.

John Kimpton evidently did believe in the power of travel to transform. He told me in self-congratulatory tones that he had come back from his travels a New Kimpton – alert, confident, intellectually enquiring, primed with vim and vigour. I was relieved not to be able to discern any difference from the old, slightly shambolic, vague, forgetful, artless Kimpton that I knew and loved.

What this journey had given me was a fervent and abiding interest in the development and make-up of the English-speaking world. Given my total inability to learn a foreign language – I belong to a very small minority, believed to be under one per cent of the population, who are unable to acquire the most basic command of a foreign tongue even by immersion – the rest of the world must necessarily lie beyond my purview. I am a firm believer that you only benefit from foreign travel if you can converse fluently with the inhabitants of other countries and expose yourself to their media outlets and their literature. That was closed for me in respect of all but those countries, mainly of the former British Empire, whose language was also my own.

I had become fascinated by the British and Irish diaspora and by the way in which the various countries that had been settled by people from these Isles, or influenced by their attitudes and culture, had developed separate and very distinct identities. There is much agonising in our post-colonial world about the rights or wrongs of Empire. I am content to let better trained minds assess this important question. My own quest was to discover how the seventy or so English-speaking countries have become as they are. To that end I decided to dedicate my leisure to collecting books on these countries, together with historic newspapers and magazines that would give me a window on to their world at different stages of their development. As for travel, I determined to revisit those countries and territories that I had so enjoyed learning about on my round-the-world tour, and explore as many new ones as I was able, especially those off the beaten track: Tonga, Saint Helena, Newfoundland, Swaziland, Brunei, the Falkland Islands....

But first I had a loan to repay and a living to earn.

# BBC to
# Backwater

# Chapter 16

. . .

# FEW OPENINGS FOR
# BEAR-CHASERS

. . .

*1964 – 1969*

It was time to take stock of my future prospects. I thought hard about my skill-set.

Knowledge base: I could recite the dates of almost anything in the last 400 years, especially 'firsts'. Sporting prowess: I had been known in antipodean poker circles as Patrick the Pommie Pot-taker, otherwise nil. Mechanical aptitude: I could operate a nineteenth-century lift, but not always with the ability to bring it level with the floor. I could also thread a silent film projector, but talkies had me baffled. Creative arts: I wrote a lovely picture postcard and I could perform a memory act standing on a table in a smoky bar. Technical accomplishments: I could lay fires the approved Canadian way and I knew the best way to clean Australian bodily fluids from bar-room floors. Nothing very marketable there, apart from the latter, maybe, in Earl's Court.

So what about professional experience for my CV? I had received a perfunctory training in the dark arts of advertising and, courtesy of the HAC, a rather more rigorous one in how to kill people. Thanks to my work experience outside the UK, I could now add: encyclopaedia salesman; librarian; lavatory cleaner; baggage-smasher; bear-chaser; waitress; pantry steward; parliamentary messenger; elevator operator; bottle dispenser; sheet-metal worker; scullion. Somehow it did not really hold together. There is a word they use in the advertising trade, synergy, which means the sum is greater than the parts. (Useful when trying to sell clients inadequate proposals.) If there had been a word meaning *less* than the sum of the parts, that would apply to my CV.

Nor did any individual item point to a roseate future in the thrusting world of London commerce. There were few openings for bear-chasers.

I had hoped for a few weeks of R and R in autumnal Gloucestershire, but it soon became apparent that having a completely broke son idling about the house all day and consuming their sherry was not what my dear parents felt should be the outcome of what looked to them like three years and four months of loafing around the world. I took the hint, touched my poor father for a further loan, and decamped to London. There I took up residence in Barnes on the rug of Charles Dyson's one-room flat. It was extraordinarily generous of him to accommodate me in this way, but it did have its downside for the three of us. The third occupant, not full-time but in and out, was Charles's sensationally attractive girlfriend Elizabeth. Her ins tended to be overnight and I felt a little *de trop* while naked bodies writhed in ecstasy on the bed. Neither of these two kind people, though, ever made me feel less than welcome.

. . .

A few weeks after my return a Parliamentary Question was addressed to the Home Secretary asking him to confirm whether it was true that British subjects who had evaded the draft in the United States could be arrested in Britain by the US military police and forcibly removed to the US without extradition proceedings. The Home Secretary confirmed that this was so. He added that the US authorities had never exercised their privilege in this regard and he believed it unlikely that they would do so in the future. It did occur to me to wonder on what advice the Right Honourable gentleman had made such an optimistic prognosis.

. . .

One day I had a call from Bob Erith, he into whose charmed circle I had been admitted under the misapprehension that my father consorted with the PM. He and the other chaps who had driven from the Cape to Cairo had taken a three-bedroom flat in Eccleston Square in Pimlico. They had invited a chum, Paul Whitfield of Christie's, to take the third room. Would I care to share it? I could not go on playing gooseberry in Charles and Elizabeth's love-nest for much longer and I agreed.

The flat was a lot more expensive than anything I was accustomed to in London living, but I had obtained a stop-gap job with a market research company in Great Portland Street and the meagre emolument would just about cover the rent provided I did not eat, drink or smoke. I saw little of my flat mates, who were busy squiring debutantes to the various diversions that made up the London season. Bob would often join me for a cup of tea when he arrived home late and regale me with stories of the *bon ton*. These often revolved round his new best friend, Prince William of Gloucester, to whom he had been introduced by the Duke of Kent, his former Commanding Officer. One evening he returned from having drinks with Prince William at St James's Palace and told me that when his host had ushered him through the private apartments, they crossed through a room in darkness. At the door the Prince turned to Bob and put his finger to his lips. 'As quietly as possible,' he cautioned, 'as my father is watching his favourite programme on television and does not like any interruptions.' Bob cast a glance at the TV screen as he and the Prince tiptoed through. The Duke of Gloucester was watching *Bill and Ben the Flowerpot Men*.

In contrast to his father, Prince William took a keen interest in the issues of the day, as did Bob himself. Moreover, he was about to embark on what he hoped would be a career in the City, becoming the first member of the Royal Family to hold a regular job outside the services when he joined Lazard Brothers at the beginning of 1965. (Yes, he is in my book.) There was another evening when Bob breezed in and announced he was dining with the Prince at a Pimlico restaurant and would Paul and I like to join them. Paul said he was busy, he needed to wash his hair. I was not going to reject what would probably be my only opportunity ever to meet a member of the royal family socially. Now I am relating this story not to impress you with my sudden meteoric rise in the social firmament, but because it gives me a chance, for the first time in my life as a scribe, to use the longest word in the English language – antidisestablishmentarianism. The Prince was not only a serious young man, but bordering on the earnest. He and Bob spent the whole of the meal discussing a threat to disestablish the Church of England, a subject on which as a Catholic I had no very strong views other than that it might be a good idea. One of my few interventions was to make a not very original remark about the Church being the Tory party at prayer. The Prince looked slightly startled and asked what I meant. It occurred to me that this was one of the ways in which being royal sets one apart from ordinary mortals. Nobody had ever used this fairly hackneyed expression in front of him before lest it should give offence to the cousin of the Head of the Church of England.

Had he survived, Prince William, who had read history at Cambridge and political science at Stanford, would have added some intellectual heft to the Royal Family. Bob's friendship with him was terminated by tragedy when the Prince was killed in an air crash in 1972. The present Prince William is named after him.

• • •

My sojourn in Eccleston Square was brief. At the end of the first month I was presented with a bill for a prodigious amount that I was informed was my share of the telephone bill, split six ways. The debs' delights had girlfriends or ex-girlfriends-now-friends-for-life in the farthest flung parts of the Empire who, so it seems, needed to be telephoned regularly and at length. Then there were current girlfriends who tended to live on sprawling estates in Scotland and needed telephonic support on a daily basis. I had overheard many of these conversations and, without taking much notice of their content, which tended to be about sheep in the case of the colonial exes or game-birds in the case of the current objects of desire, had merely noted in passing that they were protracted. It had not occurred to me that I would be paying for them. I protested that I had not made a single telephone call while I had been in residence, but was told sternly that it was share and share-alike in our Eccleston Square chummery. I paid my dues and tendered my notice and hoped that the telephone bill was not going to be followed by the drinks bill and the taxi bill. It so happened that my brother Tim was moving out of his bedsitter in Chelsea's Oakley Street and I moved in.

* * *

The market research company in Great Portand Street employed mainly out-of-work actors. Our task was to compute the data collected on the survey sheets. Not compute as in computer, because digital technology had yet to penetrate the world of marketing, but compute by recording numbers in columns and periodically adding them up. The work was leisurely, because actors are naturally convivial and tend to talk a lot. I became more knowledgeable than I needed to be about 'The Master', 'Larry', 'Dickie Darling', 'Binkie', 'Peggy', 'Sir John' and other showbiz luminaries. I also learned about what I found an altogether more compelling world, that of the upper classes. My social superiors in the chummery moved in upper class circles, but were essentially middle class boys who had more money than I or anyone in my peer group. Now it is fashionable to affect indifference to those who inhabit broad acres and decaying mansions, but as a suburban boy from the provinces I find them riveting because their lives are so different from those of the rest of us. My informant was a charming girl called the Hon. Celestine Doo-dah who occupied the desk next to me and whose family lived in picturesque penury in some crumbling Gothic edifice where they were ministered to by an underpaid or possibly unpaid butler. Celestine was in need of the £9 a week bestowed on us by our employer, the polite education she had received at Heythrop Castle not having equipped her for more gainful employment. Much has been written about upward social mobility, but downward social mobility is also worthy of attention.

One day I was instructed to deliver a parcel to the BBC. On a wall in the building where I made my delivery there was a board filled with job vacancies, each on an A5 sheet of either green or white paper. White signified open competition, green for internal applications only. I perused the white ones hopefully, but they were mainly in the engineering field and the few in production or administration demanded the kind of qualifications expected for a senior post in the Diplomatic Corps. I glanced at the green ones and one stood out. It was for a post in News Information, apparently some kind of research service, and the only qualification required was an interest in current affairs. The pay was £13 a week, not a fortune, but what job that did not require higher education would pay better?

I wrote to the BBC explaining that I was fully aware that this post was open only to internal candidates. Should they fail to fill the post internally, however, I would like to present myself as a candidate. In due course I received a reply from BBC Personnel saying that I had misunderstood the terms of the vacancy, as it was for internal candidates only. I was not sure that I wanted to work for a communications outfit that cannot do basic one-to-one communication and forgot about it. The out-of-work actors continued to regale each other with stories about what happened to the juve lead when he exited stage left instead of stage right and Celestine went on telling me interesting facts about tribal life amongst the upper classes. Then about a month later a letter arrived informing me my interview for the News Information job was on such-and-such a date. It was not that they had failed to fill the post. No, as I was to find out later, it was just routine BBC incompetence. They had simply put my application on the wrong pile, the candidates instead of the rejects. I duly presented myself for interview and, mainly on the strength of having been a Boston University librarian – News Information was part of BBC Library Services – I was hired.

. . .

I moved into the bedsitter at No. 17 Oakley Street at about the same time. It was the third floor back, with a basin and a gas fire and gas-ring and a large cupboard on the landing. Shared bathroom on the second floor. Rent was three guineas a week, gas extra via the shilling-in-the slot meter. My landlady was a sweet old lady called Mrs Linley, who transferred her affection for my brother to me. There was no such accord with Mr Linley, a cantankerous old devil who would not let his wife buy loo paper for the lodgers. We had to use squares of newspaper which Mr Linley cut out himself. He had been a socialist MP in the 1924 Parliament, which may have accounted for his misanthropy.

There were five BBC News Information units. One was at Lime Grove Studios to serve the television newsroom and another at Alexandra Palace for television features; one in Broadcasting House to serve the Home Service newsroom and another – mine – at Duchess Street, just behind BH, for radio features. The fifth was at Bush House for the World Service and coincidentally was presided over by Rubber Ears's mother, Mrs d'Arch

Smith, to whom I had now repaid the 31 shillings she lent me to complete my circumnavigation of the globe. Each one was a cuttings library, divided into People, Places and Subjects. The newspapers were 'marked up' each day by one of the senior clerks – this meant underlining key words in an article in several different copies, so that each article could be filed up to a dozen different ways – then cut up by the junior clerks, pasted on to individual backing sheets, and filed.

In effect News Information performed the same service as a search engine does today. Production staff would call up to ask for information on this, that or the other subject and the senior clerks would make a selection of cuttings, which was then dispatched through the internal distribution service. Or the broadcasters would come in personally to make their own selection. At Duchess Street our two most regular personal customers were Esther Rantzen, then a humble graduate researcher, and Roy Plomley, who would read up the cuttings file on his castaway on Wednesday, lunch him or her on Thursday, and interview them on Friday. They were both lovely people. Esther would make a theatrical entrance shrieking 'DAAAAHHHLING!!!' at me and bestow kisses on most of the male members of staff. A far remove from the stately Dame Esther of more recent times. Mister Plomley was as far opposite in manner as possible, the epitome of quiet-spoken gentlemanly restraint, always ready for a chat over a cup of tea with us humble clerks. I had the temerity on one occasion to criticise his choice of castaways. They seemed to me, I told him, a tad top-heavy on the showbiz side. Mister Plomley looked a trifle disconcerted and asked who I had in mind as an alternative. I had not actually thought of anyone in particular, but I happened to be reading a book illustrated by Edward Ardizzone, so I said how about him. 'Can't have him,' said Mister Plomley, 'it would look like nepotism. You see he's my Cousin Ed.'

The junior clerks were a motley collection of widely differing social backgrounds. Their ring-leader, primary suspect whenever there was trouble in the juniors' room, was Marek, a Polish boy whose family had settled in London after the war. Then there was Martin, a middle-class boy with a beatific smile and not a huge amount between the ears. I suspect the cutting and pasting and filing was about the limit of his abilities and I wonder what happened to him when he outgrew the juniors' room. On the whole the BBC did not sack people, so I do hope they found a niche for him somewhere. Alan came from a rambunctious family of East End gangsters. His father and uncles had all belonged to a Stepney razor gang in the 1930s. He showed me a photograph of them standing in a cobbled street in their sharp-looking suits, silk shirts and fedora hats and looking as though they owned the manor. Which they probably did, Ronnie and Reggie still being in their cradles. At the other end of the spectrum was Camilla, god-daughter of Lord Reith. (Nepotism may have worried Roy Plomley, but it seldom got in the way of appointments – the BBC was crawling with the offspring of socialist cabinet ministers.) Camilla told me that Mummy and Daddy had sent her to Paris to be finished and that she had hoped to get a job where she could use her fluent French. The only offer she received was from the British Airports Authority, making bilingual announcements over the tannoy at Heathrow. Even cutting and filing in News Information had seemed to her preferable to that.

There were perhaps half a dozen others whose names now escape me, the spear-carriers of the Corporation. The senior clerks were a fairly weird mob too and I may have been the most normal one. Ian, good-looking in a slightly sinister way, dressed entirely in black and spent most of his time perusing the files in the 'Crime: Murder' section of Subjects. He occupied whatever leisure was at his disposal between answering queries in devising foolproof means of disposing of bodies without detection. His hobby was collecting knives. Millie was a Salvation Army lass who spent as many hours working for the downtrodden and underprivileged as she did for the Corporation. She radiated goodness, in a nice way, and no one used bad words in front of her. Pauline was a mother-hen type, married to Rodge, the archetypal male chauvinist pig of that pre-feminist era. Rodge was captain of Dalston Rangers football team and every Saturday afternoon brought home eleven mud-caked football uniforms for his wife to spend the rest of the weekend restoring to a pristine state. She never complained about this, but was unable to explain to me why the other 10 players could not look after their own kit. Bernard suffered from a chronic muscle-wasting disease, which made it difficult for him to remove and replace the heavy boxes in which the cutting files were stored. This was not the ideal job for him, but no job can be easy for someone suffering from his disability. At least he was not consigned to 'disabled work'. A disability of a different sort had been suffered by bewitchingly graceful Lynette, formerly a member of the Royal Ballet, who had been dropped by her partner on the stage. Her career was ended in that instant. I asked her what had brought her to this obscure outpost of the BBC. She explained that she had not received a proper education at the Royal Ballet School, and with no educational qualifications, the BBC was the only employer that would give her a job which exercised the mind, albeit at our lowly level.

Lynette was right: it was a lowly job. So we were all very surprised when we were joined by a real graduate. Iona Rhys-Jones was not only beautiful, but she was upper class, so sophisticated that she shopped only in Paris, and a brainbox to boot. So what was *she* doing in News Information? I realised that fifty-five years later I still had no idea how she got there. Happily we are still close chums and she explained it thus. She had applied for the graduate trainee scheme after coming down from university with a first in PPE, but had just missed the intake for that year. The personnel officer in charge of the scheme suggested that she might like to mark time at News Information until the next intake and meanwhile learn how the Corporation functioned. I think in truth the personnel officer had given her the impression she would be a researcher, rather than one step up from a filing clerk. News Information Duchess Street evidently came as quite a culture shock to the poor girl, but as everybody adored her and urged her to stay, she decided to see it out for the year.

You may have gathered from the name that Iona Rhys-Jones was Welsh as well as upper-class, and that is a pretty rare combination. I do not know how many upper-class people there are in the UK and a wholly unproductive Google search suggests that nobody has tried to quantify it. My guess is the low tens of thousands. But in Wales you can, or could in Iona's youth, fit the whole lot into a single house. A fairly large house admittedly. Powis Castle is probably marginally bigger than the fictitious Downton Abbey (Highclere in reality) and the Earl of Powis would hold weekend parties to which all the gentry of Wales was invited. Provided you spoke Welsh. Iona told me that no word of English was allowed to be spoken between Friday night and Monday morning. She was all right because Welsh was her first language. She did not learn English until she was seven.

At the end of her year among we rejects, Iona decided that the BBC was not for her: the nepotism, the cronyism, the internal politicking, the need to conform to a rigid leftist mind-set, the appallingly low pay.

(In those days it was considered, by the BBC, a privilege to work for the Corporation. If you did not have a private income that was your problem.) She took herself off to a management consultancy called PA Management and was soon embroiled in reorganising the Greek economy. (This may have been the only endeavour in which Iona ever failed.) She later became speech-writer for Jeremy Thorpe.

And finally there was our boss, lovely Shelagh Finney. She was a very attractive woman of middling years who had somehow evaded matrimony and had an intellect that nowadays would have been rewarded with a position in senior management. Her principal out-of-office stimulus was music and she attended three or four concerts a week. None of these did she enjoy. 'How was the concert last night, Shelagh?' I would greet her in the morning and she would inevitably respond with a sigh or a groan. 'The third oboe played a wrong note in the second movement,' she would agonise, or some such unforgiveable solecism. It does not do to be too much of a connoisseur of the fine arts: anything less than perfection is total disaster. Shelagh's other avocation, only revealed when our professional association had blossomed into something like friendship, was writing tales of heady romance for *Woman's Own*. I was desperate to read one of these, but Shelagh would not reveal her pseudonym. I was immensely impressed by this achievement, because *Woman's Own* was known to be one of the most challenging outlets for popular literature; she thought it demeaning.

. . .

I was a useless marker. The routine was that you came in at 8 am to get a head start before the junior clerks arrived at nine to begin cutting and pasting. You were supposed to finish by 12, giving the juniors an hour to complete the job before they went off for lunch. I used to come in at seven am, but I was never finished by 12. The juniors would come and stand in the doorway, ostentatiously looking at their watches. Marek was the only one brave enough to actually cajole me, singing out 'Are you nearly finished yet?' and 'Can we go to lunch now?' until a fusillade of india rubbers and pencil sharpeners sent him into retreat.

I suppose my cognitive functions must be slower than normal; hence all the things that I cannot do as well as other people. The other part of the job, answering queries from producers, scriptwriters and researchers, was not a problem. There was only one question that I failed to solve. I was asked for a list of famous living people born out of wedlock. I probably spent longer on this one than any other question, but the subject was a closed book. Nearly all social attitudes have undergone a transformation since the sixties and it would be surprising if they had not, but the attitude towards bastardy is among those that have witnessed the most complete turn-about. It is probably safe to say that nowadays there is no stigma attached to having children outside marriage and the children themselves will not suffer any disadvantage. On the day I write this the obituary of Simonetta Puccini in the *Daily Telegraph* is sub-headed 'Illegitimate granddaughter of Giacomo Puccini'. In the sixties, even as sexual liberation blossomed, such a shameful secret was never to be divulged.

The question I was proudest of answering required no special delving. Pauline had organised a swear box in the office, with the proceeds going to good causes. (There was a certain irony in the fact that when Millie the saintly Sally Army lass was in the office, proceeds to good causes declined.) I was concerned about a drought that was ravaging Botswana, as Bechuanaland had become. There was no organised disaster appeal in Britain, so I sent our £10 worth of shilling fines direct to President Seretse Khama (the only head of an African country guaranteed not to misuse such a donation). In response I received a personal letter from his private secretary outlining what the government was doing to relieve the situation and how they proposed to spend our £10. On that same day I had a call from the Newsroom in Broadcasting House, which was unusual, asking if we had any information on famine relief in Botswana. The BH News Information had nothing up-to-date, but had told them that Duchess Street sometimes filed information from wider sources. I read the enquirer the letter I had received from Gaborone that morning and he took it down verbatim. Excerpts were quoted on the six o'clock news and in several following news bulletins.

. . .

I tell a lie. There was one other question I failed to solve, albeit an unsolvable one. Our two most frequent clients were *Woman's Hour* and the *Today* programme. In those days *Today*, presided over by the affable and disorganised Jack de Manio, was a magazine programme. It was only later, in the 1970s, that its main staple became confrontational interviews with evasive politicians (the appeal of which is lost on me, as the adversarial style simply makes the politicians clam up). The architect of this style of broadcasting, John Timpson, was also the principal critic of what I considered to be a much more informative and entertaining programme. Timpson characterised its output as 'eccentric octogenarians, prize pumpkins and folk who ate lightbulbs and spiders'.

This was perhaps partly my fault, as I sent over a folder of cuttings each day that I thought might make interesting items for the following morning. One that caught the producer's eye was about a beachcomber who lived on Brighton beach and eked out a living by harvesting the flotsam and jetsam that came in with the tide. This story had appeared in the *Sun*. The producer rang me and asked whereabouts on the beach he could locate the beachcomber, as he wanted to send someone down in a car to interview him. I rang the journo under whose byline the story had appeared and asked where we could find the driftwood hut he had so picturesquely described.

'You won't,' responded the journo tersely.

'Why not?' I asked.

'Because there isn't a hut.'

'You mean he lives somewhere else…?'

There was a sigh on the end of the phone. Then the journo said, in very precise tones as if addressing a backward child, 'No you eejit. Because he doesn't exist. I made him up. Got it?'

I was aware that tabloid newspapers sometimes embroidered stories, but I did not know that they made them up from scratch. Call me naïve, but the disappointed producer said it was a new one on him, too. Pity that *Today* became so solemn and earnest. Tell me honestly. Would you rather hear about the resourceful life of a beachcomber on Brighton beach or the Secretary of State for Brexit Brouhaha giving protracted answers that seem to have no connection to the questions he has been asked?

. . .

Much to our delight Shelagh announced her engagement. After she had married, she planned to retire from the BBC. That meant that her post would be vacant. A month or so before her departure, the job was advertised. I applied. A few days later I asked Pauline whether she had applied too. She replied that no, she had not, as the vacancy was going to her sister Pamela who worked in the BH unit.

'What do you mean?' I asked. 'What makes her think she is going to be the successful candidate?'

'She's been told by Mister Webster. He's chairing the board.'

Mister Webster was head of all the News Information units and reported direct to the Chief Librarian.

'But he can't do that!' I expostulated. 'It wouldn't be a fair board.'

'It isn't a fair board,' said Pauline. 'Don't you know that some boards are fixed in advance? This is one of them.'

I consulted Shelagh Finney. She confirmed what Pauline had said. Not all boards were open. She had also heard on the grapevine that Pamela had been selected.

I told Shelagh that I wanted to withdraw, but she said that if I did that I would have to give a reason. Was I going to tell Personnel that I knew the board had been fixed? No, clearly I wasn't, so that meant that I would have to undergo the ordeal of a board all to no purpose.

At least there was nothing to be nervous about, as I was not going to get the job however I performed. Just relax, I told myself, and try not to make a prat of yourself.

It was probably on this account that I displayed rather more confidence than would otherwise be the case. I entered the room with a smile on by face (Robin Gates would have called it 'your silly grin') and remembered to greet each member of the board by name. Nearly every advice manual on interview technique advises you to 'be yourself'. This is stupid. Obviously if you are somebody like Lord Curzon you can afford to be yourself and they will still appoint you Viceroy of India. If you are somebody like me, basically inadequate in most of the areas that fit someone for preferment, you need to present an alternative version of your true persona. It is, of course, rather easier to do this with brio if you know you are not in the running for the job anyway.

The other thing that separates sheep from goats is use of names. Greet your interlocutors by name and address them by name when you answer their questions. Now here's the clever bit. You do not address your whole answer to the person who asked the question. Like Barbara Swan in Natal you turn to the next person and the next, before completing your answer to the questioner. Everybody feels included.

Mister Webster caught me on the back foot with his first question. 'In what way is the BBC different from how you imagined it before you joined?'

As a matter of fact it was not any different from what I had expected. It was overstaffed, shambolic and disorganised, rife with nepotism, inflated with its own self-importance, and riddled with intrigue. Except that I had not reckoned on boards being fixed in advance, so that would have been the true answer. Not an appropriate one in the circumstances though.

Overstaffed – that was it. I replied to Mister Webster, 'The sheer scale of the operation is what has surprised me most.' Then I turned to the Head of Library Services, and said, 'Do you know Mr Collinson, that if the BBC was to declare a Unilateral Declaration of Independence tomorrow …' and I now addressed the personnel officer, 'there would be no fewer than six countries in Europe with a lesser population, Miss Pargeter. We employ 23,678 staff, the size of a small nation. I find that rather remarkable, Mr Webster.'

They then began to debate among themselves which six countries had fewer inhabitants than the BBC had staff, eventually turning to me for confirmation: Andorra, Monaco, Gibraltar, San Marino, Vatican State, Liechtenstein. After that the interview became more like a general conversation than a formal interrogation. Mr Collinson observed that News Information Duchess Street had run out of filing space. Had I any ideas about that? I told the board that we were adding a thousand cuttings daily, which meant that in future we must discard a thousand cuttings a day. To free up sufficient space for immediate needs we would have to jettison 3,000 boxes, totalling about a million cuttings. I had given some thought to how this could be done with the least impact on operational efficiency and would be happy to circulate a paper. Mr Collinson said he would like to see it. At interview's end I wished them all farewell with a smile and they beamed back at me. Except Mister Webster, who had a slightly worried look.

Three days later the news that Hickman-Robertson was the new Head of News Information Duchess Street swept through our small community with hurricane force. Everyone had known that Pamela was the prior selection. Nobody knew what to say to poor Pamela, least of all Mister Webster.

Nor did I know what to say to Pauline, who as our longest-serving senior clerk would now be my deputy. She knew what to say to me. She flung her arms round my neck, kissed me several times all over my face, and told me she was delighted. 'Can you imagine what it would be like having to work for your own sister?' she said. 'I was dreading it.'

Pauline was the first of a string of wonderful women who protected my back throughout my career. You will be meeting a number of them. They all had in common the fact that they could see I was essentially a hopeless case and could not survive on my own. I made them feel needed.

The other outcome of this incident was the ending of pre-fixed boards, at least as far as News Information was concerned. Elsewhere in the BBC it continued on its rampant way.

· · ·

I was now on the bottom rung of the executive ladder, with a salary almost in four figures. Charles Dyson could no longer introduce me to people at parties with 'This is Patrick. He's a filing clerk hoping to become the BBC's Head of Paperclips.' (Elizabeth: 'Shut up Charles. Patrick may surprise us all one day.')

My first act as Head of Paperclips was to circulate my promised paper on making space. Mister Collinson was evidently impressed, because he referred it up to his superior, who wrote on it 'What do you think, Tony?' and elevated it to his. Tony inscribed it 'Should we OK this?' and sent it skywards to somebody so important that my scheme was below his decision-taking level. So he noted 'Very interesting' and bounced it back down to Tony, who wrote 'I agree' and sent it downwards to his underling, who opined 'I agree too.' That did not leave Mister Collinson much leeway in the agreement stakes, so he wrote 'Thank you for letting us see this' before winging it to Mister Webster, who dropped it into my in-tray without comment. None of this had progressed with any sense of urgency, you must understand. These important managers were busy men (yes, all men). Submissions like mine would rest in an in-tray for anything from a week to a month. But I had an answer which was not 'No', even if it was not 'Yes'. I felt 'Very interesting' from such a stratospheric level was a sufficient commendation for me to proceed with my plan. But I had no illusions about who would be held responsible should it go pear-shaped.

This was not unrepresentative of the decision-making process throughout the BBC, and if the recent satirical series *W1A* guying BBC bureaucracy is as authentic as insiders say, not much has changed in half a century. I made a personal commitment to myself that should I ever rise to a position where I had decision-making powers, whether in the Corporation or elsewhere, I would do what managers are paid to do: make decisions promptly and unequivocally.

. . .

There were many strange practices in the Corporation. One day I sent for a messenger to deliver a large parcel to another outstation. The messenger who presented himself had only one arm. I said there must have been a misunderstanding and could he explain to his boss that it was a large parcel and would require a messenger with two arms. 'It ain't a problem, Squire,' the one-armed messenger assured me. 'You carry the parcel and I'll walk behind you. Then it's all square with the union.' I told him I was not worried about the union. I simply wanted a parcel delivered and I did not propose to do it myself. The messenger pursed his lips and sucked in his cheeks. 'Then we 'ave got a problem, Guv'nor,' he informed me. 'That would be discrimination against a disabled person. Union don't like that. Management don't like that. Spells trouble for everyone, like.'

The parcel was delivered by me, but I was not allowed to transport it without Mercury following me noisily in his hob-nailed boots. I was in doubt whether I should admire the Corporation for giving jobs to disabled men who could not perform them or whether I should be outraged on behalf of the licence-payer. But the BBC gave a berth to all kinds of misfits and scallywags in News Information and promoted someone like me to Head of Paperclips. What was there not to like?

. . .

There was an unforeseen benefit to my job beavering away amongst the dusty files in the basement of No 5 Duchess Street. I had resumed work on my book of firsts and here was a resource available to few other private researchers. News Information had been established during the war and so anything developed since the early 1940s, from jet aircraft to rock 'n' roll, was chronicled in detail. The files sometimes threw up tempting items from earlier times too. I found a 'looking back' feature from *The Irish Times* in the 'Women: Professional' file which described how 22-year old Miss Oonagh Keogh of Foxrock had taken advantage of a provision in the Irish Free State's new constitution to claim her right to a seat on the Dublin Stock Exchange, storming this bastion of male privilege on 9th July 1925. Now you would think that date, when the first woman stockbroker in the world took her seat, would have entered the annals of women's emancipation along with the well-known dates of the first woman doctor, woman judge and woman pilot. But there is not a single reference book other than mine that records it. Nor will a Google search reveal Miss Keogh's place in Ireland's and women's history, whereas there are literally thousands of sites recording the advent, a full forty years later, of the first woman member of the New York Stock Exchange. For me it was stimulating to discover facts that had been hidden from history.

It was an immense project that I had undertaken: to record every innovation of social or historic significance over the last thousand years, with both the first in the world and the first in Britain. This is the study I had begun at the age of 14 while hiding in the school library from my horrible fag-master. Possibly you needed to be 14 to think that such an open-ended task was even possible.

Consequently most evenings and most weekends were spent in my lonely eyrie in Oakley Street, pounding away on my 1923 Remington Portable and subsisting on whatever one-pot meals could be concocted on a single gas-ring. My fellow lodgers kept themselves to themselves, but I had been told by my brother to keep an eye out for Toby Charlton of the first floor front. Most evenings, my brother Tim explained, the bibulous Mr Charlton failed to make it up the single flight of stairs to his room. The spinster ladies of advanced years who occupied the other rooms and our landlady Mrs Linley were not able to render aid. Mr Linley would not have thrown water on you had you been on fire. It was therefore my job, said Tim, to get Mr Charlton to his room and on to his bed. I did not need to undress him.

Thus began another of those cross-generational friendships that enlivened my youth. Toby Charlton was the same age as the century and had served in the First World War as a naval midshipman. After the war he had joined the fledgling RAF and did his officer training at Cranwell, one of the earliest intakes. It was here that he achieved a first that has certainly been hidden from history. Toby, an inveterate ladies' man, became the first British member of the Mile High Club. For those unschooled in sexual shenanigans, the Mile High Club connotes that select group of couples who have done it in an aeroplane. Nowadays it is not so difficult to achieve membership if the two of you can evade the stewardess and conceal yourselves in the loo. (Of necessity it probably needs to be the proverbial quickie.) Rather more difficult in an open cockpit biplane.

At that period after the First World War any young blade who had survived the ravages of war and spoke the Queen's English would be admitted to at least the outer fringes of London Society should he so wish. Toby had established a reputation in the drawing rooms of Mayfair as someone definitely not safe in taxis and this had added to his attraction to certain young ladies of the upper crust whose attitude towards sexual gratification was, shall we say, in advance of their parents'. Among those who espoused such progressive views was the Hon. Elizabeth Ponsonby, one of the founder members of the Bright Young Things. She it was who was invited by Toby to Cranwell expressly to perform a feat of aeronautics never before accomplished in British skies. They had a dummy run in the hangar in order to work out the logistics, before heading up to 10,000 feet for the big event.

The aircraft Toby had selected was a BE2, a string and sealing wax biplane that had barnstormed the skies of the Western Front. Its peculiarity was that the pilot sat in the rear cockpit and the observer in the front. This made it possible for the lady in question to exit the forward cockpit and join Toby in the rear one by clambering down the fuselage – a hazardous operation that must have required either a good deal of courage or a conspicuous disregard for the odds on survival. Having negotiated a short stretch of slippery fabric, with a slipstream that must have felt like a howling gale, her next task was to manoeuvre herself on to Toby's lap facing him. I think we may take it as read that both parties had removed constricting nether garments in advance. The act of congress then had to be performed in double quick time, because the pilot could not see where he was going. I am not sure where he had positioned his joystick – no, the other one. Consummation achieved, the Hon. Elizabeth had to make her way back to the forward cockpit, against the slipstream and without an outstretched hand from Toby as on the inward journey.

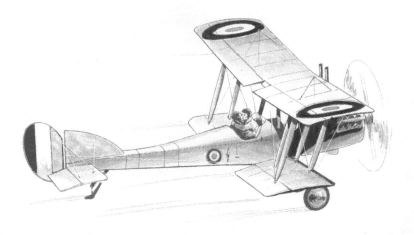

*I think we can take it as read that both parties had removed restricting*
*nether garments in advance.*

Unlike most middle-class boys allowed into the outer circle of London society, Toby actually married a member of the aristocracy, promptly resigning his commission when he did so. Lady June Charlton was the daughter of ne'er-do-well peer the Earl of Carrick, who ran a dodgy investment business with impressive premises in Berkeley Square until forced to flee to Florida with the Peelers at his heels. Any expectations that Toby and Lady June might have had of the family fortune were set at naught by this mishap and they were forced to make their own living. When Stowe School opened in 1923, they ran the tuck shop. After that venture palled, they moved to London and Toby opened a basement night club the walls of which were decorated with art deco murals of tuxedoed Negroes with saucer eyes and big blubber lips playing saxophones and trumpets – he showed me the photographs. There was also one of effeminate young men having a tug-of-war with powder puffs. Toby explained that was what they were called then, Puff – Poof ... is that where the Aussie word comes from? His wife set up her own business, 'Lady June Charlton's Beauty Preparations'. Whether it was the strain of being forced on to their own resources, or whether it was Toby spreading his favours around June's aristocratic friends I know not, but the marriage ended in 1934.

Toby joined up again in World War II, returning to the RAF. He told me an interesting story which throws some light on what might have happened had we been invaded. His initial task was to tour round the farms on the outskirts of Manchester seeking permission to set up barrage balloons for the defence of the city. Asking for 'permission' was the gentlemanly way the RAF went about things in 1939–40, though the balloons were going to be sited on these fields anyway. The hard-bitten farmers did not see it that way. Toby claimed that there was hardly an instance when he was not asked for some favour in return, additional petrol coupons or an extra allocation of fertiliser, but most often having their sons exempted from military service. They got short shrift from the fiercely patriotic Toby. He was convinced that had the Germans invaded, these farmers, and thousands of similarly minded citizens, would have willingly collaborated with the enemy for personal advantage. Thank goodness his belief was never put to the test.

Nearly half a century on, Toby's priapic adventures had yet to be concluded, despite the fact that he was virtually bedridden and could only hobble on two sticks as far as the pub on the corner. There was a very beautiful *Vogue* model called Veronica living a few doors down. She had taken a fancy to Toby, as nearly all women did, and used to sit by his bedside soothing his fevered brow or whatever it is pretty girls do in these circumstances. Myself, I could never quite grasp what it was that Toby had over chaps like me and most of the rest of my gender. If you Google John Sills Charlton (his formal name), you can find a photo of him and Lady June taken in 1925. Toby looks an archetypal lounge lizard – certainly I would not have let my daughter within miles of this louche Lothario if I had been a fond parent. But girls it seems go for that type. One day I went to visit Toby and, unusually, his barren little bedsit was empty. I strolled down to Veronica's and her front door was open. Stupidly I wandered in, calling her name. She and Toby were *in flagrante delicto*, he old enough to be her grandfather and unable to get out of bed without assistance. You had to hand it to the old roué for sheer persistence, though.

I am going to tell you one more Toby story and it is a sad one. He was making his way slowly and painfully along Oakley Street one spring day when he saw a ravishing looking girl of perhaps eighteen or nineteen on the other side of the street, accompanied by an older woman, presumably her mother. Toby gave the lass the glad-eye, probably more out of habit than dishonourable intention. The woman said something to the girl. Then to his surprise, and somewhat to his alarm, she came skipping across the street towards him. Planting herself on the pavement as he shuffled to a halt, she looked up at his face and said sweetly, 'Hello Daddy.' Toby recoiled and glanced across the street at her companion. He thought he had some dim recollection of a previous encounter. How intimate it may have been he was unsure.

The girl proceeded to introduce herself and the surname was indeed familiar. It now came back to him that he had conducted a brief affair with a lady of that name about twenty years earlier. This the girl confirmed, without a trace of embarrassment, and informed him that she was indeed his daughter. Toby said that he was delighted to make her acquaintance, but that as this was a somewhat public place in which to confront such a startling development in his personal life, would it be possible to meet somewhere more secluded? The young lady suggested tea at the Cadogan Hotel the following day. I learned all this that evening and I made considerable efforts to get Toby, who by this time looked like a walking corpse, into a fitter state for this momentous occasion. This could be a life-changer. He was estranged from his only son, but now he had the prospect of a daughter as the comfort of his old age.

Alas, it was not to be. Between her impulsive gesture in Oakley Street and the teatime meeting at the Cadogan, the young lady had learned more about her mother's relationship with Toby. He had been fully aware, her mother told her, that she was pregnant. When her child was born, Toby had already absented himself and he made no effort to contact mother or daughter in future years, nor did he make any contribution towards her upbringing or education. All this she confronted Toby with as they sat over neglected scones and sandwiches at the Cadogan, the tea in their teacups untasted. Toby heard her out and hung his head in shame. She then informed him that she had decided she did not want any relationship with him and admonished him not to make any approach to her or her mother in the future. With that she apologised for initiating the episode without fully thinking through the consequences and left the hotel. There was no parting kiss on the cheek.

Toby had behaved like a cad and reaped his just deserts. But he returned to his lonely room broken in spirit and I am not sure that he ever fully recovered from this momentary hope of finding a family that had been so abruptly torn from his grasp.

• • •

My own romantic life was constrained by the extra hours I put into selecting a million cuttings for destruction and the demands of my book. I formed an attachment with Sistie Fairweather, whom I met through the British Honduras Emergency Committee. She had been Miss British Honduras 1959 and before coming to England had worked for the telephone company in Belize City, where she was required to memorise the number of every telephone subscriber in the colony (it transpired that there were only 250). She had come to England to study ballet with a view to opening her own dance academy in Belize. She obtained a full-time job in the back office at John Lewis in Oxford Street, which she needed in order to pay her tuition fees and subsistence. John Lewis, benevolent employers as they were, let her work whatever hours fitted with her dance classes, provided she made them up in full. With this busy schedule she could only go out once a week on a weekday evening, plus the odd social occasion at weekends, usually involving jerk chicken and bongo drums. This suited my own schedule perfectly and we enjoyed a pleasant relationship that we knew would terminate when she completed her studies and returned to BH. It did so earlier than either of us had expected.

The racial discrimination practised among employers and landlords of the time is well documented and a shaming aspect of our recent history. Much less attention has been paid to the institutionalised racism that penetrated, I do believe in the light of Sistie's experience, to the heart of government. After she had completed two years of her three-year course in modern dance, the Home Office sent her a letter demanding proof that she was a bona fide student in light of the fact that she had a full-time job. She responded that, unlike most Commonwealth students, who were on generous grants or bursaries, she was wholly self-sufficient. She enclosed statements from the head of her dance school, confirming that she was a full-time student, and from the head of personnel for John Lewis stating that they had employed her in the knowledge that she was a full-time student and would be returning to her own country on completion of her dance course. The Home Office dismissed this evidence and asked for proof that she was not an economic migrant. We enlisted the support of Sistie's Member of Parliament, who knew her personally and was happy to confirm that she was in Britain temporarily as a full-time student. As he was a Conservative, we thought it would be helpful to have the testimony of a government supporter and Sistie produced Mervyn Jones, a Labour Party activist and close associate of Michael Foot. He endorsed what her MP had said, but shocked me when he remarked, in Sistie's absence from the room, 'I suppose dancing is important to those kind of people.' By 'those kind of people' this ardent socialist meant people of colour. Or perhaps Mr Jones had in mind darkies in grass skirts.

As our *coup de grâce* that we were confident would silence the Home Office once and for all, we dug out a former Governor of British Honduras, a close friend of her father (Colonel-in-Chief of the British Honduras Defence Force), who produced an affidavit to the effect that he had been privy to Sistie's intentions before she left BH and knew that she had every intention of returning home. None of this had the slightest effect on the Home Office and the socialist minister responsible for immigrants issued her with a deportation order. I am wholly confident that had she been a white Australasian or Canadian she would have experienced no problem in completing her course. (Since writing the foregoing, the Windrush Generation scandal has engulfed the Home Office. A Tory government this time; otherwise *Plus ça change....*)

A postscript. Sistie's elder brother, Flying Officer Dick Fairweather DFC of RAF Bomber Command, paid his own way to Britain to join up early in WWII. He was shot down over Germany on the Wesseling Raid of 21st/22nd June 1944 and died aged twenty-two. Thus did the British Government repay the families of her Empire war heroes.

* * *

Among our regular customers at News Information was Stephen Potter of Gamesmanship and One-upmanship fame. We established something of a rapport and one day he asked me what I was doing skulking in this backwater of BBC Radio. I explained to him that I lacked the qualifications for more elevated employment. 'But surely you could be a proper programme researcher?' he challenged. I told him alas not, much as I would love to do the kind of work that Esther Rantzen performed so energetically. In order to be considered for such a job you had to have a degree. BBC Personnel, flexible as they might be about employing people who were physically or mentally challenged, were quite unbending about this. 'Hah!' declared the Oneupmanship Meister, 'Wait till I get to work on Frank Gillard. He'll bend the rules if I lean on him a bit.' Frank Gillard, war hero and a massive all-round talent, had joined the BBC in 1936, the same year as Potter. Now he was Director of Radio and they were practically joined at the hip. Suddenly my prospects seemed more promising.

The next time Stephen Potter came in he looked chastened. Even his wicked wiles and effortless charm had failed to persuade his old friend to tweak the BBC rule-book. There were, Gillard had explained, between two and three hundred applicants for every job in programme production. It was impossible to interview them all, and so the very first elimination process was graduates only. He confided that on some days Personnel would whittle down the applications by discarding all those from people whose surname began with A-L, and the next day they would discard everyone in the M-Z category. You had to be ruthless, he asserted, and it did not do to make exceptions. Stephen pointed out that plenty of exceptions were made for the daughters of socialist cabinet ministers and others with whom the Director-General sought to ingratiate himself, but Gillard declared that the DG, being only one level of seniority below God, could do as he chose; he himself, as Director of Radio, practised no favouritism.

It was probably my bad luck that Stephen Potter's best mate was one of the few high-ups of the BBC who espoused such principles. Did he, I wonder, lose out on some useful talent by applying them so rigidly? And while many major institutions pride themselves on the fact that aspirants may rise from the bottom to the top, does the BBC still erect an impenetrable barrier for those of its staff who have not had the privilege of a university education?

. . .

The Director-General was Sir Hugh Carleton Greene, whose three brothers were respectively the celebrated novelist Graham Greene, an Everest climber, and a Japanese spy. He is largely credited with dragging the BBC out of its Reithian darkness into a shining new light of social awareness and leftist righteousness. Within the Corporation, though, he had a reputation for aloofness and elitism. Like my old headmaster at Shrewsbury, who only knew the names of his praeposters, Greene only knew the names of his directors. As a doctrinaire socialist from a privileged background he found it difficult to relate to people outside his own class.

One October day a small, untidy, chubby man came tearing into News Information with his coat-tails flapping and his hat askew. 'Hello,' he announced breathlessly, 'I'm Charles Hill and I'm the new Chairman. Just wanted to meet you all and find out what you do. Can't stay long, though, because I'm trying to get round all twenty three and a half thousand of you!'

None of us had ever set eyes on the Director-General, let alone spoken to him. Now here in our midst was the new Chairman, Lord Hill, already famous as Dr Charles Hill the 'Radio Doctor', eager to hear about our obscure corner of the Corporation. He swallowed a quick cup of tea and I gave him my ninety-second pitch on why News Information's service to producers was so indispensable, to which he made all the right responses before dashing out again with his hat still awry.

Not surprisingly there was a clash of personalities between the D-G and the Chairman, whom the effete Sir Hugh characterised as a 'vulgarian'. It concluded with Sir Hugh's not wholly voluntary departure in 1969. In the run-up to this happy event, all the senior staff were Sir Hugh loyalists. All the erks were Lord Hill supporters to a man and a woman.

· · ·

Lunching with my brother Tim one day, he asked me how I saw my future. 'In what respect?', I asked.

'Do you expect to make a career at the BBC?'

'I'd like to.'

'How far can you go up the hierarchy? Could you, in theory, rise to the top, or at least the senior echelons?'

'Er... not really. There is a ceiling for people who don't have degrees.'

'So what is your career expectancy?'

'I could become the head of all the News Information units. But at present I am the most junior of the unit heads, so that would be ten or twenty years down the line.'

'And how much does this head chap earn?'

'Hmm … about £1,500 a year I think.'

'And do you hope to marry some time?'

'Yes.'

'If you married someone from your own background, you would not be able to keep them on £1,500 a year. And you would have to send your children to the Board School.' (My brother tended to call things by archaic names. Radio 4 never stopped being the Home Service for Tim.)

I knew he was right. Much as I enjoyed working at the BBC, for all its manifest faults, I had no real future within the Corporation. Even an egalitarian like Lord Hill was unlikely to be able to change a system of elitism and patronage so entrenched. The BBC had saved me from the dole queue when I had little to offer and I was grateful for that. Now, though, it was time to move on.

. . .

But move on where? There were still woefully few openings for even the most accomplished bear-chasers.

# Chapter 17

. . .

# THE GIRL FROM GENTHIN

. . .

*1969–71*

'Were you a member of your school football XI?' asked the Brigadier. He was chairman of the Civil Service board interviewing me for a post in the Government Information Service. His tweeds were so thick they would have stood up without him inside them.

'No Sir,' I replied.

'Were you a member of your house football XI?'

'No Sir.'

'Were you a member of the school cricket XI?'

'No Sir.'

'Were you a member of your house cricket XI?'

'No Sir.'

'Were you a member of the school eight?'

'No Sir.'

'Were you a member of your house four?'

'No Sir.'

And so on through the whole catalogue of school sports. What this had to do with my ability or otherwise to be a government spokesman eluded me. The brigadier became more exasperated with every negative response. Finally he barked at me, 'What *do* you do for exercise?'

'I have walked much of the way from the Cape to Cairo,' I told him with what I thought was pardonable exaggeration in the circumstances.

Apparently, as I learned later from the Ministry of Transport representative on the board, he turned to the other two members after I had retired and harrumphed,'I don't think that boy will be any use to the Civil Service. He doesn't seem to play any sport at all.' The others were so shocked by this that they insisted I should be given the job – a job I was not even sure I wanted.

I had seen an advertisement for Government Information Officers in *The Daily Telegraph* some six months earlier and, having the principal qualification of experience in the media, I applied. There was then this long lapse before the board was held. On arriving at the Central Office of Information I was informed that there had been an error. The post they were boarding for was not that of Information Officer, but Assistant Information Officer, a training grade. Did I wish to withdraw?

I had waited six months and I had no other irons in the fire. So I said no, I would offer myself as a candidate for the more junior job. Thus I became, at the age of twenty-nine, the oldest trainee in the whole of the Civil Service, not a distinction I felt like revealing to my chums. These friends from the HAC, the Public Schools Club, the poker school etc, had mainly been office boys when I left on my travels. On my return I found that they had become junior executives. Now, five years on, some had company cars and one or two even had a wall-to-wall secretary. In ten years' time they would be jostling for a position on the board. Hopefully by then I would have completed my training.

So why did I accept? The pay, even for a trainee, was more than I had been paid as a junior manager at the BBC. (When I arrived at the Ministry of Transport I found that the office typist was earning more than my BBC salary. Not that Civil Service typists were overpaid.) And there was a prospect of advancement. The two top positions were Head of the Government Information Service and Press Secretary at No. 10. A more realistic level of attainment was Chief Information Officer of a government department. That was equivalent to a brigadier-general in the army or a junior minister in government.

And talking of brigadiers ... some time later I had a line manager, Bob Davy, who applied for promotion. The chairman of the board was the brigadier from my board. Now Bob Davy was a bit of a rough diamond who had worked as PRO for De Beers in South Africa and knocked around the world a bit. To Bob a spade was a sodding shovel. The brigadier asked him where his *father* had been educated. I am not privy to Bob's father's CV but I doubt if he had progressed beyond some backstreet Board School, round about 1905 or whenever. Bob was furious and made a formal complaint. There had already been a number of complaints about the brigadier's intrusive and irrelevant style of interrogation and this was the one that did for him. He was removed from the panel of board chairmen.

* * *

My first assignment as a trainee at the Ministry of Transport was to write a radio commercial for road safety. I was given the length of the commercial and the point to be plugged and that was all. I asked if I could hear some previous examples and was told to stop making a fuss and get on with it. It was apparent that 'training' did not involve much in the way of formal instruction in the Government Information Service. It was the sink or swim method of learning.

After a week or two of these kinds of odd jobs I was told that I was the new editor of *The Examiner*. This was not the literary weekly that numbered Byron, Keats, Shelley, Thackeray and Dickens among its contributors, but the house journal of the Driving Test Establishment. I, a non-motorist, was to edit a motoring journal. Again, there was no instruction. I was given a contact at HMSO with whom to liaise about production and told I had forty-eight pages to fill by the following week. There is a benefit to this kind of 'training'. You learn fast.

The driving-test examiners were all ex-army NCOs, salt of the earth types with real pride in their lowly-graded jobs. I greatly enjoyed touring round the driving-test centres and interviewing them about their working lives, especially the hair-raising tales of tests that had to be terminated because the candidate was a danger to other motorists, him or herself and the examiner. This was surprisingly frequent and being an examiner was a challenging as well as a hazardous job that required intense concentration. I also enjoyed talking to my client, Deputy Chief Examiner

James Coulson, who was in effect the publisher of the *Examiner*. He had just conducted Prince Charles's driving test. I asked him whether it would have been possible to fail His Royal Highness. Mr Coulson told me that they had made very certain that HRH had reached a fit standard before he applied for the test, because there would have been absolutely no question of passing him if he had not attained the required standard of safety.

Soon after he had gained his licence, it was arranged for the Prince to pay a formal visit to the Driving Test Establishment. A suave young Principal, not a member of the DTE, summoned me to his office and told me that the Prince was to be presented with a copy of *The Highway Code* – as if he had not acquired a copy during his instruction. My job was to get it suitably bound. Crushed morocco, gold tooling, that kind of thing, murmured the suave Principal airily. I consulted bibliophile Christopher Fildes (see Introduction) and he told me that the No. 1 crushed morocco man in the whole country was close by his workplace in Bath. Moreover he had just won £50 on the St Leger and he suggested that we should see if we could eat and drink our way through the whole lot at Bath's premier restaurant, The Hole in the Wall. At this date dinner at somewhere like Claridges or the Dorchester was about £5 a head, without wine, so even allowing for two or three bottles of some rare vintages we were setting ourselves quite a task. The only time I can recall eating a larger meal was when I was taken to the Randolph Hotel after an all-night poker session in Oxford and my generous host waved the menu away with a brief command to the waiter, 'Mr Hickman-Robertson will have a plate of everything.'

The book-binder took some time to recover from the request that he apply his skills, normally reserved for immensely valuable books in national collections, to a shilling copy of *The Highway Code*. Once I had explained who the recipient was to be, he entered into the spirit of the thing and drew up a set of proposals that included a slipcase and a velvet lined presentation box as well as crushed morocco and gold tooling fit for a ... well, a prince. The price would be £225.

I reported back to the suave Principal. He was delighted with the proposal and not the least fased by the price. He took it off to show to the Permanent Secretary who, he was confident, would be equally enthusiastic.

In time I was to get to know several Permanent Secretaries and in my experience they are never enthused by anything. This one was more disgusted than delighted. Such a gift to the Prince, the Permanent

Secretary intoned, would smack of rank extravagance, a reckless disregard for taxpayers' money. Crushed morocco indeed! What the Permanent Secretary wanted was something modern, stylish and inexpensive. Or at least inexpensive-looking. Like plastic. That was it. *The Highway Code* in plastic covers. What could be more 1969 than that?

I stood down the crushed morocco maestro in Bath and set off for a plastics factory in rather less elegant Shadwell. I explained the mission. There was a lot of sucking of teeth and pursing of lips. The plastic cover would require a die to be cast for this one single binding. Normally it would only be worth making a die for a run of ten or twenty thousand plastic whatevers. It wouldn't come cheap.

I reported back to the suave Principal. The cost of the die would be £350, plus the cost of binding. The Principal reported back to the Permanent Secretary. What would the *value*, not the cost, of the finished article be, asked the mandarin. The suave Principal hazarded a guess. A shilling copy of *The Highway Code* in a sixpenny binding, say 1s 6d. The Permanent Secretary, if short of delighted, was content. Nobody was likely to accuse the Ministry of Transport of extravagance.

Somewhere in the Royal Library at Windsor lies a plastic-covered *Highway Code* that cost somewhere north of £350.

· · ·

Meanwhile work on my book progressed. By now I had done all the spade-work and needed specialist sources. My weekends and leave-days were spent in the British Museum Reading Room (now the British Library) and the National Newspaper Archive at Colindale. For the 'big subjects' I sought out collections where I could talk to experts: BBC Archives and the Royal Television Society for broadcasting, the Science Museum library and Patent Office library for technology, the Veteran Car Club library for motoring, the British Film Institute for cinema, the National Army Museum for military matters, the GPO Museum & Archives for telecommunications and postal services, the GWR archives for rail transport, the Fawcett Library for the advancement of women.

Like most researchers I suffered setbacks and barriers – I went to the London University archives to identify the names of the first women in Britain to graduate and the date they did so, a significant moment in women's history that has been overlooked by historians. All that history books tell you is that London University opened its degrees to women in 1878. This information was repeated to me by the archivist. I told him I knew that, but I wanted names and the date they graduated. 'Why?' he asked brusquely.

'Because it's never been recorded anywhere outside your archives,' I told him.

'But why would anyone need to know?,' he persisted.

'I need to know and I think there are a lot of people who would like to honour the names of those pioneers.'

'Why?'

'Could you just fetch me the honours rolls for the years following 1878 please?' He gave me a long, hard scowl before retiring for an interminable length of time, then banged them hard on the desk in front of me, releasing a cloud of dust into my eyes. The answer is 17th November 1880 and those women whose names deserve to be remembered as true pioneers were Elizabeth M Creak of Redditch and Newnham Hall, Cambridge; Marianne Andrews of 73 Westwick Gardens, Hammersmith, and University College, London; and Mrs Elizabeth Hills, teacher at the East of England Girls' School in Bishop's Stortford, Herts. No thanks to that surly archivist if they are.

Every book of dates and anniversaries records that Greenwich Mean Time was adopted as standard time internationally in 1884, but when was it standardised in Britain? I called Greenwich Observatory to find out. 'Why do you want to know?' 'Because it isn't in any reference book and I am going to put it in one.' 'Why?' 'So that historians and others will know when we changed over from local time, with each big city setting its own time from the sun.' 'Why would they want to know?' 'Because it was a seminal change in how we ordered our lives.' Much laboured breathing at the other end. 'Why?'

But nowhere was quite as frustrating as the British Museum Reading Room. Readers were serviced by supercilious librarians and disgruntled old men in long brown dustcoats who did the fetching and carrying. If you put in a request at opening time, the book seldom arrived on your desk before lunch. On one occasion I needed to consult Thomas Hancock's *The Origin and Progress of the Caoutchouc or India-Rubber Industry in England* (1857). Having put in my slip at 9 am, the book arrived ten minutes before closing time at 5 pm. I took it to the supercilious librarian and asked him if he could keep it for me overnight. He refused. The following day I waited all day and finally a slip was delivered to my desk reporting that the book had been destroyed by fire damage. I asked the librarian whether there had been a fire in the stacks last night. He said it was a mistake and I should put in another request. Another whole day passed and a slip arrived at my desk declaring that the book had now been destroyed by bomb damage. This time even the supercilious one's flinty heart was softened sufficiently for him to offer to search for the book himself. He came back within five minutes bearing it aloft. 'Where was it?' I enquired. 'On the shelf where it was meant to be,' he replied. After that I decided it was quicker to take the train to Oxford and use the Bodleian Library instead.

Despite these minor upsets, things were looking up on the literary front. A *Daily Mail* journo I met in a pub did a diary piece about my quest for firsts and this caught the eye of Norris McWhirter, editor of *The Guinness Book of Records*. At this time *GBR* was published by the brewery and was Guinness's only book – later they would set up a separate publishing company. McWhirter was not able to place my book himself, but he offered to find me an agent. In the capable hands of Peter Janson-Smith, I soon had a contract with book packagers Rainbird. They in turn secured me an advance from Michael Joseph and the Ebury Press, who had agreed to publish the book in tandem.

. . .

The British Honduras Emergency Committee decided to celebrate St George's Caye Day, the colony's national day, with a fund-raiser ball at the appropriately named Empire Ballrooms in Tottenham Court Road. I could not take Sistie, as the poor girl had already been deported by a Home Office indifferent to the many services her family had performed for the Mother Country. Instead I made up a foursome with my old friend and benefactor from school, Jeremy Gould. I took an American girl called Mary-Anne who was known to both of us and JJ brought along a German girl called Karla Ehrlich whom he had recently met. We were the only white people at the ball, which was attended by nearly the whole British Honduran community in England, about 250 strong.

Miss Ehrlich looked very fetching in an exceedingly brief micro-skirted white dress and white knee socks. The rest of her, apart from her long blonde hair, was as copper-coloured as some of the British Hondurans, a hue acquired while filming in Malta. Somehow during the course of the evening JJ and I seemed to have exchanged partners.

As Miss Ehrlich, aka Karla Hickman-Robertson, will feature fairly prominently in the remainder of this memoir, I had better give you some background. Most people's family histories are pretty dull, so I hasten to tell you that this is the story of a girl brought up first under the Nazis, then under the communists, who escaped to the West and lived in dire poverty until Hollywood called and life changed forever, so it is not quite as dull as you might expect. Bear with me.

Karla Ehrlich was born in Genthin in the province of Brandenburg in 1941, daughter of Götz Ehrlich, who owned or managed (we have never been sure which) the local farmers' bank, and his wife Liselotte, known as Lilo. The first two important events in Karla's life happened in 1943. Things were going badly for the Germans on the Eastern Front and Götz was called up, along with most of the other remaining men of military age in Genthin. He was waiting with the others on the station platform for the train that would take them to the induction centre, and as it pulled in a soldier came running down the platform waving a piece of paper. As the recruits boarded, the solder cried out, 'Is there a Herr Ehrlich here?' Götz identified himself and was told he was to stay behind. His job financing farmers between harvests had been deemed essential to the war effort. None of the men who boarded the train would he ever see again.

While Götz survived, his elder brother Dr Gerhard Ehrlich, an unmarried surgeon at the Charité Hospital in Berlin, was less fortunate. His death certificate states Warsaw, Gänsestrasse, as the place of death. Present-day research has revealed this address to have been that of a concentration camp within the city. The family had come under the notice of the Gestapo because they had a Jewish name, though in fact no Jewish blood. Karla believes that Gerhard was invited to become a surgeon in the camps – Gänsestrasse was a staging post for Auschwitz – conducting medical experiments on inmates, and that he refused. If so, he is one of the unnamed and unhonoured 'Righteous Ones'.

The family lived next door to the residence of the Gauleiter in Genthin. Like many Nazis he loved animals and children. Often he would bring sweeties for the toddler Karla. She would run down the garden path squeaking 'Gauleiterchen! Gauleiterchen!' when she heard the click of the garden gate and then clasp him around his big black boots. One day in the spring of 1945 she heard the gate click, ran forward and threw her arms round the big boots and hailed her 'Gauleiterchen'. But they were brown boots, not black.... Karla's mother Lilo was watching through the window, her face frozen in horror. The Russians had arrived and this was their commander, General Filamanov. The General, though, was a man of honour. He set up his headquarters in the Ehrlichs' house and became the family's protector and friend. When he was recalled to Russia a year later, Lilo implored, 'You will write, won't you?' 'No,' he replied. 'And you must never ever attempt to get in touch with me, for both our sakes.'

In 1947 Karla's family moved to nearby Tangermünde, a small medieval walled town in what would soon become the DDR, where her father established a liqueur distillery in partnership with Lilo's brothers. This did not prove a good move. When the brothers fled to the West without informing Götz, the Russians seized the factory. Götz was left without any means of support other than Lilo's modest earnings.

By 1954 Götz had long been unemployed: there was little call for ex-bankers in the new socialist paradise of East Germany. Eventually he received an invitation to interview for the job of manager in a factory. The interview went well and he was told he could start on Monday. There was just one minor formality – he needed to show his Party card. Götz explained that he had never been a member of the Party. He was told it was most regrettable, but this responsible position in an organ of the state could only go to a party member.

Götz left, bowed down by a feeling of utter despair. Two men in raincoats and slouch hats pulled down over their eyes were standing at the entrance. 'We understand you have had a disappointment, Herr Ehrlich,' one of them ventured. 'Perhaps you would like to walk with us?' Götz was led to the banks of the Elbe, where they sat down and the two men made him an offer. As the town's former banker, he was known to all of its most prominent citizens. There was certain information about such citizens that it would be very helpful for the state to know. If Herr Ehrlich was able to keep them informed on a regular basis, they were sure some accommodation with the factory could be made and the job would be his. Götz said he needed time to think about it. The two men said of course, meet us back here in twenty-four hours. 'We are sure you will make the right decision.'

When Götz related all of this to her, Lilo said without hesitation, 'You have to leave tonight.' It happened to be her birthday. She and Götz also happened to have buried the remaining stock of schnapps from the distillery in the back garden. They dug it up and invited friends and neighbours, including the very people Götz was supposed to spy on, to a birthday celebration. And they invited the local Party bigwigs, who were never reluctant to imbibe liquor at others' expense. By midnight the *apparatchiks*, whose glasses had been constantly replenished by Lilo, were most of them comatose. Götz slipped away and walked across the fields to a small village where he caught the milk train to Berlin.

In East Berlin there was a *U-Bahn* circuit like London's Circle Line. It had a single stop in West Berlin. In every carriage there were *Stasi* operatives stationed close to the doors. The trick was to stand far enough away not to attract obvious attention, but just close enough to make your jump as the doors closed. If you mistimed your leap by a tenth of a second the next stop would be the *gulag*. Götz knew you must not look in the direction of the *Stasi* men. You must not look tense or poised to spring. Look relaxed, unconcerned, even though your heart is beating so hard you fear it must be audible. The doors began to close. He leaped. The *Stasi* men lunged towards him. He landed on the platform as the doors closed behind him. He was in the West.

Götz was ineligible for the benefits paid to refugees from East Germany because he was unable to prove that he escaped under duress. Meanwhile Lilo contrived a story that her husband was consorting with a fancy woman in Hamburg and it was she who was seducing him away from his duty to the socialist Fatherland. If Lilo could see him, and he could see his darling daughter, then he would realise that he must return to help build socialism. Amazingly the Communist authorities fell for this implausible line of reasoning, presumably because they heard what they wanted to hear. Meanwhile Lilo was dispatching parcels containing the family's household goods to a 'safe house' address in Hamburg. About half arrived, the rest purloined by East German postal workers. About a year later Lilo and Karla also left for the West. Their life in Hamburg, West Germany's most prosperous city, was to prove even more deprived than in it had been in the East.

The Ehrlichs lived in a single room in Hamburg. Not one room, plus kitchen and bathroom. Just one room. Karla went to school during Hamburg's bitter winters wearing her mother's coat; she had none of her own. She also wore her mother's shoes, shuffling to school in them because they were two sizes too big.

Eventually Götz was offered a job, a prestigious, well-paid position that would transform their lives. He was to be secretary of the distinguished Anglo-German Club that overlooks the Alster. The day before he was due to start, he had a stroke and was paralysed. Lilo obtained employment as a pharmacist (her job in East Germany). Karla worked during school vacations at the luxury food emporium run by her wealthy relatives. She was paid in kind. During the periods she had this job the poverty-stricken family lived on the kind of food we associate with Fortnum & Mason. During term-time, though, their diet reverted to black bread and potatoes. When the proprietor's sister, whom Karla has always addressed as 'Aunt', came on to the shop floor, she pointedly ignored Karla. Lilo's two brothers, Götz's partners in the defunct distillery who had brought about his ruin, were now enjoying prosperity in the West. They disassociated themselves from their sister and her family.

In the same year as I started work as a so-called 'trainee' in the advertising business, Karla secured her first job as a clerk in a coal-heaving company. Later she went to Paris as an au pair and looked after a child, born to a mother with German measles, who was blind, deaf, dumb and brain-damaged. After a couple of secretarial jobs in film companies, she joined Studio Hamburg in a similarly humble capacity and here she had her first career break. Passing an empty office she heard a telephone ringing. She picked it up and an unmistakable voice intoned, 'This is Martin Luther King Junior.' The great man was in Hamburg for a single day and wanted to get in touch with Thilo Koch, the David Frost of West German television, to fulfil a long-promised interview. Realising how important this was, Karla tracked down Koch on an out-of-town assignment and he returned immediately to Hamburg. The interview was a triumph and Koch was so delighted with his scoop that he invited Karla to join his team. Now at last she was in the front line of television news and current affairs.

Karla had learned Russian at school in East Germany and on arrival in West Germany was too far behind the other pupils to master English.

When she had an invitation from one of her mother's cousins in America, it was an opportunity to make up the deficiency. As a result, on her return to Studio Hamburg she was seconded to a Hollywood film being made out of the studio, *Heidi*. Her job was to help with basic translation between German- and English-speaking crew on set. Anxiety about her ability to cope in a strange language turned to panic when she was told that she had been reassigned to the producer of the film, a much more demanding job involving constant interaction with cast and crew as well as use of the telephone and correspondence in English. She was instructed to present herself to him at the location base, Sils Maria in Switzerland. On 27th August 1967, quaking with trepidation, she introduced herself to Frederick H Brogger in the bar of the Waldhaus Hotel. He told her that he had heard that it was her birthday. She gulped a nervous assent and he called for champagne all round. It was the first of many times that Karla would hear that joyful command emanating from the hospitable Frederick H and the start of a lifelong, if sometimes turbulent, friendship.

On set Karla met her first theatrical knight, Sir Michael Redgrave, who played Heidi's grandfather, and became an ace table tennis player in epic tournaments with Maximilian Schell and Jean Simmons. She also established a close friendship with John Williams, an unknown composer who was to become a very well-known composer, with five Oscars and a record fifty-one Oscar nominations under his belt. The film *Heidi*, little known in Britain, is notorious in America, where a Super Bowl final still remembered as 'The *Heidi* Bowl' was broken off a minute before the end to start showing the film on television. At that point the New York Jets were well in the lead and certain victors. As *Heidi*'s title credits rolled, unbeknown to the TV audience the Oakland Raiders scored two touchdowns and snatched victory from the jaws of defeat.

Karla's next film, *Bridge at Remagen* with George Segal and Robert Vaughan, also involved extraneous drama, as the crew had to flee Czechoslovakia as the Russian tanks rumbled into Prague. Fortunately they were able to bring many members of the Czech cast and crew with them, refugees who found a new life of freedom in the West.

At the conclusion of this episode Karla received a call from Frederick H Brogger, who had relocated to London, offering her the opportunity to work on *David Copperfield* in England. She had no desire to visit England, which she associated with her tyrannical English mistress in

Hamburg insisting that she speak the Queen's English and not like an American. Frederick H was accustomed to getting his own way and if he could not persuade Karla himself, he knew someone who could. Karla had a crush on John Williams. The maestro-to-be called her to say that it was absolutely essential that she came to London because the pubs had cut-glass windows. In what she later conceded is probably the stupidest reason ever for a career move, she capitulated. She did impose a condition though. She must be allowed to leave on the first plane to Hamburg after the wrap; she wouldn't be staying for the wrap party. (The particular pub with cut-glass windows that so attracted the great composer turned out to be the Salisbury in St Martin's Lane, which Williams and Brogger had adopted as their lunchtime canteen. Neither of these Hollywood honchos seemed to be aware that it was a gay theatrical pub. When Karla finally visited the cut-glass shrine, she was the only woman present.)

Karla found life in England more agreeable than she expected, living in luxurious Hans Crescent in Knightsbridge, working out at Pinewood, and on location at Southwold. She met a galaxy of British luminaries of stage and screen: Sir Laurence Olivier, Sir Richard Attenborough, Sir Ralph Richardson, Sir Michael Redgrave (again), Dame Wendy Hiller, Dame Edith Evans, Susan Hampshire, Ron Moody … Dame Edith addressed her as 'Little Girl', as in 'Come here, Little Girl'. Karla did not mind a bit. But the thing Karla liked most about England was Georgian houses. She became quite passionate about them. She confided to scriptwriter Jack Pulman (who also wrote *War and Peace*, with a little help from Tolstoy) that if she could have a Georgian house she might even stay in England, but of course that would be impossible.… Jack, unusually, was a tax inspector before becoming Britain's highest-paid scriptwriter. He explained about mortgages to her. In Germany nearly everybody rented, because mortgages are for those who already have money. In England you only needed a 10% deposit. Karla was overwhelmed. Even ordinary people could aspire to a Georgian house? 'Even ordinary people,' Jack confirmed. 'Provided they are British,' he added. Karla's face fell. Jack corrected himself: 'Or married to someone British.'

This conversation took place soon after the occasion of the St George's Caye Day Ball. A few days later I received my invitation to the royal premiere of *David Copperfield* at the Odeon, Leicester Square.

. . .

1970 was an eventful year for me because I was promoted to Information Officer, the job I had originally applied for, the Ministry of Transport was merged with two other ministries to become the Department of the Environment, and I moved out of my bedsitter at Mrs Linley's in Oakley Street and into the Omnibus Productions office in the heart of Mayfair. Frederick H had hired a residential flat in South Audley Street to serve as the production office and struck a deal with Karla that she could live there rent-free provided she did the cleaning and kept it stocked with liquor. The last proviso could have proved expensive, because this was long before Hollywood switched over to mineral water. It was an era of heavy drinkers, on both sides of the Atlantic. People would fly in from Los Angeles on the red-eye and, arriving in South Audley Street about 9 am, their first command would be 'Gemme the Coast' (Americans could never grasp the time difference) and their second would be 'Gemme the driest Martini in town'. Karla became adept at fulfilling the second command, even if she could not turn Hollywood night into day with regard to the first. Now at the rate that these big, burly men with their gravelly bass voices could tip the hard stuff down their throats, Karla would soon have been deeply out of pocket – but for a fortunate circumstance. She had a chum from Hamburg in the German Embassy, Gaby, who could obtain hard liquor brought over in the diplomatic bag at duty-free prices. Whereas a litre bottle of Gordon's gin cost £3 10s at Oddbins, for Karla the price was 13 shillings – less than one third. Scotch whisky, Hollywood's other tipple of choice, cost her about the same.

I did not reveal to my parents that I had moved: living in sin had not yet reached the provinces. So I continued to pay rent to Mrs Linley, so that if my parents called (an extravagance only warranted in emergency) she would say I had just stepped out and then call me at Karla's.

. . .

The Department of the Environment was an ill-conceived venture made in response to the universal preoccupation, much promoted by the media, for all things environmental. We occupied the three hideous tower blocks erected for the purpose in Marsham Street, Westminster, and struggled to glue together the disparate activities of three government departments that had little in common and different operating methods. These problems were compounded by the presence of no fewer than eleven ministers, under the overall command of sour, scowling Secretary of State Peter Walker, disposed in groups at the very top of the three twenty-two storey towers. For someone as scatterbrained as I, it was a nightmare. On more than one occasion I was summoned to attend a minister and went up the wrong tower. It could take a full twenty minutes to descend twenty-two storeys, wait for another lift, and ascend a different twenty-two storeys. Ministers are not accustomed to being kept waiting twenty, or indeed any, minutes.

I had ceased to be the only editor of a motoring magazine who could not drive and reassigned as a ministerial speech-writer. I had assumed that speech-writing was something of a collegiate venture. Far from it. You were not given any access to the ministers you wrote for, not even an opportunity to hear them delivering speeches in order to gain some insight into their style. The only briefing you received was whatever you could extract out of the minister's private office or the division responsible for policy on the topic. Seldom did either prove fruitful. When I had to write a speech for the minister to deliver to the Road Haulage Association, I was informed that the government had no policy on road haulage. Faced with a blank sheet of paper, I consulted my notes on firsts and found that it was the seventy-fifth anniversary of the first motor pantechnicon. So I had my opening para; now all I had to do was fill another five and a half pages.

On another occasion the speech was headed 'Anglo-French Co-operation' and was to be delivered by John Peyton, then in charge of Britain's half of the development of Concorde, to an audience of the great and the good from both sides of the Channel. I sent a note to the Private Secretary asking whether there were any particular points his minister wanted to get across. The response was succinct: 'The Minister says there is no such thing as Anglo-French co-operation.'

Public parks was another one that elicited a response from the policy wonks that there was no government policy on the issue, whatever that might be. I thought long and hard and could not think of any issues either. The blank pages stared back at me reproachfully. So I set to thinking about parks I had visited on my travels. Central Park: sheer magic so long as you do not get mugged. What I particularly liked was

413

the open-air theatre where anybody could put on a show. The only proviso, other than the usual safeguards, was that you could not charge the audience. It was free to the producer and free to the punters. What's not to like? I wrote this into the speech, recommending that all the major cultural centres of Britain should imitate Central Park in this regard. In San Francisco's Golden Gate Park it had been the Picnic Groves and the Music Concourse that attracted me. They went into the speech too. In Adelaide it was not so much the amenities that appealed, though they were fine, but the fact that the parks surrounded the city. Driving in or driving out of town your spirits were lifted by verdant lawns and swathes of flowerbeds tightly packed with glowing, iridescent blooms. I had the Minister enjoin Britain's urban planners to encircle every new town with Adelaide-style parks.

Making up government policy on the hoof was fun, but I did not expect any of it to come to pass. There was one dramatic episode at this time where fanciful policy-making of the kind I had indulged actually propelled the government into wholly unforeseen and unplanned action. Prime Minister Edward Heath had been on a state visit to Paris, accompanied by his regular speech-writer. The French had recently completed a huge programme to clean up all the public buildings and monuments of Paris. Now the city of dreams was white and gleaming and as lovely as it had been when Baron Hausmann completed his great rebuilding programme during the Second Empire. Heath was deeply impressed and as they drove into the city from the airport he remarked to the speech-writer that it would be wonderful to do the same for grimy old London, still encrusted with all the soot accumulated before the 1956 Clean Air Act.

The following week the PM was due to deliver a major speech at the Mansion House. After the early drafts had been approved, the speech-writer thought he would have a bit of a laugh and put in a declaration that the government was going to clean up London. It was not wholly a jape, because although he knew that the PM would strike the passage out, it might sow the idea in his mind for discussion in cabinet. It so happened the PM had an exceptionally heavy schedule on the day of the Mansion House speech and he never got round to checking the final draft. He simply read out what was on the paper before him and when he reached the passage about cleaning up London he froze. There was an awkward pause while his eyes scanned down the page, but precious seconds were ticking away and he could not see where to pick up the next topic. He had no choice but to carry on.

I would not have cared to have been the duty officer at the Department of the Environment that night. The press went wild. Desmond Plummer, Leader of the Greater London Council, went wilder. This was not something the government was empowered to do, he bellowed down the phone to No. 10. This was a GLC matter and the GLC had made no financial provision for such a vast enterprise. Some adroit footwork was needed to persuade the Treasury to cough up the readies and the project was presented as a joint government-GLC initiative. At DOE we were instructed to let contracts to every stone-cleaning company available, bypassing the normal tendering process. In the press office, where I was now working, we had to put up a convincing front *suggesting* that all this had long been in the planning without actually saying as much. Some of the questioning was forensic in its detail and intensity. It may surprise readers to learn that government spokesmen never lie. It is a hard and fast rule from which no exceptions are made. But there is no rule requiring a spokesman to volunteer the *whole* truth.

Edward Heath's greatest pride was getting us into the European Economic Community after years of intransigence from the French. He should have been grateful to the French though for what may not have been the most historic achievement of his career, but was certainly the most popular. The Clean Up London campaign transformed the capital and gave it a lustre that not even its oldest inhabitants could recall. It boosted pride in Britain and stimulated tourism. All this because a speech-writer took a cheeky chance and let his imagination soar.

. . .

I do not share most people's contempt for politicians. The majority of those that I encountered during thirty-one years of government service were in this usually unrewarding job because they genuinely wanted to effect change for the better. Everyone will be able to name an exception, but that is exactly what they are. And it is not only in affairs of state that politicians work on our behalf. Consider backbench MPs and their constituency work. Every constituent who attends a surgery or writes to an MP about a problem will receive a considered response and usually further action, often involving the MP writing to a minister. All letters from MPs to ministers have to be personally replied to by the minister, even if the reply has been drafted by a civil servant. The point is that the minister has to decide whether he or she approves the line the civil servant has taken. Of course it does not always result in justice being done. It did not in poor Sistie's case, where it must have been obvious to the Home Secretary that the civil servants were pursuing a personal agenda (as seems to have been the case in the recent Windrush Generation debacle). But it means that every citizen has real access to those in power in a way that exists in few other countries.

That does not mean that politicians are necessarily nice to know. Michael Heseltine, schoolmate of my brother at Shrewsbury and Kimpton's former landlord of our poker den at 29 Tregunter Road, had now cleaned up his first few millions through astute property deals in the seedier parts of Bayswater and plunged into politics with the ill-concealed intention of becoming Prime Minister. At Shrewsbury he had been the most unpopular boy in the school. At Oxford, I heard from chums like Christopher Fildes, he was the most unpopular member of his college. He was now entrenching a reputation for overbearing arrogance in the process of making himself the most unpopular of our twelve ministers, which took some doing when you had our odious Secretary of State Peter Walker as one of the contestants. Heseltine's civil servants loathed him. I was not close enough to him to harbour such an emotion. From the little bit I saw of him in action I had to concede that here was a young man who was certainly in the premier league, and by that I mean the league to become premier of the nation.

One of the duties I was least capable of performing competently was what was known as an 'agreed statement'. Ministers routinely received delegations – another manifestation of active democracy – and the press officer had to attend the meeting and write a statement of what had transpired, agreeable to both parties, and have it ready for signing off before the minister left the room. This would then be issued as a press notice. I was assigned to do one of these for a meeting between representatives of the council of a West Midlands town and Michael Heseltine for the minister to make a ruling on the siting of a pedestrian crossing in a new gyratory traffic system in the city centre. Why a minister even as junior as Heseltine was involved in such a mundane matter escapes me, but the whole scheme hung on whether the pedestrian crossing could be where the traffic engineers wanted it to be and this had been challenged.

I turned up well in advance to get the lie of the land. A heated discussion was taking place between traffic engineers, councillors and civil servants, all bent over a large plan set out on the conference room table. I listened to this escalating dispute until my head spun. I could not make head or tail of what they were talking about. Then Heseltine's Private Secretary put his head round the door and summoned we civil servants into the minister's office. 'Bring the plan with you,' he commanded. The minister had been delayed by another meeting and had not had time to read the file on this one, he explained. Would one of our chaps explain the issue please. Our chap began but after half a minute Heseltine raised his hand for silence. 'This scheme is never going to work,' he pronounced. 'Let's go next door.'

We rejoined the delegation and Heseltine wasted little time on preliminaries. He set out what it was he thought the town council and the traffic engineers were trying to achieve and sought their confirmation. Then he explained, lucidly and in detail, why it was such a crackbrained scheme and would bring the traffic of this sooty West Midlands town to a grinding halt. Heseltine had instantly detected defects in the proposal that had eluded the experts both from the council and those from within the Department. At the end of his brief peroration the traffic engineers made a half-hearted attempt to defend their professional standpoint, but it was really no contest. The young tyro with the mane of golden hair and the brain the size of Java demolished each of their arguments with ease.

I was next in the firing line. 'Is the agreed statement ready?' he demanded, extending his hand in anticipation. I had been desperately trying to write down what he had just said, at the same time as listening to what he was now saying, a feat that my fellow press officers seemed to accomplish with the minimum of effort but I found quite beyond my ability. I had also struggled to make sense of the gobbledegook spouted by the traffic engineers, but that may have been because it did not contain any. Heseltine wrested the sheet of paper from my hand, none too gently, and glanced at the incoherent scribblings I had impressed upon it. He then plucked the pen from my hand, deftly inscribed three or four perfectly formulated sentences upon the back, and passed it around the councillors and engineers for their agreement. One engineer began to expostulate, but was hushed by the lead councillor, who signed it off and handed it to me. Heseltine returned to his office and the delegation shuffled out to return to the West Midlands having enjoyed all of seven minutes of the minister's attention. I crept back to the press office to type up the statement and present it as my own. Democracy had been served.

I was interested to learn from Heseltine's private secretary that his master did not count oratory amongst his many natural talents. Aware of this deficiency, one that certainly needed to be remedied if he was to succeed in his lofty ambitions, he had set himself to acquire the art by listening to recordings of my old hero Lord Hill, he who had scuttled round all the BBC outstations in his quest to meet every member of his 23,500 staff. Heseltine could not have chosen a finer practitioner than the former 'Radio Doctor'.

Having seen the skill and brio with which Heseltine had dealt with a matter of no importance, it was revealing for me to observe him formulating what must have been the first substantive initiative of his long and distinguished political career. This was called Operation Eyesore and, given its purpose, may have been inspired by the Clean Up London campaign. If you grew up in post-war Britain, you will remember how much dereliction there was that had nothing to do with the bombing. Years of shortages of paint and building materials and the skilled labour to effect repairs and renovation meant that both town and country were blighted by eyesores, from abandoned farm vehicles to collapsing sheds of rusted corrugated iron and disused industrial and military sites with broken windows and crumbling masonry. All these blots on the landscape were far too prevalent in the 1950s and 1960s and as the seventies dawned Michael Heseltine, despite his very junior position in government, determined to do something about it. Somehow he got other ministers and the Secretary of State on side and, more remarkably, managed to prise sufficient funds out of a parsimonious Treasury for a nationwide clean-up. The results transformed the look of our nation and the effects of Operation Eyesore were permanent. Once people got used to the idea of an environment free from blemish, they started to take care not to let old buildings, vehicles and equipment rot where they stood or if they did, local authorities took enforcement action. It was one of the best things that came out of that dismal decade, the 1970s, and yet it seems to have been completely forgotten about today – no Wikipedia entry and few references via Google. What Operation Eyesore did not have within its remit was litter. If only we had made Heseltine litter czar as well.

. . .

The two ministers I liked best were Commander the Rev. Lord Sandford and Sir Eldon Griffiths. Neither of these are names with which to conjure, their political careers hitting the buffers when the Iron Lady decided they were not 'one of us'. Or maybe they were just too nice to make it up the greasy pole. The Reverend, a D-Day hero who had been earning £400 a year as a curate before assuming his ministerial role from the House of Lords, had a wide-ranging portfolio that included gypsies. He would often take me with him when he visited their encampments. In those pre-PC days most people thought of the traveller community as lawless vagabonds to be sent on their way. As a good Tory libertarian Lord Sandford championed their cause. Apart from enjoying his company on these jaunts, I admired the minister's approach to plain English. Confronted with an official document that referred throughout to 'public sanitary conveniences', he changed each usage to 'loo'.

Sir Eldon was a pig-farmer who also kept a pet lion. Anyone who likes pigs is probably on the side of the angels. His lion, Fagin, later became the last of the MGM lions. The first time I encountered Sir Eldon was when I had to escort a journo to an interview with him. As I entered his office he beamed at me and exclaimed, 'Hello, Patrick. Who have you brought to see me today?' He had bothered to find out in advance the name of the press officer and greet him as a friend. Not the kind of welcome I was accustomed to from Michael Heseltine, who would glower at press officers, a species he held in contempt. They were, he was on record as saying, 'failed hacks who couldn't make Fleet Street', an estimation probably not wholly undeserved. It was one shared by the Secretary of State, the Rt Hon Peter Walker, the only minister I met in thirty-one years of government service whom I loathed.

Peter Walker revealed his measure the very first time he penetrated the portals of our hideous new building, Marsham Towers, barking 'Do you know who I am?' at the jobsworth who barred his way demanding a pass. The Secretary of State had not considered he needed one, but unfortunately that did not concur with jobsworth's view of the way the world is ordered. 'No, I don't know 'oo you are, Squire. But if you was the Sekerty of State hisself, youze not getting' in 'ere wivout a pass,' he pronounced. It was not until his Private Secretary had been summoned from the twenty-second floor that a fuming Secretary of State obtained access to his new domain. The story was all round the vast building well before coffee-break.

Shortly after the new Department was up and running, *The Times* arranged to have one of their political correspondents embedded with the Secretary of State for a week. Our august and urbane Chief Information Officer, Henry James, later to be Press Secretary at No. 10, was sufficiently enthusiastic about this idea to agree to *The Times* running a series of articles with only checking for fact within the Department's control. I was given the job of minder: I was to shepherd the journo around, make sure he did not fall into bad company (eg Heseltine, M) and massage his ego. During that whole week the Secretary of State did not address a word to me, nor take any cognisance of my presence – on one occasion he slammed a car door in my face just as I was about to get in.

Happily I did not have to accompany Mr Walker and the journo at the weekend, as the Member for Worcester was then on constituency business and could not be attended by civil servants. On the Sunday Walker had a speech to make somewhere in the Gloucester direction. He and the journo set off in very good time, so good in fact that they were likely to arrive before the reception committee, so Walker asked journo if he had ever been to Great Malvern and would he like to see the mountain range that gave Edward Elgar so much inspiration. Journo, a music buff, was enthusiastic. When he wrote up his article on the weekend's doings he included a para about the unscheduled diversion. In my view it showed Walker in a rather more human light than was customary.

Not in the view of the Secretary of State. The morning after the article had appeared, Henry James was summoned to his office and given the biggest dressing down he had ever received in his life. Walker was apoplectic with fury. The article, he bellowed, gave the impression that he was a Secretary of State with time on his hands, with nothing better to do than go off on Sunday jaunts rather than attend to affairs of state. Why hadn't Henry James insisted that the paragraph be removed? What was he employed for if it was not to enhance the image of his employer?

There were a number of trenchant responses that Henry James could have made to this: first, that Peter Walker was not his employer; secondly, that he had not been hired to enhance politicians' images; thirdly, that he had no power to demand redaction under the terms of the Department's agreement with *The Times;* fourthly, that it presented a busy Secretary of State as a man who still found time for beauty and culture. Unfortunately Henry James, not normally a shrinking violet when it came to standing up against politicians with over-inflated egos, was cowed by the sheer venom spewing from the lips of his nemesis and said nothing in his own defence or that of the Government Information Service of which he was the Department's most senior representative. Regrettably, an arrant bully was allowed to behave in a manner wholly unfitting to a senior member of Her Majesty's Government.

Some, even of the most junior rank, were less supine than the Chief Information Officer. At Christmas I was in a crowded lift going down when the Secretary of State entered with his customary flourish. He looked around the dozen or so civil servants heading for home when his eye lit on a rather large black girl. Walker's face broke into an ingratiating smile and he addressed the black lady thus: 'Are you going anywhere exciting for the Christmas break?' She looked him up and down as if he was something alien the dog had brought in, then replied in her lilting Jamaican accent, 'Me going somewhere exciting? You must be joking, Man. You think I can afford to go anywhere on the money I get paid in this place?'

For a nanosecond I almost felt sorry for the crestfallen Secretary of State. The feeling passed as quickly as it came though.

● ● ●

Junior GIS staff like me tended to get shunted around. My next move was to Foreign Visitors, presided over by the redoubtable Miss Mueller, born and raised amongst the ex-pat community in Buenos Aires, fierce proponent of the Girls' Friendly Society, and niece of Hugh Rhind with whom I had quarrelled in Maseru. While I made it up with Mister Rhind, relations with Miss Mueller remained prickly throughout my stay under her command. Like Mister Doody at the *New Statesman*, she took an instant dislike to me, for reasons that I never fathomed since we shared the same traditional values and I treated her with the deference she demanded.

The only way I could penetrate her frosty carapace of disapproval was by enquiring after her work with the Girls' Friendly Society, or GFS as it was known to its associates (the upper middle class ladies who ran it) and members (the working-class girls whose moral welfare the associates sought to protect).

The GFS had been founded in the 1870s to provide working class girls living away from home with middle class mentors who would prevent them from getting pregnant. This did not mean birth control; it meant not going out with boys of their own class who might want to have their evil way with innocent maidens up from the country. Most of the young women cajoled and controlled by the forerunners of Miss Mueller were domestic workers. Shop girls resented being labelled as working-class, and factory girls, according to the GFS, were simply uncontrollable. What this institution was doing a hundred years later I find difficult to discern, as I learned little from Miss Mueller other than accounts of her feuds with fellow upper-middle class associates. Amazingly it is still going under its original name and, per Wikipedia, now has a mission to empower women. If this is intended to include those of humble birth, I hope for her own sake that Miss Mueller had passed on before such an alarming new concept was embraced by the GFS.

I had succeeded a delightful girl called Julia Singer in the Foreign Visitors post. Recently married to an up-and-coming young barrister (who continued rising until he became a High Court judge and Julia became Lady Singer), she was the daughter of a suburban solicitor who did not believe in education for girls. Consequently Julia, whose brain was not in the Heseltine class but approximated to a medium-sized Hebridean island, never had the opportunity to attend university. A bookish girl with insatiable curiosity, she would have thrived at the varsity. Instead, like me, she washed up in the relatively calm waters of the Government Information Service, whose requirements were sufficiently fluid to find room for people without formal qualifications like me, Julia and, indeed, Miss Mueller.

Miss Mueller adored Julia. I adored Julia. That might have given us a commonality, but alas it did not. Julia and I used to lunch together every day in the DoE canteen, but though we took care to meet up out of sight of Miss Mueller, she had agents who would supply her with intelligence reports. Julia would then receive a telephone call from Miss Mueller warning her that I was a bad influence and someone from whom to STAY AWAY. We debated together what the nature of this influence might be, but Miss Mueller remained tight-lipped on such a disagreeable topic. Perhaps Julia should have consulted Mrs Walker, mother of my school chum Nicholas, who shared Miss Mueller's negative view of my capacity to fulfil the role of a fit companion.

The role of Foreign Visitors was to take care of the large number of overseas officials and environmental specialists who wanted to visit the world's first environment ministry. Miss Mueller took the bookings while I did the leg-work. This left Miss Mueller plenty of time to devote to the many calls for her intervention from the GFS. I would arrange the itineraries, meet and greet, and either escort the dignitaries or arrange appropriate minders to do so. It would have been a relatively undemanding task but for the fact that by far the majority of visitors wanted to talk about air pollution, and that should involve an introductory session with the head of the Air Pollution Division, one Richard Adams. Regrettably Mr Adams was seldom available. Senior environment apparatchiks from Europe and North America were none too happy with being consigned instead to underlings, but Mr Adams insisted that his time was too precious to devote to these all too frequent and inevitably protracted sessions on what was then the topic of the hour.

Now I have absolutely no evidence that Richard Adams's masterpiece *Watership Down* was written in the office, nor that he had any ulterior motive for refusing my frequent overtures to meet dull and self-important people. Personally it would not amaze me if he had found the company of warrior rabbits, albeit on paper, more engaging than that of overseas environmentalists, but the records are silent on the subject.

The book was Adams's first and, like many tyro novelists, he had the devil of a job getting it into print. It was turned down by seven publishers before being taken up by niche publisher Rex Collings, who could not afford to pay Adams an advance. Nor could Collins afford a top-flight illustrator for the jacket, which did little credit to that rare type of fiction, a novel that could be read by children or adults on different levels.

The very first review copy was received by Julia in her capacity as assistant editor of that well-known literary journal *DoE World*. She received the first because Richard Adams pressed it into her hand with a shy request that it might be worthy of notice in the staff journal. Or, of course, it might not, he hastened to add. He would understand if Julia had more compelling matters to write about, like street furniture (Pelican crossings had just been introduced) or new initiatives on planning applications. Julia said she would try to squeeze in a notice and how about a profile of the author? Adams was thrilled to bits at this prospect and immediately granted Julia the access that he had so often denied to me and my visitors.

Julia's review was the very first of the hundreds, possibly thousands, of notices that *Watership Down* was to receive worldwide – the multi-award winning novel was published in eighteen foreign languages. Not all were as complimentary as Julia's, because the more earnest American literary journals, notably the *New York Times Literary Review*, took exception to the fact that the male rabbits occupied a more prominent role in the odyssey than the does. But Miss Mueller liked it, and that was an accolade unlikely to be earned by my own book when it followed *Watership Down* into the select pages of *DoE World*.

* * *

I have one more tale to tell before we leave Foreign Visitors. I was charged with escorting a Dutch planning officer to visit a newly built housing estate in East London. The Dutchman was too polite to express an opinion, but I was horrified by its gaunt, featureless towers, dimly lit stairwells, open-air corridors that acted as wind tunnels, and lack of anything decorative or on a human scale. Since it was not my place to have a viewpoint, I refrained from comment other than a single question to the architect showing us round. 'Do you,' I enquired, 'consult with the future tenants when you design an estate like this?' He looked at me with a mixture of contempt and disdain. 'Consult the tenants? What would be the point of that? What do these people know about architecture?'

* * *

James Davenport Seymour, of the illustrious New York theatrical family from whom he derived his middle name, lived on benefits in a bedsitter in Knightsbridge. Or he did live on benefits until temporarily rescued by Frederick H Brogger, who put him on the payroll as dialogue coach first for *Jane Eyre* with George C Scott and Susannah York and then on *Kidnapped* with Michael Caine (though teaching the Cockney heart-throb to speak with a Scottish accent proved beyond even his capabilities).

James, known to all as Jimbo, had not always lived in penury. During the Great Depression, when a good weekly wage was $25 pw, if you were one of the fortunate few with a job, he was working for Joe Kennedy at Paramount as a scriptwriter and taking home in excess of $4,000 pw. His credits included such classics of Hollywood's Golden Age as *42nd Street*, *Footlight Parade* and *Gold-diggers of 1933*.

When Joe Kennedy was appointed Ambassador to the Court of St James's in 1938, he invited Jimbo to accompany him as his personal assistant. Salary was not discussed but the $4,000 pw scriptwriting star was confident Joe would look after him. During the voyage over Joe suggested to Jimbo that his wife, who was due to follow later, might not cut it on the diplomatic circuit, and perhaps it would be better if he was unencumbered. Jimbo, always ready to oblige his friend and mentor, assented. By the time the ambassadorial party landed in Southampton, divorce papers had been served on Mrs Seymour by Joe's lawyers.

When Jimbo opened his first weekly pay packet as the Ambassador's aide, he found it contained £8. But he lived at the Ambassadorial residence in Regent's Park, ate and drank at either US or UK government expense, and enjoyed the hospitality of aristocratic British hosts in the whirlwind of entertaining that took place during the run-up to war. Meanwhile Joe was doing everything possible to ensure that he would be remembered with loathing by his British hosts, telling the President that Britain had no hope of surviving a war with Germany, and should receive no aid from the US, and schmoozing the German ambassador that he understood and agreed with their policy on the Jews (though he added that they were a bit heavy-handed about it). By late 1940 his position was no longer tenable and President Roosevelt ordered his recall.

Jimbo was not invited to accompany the Ambassador on the return journey. Kennedy abandoned him to sit out the war in London with no means of support. He kept himself afloat by writing B movies for British 'quota quicky' studios, but that dried up in 1947 and he went to work for the toughest bull-dyke lesbian in Soho, Sheila Van Damm, manager of the Windmill Theatre. The Windmill's speciality was nude tableaux – it was illegal for naked girls to move on stage – and it was Jimbo's job to look after the showgirls' moral welfare. Much the same as Miss Mueller's voluntary avocation, though Jimbo actually got paid – just enough to keep body and soul together – for a job that many men would have done for nothing. The girls called him 'Uncle Jimbo'.

What Karla and I found extraordinary was Jimbo's utter devotion to the whole Kennedy clan, despite the despicable way in which Joe had treated him. 'But they were all such good fun!' Jimbo would exclaim. 'I took Bobby to his first public engagement when he opened the Children's Zoo at Regent's Park and I even taught young Edward how to swim.' (Rather too well, given Edward's prowess at Chappaquiddick.)

One day Jimbo came into the office at South Audley Street and told Karla that he had a favour to ask. He had received a letter from an American Rhodes Scholar at Oxford who was deeply interested in the Kennedys and wanted to interview him about his memories of the family. The problem was, Jimbo explained, that his poky bedsitter in Knightsbridge was not really the kind of place you could entertain anyone, even a student. Could he host the young man at South Audley Street and could Karla see her way to laying on tea and cucumber sandwiches? Karla could and did. The young man arrived, Karla presented him to Jimbo, Jimbo imparted his memories of the Kennedys, the young man ate all the cucumber sandwiches and thanked Karla in effusive terms for her hospitality, and that was it.

Until 20th January 1993 when Karla's office chum Sheila called and asked if she had been watching the Inauguration. Yes, said Karla, it looked a bit nippy in Washington.

'And did it bring back memories?' asked Sheila.

'Of what?' replied Karla.

'Of the student who ate all the cucumber sandwiches?'

'Why? Does the new President like cucumber sandwiches?'

'Well, he did when he came to tea with you and Jimbo.'

I was listening to all this. 'Well?' I queried. 'Well what?' rejoined Karla. 'To think I was alone in the kitchen with William Jefferson Clinton and he didn't even try to goose me!'

. . .

By this time our relationship, Karla's and mine, had progressed to the point where we were contemplating putting it on a more permanent footing.

We were both beyond the age where gazing into each other's eyes and whispering sweet nothings seems like a good basis for half a century of life together, so we thought we should test the strength of the relationship by spending a couple of weeks isolated from familiar habitats. Yes, we were living together, but we were living in an office, with constant comings and goings of actors, producers, casting agents, scriptwriters, lawyers, future Presidents of the United States, etc etc. We needed to be properly on our own and where better than a narrow boat on the Llangollen Canal?

By this time Karla was a regular visitor to Standish Court, where my dear parents had taken an instant shine to her. My father had always wanted a daughter and, having failed to produce one himself, was hoping to acquire a surrogate by marriage. My brother had married a girl who never felt at ease in rural Gloucestershire, for her an alien world rooted in a former age. But Karla was everything he had hoped for, being glamorous, gregarious, fun-loving and, having lost her own beloved papa, in need of a father figure whom she could look up to and cherish.

*Jimbo imparted his memories of the Kennedys while the young man wolfed a whole plate of cucumber sandwiches.*

Father loved parties and he either threw one or we went to one most weekends. Karla would be summoned for inspection before these events. Father, who I may have mentioned was one of those rare heterosexual men who take an intense interest in fashion, would send her back upstairs if anything about her appearance was found wanting. Karla did not mind at all. It showed how much he cared.

We broached the subject of the holiday we had planned. At the mention of a narrow boat, Father's face clouded over. 'How many cabins does it have?' he enquired.

'Two', we lied.

'But how will people on the river bank know that you are in separate cabins?' he persisted.

'They won't', we told him. 'Why would it cross their minds to wonder?'

Father was horrified at such laxity. 'But I would wonder if I was on the river bank.'

'Tsk, tsk.', I replied. 'Now you have really shocked me, Father. On a lovely summer's day, looking at gaily painted barges rippling through the limpid water, is that really what would be uppermost in your mind?'

Father was not amused.

The expedition was a great success. Karla drove, as I was far too incompetent to manage a narrow boat, while I read to her from Margaret Powell's memoirs *Below Stairs*. Margaret Powell was a housemaid who had found fame late in life when she wrote a series of books about life as a skivvy. They were eminently suitable for reading aloud, as the upstairs-downstairs setting allowed for a profusion of accents. Karla found this captivating, having only recently been introduced to the vagaries of the English class system. (Observing life in Gloucestershire had given her some early pointers though.)

Nobody on the river bank enquired how many cabins we were occupying. I doubt whether it put their minds in a spin either.

By the end of the holiday a wedding had been arranged.

. . .

Back at Marsham Towers I had been moved again. My new berth in Parliamentary Liaison promised to be a step up from Foreign Visitors. I expected to be flashing my House of Commons pass as I passed through the St Stephen's entrance to negotiate this and that with the Speaker's office or the Clerk of the House, stopping only for a quick chat with a cabinet minister or two in the lobby. Such was the nature of the job, less the quick chats, performed by my line manager. Her two underlings, a spinster lady named Wendy and I, were consigned to the task of answering letters from schoolchildren. (No, it had nothing to do with Parliament, but the letters had to be answered by someone.) A deteriorating environment, as I have noted, was the consuming topic of the moment, and schools had rapidly joined the bandwagon. Teachers would set their classes projects and instruct them to find out background information. What they did not do was instruct their charges on the elements of conducting research, even at this level. So instead of showing them how to access sources and marshal their facts, the only instruction would be 'Write to the DoE.'

Hence we might receive twenty or thirty almost identical letters from all or most of the pupils of a class, each saying 'Please send me everything you have on transport' or 'Please send me everything you have on pollution.' Every such request was entitled to a reply.

The task would have been depressing enough in any circumstances, but it was made infinitely worse by virtue of the fact that Wendy was a compulsive talker. A lonely lady who lived on her own in Hertfordshire, she did not have many friends, nor many activities outside the office. So while I was trying to diminish the daunting piles of letters that arrived every day, it was impossible to concentrate against her incessant babble. Our daily output was far less than new letters received, so the piles grew ever higher. Added to them would be letters from teachers fulminating that their class projects were being put in jeopardy, or from head teachers threatening to write to their MPs. None of this had the slightest effect on Wendy. The torrent of words swept on, hour after interminable hour.

I could stick it out, hoping for a move in a few months' time. Or I could move to another government department. The problem about sticking it out was that it was very easy in the Government Information Service to get abandoned in an oubliette like that one. I might be left there for years.

I started to peruse the sits vac that were circulated by the GIS. Should I elect for a sideways move or try for promotion? With matrimony ahead, and earning only half as much as Karla's salary, I needed a promotion. Even a promotion to a backwater like the Department for National

Savings, which was seeking a Senior Information Officer for their press office. I had the relevant experience. Why not go for it?

In due course I was boarded. The board were chiefly concerned about the Bridgeman Report, a government paper whose recommendations were likely to radically alter the way in which the National Savings Movement was conducted. I had read the report. My guess is that other candidates had not done so. I was offered the post. I accepted.

On my last day at the DoE I was in the loo when I was joined at the next urinal by the Chief Information Officer, the imposing Henry James.

'I hear you're leaving us, Hickman-Robertson,' he drawled.

I affirmed that this was so, anticipating his good wishes for my future.

'Going to National Savings, they tell me.'

'Yes, sir. I start on Monday.'

Henry James zipped himself up, then started towards the door. Opening it, he turned towards me and intoned

'You do know you are committing career suicide, don't you?'

# Chapter 18

• • •

# CAREER SUICIDE?

• • •

*1971–79*

It may have been a government backwater I was heading to, and if Henry James was correct my career stopped there, but at least I was now earning sufficient to get married.

Karla's mother Lilo was invited to Standish Court. Lilo spoke very little English and my father no German, but they got on surprisingly well. They discovered a shared passion for ancestors and family, and would recount long and involved genealogies to each other, Lilo in broken English at the top of her voice, my father in the kind of pidgin English chaps in pith helmets use to address natives, also at a high decibel level. Why they each thought they would be easier to understand if they shouted I know not. A mutual taste for gin cemented the cross-border friendship.

My father had a deep distrust of most things foreign, as did many people of his own parents' generation – most of father's prejudices were inherited. His first trip abroad had been to visit my brother Tim when he was doing his National Service in Germany. After the ordeal of the Channel crossing – even a rowing boat made father seasick – arrival in France fulfilled his every foreboding. The French were rude, unshaven, and smelled of garlic and unwashed bodies. He was overcharged and short-changed wherever he and my mother went. Hotels were grubby. Nothing functioned properly, especially the plumbing. Then they crossed the border into Germany. Everything was sparkling clean, the Germans included. Everybody beamed at my parents in welcome. Nobody tried to cheat them. Everything worked first time. Father came back singing the praises of the country whose destruction he had spent six years in the RAF helping to bring about. All this hands-across-the-sea *bonhomie*, of course, aided the progress of my own romance.

After the shouting had died down I was summoned to Hamburg to be shown off to friends and relatives. Lilo kindly arranged what she called 'ein Cocktail' – Karla explained this was a cocktail party, something of a rarity in Germany and put on in my honour. The guests were bidden for six and I was told to be sure that I was ready in time. At five to six the bell rang. Lilo and Karla were in the kitchen, so I opened the door. Two men were standing there, so I wished them 'Guten Tag' and 'Willkommen' and asked them in English what they would like to drink, accompanied by slurping noises so that they would understand. The visitors looked slightly surprised and said they would have 'ein Bier'. As I placed the foaming steins in their hands, one of them spoke to me in German. At that moment Karla had entered the room. 'He just said,' she informed me, 'So where's the meter then, Guv?'

As the first chime of six o'clock was struck by the great clock on the Michel, the doorbell rang again. I opened the door and there were thirty-five people standing on the landing – the exact number of guests who had accepted the invitation.

It is reassuring that some nationalities live up to their stereotype.

. . .

My earnings may have increased, but we were not going to begin married life sitting on a pile of cash. I had started doing a syndicated newspaper feature on firsts and I put the proceeds into the kitty. My contribution towards our joint assets was £120. Or it would have been £120, had I not passed Norman Stone's bookshop in Church Walk, Kensington, when he had the Bradbury Collection for sale. Bradbury & Evans were the publishers and printers of *Punch* from its inception in 1841. William Bradbury had collected all the different cover variants before the famous

Dickie Doyle cover of 1849, destined to remain unaltered for over a century, together with various special numbers and one-offs, and also parodies and imitations of the magazine. There was a *Judy* and a *Toby* and a *Punch & Judy* and a *Penny Punch* and *Sunday Punch*, while from the colonies were *Canadian Punch*, *Melbourne Punch*, *New Zealand Punch*, *Hong Kong Punch*, *Cape Punch*, *Rhodesian Punch*, *Singapore Punch* and *Hindi Punch* as well as a *Japan Punch* and a *Punch* in Danish. Other curious variants included a *Shorthand Punch* and a *Braille Punch*.

The only really important item missing from the collection was Volume 1 Number 1 of *Punch* itself. But a few years earlier I had seen a copy advertised in *Exchange & Mart*. The vendor told me that he did not know whether it was genuine or not (there had been several reprints at anniversaries), so he was asking a modest two guineas for it. If it was a reprint, I would lose out. If it was the real thing, he would lose out. He lost out.

Norman Stone was asking 100 guineas for the collection, but accepted £100. Before the deal was struck, though, I had to put the proposition to Karla. What finer wife could any man wish for than one who was prepared to enter the matrimonial state on £20? We still have the Bradbury Collection, augmented over the years, and eventually it will join the *Punch* archive in the British Library.

. . .

Karla explained to my father that the wedding would not be like an English wedding. There would be about twenty guests, mainly relatives, and the after-church celebration would be a sit-down meal in a restaurant.

My father, as I may have mentioned, loved parties. He liked funeral wakes best, but after that came weddings. He derived immense pleasure from finding fault with what his fellow guests were wearing, but over and above that he did have a genuinely romantic streak and he revelled in the whole glorious spectacle of two young people setting out on life's journey together, along with the lovely flowers, the transcendent music, the floating fashions, the scrumptious eats, even the endless, banal speeches. So when Karla recounted to me their conversation, I could surmise that father's heart had sunk. 'He then offered to have the wedding here at Standish,' she told me. 'But he was a bit hesitant about it and I told him I could not possibly accept that. It would be lovely, but quite impossible.'

'My dear girl!' I exclaimed. 'He was only hesitant because he was afraid you might take offence. There is nothing that would give him greater pleasure. He has always regretted not having a daughter to give away. He loves weddings, but knew he would never have the opportunity to arrange one himself. Until now. And you said *no*?'

The next morning Karla reopened the matter of the wedding feast. When I entered the room I could tell from father's beaming face that matters had been brought to a satisfactory conclusion.

Standish Court, to which my parents had moved from our Gloucester suburb in 1960, lay halfway between Gloucester and Stroud. It was a thirteenth century monastery that had been converted into a manor house after the Reformation. It had been occupied by the US Army in World War II and they had made such a mess of it that the disheartened owners could not bear to return after the war. Instead they decided on the then novel idea of making it into separate dwellings, since the absence of domestic staff in Attlee's new Britain meant that large country houses were almost impossible to maintain in their former state. It is reputedly the first country house in Britain to have been converted to multi-occupancy in this way. My parents occupied half of one wing, the refectory in monastic days, while the other was a lesbian love-nest in which an English hockey champion and her swain lived lives of the utmost outward respectability. Next door to my parents in the main part of the house were the Nairacs, he a Mauritian eye surgeon with a huge extended family all of whom addressed him as 'Oncle Maurice'. As did Karla and I.

The son of the house, Robert, had the the misfortune to look Irish, profess the one, true and only faith, represent the varsity at boxing and sing like John McCormack. I say it was his misfortune because these characteristics, coupled with reckless bravery and an easy, flamboyant charm, made him ideal material to go undercover in Northern Ireland during the Troubles. At one of father's frequent parties he started to spill it all out to Karla and me, revealing things about his secret life attached to the SAS that he had never revealed to his parents or his beloved sister. I suppose we were sufficiently detached to be confidants. It was the last time we saw him. When he returned to duty he was captured after singing rebel songs in an IRA pub in Antrim, dragged into a field and tortured, then shot. He was denied a priest for the last rites because his killers refused to believe he was Catholic.

The other wing was occupied by two more families and there were also dwellings in the tithe barn, the cow-sheds and the stables – eight in all. Next door was the home farm. Entrance to the property was through a Norman arch, which my father found to his alarm was, for obscure reasons, his sole responsibility to maintain. Though highly picturesque, it looked as if it might collapse at any moment. Father fretted about this for several months after moving in, until one day he visited the pub and saw on the wall a 17th century print of the arch looking exactly the same as it did now. Outside the arch stood an exquisitely preserved Elizabethan village school, probably one of the few schools of such antiquity to look exactly as it had been when first opened. Beyond that was a 12th century church and a churchyard in which lay the mortal remains of 900 years of succeeding generations of villagers. There was one other feature that made Standish Court the most desirable setting for a wedding it is possible to imagine. This was a sunken garden, belonging to the owner of the tithe barn, whose avocation was nurseryman. It was, therefore, maintained to a pitch of perfection. Here, courtesy of kind Bonham Bazely, we sited the wedding marquee.

Karla had invited her wicked uncle to give her away, he who escaped from East Germany leaving her father stranded and without resources. The same he who did nothing to aid the penniless family when they made their own escape. He replied that he thought England was too far to come just for a wedding. So father achieved what he had so long regretted could never happen: to walk a beautiful daughter down the aisle. I hope it was the happiest day of Karla's life, but I know for certain that it was the best that father had ever enjoyed, at least since his own wedding.

Father told all his friends that he and Lilo were splitting the wedding between them, a white lie to explain the somewhat unusual circumstance of the wedding taking place at the groom's home. The other peculiarity was that of a Catholic marrying a Lutheran in an Anglican church. This was only the second wedding of a Catholic in an Anglican church with the hierarchy's blessing. It had necessitated a personal dispensation from Cardinal Heenan, Head of the Catholic Church in England. Had it been the first I could have included myself in my own book.

Karla had no relatives at the wedding except her mother and a cousin, but was supported by a cohort of Hollywood apparatchiks looking a little uncomfortable on that radiant July day in their unaccustomed tail-coats and grey toppers. Jimbo's outfit dated from his days on the diplomatic circuit and he looked as pleased as Punch to be togged up again, probably for the first time since the Kennedys headed for home. The presence of Delbert Mann, winner of the Best Director Oscar for *Marty*, bespoke Karla's elevation in this strange world in which everybody, of either sex, was addressed as 'baby' (by Americans) or 'duhling' (by English movie makers). Frederick H Brogger had arrived in his chauffeur driven top-of-the-range Rover, which was then put at our disposal for the honeymoon. Karla was attended by Mary-Anne, the American girl I had escorted to the St George's Caye Day Ball, and Gaby, purveyor of gin at 13 shillings the litre bottle, who was now able to meet for the first time some of the beneficiaries of the diplomatic bag. She also met the dashing undercover agent Robert Nairac, one of my ushers, and instantly fell under his spell, but most of Gloucestershire womanhood was under the same spell, as well as an unknown quantity of Irish colleens. A lot of hearts were broken when heroic Robert met his tragic end. My Best Man was my dear friend Jeremy 'JJ' Gould from school, who had saved me from the fate of leaving Shrewsbury tagged as 'the thickest boy in the school', had introduced me to the girl I was about to marry, and hastening forward a few decades, found us our retirement home in the country. He has been what you might call a long-term Best Man.

As a child I used to declare that when I was married I would go away in a horse-drawn carriage. Grown-ups smiled sweetly and forbore to point out that there weren't many around by the second half of the twentieth century. Indeed by 1971 there were only two livery stables hiring out carriages (mainly for film and TV productions) in the whole country. One was in London. The other was in Stroud, the nearest town to Standish. Karla and I went away in an 1898 canoe landau with a silk-hatted coachman on the box, bearing a long whip decorated with white satin bows.

* * *

We started married life in the Omnibus Productions office in South Audley Street. Soon I was there on my own, because Karla went off to California to work on Frederick H Brogger's latest production, an adaptation of John Steinbeck's *Red Pony* for which he had signed Henry Fonda and Maureen

O'Hara. I was able to visit because the US Government had announced an amnesty for draft dodgers over the age of thirty. I bought a Greyhound ticket and crossed America, Washington to LA. On the first leg of the journey I sat next to a girl who informed me that her boyfriend was English. She wanted to visit him and thought she might go by Greyhound. I was a bit confused. 'Do you mean you would go by Greyhound to the airport?' I asked. 'No,' she said. 'I can't afford to go to London by air. I'll go all the way by bus.' I muttered something about the Atlantic Ocean and she looked at me wide-eyed. 'Isn't England in America?' she gasped.

On arrival in Hollywood I found the production in crisis. Frederick H had run out of money. Henry Fonda had gallantly paid the wages for the whole cast and location crew in Sonora for a week, in order to give Fred time to do some hustling. So far this had produced only a single offer of aid. An Italian-American driver on the production had asked to see Fred in private. He knew the production was in trouble from snippets of conversation he had picked up while driving the producers and told Fred that he had friends in the industry who could help. Fred talked this over with his partners. They knew what it meant. The Mafia had been trying to get a foothold in Hollywood for years, but had always been resisted by those who knew that any breach would eventually mean a total takeover of the industry. The partners told him he had to refuse, even if it meant shutting down the production at the end of the week.

That Friday, the day that the crew would walk off the set in Sonora if they were not paid, Fred received a legitimate offer. Now the problem was how to get the payroll up to Sonora, a distance of 330 miles, by the final deadline of 10 pm. Karla started ringing round air charter companies, but none of them could provide a plane at that short notice. At six pm she found a stunt pilot called Slim who said he had been flying helicopters all day, so was legally barred from putting in any more hours, but was willing to fly Fred up there in his private plane if it was made worth his while. A deal was struck and Fred and I, who had been volunteered by Karla as bagman, rushed to Burbank Airport. She set off for Sonora by car. When we arrived the pilot was already in the cockpit with the engine idling. We clambered into the only two passenger seats, one behind the other, and were in the air before we had recovered our breath, me clutching a briefcase stuffed full of $10 and $20 bills – just like in the movies.

*I hissed in Fred's ear 'Check whether Slim's eyes are open'.*

Darkness fell and clusters of lights twinkled beneath us. I was sitting behind Fred, but was alarmed to see that the pilot's chin was slumped on his chest. I tapped Fred on the shoulder and hissed in his ear 'Check whether Slim's eyes are open.' Fred leant forward towards Slim, then backwards towards me and whispered, 'No. He's asleep. Do you think I should give him a shake?'

'Don't,' I replied. 'If he wakes up with a start the plane may spin out of control.'

There followed the longest twenty minutes of my life and I think Fred's too. Eventually Slim raised his head, peered around him, and grunted 'Where are we?'

Probably over the Sierra Nevada, we told him. If we had kept going straight.

'Either of youse guys know what Sonora looks like?' Slim asked laconically.

'I was rather hoping you would know the way,' I replied, my voice rising so that I sounded like the silly ass Englishman of popular imagination. 'Can't you radio ahead to the airport and get a bearing?'

'Airport's closed this time a night,' growled Slim in the unmistakeable tone of one who would ask for my advice when he wanted it.

Frederick proffered the information that Sonora had one long main street with a couple of other principal streets crossing it. We circled around a fairly large area of central California in which most of the patches of light looked like there was a main street bisected by a couple of principal streets. If we headed for Sacramento Airport for a safe landing we would never make the payroll deadline. If we tried landing in an alfalfa field ... forget it.

Then the miracle happened. Directly below us was a cluster of lights signifying a main street and two bisecting streets. Suddenly a whole avenue of lights snapped on adjacent to it. 'Them's the airport lights goin' on' grunted Slim. 'Guess that could be Sonora.'

It was not a miracle, it was clever Karla. Heading up Highway 101 she had suddenly had a dreadful thought that Sonora Airport, not one of America's major transportation hubs, might close when darkness fell. She stopped at a motel and called Directory to find the number of the Seven-Eleven in Sonora. She rang the counter clerk there and asked if he knew who ran the airport. 'That's Ma Timmins,' she was told. 'I'll give you her home number.' Ma Timmins had just sat down to a pot roast with Pa Timmins but said she would put it back in the oven and send Pa over to turn on the runway lights. Only in America....

The plane landed safely. I paid out the monies due in the bar of the Sonora Inn. That night the bar stayed open until the first rosy streaks of dawn.

. . .

When Karla arrived home from Hollywood, house-hunting began in earnest. The Georgian house was out of reach, but we found a quiet, leafy street in Kew called Ruskin Avenue lined with pleasant and commodious Edwardian villas. The average price of £10,500 was too much, but there was one for sale that had been lived in by the same woman since she was born there in 1904. She had gone doolally some twenty years earlier and the house had not been redecorated since then. Nor had it been cleaned and the smell was repellent. But Karla knew that it was surface dirt and a good Saxon girl is never loathe to get down on her hands and knees.

After some hard bargaining with the agent, it was ours for £8,250, of which £1,250 was the deposit. I had received the advance on my book, so that helped with the down payment. Karla contributed the money she had saved by not paying rent, and Frederick H Brogger the copper coins that were probably the only thing he disliked about England. Every evening he left all his threepenny bits, pennies and halfpennies on his desk rather than having them weigh down his pockets the next day. They were Karla's perk and by the time of decimalisation added a three-figure sum to our savings for the deposit.

· · ·

Before joining National Savings, I had invited my predecessor in the post to lunch in order to find out about the nature of the job. All that I could ascertain from him was that he spent much of his time organising beauty contests. It was a somewhat unexpected aspect of government service.

Once in post I found out more. National Savings had three outstations, the National Savings Bank at Glasgow, the Savings Certificate Office at Durham and the Premium Bond Office at Lytham St Annes on Lancashire's Fylde Coast. Each employed several thousand staff, mainly in clerical operations, and it was as a morale booster for those working in low-paid, dull and repetitive jobs that the beauty contests were held.

Just how dull and repetitive much of the work was I learned on my first visit to Durham. This medieval city is one of the gems of urban England. If you have never been, go. Built on hills, it has probably the most spectacular townscape of any city in the nation. Provided, that is, you view it from the top of the National Savings building. From anywhere else in Durham the view is marred by this hideous concrete manifestation of the new brutalism of the early sixties. Needless to say it won every RIBA award going. It is truly one of the most vile buildings I have seen anywhere in the world.

But back to the work carried out within the monstrosity. During the sixties National Savings had been in the forefront of financial institutions computerising their operations. Although we still employed about 16,000 staff, this was a huge reduction on the numbers who had been engaged on manual operations. The scale was vast as there were over 60 million National Savings Bank Accounts and nearly 40 million Premium Bond holdings. There were also several tens of millions of Savings Certificate holdings, for which all transactions were conducted by huge mainframe computers. The votaries of these great, gleaming machines were hundreds of data processors. Their job it was to input the data for the computers to process, which they did by keying in transaction details at the rate of 40,000 digits an hour. Those who fell short of the norm were penalised. All the data inputters were female except one. This lone male must have been exceptionally brave to take on the job, for County Durham was still one of those northern regions where a man seen pushing a baby stroller was likely to get half a brick heaved at him and would be the butt of lubricious ribaldry down at the working men's club. Most of the girls who keyed their 40,000 depressions an hour were the daughters of miners or out-of-work miners. Some were the principal breadwinner of the family.

None of the girls or their single male colleague looked up as I was conducted round by their supervisor. They could afford no interruptions or distractions. Impressed with this seeming dedication to the relentless task – relieved only by a ten-minute break every two hours – I asked the supervisor what was the principal characteristic he looked for when he recruited new hands. I expected him to say 'dexterity' or 'nimbleness', so his response startled me. What he sought above all else, he told me without a hint of levity, was stupidity. Any girl with the slightest imagination, he explained, would find their thoughts drifting away to something more pleasurable than key depressions. The fastest, most accomplished, least distracted data processors, he declared, were the ones who had nothing to say for themselves at the job interview. 'And save me from the ones with a GCE to their name,' he concluded.

. . .

The data prep girls, though, were amongst the most enthusiastic competitors in the Miss Savings Certificate contest. This was conducted to the accompaniment of an oompah-oompah colliery band while a copious amount of ale was poured down the throats of the male spectators. The Glasgow contest was also a spirited affair, with Highland dancing among the skills expected of any girl vying for the title of Miss Savings Bank. The cream of the contests, however, was Miss Premium Bond. Most of the staff came from Blackpool, a resort with a long tradition of professional entertainment, and the contest was organised to exacting production standards. Unlike the canteen festivities of Durham and Glasgow, Blackpool's show was held in a proper theatre on one of the piers and was open to the paying public. The first year I was in charge, the compère – booked long before my arrival – was the incomparable Frank 'It's the way I tell 'em' Carson. The prize was also a cut above the 'Dinner for two at Berni Inn and a free hairdo' of the other contests. Miss Premium Bond was to have two nights in London at a luxury hotel and would be taken on to the set of the latest James Bond picture at Pinewood Studios. There she would be introduced to 007 himself, Roger Moore of the raised eyebrow, and would be photographed with him for a poster declaring ours to be 'The Biggest Bond of All'.

The victor was a girl from New Purchase Registrations called Sandra Benson, who had won over the judges – Karla being one of them – more for her personality and peppy replies to Frank Carson's jokey questions than for outstanding looks. This gave me a bit of a problem, because I needed a girl who could measure up against heart-throb Roger Moore. On her arrival in London – her first visit to the metropolis – Sandra was whisked off to Bond Street by Karla and attired in the best *prêt à porter* that tax-payers' money could buy. The matching shoes were found at Ferragamo. First thing next morning we escorted her to Vidal Sassoon and had her hair styled to the look of a star. After that it was a two-hour session at Elizabeth Arden, which completed the transformation. Sandra Benson, clerical assistant from the Fylde, emerged as a sophisticated, beautiful young lady. We took her to lunch at Strand-on-the-Green and every head turned when she walked into the restaurant.

I had expected Roger Moore to spend a couple of minutes posing with Sandra, then make a rapid exit. Not a bit of it. He kissed her on both cheeks, kidded around while they posed for the poster, then went off to get her a cup of tea and a sticky bun. They spent the next forty-five minutes sitting side by side in director's chairs chattering away as if they were family, until a minion arrived to summon the great man on to the set. He gave her a big wink and a raised eyebrow between takes.

It was, Sandra told me when we saw her off on the train next morning, the best time she had ever had in her life. Maybe she had too good a time. The Americans have a catchphrase, derived from a popular song, 'How you gonna keep her down on the farm now that she's seen Paris?' The next I heard of Sandra she had given up her job at the Bonds Office and headed south to start a new life in London. I never knowingly saw her again, though if I had passed her in the street at any time over the next thirty years would I have recognised her without the Elizabeth Arden slap and the Vidal Sassoon blow-wave? She must have come to London with high expectations, but it can be a lonely, unwelcoming city. I do hope that at least some of her dreams came true.

. . .

I soon discovered that the reason my predecessor had been so vague about the duties of the post is that there was no job description. Neither my line manager nor the Chief Information Officer did any work at all. The latter, a portentous Scotsman called Wallace King, spent his mornings doing the *Daily Telegraph* crossword and his afternoons talking to anyone who would listen about his glory days in the Auxiliary Fire Service during the war. His own staff were not offered an option in this regard. My line manager, Bob Davy, liked talking about *his* glory days working for De Beers in South Africa, but as he spent very little time in the office this did not detain me unduly. There was some mystery about where it was Bob went off to at 9.30 every morning, after he had enjoyed his morning cup of coffee, and from whence he returned at five o'clock for a quick cup of tea and a chat about the diamond industry before heading home to his rather spectacular live-in girlfriend. This was solved after a call from *Private Eye* asking him to get in touch. The caller was my fellow Old Salopian Paul Foot, socialist firebrand and the *Eye*'s principal investigative journalist. Foot was not a chap of whom to fall foul. A piece he had written excoriating Anthony Chenevix-Trench, his old Shrewsbury housemaster, exposing him as a flagellomaniac, may have contributed to his removal as headmaster of Eton. I had fielded the call without revealing our former connection. I recommended to Bob that he should return the call pronto, as Footy sounded as though he was on the warpath.

For once Bob spent an afternoon in and it was the only time I ever saw this normally ebullient, loquacious self-believer downcast. He told me all, following a two-and-a-half-hour grilling from the scourge of the bourgeoisie. Footy had discovered that Bob was running a financial PR company from an office in the City. His efforts to deny it had sounded increasingly unconvincing as Foot piled up more and more evidence. Bob was convinced that this was the end of his Civil Service career, along with the loss of all his pension rights. But when *Private Eye*'s next issue came out, there was nothing in it about his moonlighting activities. He continued to look a very worried man for several weeks after that, but Foot's piece never appeared. I can only surmise that it got pushed out of the issue for which it was intended by something more significant, and that after that Foot lost interest in what to him was a minor story.

I was in charge of the Press Office, so that gave me something to do in between beauty contests, but it soon became apparent that the job was what you made of it. Unlike most government press offices, we did not deal in anything controversial (other than Bob's work habits), so to justify its existence it needed to be proactive. The organisation's main problem was that its image set it apart from the other mainstream savings institutions, mainly the banks and building societies. Its function, originally to promote thrift amongst the improvident poor, had shifted over the years, and particularly during two World Wars, to providing an alternative form of government borrowing from that offered by the Bank of England through the sale of gilts. The problem was that while the Bank was dealing in a very small volume of transactions of a very high value, which was the cost efficient way to manage government debt, National Savings was attracting literally millions of transactions of low average value. This made the operation expensive to run, reducing our ability to offer competitive interest rates. In effect we were trading on the ignorance of our investors. It was not a good way to run one of the largest financial institutions in the country, especially one operated by the state ostensibly in the public interest.

I promise you that this is the last you will hear about National Savings' strategic issues, but it is important to explain why I was prepared to spend the next three decades labouring in what could have been such an unpromising vineyard. There was a real job to be done and one that would benefit government and people: to turn the organisation round from one fulfilling an essentially nineteenth century function of promoting orderly habits amongst the proletariat to offering the Treasury a properly costed retail alternative to the wholesale funding carried out on its behalf by the Bank of England. This meant changing attitudes as well as policies. So the Press Office began to assume the role of a public relations outfit, to persuade journalists and the public they addressed that our primary market had ceased to be children's savings and the unbanked. The change I and my colleagues were promoting had to be real. Fortunately it was not a party issue, and successive governments of both parties bought into the scenario. The Treasury's attitude veered between supportive and obstructive, but that is always the Treasury's way.

My job, therefore, involved talking to journalists, setting up press conferences, writing articles for publication and letters to the press, and touring the broadcasting studios. In time Bob Davy made a sideways transfer to another department and I was appointed in his place. I was able to leave the beauty contests in other, receptive, hands.

●　●　●

Soon after buying the Edwardian villa in Kew, and struggling to meet our interest payments and other outgoings, we had a call from Granada Television saying that they had heard that we had a collection of vintage magazines and newspapers. They were making a drama series called *Sam*, set in the Yorkshire coalfields in the 1920s, and could we hire them working-class publications of that period? We had no idea how much to ask, and let them have about a dozen for 30 shillings. After that we wised up and started to charge first £2 per item, then £3. Over the years this paid for new acquisitions to the collection, so it washed its own face. As all the purchases were tax-deductible, we turned a small but useful profit. We registered our little business as Backnumbers.

This was the golden age for period TV drama, the source of most of our orders, but there were sometimes big Hollywood movies too. Steven Spielberg's *Indiana Jones and the Last Crusade* had scenes set in America, Britain and Germany in the 1930s. We were asked for American and British publications, but when I offered to provide German material as well I was told there was no need, as they would source these when the shoot moved to Germany. 'You do know that trading in Nazi memorabilia is banned in Germany, don't you?' I asked the props buyer. 'Yeah, yeah. Rules are meant to be broken' he chuckled confidently. Not in Germany, they aren't, I thought to myself. I waited for a plaintive call from Berlin. Sure enough it came. They had not been able to source a single magazine or newspaper, the props buyer wailed, and Mister Spielberg wanted an entire bookstall at the Anhalter Bahnhof dressed for 1937. What could we do to help? I told him we could dress the whole thing, if we padded out the German material with magazines and newspapers from other European countries – Berlin was a cosmopolitan city even under the Nazis. A deal was struck, the most lucrative of Backnumbers' whole thirty years of trading.

Less lucrative were the orders we received from Michael Winner, the only director who used to negotiate with us in person. He would come to our house, sit in the basement swilling copious amounts of our best claret, and relentlessly drive down the price on every item. It was a game to him and one we were happy to indulge, having hiked the asking price in anticipation of his love of getting the better of us on the deal.

I derived personal satisfaction from the authenticity that Backnumbers' modest contribution brought to innumerable films and television dramas, but the greatest single pleasure Karla and I both experienced in running our small business had nothing to do with props. The *Sunday Times* had asked to do a feature about the collection and sent along a photographer called Dmitri Kasterine. Not only was he charming, but turned out to be a former colleague of Karla's then business partner Tony Mayer and so naturally he had to stay for supper. Over the meal we enquired about his Russian name.

Dmitri explained that he had been named after the Grand Duke Dmitri, first cousin of the last Tsar of Russia and one of the plotters who assassinated Rasputin. In 1918 he had been accompanied into exile, the only Romanov given leave to settle in Britain, by his *aide-de-camp*, Dmitri's father. Dmitri never knew him, because when he was still an infant his parents separated and in 1938 his father was killed in a car crash. Nor had he ever seen a picture of him, because his mother, stricken by her husband's dalliances with other women, had destroyed every photograph. As he grew up Dmitri became obsessed about his father's appearance, interviewing everyone still alive who had known him. He even located the gravedigger who had dug his father's grave at Brookwood Cemetery. This worthy told Dmitri that his father had been a very tall man, because he remembered how long the coffin had been.

It was at this somewhat macabre juncture of the story that something switched on in my mind. 'Your father was not a tall man, Dmitri,' I told him. 'In fact he was below average height.'

Dmitri was transfixed. 'What do you mean? How do you know?' he exclaimed. 'Was your father called Nikolai Kasterine, Nikki for short?'

I enquired. Dmitri confirmed that he was. 'Then I have a photograph of your father,' I told him. 'It was published in the *Bystander* shortly before his death and the reason I know he was a small man is because it was taken on the front at Deauville and shows him standing next to a beautiful girl several years younger but a number of inches taller.' Dmitri was thrilled. 'Can you find it?' he urged.

But I could not find that elusive copy of the *Bystander* and Dmitri, previously elated, now left the house deeply disappointed.

Several months later the *Bystander* with Nikki Kasterine's photgraph reappeared. We had hired it out for ITV's drama series of *Brideshead Revisited* in 1979, but a technicians' strike had brought the production to a halt. Expecting the strike to be settled quickly, the production company held on to all the magazines they had hired from us. In the event the strike continued for several months and then there were further delays because the original director was no longer available. By the time Dmitri visited us in 1981, we had completely forgotten about them. When they finally arrived back, we took the *Bystander* to a photographic studio and had the diminutive lothario's picture blown up as large as was possible without losing definition. We then found a silver frame for it and invited Dmitri to dinner without telling him why. We set the photograph on a table with a lamp shining directly on to it, sat Dmitri down in an armchair opposite, and made a rapid exit having asked him what he would like to drink.

After a sufficient interval we returned to the room. Dmitri was sitting with the photograph cradled in his hands, tears streaming down his cheeks. But of course he was Russian, so we knew they were tears of joy.

. . .

As Karla was moving about so much, we had to use my direct line number at National Savings as the Backnumbers contact point. My movie-mad secretary Marion found talking to film and TV studios much more fun than talking to the Treasury or the Bank of England, so she never minded this extracurricular duty. I just prayed that wind of it did not come to Paul Foot's ears. The business continued until Karla and I retired to the country. Our last ever order was for Robert Altman's 2001 production *Gosford Park*. If you download this wonderful BAFTA-winning, Oscar-nominated evocation of pre-war life in a great country house, look for the profusion of sporting, social and fashion magazines on the big table in the drawing room. Those are ours. And look for the scene of Dame Maggie Smith making waspish remarks as she reclines in an armchair flicking through the pages of *Country Life*. That's ours. Or was ours. After we moved to the country Karla spent four years putting the 20,000 magazines and newspapers of the collection on eBay. Altogether they fetched nearly £75,000, which became our Retirement Travel Fund. That way I got to see the bits of the former Empire that I had missed out.

. . .

Twenty years on from taking refuge from dreaded fagmaster David Walker in the school library at Shrewsbury and starting my book of firsts, it was at last complete. Norris McWhirter, dear man, had continued to be supportive and had brokered a deal with Shell to sponsor the book, just as Guinness had sponsored the book that will be forever associated with the McWhirter Twins. This enabled it to be sold at a margin below market price, £3.50 at a time when similar books were priced at £3.95. This undoubtedly gave it a boost, though Shell had regretted their decision when they found that the book was not, as they had fondly imagined, a chronicle of developments in the transportation and petro-chemical industries, but a much more wide-ranging review of social as well as technological innovation. The very first of the alphabetical entries was on abortion and there were a number of articles relating to the sexual revolution. About a month before publication date Shell tried to have the book suppressed, but after their lawyers had trawled through the contract seeking loopholes, were advised they had no powers to have it withdrawn. They had to settle for a gritted-teeth disclaimer at the front declaring that Shell accepted no responsibility for the author's selection of subject matter. Readers may have idly wondered why in that case they had chosen to sponsor it.

Reviews were almost universally favourable, with a whole page in *Time* magazine – a singular accolade for a first-time author and a Brit at that – and there was a flattering profile piece in the *Guardian*. The single exception in this chorus of praise was Auberon Waugh, who denounced *The Shell Book of Firsts* in the *Sunday Times* on the grounds that there was insufficient evidence that what I claimed to be the first of this or that had no precedent. Well no, Bron – still making mischief up there in heaven

I dare say – I do not claim to be definitive: in many cases what I have identified is the earliest *known* example of something. If readers can find earlier examples, I am open to challenge. Though I hesitate to compare my humble efforts with the magisterial *Oxford English Dictionary*, the principle is the same. The citation for first use of a word in print is similarly the earliest that the *OED* has been able to identify. Find an earlier one and they will amend the entry. As I will amend mine.

I did not receive another stinker of a review for any of my books until the publication by Bloomsbury of New York in 2011 of *Robertson's Book of Firsts*, which dealt with the first in the world followed by the first in the US – matching the first in the world followed by the first in the UK of *The Shell Book of Firsts*. This was eviscerated in the *Washington Post* by none other than Bron's son Alexander Waugh, who had checked a number of entries against comparable Wikipedia articles and found earlier manifestations cited by the latter. For example, I gave the earliest public park as Bowling Green Park in New York in 1733, but Wikipedia claims that the first was a sixteenth century park in Seville. No, Alex, that park was a private park when it was founded and did not become public until well after 1733. What is it about these Waughs? Why have they got it in for me when I venerate their father/grandfather so much that I have on my library shelves not only every book he wrote but every one of the sixty or so works written about him?

Is there anything worse than authors moaning about their reviews? Only authors whingeing about their publishers. So let me get it off my chest. *The Shell Book of Firsts* was published three months before Christmas to allow time for it to build up a full head of steam for the Christmas market. But the whole first impression of 30,000 copies sold out in six weeks. So just as people started buying books for Christmas, there were none in the shops. Next up those clever marketers at Michael Joseph and the Ebury Press got together and decided that this book was a cash cow, so why not use cheap gungy paper for the reprint and hike the price from £3.50 to £4.50. And if they had it printed in Hong Kong that would save even more on costs, even if it did take four months to ship on what was literally a slow boat from China. So the book reappeared in the shops a full six months after it had sold out, looking and feeling a much more lightweight job at a price that was no longer well below average but now well above. Not to anyone's great surprise, except the suits at Michael Joseph and Ebury Press, it tanked.

Never mind: there was a book-club edition that did well, an American edition, serialisation in the *National Enquirer* in the US and by Axel Springer in Germany, and foreign language sales to Germany, Austria, Denmark, Poland and Japan. Sometime later David Frost bought an option on the TV rights and, though that never reached fruition, he renewed twice, so it was a nice little earner. The book was eventually republished by Hodder Headline in both hardback and paperback editions. I suppose in a way I should feel grateful to that brute David Walker.

* * *

Karla's career took a new direction, also involving David Frost. She embarked on what would be the first of several big-budget documentary series, this one an exploration of Iranian history titled *Crossroads of Civilization* in seven one-hour episodes. Frost was the presenter and executive producer. When he and his team were summoned to the Palace in Teheran, Karla as the sole woman present was the only one not presented to the Shah. He came up to her, stuck out a bejewelled royal paw and said, 'My name is Pahlavi. What's yours?'

I used my annual leave to join Karla in Persepolis for the shooting of dramatic reconstructions, including full-scale battles, for which the Shah had lent them the whole of his crack Parachute Regiment. Part of the deal with the Iranian authorities was that each member of the very large English crew would have an Iranian counterpart. Some, indeed most, of these people seemed to have very little knowledge of film-making. Karla's shadow was a woman fluent in German called Maryam Razhavi. One day Karla was trying to make a call to her mother in Hamburg and, as was customary, had been trying to get a connection for nearly an hour without success. Maryam came into the room and asked Karla why she was so hot and bothered. She then took the phone from Karla and dialled a number in Teheran. She spoke rapidly in Farsi. There was a brief pause followed by some crackles and blips and she handed the phone back to Karla. 'Guten Tag' said Lilo at the other end. This is how Karla learned that her shadow worked for Savak (the Iranian Secret Service).

When Frost interviewed the Shah he asked how many people worked for Savak. 'Sixty-five,' replied the Shah without hesitation. Frost shot back. 'And how many work for the sixty-five?'

The food at the 5-star Darius Hotel at Persepolis, main base for the location shooting, was an unremitting choice of lamb kebab, shish kebab or kebab kebab. The Cockney horse-boys, in charge of the equine stunts in the battle scenes, soon tired of this 'furrin muck' as they called it, and found themselves a restaurant in Shiraz that would do them something tasty with chips on the side and Bisto gravy. They took a taxi the forty miles into Shiraz every night, kept it waiting an average of five hours while course followed course at glacial pace, then taxied back again. Producer Martin Hall, a chum from Arnold Ellis's History Lower VIth at Shrewsbury, had kindly given me a temp job as cashier on the production, enabling me to share Karla's room and eat with the crew without charge. Each morning the horse-boys would present an astronomical tab for the taxi and the East End nosh. As they could not read or write, their collective girlfriend Frances, ex-Roedean, had to sign for them.

The shoot went on for seven months and the Persepolis Hotel was a hot-bed of sexual activity, in every combination imaginable. I think Harvey Weinstein would have been genuinely shocked. It was the horse-boys who organised a sweep on who could get Karla into bed first, eagerly abetted by the grips. Neither she nor I were aware of this at the time, though I suppose the furtive sniggering in the background every time she spoke to anybody male in the bar should have alerted us that something was up. Back in London Martin Hall revealed that at the end of the shoot the whole kitty had been donated to the horse-boys' favourite charity for retired stunt horses.

*Crossroads of Civilization* should, I believe, have been a notable documentary remembered and extolled a generation on. It was not to be. The *New York Times* condemned it, sight unseen, as propaganda for the Shah's regime, despite the fact that seven of the eight episodes were historical. Certainly the Shah had supported what was principally a cultural endeavour, but David Frost was far too canny a film-maker to lend his name and reputation to anything on which he did not enjoy editorial control. As a result of the *New York Times*'s virulent campaign, none of the American networks would touch the series. In London *The Times* parroted the same line as its New York namesake, again sight unseen, with the result that both the BBC and ITV rejected it without a showing. Only ABC in Australia had the courage to pick it up.

A few months later the Shah had lost his throne and many of our Iranian colleagues on the shoot would suffer the revenge of the Ayatollah and his henchmen. Savak was not an institution that anyone could defend, but it bore no comparison to what replaced it. Under the new dispensation fourteen-year-old schoolgirls were publicly hanged from cranes in the street.

And Maryam Razhavi? She escaped to London. One day as I was walking down Kensington High Street, centre of the Iranian diaspora, I saw portraits of her stuck to every lamp post. She had just been proclaimed President of the Iranian Government-in-Exile.

. . .

While my personal fortunes were rising in the seventies, the nation's were plummeting. When I had worked for the BBC in the sixties, nearly every news bulletin led with a story about a strike threatened, a strike already happening, or a strike concluded, usually to the detriment of the employers. Sometimes the second and even third stories would be about other strikes. While hippies disported themselves in a haze of cannabis smoke, and talked of peace and love, the workers of the world, and particularly those of France and Britain, were girding their loins for a final showdown with capitalism. As the seventies advanced, there seemed to be a real prospect that parliamentary democracy would be ceded to union rule.

At National Savings our unions were divided between Militant Tendency, essentially Trotskyists, and old school Stalinists, adherents of the Communist Party of Great Britain. The latter faction was led by a charismatic firebrand called Peter Copeland, whose intelligence and organising ability easily matched that of anyone on our Board of Directors. He was far easier to deal with than his opponents on the far left, because he was rational in his arguments and, as a true believer in state ownership, a fervent supporter of the National Savings Bank and our other operations. The Militants wanted to undermine National Savings, seeing the prospect of its destruction as one more nail in the coffin of capitalism. They succeeded in bringing the National Savings Bank, located on Red Clydeside, out on strike. For six weeks we were unable to repay our depositors, the worst fate this side of bankruptcy that can befall any bank.

One day in late 1978, during the Callaghan government's 'Winter of Discontent', our CEO, Director of Savings James Littlewood, came back from a luncheon with the Chairman of the Post Office and immediately summoned a meeting of his senior headquarters staff. What he was about to impart, he told us gravely, must not go beyond the walls of the board room except on the strictest need-to-know basis. The Chairman had told him that the Post Office was privy to secret intelligence to the effect that the government expected a breakdown in social order. At its worst this could mean that public services ceased to function amidst widespread civil unrest, which might or might not be controlled by the police and armed forces depending on their loyalty. The Post Office was preparing for a scenario in which there would be no postal services; telecommunications would be gravely impaired. Mr Littlewood reminded us of the recent strike at the National Savings Bank and pointed up the prospect of people who had all their savings invested with us having no recourse to them over a protracted period of time. A strategy would be prepared, he told us, to mitigate the effects of such a catastrophe as far as we were able.

Of course none of this came about. The government capitulated to the unions, the economy took another dive, and the subsequent general election brought Britain's first female Prime Minister to power. I do find it surprising, though, that so little of this episode, with government preparing for revolution, was leaked to the media, and that even now it goes unrecorded in the many histories of the period. Probably only when still classified files of the Cabinet Office's Civil Contingencies Unit are released into the public domain will we know the full extent of the threat the nation faced as the government vaccilated about whether to declare a State of Emergency and mobilise the army.

* * *

One spring day we invited Julia Singer and her husband Peter over for dinner. She told me they would have to take a rain-check, as they had put their house on the market. I informed Karla. 'That Georgian house in Islington?' she queried. 'That Georgian house' I confirmed. 'Did you check the asking price?' Karla asked. I told her they wanted £35k. The following evening, after much deliberation, I called Julia again. 'If we were to buy your house, would you come for dinner?'

They came for dinner.

The house was 81 Theberton Street, a four-storey 1820s house just off fashionable Gibson Square. Karla's gamble with the villa in Kew had paid off. In less than three years, London house prices had doubled. But Karla had done such a fine job of redecorating that smelly, neglected house that it fetched three times as much as we paid for it. With Karla's savings from seven months in Iran, added to my book money, and a bit off the asking price, we were just able to afford the Islington house. The Georgian house.

Shortly after moving in, Nicola Karoline Antonia Hickman-Robertson was born at Queen Charlotte's Hospital. We were a family, one of those fortunate families that live in Georgian houses.

. . .

When Wallace King retired as Chief Information Officer, his place was taken by another Scotsman, James Mackenzie. Unlike the idle, affable Wallace, he was an unsmiling, lugubrious man with an intense work ethic. Each day he would summon me and his other deputy, Peter Hutchings, head of paid publicity, for a detailed account of what we had been doing. There was seldom any reaction, but I always left his enormous office feeling as I had after an interview with my housemaster Alec Binney. It was not so much that you had necessarily done wrong, but you had not done much that was right either.

And then suddenly James Mackenzie was dead. I suppose he must have been in his mid-fifties and it was, of course, a terrible shock to his family and his associates. I will not pretend that I felt deep sorrow, but such a premature death is not a fate one would wish on any man.

So there was a vacancy for the post of Chief Information Officer. As it was graded at two levels above my present post of Principal, and as Peter Hutchings had several years' seniority over me, there was no real prospect of securing the job. It was necessary to apply, though, if only to show my face to the Head of the Government Information Service. He would be one of the three members of the board, together with the Director of Savings James Littlewood and an outside chairman.

Word around Whitehall was that the Head of GIS had long wanted to appoint a Chief Information Officer who was under fifty. There had never been a CIO of any department in his or her forties. Peter Hutchings was just under 50, as was another candidate, my former boss Bob Davy. I was a stripling of 39. It was also known that the Head of GIS sought an energetic ideas man or woman prepared to bring about innovative change. This was not just about National Savings, certainly in need of a shake-up. It was his belief that the whole GIS remained a legacy of wartime Ministry of Information days.

The problem about this was that James Littlewood was deeply resistant to any form of change unless it involved computers. I remember him saying at a retirement do for his deputy 'The great thing about Barbara is that whenever I have felt tempted to alter anything in National Savings, she has always convinced me I shouldn't. And she was always right.' Also he was only two years off his own retirement and wanted a quiet life, lulled by the gentle hum of his beloved mainframes.

I thought long and hard and then I decided how I was going to play it. I had no hope of being selected, but I needed to make a good impression. The Head of GIS started the questioning, and I set out an ambitious programme for how I thought National Savings could be made relevant to present-day needs and the role that information services would play in that. I could see James Littlewood looking deeply troubled as radical plan followed on radical plan. Then I turned to address the Chairman. 'That is my programme, sir' I told him. 'But I would not start to implement it immediately. Our flagship National Savings Bank was closed for six weeks by strike action and we need a period of recovery. If my plans for reform are accepted, I recommend that we spend the next two years preparing for these changes.' I stole a glance at James Littlewood. He looked as if he had just been reprieved from some particularly harsh fate.

Bob Davy blotted his copybook by holding forth on the failures of National Savings' management, not something that was likely to endear him to Mr Littlewood. Peter Hutchings failed to persuade the Head of GIS that he was a Young Turk ready to propel National Savings into the last quarter of the twentieth century. There were half a dozen other candidates and I do not know how they performed. But the advice on job interviews that I offered earlier – do not be yourself, be the person they want in the job – worked in this case. At thirty-nine I became the youngest Chief Information Officer in government service, ten years on from being its oldest trainee.

# Chapter 19

· · ·

# ADVENTURES IN A
# BACKWATER DEPARTMENT

· · ·

*1979–89*

At very long last I had become a prefect, or something very like it, a position of authority and status and privilege that had never been accorded to me at either St Peter's or Shrewsbury. With my new status as a board director (National Savings was the only government department other than the Ordnance Survey to operate as a commercial entity) went the trappings of material success. First there was the enormous office, in which I had felt overwhelmed when I was summoned there by James Mackenzie, but was now all mine in which to play Mussolini should I be so inclined. It had a television set, a drinks cabinet (furnished at my own expense – dispensing hospitality was not a charge on the taxpayer), a deep pile carpet, a conference table, a tree that nearly touched the ceiling and original artwork on the walls ranging from Lawson Wood to Rowland Hilder. The latter was so stunning – an autumn landscape of the English countryside commissioned by National Savings during World War II to show people what we were fighting for – that I had it valued: an estimate (1979 prices) of £16,000. It now hangs in our drawing room, on permanent loan from the government until my death.

My job title was Director of Marketing, which meant that I had overall responsibility for delivering sales averaging around £1 billion a month towards the Government's public sector borrowing requirement. This did not represent a net increase to the National Debt, because we needed to refinance maturing debt. It was still a prodigious amount. Think of it, about £48 million each working day. One of the appealing aspects of the job was dealing with such vast sums of other people's money. When we talked to the Treasury, it was in units of £250 million. Anything less was, to them, like the coppers that Frederick H used to leave for Karla every night.

So I now had charge of paid publicity, a field in which I had not worked since I was an office boy at S.H. Benson, and public relations. My first task in the former field was to hold a competition to unify our advertising account, until then split between two agencies, Saatchi & Saatchi and Dorland Advertising. I did not take to Saatchi's, who held the lion's share of our business. They struck me as an arrogant bunch who seemed so confident of winning the whole of it that they made little effort to convince me, a newcomer, of their credentials. The aloof Saatchi brothers did not deign to meet me, which must have been unprecedented amongst agency proprietors pursuing a blue-chip account of our magnitude. Dorland's, on the other hand, in the knowledge that they were the rank outsiders in the race, pulled out every stop. Their CEO, Jack Rubins, who was like a caricature of a Jewish wheeler-dealer, was a hugely engaging character who treated his agency and its clients like extended family. (He gave James Mackenzie's son a job, because that's what a Jewish patriarch does for a boy who has lost his father.) Me, I have always had a regard for the underdog, having spent most of my time being one. So National Savings became one of Dorland's major accounts instead of one of Saatchi & Saatchi's minor ones.

·  ·  ·

This was an era of unbridled hedonism in the corporate world. The advent of Margaret Thatcher as PM had put new heart into British business after years of decline during the sixties and seventies. Manufacturing was never to recover, but service industries revived a moribund economy, led by the financial sector. Entertaining was lavish, with the traditional events of the

London Season, expected to wither and die in the atmosphere of post-war austerity, now given a new lease of life by a huge injection of corporate funds. Karla and I were beneficiaries of this fairly shameless new order, enjoying the delights of Henley, Wimbledon, Ascot, Covent Garden, the Royal Academy, Glyndebourne, the Chelsea Flower Show and the Last Night of the Proms, as well as polo, yachting in the Solent, and various West End first nights. There were lunches and dinners at Langan's Brasserie, L'Escargot, Harvey's, Le Caprice, the White Elephant, Quaglino's, the Greenhouse, the Roux brothers' Le Gavroche, and also many of those smaller, trend-setting restaurants frequented by the art and literary world as well as admen and their clients, like Alastair Little's 192 in Notting Hill and the similarly named 435 in the King's Road. Fine dining might also take place in more exotic locales, because conventions were held at alluring destinations like Berlin, Paris, Monte Carlo, Copenhagen, the French Riviera and as far away as Buenos Aires. Long-distance travel was Business Class. There was also an inter-agency poker school that rotated around members' London homes for the regular weekly game, but took off for places like Malaga for the odd weekender marathon. On these occasions play would begin late on Friday night and, interrupted only for excursions to local restaurants, continue until time to leave for the airport on Sunday night.

Was all this carousing necessary in order to conduct business? Of course not. When the entertainment was offered by other agencies or suppliers of services, it was of course in the nature of a soft bribe. The recipients of these favours found it easy to justify on the grounds that nobody ever moved their account for the sake of a good lunch. The lavish hospitality offered by the incumbent agency and ancillary suppliers was explained away as an opportunity to talk about strategic issues, as opposed to the nuts and bolts of day-to-day activity, in a relaxed atmosphere. There was a modicum of sense in this, because it was beneficial for senior people on both sides of the fence to talk over the wider issues without the formality of a set agenda. But as Jack Rubins used to say, let's get the boring stuff over with our soup, then we can talk about girls with our mains. (I doubt he said that to James Mackenzie.)

Another aspect of this playful eighties approach to big business was the exploitation of famous names, on the basis that nothing impresses a client more than wheeling out a celebrity. This could be done with finesse, as in the case of the advertising agency Benton & Bowles, who had a lecture programme to which they would invite people like me who might be induced to confer future favours. CEO Bruce Rhodes used to select deliberately provocative speakers in order to shake us all up a bit. For instance, Ken Livingstone delivered a denunciation of capitalism with such charm and erudition that he had his audience of capitalist hyenas believing maybe there could be such a thing as a benign socialist regime. Until we recovered from Bruce Rhodes's generous hospitality and reality impinged.

Less finesse went into pairing off slebs with prospective clients at charity do's, which were frequent and lavish. On one occasion the entertainment was a horse race shown on a screen while Peter O'Sullevan gave a live commentary in person. All the punters had been issued with tickets bearing the names of three horses in the race and the winner was the ticket holder with the names of the first, second and third horses past the post. For the first time in my life I found myself winner of what was, in reality, a raffle. They then wheeled Jeremy Beadle on to the stage to present the prize. I knew Beadle because he did a late night show on LBC and whenever he ran out of interviewees willing to yakker for three hours till two in the morning he would send for me. I did a memory act, with listeners ringing in asking the first of this or that. When I pranced on to the stage waving my winning ticket Beadle did a double-take and exclaimed, 'Good heavens! It's my old chum Hickman-Robertson.' Perhaps not the wisest reaction in the circumstances. A cry of 'Fix! It's a fix!' rang round the hall.

On occasion the slebs, in the form of media moguls, were themselves the hosts. In this way I lunched with Rupert Murdoch and dined with Robert Maxwell. On the Murdoch occasion there were seven guests at the table, of whom two were female executives, one of them my account manager Mary Hargreaves, both ardent feminists. After we were seated, and introductions had been made, the Australian titan cast a vulpine leer at them, before opening the batting with 'Well, then. What have the liddle lidies to say for themselves?' Mary's face was a mask of barely suppressed fury. I gripped her knee hard under the table. 'Don't!' I commanded out of the side of my mouth. 'It isn't worth it.' Mary bit her lip, but she was quivering. Fortunately the other 'liddle lidy' spoke up. She smiled at the roguish tycoon sweetly and said 'Nothing that would engage your attention, Mr Murdoch. I am sure we would all rather listen to you.' This was met with a rasping chuckle. Like the Americans, Australians don't do irony much.

The Robert Maxwell *feste* was the old villain's sixty-fifth birthday, held at his Oxford mansion Headington Hill Hall. This was a very big do, so big that it had to be held over two nights. We went on the first night. The guests were a mixture of slebs and fellow tycoons on the one hand and humbler folks on the other. Richard Branson was on the table next to us, but Karla and I, present only because I spent a lot of taxpayers' money in Cap'n Bob's papers, were part of a motley group that included an Indian couple who introduced themselves as 'Mister Maxwell's newsagents'. How nice of Cap'n Bob to invite the man who delivers his papers in the morning, I thought to myself. Perhaps he was not such a bad old stick after all. Mrs Patel, the newsagent's wife, confided to me that they had been in a huge pickle about what to buy the great man as a birthday present. Surely he had everything he could ever need? She had never been to a social function in England before, although she had lived here for thirty years. Her husband was head of the family, so it was her duty to entertain his siblings and their spouses every Saturday. I asked if she and Mr Patel were entertained in turn by them, but apparently that was not the done thing. So she seldom left her own house and the visit to Headington Hill Hall and mixing with the rich and famous was, she admitted bashfully, a somewhat overwhelming experience for her.

The principal speech lauding the birthday boy was delivered by Kevin Maxwell, later notorious as Britain's biggest ever bankrupt. It was as fulsome as might be expected from a favourite son who expected to assume his father's mantle. But after about ten minutes of lavish praise, Kevin was interrupted as the massive form of his father rose majestically from his chair. Kevin stumbled to a halt. Cap'n Bob raised his arm in the air and his hand contained what looked like a telegram. He craved our pardon, he boomed, but an important communication had just arrived from Number 10 Downing Street. He then read the message of good wishes in sonorous tones, pausing before the name of the signatory 'Margaret'. Kevin was then allowed to resume his speech. Five minutes on and the enormous presence once again rose to its feet. Another raised arm, another piece of paper. A further apology, but he felt we would wish to know that this message had just come in from Washington.

More sonorous words. Another pause. Then the name reverberated around the hall ... 'Ronnie'.

It was a pretty impressive performance. But what I enjoyed most was the revelation, when I compared notes with a guest from the following evening's entertainment, that the whole charade had been performed again, word for word, gesture for gesture, on that occasion too.

As for my modest Indian table companion, more was revealed when the *Sunday Times* published its annual Rich List. Her husband did not own 'a newsagents', as I had understood, but 750 of them. His fortune was estimated at £40 million, less than National Savings sold on a good day but better than a bat in the eye with a burnt stick.

I do not think Mrs Patel should have suffered such anxiety over the choice of appropriate gift. There must have been about 500 of them and I suspect they were opened and listed by Maxwell minions. Then perhaps they were laid out for his inspection, so that he could ask who had given something that particularly took his fancy. Like *Everything You Never Ever Needed to Know about the Movies*, signed by the author (*moi*). Or the solid gold Indian serving dish that had been Mrs Patel's eventual choice. (It had worried me how a newsagent could afford this when she told me.) I dare say all these tributes to Cap'n Bob were sold up when Kevin filed for bankruptcy. Mrs Patel's solid gold platter probably fetched a quid or two, a bit more than the signed copy of my book anyway.

* * *

These encounters with the rich and famous tended to be group affairs. I did, however, enjoy a series of one-on-one lunches with Tim Bell, co-founder of Saatchi & Saatchi and the mastermind behind the transformation of Mrs Thatcher from shrill suburban housewife to Iron Lady. I cannot now remember what these lunches were about, as by then he had moved on from the agency I had fired. Rather a lot of wine used to be taken, I recollect, and there was mirth and ribaldry.

One day I had an unexpected call from the Cabinet Office. It was their intention to appoint a deputy to Bernard Ingham, Press Secretary at No. 10. Would I wish to be considered as a candidate?

This was unusual in a number of ways. Ostensibly all government posts were filled by open competition. This had to be one of those rare, highly sensitive posts to which recruitment was by the 'tap on the shoulder' of John Le Carré spy novels. Such posts went to Whitehall insiders, not to people who skulked in government backwaters in *terra incognita* like Hammersmith. I was the most unknown Chief Information Officer in the Government Information Service. I was not even invited to the weekly meeting of CIOs because whatever it was we did out in Hammersmith was considered irrelevant to the mainstream business of government.

It was, of course, very flattering to be invited to compete – I knew enough of the byways of government by now to realise that in such a situation there were probably not more than two or three carefully screened candidates. But did I really want to do this job? There were several very good reasons to hesitate. I would have to give up all my extracurricular activities – chairing the Ephemera Society, running Backnumbers, broadcasting and lecturing on this and that, writing books on the side. We had just bought a country cottage in Wiltshire, and I would not be seeing that again while I was at No. 10. Nor would I see hardly anything of Karla or watch my adorable daughter Nikki growing up. Bluff Yorkshireman Bernard Ingham did not suffer fools gladly and particularly fools from the soft suburban south who had been educated at poncey public schools. And Mrs T? It was well known that within five minutes of meeting she had decided whether you were 'one of us'. If not, outer darkness. In favour: I would watch history being made and might even become a footnote to history myself. There were no other discernible advantages and so, comfortable in my berth in one of government's remotest backwaters, I declined.

Of course I have often wondered how different my life might have been had I accepted. And I have always speculated how it was that he who was probably the most obscure Chief Information Officer in the Service came to be on this very exclusive list. Certainly not by recommendation from Bernard Ingham's predecessor at No 10, the august and urbane Henry James who had warned me that I was committing career suicide when I exited Whitehall. Only when I was writing this chapter did light finally dawn. I now know who had whispered in Mrs T's ear. Step forward the Rt Hon. The Lord Bell!

◆ ◆ ◆

Another professional relationship that ripened into friendship was with the director of several of our television commercials, Richard Collin. Athletic, erudite and engaging, Richard had an unusual background for one of his creative talents, having joined the army as a Boy Soldier at the age of 15 and served as a 'squaddie'. He and his wife entertained an eclectic group of friends at their elegant, white-fronted Georgian house in Pimlico and idyllic thatched cottage in the Cotswolds. I particularly recall one luncheon at the house in Ponsonby Place at which Erin Pizzey, founder of the Chiswick Women's Refuge, was amongst the guests. I had assumed that this combative activist on behalf of battered women was a strident feminist and pillar of the left. On the contrary, she told us, she had been put off feminism at an early age by her mother's example. She utterly rejected the proposition that only men were inherently given to violence; many of the women she sought to aid had themselves a record of violent behaviour. Her support was frequently sought for the kind of movements espoused by privileged members of the arts and media elite, especially actresses who believed that their ability to emote also entitled them to impose their political beliefs on the undereducated. Erin Pizzey deeply resented their assumption that compassion was a preserve of the fashionable left.

Also present was a young Indian who contributed little to this conversation, but did reveal to me that he was engaged on a work of fiction. As a published author, albeit of a single non-fiction work, I felt an obligation to give him the benefit of my experience. If he needed any help finding an agent, I could put in a word. Mebbe he would like me to run my eye over the manuscript? These well-meant overtures were received by my table companion with less enthusiasm than I had expected, but I consoled myself with the thought that the fellow might be a bit shy.

As it turned out, Salman Rushdie did not require my intervention to find an agent or a publisher. Furthermore the novel of which he spoke, *Midnight's Children*, won the Booker Prize without any input from me.

* * *

I was at Heathrow meeting Karla off a plane from one of her many overseas assignments when I saw amongst the crowd of meeters and greeters a girl of jaw-dropping beauty. Slender, blonde, blue eyed, flawless complexion, fairly scruffy in an enticing way in her ripped jeans and loosely worn fraying T-shirt. Then my own lovely wife appeared and I dismissed the apparition from my mind.

Two days later we were in the Balcony Bar at the Royal Court when Karla exclaimed 'Oo look, there's Simon Perry.' 'Who Simon Perry?' I asked. 'Hot new producer. That's him over there. Next to the blonde girl in the torn jeans and the grubby T-shirt.'

I looked. I saw a tall, handsome man with 'Old Etonian effortless superiority' stamped all over him. And next to this Adonis sat the apparition. Karla said, 'Shall we go over and say hello? Or would you rather not?' I made some kind of gurgling sound that Karla accepted as assent.

Simon Perry introduced the apparition as Monday Ellis. There was conversation. We agreed to meet for supper afterwards. Over this repast, Monday revealed that it was her ambition to write a film book. 'Good heavens,' I exclaimed. 'That's what I want to do too! Fancy that. Mebbe we could find a topic to collaborate on?'

I have a somewhat detached relationship with the cinema. I am interested in its history, not the arty, auteur theory side, but how it became a mass medium. On the other hand I have never enjoyed Hollywood films (with rare exceptions). I find them artificial and contrived, since neither what people do nor what they say to each other bears any relationship to how people comport themselves in real life. Ah, but it is all about escapism, you will tell me. Well, it may be for you, and for the millions who worship at Hollywood's altar, but not for me. I like film, theatre, journalism, literature, photography, art to show me why things are the way they are. So I was probably not the ideal person to write a book about cinema.

Not that I had any real intention of doing so. I simply saw this as a means of spending some quality time with Monday.

Now at the risk of sounding defensive, I must briefly explain my motives. Yes, I was a happily married man with a lovely child. No, I was not trying to get into Monday's knickers. She had this lovely bear-like Old Etonian hunk of a movie-maker lover and there was no reason why she should have any preference for a balding, close to middle-aged civil servant who could not dance or drive. I thought we might have a few lunches together, ostensibly to talk about a book that would never materialise, and I would gaze into her iridescent blue eyes and marvel at her wondrous sylph-like beauty.

So we did. That is, we met for lunch and had lots of laughs and completely forgot to discuss the book, so that meant meeting up again the following week when much the same happened, so we made a date for the following Wednesday, and after that we made it every Wednesday. The only occasions we met otherwise were with Simon and Karla, usually supper at ours or theirs.

This pleasant relationship continued for several months, until one of our lunchtime trysts when Monday suggested that perhaps it was time we should put a proposal together for a publisher. By this time Guinness had set up a publishing company separate from the brewery, presided over by the McWhirter Twins. As a spin-off to the *Guinness Book of Records* they were publishing a series of books under the rubric *Facts & Feats*. I suggested to Monday that we should propose a *Film Facts & Feats*, to which she assented.

I rather assumed that our proposal would receive a polite response saying that a *Film Facts & Feats* was not within their future programme of titles or, if it was, that they had already commissioned someone to do it. Then we could revert to Wednesday lunches to discuss other unlikely propositions.

But rather to my surprise the reply was that Guinness had indeed scheduled a *Film Facts & Feats* in their plans for the series, but did not have an author. Would Monday and I like to make a presentation to the editorial board on such-and-such a date.

Monday was a free spirit and dressed the part in clothes that may have been rejected by Oxfam. I explained to her that the McWhirter Twins espoused traditional values and asked whether she possessed a frock to wear for the presentation. She thought she had owned one in the sixties and that it might still be in a wardrobe somewhere.

I met Monday on the platform at Enfield, nearest station for the Guinness office. She had found the frock. It must have dated from 1968 or 1969 when hemlines reached their ultimate level of revelation. This one ended where Monday's shapely thighs began. Her legs, which seemed to travel a great distance to the ground, were bare. She wore no makeup, nor did she need to. Her hair, untroubled by the attentions of a hairdresser, was an aureole of spun gold.

*I became aware that I had lost the attention of my audience ...*

There were about eight or nine suits around the boardroom table. Monday and I were seated at a slight distance and I was invited to open the presentation. After I had been speaking for less than five minutes, I became aware that I had lost the attention of my audience. Most of the men, apart from the Twins, were craning over the table to catch a glimpse of Monday's honey-hued legs. I struggled on for a few more minutes before throwing in the towel. Perhaps it would be better if we did the rest as a question and answer session, I ventured.

At first the chairman of the editorial board seemed unaware that I had finished speaking. Then he turned to Monday and asked, 'Are you free to have lunch with us? There's a rather nice little pub out in the country that we sometimes go to.' Monday said she was and there was an immediate collective move towards the door. Nobody enquired whether I was free for lunch.

Lunch passed in general conversation and little was said about the prospective book. Monday kept the editorial board entertained while I chatted with the McWhirters. It was not apparent whether the book was still on the agenda or not.

Two days later my agent sent me a draft contract. Guinness Superlatives wanted delivery in two years, having estimated that the research involved would take four man-years for two authors. The remuneration offered was, in my agent's opinion, favourable. I rang Monday, passed on this information, and asked whether she was ready to sign. There was rather a long pause. Then she asked me if we could discuss it at her place.

I had never been to Monday's flat before. I suppose the fact that it was empty of furniture should have come as no surprise. Nor were there any carpets. We sat on the bare boards and drank warm *Asti Spumante* while Monday explained that she was suffering from what she described as 'a crisis of confidence'. She was not at all certain that she could find the kind of material suitable for the kind of books Guinness published, nor how it could be presented in a way that was readable and arresting and not merely a recitation of facts and figures. We talked this through for two or three hours, but it was clear that her heart was not in the project. I did not press her to undertake something that she did not think she could deliver to her own exacting standards.

This left me in a bit of a pickle. I did not think I could go back to my agent and to the McWhirters and tell them that I was not very keen on films, not the Hollywood kind anyway, and that the project had really been an excuse to chat up an exceptionally charming and pretty girl. No, I was stuck with doing four man years of research in only two and producing a book that would justify the McWhirters' faith in me. At the same time as doing a full-time and quite demanding job for the Government. I had got myself into this jam for reasons which, while not dishonourable, were certainly not commendable, and I must make the best of it.

I have remarked earlier on the tendency of authors to complain about their publishers. Fortunately Guinness were ideal taskmasters. The editor they assigned me, Ann Marshall, was sweetness and light. Nobody insisted, as I had feared, that the book fit a *Facts & Feats* template. And I was even allowed to indulge my aversion to Hollywood schlock and European art film pretentiousness by writing about the most obscure movies from the most improbable film-making nations. These were films nobody had heard of outside their own countries and which few will ever see, but their existence demonstrated that there is a movie world beyond Hollywood, Paris and Rome.

Such books are often dismissed as trivia and I wanted this one to be both an entertaining read and a useful work of reference. The many charts illustrating various facets of the movie-making business, with accompanying analysis, were based on original research and therefore available nowhere else. I also attempted to range much wider than the usual concentration on directors and stars. There were chapters on extras, titles, shorts and docs, publicity, cinemas, colour, sound, music, literature of film, animation, effects etc. There were lists not just of the top ten of this or that but complete lists: everyone who had ever played themselves in a film or all the portrayals of US presidents. When I listed all the Tarzan movies or all the Sherlock Holmes movies, it was not just the Hollywood versions but those made in India, the Far East, Russia and various parts of Eastern Europe. For light relief there were what I termed 'out-takes': anecdotes about the very strange world of movie-making set in separate boxes that had to be, if not proven, at least credible. One way of testing veracity is to insist on a precise date. Apocryphal stories tend to be set in some nebulous 'golden age'. True events happen on a named film or in a named place, about named people, in a specific year.

It seemed to work. I completed the book in two years, just. *The Guinness Book of Film Facts & Feats* (later *Movie Facts & Feats*) became the most popular of the *Facts & Feats* series and Guinness's biggest seller (apart from *GBR*) after *The Guinness Book of Hit Singles*. Every two or three years Guinness asked for a new version and this was comparatively easy to do. I subscribed to *Variety*, known as 'The Hollywood Bible' but actually global in its perspective, as well as *Screen International* and to British Film Institute publications that reviewed every film released in Britain, including porn films. Most of the updates could be culled from these sources and I would add three or four wholly new features for each edition. *Variety* did not seem to mind me mining their columns in this way, because when the book was published in America they gave me one of the most generous reviews I had ever had. They said it seemed inconceivable that such an assemblage of facts and figures could be the work of one person. Well, they themselves had helped.

Which brings me back to Monday. She became press officer at the British Film Institute. As much of my original research was done in the BFI Library, I continued to see her from time to time. She was not the least resentful about the success the book had attained. When she moved on from the BFI after ten years, *Variety* said she was 'the best press officer in the world'. Always very pro-Brit is *Variety*, though in this case I am sure the accolade was fully deserved.

\* \* \*

There are a number of well-known scenarios for nightmares, for example you are hurtling towards a cliff in your car and your foot will not reach the brake pedal. Another is you are standing in the wings of an enormous stage – at the Albert Hall for instance – and someone says 'You're on next.' But you have no idea what you are supposed to do.

When I started on *The Guinness Book of Film Facts & Feats* I naturally combed through the movies section of the *Guinness Book of Records* to ensure we were singing from the same hymn sheet. One of the entries was for the performer with the most film credits, claimed to be for the Gujarati singer Lata Mangeshkar with 'about 3,000 films'. This worried me on two counts. If you claim a record, surely it must be exactly quantified? And although Lata Mangeshkar had enjoyed a very long career, spanning forty years, 3,000 film credits works out at seventy-five films a year. In India big stars work on several films at once and a backing singer like Lata might conceivably be able to perform for more than one film a week, but I needed verification. When I heard that Lata Mangeshkar was performing in London, I called up her manager to ask him if he knew her exact tally of films. He said he didn't, but if I would like to ask her in person I could come along to the Royal Albert Hall that evening. Just ask for him at the stage door.

The manager explained that the star would receive me in her dressing room after the show. He had arranged a seat for me to watch her performance from the choir stand. Accordingly I found myself sitting on the stage itself, in full view of the audience. It was certainly a novel perspective. The concert was a sell-out, with all 5,272 seats taken. Lata Mangeshkar performed a routine of her Bollywood hits and the audience went wild with delight. After forty-five minutes or so she left the stage and I felt a poke in the lumbar region. It was the manager.

'You're on next,' he whispered.

'Waddayamean I'm on next. Doing what?'

'Just tell the audience how much the diva means to you.' Before I could protest further he had slipped away into the darkness.

At that point the MC strode on to the stage and made an announcement in Hindi. There were only two words I recognised. One was 'Hickman' and the other was 'Robertson'. He then turned to me and gestured. The expectant audience fell completely silent. I wondered at what point I would wake up and know that none of this had actually happened. I didn't.

There was no choice but to advance to the front of the stage. What on earth could I find to say? And then I realised that in a rush of blood to my head I had forgotten the diva's name. How do you make a speech to an audience that doesn't speak English – not many of them, anyway – about a woman you have never met and whose name you cannot remember?

Then I had an inspiration. The diva's first name came back to me. Lata. I could not just refer to her as Lata though, any more than you refer to Maria Callas simply as 'Maria'. Madame Lata, that was it. I began hesitantly, but as soon as I spoke the words 'Madame Lata' there was an immense cheer that filled the cavernous hall and reverberated against those acoustic discs hanging from the ceiling. I realised that it did not actually matter what I said, as little of it was understood anyway, but the important thing was to repeat 'Madame Lata' in every sentence. Each time I did so there was an ovation. I had never been cheered by 5,000 people before, nor have I since. It is quite a heady experience and I can understand why showbiz people become addicted to playing an audience. I was a hit! No, of course I wasn't. Madame Lata was a hit and I was receiving the applause on her behalf. Still, as nightmares go, it felt pretty good.

Afterwards in a dressing room looking like Chelsea Flower Show I was received graciously by the diva herself. She spoke no English, so the manager interpreted. After an exchange of courtesies, and mutual compliments on our respective performances, I was able to deliver the key question. How many movies had she sung for or in?

There was a rapid burst of Hindi and much jangling of bangles as Madame waved her arms. The manager spoke. 'Lata says many, many films. Lots of films. She has never counted them. But oh so many!'

I persuaded Norris McWhirter that the *Guinness Book of Records* needed some harder evidence before they repeated the claim for the record number of film credits. And while he was about it, the bizarre assertion that the Falkland Islands had the world's highest number of cinema seats per capita had to go too. (There were no cinemas in the Islands at the time.)

. . .

James Littlewood was succeeded as CEO of National Savings by Stuart Gilbert, a highly intellectual Treasury man. Unlike his predecessor he took a close interest in the promotion of National Savings, which meant that I dealt with him on a daily basis. He insisted on personally signing off everything put out in National Savings' name, which gave the advertising agency a fair amount of grief. 'This is second-rate crap,' he said to Mary Hargreaves, our account manager at Dorland's, of one press advertisement she was presenting. 'But it is an improvement. You usually show me third-rate crap.'

Stuart, like a lot of very clever people, did not think like the rest of us. One day Mary had to present a poster for National Savings Deposit Bonds, which for perfectly cogent reasons that escape me was illustrated by a field of wheat. The Director of Savings tugged at his moustaches and said it would not do. Wheat produced bran. Bran produced a deposit. If he approved this poster, National Savings would be exposed to ridicule. Neither Mary nor I felt able to tell this Oxford double first that while his brain might run along such channels, very few others' did. Except possibly primary school kids with minds as grubby as their knees.

On another occasion the offending piece of work was a television commercial featuring a large symphony orchestra. At the start the orchestra is seen and heard in full swing, but every few seconds one or another set of instrumentalists ceases to perform, until it is down to only the string section. Then each of the strings ceases until there is but a single player in the spotlight. Again I have no recollection of how this connected with a judicious choice of investment, but whatever it was it worked for me and for all my colleagues. Except one. Stuart did not like the choice of music, which was a piece by Tchaikovsky that the creative director had specially chosen because it happened to work well with the withdrawal of each instrumental section. 'Nobody of any taste listens to Tchaikovsky,' pronounced the Director of Savings. This time I did argue the agency's case. We had tried several other symphonies and it only really worked with the Tchaikovsky. Stuart was adamant. The London Symphony Orchestra was hired at vast expense. The commercial was made using an alternative piece of music by a composer of whom Stuart approved. Bartok if I remember rightly. It was an utter disaster. We should have simply scrapped the idea when Stuart made his initial objection. As it was tens of thousands of taxpayer pounds were wasted.

There were occasions when I was the one making objections, so the agency did not enjoy an easy ride. I was particularly concerned with the low standard of copy-writing, a defect by no means unique to Dorland's as I was to learn when I worked with other agencies. Most copy-writers appeared to be failed art-school students who had wanted to be art directors but found themselves stuck with the boring business of putting words on paper instead. It was not that we as civil servants wanted the copy to be written in officialese, but rather the opposite. Financial copy required precision, but to be readily understood it also demanded the ability to express relatively complex ideas in short sentences and simple language. This seemed to be beyond the ability of the art-school drop-outs and most of their prolix copy I had to rewrite myself.

I made a particular nuisance of myself when we were shooting a commercial on a golf course with Norman Lumsden, who had played JR Hartley in the much-loved Yellow Pages ad about a wistful old gentleman seeking a copy of *Fly Fishing* by JR Hartley. The setting was supposed to be a Scottish golf course, but the agency declared it too risky to shoot in Scotland in April and assured us that the only place in Europe with guaranteed sunshine at that time of year was Malaga. The agency's reasons for shooting commercials in exotic, warm locales were sometimes more inventive than the commercials. They even managed to find a golf course with fir trees on the Costa del Sol. Off we all trooped slathered in sun-cream, only to be met with an arctic blizzard blowing down from the Pyrenees. It was, we were told, the worst April weather ever experienced in Spain and the first time in living memory that snow had fallen on the Costa del Sol. Out of interest I checked the weather in Scotland. The whole country was bathed in sunshine and the Glasgow *Daily Record* had dug out its rarely used 'Phew What a Scorcher!' headline.

But that is not the point of this tale. After four days of huddling in unheated hotel rooms, the snow melted and we were able to start work. In the commercial Norman Lumsden was playing the role of a golfer who needs a hole-in-one to win the match. When he does his final drive he executes a wayward slice and the ball sails off to the left of the fairway where it hits a parked car and bounces against a telegraph pole from whence it lands in a fountain just as the jet is switched on, propelling it high into the air and on to the roof of the club-house, from which it rolls down and hits the seat of a child's see-saw that flings it on to the green where it trickles towards the hole....

Standing on the green, watching its progress, are Norman and his opponent Charlie. 'Wait a minute,' screeched the client (me) as the director called 'Action!' 'What's the problem?' the director sighed. 'How did Norman and Charlie get on to the green?' I asked. 'They walked,' hissed the director through clenched teeth. 'A golf ball takes an average of five or six seconds to travel the length of a par 3 fairway in settled conditions,' I expounded. 'This one took a circuitous route, so let us say nine or ten seconds. You're telling me that Norman and Charlie walked the length of the fairway in less than that time?'

The director plucked a spotted bandanna handkerchief from a back pocket and mopped his brow theatrically. He spoke slowly and distinctly as to a half-witted child. 'It's fantasy. None of this could really happen. It's what people enjoy. Don't you ever go to the movies?' I resisted the temptation to say No, I just write books about them. 'There are two types of fantasy,' I told him as he stared at the sky as though seeking an opportune thunderbolt. 'The kind that is wildly improbable, but just within the bounds of possibility. That's the kind of fantasy represented by the flight of the ball. It wouldn't happen but it could happen. Then there is fantasy that simply defies the laws of nature and to no purpose. That is represented by Norman and Charlie being on the green when the ball arrives. It is impossible. And if they have magic powers that make it possible, then Norman could get a hole-in-one the same way.'

The director turned to the agency producer. 'You agree that Norman and Charlie should be on the green, don't you?' The producer looked like a startled rabbit and muttered something unintelligible. 'No,' I said to the director. 'He's not paying for this shoot. The taxpayer is. Now I want the ball to enter the hole and then cut to Norman and Charlie hoving into view.'

Clients are not supposed to interfere on set. They are there, as Mary Hargreaves would remind me fairly forcefully, simply to approve script changes. Personally, though, I think they are also there to stop preening prima donna directors getting above themselves.

. . .

There was always potential for the unexpected when shooting abroad. The agency came up with another good idea for a bit of sun worshipping in winter. They devised a commercial set in a lush English garden in summertime. It was now November. So of course we would need to shoot it in South Africa and they even managed to concoct a set of dubious figures that showed it would actually be cheaper than shooting in England.

Everything was well prepared and we even flew out a scarlet pillar-box for a street scene. It was only when we went to inspect the glorious garden in Constantia we had hired for a day that a botanically-minded member of the crew pointed out that many of the flowers and shrubs were tropical growths unknown in English gardens. We had just enough time to scour the garden centres of Cape Town to assemble sufficient English flowers for replanting. We then had to negotiate with the owners of the garden to let us dig up their precious tropical growths, which involved a further expenditure of taxpayers' money, and then hire a horticultural expert from Cape Town University to supervise the extraction and careful nurturing of the plants while they were out of the ground. This gentleman warned us that they must be restored to their habitat within four hours, which gave the director exactly half the time he had estimated it would take to shoot the garden scenes. Not all directors are poncey, self-regarding *auteur* types. This one completed the shoot in half a day without whingeing about it and delivered a lovely little English drama under cloudless, blue southern skies that might well have been shot in a Jane Austen rectory garden. But not in November.

Another shoot we did abroad was a Premium Bonds poster with the slogan 'Escape with £250,000!' showing an attractive young couple aboard a yacht and a pirate's chest full of money. We had tried shooting it off the Norfolk coast, but slate-grey skies and leaden seas rendered the pictures unusable. We decided to shoot in Australia instead, as I was going anyway to research *The Guinness Book of Australian Firsts*. We hired a magnificent sloop with teak decks and then held a casting call for an English-looking couple. A suitable male model was chosen easily, but selection of his partner presented a problem. The man was of average height, about 5ft 9 in, but at the audition for female models the first forty-nine we saw were all six feet tall or over. The fiftieth and final candidate was an exceedingly pretty girl about 5 ft 6 in. She was ideal.

The only drawback was that Lisa, our model, had to fly to Melbourne on the evening of the shoot and would have to leave before five. We agreed to accommodate this. On board the yacht I asked her if she did much work in Melbourne – I would have thought they would have their own stable of photographic models. She told me that all the models in Melbourne were six foot or over. 'It's the same in Adelaide and Brizzie,' she told me. 'I'm the only model under six foot, so I'm in constant demand. I fly all over Australia and while it's good to have the work, it's pretty exhausting. I wouldn't mind a few other shorties in the game.' I asked her why, if there was such demand for her services, the model agencies clung to their six-foot shibboleth. 'I blame it on Elle Macpherson,' she replied. 'She was Australia's first real supermodel, she's on covers all over the world. Our agencies think that if they want a winner like Elle, they have to go for tall. And now everyone overseas thinks that all Ozzie birds are over six feet. So I'll never get work abroad.'

What Lisa said is quite true. There is a perception, not only in the modelling business, that all Australian girls are long and willowy. It is, in fact, a myth. There was a report in the *Sydney Morning Herald* on the day we left that the average height for Australian women was 5 ft 4½ in, according to a new survey. That made them just half an inch shorter, on average, than British women. Incidentally Lisa's career as Australia's only mini-model went from strength to strength. A year or so later we had an Australian intern at National Savings and when she saw the poster on my wall, she told me that Lisa was now a household name in Australia.

On another occasion the south of France was the chosen setting, this time for a set of photographs for National Savings Gift Tokens. I had acquired a regular model by now, more or less accidentally. We had been doing a guide to children's savings, an area of our work I wanted to see diminished. I gave the job to my head of studio with instructions to commission a cover portraying four children in different settings, a two-year-old, seven-year-old, twelve-year-old and seventeen-year-old. He made the basic mistake of leaving the selection of models to the photographer. The 17-year old, I had emphasised, needed to be on this side of adulthood, given the subject matter. The photographer picked a large, athletically-built young lady with an impressive chest measurement. She looked closer to twenty-seven than seventeen and, juxtaposed to the other children on the guide's cover, might well be mistaken for their mother. The head of studio was one of those for whom second best will do, so I told him I would select a model.

More urgent matters intervened and two days before the rescheduled shoot I still had not found a seventeen-year old model who looked seventeen. Then I saw her in the street, a girl of winsome beauty who walked with the grace of a ballet dancer. I introduced myself and enquired whether she was a model. No, she said, she was a student at the Royal Ballet School. I outlined what we required and, as she seemed hesitant, I gave her my card and asked her to ring if she would like the job.

The following morning my secretary Marion told me she had the Royal Ballet School on the line. 'Ah, that will be Dido Nicholson,' I said. It wasn't.

'This is Barbara Fewster, Director of Balletic Studies,' said a frosty voice. 'I understand you accosted one of our gels in the street yesterday.'

'I do not accost, Miss Fewster. I introduced myself to Miss Nicholson and asked if she would like to model for us.'

'Are you aware, Mr Hickman-Robertson, that we do not allow our gels to be exploited for commercial purposes?'

'Very commendable. But this would not be commercial, Miss Fewster. Miss Nicholson would be providing a service to the British Government.'

There was a pause before Miss Fewster spoke again. 'Oh, I see ... the Government. I suppose that does make a difference. Would she be chaperoned?'

'She will be accompanied by a responsible adult at all times, Miss Fewster.'

'And would she be paid for her services, Mr Hickman-Robertson?'

'She will be paid £5 per hour.' I did not believe in extravagance when it came to promoting children's savings.

'£5 an hour! It sounds a great deal of money for a seventeen-year old girl to earn' said Miss Fewster.

I agreed that the world was going to hell in a handbasket, but what could you do with all these modern notions about. Like paying children for their labour. Miss Fewster and I parted the best of friends. Dido did the shoot, then several others, and became our regular teenage and, later, young adult model. She left the Royal Ballet School and joined Sadler's Wells, where she rapidly became a coryphée. Then came a dreadful day when a male partner dropped her on the stage, breaking her foot. The

Royal Ballet sent her to a specialist unit in Monte Carlo for remedial treatment.

Along the coast at St Tropez was the photographer David Hamilton, well known for his soft-focus studies of beauteous girls in diaphanous dresses. It seemed an opportunity too good to miss and I asked the agency to negotiate with him. Hamilton was not the easiest of photographers to do business with. His fee was $5,000 an hour, he would only shoot at the location of his choice, and he would not shoot any model over the age of seventeen. Dido was in her twenties by now, but I knew that she was exactly the type that Hamilton liked to immortalise in the glossy coffee-table books that he specialised in. I sent him a recent poster we had featured her on. He replied within minutes of receiving it that he would accept the assignment.

Mary Hargreaves and I flew down to the location Hamilton had chosen, Cap d'Agde. We hired a car at the airport and set off to find the location. Every time we stopped for directions there were smirks and sniggers. All was revealed – in more than one sense – when we discovered on our arrival that Hamilton had chosen a naturist resort as our base. We had expected Dido to appear the following day, but found that she was already there. Hamilton had found out her whereabouts from the Royal Ballet and given her instructions to arrive the previous day in order to 'get to know her'.

The resort was probably the largest naturist centre in Europe. It had hotels, bars, leisure centres and shops, in all of which the staff were stark naked. Seeing a supermarket check-out girl performing the routine tasks of her trade without a stitch on was a somewhat startling sight. In these commercial areas nakedness was optional for guests. I stayed put in them while my companions took themselves off to the beach area reserved solely for the unclothed. I did not wish to become known at Dorland's as the Naked Civil Servant.

The shoot was held in an olive grove and Hamilton's photographs were redolent of a hazy sun-dappled afternoon in *le Sud*. He asked Dido if she would recruit teenage girls who looked 'just like herself' in London and send them down to him. She would be well rewarded. In view of the scandal that later engulfed David Hamilton, resulting in him taking his own life, I sincerely hope that Dido failed to carry out the commission.

• • •

There were other excursions on behalf of National Savings, to the US and Canada, to Brazil and Argentina, to Monaco, Czechoslovakia, Denmark, Gibraltar, Lithuania, Morocco and Mauritius. During leaves I continued to explore the English speaking world, visiting Barbados, the Bahamas and Bermuda, BVI, Malaysia, Brunei, Singapore, India, Hong Kong, Namibia, Botswana, Tonga, Samoa and Swaziland. Karla's documentary series – *The Commanding Sea* with Clare Francis, *Wine* with Hugh Johnson, *Oil, Africa* with Basil Davidson, *Hardy Kruger Globe Trotter, Listening to Volcanoes* with Madhur Jaffrey, *Secrets of Calcutta, Children in Need* – took her to India, Zimbabwe, Kenya, Ethiopia, Uganda, Sri Lanka, Dominican Republic, Philippines, Austria, Romania, Turkey, Lebanon, Russia, Ukraine, Iceland and Spitzbergen, among others. Shot rather closer to home, in Paris, was Karla's first film as a producer, *Chasing a Rainbow: The Life of Josephine Baker.* This won the Emmy for Best International Documentary.

People sometimes ask us what is the remotest place we have visited. The Falkland Islands involved flying to Lima, taking a boat down the coast to Santiago, then flying via Terra del Fuego to Port Stanley. The return flight (without the boat trip) took exactly forty-eight hours. St Helena is pretty remote by virtue of the fact that until 2018 it was the only country in the world that could not be reached by air. We flew to the Canaries, boarded the RMS *St Helena*, the world's last ocean liner to ply a regular, scheduled route, and travelled via Ascension Island to Jamestown, the lovely little Georgian capital (pop. 750) of St Helena. But the remotest of all has to be the Marquesas, a French Overseas Département (pop 8,300) in the South Pacific. Karla had been asked by Michael Gill, producer of Lord Clark's *Civilisation* and father of AA Gill, to accompany him to Tahiti and the Marquesas with a skeleton crew to film *Paul Gauguin: the Savage Dream* for the National Gallery in Washington DC. I was hired as Sound Recordist and Chief Cook and Bottle Washer (unpaid).

Tahiti is a fairly sophisticated place, but the Marquesas, where Gauguin died in 1903, were over 1,000 miles away and not accessible by any form of public transport, whether by sea or air. Assuming that the inhabitants would lean towards the primitive, Karla went off to Oxford Street to buy beads for barter, in particular to pay the bare-breasted natives she needed to hire for dramatic reconstructions.

The Gauguin Gallery in Tahiti did not have any Gauguins, but they did have his shopping lists. The island is almost wholly mountain, with only the narrowest coastal fringe. In Gauguin's day the natives lived mainly on fruit that grew wild on the slopes, but the artist was in ill-health and could not follow them. An unfriendly lot, they were unwilling to share. (They have not changed much.) The shopping lists testify that he lived almost entirely on tinned food, which he imported direct from Paris. Tinned asparagus was his favourite.

Karla hired a plane for the six-hour flight to Atuona, the mighty capital (pop. 600). This was a replacement for the charter plane that had been lost in the drink returning from Atuona the previous year. Happily the two French pilots had been rescued. Less happily, one of these would be flying the new plane too. (Only later did we learn that his 'co-pilot' was a chum who fancied a free ride to the Marquesas, but had never flown a plane in his life.) Hiva Oa, the island on which Gauguin lived, has the shortest airstrip in the world, terminating on a precipice. It was something of a white knuckle flight and a terrifying descent, but I am here to tell the tale.

There were no hotels in the whole group of islands and only two restaurants, 300 miles apart. We stayed at the Government Rest-house, which was self-catering but with no crockery, cutlery or kitchen utensils provided. I bought what we needed from Atuona's general store, where a very basic frying pan cost $25. The native maidens Karla sought to recruit for the bare-breasted scenes representing Gauguin's inspiration were unimpressed with her beads and baubles from Oxford Street. They would work for Equity scale or not at all. There was not a bare breast in sight and they were arrayed in what looked like the latest Paris fashions. Their clothes were indeed Paris fashions, albeit not quite the latest. It took three to six months for the mail order catalogues to arrive from the French capital, another month or so for the girls' orders to reach Paris via Tahiti by airmail, and a further three to six months before the garments arrived.

The native interpreter, Monsieur Charming, told Karla he had only met two other Germans. It transpired that Karla knew them both.

At Atuona's single restaurant, which only opened if someone had booked a table, our team was served by a waitress who bore a striking resemblance to Gauguin's *Lady with a fan*. Karla remarked on the fact to her. She said she had never seen the painting, not even a reproduction, but she had been told about it by her grandmother – daughter of the 'Lady with a fan'. There followed a two-day tussle with her surly boyfriend while we tried to persuade him to let her be filmed – men still called the shots in the Marquesas. In the end she agreed to be filmed secretly, on the basis that Monsieur Miseryguts would never see the film anyway. The Marquesas had no cinemas and no television.

*Paul Gauguin: The Savage Dream* was premiered in association with the sell-out Gauguin exhibition at the National Gallery of Art in Washington DC and was a huge success, apart from my sound. That had to be re-recorded.

• • •

Elsewhere in the film world, Karla's former mentor Frederick H Brogger was having a trying time. Following a disastrous shoot in Ireland, never completed because the money ran out again, he was arrested by City of London Police on thirteen charges of fraud, forgery and perjury. Released on bail, he had to surrender his passport, but doctored an expired passport by the simple expedient of writing 'Extended' under the expiry stamp and signing it with the name of a fictitious State Department official. He hired a car which he drove to Scotland, abandoning it at the airport, and flew out of Glasgow (passport control being laxer there than at Heathrow) to an unknown destination in America. Karla and I received a single communication – posted in transit – informing us that he was safe, but we would hear nothing further for four years.

• • •

You can have a barrel of fun if you have enough money. As I had several million pounds of your money to spend every year, there were all sorts of exciting things I could do with it. I once hired Wembley Stadium to shoot a commercial. That was a bit pricey. I hired the private gardens of lovely, elegant Regency Edwardes Square in Kensington to take some pictures of Dido contemplating a rose for a poster. That wasn't. I asked my Irish assistant Philomena to negotiate with the garden trust and to come back to me if they wanted more than £1,000. She reported back that they had asked for £100. 'That's all right then,' I said. 'No, it isn't,' retorted Philomena. 'I said to them, do you know who you are talking to?

This is the British Government. And we'se doin' the payin'. Do you think the Government's made of money? So I got it for £50.'

I had been attracted to Edwardes Square as a location after we ran a competition in partnership with the *Evening News*, a venture suggested by the paper's financial editor Christopher Fildes, now moved on from the manufacture of ladies' underwear in Bath. The prize was dinner at the Savoy with *Up Pompeii* comedian Frankie Howerd. We had been using him for some advertising work, and when I put Philomena on the job she persuaded him to render this additional service for free. The winners were a shy elderly couple from the outer suburbs and I feared for a difficult evening. Frankie Howerd kept them in howls of laughter from the soup to the cheese. Afterwards he and I set off down the Strand looking for a taxi. He had now stopped being the funster and started telling me the story of his life. The taxi forgotten, we walked the length of Piccadilly and he started to relate to me his inner torments as we progressed up Kensington Gore. He was the archetypal tortured clown and I suppose he was able to reveal so much of himself because I was a stranger he was unlikely to encounter again. More than anything he was concerned about his legacy and whether he would be remembered as an artist rather than as a funny man. It took us two hours to reach his home at No. 27 Edwardes Square and I felt that I had been privileged to have received these confidences.

All kinds of doors open if you have a cheque-book to hand and I had a wonderful few days touring the provincial art galleries of England looking for works of art that had not been reproduced before. This was for a new series of our gift tokens. It is remarkable, indeed shocking, how much valuable art is secreted away in basements and never gets exhibited. I was looking at paintings by prominent artists that may never have been seen by anyone other than the gallery staff since their acquisition. I also had my own art exhibition, or rather my own exhibition of original artwork for National Savings posters. We had been commissioning first-rate poster artists for over seventy years and, like the art galleries, had a wealth of distinguished work languishing unseen. So I did a deal with the magnificent Kelvingrove Art Gallery in Glasgow and we put on a show that told the history of National Savings in popular art. Maurice Rickards, founder of the Ephemera Society, himself a commercial artist of distinction, produced an erudite catalogue.

There was another happy result of what I think of as cheque-book power (and I never forgot whose account the cheques were drawn on). A former Financial Director of National Savings called Ken Burton had devoted the early years of his retirement to writing a history of National Savings in World War I. He told me about this at some reunion do and I asked him what he was going to do with it now that it was finished. He said he had put the manuscript in his sock drawer and he thought it would probably be archived in a skip after he died. I asked him if I might read it. Now the history of National Savings is, I grant, of somewhat specialist interest, but Ken's book was well written and told a story that actually contributed something of substance to our knowledge of how Britain met the prodigious cost of the First World War. The reason that most people in 1914 thought the War would be over by Christmas was not about force of arms, but because economists said that the combatant nations would run out of money well before they ran out of men. That it did not happen like that was because of public borrowing on a scale never known before, and not least the important innovation of borrowing direct from the public. How this was done, using government propaganda techniques still current today, was the subject of Ken's labour of love. So I offered to publish it for him.

Ken and I spent many fruitful hours researching picture material at the Imperial War Museum. The layout and design, including a very striking cover, were the work of my studio (whose truculent head had moved on). The book was printed by HMSO. I made every effort to contain costs and sought a place where we could have the book launch for nothing. When I mentioned my quest to Professor Michael Twyman of Reading University, a fellow Ephemera Society council member, he invited us to have the launch at Reading's Department of Typography. This resulted in a remarkable coincidence. The Department was housed in flat-roofed bunker-style buildings that had been erected on Reading's campus during World War II to house various government agencies. When I ushered Ken into the particular room where we were hosting the event, he looked round in wonder and exclaimed, 'This is the old National Savings Committee office. It is where I worked during the war – my desk was over there, where you have the display of my book!'

My brother Tim and I would meet for lunch in the City three or four times a year. On one of these occasions he was uncharacteristically subdued. I asked him whether he was under the weather.

He gave a long-drawn-out sigh. 'I was doing a calculation this morning. It is exactly twenty-five years since I qualified as a solicitor. I thought it would be a wonderful profession to be in. But every day is the same. Same faces, same kind of work. Torts, wills, conveyancing. I never go anywhere outside London. I've got at least another fifteen years to go before I can retire and I know that those years will be no different from these years.'

He took a pull on his ale and wiped his mouth. 'Still, I shouldn't be going on like this to you. Stuck in an office in Hammersmith, doing the same old same old. It must be even duller than my job, being a civil servant in a backwater department like yours. I don't expect you get out much either, do you?'

Just now and again, I told him. Here and there, now and again.

# Chapter 20

. . .

# CRISES MINOR AND MAJOR

. . .

*1989–2000*

Index-linked Savings Certificates were a form of investment that maintained their value in line with the Retail Prices Index (RPI), introduced at the time of Britain's highest ever annual rate of inflation of nearly 25% in 1975. This guarantee was enshrined in the Prospectus, a legally binding document. The idea of an investment prospectus is primarily to protect the interests of the investor. Just occasionally, for reasons wholly unforeseen, it can do exactly the opposite.

Hence several hundred thousand of our investors were disadvantaged when the Department of Trade published the incorrect RPI in the *London Gazette*. Now you would think that all the Government needed to do to provide restitution was simply publish a correction in the following issue. They did, but that did not restore the value of people's Index-linked Savings Certificates because the Prospectus stated that the published RPI would be used to calculate the value. And the Prospectus had the force of law.

You and I and Michael Fawcett might say that the *intention* was to keep pace with inflation and that should override any mistakes made in calculating the RPI. The Treasury decreed otherwise. Michael Fawcett, who he? Michael was a holder of Index-linked Savings Certificates who took grave exception to the fact that he had lost £2.74 by the error in the RPI and wanted National Savings to pay him that sum. He also happened to be a clerk at the Savings Certificate Office in Durham, so he knew how index-linking worked. Michael decided to sue the employer to whom he had lent his savings for the money he considered was owing.

The judge listened carefully to Michael's argument that an *intention* to pay the full amount of any increase in inflation was inherent in the Prospectus and agreed with Michael that this principle should apply regardless of the actual figure published in the *London Gazette*. Considering that National Savings was represented by a battery of highly paid lawyers, and that Michael was representing himself, it was a triumph for the individual against the Establishment.

Until National Savings decided to take the case to appeal.

Now you may wonder why we were prepared to go to so much effort and expense to avoid paying £2.74. There is an established principle in government – a facet of our democracy for which we should be forever grateful – that if the law finds against the powers that be in any individual case, then everyone else who has a similar claim must be given restitution automatically without having to apply for it. (And this is one reason why we should also be so thankful that we have an independent judiciary.)

As I said, several hundred thousand investors were affected. Had it been simply a matter of paying £2.74 to each of them, we would have done so. But every holding was different, the amount owing depending on when the Certificates had been bought and how large the holding. Individual calculations would have to be made for each of several hundred thousand holdings. There was no computer program designed to deal with such an unforeseen contingency and we simply did not have sufficient clerical staff to cope with the task. It had already generated a vast correspondence from those affected, placing a huge pressure on resources.

It was at this stage that I became involved, as one of the National Savings team charged with securing a judgement on appeal in favour of the Government and against Michael Fawcett. I found myself in an equivocal position, because secretly I wanted the judgement in his favour to be upheld. It seemed to me a clear case of 'the law is an ass' and of natural justice needing to triumph over bureaucracy.

We engaged the services of one of the highest paid QCs in London, an advocate with a formidable record of successes in lost-cause cases taken to the Court of Appeal. He held a case conference in his chambers at Lincoln's Inn. I was fascinated to find that such an eminent practitioner should occupy an office no larger than my secretary Marion's and that it was filled floor to ceiling with bundles of papers in no apparent order. How did he ever find anything? There was but one small aperture between these stacks and that revealed a framed certificate on the wall proclaiming the undermentioned to be a Member of the Falkland Islands Bar. The conference was brief. Our QC had no need to refer to papers, as he had all the particulars of the case front of mind. He asked a few questions of a technical nature and did not trouble to note down the answers. They were firmly lodged within a brain so formidable that it must surely have been the nemesis of any who had the misfortune to oppose him in the High Court at Port Stanley.

National Savings had offered to pay for any counsel of Michael Fawcett's choice, but he preferred to represent himself. I think this can only have been actuated by a belief that the rightness of his cause was self-evident, and required no exposition, because he did not plead very effectively. The judge took great pains to draw out of him his line of argument, without much success. He simply asserted that he and others like him had been assured in the literature promoting Index-linked Certificates (written by me) that they would keep pace with inflation and that this had not been fulfilled. Our QC contended that the sales literature was not contractually binding if it was negated by the terms of the Prospectus.

There was an argument that I think Michael might have deployed to effect. The RPI in this case had been miscalculated, but it could just as easily be misprinted. Suppose, for the sake of argument, the decimal point had been shifted two places to the right or even omitted altogether. That would have been an error in the investor's favour, and to the power of a hundred, a thousand, or ten thousand. Would the argument that the figure printed in the *Gazette* applies regardless have been sustained if it had meant that every person holding Certificates to a true value of, say £120, would be entitled to a repayment of £1,200 or £12,000? I suggest not.

Our QC and the judge engaged in a lengthy and arcane deliberation across the courtroom floor in which there was constant repetition of 'a tap on the shoulder'. As far as I could make out, this equates in legal parlance to what the man in the street might understand by any particular phraseology, in this case presumably the terms of the Prospectus. It was all way above my head and probably Michael's as well. While I had been impressed with the judge's patient attempts to give Michael a fair hearing, I was less so by what seemed to me to be a fairly opaque exchange between highly-trained lawyers in language that was certainly not couched in terms readily understood by the man in the street. After all, the issue at stake was whether, in the case of error, the Prospectus should be interpreted literally or in the manner a reasonable person might expect. ('Reasonableness' is a concept recognised in English law, though not in European law.)

The judge overturned the original judgement on grounds that the law could recognise no factors other than the primacy of the wording of the Prospectus, *irrespective of what it might have been intended to mean.* Michael was deeply disappointed. So was I, on behalf of hundreds of thousands of investors and in the name of common sense and natural justice.

· · ·

My only other, peripheral, engagements with the law involved my publisher, Guinness. One day, shortly before the deadline for a new edition of *The Guinness Book of Movie Facts & Feats* to go to press, an anguished picture researcher rang to say he was six pictures light and could I produce anything that would relate to the text. I told him that I had an American book of historic front-of-house stills – for the benefit of younger readers, cinemas used to have stills from the current attraction displayed outside – and that there were at least half a dozen that matched films mentioned in the book. It would be up to him to clear the rights, though, before the imminent deadline.

He used the pictures that I had supplied, but he did not clear the rights. The next we heard on the matter was a letter from a firm of New York attorneys, representing the author of the stills book, demanding $18,000 in reparation for breach of copyright. The stills we had used dated from the teens and twenties and were in the public domain. I assumed that the copyright they were asserting was for the photographs the author had taken of the original stills for reproduction. When Guinness asked me what I thought they should do, I advised that they should offer to pay the maximum reproduction fee for this kind of material, say $75 an image or $450 in total. They might round it up to $500 to show goodwill.

Guinness then consulted their own lawyers, whose advice was succinct. Pay up. You do not want to get entangled in a lawsuit in the American courts where the plaintiff is American, they counselled.

Roll on a few years and I met a charming young lady at a party who revealed that she was an international copyright lawyer. At the risk of sounding like a party guest button-holing a doctor about his ailments, I recounted my story. She was in fact very interested, because the question of reproduction rights – as opposed to copyright – had never been tested, to her knowledge, in the American courts. The author of the stills book had not acquired a new copyright by virtue of photographing the out-of-copyright images. This was because he had not contributed to the artistic expression of the work by so doing. Had he altered the image in any way, though, for example by drawing a moustache on Greta Garbo's lip, or even by inscribing a simple cross in one corner, he could then assert copyright in this, a newly-created image to which he had contributed. It would be up to the courts, though, to decide whether the copyright was valid. The most he could claim for the unauthorised use of unaltered, out-of-copyright images in his personal collection was a reproduction fee at the going market rate. A punitive rate, like the sum that Guinness had paid, would have had no legal backing.

The moral of this story is: don't go to Sue, Grabbit & Runne if you have a claim made against you of a technical or specialist nature. Go to a technical or specialist lawyer.

. . .

My relationship with Guinness, as I have explained, was an exceptionally happy one. Their contracts were simple and straightforward, they paid on time, and they did not interfere. I even got away with inserting a wholly fictitious record ('The most frequently used cliché in movie dialogue', which I claimed to be 'Let's-get-outta-here') and with using a made-up word in the hope of it acquiring common usage ('spondurgle' meaning when you open your mouth to say one thing and another word comes out; please feel free to use it). For my part I always delivered by the due date and my manuscripts never over-ran. So it was something of a love-in between Guinness and me.

Until the bean-counters took over.

Guinness Superlatives the publisher had already become independent of Guinness the brewery, but now it was sold by the holding company to an outfit run by accountants who had no experience of publishing. Their remit was to cut costs and take *The Guinness Book of Records* downmarket with a view to maximising its sales amongst people who cannot read without moving their lips. The cost-cutting exercise involved sacking 85% of the loyal, clever, accomplished staff and 100% of Guinness's stable of authors. In future the books would be commissioned from hack writers at so much a line. They suggested to me that I might like to do a *Great Days of Hollywood* book for them on these terms. I passed.

Not only was I deprived of a useful source of income – my Guinness books paid a fair amount of Nikki's school fees – but I was halfway through a new edition. My agent banged in a claim for compensation. The bean-counters offered £3,000. I took advice from the Society of Authors and they assessed my potential loss at £10,000. Armed with this information, I suggested to my agent that we should run through the contract to make sure there were not any bits of small print that might inhibit our claim. He rang back a few minutes later sounding unsettled. 'There is nothing in the file for this edition,' he said. 'Have you got anything in your personal files?' I had not. The truth of the matter was that my relationship with Guinness had become so easy-going that on this occasion all parties had forgotten to sign a contract. The bean-counters did not owe a penny.

A day or two later my agent called me again. The bean-counters would undoubtedly ask their minions to produce the contract, he said. The minions would have to reveal that it could not be found. It was so unheard of for a book to be commissioned without a contract that the bean-counters would assume that Guinness – or some factotum long since departed clutching their P.45 – had simply lost it. They would be too embarrassed to admit this, so they would be unlikely to ask to see ours.

We banged in the claim for £10,000. Doubtless they consulted their lawyers, the same ones who had previously advised 'don't argue, pay up'. They paid up.

The moral of this story is 'don't let the bastards grind you down'. Or something like that.

* * *

Stuart Gilbert was succeeded as Director of Savings by John Patterson, a very strange man indeed. He had been head boy at Epsom College and ran the Department as if he still had a duty to keep the fags in order and win the House Cup for Orderly Behaviour. Like most head boys, he had favourites. One of these was me, for reasons I could never quite discern as I was still an unruly, inky schoolboy at heart and the kind who would have been regularly bending over his study chair had I been at Epsom. Maybe it was because I shared his addiction to Plain English, which to John Patterson was something of a crusade. Contrary to popular view, both the internal and external communications of most Government Departments were much superior to those of commercial organisations and John's ambition was that National Savings' written output, both correspondence and publications, should be the best of all. So he sought me as an ally.

John Patterson's other principal favourite was my deputy Mrs Culham, a winsome lady from mining stock in Blairgowrie in Scotland, one of a succession of delightful gels who covered my back for me. Like her several predecessors in this role, she knew all my faults, forgave most of them, and covered or rectified the many mistakes I made through absentmindedness, impulsiveness or plain stupidity. She and I made something of a triumphant partnership until it was broken up by Headboy, who wanted to promote her into my job. I was moved sideways into a new directorial post, Head of Policy.

This job involved liaison with Treasury and submissions to Ministers, customer service standards, all written communications, and product development. The latter was a much-needed discipline which had not in the past been any particular director's responsibility. I embraced it with enthusiasm, thereby precipitating a national crisis. Literally.

It all began when I had a brainwave in the back of a taxi in Kensington Gore returning from a convivial and bibulous business lunch. National Savings rates were set by reference to the yield curve, the general principle being that savers would receive a better rate for tying their money up for a period of years. I pondered whether it might be possible to retain people's money for longer while paying short-term rates. (If that sounds inimical to the interests of the saver, it is. I was employed to serve the interests of the Treasury by borrowing cheaply, thereby benefiting taxpayers.)

The cunning notion I came up with was launched as the FIRST Option Bond, a perpetual bond that paid the saver a guaranteed rate for one year.

*I was rewarded with a glower of disavowal from beneath 'Badger' Lamont's bushy eyebrows.*

Instead of repaying at the first anniversary, National Savings would write to savers with an offer of a new one-year rate. To accept the rate, the saver did not have to do anything. The bond rolled over automatically. Inertia, I was confident, would ensure that the majority of the investments were retained.

I impressed on our Treasury Minister that the Bond must be launched with a generous rate to attract a large initial investment, most of which we expected to hold on to after the first anniversary, even at a less competitive rate. The Minister agreed and the Bond was a runaway success. Unfortunately it proved rather too successful, because the building societies cried foul and protested that it was drawing funds away from them. Led by the vociferous chairman of the Cheltenham & Gloucester, they threatened all sorts of unacceptable actions that would have upset the housing market, increased mortgage rates and put quite a lot of home-owners into negative equity.

The Chancellor of the Exchequer, Norman Lamont, called a crisis meeting and never before had I sat at a table shoulder to shoulder with so many names that would become eminent: Gus O'Donnell, future Cabinet Secretary and now a peer, Jeremy Heywood, who succeeded Lord

O'Donnell as Cabinet Secretary and was Permanent Secretary at David Cameron's No 10, and a young David Cameron himself, then a political adviser to the Chancellor. Norman Lamont proposed that the rate on offer for FIRST Option Bonds should be withdrawn for new savers. I complained that this would strangle my infant at birth and was rewarded with a glower of disavowal from under 'Badger' Lamont's bushy eyebrows. The rate was slashed.

Now in order to keep us ticking over in Europe's Exchange Rate Mechanism (ERM), the Chancellor had given a commitment to the IMF and European finance ministers to maintain a high base rate. Across the pond, arch currency manipulator George Soros read about the cut to the FIRST Option Bond rate (probably alone of American financiers to have noted this) and concluded that the Chancellor might renege. Accordingly he moved against sterling. The rest of the currency market followed.

There was now a major crisis in Whitehall, because the only way Lamont could keep sterling within the ERM was by raising rates. This he reluctantly did. When that failed he raised rates again ... and again ... and again, thirteen times in all during Black Wednesday. At last the market could no longer sustain such an impact and Britain crashed out of the Exchange Rate Mechanism, allowing base rate to drop back to a sustainable level.

Fortunately Lamont did not link George Soros's actions to my brainwave for cheap public borrowing – that was revealed later in the *Guardian*. He said that he 'had sung in his bath', such was his relief to be out of the stranglehold of the ERM, so he was happy. I kept my job, so I was happy. George Soros made an extra billion or so, so he was ecstatic. And Britain learned to keep away from European currency initiatives like the Euro. Had we joined, there would have been no Brexit.

When I had been too much of a scaredy-cat to work for Mrs Thatcher at No. 10 I thought I had sacrificed my chance to became a footnote to history. I seem to have achieved it anyway.

. . .

In 1991 Frederick H Brogger re-entered our lives. He had not been heard from for four years, ever since being arrested in Britain on charges of fraud, forgery and perjury, then breaking bail and fleeing the country on a false passport. In the meantime his eldest daughter Chrissie had been in therapy and had been persuaded by an unqualified psychotherapist that all her many problems in life were the fault of her father. She contacted the City of London Police and revealed that Frederick was living under an assumed name, with a new woman in his life, at Carmel, California.

25th December 1990 was a slow news day like most Christmas Days. When NBC, CBS and ABC News each got a tip-off from the Feds that they were going to make an arrest on Carmel Golf Course, they leaped at the opportunity. The Federal Marshal waited until Fred reached the eighteenth hole, which he let him play, before moving in and handcuffing him. The arrest of such a dangerous international criminal in a playground of the rich made all three national news bulletins. Fred had belatedly achieved the celebrity that had eluded him as a film-maker.

After six months in Oakland Maximum Security, Fred was extradited. The City of London Police detective to whom Chrissie had shopped her father flew to New York to accept the prisoner for transport back to Blighty. He was shocked when Fred shuffled off the Oakland plane in shackles and asked the prisoner escort to remove them. 'Not until he is on the London plane, Bub,' was the response. 'He's ours till then.' The kindly detective removed the chains the instant Fred was boarded, watched by 200 enthralled, rubbernecking passengers and crew.

On arrival Fred was banged up in Pentonville. On the first night there were kidneys and Brussels sprouts for dinner. There are two things Fred cannot eat: kidneys is one, Brussels sprouts is the other. 'I think I'll pass,' he said politely to the trusty dishing up the food. Suddenly he felt himself lifted off the ground as an enormous warder grabbed him by the collar. He was dragged down a long flagstoned corridor and thrown on to the floor of an empty cell. There the gorilla warden was joined by three equally strapping colleagues. They proceeded to kick the shit out of the poncey middle class Yank who wouldn't eat up his greens.

The two nights Fred spent in Pentonville he said were worse than the whole six months in Oakland, one of the most violent jails in America. When Karla and I saw his bruised and battered face, we were determined to get him out. At the bail hearing, the judge set bail at £150,000. 'Otherwise,' he declared, 'it could be just an expensive ticket back to America.' And half of it must be from a British source, he added, looking meaningfully at Karla. Fred's inamorata Betsy stumped up $100,000. Karla emptied her building-society account for the other half. The condition of release was that Fred would live at 81 Theberton Street under Karla's personal supervision. Karla got this order amended so that Fred could live in our weekend cottage at Collingbourne Ducis in Wiltshire, and lied through her back teeth that she would be in permanent residence there.

Fred had to report to Andover Police at nine every morning. He took the female desk-sergeant flowers on the first day and chocolates on the second. Within a week he was the darling of the station. After spreading sweetness and light amongst Andover's finest, he proceeded each morning to Andover Golf Club, where his cover story was that he had come to the English countryside to write a film script. In no time at all he was the most popular member of the club and there was talk about an international tourney between Carmel GC and Andover.

Every Friday night Karla and I would trundle down the M4 to Collingbourne. As we opened the garden gate, we would hear the pop of a cork leaving a champagne bottle. The table was laid and dinner, always delicious, was in the oven. Several months passed in this way before a date was set for the court case. There were sad farewells at Andover Police Station and Andover GC threw a goodbye banquet. Not only did the members club together for a gift to remember them by, so did the club's waiters and waitresses.

The trial was an impressive affair. It took the clerk of the court twenty-three minutes to read out the list of charges. Afterwards I overheard him tell an usher that it was the longest indictment he had ever delivered. I was called as a character witness, but the judge had the mistaken impression that I was an expert on film finance. I found myself struggling to explain that it is fairly normal in Hollywood, if not strictly legal, to attempt to complete film A from the budget raised to shoot film B. Such an arrangement usually works out, even if it means completing film B from the budget of film C. In Fred's case there had, regrettably, been no film C.

Whether this inexpert testimony helped or hindered it is hard to say, for Fred was found guilty on all thirteen charges but, to his and Betsy's and Karla's huge relief, given a two-year suspended sentence and a deportation order. It seems that Fred had managed to exert his charm even on the judge, one not noted for lenient sentencing. Afterwards Fred asked me if I thought the case would be reported in the press, as he didn't want the chaps at Andover Golf Club to hear about it. I reassured him that he was not nearly famous enough for the case to be reported (at which he looked slightly crestfallen). Next day *The Times* carried a front-page headline 'Hollywood Producer Guilty of Fraud, Forgery and Perjury'.

A couple of weeks after Fred's return to Carmel, Betsy took a call and it was the Secretary of Andover Golf Club on the line. Fred cringed. This must be the call to tell him never to darken the doors of Andover Golf Club again. Hesitantly he took the phone. 'So, Fred, have you talked to the guys at Carmel Golf Club yet about our International? We're ready to fly over to California whenever.' Fred could scarcely believe what he was hearing. 'Did you see the piece on the front page of *The Times*?' he warbled. 'Of course we did,' laughed the secretary. 'We always knew you were up to something, you old rogue. We just weren't sure what.' (Andover beat Carmel in the initial tournament, but American pride was restored when a return match was played in England.)

*   *   *

Eventually Mrs Culham found the strain of being the favourite of Director of Savings John Patterson too stressful and made a sideways move to the poisoned chalice post of Chief Information Officer at Inland Revenue. When he retired John Patterson became head of a newly created foundation for fostering financial education in schools. Mrs Culham was appointed a trustee and became, in effect, John's boss. She told me ruefully that she found him no easier to deal with as an employee than he had been as her employer.

On taking up my post as Head of Policy I had acquired a new deputy, Jack Tocock. Jack was an East End lad who had left school at fifteen to join National Savings as a postboy. Without academic qualifications, his career expectancy did not exceed the level of Clerical Officer, but he had attained the level of Principal (equivalent in salary terms to an MP) by application, quick-wittedness, ingenuity and being a thoroughly nice guy. A well-tailored three-piece suit with the sharpest trouser creases in Hammersmith may have helped as well.

Everybody liked Jack. I liked Jack because he immediately sussed that his principal function was to take over Mrs Culham's role as my protector and fixer. Whenever I got into a scrape, which was fairly frequently, I would go and wail about it to Jack. However bad the situation, Jack would weigh up the facts, assess at whose door the blame might be laid, and work out a plan for my salvation. 'Leave it to me, Squire,' he would say. 'I know a bloke in – whatever the relevant outstation or division it might be. I'll call in a couple of favours. Say no more.' I would wait a couple of days and then hesitantly ask Jack whether there had been any progress. Invariably the answer would be 'All fixed, Squire. Nobody need know where the skellingtons lie. Know what I mean?' And Jack would tap the side of his nose meaningfully. No recompense was ever sought for these services. Jack reckoned that posh gits like his new boss could not do up their own shoelaces and it was up to blokes like himself who had been round the block a couple of times to bail them out when needed.

Not even Jack, though, could solve the Great Premium Bond Crisis of nineteen ninety whenever-it-was. Bear with me if I sketch in a little essential background. The chief concern of Premium Bond holders, as I was only too aware as Head of Customer Services, was whether their Premium Bonds had been fed into ERNIE, the electronic maestro that draws the winning numbers. Those who had failed to win as many prizes as they felt they deserved were sure that we had mislaid their bonds.

You are quite right, Sir or Madam, I would inform them, your bonds have *not* been fed into ERNIE. This is because NO bonds are fed into ERNIE. The Electronic Random Number Indicator Equipment (ERNIE) is not a computer, I would explain, it is simply a machine that draws numbers at random. Unlike a computer, which can be programmed to do this or that, ERNIE has only two controls: the ON/OFF switch, and the control setting the highest number that can be drawn – the same number as the total of all the bonds that have ever been sold. That means ERNIE can draw the numbers of bonds already encashed – if so, the prize goes to the next eligible number. No bonds are fed in, so no bonds can be left out.

It was not until I had been repeating my mantra that ERNIE was not a computer for the better part of thirty years that I learned that the man who built our electronic wonder box, Tommy Flowers, was the man who had earlier invented the electronic computer. So why, you may ask, should the name of such an illustrious innovator, father of a device that has changed the course of history, be so unknown? Simply because when he built the Colossus series of computers for Bletchley Park in World War II they were Top Secret. These were the devices that broke the Germans' Ultra Code – the code used by Hitler to communicate with his commanders in the field.

At the end of the War Churchill commanded that they should be broken up into parts 'no larger than a man's fist' and that no one who had worked on them should ever divulge the secret. So Tommy Flowers lived out his life in obscurity, unhonoured and unrewarded for shortening the war by two years (in Churchill's assessment). I know whose statue I would put on that empty plinth in Trafalgar Square.

Forgive the digression – this story is supposed to be about the man who wrought the biggest cock-up in National Savings' history, not the man who gave us all the benefits of the digital world. Tommy, stand aside.

It began innocuously enough with a droll piece in the *Financial Times* comparing ERNIE with George Clooney. As the words 'droll' and '*Financial Times*' seldom appear in conjunction, this was in itself worthy of note. I forget exactly in what ways Gorgeous George resembled our hefty piece of electronic gadgetry whirring away at Lytham St Annes, but it was sufficiently flattering to both parties that I had the brainwave of using it to promote Premium Bonds. More precisely, as the basis for a piece of junk mail. I *love* junk mail. No, I am sure you don't. Not many recipients do. But those of us who send out junk mail in millions – and this mailshot was going out to two million people – really do love it for the phenomenal results it can bring if you do it properly.

I asked Jack to get on to the *FT* and negotiate a price for the right to reprint the article and use it as a sales aid. They came back with a demand for £25,000. I told Jack to play hard-ball and he eventually worked it down to £17,500. (I suppose I should have put Philomena on the job. She would probably have got the *FT* paying *us* for the publicity we were giving them.) After the mailshot had gone out, I received a furious telephone call from the authoress of the article. She was really abusive. She said I had ruined her reputation in Fleet Street, as all her colleagues thought she had prostituted her talent for commercial ends. I pointed out to her that it was her employer who was doing the pimping and if she was upset about it she should complain to the suits at the *FT*. As far as I could ascertain she had not seen any of the £17,500, which I would have thought was a rather stronger basis for complaint.

I always insisted that our junk mail should look as boring as possible. No golden stars and rattle-tattle slogans on the envelope, no multi-colour splash-dash inside. I wanted our mailshots to look like official government communications. That way they got opened and got read.

I think this worked, because our response rates were way ahead of the industry average. The George Clooney mailshot beat all our own records, with sales of over £100 million. It was a triumph and I basked in as much glory as can be conferred by such a despised form of marketing activity. Until the fateful day we learned that for the first time in forty or so years had happened that which we had always sworn could not happen. Not all the bonds sold had been included in the draw.

People who complained about not winning were normally people with holdings of a few pounds who failed to understand that their odds of winning anything were fairly remote. My George Clooney mailshot, though, had been targeted at well-off investors and had sought to persuade them to buy maximum holdings of £20,000. For such investors, the odds of winning any prize were about evens in each monthly draw. When we began to receive complaints from these holders that they had won nothing over several months, warning bells began to ring. Our statisticians confirmed that the odds against this were improbable to the point of almost impossible. We set the technical bods to work and they came back with the news we most dreaded. A significant proportion of the sales from the George Clooney mailshot had not been registered. Therefore the highest number that ERNIE could draw had been set too low. Bonds had indeed been 'left out' of the draw.

This news arrived at Headquarters from Lytham St Annes by about 11 am. Our then Director of Savings Peter Bareau, the first ever appointed from outside the Civil Service, knew exactly what his first step should be – one that I doubt would have been taken by a career civil servant. He called in crisis-management consultants and by 12 noon they were gathered round the board table together with key players who would need to carry out their recommendations. The Draw Supervisor, on conference call from Lytham, explained what had happened. Each month's purchases of Premium Bonds were registered by a computer that ran in tandem with another computer associating them with existing holdings. What nobody knew when this system had been introduced was that it would only function to a certain maximum of transactions. Over that volume of sales, the second computer would cancel the data recorded by the first computer. The success of the mailshot had tipped this critical balance, with the result that the highest random number ERNIE could draw was below the cumulative number of bonds sold.

It was fascinating to watch the responses of the crisis management experts. Led by a very savvy lady in her mid-thirties, they were adept at getting to the heart of the problem without diversion or distraction, fully comprehending that what was at stake was public confidence in £50 billion of investment in Premium Bonds. Ancillary to this was the massive administrative costs that would be incurred if loss of confidence resulted in a level of repayments and correspondence beyond our ability to handle. They stressed the need to explain the situation fully, holding nothing back, and to do so that day. There was no time for consultations with the Treasury or our Minister; we must be able to tell our customers that we informed them as soon as we knew what had happened.

All government departments make cock-ups and some have to 'fess up before their cack-handedness is dragged out of them by a Parliamentary Committee or press exposure. Our debacle was exacerbated by the fact that we had spent 40 years assuring our customers that this was something that could not happen. It was made much worse again by virtue of our still not knowing why one computer cancelled out the other if the volume of transactions was too high.

That was not the end of our failures. The unregistered bonds had missed out on half a dozen monthly draws. I had hoped that we would be able to run six extra draws, confined to these bonds but at the prevailing odds of winning. But Premium Bonds operate under an Act of Parliament that prescribes how and when draws are made. It does not allow for supplementary draws in any circumstances. So the only recompense we could make to our disadvantaged bond-holders was to pay them a rate of interest that matched the rate paid into the prize fund. At that time the rate was about 8%. So someone who had purchased £100 worth of bonds as a result of my mailshot, and missed out on six draws, would receive £4 compensation. As they had invested in the hope, however remote, of winning the £1 million monthly jackpot, four quid was unlikely to fill their hearts with gladness. Nor did it, as a voluminous postbag testified.

As head of customer relations, I was given the challenging task of writing the form letters for response to the several hundred thousand letters of complaint, query and outrage that we received over the next few weeks. Following the advice of our crisis consultants, we carried out an analysis of the initial correspondence and divided the questions and comments into fourteen principal categories. The form letters could be edited to respond to any combination of these. Common to nearly every letter was a demand to know what had happened and why, and I wrote an explanation of 'what' drawing on the depths of my ignorance of technical matters. I was the ideal person for the task; I could express it in terms that would be readily understood by recipients who were equally ignorant. For the minority of respondents who were digitally literate, we had an explanation drafted by our computer engineers in impeccably incomprehensible technobabble. The 'why' of the matter was left unaddressed, other than the fact that it had been triggered by record sales. The reason for those sales being way-above-average I deemed irrelevant.

A few letters, mainly from MPs or VIPs, came to me for personal reply, together with those not covered by the form letters. Among the latter was an irate letter from somewhere not far distant from Tunbridge Wells demanding to know whether the individual responsible for precipitating such a catastrophe had been identified and dismissed the service. I replied in mock indignation, informing my correspondent that the culprit was indeed known but that we did not operate a 'blame culture' in National Savings. I was sure, I concluded, that she was of the forgiving nature extolled in all the world's great beliefs and that she would wish the miscreant to be given the opportunity to redeem himself. The miscreant then poured himself a large gin and tonic before turning to the next tirade of vituperation.

. . .

Director of Savings Peter Bareau had come to us from the world of international banking. A violin-playing Old Etonian, he had the air of effortless superiority and the arrogance associated with alumni of his old school, but that is no bad thing in a chief executive, especially one called in with the remit he had been handed by the Treasury. Unbeknown to any of his Board of Directors, it was to decide whether National Savings, an organisation that represented 20% of the National Debt yet 'had lost its way' (in Bareau's own words), should be reformed or abolished. We only heard about the reform part, the subject of a strategic review he launched immediately upon his arrival.

Once he had the review under way – carried out by one of the top firms of management consultants at an eye-watering fee – Bareau's next step was to make all his directors resign and reapply for their own jobs. As part of this process he rewrote the job description of each director. I read mine with mounting alarm. What was demanded of the Head of Policy, not unreasonably, was extensive experience of financial markets on a broad front. My experience of financial markets was confined to the very narrow front of National Savings.

I was four years off from retirement. If I got the push, it was highly unlikely that any Whitehall department would employ me. I could not afford to take early retirement on a reduced pension with Nikki, a teenager with the expensive habits of her kind, heading off to uni. I was unlikely to find much support from my own colleagues on the Board, who resented not only the fact that I had more fun in my job than they did in theirs, and that I had a bigger office and two secretaries, and that I had, until the advent of Mr Bareau, enjoyed warm and close relationships with the previous four Directors of Savings. I did, however, have one friend at court. Of recent years our Board had enjoyed the services of two non-executive directors, bringing in some much-needed knowledge of the private financial sector with which we were competing.

One of these was non-execs was called Howard. I hardly knew him until a strategic 'away-day' held at a large hotel in York. I confess that I often found these prolonged jaw-fests very tedious, especially as they were largely conducted in management-speak, a language that I do not understand. The only part I enjoyed was the free lunch, served while my colleagues wittered on about leveraging our synergies and actioning the key deliverables. On this occasion the lunch trolley exposed a veritable cornucopia of delicious-looking cold comestibles. I was just about to help myself to a particularly enticing dressed crab when a waiter shimmered in and, without a word of explanation, wheeled the trolley out again.

There followed a very long interval of lunch deprivation while the discussion moved on to incremental improvements to the ongoing paradigm shifts, so I slipped out to find out what was happening. A replacement trolley was promised. After a further protracted interval a much smaller trolley was wheeled in containing a single platter of what looked like British Rail sandwiches circa 1947 on an off-day. I told the waiter, sotto voce, that I wished to interview the duty manager. This functionary confessed to me that the first trolley had been intended for a meeting of investment bankers in the room immediately above ours

– it had been delivered to the wrong floor. The sandwiches were what they generally served to civil servants. I pointed out that they had been standing so long that they were curling at the corners and suggested he make a proper recompense for such poor service by providing us with the same spread as the investment bankers.

None of this exchange was noted by my colleagues, earnestly engaged in discussion of refreshing our brand values, except Howard. He leaned over and whispered, 'My! You handled that one well. I like your management style.' Gratified as I was by his compliment, management style did not come into it. I was bored out of my mind and starving. After that Howard never omitted to greet me with a few cheerful observations at board meetings.

. . .

Peter Bareau was a difficult man to please. The only time I succeeded in impressing him – that is probably too strong a word; satisfying him – was at a large meeting of senior staff to talk about the public-sector borrowing requirement. I was not paying much attention (thinking about lunch probably) when he suddenly shot at me, 'How much of the National Debt comprises privately held gilt-edged securities, Hickman-Robertson?' Believe me, this is a figure retained in the minds of probably not more than half a dozen people in the whole country, most of them employed by the Bank of England. But I had happened to read it in the *Economist* the previous evening. If Bareau had asked me the question a day later, I would probably have forgotten it.

'£9.3 billion, Director of Savings,' I replied without missing a beat.

'What percentage of the National Debt does that represent?' Bareau queried.

'Well, Director, the National Debt stands at £352 billion, so as a percentage £9.3 billion represents … er … er.' The idiot boy who had scored 2% in Maths O-level spluttered into silence as Bareau snapped back '2.64%'. He may have been deficient on the charm front, but he had a mind like a steel trap.

If only Howard had been there. Now he *would* have been impressed by my command of the figures. Some of them.

. . .

Knowing that I had no chance at the interview board for my job, nevertheless I still applied. I had hatched a plan, a fairly risky one.

The board was presided over by Peter Bareau, assisted by Howard and a mandarin from the Treasury. After a few desultory openers, Bareau asked me the question I had prepared for.

'What makes you think you are the best candidate for the job?'

'I don't, Director of Savings,' I replied.

My reply had the desired effect. All three faces before me bore a startled expression.

'Did I hear that correctly, Hickman-Robertson? You don't think you are the right man for the job? Why not?'

'We are entering a new phase of National Savings' progress. We are developing a strategic plan that will ensure greater value for the taxpayer while responding more cogently to changing market conditions. You need a Head of Policy with the kind of outside experience that will inform the difficult decisions that this will entail.'

They digested this, then Bareau asked, 'Why did you apply, then?'

'The strategic plan promises to be a bold and venturesome new initiative. I want to be part of it and to use my extensive internal experience to assist in taking it forward. Had I not applied, it would have looked as if I lacked commitment.'

Bareau rubbed his chin. 'Yes, hmm, I see your point. But you do realise, don't you, that you have effectively ruled yourself out of consideration for this post? I think, if my colleagues agree, we should terminate the interview here.'

The colleagues assented and I withdrew as gracefully as I was able in the somewhat unusual circumstance of an interview that has failed to run its course. Howard looked concerned.

What happened after I had closed the door I learned later from the Treasury representative. Howard had said to Bareau: 'You can't afford to lose that chap. He's been on the Board longer than any other director and he knows the system you want to change. If you are going to alter something root and branch, you need a thorough understanding of what it is you are replacing. He won't oppose you – he's already signified that he wants to enable the process. And he's a problem solver.'

I think the last bit was a reference to my ability to solve commissariat problems, but anyway Howard seems to have convinced Bareau, for he created a new post in marketing for me, deputising for a new Director of Marketing. Replacing Mrs Culham's female successor, this functionary had been recruited from the banking sector at a six-figure salary – Bareau had somehow persuaded a parsimonious Treasury to give him the freedom to pay market rates, rather than the civil service scale, for key positions. The incumbent, unfortunate lady, had failed to persuade Bareau or the interview board that she had the requisite experience of the world outside. As an ardent feminist and a militant socialist, she was not a supporter of Bareau's ambition to bring our state-run institution in line with titans of the capitalist universe. I admire Bareau's courage in disposing of the only female director on the Board. At her last board meeting he gave a gracious speech thanking her for her services. In response she stood up and denounced him in shrill and strident tones. Bareau handled this tense situation with the aplomb that propels OEs like himself to the top of whatever institutions they favour with their services.

I retained my salary – civil service, not market rate – and was allowed to keep my outsize office with its original works of art and my drinks cabinet and my two secretaries. Bareau had made a pitch for Marion's services, but she said that if she had to work for anyone other than Mr Hickman-Robertson she would resign. And best of all I was permitted to take dear Jack with me as my deputy. 'How did you swing that one then?' he asked when I told him of our new assignments. 'No, don't tell me, Squire. Called in a couple of favours, did you? Saynomore.'

. . .

I mastered the ability to drive a car at the age of forty-seven – under some duress as Nikki arrived at school-run age – and at about the same time acquired one of the first mobile phones in the country, the infamous 'brick' costing £1,500 or thereabouts. That I never mastered, but as Mrs Culham and later Jack were usually on hand to make my calls for me whenever we were out in the field, it scarcely mattered.

Soon after I retired in February 2000, Karla and I were sitting in a café somewhere in Germany, having been away from England for a number of weeks. Karla needed to powder her nose and handed me the mobile phone that was technically mine, though nobody had ever phoned me on it. (I was careful to restrict knowledge of its number.) 'If anybody calls you, press that and that and that,' she instructed. 'It won't ring,' I assured her. 'It's not as if I'm expecting a call from the Prime Minister.'

As if to defy me, as soon as Karla had exited the damn thing rang. I pressed the various buttons as instructed and rather to my surprise heard a voice – I was more accustomed to a series of beeps and crackles followed by silence.

'This is No 10. Downing Street,' said the voice. Having established that I was indeed P Hickman-Robertson, it continued, 'The Prime Minister is disappointed not to have received a reply to his letter of three weeks ago.'

Now I was not in regular correspondence with Tony Blair, so some further elucidation was needed. The letter, it transpired, contained the offer of an honour, and the PM would like to know whether I would accept it. An OBE for services to Government. What a nice gesture, I thought, though I was somewhat bemused as to what services Mr Blair had in mind. Not that I proposed to challenge the PM on the point. I told the voice that Tony could get back to running the country, as I was happy to accept. Or words to that effect.

Karla returned from the washroom. 'Did the PM call?' she asked. 'Yes,' I said. 'Well, not in person. Some dogsbody in the Private Office.' 'Yeah, yeah,' said Karla. 'Very funny.'

The matter of what services to Government did not become much clearer when I was summoned to the Palace, accompanied by Karla and Nikki, to receive the award. Having bestowed the medal, the Queen remarked, 'I understand you did a lot of work for the Government overseas, Mr Hickman-Robertson?' I was a bit nonplussed by this. National Savings was one of the few government departments that had absolutely no interaction with counterparts in other countries. It is true that I had made a number of visits abroad on behalf of NS, but can Her Majesty have been referring to my partying on Copacabana Beach, getting mugged while book-hunting in Buenos Aires, enjoying the high life in Paris, Berlin, Nice and Geneva, attending a live porno show in Copenhagen, travelling the back roads of Virginia, touring the bookshops of Ontario, lounging around at the San Geran in Mauritius, exploring Constantia at the Cape, enjoying winter sun in Malaga and Morocco, attending the national opera in Prague, sailing a vintage, teak-decked yacht for a photoshoot with Australia's most beauteous models in Sydney Harbour, or playing illegal poker in Monte Carlo? Nor surely does she mean the sacrifice of my dignity and decorum at a nudist colony along the coast from St Tropez?

Apparently not, as I learned when I bought Jack lunch to see what he knew of the matter. Quite a lot, as it happened, as he had been given the unenviable task of writing the citation. 'It wasn't easy,' he told me. 'After all, whenever you had one of your brainwaves it seemed to involve National Savings in some kind of disaster. So I had to put in quite a lot of stuff that I had done myself – well, it was on your behalf.' I told him I thought this was wholly right and proper. There is a time-honoured tradition throughout the public service that bosses take the credit for the achievements of their underlings. 'Well, you'd know about that, Squire,' said Jack. He chuckled. 'OBE – Other Buggers' Efforts they call it, don't they? No wonder they gave you that one.'

Happily I am not quick to take offence. I asked him if he had any idea what the Queen had meant about my sterling deeds overseas. 'Oh, that!' said Jack. 'No, she must have got it a bit wrong. I soon ran out of things to say in your favour, so I padded it out a bit with some guff about overseas visitors. We used to have those seminars for delegations from places like Bulgaria and you would talk a lot. Hard to get you to stop. And you were always skiving off to give lectures – or so you said. Probably in a lap-dancing club somewhere if the truth be told.'

If the truth be told, Jack, I was *not* in a lap dancing club. I was at Crown Agents, which held courses in public administration for people from the bits that used to be coloured red on the map, or I was at the Bank of England's Central School of Banking, where I used to lecture to visiting dignitaries on public sector debt management in the retail sector. (You're right, I don't know how they kept awake either.) I even had the Chancellor of the Exchequer of Eritrea in my class once. What the Queen had doubtless taken in from reading the citation was that I dealt with a lot of foreigners. My adventures overseas might have made for a more picturesque account of my career in government, but hardly one likely to have been rewarded with a gong.

When the New Year's and Birthday Honours lists are published, there are usually a few dissenting voices complaining that the wrong people are being honoured. I am sure it does happen. This was only the fourth honour bestowed on civil servants from National Savings in living memory. My first boss there, Wallace King, had an OBE too. This can only have been for his skill in solving the *Daily Telegraph* crossword puzzle, since his working days were seldom occupied with any other activity. Then there was a very pretty waitress called Winkie in the executive dining room we used to have at National Savings before egalitarianism decreed canteen meals for all. Director of Savings James Littlewood, though the very soul of propriety, was nevertheless as susceptible as the next man to a slender waist and a well-turned ankle, and Winkie had both, along with a mane of russet hair reminiscent of Maureen O'Hara. Mister Littlewood enjoyed Winkie's lunchtime attentions so much – attention with the silver service, don't get me wrong – that he arranged for her to be awarded the BEM. She was over the moon. Then there was a Director of Savings, like most of them before Peter Bareau on secondment from the Treasury, whom the Treasury did not want back at the end of his term. They eased him out on early retirement and bunged him a CBE in recompense. After that there was me.

I don't think the dissenters should get too het up about it. No system of awards or honours can be wholly fair. Consider the Oscars. Often an acting award seems to have been made for the role – someone disabled or someone black and persecuted – rather than the performance. There was a lovely scene in Ricky Gervais's satiric series *Extras* in which a chain-smoking Kate Winslet – playing herself in the habit of a Sister of Mercy – says to Gervais between puffs, 'They give you an Oscar if you play a nun in a holocaust movie.' Not far from the truth. Even awards for gallantry may not always go to the bravest. Generally the act of heroism needs to be attested by two witnesses – some of the most heroic acts of the battlefield are not seen by any survivor. That, though, is a bit different from unworthy people getting awards. All I can say is: lighten up. Honours are supposed to give pleasure to the recipients and those whose services to the public good might be judged to be, shall we say, marginal, may enjoy their awards even more than the truly worthy.

I know I do.

# L'Envoi

In 2018 our daughter Nikki achieved a lifelong ambition. Twenty-five years earlier when the careers mistress at Downe House had asked her what she wanted to be in life, her reply had been a housewife. Shock, horror. That was not an option at this posh but then fairly academic school. Downe House gels became diplomats, surgeons, lawyers, captains of industry, stars of stage and screen (Geraldine James, Miranda Hart, acclaimed novelists (Elizabeth Bowen), literary supermodels (Sophie Dahl), broadcasters (Clare Balding) or royalty (Lady Gabriella Windsor, HRH the Duchess of Cambridge). So Nikki dutifully became a lawyer, married fellow lawyer Jim, bought a big dilapidated house in Herne Hill on a frighteningly large mortgage, had three wonderful children (Henry, Chloe, Emilia), gave the big house in Herne Hill a makeover and sold it at a substantial profit, abandoned the law, which she had found as soul destroying as did my poor brother, and moved to the country to fulfil her original goal of being a happy housewife. What is it with these upper-crust feminists that women can be anything they want but only so long as it is something that the sisterhood approves?

Karla and I had long since retired to the country, moving to the Lambourn Valley in West Berkshire soon after my retirement. One of my life's ambitions had been to have my own library, and our choice of location was dictated by where we could afford a house commodious enough to house the books. Other people downsize when they retire; we upsized. After we had moved in, the Kansan and his lovely Texan wife Toni visited from Kansas City. We schlepped them around hill and dale along country lanes with infrequent passing places, our colonial visitors making the appropriate 'Ooh!' and 'Aah!' noises. 'Is this the most boodiful part of the whole of England?' enquired Toni. I told her that there are many celebrated areas of outstanding natural beauty, such as the Cotswolds, the Lake District, the Derbyshire Dales, the Sussex Downs, the Yorkshire Wolds, the Cornish Riviera, but it is possible that this is the most beautiful area that has no name. May it long resist being dubbed the Kennet Country and that way we may preserve its attractions without the onslaught of mass tourism.

Retirement gave us new opportunities for extended travel. In 2001 I teamed up with a fellow member of the Ephemera Society and book collector, Tim Nicholson, to drive round the perimeter of Australia, Darwin-Darwin. Together with explorer John Blashford-Snell, Tim had been the first to drive the length of the American continent, crossing the hitherto impassable sixty-six-mile swamp the Darien Gap, so he knew a thing or two about driving in harsh conditions. We did the circuit in fifty-five days, stopping at every second-hand bookshop on the route and arriving back in Darwin laden with literary treasures. On completion of our odyssey Tim called the hire company in Melbourne asking what we should do with the car. 'How about you push it off a cliff, Sport,' was the laconic Australian response.

In 2004 Karla and I spent six months in North Carolina while I researched *Robertson's Book of Firsts*, the American version of the book I had started writing in the school library exactly half a century earlier. (That was world and British firsts; this was world and American firsts.) The University of North Carolina at Chapel Hill was kind enough to confer on me Visiting Scholar status, giving me the run of its library of 7½ million books (one of the largest in the US) and nearby Duke University's 5½ million. The town may have been known as the Soviet Republic of Chapel Hill to its staunch Republican neighbours, but it had two inestimable advantages: free public transport (one of only three places in the US to offer this genuine benefit of socialism) and the best Eggs Benedict in the Carolinas (made with cheese sauce instead of hollandaise) at the Franklin Street Diner.

There were other expeditions, accompanying Mark 'God's-Gift-to-Women' Shand and Hollywood diva Goldie Hawn to make a film about Tara the Elephant in a tiger reserve in Madhya Pradesh (hot gossip – Goldie is terrified of elephants); aboard the *RMS St Helena* to remote Ascension Island and St Helena; with John Kimpton across the desert country of Namibia; to a 600-room six-star hotel in Brunei where there was only one other guest; to the Viking settlement at l'Anse aux Meadows in Newfoundland and across Canada by train; and, fulfilling another lifetime ambition, to the mystic, magical Falkland Islands. There were a number of trips to renew friendships in Australia and New Zealand, to America to see Frederick H Brogger, now back with his first wife, and to South Africa to attend Mary Hargreaves's second wedding, held under a baobab tree with feasting to follow beneath a canopy of stars. But travel in retirement is not like the travels of our youth, for it is seldom attended by risk or enlivened by adventures, and any upsets along the way can usually be put right with the flourish of a credit card. So these latter-day excursions need not detain us here.

Back here in the Lambourn Valley, Karla potters in her garden and I potter in my library. She attends U3A seminars by Michael Hart on German current affairs and I amuse myself with writing the odd book or article and firing off squibs to the *Daily Telegraph*, the *Spectator* and the *Oldie*. One result of these letters is that people I have not seen in decades, old HAC chums, girlfriends, long lost cousins, get in touch. But I have lost contact with two of the most cherished companions of my youth, Norman Davies and Maggie. If either of you is out there....

There are compensations for growing old. As a young person the reaction to my general incompetence ranged from impatience to contempt. As I approach my ninth decade it is indulged, even treated as endearing (except by the competent member of our household).

So we move towards what I hope will be the uneventful conclusion of a mainly uneventful life. When I tell people that I am writing a memoir, I can read their thoughts even as they exclaim brightly, 'How nice!' *He was a middle class boy from an undistinguished family who grew up in the suburbs of a provincial town, was the despair of his teachers and a disappointment to his parents, never got any qualifications and frittered away his youth travelling here and there until washing up in a backwater government department for the next thirty years. And all that's going to be in a BOOK?*

I have always treasured the ordinary, the quiet passage of everyday lives. I believe they deserve to be chronicled, because the unexceptional is more representative than the distinctive or distinguished. My only difference from thousands of my peers is that I was below the average in almost every field of endeavour. That I prospered in spite of this is a matter of good fortune. I never had to fight in a war. I live in a country with the blessing of the rule of law and with a tradition of tolerance. I worked in an environment in which I was enabled to exploit some very modest talents to advantage. All this I have put down in writing, because lives so ordinary are the warp and weft of the age in which we live. Here is my personal testament of what it has been like to live through the second half of the 20th century in this our island nation as it sought a place in the new global order, and in those other nations of the far-flung English-speaking world that gave me welcome. It is remarkable only for being so unremarkable and for that I am profoundly thankful.

Lightning Source UK Ltd.
Milton Keynes UK
UKHW021816171019
351803UK00001B/8/P